The Periglacial Environment

Second Edition

The Periglacial Environment

Second Edition

HUGH M. FRENCH

LONGMAN

Addison Wesley Longman Limited
Edinburgh Gate, Harlow
Essex CM20 2JE, England
and Associated Companies throughout the world

First edition 1976
Reprinted 1983, 1988
Second edition 1996

British Library Cataloging in Publication Data
A catalogue entry for this title is available from the British Library.

ISBN 0-582-30536-5

Library of Congress Cataloguing-in-Publication Data
A catalogue entry for this title is available from the Library of Congress.

Set by 30 in 9/11 pt Times
Produced by Longman Singapore Publishers Pte
Printed in Singapore

Contents

List of Figures   xi
List of Tables   xxiii
Preface to first edition   xxvii
Preface to second edition   xxix
Acknowledgements   xxxii

Part 1   **The periglacial domain**   1

Chapter 1   Introduction   3

1.1   The periglacial concept   3
1.2   Periglacial processes   5
1.3   The growth of periglacial geomorphology   7
     Further reading   8
     Discussion topics   9

Chapter 2   Periglacial landscapes   10

2.1   Introduction   10
2.2   Proglacial, paraglacial or periglacial?   10
2.3   Never-glaciated periglacial terrain   13
2.4   Implications   18
     Further reading   18
     Discussion topics   19

Chapter 3   Periglacial climates   20

3.1   Boundary conditions   20
3.2   Periglacial climates   20
3.3   Periglacial climates and the cryosphere   26
     Further reading   28
     Discussion topics   28

Part 2   **Present-day periglacial environments**   29

Chapter 4   Frost action and cryogenic weathering   31

4.1   Introduction   31
4.2   The freezing process   31

4.3	Ice segregation and frost heave	33
4.4	Freezing and thawing indices	34
4.5	The ground temperature regime	35
4.6	Frost cracking	39
4.7	Cryogenic weathering	40
4.8	Salt weathering	45
4.9	Solution and karstification	47
	Further reading	50
	Discussion topics	50

Chapter 5   Permafrost — 51

5.1	Historical perspective	51
5.2	Moisture in permafrost	52
5.3	Geothermal regimes of permafrost	54
5.4	Distribution of permafrost	56
5.5	Permafrost and terrain conditions	65
5.6	Surface features of permafrost	69
5.7	Permafrost hydrology	73
	Further reading	78
	Discussion topics	79

Chapter 6   Ground ice — 80

6.1	Ground ice description	80
6.2	Types and amounts of ground ice	87
6.3	Ice wedges	89
6.4	Massive ice and massive icy bodies	98
6.5	Ice-cored mounds and pingos	101
	Further reading	108
	Discussion topics	108

Chapter 7   Thermokarst — 109

7.1	Causes of thermokarst	109
7.2	Thermokarst subsidence and thermal erosion	112
7.3	Alas thermokarst relief	113
7.4	Ice-wedge thermokarst terrain	117
7.5	Retrogressive thaw slumps	119
7.6	Thaw lakes and depressions	121
7.7	Fluvio-thermal erosion	124
7.8	Thermokarst involutions	126
	Further reading	126
	Discussion topics	126

Chapter 8   The active layer — 127

8.1	Definition	127
8.2	Thermal regime of the active layer	127

8.3	Unfrozen water in freezing and frozen soils	130
8.4	Frost heave	131
8.5	Thaw consolidation	139
8.6	Thermally induced mass displacement	139
8.7	Cryoturbation and patterned ground	140
8.8	Active layer hydraulics and mud boils	147
8.9	Conclusions	148
	Further reading	148
	Discussion topics	148

Chapter 9 Hillslope processes 149

9.1	Mass wasting	149
9.2	Solifluction	151
9.3	Slopewash	157
9.4	Rapid mass movement	161
9.5	Frozen slopes	167
	Further reading	169
	Discussion topics	169

Chapter 10 Slope morphology 170

10.1	The free-face model	170
10.2	Rectilinear debris-mantled slopes	172
10.3	Convexo-concavo debris-mantled slopes	172
10.4	Pediment-like forms	175
10.5	Stepped profiles	177
10.6	Slope evolution	180
10.7	General reflections	183
	Further reading	183
	Discussion topics	184

Chapter 11 Fluvial processes and landforms 185

11.1	Introduction	185
11.2	Major rivers	186
11.3	Channel hydrology	186
11.4	Basin hydrology	190
11.5	Sediment flow, surface transport and denudation	194
11.6	Fluvio-thermal erosion	197
11.7	Channel morphology	198
11.8	Valley asymmetry	202
	Further reading	203
	Discussion topics	203

Chapter 12 Wind action and coastal processes 204

12.1	The role of wind	204
12.2	Loess-like silt	206
12.3	Sand dunes and sand sheets	207

12.4   Coastal processes   209
12.5   Cold-climate deltas   213
        Further reading   214
        Discussion topics   214

Part 3   Pleistocene periglacial environments   215

Chapter 13   Pleistocene periglacial conditions   217

13.1   Introduction   217
13.2   The time scale and climatic fluctuations   217
13.3   Geomorphic considerations   221
13.4   Problems of reconstruction   224
13.5   Extent of late Pleistocene periglacial conditions   226
        Further reading   231
        Discussion topics   232

Chapter 14   Relict periglacial phenomena   233

14.1   Introduction   233
14.2   Perennial or seasonal frost?   234
14.3   Evidence for frost action   235
14.4   Evidence for frozen ground   242
14.5   Pleistocene frost fissures   243
14.6   Frost mounds   249
14.7   Thermokarst forms and structures   253
        Further reading   256
        Discussion topics   256

Chapter 15   Pleistocene wind action, tundra rivers and periglacial
              landscape modification   257

15.1   Wind action   257
15.2   Tundra rivers   262
15.3   Asymmetrical valleys   264
15.4   Periglacial landscape modification   264
15.5   Summary   276
        Further reading   276
        Discussion topics   277

Part 4   Applied periglacial geomorphology   279

Chapter 16   Geotechnical and engineering aspects   281

16.1   Introduction   281
16.2   Human-induced thermokarst and terrain disturbance   281
16.3   Engineering and construction problems   285
16.4   Hydrological problems   291

| | Further reading | 294 |
| | Discussion topics | 294 |

| Chapter 17 | Global change and periglacial environments | 295 |

17.1	Global change and cold regions	295
17.2	Evidence from the present day	296
17.3	Future responses	298
	Further reading	304
	Discussion topics	304

| References | | 305 |

| Index | | 335 |

List of Figures

1.1 Regional extent of different periglacial zones in the northern hemisphere, according to J. Karte (1981)

1.2 Diagram illustrating limits of the periglacial domain: (a) high-latitude domain; (b) alpine domain

1.3 Distribution of permafrost in the northern hemisphere (from Péwé, 1991)

2.1 Temporal relationship between glacial, periglacial and temperate landscapes under changing energy conditions (modified from Thorn and Loewenherz, 1987)

2.2 Limits of Quaternary continental ice in northwestern Canada

2.3 Vertical air photo of the Beaufort Plain, NW Banks Island showing never-glaciated terrain dissected by streams

2.4 Vertical air photo of area adjacent to Sleepy and Welcome Mountains showing main elements of geological structure and dissected pediments of Caribou Creek. Geology after Norris (1977)

2.5 Landscape elements of the Barn Mountains, northern interior Yukon: (a) synclinal ridges and outliers form upland massifs and inselberg-like hills near Sleepy Mountain; (b) pediment-like surfaces surround the upland massifs in Canoe Creek

3.1 (a) Potential insolation expressed as a percentage of the potential insolation at the equator (according to Dingman and Koutz, 1974). (b) Variation of actual incoming solar radiation over a year at the same latitude (34°N) but different altitudes: Fenghuo Shan at 4800 m a.s.l., and Xi'an at 1300 m a.s.l. (source: from Wang and French, 1994)

3.2 Freezing and thawing conditions in various periglacial environments of the world: (a) Yakutsk, Siberia; (b) Tuktoyaktuk, Mackenzie Delta; (c) Spitsbergen; (d) Fenghuo Shan, Qinghai-Xizang (Tibet) Plateau, China; (e) El Misti (Mont Blanc Station), South Peru; (f) El Misti (Summit Station), South Peru; (g) Sonnblick, Austrian Alps; (h) Kerguelen Island (sources: (a), (c), (e) and (f) from Troll, 1944; (b) from AES records, Canada; (d) constructed from monthly means of air temperatures recorded at Fenghuo Shan by Northwest Railway Institute personnel)

4.1   Schematic diagram illustrating how the lower free energy of soil water, a weak solution, leads to a depression of the freezing point (from Williams and Smith, 1989)

4.2   Diagram illustrating the different amounts of unfrozen water existing in different soils at temperatures below 0 °C (from Williams and Smith, 1989)

4.3   Schematic illustration of two mineral soil particles with ice and water: (a) general conditions for segregated or pore ice formation in freezing soil; (b) growth of pore ice; (c) growth of segregated ice + frost heave

4.4   The annual ground temperature regime recorded at Fenghuo Shan, Tibet Plateau, 1991–93 (from Wang and French, 1995c)

4.5   Fall freeze-back and the 'zero curtain' phenomenon at Inuvik, NWT, Canada, 1971–2 (from Heginbottom, 1973)

4.6   Air and ground temperatures at Signy Island, South Antarctic, 3–10 January 1963, and their relationship to cyclonic and diurnal conditions (from Chambers, 1966)

4.7   An example of bedrock weathering by frost action, Prince Patrick Island, NWT, Canada

4.8   Cracks in quartz particles, formed as a result of freezing in gas–liquid inclusions. Photos courtesy of V. Konishchev

4.9   Types of cavernous weathering, taffoni structures and wind erosional features occurring in Antarctica (modified from Selby, 1971a)

4.10   Karst morphologies associated with discontinuous permafrost terrain: (a) Nahanni karst, NWT (from Ford, 1987); (b) Akpatok Island, NWT (from Lauriol and Gray, 1990)

5.1   Terms used to describe the state of the water relative to ground temperature in soil materials subjected to freezing temperatures (modified from van Everdingen, 1985)

5.2   Permafrost terminology: (a) terms used to describe the ground temperature relative to 0 °C, and the state of the water, versus depth (modified from van Everdingen, 1985; from ACGR, 1988); (b) relationship between permafrost, the permafrost table, the active layer and supra-, intra- and sub-permafrost taliks (modified from Ferrians *et al.*, 1969)

5.3   Distribution of permafrost in Canada, with extension into Alaska and Greenland (from ACGR, 1988)

5.4   Schematic representation of the relationship between permafrost, landforms and vegetation in the discontinuous zone of Canada. The diagram illustrates a cross-section through a peat-plateau – collapse scar with a young palsa in summer (modified from Tarnocai, 1973)

5.5   Graph showing relationship between latitude and altitude of reported localities of existing mountain permafrost in the cordillera of North America (from Péwé, 1983a)

5.6   Permafrost in the Former Soviet Union (after Kudryavtsev *et al.*, 1978)

5.7   Permafrost distribution in the People's Republic of China (after Shi, 1988)

5.8   Graph showing changes in permafrost thickness, mean annual ground temperature (MAGT), mean annual air temperature (MAAT), and topography across the northern part of the Tibet Plateau (from Wang and French, 1995c)

5.9   The lower limit of mountain permafrost: (a) permafrost lower limit in the Andes compared with the average for the northern hemisphere; (b) altitude of some geographical boundaries plotted against latitude; (c) relations between lower limit of permafrost, treeline and glaciation in central Scandinavia (source: (a) and (b) modified from Cheng and Dramis, 1992; (c) from King, 1986)

5.10   Numerical simulation of geothermal disturbances resulting from water bodies in the Sachs River lowlands, southwest Banks Island, Canada. Simulation performed by D. G. Harry in 1982

5.11A   Mature palsas on the Varanger Peninsula, northern Norway. The palsa is 4–5 m high and undergoing block collapse around its edges

5.12   The influence of repeated snow clearance on the development of ground freezing during two winters in Finnish Lapland is compared with an uncleared control plot (after Seppälä, 1982)

5.13   Talus rock glacier, Ogilvie Mountains, North Klondike Valley, Yukon, Canada. The feature is largely inactive

5.14   Types of rock glaciers, acording to Barsch (1988). (a) Talus rockglaciers are formed below talus slopes. (b) Debris rockglaciers are formed below glaciers

5.15   Occurrence of groundwater in permafrost areas

5.16   Icings and related phenomena. (a) The Babbage River Icing, Barn Mts, northern Yukon. (b) An icing mound on the Big River, central Banks Island. Photo courtesy of David Nasagaloak, Sachs Harbour

5.17   Sequence of events in the formation and decay of frost blisters (modified from van Everdingen, 1978)

5.18   Remnants of a seasonal frost mound, North Fork Pass, Ogilvie Mts, interior Yukon, Canada (August 1983)

6.1   Examples of cryostructures in frozen ground: (a) inclined ice lenses, 30–80 cm long and 5–10 cm thick, formed by subaqueous syngenetic freezing of glaciolacustrine silty clay near Mayo, Yukon Territory; (b) fine reticulate network of ice veins formed in silty clay diamicton, Pelly Island, Pleistocene Mackenzie Delta, NWT. Photo courtesy of D.G. Harry

6.2   Classification of cryostructures. (a) Ice is shown in white and sediment in grey or black. In lenticular and layered cryostructures, lenses and layers may comprise either ice or sediment. (b) Terms describing layered and lenticular cryostructures (from Murton and French, 1994)

6.3   Cryostratigraphy at Crumbling Point, Pleistocene Mackenzie Delta, Canada. (a) Sand wedge penetrating both a layered and a sand and diamicton cryofacies assemblage. (b) Generalized cryofacies log.

(c) $\delta^{18}O$ profile of ground ice within both cryofacies assemblages (from Murton and French, 1994)

6.4   Diagram illustrating the formation of a thaw unconformity: (a) initial permafrost conditions with ice wedges and reticulate cryostructures; (b) degradation of permafrost, formation of primary thaw unconformity (T/U_1) and residual thaw layer; (c) aggradation of permafrost, formation of lenticular cryostructures. The thaw unconformity becomes a secondary thaw unconformity (T/U_2) marked by the ice wedge truncation and a change in cryostructures

6.5   Cryostructural discontinuity between aggregate-rich ice that has melted out from underlying aggregate-poor ice. The contact is a secondary thaw unconformity

6.6   A genetic classification of ground ice (after Mackay, 1972b)

6.7   Typical distribution of ground ice with depth, Richards Island, Pleistocene, Mackenzie Delta, Canada (from Pollard and French, 1980)

6.8   Large epigenetic ice wedge formed in silty diamicton, Pleistocene Mackenzie Delta, Canada

6.9   An example of a small relict syngenetic ice wedge (vein), Sachs Harbour lowlands, Banks Island, Canada

6.10   Typical terrain and instrumentation at the ice-wedge monitoring site of J. R. Mackay at Garry Island in the Mackenzie Delta region

6.11   Diagram illustrating the growth of ice wedges and how crack initiation must commence in wedge ice at the top of permafrost and then propagate upwards and downwards (from Mackay, 1989b)

6.12   Types of polygonal nets in permafrost terrain

6.13   Oblique air view of oriented orthogonal ice-wedge pattern in an abandoned channel, Mackenzie Delta region, Canada

6.14   The growth of the polygonal net: (a) a successive growth of fissures of higher orders; (b) a newly-born ice-wedge system at Illisarvik (from Mackay, 1986d)

6.15   Data on polygon deformation, Garry Island, Mackenzie Delta region (Mackay, 1980a): (a) plan of experimental site indicating locations of steel tubes and 1966–78 rate and direction of movement of active layer; (b) cross-section between tubes 1 and 18 indicating changes in distances between tubes, 1966–78

6.16   The relationship between mean annual ground temperature, the formation of ice and soil wedges, and the nature of the substrate: (a) clay; (b) sand and gravel (from Romanovskii, 1985)

6.17   Deformed massive ground ice near Nicholson Island, Pleistocene Mackenzie Delta, Canada

6.18   A classification of massive ground ice proposed by J.R. Mackay at a GSC Workshop in 1989

6.19   Features commonly seen in detailed observation of massive ice (from Mackay, 1989a)

6.20   Diagram illustrating the various types of frost mounds and their origin (from Mackay, 1986c)

6.21   Large bulgannyakh (pingo) in Olong Erien alas, central Yakutia, Siberia. A 'flat' bulgannyakh is just visible in near left of the photograph

6.22   Collapsed closed system pingo occurring in Sachs River Lowlands, southern Banks Island, Canada

6.23   Illustration of the growth of a closed-system pingo (modified from Mackay, 1979a). (a) The initial condition. (b) The growth of segregated ice. (c) The formation of a subpingo water lens and the accumulation of intrusive ice

6.24   Seasonal growth bands in pingo ice, observed in Pingo 20, Tuktoyaktuk Peninsula, Pleistocene Mackenzie Delta (see Mackay, 1990b): (a) general view of the pingo showing partial collapse and exposure of the ice core; (b) seasonal ice banding in the ice core

7.1   Diagram illustrating how terrain disturbance of an ice-rich tundra soil can lead to thermokarst subsidence (source: Mackay, 1970)

7.2   Diagram illustrating how geomorphic, vegetational and climatic changes may lead to permafrost degradation (modified from French, 1987c)

7.3   The sequence of development of alas thermokarst relief in central Yakutia, according to P. A. Soloviev (1973b)

7.4   A small human-induced alas depression which has developed in historic time near Maya village, central Yakutia. Deforestation was probably the cause of thermokarst

7.5   Map showing extent of alas thermokarst terrain in the vicinity of the Abalakh settlement, central Yakutia, FSU (from Soloviev, 1973a)

7.6   Typical relief and vegetation of low- and high-centred ice-wedge polygons

7.7   Oblique air view of degradation polygons or 'graveyard mounds' occurring on sloping terrain, eastern Banks Island, Canada

7.8   Oblique air view from 50 m elevation of terrain undergoing rapid thermal melting and erosion operating preferentially along ice wedges, eastern Banks Island, Canada

7.9   A retrogressive thaw slump, eastern Banks Island, Canada

7.10   Vertical air photo of part of the Sachs River lowlands showing thaw lake terrain

7.11   A thermo-erosional niche developed in sand and gravel, Ballast Brook, northwest Banks Island, Canada

7.12   Examples of lateral and thermal river-bank erosion in Siberia (modified from Czudek and Demek, 1970)

8.1   Ground thermal regimes at four closely spaced sites near Thompson, Manitoba, 1968–71 (data from Brown and Williams, 1972)

8.2   Seasonal changes in the active layer (source: ACGR, 1988)

8.3   Seasonal changes in moisture content in the active layer, as reported from China, Siberia and North America (from Mackay, 1983)

8.4   Relationship between ground temperature envelopes and curves of unfrozen water content versus temperature of frozen soil: (a) region of positive ground temperature gradient: (b) region of negative ground temperature gradient (from Cheng, 1983)

8.5   Diagram showing the relative positions of the frozen fringe, the freezing front and the cryofront during freezing of a fine-grained, frost-susceptible soil (source: ACGR, 1988)

8.6   Bedrock heave in Palaeozoic greywacke, near Churchill, Manitoba

8.7   Examples of bedrock heave (from Dyke, 1984)

8.8   Stone tilting: (a) uptilted siltstone and sandstone slabs of Weatherall Formation (late Devonian age) near Rea Point, eastern Melville Island; (b) diagrammatic illustration of the mechanism by which a stone becomes tilted through frost heaving of the ground (from Pissart, 1970)

8.9   Section through extrusion features developed after repeated freezing and thawing in a tray of layered sediments: (a) crushed quartz was the middle layer; (b) silt was the middle layer (from Corte, 1971)

8.10   Examples of rapid mass movements occurring in summer and confined to the active layer, western Canadian Arctic: (a) detachment failure occurring on very low-angled slope, eastern Melville Island, NWT; (b) skin flows and multiple mudflows, Masik Valley, southern Banks Island, NWT

8.11   Diagram illustrating the change from circles to stripes as slope angle increases, according to J. Büdel (1960)

8.12   Examples of patterned ground: (a) non-sorted circle surrounded by tussock rim, eastern Banks Island, NWT; (b) sorted circles, Resolute Bay, NWT, site of experimental studies by A.L. Washburn (see Washburn, 1989)

8.13   Examples of stripes: (a) non-sorted, central Banks Island; (b) sorted, eastern Prince Patrick Island, NWT, Canada

8.14   The formation of non-sorted circles (mud/earth hummocks) in the Mackenzie Valley, Canada: (a) mud hummock in the boreal forest (*Picea mariana*) near Inuvik, NWT; (b) section through earth hummock showing cryoturbated organic material in centre, Hume River region, near Fort Good Hope, NWT (photo courtesy of S. C. Zoltai); (c) equilibrium model of hummock growth (from Mackay, 1980b)

8.15   Non-sorted circles, western Spitsbergen: (a) surface relief; (b) inferred soil circulation patterns according to Hallett *et al.* (1988)

8.16   Formation of mudboils: (a) mudboils formed on lower slopes near Rea Point, in silty sandy sediment, eastern Melville Island, NWT; (b) schematic evolution of a mudboil with rupture of a surface carapace according to Egginton (1986)

9.1   Nature of frost creep and solifluction movement: (a) conventional frost-heave diagram; (b) typical movement profile associated with one-sided freezing; (c) typical movement profile associated with two-sided freezing; (d) peg profile resulting from frost creep (one-sided freezing), Tarfala, northern Sweden, 1982–90. Photo courtesy of A. Jahn

9.2   Gelifluction movement, Garry Island, NWT (data from Mackay, 1980). (a) Vertical velocity profile, illustrating plug-like flow. (b) Site 2 slope profile and mean annual movement (1965–76). (c) ^{14}C dates for organic material along the bottom of late summer active layer at site 2

9.3   Typical plasticity values for solifluction sediments (from Harris, 1987)

9.4   Typical fabric diagram of gelifluction (colluvium) deposit on the gentle slope of an asymmetrical valley, Beaufort Plain, northwest Banks Island, Canada (from French, 1971b)

9.5   Solifluction sheet, northwest Banks Island, NWT, Canada

9.6   Typical pattern of snow ablation and associated runoff and active layer conditions near Resolute, high Arctic, Canada (from Woo and Steer, 1983)

9.7   Snowbank runoff plot and portable weir with water level recorder used to monitor surface wash, Thomsen River area, north central Banks Island, Canada

9.8   Different mechanisms of active layer failures (from Lewkowicz, 1990)

9.9   (a) Debris flow tracks on talus slopes, Sleepy Mountain, northern interior Yukon, Canada. (b) Debris flows, Longyeardalen, Spitsbergen

9.10   Failures of frozen slopes: (a) schematic diagram illustrating permafrost conditions on Mackenzie River banks, NWT; (b) typical method of slope failure; example of Mountain River site (from McRoberts and Morgenstern, 1974)

10.1   Typical slope forms found in present-day periglacial regions

10.2   Theoretical development of slopes proposed for the McMurdo dry valleys, Antarctica (from Selby, 1974)

10.3   Examples of convexo-concavo debris-mantled slopes: (a) smooth convexo-concavo debris-mantled slope with bedrock outcrop (summit tor), Prince Patrick Island, NWT; (b) smooth, predominantly convex debris-manted slopes, Ogilvie Mountains, northern Yukon, Canada

10.4   Examples of hillslope tors associated with debris-mantled slopes: (a) hillslope tor developed in Upper Jurassic-age sandstone, surrounded by frost shattered angular debris, Prince Patrick Island, NWT; (b) hillslope tor in quartzite, unglaciated Klondike Plateau, Yukon Territory

10.5   Topographic profile of a pediment in the Barn Mountains, unglaciated northern Yukon (from French and Harry, 1992)

10.6   Schematic diagram illustrating possible relationship between Pleistocene climatic fluctuations and enhanced pediment activity in the Barn Mountains (from French and Harry, 1992)

10.7   Bedrock (i.e. cryoplanation) terrace at a high elevation in the Buckland Hills, Yukon Territory on argillite and chert of the Neruokpik Formation (Precambrian)

10.8   Stages in the development of cryoplanation terraces in resistant rock, according to J. Demek (1969b)

10.9   Schematic illustration of the cycle of periglacial landscape modification suggested by Peltier (1950)

10.10   The evolution of a free face and talus slope under conditions of basal removal from a fixed point (from Carson and Kirkby, 1972)

11.1   The Mackenzie River, northern Canada: (a) extent of drainage, with major tributaries; (b) daily discharge, 1986, above Arctic Red River, and, of Camsell, Liard, and Hay River tributaries

11.2   Cross-section through a typical ice jam on a large northern river in Canada: (a) longitudinal; (b) channel cross-section (source: Gerard, 1990)

11.3   River freeze-up processes: (a) growth of ice cover at freeze-up and associated water level changes (from Gerard, 1990); (b) formation of river icings (*naledi*) in shallow sections of multiple-channel systems

11.4   Hydrographs representing typical streamflow regimes in periglacial areas (from Woo, 1986, 1990b)

11.5   (a) A small stream in eastern Banks Island in late June; towards the end of sprin snowmelt (b) the same stream in mid August

11.6   Daily water balance for McMaster River basin, Cornwallis Island, NWT, during the summer of 1978 and the annual water balance for 1975–78 (data from Woo, 1990)

11.7   Oblique air view from 150 m elevation of small box-shaped valley with braided stream incised within fluviatile terrace, eastern Prince Patrick Island, Canada

11.8   The Ballast Brook, northwest Banks Island, Canada; an example of a large braided channel with periglacial valley sandur

11.9   Asymmetrical valleys on the Beaufort Plain, northwest Banks Island, Canada

12.1   Examples of wind erosion and deposition: (a) niveo-aeolian deposits on melting snowbank, central Banks Island, Canada; (b) blow-out adjacent to Qinghai-Xizang Highway, China

12.2   Typical grain size distribution for loess (a) and cover sand (b)

12.3   Recurrence interval of annual maximum onshore storm events during open water conditions at Sachs Harbour, 1971–80 (from Harry *et al.*, 1983)

12.4   Sequential development of the Sachs Harbour spit, 1950–79 (from Clark *et al.*, 1984; Harry *et al.*, 1983)

12.5   Sea ice pushed onshore in July 1984 at Thesiger Bay, southern Banks Island, NWT, Canada

12.6   Cliff erosion in unconsolidated ice-rich sediments: (a) thermo-erosional niche formed at base of cliffs, 5.0 m deep, Sachs Harbour, Banks Island, Canada; (b) cliff failure by block detachment along ice wedge oriented parallel to the cliffline, Maitland Bluffs, Mackenzie Delta region, NWT, Canada

13.1   Climatic variations in the last 150 000 years expressed as changing δ^{18}O/^{16}O ratios, and July temperatures, together with generalized late Quaternary stratigraphies for Europe, North America and the UK (modified from West, 1977, figure 10.10; Lowe and Walker, 1984; Ballantyne and Harris, 1994, Table 2.1; Vandenberghe and Pissart 1993, Figure 6.5)

13.2   Generalized Quaternary climatic curve, the palaeo-magnetic time scale, the East Anglian stratigraphic record, and the occurrence of various periglacial phenomena in south and east England (data from West, 1977)

13.3   Stratigraphic positions of Weichselian periglacial structures in central Europe (from Karte, 1987)

13.4   Climatic reconstruction and regionalization of Europe during the Weichselian stage, according to J. Büdel (1951; 1953)

13.5   Map of western and central Europe showing the southern permafrost limits as proposed by Poser (1948), Kaiser (1960), Maarleveld (1976) and Velichko (1982), according to the distribution of periglacial phenomena dated from the last cold maximum

13.6   Tentative reconstruction of the maximum extent of late Wisconsinan periglacial conditions in the United States south of the ice sheet limits (based upon Péwé, 1983b; Clark and Ciolkosz, 1988; Braun, 1989; Washburn, 1979)

13.7   Simplified relation between growth and decay of permafrost and (a) cold/warm-based ice-sheets and (b) climatic fluctuations (from Romanovskii, 1993; Dostovalov and Kudryavtsev, 1967)

13.8.   Changes in permafrost distribution since the Pleistocene in northern China (from Qui and Cheng, 1995)

13.9   Quaternary sea-level changes

14.1   Cave drawings in the Dordogne region, southern France: (a) woolly mammoth, Cave of Les Combarelles; (b) woolly rhinoceros, Cave of Font de Gaume (from Sutcliffe, 1985)

14.2   Distribution of frozen Pleistocene mammalian carcasses and parts of carcasses in Siberia, Alaska and Canada (from Sutcliffe, 1985)

14.3   Frost-weathered bedrock features, southwest England: (a) hillslope tor, 10 m high, near Lynton, N. Devon; (b) frost-riven scarp, 4–5 m high, on Cox Tor, Dartmoor, N. Devon, developed in metadolorite. Both photographs courtesy of D. N. Mottershead

14.4   *Grèzes litées* near Sonneville, Charente region, southwest France

14.5   Pleistocene frost-disturbed structures. (a) Cryoturbated surface layer in Chalk, Pays de Caux, northern France, resulting from intense frost action within the seasonally frozen layer. (b) 'Bird-foot' involutions, northern Belgium, related to loading and density differences in water-saturated sediments

14.6   The most frequent deformation structures in the Pleistocene seasonally frozen or active layers (according to L. Eissmann, 1994)

14.7   Oblique air photograph showing Weichselian ice-wedge polygons as revealed by differential crop markings. Photo courtesy of H. Svensson

14.8   Examples of different types of Pleistocene frost fissures, Lódź region,
        central Poland: (a) wedge of secondary infilling (i.e. old ice wedge);
        (b) wedge of primary infilling (i.e. old sand wedge); (c) composite wedge
        (from Gozdzik, 1973; Harry and Gozdzik, 1988)

14.9   Pseudomorph and U-shaped involution above a partially thawed ice
        wedge, North Head, Richards Island, Pleistocene Mackenzie Delta,
        NWT, Canada (from Murton and French, 1993b)

14.10   Ice-wedge pseudomorph, or wedge of secondary infilling, Belchatow,
        Poland

14.11   Composite wedge developed beneath fossil soil within loess, Miechow
        Plateau, southern Poland

14.12   Distribution of Pleistocene frost fissures and other evidence of
        permafrost at the maximum of the last glaciation in Central Europe
        (from Karte, 1987)

14.13   Distribution and age of ice wedge casts in North America (exclusive of
        Alaska) in relation to position of Wisconsinan glacial ice fronts (source:
        Péwé, 1973, and others)

14.14   Oblique air view of part of Walton Common, Norfolk, England, showing
        ramparts and enclosed depressions associated with the formation of frost
        mounds, probably seasonal in nature. Photo by permission of University
        of Cambridge

14.15   Plan of frost mound ramparts in the Brackvenn, Hautes Fagnes region,
        Belgium, as identified by A. Pissart (1965)

14.16   Types of non-diastrophic structures associated with Pleistocene
        permafrost in central England (after Hollingworth et al., 1944; Dury, 1959)

14.17   Non-diastrophic structures in unconsolidated sediments (according to
        L. Eissmann, 1994, following observations in central Germany)

15.1   Rounded mat grain caused by wind action from Pleistocene dunes,
        Belchatow, Poland. Photo courtesy of J. Gozdzik

15.2   The distribution and frequency of occurrence of wind-modified sand
        grains in Europe (from Cailleux, 1942)

15.3   Global distribution of major loess occurrences (after Pye, 1984)

15.4   Distribution of Pleistocene cold-climate dune fields and sand sheets
        in Europe and North America, together with glacial limits (from
        Koster, 1988)

15.5   The pradolinas (Urstromtaler) of the North European Plain together
        with ice-marginal limits (from Jahn, 1976)

15.6   The Pleistocene periglacial fluvial cycle: (a) late Weichselian incision and
        infilling sequence, Maastricht, southern Netherlands; (b) the generalized
        fluvial cycle during a glacial (cold) period (from Vandenberghe, 1993)

15.7   Extent of Chalk outcrops and Chalky Drift materials in southern
        England and the maximum extent of the last glaciation. Also shown are
        locations of various periglacial phenomena reported in the literature
        (source: Rose et al., 1985a)

15.8 The sarsen 'rock stream' in the Valley of Stones, near Blackdown, Dorset, southern England

15.9 Possible development of Clatford Bottom, Wiltshire, according to Small *et al.* (1970)

15.10 Map showing the limits of the last glaciation and the periglacial zone of central Poland

15.11 Periglacial dells, northern edge of the Lódź Plateau near Swardzew, central Poland

15.12 Pleistocene periglacial slope evolution at Gora Sw Malgorzata, central Poland (from Dylik, 1963, 1969a)

15.13 Pleistocene periglacial slope evolution at Walewice, central Poland (from Dylik, 1969b)

16.1 Human-induced thermokarst in borrow pits adjacent to the Sachs Harbour airstrip, Banks Island, Canada (see French, 1975a)

16.2 Terrain disturbance associated with vehicle movement over ice-rich tundra: (a) old vehicle track, probably created in late 1940s or early 1950s in area of old United States Navy Petroleum Reserve-4 (NPR-4), Alaska North Slope; (b) gully erosion along an old vehicle track made in the summer of 1970 near the site of Drake Point blow-out, Sabine Peninsula, Melville Island

16.3 Terrain disturbances adjacent to a staging area in the Bovanyanka gas fields, Yamal Peninsula, western Siberia

16.4 Diagram illustrating the effects of a gravel fill upon the thermal regime and thickness of the active layer: (a) too little fill; (b) too much fill; (c) effects of cases (a) and (b) upon the thermal regime (source: Ferrians *et al.*, 1969).

16.5 At Inuvik, NWT, buildings are placed upon wooden piles. Services such as water and sewage are effected by a utilidor system which links each building to the central plant

16.6 Dawson City, Yukon. (a) An abandoned building illustrating severe settlement due to permafrost degradation. (b) In May 1980, installation of new municipal services was by means of trenches excavated to a minimum depth of 2.0 m and backfilled with coarse gravel

16.7 Modern construction techniques, Yakutsk, Siberia

16.8 Ross River school, Yukon, Canada: (a) design of insulated building using heat pump chilled foundation; (b) calculated temperatures; (c) measured temperatures (from Baker and Goodrich, 1990)

16.9 The Eagle River bridge, Dempster Highway, Yukon, is a single-span structure with minimal pile support in the river

16.10 Plan and profile at Eagle River bridge, Northern Yukon, with stratigraphic and permafrost information determined by drilling during the 1976–77 winter (from Johnston, 1980)

16.11 The Trans-Alaska Pipeline near Fairbanks, Alaska. Note the elevation of the pipe, the cooling devices in the VSMs and the gravel access pad

16.12   Conceptual illustration of the freezing and thawing effects of a pipeline crossing from unfrozen to frozen terrain, or vice versa, in the discontinuous permafrost zone in Canada (from Nixon, 1990)

16.13   View of the frost heave test facility owned and operated by Northwest Alaskan Pipeline Company, at Fairbanks, Alaska

17.1   Global surface air temperatures (1900–88) plotted against 1950–79 average (from Slaymaker and French, 1993)

17.2   Regional variability of climate, Mackenzie Valley, NWT: (a) winter mean temperature, Norman Wells, NWT (1944–87) and five-year running means; (b) time series of temperature for Inuvik, NWT and of precipitation for Yellowknife, NWT over 1988 summer (from Slaymaker and French, 1993)

17.3   Equilibrium ground temperature profiles showing the long-term effect of a climatic warming of 4 °C in (a) continuous permafrost zone; (b) discontinuous permafrost zone

17.4   Predicted changes in permafrost in Canada as the result of a surface temperature increase of 4 °C (source: Atmospheric Environment Service, Canada)

17.5   Predicted changes in permafrost distribution in Siberia as the result of a surface temperature increase of 2 °C (source: Anisimov, 1989; quoted in Street and Melnikov, 1990)

17.6   Predicted changes to the boreal forest following global climate warming. (a) Western Canada, based on a mean annual growing degree days (above 5 °C) (from Wheaton and Singh, 1988). (b) Sweden, based upon a 3 °C mean annual temperature increase (from Boer et al., 1990)

List of Tables

2.1 Selected climate data for (a) western Canadian Arctic and (b) stations closest to the Barn Mountains, Interior Yukon

3.1 Climatic data for selected localities in different types of periglacial environments

3.2 Relative extent of terrestrial areas of seasonal snow cover, ice and permafrost

3.3 Simulated climate change in the Fennoscandian region due to a doubling of the atmospheric CO_2 content, according to a scenario derived from the GISS model

4.1 Some typical freeze–thaw cycles, variously defined, as recorded in different periglacial environments

4.2 Some Russian data concerning rates of bedrock weathering by frost action: (a) average thickness of disintegration layer for one freeze–thaw cycle in various rocks of different water saturation; (b) data on fissuring of feldspar sandstones in opencast mine, Taimyr, Siberia

4.3 A comparison of the volume expansion and segregation ice models of frost weathering

4.4 Experimental data which demonstrate the instability of quartz particles under cryogenic weathering

4.5 Chemical changes observed following repeated freezing and thawing of clay minerals

4.6 Reports of honeycomb weathering in Antarctica

4.7 Some typical rates of limestone solution under periglacial and non-periglacial conditions

5.1 Permafrost depths and mean annual air temperatures at selected localities in the northern hemisphere

5.2 Global distribution of permafrost according to I. Ya. Baranov (1959) and Shi (1988)

5.3   Some typical values of thermal conductivity of various materials

5.4   Ground temperature conditions at four adjacent sites near Churchill, Manitoba (lat. 59°N)

5.5   Various types of taliks occurring in permafrost regions

6.1   Cryofacies types applicable to ice-rich sediments in the Pleistocene Mackenzie Delta

6.2   Isotopic and geochemical composition of water (ice) at two drained lake sites in the Mackenzie Delta region, Canada

6.3   Ground ice volumes in upper 5 m of permafrost in selected areas, western Canadian Arctic

7.1   Active layer thickness under different terrain conditions: (a) depth of the active layer in ice-wedge polygon terrain in the Yana-Indigirka lowlands of northern Siberia, illustrating thermal effects of standing water bodies; (b) increase in active layer depth, thickness of permafrost thawed and ground subsidence at the site of the 1968 forest fire at Inuvik, NWT, Canada

8.1   Typical values of soil diffusivity

8.2   Some typical frost heave values recorded in a number of different localities

8.3   Values of upfreezing of wooden stakes and stones inserted to various depths

8.4   A genetic classification of patterned ground

9.1   Slope movement data for hummocks at two sites, Garry Island, NWT, Canada

9.2   Some recorded rates of solifluction movement

9.3   Summary data on three active layer failures, Fosheim Peninsula, Ellesmere Island, NWT, Canada

9.4   Ranked list of major slope processes in Kärkevagge, Lappland, 1952–60

9.5   Cases of alpine debris slides and flows in Scandinavia and Spitsbergen and estimated indices of their denudation impact

9.6   Tentative rates of denudation due to avalanche activity in glacial cirques from Spitsbergen

9.7   Some rates of cliff recession under periglacial and non-periglacial conditions

9.8   Permafrost creep data from a number of localities

9.9   Summary data of reported failures in thawing soils

11.1   Mean freeze-up and breakup dates, Mackenzie River, NWT, 1946–55

11.2   Ice-jam damage events on Yukon and Mackenzie Rivers, Canada, 1960–85

11.3   Mean annual discharge ($\bar{Q}$) and standard deviation of flow (S) of selected rivers in northern Canada

11.4   Sediment movement in some Baffin Island streams

11.5   Some selected values of total sediment yield from periglacial catchments

11.6   Typical volumes of suspended and solute sediment transport in periglacial regions

11.7   Dissolved organic carbon transport for periglacial and non-periglacial rivers

11.8   Proportional distribution of discharge and sediment for the highest flow events in nival and proglacial streams, Baffin Island, Canada

11.9   Some characteristics of valley asymmetry in northern regions

12.1   Major cold-climate dune fields in Arctic Canada, Alaska and northern Scandinavia

12.2   Some roundness values for beach materials in various periglacial and non-periglacial regions

13.1   Generalized sequence of Late Glacial and Postglacial (Flandrian/ Holocene) vegetational successions in the British Isles, New England and southwestern Québec

15.1   Some examples of slope asymmetry attributed to Pleistocene periglacial conditions in Europe

16.1   Some examples of the effects of human-induced vegetational change upon permafrost conditions in Siberia, according to P. I. Koloskov (1925)

17.1   Recent trends in ground thermal regimes, Qinghai-Xizang Plateau, China: (a) rise of mean annual ground temperature at Fenghuo Shan, 1962–89; (b) decrease in permafrost thickness along northern boundary of permafrost zone adjacent to the Qinghai-Xizang Highway

17.2   Predicted changes in vegetation zonation for western and northwestern Canada, as implied by GISS and GFDL-based climate change models

Preface to First Edition

This book is intended for use by second- and third-year level geography students in universities or colleges of higher education in the United Kingdom. It is also suitable as a text for an undergraduate course on periglacial geomorpology at the honours level in Canada and the United States. On a more general level, the book may prove useful to high-school teachers and other individuals interested or specializing in the physical geography of cold regions. I have assumed, however, that the reader will already possess some understanding of the physical environment, such as might be provided by a first-year physical geography or elementary geomorphology course.

In writing this book I had two aims in mind. The first was to give a realistic appraisal of the nature of geomorphic processes and landforms in high-latitude periglacial environments. The second was to provide some guide to the recognition and interpretation of periglacial features in the now temperate regions of North America and Europe. The regional emphasis is oriented towards areas of which I have personal field experience, notably the western Canadian Arctic, central Siberia, southern England and central Poland. Thus, the overall focus is more towards lowland, rather than alpine, periglacial conditions. Notwithstanding this comment, I have attempted to give a balanced world picture; important literature pertaining to other areas has been incorporated.

The reasons for writing this book are also twofold. First, the majority of students will never have the opportunity to experience, at first hand, high-latitude periglacial environments. However, since cold conditions prevailed over large areas of middle latitudes at several times during the last one million years, the appreciation of such conditions is essential for a balanced interpretation of these landscapes. Second, the vast northern regions of North America and Siberia are assuming an ever-increasing importance in man's quest for natural resources. Their development will be possible only if we understand the terrain and climatic conditions of these regions. For both these reasons, I hope this book will serve a useful purpose.

I have divided the book into three parts. Part 1 is a general introduction to periglacial conditions in which the extent of the periglacial domain and the variety of periglacial climates are briefly considered. Part 2 presents a systematic treatment of the various geomorphic processes operating in present-day periglacial environments. Wherever possible, I have attempted to show the relationship between process and form and to stress the multivariate nature of many landforms. The sequence of chapters is important since they are planned to be read successively. Part 3 serves only as an introduction to Pleistocene periglacial phenomena. Emphasis in this part is upon forms rather than processes and their interpretation in the light of our understanding of similar phenomena in present-day periglacial environments.

I have not attempted to be comprehensive in my treatment of the literature. By selecting information, I have attempted to give a viewpoint. Inevitably, this viewpoint is biased to reflect my own prejudices and field experience. For example, if I had worked extensively in alpine rather than high-latitude lowland environments, probably I would not have given the same emphasis to permafrost, ground ice and thermokarst as I do. However, I believe a viewpoint is necessary since my experience with students is that they require some guidance in coping with the increasing volume of literature which appears each year.

I would like to acknowledge the help and encouragement given me by a number of individuals and organizations, without which this book would not have been written. The late Professor Jan Dylik of the University of Lódź, Poland, provided me with much inspiration and encouragement in the early stages, as well as friendship and hospitality. He was instrumental in planning the organization of many of the chapters and it is to be regretted that his untimely death in 1973 did not permit him to see the final product. Professors Ron Waters and Stan Gregory of the University of Sheffield, England, were also extremely helpful in encouraging me to write this book and identifying its basic thrust. In Canada, the opportunity to work in the Arctic since 1968 has been made possible by the active support of the Geological Survey of Canada and the Polar Continental Shelf Project. Numerous individuals both in Canada and the United Kingdom have helped in many ways, by discussion, providing material, and reading some of the early draft chapters; they include R. J. E. Brown, M. J. Clark, J. G. Fyles, P. G. Johnson, D. Mottershead, A. Pissart, D. A. St-Onge, R. J. Small and P. Worsley. To all, I extend my thanks.

Last, and most important of all, the unfailing encouragement and support of my wife, Sharon, is acknowledged with deep gratitude and affection.

Hugh M. French
Ottawa, 1976

Preface to Second Edition

When I drafted the first edition of *The periglacial environment* over 20 years ago, I had worked in the cold, non-glacial regions of the world for only 6 years, mostly in the Canadian Arctic. Having previously completed my graduate studies upon the Pleistocene periglacial phenomena found on the Chalklands of southern England, I looked to the polar region of North America as a natural analogue for the cold-climate conditions which had largely fashioned the Chalk landscape. Now, after nearly 20 more years of field work in many of the so-called periglacial regions of the world, I am not sure that a simple analogue exists. Instead, I am impressed by the complexity and diversity of periglacial environments, both today and in the past.

The past 20 years have also seen a dramatic expansion in our understanding of the geomorphic conditions, especially permafrost, which typify these environments. A distinct process-oriented geomorphology, termed *geocryology* or *permafrost science*, has developed in North America and elsewhere, building largely but not exclusively upon Russian concepts and principles. There has also been an integration into periglacial geomorphology of modern instrumentation and technology. At the same time, rapid advances in Quaternary dating techniques mean that our understanding of Pleistocene events is now more precise.

Underlying much of our interest in the cold non-glacial regions of the world is an appreciation of the natural resources known to occur in such regions. For example, the oil and gas resources of the Western Siberian Plain, some of the largest in the world, necessitate an understanding of the tundra and taiga environment. Modern environmental protection attitudes dictate that the exploitation of these resources is undertaken in a manner which minimizes harmful impacts upon the terrain, flora, fauna and indigenous peoples of these regions. The same is true in North America, and in many of the alpine periglacial regions of the world. Finally, the significance of the cryosphere, of which the periglacial domain is an important component, is now being examined in the context of ongoing and predicted global changes. For various reasons, it is thought that global climate changes will be first apparent and most magnified in the high latitudes. Hence, there is an urgent need for the monitoring of change in the boreal forest, tundra and polar desert environments.

For all these reasons, a second edition of my earlier work is justified. My aim has been to incorporate the results of these new developments while at the same time not altering the overall level, scope and organization of the book. I have tried to maintain the original flavour and style; however, many chapters are new and others have been entirely rewritten. The volume also looks different since I have deliberately tried to incorporate a large number of new or different diagrams and photographs. As with the first edition, my selection of material is deliberately subjective; I have not attempted a comprehensive coverage of the literature, and the book is certainly not meant to be a reference text. Rather, the second edition continues to be my own personalized view of the cold non-glacial environments of the world. There is a heavy emphasis upon those areas with which I have familiarity, such as the North American and Eurasian polar and mid-latitude lowlands. The alpine, high-altitude periglacial environments of middle and low latitude are not neglected but, because there is a relative abundance of accurate up-to-date information available elsewhere, I feel justified in my lack of emphasis in this area. A second omission in the coverage of this book, also apparent in the first edition, is the relative lack of examples from the southern hemisphere, especially the ice-free areas of Antarctica. Here, I plead my partial ignorance. Finally, the extensive periglacial region of the Qinghai-Xizang (Tibet) Plateau has so far not been adequately described in the Western literature, yet it is of the same size as the North American or Eurasian periglacial regions. Thus, I have attempted to incorporate, wherever appropriate, data from this unusual environment.

Throughout my academic career I have taught in the Departments of Geography and Geology at the University of Ottawa. This has been a fruitful and productive milieu for pursuing my periglacial interests. I have been fortunate in supervising, over the years, a number of talented and energetic graduate students and employing undergraduate field assistants, all without whom my visits to the Arctic would have been much lonelier and certainly less productive. In this regard, special mention and warm appreciation must be given to the stimulus provided by Paul Egginton, Toni Lewkowicz, David Harry, Wayne Pollard, Dana Naldrett, Lorne Bennett, Julian Murton and Baolai Wang. They have contributed much to my understanding of the geomorphology and Quaternary geology of the cold non-glacial regions of the world. At the same time numerous colleagues, both in Canada and elsewhere, have encouraged me, or collaborated with me; these include Mike Clark, Jan Gozdzik, Cheng Guodong, Charlie Harris, Stuart Harris, Alan Heginbottom, Alfred Jahn, Johannes Karte, Vyacheslav Konishchev, Eduard Koster, J. Ross Mackay, Derek Mottershead, Troy Péwé, Albert Pissart, Anders Rapp, Nikolai Romanovskii, Mike Smith and Link Washburn. Several colleagues, sadly no longer alive, have also influenced me: the late Roger J. E. Brown was instrumental in encouraging me to become more involved in the geotechnical aspects of permafrost, and in the administration of permafrost science and engineering in Canada; the late Brian Rust, my longtime friend and colleague in Geology at the University of Ottawa, always provided critical support and fostered in me an appreciation of Pleistocene and Recent sedimentation. Finally, the Natural Sciences and Engineering Research Council (NSERC) and the Polar Continental Shelf Project (PCSP) have generously provided operating grants and Arctic logistics respectively over a 25-year period, and I have received close support and cooperation from many officers of the Geological Survey of Canada and from the Department of Indian and Northern Affairs, both agencies located in Ottawa.

My secretary, Pierrette Gouin, has provided outstanding service in the preparation of the text.

To all mentioned above, I owe a debt of gratitude since this second edition is as much their work as it is mine.

Hugh M. French
Ottawa, 1996

Acknowledgements

We are grateful to the following for permission to reproduce copyright material:

Fig. 1.1 *Bochumer Geographische Arbeiten*, **35**, p149, Abb.20. Germany (Karte, 1979); Figs 1.2b and 5.9c *Geografiska Annaler*, **68**A, p131–140 (King, 1986); Fig. 1.3 courtesy of T.L. Péwé and The International Permafrost Association; Fig. 2.1 from *Periglacial processes and landforms in Britain and Ireland*, Boardman (ed.) Cambridge University Press (Thorn & Loewenherz, 1987), partially derived from *AMJ Sci.*, **277**, p178–91 (Graf, 1977); Fig. 2.3 © A 17381–137 (August 29, 1961), Fig. 2.4 © A 24502–160 (July 13, 1976) and Fig. 7.10 © A 15980–25 (July 14, 1958), aerial photographs from Her Majesty the Queen in Right of Canada, reproduced from the collection of the National Air Photo Library with permission of National Resources Canada; Fig. 3.1 *Permafrost and periglacial processes*, **5**, p87–100, reprinted with kind permission of John Wiley and Sons Ltd (Wang & French, 1994); Figs 4.1 and 4.2 from *The frozen earth: fundamentals...* Cambridge University Press (Williams & Smith, 1989); Figs 4.4 and 5.8 *Quaternary Science Reviews*, **14**, p255–274, reprinted with kind permission of Elsevier Science Ltd, The Boulevard, Langford Lane, Kidlington, Oxford 0X5 19B (Wang & French, 1995); Figs 4.10a, 17.1 and 17.2, *Canada's Cold Environment*, McGill Queen's University Press (Slaymaker & French, eds. 1993); Fig. 4.10b *Permafrost and periglacial processes*, **1**, p129–144, reprinted with kind permission of John Wiley and Sons Ltd (Lauriol & Grey, 1990); Figs 5.1, 5.2a, 5.3, 5.4 National Research Council of Canada (ACGR, 1988); Fig. 5.5 *Arctic and Alpine Research* **15**, No. 2, p152, reproduced by permission of the Regents of the University of Colorado (Péwé, 1983); Figs 5.9a and 5.9b *Permafrost and periglacial processes*. **3**, p83–91, reprinted with kind permission of John Wiley and Sons Ltd (Cheng & Dramis, 1992); Fig. 5.12 French (ed.) National Research Council of Canada (Seppälä, 1982); Figure 5.14, *Advances in periglacial geomorphology*, Clark (ed.) reprinted with kind permission of John Wiley and Sons Ltd (Barsch, 1988); Fig. 5.17 *Canadian Journal of Earth Sciences*, **15**, 263–276, National Research Council of Canada (van Everdingen, 1978); Figs 6.2 and 6.3 *Canadian Journal of Earth Sciences*, **31**, p737–747, National Research Council of Canada (Murton & French, 1994); Fig. 6.6 *Annals of the Association of*

American Geographers, **64**, p4, Blackwell Publishers, Cambridge, MA 02142 (Mackay, 1972); Fig. 6.7 *Canadian Geotechnical Journal*, **17**, p509–516, National Research Council of Canada (Pollard & French, 1980); Fig. 6.11 *The Canadian Geographer*, **33**, p367, Canadian Association of Geographers (Mackay, 1989), Fig. 6.20, **30**, p361–365 (Mackay, 1986), Fig. 8.7, **30**, p358–366 (Dyke, 1986) and Fig. 8.16b, **30**, p358–366 (Egginton, 1986); Fig. 6.16 *Field and Theory: Lectures in Geocryology*, reprinted with permission of University of British Columbia Press, all rights reserved (M. Church & O. Slaymaker eds.) (Romanovskii, 1985); Fig. 6.19 *Geological Survey of Canada*, 89–1G, 5–11, Energy, Mines and Resources Canada (Mackay, 1989); Fig. 6.23 *Géographie Physique et Quaternaire*, **33**, No. 1, p3–61, Université de Montréal Press (Mackay, 1979); Fig. 7.2 Gregory & Walling (eds.) reproduced with kind permission of John Wiley and Sons Ltd (French, 1987c); Figs 8.2 and 8.5 National Research Council Canada (ACGR, 1988); Figs 8.3 and 8.4 Clark (ed), John Wiley and Sons Ltd (French, 1988); Fig. 8.14c *Canadian Journal of Earth Sciences*, **17**, p996–1006, National Research Council of Canada (Mackay, 1980); Fig. 9.2 *Canadian Journal of Earth Sciences*, **18**, p1666–1680, National Research Council of Canada (Mackay, 1981); Fig. 9.3 Anderson and Richards (eds.), reproduced with kind permission of John Wiley and Sons Ltd (Harris, 1987); Fig. 9.8 from University of Laval in *Nordicana*, **54**, p112, Lewkowicz, Proceedings of the Fifth Canadian Permafrost Conference, 1990; Fig. 9.10 *Canadian Geotechnical Journal*, **11**, p447–469, National Research Council of Canada (McRoberts & Morgenstern, 1974); Fig. 10.2 *New Zealand Geographer*, **30**, p18–34, Geographical Society of New Zealand (Selby, 1974); Figs 10.5 and 10.6 *Geografiska Annaler*, **74**A, p145–157 (French & Harry, 1992); Figs 11.2, 11.3a Northern hydrology, Canadian perspectives, *Science Report* **1**, Prowse & Ommanney (eds.), National Hydrology Research Institute (Gerard, 1990) and Fig. 11.6 (Woo, 1990); Figs 12.3 and 12.4b *Zeitschrift für Geomorphologie*, Supplementband **47**, p1–26, courtesy of E. Schweizerbart'sche Verlagsbuch-handlung, Stuttgart, Germany (Harry, French & Clark, 1983); Fig. 13.3 Boardman (ed.), Cambridge University Press (Karte, 1987); Fig. 13.8 *Permafrost and periglacial processes*, **6**, p3–14, reprinted with kind permission of John Wiley and Sons Ltd (Qin & Cheng, 1995); Figs 14.1 and 14.2 *On the rack of Ice Age mammals* (A.J. Sutcliffe, 1995, courtesy of the Natural History Museum, UK; Figs 14.6 and 14.17 *Altenburger Naturwissanschaftliche Forschungen,* **7**, courtesy of Mauritianum Altenburg, Leipzig (Eissmann & Litt eds. 1994), Abb 33, 34; Fig. 14.14 for photographs AWD 68 and ZC 92 from Cambridge University Collection of Air photographs, copyright reserved; Fig. 14.9 *Journal of Quaternary Science* **8**, p185–196, reprinted with kind permission of John Wiley and Sons Ltd (Murton & French, 1993); Fig. 14.12 Boardman (ed), Cambridge University Press (Karte, 1987); Fig. 15.4 *Journal of Quaternary Science*, **3**, p69–84, reprinted with kind permission of John Wiley and Sons Ltd (Koster, 1988); Fig. 15.6 *Zeitschrift für Geomorphologie*, Supplementband **88**, p17–28, courtesy of E. Schweizerbart'sche Verlagsbuch-handlung, Stuttgart, Germany (Vandenberghe, 1993) and **47**, p1–26 (Harry, French & Clark); Fig. 16.10 National Research Council of Canada (Johnston, 1980).

I am also indebted to the following for permission to reproduce photographs:

Professor V.N. Konishchev, Moscow State University for Figs 4.8a and 4.8b; Dr. S.C. Zoltai, Canadian Forestry Service, Natural Resources Canada for Fig. 8.14c; Professor A. Jahn for Fig. 9.1; Dr. D. Mottershead for Figs 14.3a and 14.3b; Professor H. Svensson, University of Lund, for Fig. 14.7; Dr. J. Gozdzik, University of Lódź, Poland for Fig. 15.1.

Whilst every effort has been made to trace the owners of copyright material, in a few cases this has proved impossible and we take this opportunity to offer our apologies to any copyright holders whose rights we may have unwittingly infringed.

PART 1

The periglacial domain

1 Introduction
2 Periglacial landscapes
3 Periglacial climates

CHAPTER 1

Introduction

This chapter aims to provide a background to the 'periglacial' concept and to the so-called 'periglacial' processes. It concludes with a summary of the growth of periglacial geomorphology, both within the International Geographical Union (IGU) and the International Permafrost Association (IPA).

The two diagnostic criteria for periglacial designation are (a) intense frost action and (b) perennially frozen ground, or permafrost. The spatial extent of the periglacial domain is then outlined. Approximately one-quarter of the Earth's land surface currently experiences periglacial conditions. During the Pleistocene an additional one-fifth was affected to a greater or lesser extent.

1.1 The periglacial concept

The term 'periglacial' was first proposed by a Polish geologist, Walery von Lozinski, to describe frost weathering conditions associated with the production of rock rubbles in the Carpathian Mountains (Lozinski, 1909). Subsequently, at the Xl Geological Congress in Stockholm in 1910 he introduced the concept of a 'periglacial zone' to describe the climatic and geomorphic conditions of areas peripheral to the Pleistocene ice sheets and glaciers (Lozinski, 1912). Theoretically, this zone was a tundra region which extended as far south as the treeline.

For several reasons, Lozinski's initial definition is unnecessarily restricting. First, frost-action phenomena are known to occur at great distances from ice margins and can be unrelated to ice-marginal conditions. For example, parts of central Siberia and the interior of Alaska are commonly regarded as being 'periglacial' in nature. They owe their distinctive nature, however, not to their proximity to ice sheets but rather to factors such as permafrost or low mean annual temperatures. Second, although Lozinski used the term to refer primarily to areas and not to processes, it has increasingly been understood to refer to a complex of geomorphic processes. These include not only the relatively unique frost-action and permafrost-related processes but also a broad range of processes which demand neither a peripheral ice-marginal location nor a cold climate for their operation.

Thus, modern usage of the term 'periglacial' refers to a wide range of cold, non-glacial conditions, regardless of their proximity to a glacier, either in time or space (e.g. Jahn, 1975; French, 1976a; Washburn, 1979). For our purposes, periglacial environments may be defined simply as those in which frost-action and permafrost-related processes dominate. The periglacial domain refers to the global extent of the associated climatic conditions.

The extent of the periglacial zone in the northern hemisphere is illustrated in Fig. 1.1. Based upon the spatial association of certain microforms and their climatic threshold values, several different periglacial zones can be recognized. They occur not only in high latitudes and tundra regions, as defined by Lozinski, but also below the treeline and in high altitude

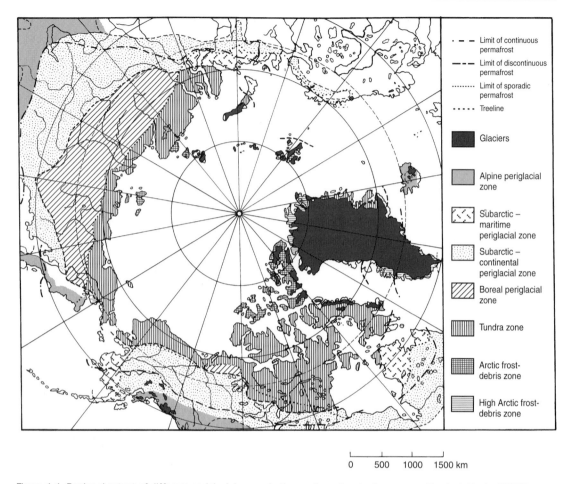

Figure 1.1 Regional extent of different periglacial zones in the northern hemisphere, according to J. Karte (1979).

(alpine) regions of middle latitudes. They include (a) the polar desert and semi-deserts of the high Arctic; (b) the tundra zone; (c) the boreal forest zone; and (d) the subarctic zones of (i) maritime and (ii) continental nature. To these we must add the alpine periglacial zones of mid and low latitudes, the largest of which, by far, is the Tibet Plateau of China. These areas are not included on Fig. 1.1.

There are two diagnostic criteria, one or both of which are common to all periglacial environments. The first is the freezing and thawing of the ground, often in association with water. According to J. Tricart, 'the periglacial morphogenetic milieu is that where the influence of freeze–thaw oscillations is dominant' (Tricart, 1968, p. 830). The second is the presence of perennially frozen ground or permafrost. For example, T. L. Péwé considers all areas currently underlain by permafrost to be the modern periglacial zone; 'permafrost is the common denominator of the periglacial environment, and is practically ubiquitous in the active periglacial zone' (Péwé, 1969, p. 4).

It should be emphasized that there is no perfect spatial correlation between areas of intense frost action and areas underlain by permafrost, although the coincidence of the two is high. There are certain subarctic, maritime and alpine locations which experience frequent freeze–thaw oscillations but lack permafrost. Furthermore, the fact that permafrost underlies extensive areas of the boreal forest in Siberia and North America and is unrelated to present climatic conditions complicates any simple delimitation of periglacial environments. In practice, the relict permafrost of Siberia and North America extends the periglacial domain beyond its normal (i.e. frost action) limits.

Using the diagnostic criteria, an estimate is that approximately 25 per cent of the Earth's land surface currently experiences periglacial conditions. There are all gradations between environments in which frost processes dominate, and where a whole or a major part of the landscape is the result of such processes, and those in which frost action processes are subservient to others. A complicating factor is that certain lithologies are more prone to frost action than others, and hence more susceptible to periglacial landscape modification.

During the cold periods of the Pleistocene, large areas of the now-temperate middle latitudes experienced intense frost action and reduced temperatures because of their proximity to the ice sheets. Permafrost may have formed, only to have degraded during a later climatic amelioration. In all probability, an additional 20–25 per cent of the Earth's land surface experienced periglacial conditions at some time in the past.

Thus, the actual periglacial domain extends over two major vegetation types: (a) the subarctic and northern forests and (b) the Arctic tundra and ice-free polar desert zones. In addition, the periglacial domain includes the various high-altitude or alpine zones which exist in many of the larger mountain ranges of the world. The largest of these is the Tibet Plateau. Figure 1.2 summarizes the various concepts of the periglacial domain.

1.2 Periglacial processes

Ever since Lozinski first defined the periglacial zone, it has been widely accepted that frost action was the most important weathering process in periglacial environments. Since the effectiveness of chemical weathering generally decreases with decreasing temperatures, chemical weathering was assumed to operate at a slow pace in periglacial environments and to play a secondary role. While this is true in most instances, one must not infer that mechanical weathering is greater in periglacial environments than in non-periglacial environments. This has yet to be proven since recent Russian laboratory investigations cast doubt upon some of the traditional weathering concepts when applied to cold regions. Rather, it seems best to regard the prevalence of physical weathering as merely reflecting its dominance over chemical weathering. Alternatively, it may be a unique complex of physico-chemical weathering processes that distinguishes cold regions from temperate and tropical regions.

A second assumption has been that periglacial processes possess a unique and distinctive nature, giving rise to a readily definable periglacial morphogenetic region. This may be the case in certain instances. However, many of the so-called periglacial processes are little different from those operating in other non-glacial regions of the world, and differ only in their frequency and/or intensity.

Processes which are clearly unique to periglacial environments include the formation of permafrost, the development of thermal contraction cracks, the thawing of permafrost (thermokarst), and the formation of wedge and injection ice (Dylik, 1964a, pp. 116–17). Cryogenic weathering is problematic given our limited understanding of this process. Other processes, not necessarily restricted to periglacial regions, are important on account of their high magnitude or frequency. These include ice segregation, seasonal frost action and rapid mass movement. Nearly all frost-action processes operate in conjunction with the freezing of water.

Probably the most fundamental of periglacial processes are those associated with frost heaving and ice segregation. The engineering and geotechnical hazards due to the ground displacements and pressures generated by ice segregation and frost heaving, together with the accumulation of segregated ice in freezing soil, are well known throughout most of North America, Europe and Asia (e.g. Ferrians *et al.*, 1969). The process of ice segregation involves complex interrelationships between the ice, an unfrozen liquid phase, and the bulk pore water. Complex latent heats of phase change as well as variable interfacial energies between phases are involved, and these are not fully understood.

The formation of permafrost is probably the most diagnostic of the periglacial processes and, along with ice segregation, is by far the most important on account of its geotechnical significance. The term 'permafrost' was first introduced into the English literature by S. Muller (1945) as a shortened form of permanently frozen ground. Modern usage in Canada and the United States defines permafrost as 'ground (soil and/or rock) that remains at or below 0 °C for at least two years'. However, permafrost is not necessarily synonymous with 'frozen ground', since earth materials may be below 0 °C in temperature but still be essentially unfrozen on account of

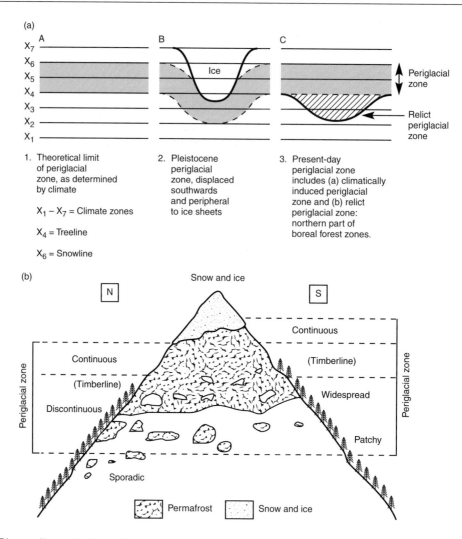

Figure 1.2 Diagram illustrating limits of the periglacial domain: (a) high-latitude domain; (b) alpine domain.

depressed freezing points due to mineralized ground-waters or other causes. Furthermore, significant quantities of unfrozen water can exist in frozen ground. To accommodate these subtle terminological difficulties, recent usage sometimes regards permafrost as being synonymous with perennially cryotic ground (e.g. see ACGR, 1988).

The global extent of permafrost in the northern hemisphere is illustrated in Fig. 1.3. Permafrost of varying sorts underlies between 20 and 25 per cent of the Earth's land surface including 80 per cent of Alaska, 50 per cent of Canada, 50 per cent of the former Soviet Union (FSU) and 20 per cent of the

People's Republic of China. Not surprisingly, it is in these countries that permafrost science (geocryology) and periglacial geomorphology are most closely linked. In general terms, the congruence between the extent of the periglacial domain (Fig. 1.1) and the global extent of permafrost is remarkably high.

The recognition of the previous existence of permafrost is an important tool in Quaternary studies involving palaeo-environmental reconstruction. However, it must be emphasized that deep seasonal frost rather than permafrost may have characterized certain periglacial regions during the Pleistocene and, following the disappearance of the cold-climate

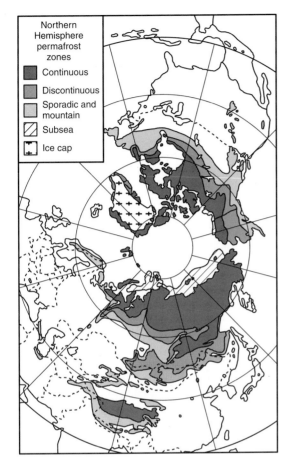

Figure 1.3 Distribution of permanfrost in the northern hemisphere (from Péwé, 1991).

wedging and/or a complex of physico-chemical weathering processes.

In addition, and bearing no order of importance or magnitude, are the following:

3. A complex of frost activity operating within the seasonally frozen layer, such as frost heaving, soil churning, soil creep, stone tilting, upfreezing, mass displacement and particle size sorting.

4. Rapid mass movement; either the relatively slow flow of water-saturated soil (solifluction) aided by slopewash processes, or gravity-controlled rockfalls, slumps or failures, all of which can lead to the active development of slopes.

5. Fluvial regimes, of predominantly snowmelt origin, characterized by marked seasonal discharge patterns and by a high level of suspended and bedload sediments.

6. Strong wind action processes, including nivation or snowpatch effects, which are accentuated by lack of vegetation, and by large amounts of glacially derived and/or frost-comminuted debris.

All these processes are discussed in Part 2. Some are distinct to the periglacial domain, or zonal in nature; others are clearly azonal and operate equally well in areas outside the periglacial domain. Those processes unique to periglacial environments relate to the formation of permafrost. In a second category are those processes that are unique by virtue of their high intensity and efficacy under periglacial conditions. These are the processes of ice segregation, seasonal frost action and frost/cryogenic weathering, and the various forms of mass movement. In a third category are all the other processes which operate in an azonal fashion throughout the world, such as running water, and wind action. While geomorphologically significant within the periglacial domain, this final group of processes is equally, if not more, effective outside it.

conditions, it may be difficult to distinguish between the two. Moreover, permafrost conditions can vary spatially, being either continuous, discontinuous or sporadic in nature. A further complication is that taliks and groundwater flow are an important but often complex part of any permafrost system.

In summary, one can list the various groups of processes which are thought typical of the periglacial environment. Two are of primary importance:

1. The development of perennially cryotic ground with ice segregation, combined with the thermal contraction of the ground under intense cold, the creep of ice-rich permafrost, and the thawing of such ground.

2. The frost weathering of soils and bedrock, including the disintegration of surface rock by frost

1.3 The growth of periglacial geomorphology

Although geologists in Europe and Russia were aware of the existence of cold-climate phenomena and related sediments in the nineteenth century, the growth of periglacial geomorphology dates from the twentieth century. The XI International Geological

Congress field excursion to Svalbard in 1910 allowed scientists to observe and discuss (for many, for the first time) the landforms and processes of cold non-glacial environments. A number of pioneer papers appeared shortly afterwards (e.g. Meinardus, 1912; Högbom, 1914). At this time, Lozinski (1909, 1912) proposed his concept of the 'periglacial zone' and, earlier, Andersson (1906) formulated the first definition of a periglacial climate and a periglacial 'facies'. Other developments in this early growth phase of periglacial geomorphology were the many casual observations upon frozen ground phenomena made in North America consequent upon the Klondike Gold Rush of 1896–8, and the subsequent expansion into Alaska in the early 1900s.

The nature of frozen ground was already well known in Russia by the turn of the century, since early ground temperature observations had been made by A. von Middendorf in 1844 at Shergin's Well, Yakutsk, Siberia. However, the internal political system and then the upheavals following the 1917 revolution led to little dissemination of that information. In northern Alaska, regional geological reconnaissance studies by Leffingwell (1919), Capps (1919) and others provided some of the few integrated views of periglacial landform processes. Earlier, in the nineteenth century, scattered observations in North America were made during Alexander Mackenzie's trips of exploration down the Mackenzie River, by employees of the Hudson's Bay company, and by search parties of the Franklin Expedition (e.g. Richardson, 1839; Lefroy, 1889).

Given the inaccessibility of most northern regions, it was inevitable that periglacial geomorphology subsequently developed in Europe after the Stockholm Congress of 1910 as a branch of climatic geomorphology, emphasizing Pleistocene and Quaternary studies aimed at palaeo-geographic and environmental reconstruction (e.g. Büdel, 1944, 1953; Cailleux, 1942; Dylik, 1953, 1956; Edelman et al., 1936; Poser, 1948). Following the Second World War, this trend continued, although with an increased emphasis upon polar regions (e.g. Büdel, 1963; Tricart and Cailleux, 1967; Jahn, 1975) and global regionalization (e.g. Troll, 1944). In the late 1960s and early 1970s there was a dramatic increase in awareness of the high latitudes of the world, especially in North America and the USSR. This was partly the result of the search for natural resources. Increasing engineering and geotechnical activities prompted an upsurge in the study of cold-climate and permafrost-related processes. Permafrost science, or geocryology, with all its engineering applications, became a priority research discipline in the United States, Canada and the USSR, often with substantial government involvement. As a result, the traditional Quaternary-oriented periglacial studies became overshadowed. Textbooks by Jahn (1975), French (1976a) and Washburn (1979) document the growth of periglacial geomorphology and permafrost studies in this period. In the Soviet Union, the textbook by Kudryavtsev (1978) summarized Soviet perma-frost science; in China, the Desert Research Institute of the Academy of Sciences initiated systematic study of permafrost in western China (e.g. Academica Sinïca, 1975).

Over the past 30 years, a series of international permafrost conferences, first in 1963 at Purdue University, USA, and every five years since 1973, has provided an in-depth record of the scientific advances in our understanding of permafrost. Two recent summaries of periglacial geomorphology are provided by French (1987a), Pissart (1994) and Thorn (1992).

Specifically in the last decade, there have been two developments or trends. First, there has been the emergence of periglacial and permafrost studies in the People's Republic of China, centred upon the Lanzhou Institute of Glaciology and Geocryology, and culminating in the Sixth International Conference on Permafrost being held in Beijing, China, in 1993. Second is the formation of the International Permafrost Association (IPA) in 1983, and the close links between it and the International Geographical Union (IGU) periglacial community. This has led to an integration of traditional climato-genetic periglacial geomorphology with process geomorphology, permafrost science and geocryology.

Further reading

Barsch, D. (1993) Periglacial geomorphology in the 21st century. *Geomorphology*, **7**, 141–163.

French, H.M. (1987) Periglacial geomorphology in North America: current research and future trends. *Progress in Physical Geography*, **11**, 569–587.

Karte, J. and Liedtke, H. (1981) The theoretical and practical definition of the term 'periglacial' in its geographical and geological meaning. *Biuletyn Peryglacjalny*, **28**, 123–135.

Pissart, A. (1990). Advances in periglacial geomorphology. *Zeitschrift für Geomorphologie, Supplementband,* **79**, 119–131.

Thorn, C. (1992) Periglacial geomorphology. What? Where? When? In: J.C. Dixon and A.D. Abrahams (eds), *Periglacial Geomorphology*. Chichester: J. Wiley and Sons Ltd, pp. 1–30.

Discussion topics

1. What constitutes the periglacial domain?
2. What is the relationship between glacial and periglacial?
3. Distinguish between periglacial geomorphology and geocryology.

CHAPTER 2

Periglacial landscapes

In this chapter, the concept of a 'periglacial landscape' is critically examined. It is suggested that many present-day periglacial regions do not necessarily represent typical periglacial landscapes since they have recently emerged from beneath Quaternary glaciation. As such, periglacial processes are merely modifying already-existing glacial landscapes.

The landforms of two cold, never-glaciated regions are then briefly described from the western Arctic of North America. They can be regarded as models to which, over time, periglacial landscapes might evolve.

2.1 Introduction

It is commonly assumed that the periglacial landscape is unique. This is because the most distinct periglacial landforms are usually associated with permafrost. The most widespread are the tundra polygons formed by thermal contraction cracking. Ice-cored hills, or pingos, are a less widespread but equally 'classic' periglacial landform. Other aggradational landforms, such as palsas and peat plateaux, are also associated with permafrost, while ground ice slumps, thaw lakes and irregular depressions result from the melt and erosion of ice-rich permafrost.

In a second category are all the periglacial phenomena resulting from frost wedging and the cryogenic weathering of exposed bedrock. Coarse, angular rock debris, normally attributed to frost wedging or cryogenic weathering, occurs widely over large areas of the polar deserts and semi-deserts. Angular frost-shattered bedrock protuberances (tors) may stand out above the debris-covered surfaces reflecting more resistant bedrock. Superimposed upon this 'typical' landscape is the occurrence of various patterned ground phenomena. Most are thought to be related to the lateral and vertical displacement of soil that accompanies seasonal or diurnal freezing and thawing.

A final assumption relates to the overall flattening of landscape and smoothing of slopes, thought typical of many periglacial regions. This is generally attributed to mass wasting. Cryoplanation is the term sometimes used to describe this landscape modification. Agents of transport include frost creep (the movement that occurs when soil, during a freeze–thaw cycle, expands normally to the surface and settles in a more nearly vertical direction) and solifluction (the slow downslope movement of water-saturated debris).

It is important that we establish the accuracy of these widely held impressions and determine, if possible, the exact nature of 'true' periglacial landscapes.

2.2 Proglacial, paraglacial or periglacial?

Given the fluctuating climates of the Pleistocene, and the fact that many areas of current periglacial conditions have only recently emerged from beneath continental ice sheets, relatively few periglacial regions can be regarded as being in geomorphic equilibrium. Probably the most extensive of such areas exists in central Siberia. In North America, also, parts of interior Alaska and northern Yukon Territory lay beyond the ice limits, and certain of the Canadian Arctic islands may never have been glaciated. In most other areas of current periglacial activity, the legacy of glacial conditions must be considered.

In middle latitudes, the major problem is to identify the degree to which the effects of Pleistocene periglacial conditions have been eliminated. Often, lithology is an important variable controlling the preservation of periglacial landforms, and careful field investigation is required before the nature and magnitude of the periglacial legacy can be established.

It is useful at this point to distinguish between proglacial, paraglacial and periglacial conditions. *Periglacial*, as defined in Chapter 1, refers to the geomorphic processes and landforms of cold non-glaciated landscapes irrespective of their relationship to ice sheets or glaciers. *Paraglacial*, as defined by Church and Ryder (1972), refers to the widespread disequilibrium that occurs as a geomorphic environment moves from one equilibrium condition to another. In the case of the periglacial environment, the transition has usually been either to or from a glacial or temperate environment, the so-called glacial and interglacial periods of the Pleistocene. The

proglacial environment, which refers specifically to ice-marginal conditions, is a periglacial environment in the original sense of Lozinski.

Bearing these concepts in mind, one can illustrate the temporal relationships which might exist between the glacial, periglacial and temperate landscapes (Fig. 2.1). Whether it is correct or not to assume that glacial landscapes are relatively high energy and temperate latitude landscapes are low energy is open to debate. What is more relevant to our discussion is the assumption that the periglacial landscape reflects a constant energy condition, or equilibrium. What is certainly debatable is whether or not such an equilibrium characterizes periglacial regions today. For example, the 'classic' periglacial terrain visited in 1910 by the participants on the International Geological Congress fieldtrips to Svalbard, a heavily glaciated island undergoing isostatic rebound, were examining either a paraglacial or proglacial environment, rather than a periglacial landscape as defined above.

One perspective on this dilemma may be found in the cold regions of the world which have remained unglaciated throughout the majority, if not all, of the Quaternary. Such environments may reasonably be regarded as being in geomorphic near-equilibrium, although the rate of efficacy of the processes involved may not have remained constant, and the possibility still exists that certain landforms may be inherited from earlier, warmer times. In the northern hemisphere, the most extensive areas of such terrain occur

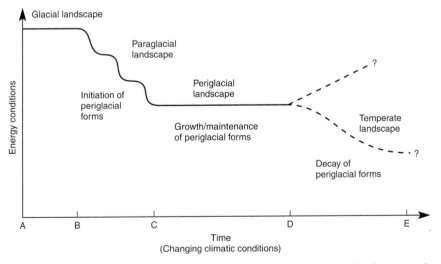

Figure 2.1 Temporal relationship between glacial, periglacial and temperate landscapes under changing energy conditions: (modified from Thorn and Lowenherz, 1987.) A–B, glaciation; B–C, deglaciation; C–D, periglacial equilibrium; D–E, climatic amelioration

Table 2.1   Selected climate data for (a) western Canadian Arctic and (b) stations closest to the Barn Mountains, Interior Yukon

(a) Physiographic Region	Mackenzie Delta	Low Arctic		High Arctic
Location:	Inuvik	Tuktoyaktuk	Sachs Harbour	Resolute Bay
Latitude:	69°N	69° 30'N	72°N	74°N
Ecological region:	Northern subarctic	Low Arctic	Low Arctic	High Arctic
Elevation (m):	60	18	84	64
Mean temperature (°C):				
Annual	−9.6	−10.7	−14.5	−16.4
January	−29.0	−27.2	−29.0	−32.6
July	+13.2	+10.3	+5.0	+4.3
Average frost-free period:	45	55	15	9
Average precipitation:				
Annual (mm)	260	130	102	136
June–August (mm)	93	64	49	69
Snowfall (cm)	174	56	47	78

(b)	Temperature (°C)			Precipitation (mm)				
	Mean Daily Year	Extreme Max.	Extreme Min.	Rain	Snow	Days With	Total	No. of Days with Frost
Shingle Point 55 m a.s.l. 68°57'N 137°13'W	−10.6°C	31.0°C	−52.2°C	110	86	63	196	286
Eagle Plain 116 m a.s.l. 66°26'N 136°45'W	-6.9°C	27.5°C	-48.0°C	277	166	105	441	n/a
Old Crow 253 m a.s.l. 67°34'N 139°43'W	−10.5°C	31.6°C	−59.4°C	108	104	71	212	302

Source: Wahl et al. (1987)

in central and eastern Siberia, and in the northwestern Canadian Arctic and central Alaska. The Tibet Plateau, thought to have been unglaciated by most Chinese scientists, cannot be regarded as an equilibrium periglacial landscape since it is very young, the result of exceptionally rapid uplift during the late Pleistocene (≈ 10 mm/year for the last 130 000 years).

Thus, the permafrost and frost action which currently characterizes the plateau is the result of the ever-increasing elevation of the plateau. Geologically speaking, the Tibet Plateau landscape is definitely *not* in equilibrium. Equally, most alpine periglacial environments are, by definition, proglacial in nature (i.e. periglacial in the original sense of Lozinski). As for the boreal forest, tundra and high Arctic regions, the majority have only recently emerged from beneath continental ice sheets; these regions have moved temporally and spatially from being proglacial to paraglacial, and the degree to which they are in balance with current cold-climate conditions varies, depending largely upon the susceptibility of local bedrock to cryogenic weathering and landscape modification.

A second perspective is to examine landscape where it is clear that there is no historical legacy. The Holocene deltaic environments of the large northern rivers, such as the Ob, Lena, Yenesie, Yukon and Mackenzie, or the emergent coastal relief of many of the high Arctic islands, are obvious examples. But it is also clear that these are special cases which do not easily permit historical insight of the time scale required. Accordingly, our attention must focus upon the cold and never-glaciated regions of the world.

2.3 Never-glaciated periglacial terrain

In this section, two never-glaciated cold regions are briefly described, as possible illustrations of periglacial terrain. One is an upland, the other is a lowland. Both are located in the western Canadian Arctic. The prevailing climatic conditions are summarized in Table 2.1, while Fig. 2.2 outlines the limits of Quaternary glaciation in this part of the Canadian Arctic.

2.3.1   The Beaufort Plain of northwest Banks Island, Canada (latitude 73°N; longitude 124°W)

The northwest corner of Banks Island fulfils several essential requirements for periglacial designation *senso stricto*. First, although climatic data are unavailable for this remote and uninhabited area, it is reasonable to assume that conditions are in between those recorded at Sachs Harbour (71°N) and Resolute Bay (74°N) (Table 2.1(a)). The climate is very cold, with a mean annual air temperature of approximately –12 to –15 °C. Winter extremes may be as low as –50 °C. The region is also arid, with less than 200 mm of rain or snowfall equivalent a year. The frost-free period does not exceed between 10 and 30 days a year.

Second, following detailed Quaternary geology mapping of Banks Island in the 1970s, it was concluded that this northwest corner of the island

escaped glaciation throughout the Quaternary, despite evidence of at least four major glaciations affecting other parts of the island (Vincent, 1982). The most recent glaciation, the late Wisconsinan, impinged upon the north coast of Banks Island when a major ice lobe extended west through McClure Strait, to leave a distinct coastal moraine system. A series of well-developed ice-marginal meltwater channels came into operation at this time (French, 1972b).

Third, a detailed Quaternary record is available from a thick sequence of sediments exposed at Duck Hawk Bluff, on the southern tip of Banks Island (Vincent, 1989). Their study has revealed a sequence of climatic oscillations throughout the Quaternary which indicates that, even in the interglacials, the climate was cool in this part of the Arctic. The oldest sediments, known as the Worth Point Formation, are found in a channel incised within late-Tertiary-age gravels of the Beaufort Formation. Macrofossils of larch and various shrubs and herbaceous plants suggest that an open subarctic forest–tundra environment existed in the early Quaternary. Because the sediments are magnetically reversed the sediments are older than 790 000 years BP.

One can conclude with reasonable confidence that this northwest corner of Banks Island experienced uninterrupted, but variable, cold non-glacial conditions throughout the last 1 000 000–2 000 000 years.

It is informative, therefore, to describe the landforms of this region. J. G. Fyles was the first to undertake a systematic study of the geomorphology (in Thorsteinsson and Tozer, 1962, pp. 1–17). He describes the Beaufort Plain in these terms:

'Northwestern Banks Island is a fluvial plain . . . underlain by thick gravels and sands. The Beaufort Plain rises gradually from sea level at the west coast to an altitude of about 800 feet at its eastern boundary. It is drained by more or less parallel, west-flowing, consequent major rivers and by dendritically arranged tributary streams . . . River valleys are cut a few feet to 500 feet below the plain surface. The larger valleys . . . have flat floors and steep walls. Some are asymmetrical in cross section, with a steep undercut north wall. Many of the rivers are strikingly braided . . . Large abandoned valleys just south of the morainal belt appear to be ancient, west-draining courses of the rivers that now flow to the north coast . . . The valleys are separated by broad areas of flat plain, and dissection has only locally progressed beyond early youth. The plain surface is remarkably uniform and completely free of lakes . . . The plain has not yielded clear evidence of having been overridden by glacial ice. (pp. 15–17)

An annotated aerial photograph (Fig. 2.3) illustrates the nature of the Beaufort Plain. The contrast between the never-glaciated terrain and the adjacent

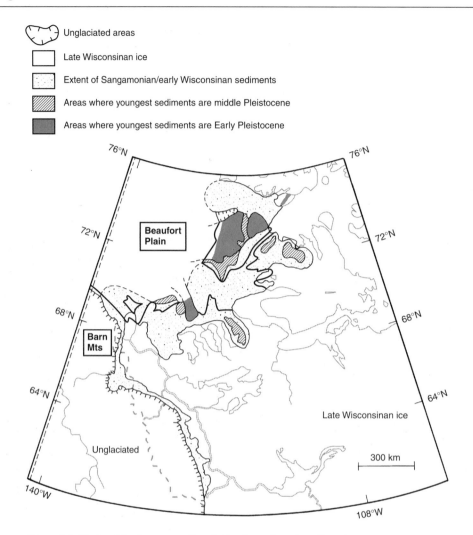

Unglaciated areas

Late Wisconsinan ice

Extent of Sangamonian/early Wisconsinan sediments

Areas where youngest sediments are middle Pleistocene

Areas where youngest sediments are Early Pleistocene

Figure 2.2 Limits of Quaternary continental ice in northwestern Canada.

terrain affected by the youngest glaciation (the Amundsen–Wisconsinan glaciation) can be seen. The aerial photograph should be examined carefully. It suggests that never-glaciated periglacial terrain is not much different from terrain existing in the non-periglacial regions of the world.

The Beaufort Plain suggests that a periglacial land-scape is a fluvial one of low relief. Evidence of the prevailing cold conditions is found in the occurrence of thermal contraction cracks, asymmetrical valleys and mass wasting beneath snowbanks. Braided rivers indicate highly variable and seasonal (nival) dis-charges. There is a notable absence of pingos or thermokarst phenomena.

Let us now turn to a second example of never-glaciated periglacial terrain.

2.3.2   The Barn Mountains, interior northern Yukon, Canada (latitude 68°N; longitude 138°W)

The Barn Mountains form uplands, part of the British Mountains, and rise from near sea level to ele-vations in excess of 1200 m above sea level (a.s.l.). The dominant control over relief is bedrock structure. In the foothills sequences of gently folded Mesozoic-age shale and sandstone produce anticlinal escarpments and synclinal ridges. The main range of the Barn Mountains consists of faulted Palaeozoic shale and limestone interbedded with quartzite, chert and conglomerate.

The Barn Mountains, like the Beaufort Plain, fulfil the requirements for periglacial designation. First, the mountains lie beyond the maximum limit of Pleistocene glaciation. According to Hughes (1972b)

and Rampton (1982), the last major ice advance, the Buckland Glaciation, was northwestwards from the Mackenzie Delta along the coastal plain to the north. Evidence of glaciation, in the form of either till deposits or glacially sculptured landforms, is absent from the Barn Mountains. Second, the present climate is extremely cold and dry. Again, no climatological records are available for the Barn

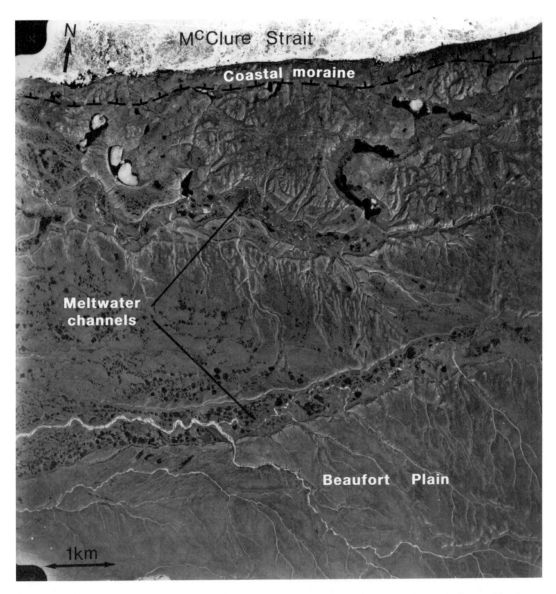

Figure 2.3 Vertical air photo of the Beaufort Plain of NW Banks Island showing never-glaciated terrain dissected by streams. Large meltwater channels are aligned approximately parallel with the glacial topography adjacent to the north coast. (Air photograph A 17381–137, National Air Photo Library, Natural Resources Canada, Ottawa)

Mountains but data from Shingle Point on the Beaufort Sea coast, and from Eagle Plain, 150 km inland, provide some indication of local conditions (Table 2.1(b)). In winter, because of inversion effects, temperatures in the mountains are probably not as low as at Shingle Point and the Eagle Plain data are more representative. In summer, elevation considerations suggest that the Barn Mountains are slightly cooler than either Shingle Point or Eagle Plain. Precipitation, in the form of both rain and snow, is higher than at Shingle Point because of orographic effects and is probably similar to Eagle Plain. More than half the precipitation in the Barn Mountains falls as rain, between June and September.

In the context of periglacial terrain the landscape of the Barn Mountains is also instructive. It consists of structurally controlled upland massifs surrounded by extensive pediments, dissected by streams and larger rivers draining towards the Arctic coast (Fig. 2.4). The pediments, first reported by Hughes (1972b) during surficial geology mapping, have been termed cryopediments and similar surfaces occur elsewhere in the unglaciated interior Yukon (e.g. Priesnitz, 1981; Priesnitz and Schunke, 1983). The pediments are best developed where relatively less resistant Mesozoic-age shale outcrops adjacent to more resistant sandstone. In places, sandstone outliers are completely surrounded by gentle pediment surfaces, forming isolated inselberg-like hills (Fig. 2.5(a)). The pediment surfaces truncate dip of the underlying rock (Fig. 2.5(b)), are dissected, occasionally cross fault lines (see

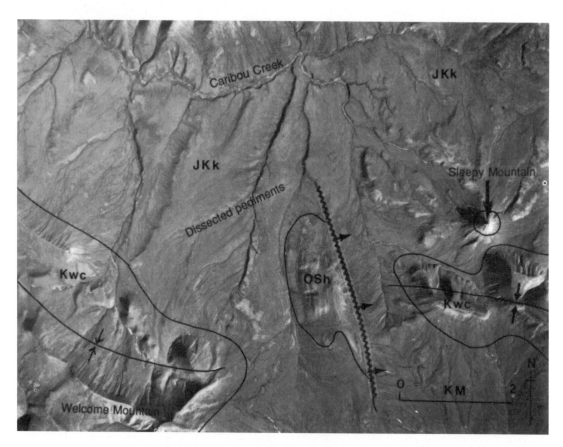

Figure 2.4 Vertical air photo of area adjacent to Sleepy and Welcome Mountains showing main elements of geological structure and dissected pediments of Caribou Creek. Geology after Norris (1977). OSh, Ordovician shale; JKk, Kingak Formation shale (Lower Cretaceous); Kwc, Lower Cretaceous sandstone and quartzite, ridge-forming. Latitude 68°24'N; longitude 138°16'W (Air photograph A24502–160, National Air Photo Library, Natural Resources Canada, Ottawa).

Figure 2.5 Landscape elements of the Barn Mountains, northern interior Yukon: (a) synclinal ridges and outliers form upland massifs and inselberg-like hills near Sleepy Mountain; (b) pediment-like surfaces surround the upland massifs in Canoe Creek.

Fig. 2.4), and sometimes encroach upon the adjacent sandstone. For the most part, they are 'covered' pediments (Twidale, 1987); that is, they are cut in weak bedrock and carry a protective veneer of detritus derived from upslope. In the European literature, such features are commonly termed 'glacis' (e.g. Dresch, 1982, p. 90) or 'erosion glacis' (e.g. Joly, in Demek, 1972b, pp. 189–92). Closely related features are large terraces or steps carved in bedrock and occupying upper hillslope positions.

These are generally referred to as cryoplanation terraces (e.g. Priesnitz, 1988).

In all probability, the landscape is very old, dating from the middle to late Tertiary. The pediments, probably in existence prior to the onset of the Quaternary, would have been effective slopes of transportation of waste material only under certain cold-climate conditions. For example, French and Harry (1992) speculate that (a) they would have been active only during periods of intense weathering and high sediment removal, and (b) they would have been inactive whenever moisture levels fell below a critical (undefined) level.

At the micro-scale, angular rock rubble veneers many of the upland surfaces of the Barn Mountains, and large non-sorted polygons are common. At the meso-scale, tors and bedrock (i.e. cryoplanation) terraces exist at higher elevation but there is no obvious relationship between the tors and the terraces. A striking observation is that these features and the angular rock rubble surfaces show little sign that they are forming under today's climate.

In summary, the landscape of the Barn Mountains contains a distinct suite of landforms, quite different from that of the Beaufort Plain. To some degree, the difference is one of geology. However, the terrain also suggests that landscape evolution is slow and certain elements bear a striking resemblance to those of hot, semi-arid regions.

2.4 Implications

Even though the landscapes of never-glaciated cold regions, such as the Beaufort Plain and the Barn Mountains, are typical of periglacial terrain, such environments do not constitute the majority of the periglacial domain. It follows that many regions that currently experience periglacial climates do not necessarily possess true periglacial landscapes. This important qualification must always be borne in mind in Part 2. A basic advance in our understanding of periglacial environments is to recognize that the geomorphic footprint of periglacial conditions is not always achieved, and most periglacial environments possess some degree of inherited paraglacial or proglacial characteristics.

Further reading

General

Büdel, J. (1982) *Climatic geomorphology*. Princeton, NJ: Princeton University Press, 443 pp. (translated by Lenore Fischer and Detlef Busche). Especially sections 2.2, The polar zone of excessive valley-cutting (the active periglacial zone), and 2.3, The peritropical zone of excessive planation.

Dylik, J. (1957) Tentative comparison of planation surfaces occurring under warm and cold semi-arid conditions. *Biuletyn Peryglacjalny*, **5**, 175–186.

Peltier, L. (1950) The geographic cycle in periglacial regions as it is related to climatic geomorphology. *Annals, Association of American Geographers*, **40**, 214–236.

Thorn, C. and D.S. Loewenberz (1987) Spatial and temporal trends in alpine periglacial studies: implications for paleo-reconstruction. In J. Boardman (ed.), *Periglacial processes and landforms in Britain and Ireland*, Cambridge: Cambridge University Press, pp. 57–65.

Northwest Banks Island

French, H. M. (1971) Slope asymmetry of the Beaufort Plain, northwest Banks Island, N.W.T. Canada. *Canadian Journal of Earth Sciences*, **8**, 717–731.

French, H. M. (1972b) Proglacial drainage of northwest Banks Island, District of Franklin, N.W.T. *Muskox*, **10**, 26–31.

Fyles, J. G. (1964) in R. Thorsteinsson and E.T. Tozer, *Banks, Victoria and Stefansson Islands, Arctic Archipelago*, Geological Survey of Canada, Memoir 330, pp. 8–17.

Vincent, J. S. (1982) The Quaternary history of Banks Island, N.W.T., Canada. *Géographie Physique et Quaternaire*, **36**, 209–232.

Vincent, J. S. (1989) Quaternary geology of the northern Canadian Interior Plains. In R. J. Fulton (ed.), *Quaternary geology of Canada and Greenland*, Geology of Canada, No. 1. Geological Survey of Canada, pp. 100–137.

Barn Mountains, northern Yukon

Hughes, O. (1972) *Surficial geology of northern Yukon Territory and northwestern District of Mackenzie, Northwest Territories.* Geological Survey of Canada, Paper 69–36, Map 1319 A.

Rampton, V. N. (1982) *Quaternary geology of the Yukon Coastal Plain.* Geological Survey of Canada, Bulletin 317, 49 pp.

French, H. M. and D. G. Harry (1992) Pediments and cold-climate conditions, Barn Mountains, unglaciated northern Yukon, Canada. *Geografiska Annaler*, **74 A**, 145–157.

Discussion topics

1. Distinguish between periglacial, proglacial and paraglacial environments.

2. What are the main landscape elements of (a) the Beaufort Plain and (b) the Barn Mountains?

3. What is the evidence of current cold-climate modification of the landscapes of (a) the Beaufort Plain and (b) the Barn Mountains?

4. How different are these landscapes from those of (a) humid temperate and (b) hot arid regions of the world?

CHAPTER 3

Periglacial climates

A number of distinct climatic environments exist in which frost-action processes dominate. Their combined spatial extent constitutes the periglacial domain. The extent of this domain is somewhat difficult to establish, however, since there are all gradations from climatic environments in which frost-action processes dominate and where the whole or a major part of the landscape depends upon such processes, to those in which frost-action processes occur but are subservient to others.

The periglacial domain is an important component of the cryosphere. Global climate models (GCMs) predict warming will be greatest in high latitudes and that periglacial climates will be significantly affected.

3.1 Boundary conditions

Boundary conditions between periglacial and non-periglacial conditions are arbitrary to a large extent, and will vary considerably depending upon the criteria used.

The presence or absence of perennially frozen ground is a reasonably easy boundary definition, although the outer boundaries of the discontinuous permafrost zone are often hard to delineate. The location of the treeline is a second relatively unambiguous boundary definition, since most investigators equate severe periglacial conditions with tundra or polar desert ecozones. However, the treeline is not static but either advancing or retreating depending upon environmental and regional climatic conditions. Moreover, the treeline is not a line but rather a zone, over 50–100 km wide in places, lying between the biological limit of continuous forest and the absolute limit of tree species.

For our purposes, and in keeping with a simple frost-action definition of a periglacial environment, we can adopt an empirical definition of the boundary condition for the periglacial domain. It is defined to include all areas where the mean annual air temperature is less than +3 °C. This definition closely follows the limits proposed by Williams (1961) for the development of solifluction and patterned ground of a frost-action nature. Since it includes not only areas where frost-action conditions dominate but also areas which are marginally periglacial in character, it gives some idea of the maximum extent of the periglacial domain. We may further subdivide the periglacial domain by the –2 °C mean annual air temperature into environments in which frost action dominates (mean annual air temperature less than –2 °C) and those in which frost-action processes occur but do not necessarily dominate (mean annual air temperature between –2 °C and +3 °C).

3.2 Periglacial climates

The concept of a distinct periglacial climate was first proposed by Troll (1944) in his global survey of frost-action conditions. It was subsequently incorporated by Peltier (1950) into a scheme of morpho-genetic regions. According to Peltier, the periglacial climate was characterized by mean annual air temperatures of between –15 °C and –1 °C, precipitation of between 120 and 1400 mm/year, and 'intense frost action, strong mass movement, and the weak importance of running water'. Today, this definition is not regarded as being very useful. By masking a wide range of climatic conditions, it favours the assumption of a regular, uniform type of periglacial climate. This is misleading since it is more realistic to stress the variety of cold climates that exist and in which frost action dominates.

Some of the first to appreciate this were the French climatic geomorphologists J. Tricart and A. Cailleux (Tricart, 1970; Tricart and Cailleux, 1967, pp. 45–67). They distinguished between three types of periglacial climatic environments. The first type (Type I: Dry climates with severe winters) experiences seasonal and deep freezing while the third type (Type III: Climates with small annual temperature range) experiences shallow and predominantly diurnal freezing. The second type (Type II: Humid climates with severe winter) is intermediate. Another differentiating factor is that permafrost is characteristic of the first type, is irregular in occurrence and distribution in the second type, and is absent in the third type. One problem of this threefold division of periglacial climates is that the first two types are identified primarily in terms of humidity while the third is identified in terms of temperature. As a result, Type I includes the two rather different climatic environments of the Canadian high Arctic and the subarctic continental areas of central Siberia. Moreover, an Arctic subtype of Type II, as typified by Spitsbergen, is more similar to the environments of other high latitudes than to a mountain variety, which is the other subtype of that category.

In a rather more pragmatic fashion, Barsch (1993) suggests that periglacial environments simply exist in areas with polar climates. In other words, they exist in those areas dominated by the E (Ef and ET) climates of Köppen (1923). As regards alpine periglacial climates, the boundaries are similar but problems arise in arid to semi-arid mountains where the upper timberline (i.e. the lower limit of periglacial conditions) does not exist. As regards the upper limit of periglacial conditions, the existence of glaciers and permanent snow and ice for both the polar and alpine periglacial environments is relatively unambiguous. Unfortunately this approach fails to recognize the important boreal forest component of the periglacial domain, and the fact that relict permafrost can be just as important as contemporary frost action in determining the character of the periglacial landscape.

In the first edition of this book four periglacial climatic environments were proposed. In an attempt to incorporate the relatively unique climatic conditions of the Qinghai-Xizang (Tibet) Plateau, this earlier classification is now modified slightly to include elevation as well as insolation and temperature. Five broad categories of periglacial climates are now identified.

Basic to the classification is the fact that radiant energy from the sun influences both air and ground temperatures. For example, Fig. 3.1 shows potential insolation, expressed as a percentage of the amount

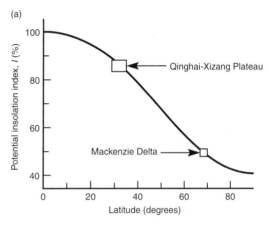

(a)

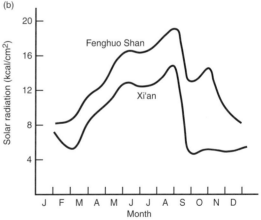

(b)

Figure 3.1 (a) Potential insolation expressed as a percentage of the potential insolation at the equator (according to Dingman and Koutz, 1974). (b) Variation of actual incoming solar radiation over a year at the same latitude (34°N) but different altitudes: Fenghuo Shan at 4800 m a.s.l., and Xi'an at 1300 m a.s.l. (source: from Wang and French, 1994).

received at the equator, as a function of latitude. If one assumes potential insolation at the equator to be 3.12×10^5 ly/year (Dingman and Koutz, 1974), then the potential insolation of a horizontal surface on, say, the Qinghai-Xizang Plateau at latitude 29–38°N, is approximately 2.68×10^5 ly/year. This can be compared with the comparable value for the Mackenzie Delta, Canada (latitude 68–69°N) of 1.58×10^5 ly/year.

Elevation also influences the amount of solar radiation received. For example, Fenghuo Shan, on the Tibet Plateau, is at the same latitude as, but 3500 m higher than, Xi'an in central China. However, the actual solar radiation received at Fenghuo Shan is much higher than at Xi'an (Fig. 3.1(b)) because the water vapour and aerosol content in the atmosphere decrease with increasing elevation. This in turn causes less cloud cover and a greater transparency in the atmosphere at high elevations. Therefore, the combination of low latitude and high elevation makes the Tibet Plateau a strong solar receiver. This effect is still present, but less marked, in the alpine environments of mid latitudes.

Based upon elevation, insolation and temperature, the various periglacial climatic environments can be summarized as follows:

1. *High Arctic climates* – in polar latitudes; extremely weak diurnal pattern, strong seasonal pattern. Small daily and large annual temperature range. Examples: Spitsbergen (Green Harbour, 78°N); Canadian Arctic (Sachs Harbour, 72°N).

2. *Continental climates* – in subarctic latitudes; weak diurnal pattern, strong seasonal pattern. Extreme annual temperature range. Examples: central Siberia (Yakutsk, 62°N); interior Alaska and Yukon (Fairbanks, 65°N; Dawson City, 64°N).

3. *Alpine climates* – in middle latitudes in mountain environments; well-developed diurnal and seasonal patterns. Examples: Colorado Front Range (Niwot Ridge, 40°N); Alps (Sonnblick, 47°N).

4. *Qinghai-Xizang (Tibet) Plateau* – a high-elevation, low-latitude mountain environment. Well-developed diurnal and seasonal patterns. Above normal insolation due to elevations of 4200–4800 m a.s.l. Example: Fenghuo Shan (34°N).

5. *Climates of low annual temperature range* – in azonal locations:
    (a) Island climates in subarctic latitudes. Examples: Jan Mayen (71°N); South Georgia (54°S).

(b) Mountain climates in low latitudes. Examples: Andean summits, Mont Blanc Station and El Misti, Peru (16°S).

Climatic data for some of the locations mentioned above are given in Table 3.1 and the nature of their typical frost-action conditions is graphically illustrated in Fig. 3.2. The number of frost-free days, days of alternating freezing and thawing, and days in which temperatures remain below 0 °C are plotted for eight localities. The graphs clearly show that the least number of freezing and thawing days occur in the high Arctic and continental climates, which are dominated by seasonal patterns, while the greatest number occur in the climates of low annual temperature range, which are dominated by diurnal or cyclonic (i.e. short-term) fluctuations. In more detail, the characteristics of each climatic type are described below.

3.2.1 High Arctic climates

Several characteristics make these the most distinctive of periglacial climates. First, extremely low winter temperatures occur for periods of several months, when there is perpetual darkness and temperatures may routinely fall to –20 °C or even –30 °C. The ground freezes to form permafrost and the ground surface contracts under the intense cold. Second, temperatures rise above freezing for only two or three months of the year, when the surface thaws to depths varying between 0.3 and 1.5 m and average air temperatures rise 4–6 °C above zero. Third, precipitation amounts are low. In parts of the Canadian Arctic, precipitation is less than 100 mm/year, of which approximately half falls as rain during the summer period. Because of low evaporation rates, and the inability of the water to percolate through the soil on account of permafrost, the effectiveness of this precipitation is high. As a consequence, although arid in terms of total precipitation, these regions are surprisingly wet during the summer. In more maritime locations, such as Spitsbergen, precipitation amounts increase considerably to as much as 250–400 mm/year. In these regions, snow assumes importance in protecting the ground surface from the extremes of cold and increases the magnitude of the spring runoff. The ice-free areas of Antarctica represent a unique type of *High Arctic* climatic environment. Temperatures are exceptionally low and precipitation is often negligible.

Table 3.1 Climatic data for selected localities in different types of periglacial environments

(a) Temperature (°C) and precipitation (mm) data

		J	F	M	A	M	J	J	A	S	O	N	D
High Arctic climates													
Spitsbergen, Green Harbour	T (°C)	−16	−19	−19	−13	−5	+2	+6	+5	0	−6	−11	−15
	P (mm)	35	33	28	23	13	10	15	23	25	30	25	38
Canadian Arctic, Sachs Harbour	T (°C)	−29	−31	−27	−20	−8	+2	+5	+4	−1	−10	−24	−27
	P (mm)	2	2	3	2	5	4	24	16	16	12	4	3
Continental climates													
Central Siberia, Yakutsk	T (°C)	−43	−36	−22	−7	+6	+15	+19	+15	+6	−8	−28	−40
	P (mm)	11	9	6	11	18	33	43	42	26	20	16	12
Yukon, Canada, Dawson City	T (°C)	−31	−23	−16	−3	+8	+13	+14	+12	+6	−4	−17	−25
	P (mm)	20	20	12	18	23	33	40	40	43	33	33	28
Alpine climates													
Alps, Sonnblick, 3060 m	T (°C)	−13	−14	−11	−9	−4	−1	+1	+1	−1	−5	−9	−11
	P (mm)	124	124	160	167	157	140	142	129	116	129	117	134
Rockies, Niwot Ridge, 3750 m	T (°C)	−10	−10	−8	−4	+3	+9	+12	+11	+7	+2	−5	−9
	P (mm)	137	91	105	102	68	70	80	57	72	39	112	88
Qinghai-Xizang Plateau (Tibet)													
Fenghuo Shan, 4800 m	T (°C)	−18.2	−14.7	−11.6	−6.5	−2.2	1.6	4.2	4.8	1.5	−5.1	−13.5	−18.5
	P (mm)	1.4	2.2	4.4	6.2	35.1	109.6	86.3	47.2	47.0	5.4	0.0	0.5
Climates of low annual temperature range													
Jan Mayen	T (°C)	−3	−3	−4	−2	−1	+3	+5	+5	+3	−1	−2	−4
	P (mm)	40	38	30	29	13	15	23	23	48	43	33	30
South Georgia, Gruytviken	T (°C)	+5	+5	+4	+2	0	−2	−2	−2	+1	+2	+3	+4
	P (mm)	84	104	129	134	139	127	139	129	86	66	86	86

(b) Summary data

			Mean annual temperature (°C)	Annual range	Total precipitation (mm)
High Arctic climates	Spitsbergen	78°N	−8	25	298
	Sachs Harbour	72°N	−14	36	93
Continental climates	Yakutsk	62°N	−10	62	247
	Dawson City	64°N	−5	45	343
Alpine climates	Sonnblick	47°N	−7	15	1 638
	Niwot Ridge	39°N	−3	22	1 021
Qinghai-Xizang Plateau (Tibet)	Fenghuo Shan	34°N	−6	23	345
Low-temperature range	Jan Mayen	71°N	0	8	365
	Gruytviken	54°S	+2	7	1 309

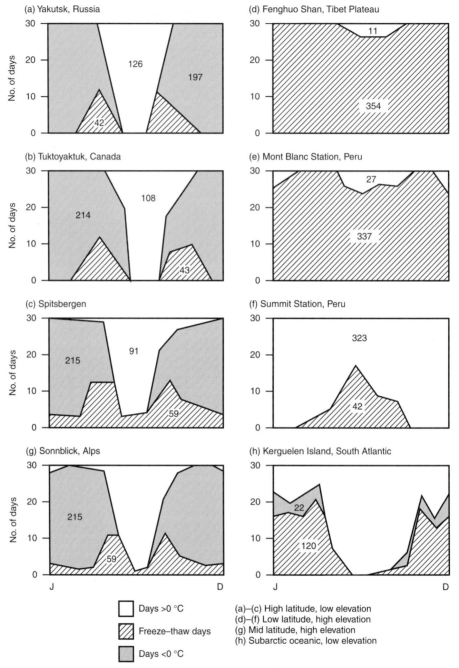

Figure 3.2 Freezing and thawing conditions in various periglacial environments of the world: (a) Yakutsk (lat. 62°01'N, long. 129°43'E, altitude 108 m): (b) Tuktoyaktuk (lat. 69°27'N, long 133°02'W, altitude <10 m); Mackenzie Delta (c) Spitsbergen (lat. 78°02'N, long. 14°14'E, altitude 7 m); (d) Fenghuo Shan Qinghai-Xizang (Tibet) Plateau, China; (lat. 34°20'N, long. 92°52'E, altitude 4800 m); (e) El Misti (Mont Blanc Station), South Peru (lat. 16°16'S, long. 71°25'W, altitude 4760 m; (f) El Misti (Summit Station), South Peru (lat 16°16'S, long. 71°25'W, altitude 5850 m). (g) Sonnblick, Austrian Alps (lat. 47°03'N; long. 12°57'E; altitude 3060 m); (h) Kerguelen Island (lat: 49°30'S; long. 69°30'E; altitude sea level). (Sources: (a), (c), (e) and (f) from Troll, 1944; (b) from AES records, Canada; (d) constructed from monthly means of air temperatures recorded at Fenghuo Shan by Northwest Railway Institute personnel).

In all high Arctic climates, the snowcover during the winter is thin and often discontinuous, even in the moister regions. Upland surfaces and exposed areas are swept bare by wind, allowing frost to penetrate deeply and snowbanks to accumulate only in hollows and lee-slope positions.

In the northern hemisphere, the approximate spatial limits of these climatic conditions may be arbitrarily defined by the glacial limit to the north and by either the treeline or the 8–10 °C annual July air isotherm to the south. For the most part, these areas are referred to as the tundra or polar regions of the world.

3.2.2 Continental climates

South of the treeline in subarctic and continental locations are large areas which experience a wider range of temperatures than high Arctic areas. Although mean annual air temperatures are approximately the same or slightly higher than in areas north of the treeline, these mean values disguise extremely low temperatures in winter and remarkably high temperatures in summer. Yakutsk, in central Siberia, and Dawson City, in the Yukon Territory, illustrate this phenomenon (Table 3.1). At Yakutsk, for example, January temperatures of –40 °C and July temperatures of +15 to +20 °C are quite common. At Yakutsk, the annual average range of temperature is 62 °C. This may be compared with that of Sachs Harbour, where the annual range is only 36 °C.

Besides being hotter, the summers are longer than in high Arctic climates, and above-freezing temperatures occur for five or six months of the year. Seasonal thaw may penetrate over 2.0–3.0 m. Precipitation amounts are also greater than in high Arctic regions since disturbances associated with the Arctic and polar fronts are more frequent at these latitudes. Between 250 and 600 mm/year are typical, with the majority falling during the summer months. However, evaporation rates are also high during the summer and there is usually a soil moisture deficit.

The summer dryness of the northern forests, together with their high air temperatures, constitutes a favourable environment for forest fires. The boreal forest is regarded by some as a fire climax in terms of vegetation successions. According to Veireck (1973), wildfires in Alaska alone burn an average of 400 000 ha/year. They constitute, therefore, a distinct feature of the continental periglacial environments and have no counterpart in the treeless and cooler

high Arctic climatic environments. Winter snowfall is another differentiating characteristic of continental climates since amounts are considerably greater than in high Arctic climates. The snowfall and forest cover interact to determine whether permafrost forms or not; in open areas where snow accumulates, it protects the ground from deep frost penetration and permafrost may not occur. Beneath trees, where snow depth is less, there is deeper frost penetration and a greater probability of permafrost occurrence. Where continuous and thick permafrost is present, there is reason to believe that this is relict and unrelated to present climatic conditions.

3.2.3 Qinghai-Xizang (Tibet Plateau)

Because the Tibet Plateau has low latitude and high elevation, its climate experiences both diurnal and seasonal rhythms. The mean annual air temperature ranges between –2.0 and –6.0 °C and the annual range of monthly air temperatures is relatively low when compared to continental and high Arctic climates. In contrast to alpine environments, however, precipitation is low, being more similar to high latitudes. Because evaporation rates of between 1200 and 1800 mm/year are typical and annual total precipitation ranges between 200 and 600 mm, most of it concentrated in the June–September period, the Plateau has a marked water budget deficit. As a consequence, vegetation is steppe-tundra in nature and more barren than the low Arctic tundra. Snow cover is also generally thin, <6 cm on average. It often disappears two to three days after deposition when air temperatures rise above 0 °C in mid-afternoon, or when evaporation and/or sublimation processes occur. In general, the mean annual air temperature on the Plateau changes with both latitude and altitude: lapse rates range between 0.44 and 0.55 °C per 100 m.

The annual fluctuations in solar radiation and air temperature create a distinct freeze–thaw regime. Data for Fenghuo Shan are illustrated in Table 3.1 and in Fig. 3.2; these are typical for most stations on the Plateau. Although the Plateau experiences approximately the same number of freeze–thaw cycles as other localities of similar latitude and altitude (e.g. Mont Blanc station, Peru, see Fig. 3.2), the number of frost-free days is approximately one order of magnitude less on the Plateau than at high latitudes. For example, the average number of frost-free days at Fenghuo Shan is only 11, while at Tuktoyaktuk, in the Canada Arctic, it is 108, despite the fact that the mean annual air temperature at Tuktoyaktuk is about 4–5 °C lower than at Fenghuo Shan. This apparently anomalous situation reflects the fact that the Tibet Plateau has a much smaller temperature range than the high latitudes where seasonal rhythms dominate over the diurnal ones.

In summary, the distinct and unique climate of the vast Tibet Plateau justifies its recognition as an important periglacial climate.

3.2.4 Alpine climates

Alpine periglacial climates are characteristic of tundra regions lying above the treeline in middle latitude locations. They are not as extensive as either of the three previous climatic environments. In the European Alps and the Rockies, the treeline occurs at elevations varying between 2000 and 4000 m, but in other localities, such as northern Scandinavia, Iceland and northern Labrador-Ungava, the treeline approaches sea level. Irrespective of elevation, however, all these climatic environments experience a seasonal and diurnal rhythm of both temperature and precipitation.

None of the alpine climates experiences the severe winter cold of either high Arctic or continental climates. On the other hand, the diurnal and seasonal rhythm imposed by their middle latitude locations results in a higher frequency of temperature oscillations around the freezing point. Precipitation is also heavy, the result of either orographic or maritime effects. Total amounts often exceed 750–1000 mm/year, much of which occurs as snow. Permafrost is often lacking or discontinuous, the result of the higher mean annual temperature and the protection given to the ground surface by the winter snow cover.

3.2.5 Climates of low annual temperature range

There are certain very restricted areas of the world which experience not only a mean annual air temperature below +2 °C but also a remarkably small range of temperatures. These unique climatic conditions occur in two types of locality.

The first is a subarctic oceanic location, where the thermal influence of the surrounding water bodies exerts a moderating influence upon temperatures. In the northern hemisphere, Jan Mayen and Bear Islands experience this climate, while in the southern hemisphere, the islands surrounding Antarctica, such as Kerguelen, South Georgia and the South Orkneys, are similar. In these climatic environments, the mean annual amplitude of temperature is in the order of only 10 °C. Not surprisingly, these areas experience a high frequency of freeze–thaw cycles of short duration and shallow penetrability into the ground. Because of their maritime locations, these islands experience considerable precipitation, often varying between 1000 and 2000 mm/year, and unstable cyclonic weather, with much low cloud and fog.

The second is an alpine location in low latitudes where diurnal temperature variations dominate the weak seasonal influences. Numerous shallow freeze–thaw cycles occur throughout the year and precipitation may vary from near-arid to humid, depending upon location. These climatic conditions exist towards the summits of the various mountain ranges in the Andes of South America, and in East Africa, but clearly are not extensive.

3.3 Periglacial climates and the cryosphere

The periglacial domain is an important component of what is generally termed the cryosphere. Terrestrial components include seasonal snow cover, mountain glaciers, ice sheets, perennially frozen ground (permafrost) and seasonally frozen ground. The other important component of the cryosphere is the Arctic sea ice. Table 3.2 lists the relative extent of the terrestrial components of the cryosphere.

The cryosphere is generally recognized as being particularly sensitive to global warming. Most global climate models (GCMs) predict warming to be greatest at high latitudes. In particular, winter warming is expected to be more than the global annual average. In addition, and also in high mountain regions, climate change will occur through the alteration of freeze–thaw processes and changes in the occurrence of glacier ice, ground ice, sea ice and lake ice. The reasons for these changes, and their geomorphic consequences, will be discussed at greater length in Chapter 17. Here, it is important to stress, in general terms, the roles which the periglacial domain, and the cryosphere, play in global change.

To illustrate the extent of these changes, Table 3.3 lists the changes which might occur in the Fennoscandian region owing to a doubling of the CO_2 content, according to the GCM developed by the Goddard Institute for Space Studies (GISS). The

Table 3.2 Relative extent of terrestrial areas of seasonal snow cover, ice and permafrost

	Area (million km²)	Volume (million km³)
Land ice		
Antarctica	13.9	30.1
Greenland	1.8	2.7
Small ice caps	0.35	0.2
Mountain glaciers	0.2	0.03
Major permafrost regions		*Percentage underlain by permafrost*
USSR (FSU)	16.84	50
Canada	9.38	50
China	9.38	22
Greenland	2.18	100
USA (Alaska)	1.52	82
World land area	140.7	20–25
Northern Hemisphere		
Continuous	7.6[1]	
Discontinuous	17.3[1]	
Alpine permafrost	2.33[1]	
Land ice and seasonal snow	*Area*	*Volume*
Northern Hemisphere		
Early February	46.3	0.002
Late August	8.7	
Southern Hemisphere		
Late July	0.85	
Early May	0.07	

[1] Approximate
Source: after Washburn (1979); Rott (1983)

model predicts mean winter temperatures to increase by 5–6 °C, the mean annual temperature to increase by 4–5 °C, the growing season (daily mean temperature ≥ 5 °C) to increase by 70–150 days, and precipitation to increase by 150–300 mm. Clearly, if the changes predicted for Fennoscandian are typical of those predicted for other high-latitude regions, then the periglacial climates and, by extension, the extent of the periglacial domain, will change radically. In Canada, for example, it is predicted that the southern limit of permafrost will shift northwards by distances ranging between 100 and 200 km. Even in low latitudes, the effects of global warming will be important. For example, a recent rise in the mean annual ground temperature on the Tibet Plateau between 1962 and 1989 suggests, if this trend continues, that permafrost will disappear from the Tibet Plateau in approximately 150 years.

The majority of the so-called periglacial regions of the world have a high negative radiation budget. Changes in that budget will prompt major global changes in atmospheric and oceanic circulation. For example, the melt of sea ice and ice shelves promotes the formation of cold bottom waters that drain equator-ward and influence circulation patterns in oceans around the world. The polar seas are also large sinks for CO_2 and play an important role in the exchange of CO_2 between the ocean and the atmosphere. Any increase in their extent will have worldwide consequences. There are several other positive feedback mechanisms which will specifically accelerate the global warming in cold regions. For example, the melt of sea ice and seasonal snow cover will reduce albedo and increase solar radiation inputs at the ground surface. In boreal forests and tundra or wetland regions there are large terrestrial CO_2 and CH_4 (methane) reservoirs that will be released as temperatures rise and permafrost thaws. The greenhouse warming caused by the release of increasing amounts of CO_2, CH_4 and other gases into the atmosphere may affect the Greenland and Antarctic ice-sheets which, between them,

Table 3.3 Simulated climate change in the Fennoscandian region due to a doubling of the atmospheric CO_2 content, according to a scenario derived from the GISS model

Climate Parameter	Climate Change Increase (+) decrease (−)		Magnitude
Mean annual temperature	+		4–5 °C
Mean winter temperature	+		5–6 °C
Mean summer temperature		+	2–3.5 °C
Annual temperature amplitude		+	2–4 °C
Length growing season (daily mean temp. ≥ 5 °C)		+	70–150 days
Effective temperature sum (threshold ≥ 5 °C)	+		500–1000 degrees
Length thermal winter (daily mean temp. ≤ 0 °C)	−		2–4 months
Length thermal summer (daily mean temp. ≥ 10 °C)	+		2–3 months
Number of heating degree days (daily mean temp. ≤ 17 °C)	−		30–40%
Mean annual precipitation	+		150–300 mm
Precipitation excess		+	10–50%

Source: Boer *et al.* (1990)

contain enough water to raise global sea level by at least 60 m.

In summary, the periglacial domain is susceptible to significant change, both in its nature and its extent, if present and predicted global warming trends continue. Second, the cryosphere, of which the periglacial domain is a major component, will play an important role in promoting global change. For both reasons, a better understanding of periglacial conditions is warranted. These are now examined in Part 2 (Chapters 4–12).

Further reading

Boer, M.M., E.A. Koster and H. Lundberg (1990) Greenhouse impact in Fennoscandian – Preliminary findings of a European Workshop on the effects of climatic change. *Ambio*, **19**(1), 2–10.

Street, R.B. and P.I. Melnikov (1990) Seasonal snow cover, ice and permafrost. In W.J.McG. Tegart, G.W. Sheldon and D.C. Griffiths (eds), *Climate Change, the IPCC Impacts Assessment*, Chapter 7. Report prepared for IPCC by Working Group II, WMO-UNEP, Australian Government Publishing Service, pp. 7-1 to 7-33.

Street, R.B. and P.I. Melnikov (1993) Terrestrial component of the cryosphere. In: W.J. McG. Tegart and G.W. Sheldon (eds), *Climate Change 1992, The Supplementary Report to the IPCC Impacts Assessment* WMO–UNEP, Australian Government Publishing Service, pp. 94–102.

Troll, C. (1958) *Structure soils, solifluction and frost climate of the Earth*. Translation 43, US Army Snow Ice and Permafrost Research Establishment, Corps of Engineers, Willmette, Illinois, 121 pp.

Discussion topics

1. Describe the variability of periglacial climates.
2. What is the importance of the cryosphere in global change scenarios?

PART 2 Present-day periglacial environments

4 Frost action and cryogenic weathering
5 Permafrost
6 Ground ice
7 Thermokarst
8 The active layer
9 Slope processes
10 Slope morphology
11 Fluvial processes and landforms
12 Wind action and coastal processes

CHAPTER 4

Frost action and cryogenic weathering

Frost action in soils describes the two processes of (a) frost heave that occurs as water changes state during the freezing period and (b) thaw weakening and settlement that occur as seasonally frozen ground thaws. Frost action contributes to the mechanical weathering (i.e. disintegration and breakdown) of soil and rock material.

Frost action is one component of cryogenic weathering, a poorly understood group of physico-chemical processes that operate in cold climates. Other specific weathering processes influenced by cold climate conditions include salt weathering and solution.

4.1 Introduction

Frost action is a collective term used to describe a number of distinct processes which result mainly from alternate freezing and thawing in soil, rock and other materials. Frost action also refers to the effects of frost on materials and on structures placed on, or in, the ground. The latter are dealt with in Part 4; here we deal with the geomorphic processes associated with the repeated freezing of ground and the manner by which the destruction of rock and soil proceeds under these cold-climate conditions.

It is widely believed that frost action is the fundamental characteristic of present-day periglacial environments. Frost-action processes probably achieve their greatest intensity and importance in such areas. It is this belief which leads to the presentation of this chapter at the beginning of Part 2. The chapter begins by describing seasonal freezing and thawing and the various processes associated with these temperature variations. Then, the complex of physico-chemical weathering is examined and, finally, several specific weathering processes are discussed within the context of cold conditions.

In Chapter 5 we examine perennially frozen ground (permafrost), since its formation reflects the duration and intensity of the annual ground temperature regime. The existence of ground ice, and related thermokarst processes, which are described in Chapters 6 and 7 respectively, depend upon the presence of either seasonally or perennially frozen ground. Frost action, through cryoturbation and the physico-chemical weathering complex, also influences the nature of the near-surface soil mantle, or regolith. This is considered in Chapter 8 under the heading of 'The active layer'. Finally, frost action and seasonally or perennially frozen ground influence the nature of various weathering and transporting processes operating on hillslopes and in river channels. These processes, and the landforms that result, are described in Chapters 9–11.

Wind action and coastal processes are not directly related to either frost action or frozen ground, yet, because they assume a distinct characteristic in periglacial environments, merit separate attention in Chapter 12.

4.2 The freezing process

The nature of the freezing process has attracted much attention from research agencies such as the US

Army Cold Regions Research and Engineering Laboratory (CRREL), the US Highway Research Board and the National Research Council of Canada.

The detailed physics of the freezing process need not concern us; the text by Williams and Smith (1989) includes a good discussion (e.g. Williams and Smith, 1989, pp. 1–8 and 174–201). On the other hand, a few comments are necessary to preface this chapter. First, the freezing process is complex since different soils cool at different rates depending upon heat conductivity and moisture content, and thus freeze at different rates. Second, soils do not necessarily freeze when their temperatures fall to 0 °C since they are known to exist in a supercooled state. A common condition is for saline groundwater to lower the temperature at which the soil freezes. Third, the duration and intensity of a temperature drop below 0 °C will affect the rate and amount of freezing of the soil. For example, a question commonly asked is whether the effect of a ground temperature remaining just below 0 °C for a certain length of time is the same as that of a more extreme drop but of a much shorter duration. It is clear therefore, that in discussing frost action one is dealing with a complicated process, the details of which are still not fully understood.

Bearing this in mind, one should understand a few basic freezing relationships, especially as they relate to soils and bedrock.

First, pure water freezes at 0 °C and in doing so expands by approximately 9 per cent of its volume. This phase transition, between liquid and solid, is fundamental to our understanding of frozen and freezing soils. The most obvious result of freezing is the volume increase in soil which results; this is commonly known as 'frost heave' and has considerable geomorphic and practical significance, the latter by displacement of buildings, foundations and road surfaces (see Part 4), the former by heaving of bedrock, uplifting of stones and objects, and frost sorting (see Chapter 8). However, it must be emphasized that the 9 per cent expansion associated with the change from water to ice is not what permafrost scientists normally regarded as frost heave (Williams and Smith, 1989, p. 193). For the soil to heave, the ice must first overcome the resistance to its expansion caused by the strength of the overlying frozen soil. This usually occurs only when segregated ice lenses form.

Frost heave relates to the occurrence of freezing at temperatures below 0 °C. In understanding this process, we need to consider the phase transition of substances. Two phases of a substance can coexist only when the free energies of the phases are equal. This occurs when H_2O is at the freezing (or melting) point. However, at temperatures below the freezing point, the free energy of the liquid exceeds that of the solid. The result is an unstable condition in which the phase of lower free energy is increased at the expense of the higher energy phase. In other words, as the temperature drops below 0 °C, water changes to ice.

In soils, however, water commonly contains dissolved salts. This results in depression of the freezing point. Usually, because the concentration of dissolved salts is weak, this freezing point depression is only 0.1 °C or so below 0 °C. This concept is illustrated in Fig. 4.1.

A second important process relates to the molecular forces existing between phases when the interface is confined. This is known as capillarity. In soils, the capillarity between soil particles increases as the soil particles become smaller. Moreover, during soil freezing, the formation of ice also results in water being confined progressively in a smaller space. Accordingly, the free energy of the water falls as freezing takes place and this is most apparent in fine-grained sediments. This effect is termed cryosuction and is the cause of water migration to the freezing zone.

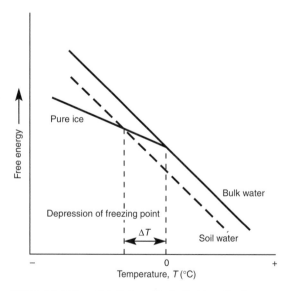

Figure 4.1 Schematic diagram illustrating how the lower free energy of soil water, a weak solution, leads to a depression of the freezing point (from Williams and Smith, 1989).

The amount of water which freezes at any one particular temperature will also depend on the nature of the soil in question. This is because different mineral particle surfaces have different adsorption properties. Adsorption refers to forces emanating from the particle surface which lower the free energy of water in a thin layer near the surface of the particle. For freezing to continue, this moisture needs to be converted to ice, and consequently lower temperatures are required. Usually, a film of water separates soil ice from solid particles. Thus, 'frozen' soil still contains unfrozen water. However, as temperatures fall, these films become thinner. This explains why, in a series of laboratory experiments, Williams (1976) and others have been able to demonstrate that different soils retain varying amounts of unfrozen water at temperatures below 0 °C (Fig. 4.2).

Several other soil–moisture freezing relationships need brief mention. First, latent heat is involved in the phase change of H_2O. For example, when ground freezes and ice segregation occurs, temperatures remain constant owing to latent heat flux. This is the so-called 'zero-curtain' effect (see Fig. 4.5). It should be emphasized that heat flow always takes place in response to a thermal gradient. The latent heat released at the freezing front flows upwards along the thermal gradient, so temperatures do not rise; rather, they remain constant for as long as sufficient latent heat is released to satisfy the thermal gradient and thermal conductivity. When ice formation decreases, owing to reduced supply of water, less latent heat is released and the soil cools down, allowing the freezing front to advance once again.

Second, the progressive freezing of soil water helps determine the thermal properties of the soil. For example, the apparent heat capacity will rise and the thermal conductivity of frozen soils change as the ice and water contents change. Third, pressure lowers the freezing point of water and this can result in unfrozen conditions because of high overburden pressures (as beneath advancing glaciers) at depth.

4.3 Ice segregation and frost heave

As soil freezes, any water present within the soil segregates into ice lenses. Early work carried out upon the mechanism of segregated ice formation by Taber (1929, 1930) led to two important conclusions: (a) ice segregation is favoured in materials having a grain size composition of 0.01 mm diameter or less, and (b) ice crystals grow within the material in the direction in which heat is being most rapidly conducted away, i.e. normal to the surface. These conclusions have been verified by a number of later studies.

The cryosuction resulting from capillarity increases by approximately 1.2 MPa per °C below 0 °C (Williams and Smith, 1989, p. 190). Cryosuction is usually expressed using the terms P_I (pressure of ice) and P_W (pressure of water):

$$P_I - P_W = \text{soil constant } (2\theta/r) \qquad (4.1)$$

The soil constant is a function of θ, the surface tension and soil particle volume, and r, the radius of curvature of the soil particle surface (i.e. grain size). This relationship determines whether segregated ice or pore ice will form. For example, Fig. 4.3 considers two soil particles as representing a section of soil located approximately at the freezing level. When the ground freezes, the freezing plane may either remain stationary above the soil particles, or tongues of ice may descend through the pores. If the freezing plane

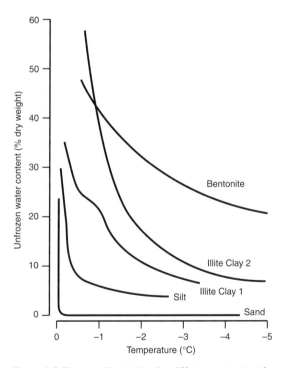

Figure 4.2 Diagram illustrating the different amounts of unfrozen water existing in different soils at temperatures below 0 °C (from Williams and Smith, 1989).

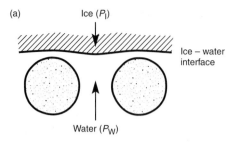

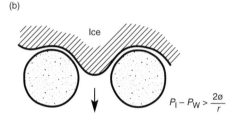

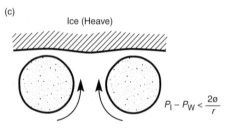

Figure 4.3 Schematic illustration of two mineral soil particles with ice and water: (a) general conditions for segregated or pore ice formation in freezing soil; (b) growth of pore ice; (c) growth of segregated ice + frost heave.

remains above the soil particles, water will move upwards through the soil pores from the unfrozen ground beneath and towards the freezing plane. Ice crystals will develop therefore, and, as long as the supply of water is maintained, an ice lens will develop. This, in turn, promotes an upward heave of the overlying sediment.

The main control over whether the freezing level will remain stationary or descend is cryosuction since this controls the supply of water to the freezing plane. If this tension is high, then it will maintain the freezing plane at its original level; if it is low, then a tongue of ice moves down through the soil by progressively freezing the pore water in place. This forms pore ice as opposed to segregated ice. When it is appreciated that fine-grained soils possess small interstices, and that cryosuction can be more easily maintained in

such a situation, it is clear that segregated ice formation is favoured in fine-grained materials. Such sediments are often termed 'frost-susceptible' by engineers. Pore ice, by contrast, commonly develops in coarser-grained material, often sand, where it is harder for cryosuction to be maintained in the correspondingly larger soil interstices. These 'non-frost-susceptible' materials, usually sandy gravels, are in high demand for building and construction purposes, wherever heaving must be minimized. An additional consideration is that pore water expulsion ahead of the freezing plane in coarse, saturated, non-frost-susceptible soils is commonly cited as the cause of massive ice lenses and the growth of closed system pingos. This is discussed in Chapter 6.

It is also useful to distinguish between primary and secondary frost heave. Primary heave usually refers to the heave that occurs near the frost line, while secondary heave refers to heave that occurs within frozen layers at various temperatures. The latter is explained by the presence of unfrozen films which allow water to slowly migrate through frozen soil. Several experiments have demonstrated that moisture migration through frozen soils is possible (e.g. Hoekstra, 1969; Burt and Williams, 1976). The importance of secondary heave lies in the large heaving pressures that may develop over time. In spite of the fact that frost heave pressures are relatively easily explained, prediction of their amounts appears difficult and controversial, as in the case of chilled gas pipelines (e.g. see Williams, 1986). Although frost heave pressures up to 100–300 kPa may develop relatively quickly (Williams and Smith, 1989, p. 197) there is still no widespread agreement upon the basis for quantitative predictions of heave.

4.4 Freezing and thawing indices

Two quantitative indices are frequently used by geomorphologists in discussing frost-related processes. For convenience, they are briefly outlined here.

First, the calculation of thawing and freezing degree days is based upon the cumulative total air temperatures above or below zero for any one year (Thompson, 1966). Mean daily air temperatures provide the basic data. Degree days provide an index of the severity of the climate and the magnitude of the thaw and freezing periods. Their calculation is useful, therefore, when comparing such parameters as depths of seasonal frost penetration or rates of thermokarst development.

The frequency of freezing and thawing is of particular significance with respect to frost wedging and rock shattering. Degree days give no indication of this and instead, the number of freeze–thaw cycles is more relevant. Unfortunately, several problems limit the usefulness of freeze–thaw cycles as a measure of frost-action effectiveness. First, there is the basic difficulty of defining the exact point of freezing across which the oscillations should be measured. Second, the use of air temperatures to define cycles (e.g. Fraser, 1959) is not completely satisfactory, since significant differences may exist between air and ground temperatures. Third, even when direct ground temperature measurements are available, just what constitutes a freeze–thaw cycle is debatable. Each separate occasion of freezing and thawing requires a different degree of heating and cooling, dependent upon such factors as the ambient temperature and water content of the soil, the duration of the fluctuation, the intensity of solar radiation, and the character and depth of any snow cover. Fourth, cycles may be of different intensities (i.e. different temperature ranges) and this makes any comparison of cycle frequencies difficult. Finally, the duration of any cycle may range from a few minutes to several days, and it is probably unwise to assign equal significance to the various cycles.

4.5 The ground temperature regime

The majority of periglacial environments experience some form of seasonal change through the year. It is possible, therefore, to recognize a summer thaw period of limited duration and a longer winter period during which temperatures remain below 0 °C. The exception to this is the alpine periglacial environment of low latitudes which experiences a diurnal rather than a seasonal cycle.

4.5.1 The annual regime

Numerous data sets now exist which record the annual ground temperature changes. One such data set is illustrated in Fig. 4.4, from Fenghuo Shan on the Tibet Plateau. A number of important characteristics of the seasonal freezing and thawing regime are illustrated. The most obvious is that, at a depth of 1.2 m, the ground remains frozen throughout the year at this locality. Second, the deeper sections of the

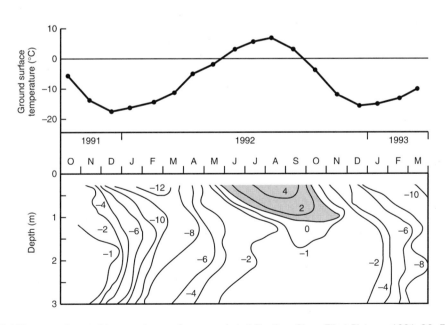

Figure 4.4 The annual ground temperature regime recorded at Fenghuo Shan, Tibet Plateau, 1991–93. Elevation 4850 m a.s.l. (from Wang and French, 1995c).

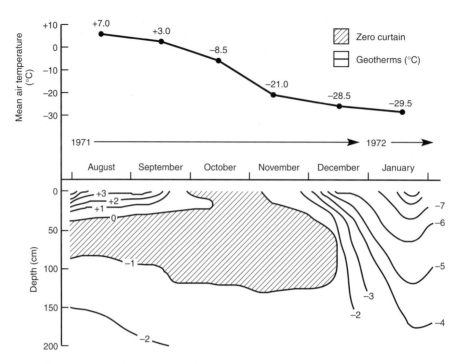

Figure 4.5 Autumn freeze-back and the 'zero curtain' phenomenon at Inuvik, NWT, Canada, 1971–2 (from Heginbottom, 1973).

seasonally thawed layer are in a transitional freezing zone for a large part of the year. At Fenghuo Shan, for example, the temperature at a depth of 1.0 m remains in this transition zone (–4 °C to +2 °C) for over seven months. A third observation is that the length of time during which the ground temperature remains within the transitional freezing boundary progressively decreases towards the ground surface. Thus, the near-surface experiences an increasing number of short, shallow temperature fluctuations related to diurnal, cyclonic or other short-term influences. These are discussed below.

From a geomorphic viewpoint, the nature of the spring thaw is of interest since it influences the nature of spring runoff. Usually, the spring thaw occurs quickly and over 75 per cent of the soil thaws within the first month or five weeks of air temperatures rising above 0 °C. This rapidity of thaw is the result of the percolation of meltwater through the soil under gravity processes, transferring heat to the frozen material beneath. Coarse sediments are particularly suited to rapid thaw since percolation is easy and thermal conductivity of such sediments is generally high.

The autumn freeze-back is much more complex and may extend over eight to ten weeks. This is best illustrated with data from Inuvik, NWT, Canada (Fig. 4.5). Freezing occurs mostly from the surface downwards but also, to a lesser extent, from the permafrost surface upwards. At Inuvik, freezing begins in late September and ends in mid-December. During most of this time, ground temperatures remain remarkably constant in the range of –2 °C to 0 °C. This transitional temperature zone is sometimes referred to as the 'zero curtain'. It occurs because the onset of freezing during the autumn releases latent heat to the soil which temporarily compensates for the upward heat loss associated with the drop in air temperatures.

A second feature of interest in the freeze-up period is the initially slow rate of freezing from the surface downwards and then the dramatic speed-up in freezing at depth. For example, at Inuvik the top 25.0 cm takes over six weeks to drop below the freezing boundary but the remaining 100.0 cm takes only four weeks. This increase in the rate of freezing at depth is the result of two factors. First, there is a decrease in soil moisture with depth since it has already been drawn upwards towards the freezing plane to form segregated ice lenses. Therefore, the amount of latent heat released as a result of the water–ice phase change at depth is reduced and no longer offsets the temperature fall. Second, upfreezing from the perennially frozen ground combines with downfreezing from the surface to quicken the overall movement of the freezing plane at depth.

The implications of these observations with respect to weathering processes are still uncertain. It is clear that much of the soil profile remains within a transitional freezing boundary (−2 °C to 0 °C) for a long and continuous period. The restriction of short-term temperature fluctuations to the surface layers implies that they are incapable of inducing mechanical weathering at depth. It follows that the freezing boundary conditions, which are related to the annual cycle, are probably more relevant when considering weathering at depths in excess of 10–15 cm. However, it is an open question whether mechanical or chemical weathering is more important within a zone of near-zero constant temperatures combined with high moisture content.

There are certain areas for which the annual cycle, as described above, is not entirely representative. Alpine environments of low latitudes are the obvious example since they experience diurnal rather than seasonal conditions. A second example is that of the subarctic locations which experience seasonal freezing and thawing but which are not underlain by permafrost. In such areas, the absence of an impermeable frozen layer beneath results in (a) meltwater percolating to the groundwater-table and (b) an absence of upfreezing in the autumn freeze-up period. The net effect of both is to reduce the importance of the zero curtain.

4.5.2 Short-term fluctuations and freeze–thaw cycles

Short-term temperature fluctuations are frequently imposed upon the long-term temperature cycle previously described. Although it is often difficult to distinguish between the two, these fluctuations may be classified as being either diurnal or cyclonic in nature.

Diurnal variations usually relate to changes in insolation and surface heating brought about by the variations in angle and azimuth of the sun. In high latitudes, however, the diurnal influence is relatively weak in comparison to lower latitudes since the sun is above the horizon for much of the Arctic day. Furthermore, although south- and west-facing slopes should receive greater insolation than slopes of other orientation, these differences are so weak that they are sometimes over-ridden by local factors.

In the temperate latitudes diurnal ranges are much better developed. For example, the range between mean daily maximum and minimum air temperatures, at 3050 m in the Colorado Front Range, can reach 15 °C in July (Fahey, 1973). It is also in alpine environments that the effects of orientation become well developed, with south- and west-facing slopes in the northern hemisphere experiencing significantly higher soil temperatures.

Local climatic events of a cyclonic nature may also produce marked fluctuations in soil temperature. This is especially the case in high Arctic regions where periods of direct solar radiation may heat the ground surface to give a 20–30 °C temperature difference between the air and the ground surface. In Antarctica, for example, Souchez (1967a) observed thawing of snow when the air temperature was −20 °C caused by the localized heating of dark rock surfaces. On Signy Island, Chambers (1966) documented an instance when daytime air temperatures were −0.6 °C but ground temperatures were +5.6 °C, as a result of direct solar insolation. The passing of a cloud or the falling of a small amount of precipitation will also affect soil temperatures. For example, on Banks Island, the author has documented the rapid changes in soil temperatures which follow a summer snowfall of 2.5 cm (French, 1970); within three or four hours, the entire active layer had attained a near-isothermal state owing to rapid percolation downwards of the snowmelt. A final example is provided by the effects of a period of predominantly sunny days followed by several days of dull, overcast and cyclonic weather on Signy Island (Fig. 4.6). During the sunny days, there were distinct diurnal soil and air temperature cycles, with temperatures rising to +14.6 °C at the 1.0 cm depth at one point. On the last two days, when there was almost continuous low and medium cloud cover, the 1.0 cm soil temperature did not rise above +3.4 °C, and the heating and cooling of the soil were far less dramatic. Similarly, on the Tibet Plateau, at altitudes in excess of 4800 m a.s.l., air temperatures fluctuate significantly during the day in accordance with periods of direct sunshine.

Because of their supposed geomorphic significance with respect to frost wedging and cryogenic weathering, the frequency of short-term freeze–thaw cycles has been investigated by many workers. For example, Fraser (1959) used air temperatures to estimate average frequencies of freeze–thaw cycles in northern Canada and concluded that freeze–thaw cycles

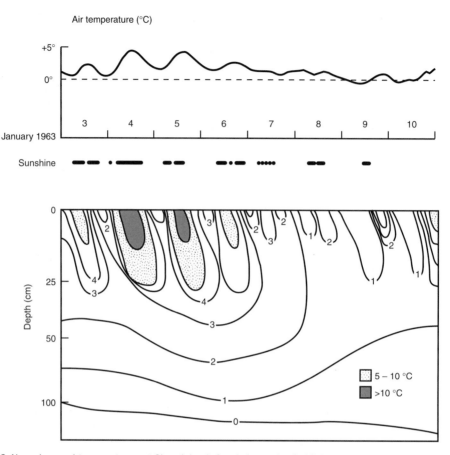

Figure 4.6 Air and ground temperatures at Signy Island, South Antarctic, 3–10 January 1963, and their relationship to cyclonic and diurnal conditions (from Chambers, 1966).

increased southwards from approximately 15 per annum in the Arctic islands to near 50 in southern regions. Not surprisingly, he questioned the effectiveness of freezing and thawing as a geomorphic agent in high latitudes. More recently, numerous direct ground surface measurements in a number of different climatic environments throw increasing doubt upon the assumption that numerous freeze–thaw cycles exist. Observations indicate the number of freeze–thaw cycles to be surprisingly few (Table 4.1). The greatest number occur at the ground surface and these cycles are twice as numerous as air cycles. With depth, however, there is a rapid drop in frequency such that beneath 5.0–10.0 cm often only the annual cycle takes place.

Oceanic periglacial environments have traditionally been assumed to be the most suited for freeze–thaw processes. Even here, however, it has been found that freeze–thaw cycles are not very numerous. For example, on Signy Island, where air temperatures fluctuate constantly within a few degrees of zero, a total of only 42 freeze–thaw cycles were recorded at the 1.0 cm depth during the two years of 1962 and 1963 (Table 4.1). At the 2.5 cm depth the number fell to 25, at the 5.0 cm depth the number was 13 and at depths in excess of 10.0 cm only the annual cycle occurred. According to Chambers, the freeze–thaw cycles on Signy Island are usually caused by cyclonic disturbances leading to a drop in surface temperatures. They rarely last more than a few hours.

Mid-latitude alpine environments are also regarded as being particularly suited to numerous freeze–thaw cycles since they experience marked diurnal temperature fluctuations. In the Japanese Alps, Matsuoka (1990) observed an annual average of 88 cycles at a depth of 1.5 cm over a five-year period, while in the

Table 4.1 Some typical freeze–thaw cycles, variously defined, as recorded in different periglacial environments.

Location	Climatic Type	Ground Cycles	Cycles at 1.0–2.0 cm	Cycles at 5.0 cm	Cycles at 20 cm	Definition of Cycle
Resolute Bay, Canada, 74 °N	High Arctic	23	n.d.	0	n.d.	–2 to 0 °C (28–32°F) (Cook and Raiche, 1962)
Mesters Vig, Greenland, 72 °N	High Arctic	23	n.d.	18	n.d.	Amplitude $\geq 0°$ C (Washburn, 1967)
Siberia (a) Kolyma, 67 °N	Continental – tundra	50	n.d.	n.d.	2	Temperature transitions across 0 °C (Ushakova, 1986)
(b) Vilyusk, 63 °N	Continental – taiga	94	n.d.	n.d.	2	
(c) Krasnoyarsk, 56 °N	Continental – taiga/steppe	59	18	14	4	
Signy Island, 61 °S,	Low temperature range		19	4		+0.5 to –0.5 °C (Chambers, 1966)
Front Range, Colorado, 39 °N	Alpine (3750 m)	n.d.	9	n.d.	n.d.	>0 °C and < 0 °C within 24 hours (Fahey, 1973)
	Subalpine (3000 m)	n.d.	50	n.d.	n.d.	
Japanese Alps, 35 °N	Alpine (2800 m)	n.d.	88	n.d.	n.d.	–2 to +2 °C (Matsuoka, 1990)

n.d., not determined

Colorado Front Range, USA, Fahey (1973) monitored over 50 fluctuations across the 0 °C threshold within 24 hours at two sites in one year. But even these frequencies are relatively low and they certainly do not automatically justify the assumption that freeze–thaw weathering is the dominant process of rock disintegration in periglacial environments.

4.6 Frost cracking

The lowering of temperature of ice-rich frozen soils can lead to a thermal contraction of the ground and the development of fissures. These are called frost fissures or frost cracks. They develop because pure ice has a coefficient of linear expansion of 52.7×10^{-1} at 0 °C and only 50.5×10^{-1} at –30 °C, and because the rates of contraction and expansion of ice-rich sediments are probably little different from those of pure ice.

Thermal contraction cracking is an important frost-action process. The conditions for cracking are discussed in detail in Chapter 6. Here, it is useful to discuss the different types of frost cracks that can occur and their physical appearance. First, there are

cracks which are filled with ice. These are termed ice wedges. Second, there are frost cracks which are filled with sand, known as sand wedges. Third, there are frost cracks filled with mineral soil, known as soil wedges. While ice wedges and sand wedges develop only in permafrost and may extend downwards for several metres, soil wedges are usually confined to the seasonally frozen layer.

4.6.1 Frost cracks filled with ice

The infilling of frost cracks with water and snow which percolates down the cracks results in the development of ice wedges. These are wedge-shaped bodies of vertically foliated ice which build up over a number of years. They are discussed more fully in Chapter 6.

4.6.2 Frost cracks filled with sand

Sand wedges are a second type of frost fissure that develops from thermal contraction of the ground. In this case, no moisture is available to penetrate the crack. Instead, the crack is filled with windblown sediment or other material. Péwé (1959) first described sand wedges at McMurdo Sound in Antarctica which he termed 'tesselons', and, subsequently, similar features have been described from other polar regions (e.g. Nichols, 1966; Ugolini *et al.*, 1973; Pissart, 1968). They usually occur in the more arid permafrost regions, with less than 100 mm of precipitation per year. Typically, the infilling material in sand wedges is in the loess size range. It presents a vertical stratification, with a tendency for a decrease in particle size with increased depth in the wedge, since only the smaller particles are able to penetrate the very narrow tip of the wedge. Some of the most striking sand wedges described to date are from a locality in the Pleistocene Mackenzie Delta, Canada, where wedges, 4–6 m deep, penetrate massive ice (Murton and French, 1993a; see Chapter 6, Fig. 6.3).

4.6.3 Soil wedges (seasonal frost cracking)

Frost cracks which develop primarily in the seasonally frozen layer have been described by a number of workers, notably Dylik (1966), Freidman *et al.* (1971), Jahn (1983) and several Russian investigators (e.g. Danilova, 1956; Katasonov, 1973; Katasonov and Ivanov, 1973). These cracks, which are infilled with mineral soil, are termed 'soil wedges', 'ground veins' or 'seasonal frost cracks'.

Soil wedges are particularly well developed in continental periglacial regions such as parts of central Yakutia, Russia, possibly on account of the thickness of the seasonally thawed layer in that area. However, they have also been described from Iceland, Svalbard and Scandinavia. In Siberia ground veins rarely exceed 1.5 m in depth and are usually found in sand and gravel. The surrounding sediments often show distinct deformation. In many instances there is a 'turning-down' of the enclosing sediments; in others, flame structures and other deformations are present. The frost cracks described from Iceland are similar to the Siberian structures since they are also vein-like structures with a downturning of the enclosing sediments.

Soil wedges pose a number of problems. First, it is not known what type of frost action environment is necessary for them to form, and whether perennially frozen ground is necessary. Instances of seasonal frost cracking have even been reported from middle latitudes (e.g. Washburn *et al.*, 1963). Second, as stressed by Dylik (1966, p. 260), the reason for the downturning of some of the sediments adjacent to the soil wedges is not well understood. It may be that some of the Siberian features are ice-wedge pseudomorphs and result from the thawing of ice wedges formed in an earlier period. Finally, the differing spacings between fissures, as reported from Siberia and Iceland, are difficult to explain. Clearly the interpretation of soil wedges is not complete, and their use as indicators of perennially frozen ground not justified.

4.7 Cryogenic weathering

Cryogenic weathering refers to the combination of mechanico-chemical processes which cause the *in situ* breakdown of rock under cold-climate conditions. In the last 15 years the inadequacy of the simple freeze–thaw cycle, as outlined above, led to studies that have questioned the basic fundamentals of cold-climate weathering. Several different approaches can be recognized. First, detailed field studies have been undertaken with the aim of increasing the availability of data upon rock temperatures, rock moisture contents and rock moisture chemistry (e.g. McGreevy and Whalley, 1982, 1985; Hall *et al.*, 1986). Second, a number of studies have attempted to actually measure the rate of rock disintegration in the field and to develop predictive models (e.g. Matsuoka, 1990, 1991; Douglas *et al.*, 1991). Third, laboratory simulation and modelling, notably in France (e.g. Lautridou, 1982; Lautridou and Seppälä, 1986), Japan (e.g. Matsuoka, 1989) and Russia (e.g. Konishchev, 1982; Grechishchev *et al.*, 1992; Konishchev and Rogov, 1993), have emphasized the role of granulometry, mineralogical composition, and micro-structures in rock weathering. Finally, the role of ice segregation as a weathering mechanism has been examined both theoretically and experimentally (e.g. Hallet *et al.*, 1991; Akagawa and Fukuda, 1991).

To complicate the situation, several weathering processes other than freeze–thaw are now recognized to be significant under cold-climate conditions. These include (a) the interaction of freeze–thaw with salt weathering (e.g. Williams and Robinson, 1981, 1991), (b) the role of wetting and drying (e.g. Pissart and Lautridou, 1984; Prick *et al.*, 1993), (c) thermal fatigue (e.g. Hall and Hall, 1991) and (d) the role of chemical (e.g. Dixon *et al.*, 1984) and biological (e.g. Hall and Otte, 1990) weathering.

Figure 4.7 An example of bedrock weathering by frost action, Prince Patrick Island, NWT, Canada. The rock is a fissile sandstone of Upper Jurassic age.

It is not possible within the space constraints of this chapter to summarize all of the recent literature on cryogenic weathering. Here, attention focuses upon, first, the rate of bedrock weathering by frost action, and, second, experimental and theoretical studies aimed at understanding the fundamental processes behind frost weathering. This is followed by a discussion of some of the other weathering processes which operate in cold climates.

4.7.1 Bedrock weathering by frost action

The disintegration and mechanical breakdown of rock by the freezing of water present within the pore spaces, joints and bedding planes is widely regarded as a particularly potent geomorphic agent in periglacial environments (Fig. 4.7). Extensive surfaces of angular rock fragments commonly referred to as 'block fields' in the European literature and '*kurums*'

in the Russian literature (e.g. Romanovskii *et al.*, 1989), are the most dramatic features, but others include hillslope and summit tors, and near-vertical rockwalls with extensive debris slopes beneath.

Several investigators stress the role of microfractures in bedrock as the method by which water penetrates bedrock and subsequently freezes to cause rock disintegration. However, when this cracking takes place and what causes it are still not clear. For example, using sandstone samples, Hallet *et al.* (1991) inferred, from experiments monitoring acoustic emissions, that freezing-induced microfracture propagation occurred at temperatures between $-3\,°C$ and $-6\,°C$. Thus, microfracturing may not require freeze–thaw cycles or even falling temperatures but a constant sub-zero temperature. Earlier, Walder and Hallet (1985, 1986) emphasized that a high frequency of freeze–thaw cycles is not necessary for crack propagation, which can occur at temperatures anywhere between $-4\,°C$ and $-15\,°C$.

In other experiments reported by Konishchev and Rogov (1993) it has been found that the speed of crack growth in water (ice) saturated samples far exceeds that of dry samples when subject to numerous freeze–thaw cycles. These data (Table 4.2(a)), for different rock types, give some indication of the approximate maximum speed of frost weathering. The average thicknesses of the disintegration layer for ice-saturated rocks during one freeze–thaw cycle ranged from a high of 3.5 mm in marl to a low of $30–50 \times 10^{-5}$ mm in sandstone and porphyry. Clearly, rock type is an important variable in addition to whether or not the rock is dry or saturated.

Some recent field observations, also summarized by Konishchev and Rogov (1993), provide insight into the nature of bedrock disintegration by frost. For example, in an engineering study in Tashkent, Tadjikstan, numerous microcracks appeared in granite as the result of sharp temperature changes and large temperature amplitudes, and in connection with heterogeneous mineralogical composition. In the Ukraine, the speed of frost weathering of water-saturated limestones on buildings in Simpheropol City has been 1–10 mm/year, while on dry or only locally saturated limestone, rates were lower, between 10^{-1} and 10^{-2} mm/year. Finally, in the Taimyr region of northern Siberia, arcose sandstone exposed in an opencast mine showed a marked increase in cracks and fissures in the years immediately following exposure to periodic freeze–thaw (Table 4.2(b)).

Table 4.2 Some Russian data concerning rates of bedrock weathering by frost action: (a) average thickness of disintegration layer for one freeze–thaw cycle in various rocks of different water saturation; (b) data on fissuring of feldspar sandstones in opencast mine, Taimyr, Siberia

(a)

Rock, deposits	Average Thickness of Disintegration Layer (mm)			
	Dry Samples		Water-saturated Samples	
	Range (mm)	Average (mm)	Range (mm)	Average (mm)
Granite	$(6.4–8.6) \times 10^{-5}$	8.0×10^{-5}	$(6.4–34.9) \times 10^{-5}$	14.5×10^{-5}
Weathered granite	$(8.7–11) \times 10^{-5}$	10×10^{-5}	$(10–32) \times 10^{-5}$	20×10^{-5}
Gneiss-granite, gneiss	$(7.0–9.2) \times 10^{-5}$	8.0×10^{-5}	$(7.0–9.9) \times 10^{-5}$	9.0×10^{-5}
Porphyry	$(8.1–25) \times 10^{-5}$	11×10^{-5}	$(3.1–92.4) \times 10^{-5}$	30×10^{-5}
Diabase	$(0.8–8.3) \times 10^{-5}$	4.5×10^{-5}	$(1.1–8.3) \times 10^{-5}$	4.5×10^{-5}
Metamorphic shale	$(2.8–27) \times 10^{-5}$	12×10^{-5}	$(8–35) \times 10^{-5}$	18×10^{-5}
Limestone	$(3.8–7.3) \times 10^{-5}$	5.5×10^{-5}	$(22.3–24.7) \times 10^{-5}$	23.5×10^{-5}
Sandstone	$(4.0–7.1) \times 10^{-5}$	6.0×10^{-5}	$(4.0–160) \times 10^{-5}$	48×10^{-5}
Limestone, dolomite	$(400–1000) \times 10^{-5}$	600×10^{-5}	1–8.7	1.0
Marl	$(400–1000) \times 10^{-5}$	600×10^{-5}	1–8.7	3.5

(b) Fissures	Year of Openpit Stripping	Width of Fissures (mm)	
		Min.	Max.
Horizontal	1973	15	1
	1977	18	0.5
Vertical and subvertical	1973	50	3
	1970	60	1

Source: from Konishchev and Rogov (1993)

The factors influencing cold-climate rock disintegration have been examined in several studies. One of the most recent is based on field observations in the Japanese Alps, Svalbard and Antarctica (Matsuoka, 1990, 1991). The conclusion is that the annual frost shattering rate is not only a function of freeze–thaw frequency per year, but also of the degree of water (ice) saturation, and bedrock tensile strength. Because shattering rates were lowest at the Antarctica and Svalbard sites, it was further concluded that moisture content is the most effective environmental factor controlling the shattering rate. Such a conclusion may be an oversimplification however, since elsewhere in Antarctica Hall (1990) found that rates of wet rock disintegration on Signy Island, an environment of numerous freeze–thaw cycles and high humidity, were very slow, of the order of only 2 per cent mass loss per 100 years. In another study aimed at understanding the controls over rock weathering, Douglas *et al.* (1991) found that microfracture density and crack width on basalt rockwalls correlated best with the overall pattern of annual rock removal. Although peaks did occur in spring and autumn, presumably due to frost, other factors such as tensile strength of the rock were equally important.

4.7.2 Frost weathering models

The conventional view has been that frost weathering (i.e. frost shattering) is the result of the 9 per cent volumetric increase which occurs during the water–ice phase transition. Theoretically, the maximum pressure set up by the freezing of water is 2100 kg/cm^2 at -22 °C. At temperatures below this, the pressure decreases because the ice begins to contract. In reality, however, this maximum value is almost certainly never reached or even approached since a number of factors operate to reduce the pressures developed. First, the water or ice must be contained within a closed system for high pressures to develop; this usually means conditions of extremely rapid freezing from the surface downwards which seals the pores and cracks in the rock. Second, air bubbles in the ice, and pore spaces within the rock reduce pressures considerably. Third, and probably most important of all, the rock

Table 4.3 A comparison of the volume expansion and segregation ice models of frost weathering

Volumetric Expansion Model	Segregation Ice Model
1. No frost weathering if pore fluid contracts upon freezing.	1. Frost weathering does not depend on the volumetric expansion of water during freezing. Frost weathering results from heaving pressures that are universal in freezing porous solids whether the pore fluid expands or contracts upon freezing.
2. No frost weathering under conditions common in nature: saturation level less than about 91%, and pores not effectively sealed off (hydraulically closed system).	2. Saturation level influences rate of water migration in hydraulically connected pores (open system). Low saturation does not preclude water migration and crack growth.
3. Water may be expelled from freezing sites, but never drawn towards such sites.	3. Water attraction to freezing sites, owing to chemical potential gradients, is a key factor in frost weathering. If crack growth cannot accommodate water-to-ice expansion, water is expelled from freezing sites.
4. Crack growth should occur in bursts as water freezes and expands	4. Slow, steady crack growth should occur as water migrates towards ice bodies within cracks. Predicted crack-growth rates are compatible with values inferred from experimental data.

Source: from Hallet *et al.* (1991)

itself and certainly the soil mantle, is not strong enough to withstand such extreme pressures, especially since it is a tensile force rather than a compressive force which is being considered. As a result, the actual pressures developed by the freezing of water in rocks are much less than the theoretical maximum. For these reasons, the conventional interpretation of frost shattering as the cause of cryogenic weathering is largely inadequate.

A more realistic model, especially applicable to soils, is a segregation ice model of frost weathering. This was first proposed by Walder and Hallet (1985). The model treats freezing in water-saturated rock as closely analogous to slow freezing in fine-grained soils. Expansion is primarily the result of water migration to growing ice lenses and only secondarily the result of the 9 per cent volumetric expansion (Hallet *et al.*, 1991). Frost weathering is the result, therefore, of the progressive growth of microcracks and relatively large pores wedged open by ice growth.

Although this model is largely theoretical, there is substantial circumstantial evidence which supports it. This includes (a) direct studies of water migration towards the freezing front in freezing rocks (Fukuda, 1983), (b) dilametric studies of freezing and thawing calcareous rocks (Prick *et al.*, 1993) and (c) laboratory data from freeze–thaw experiments (e.g. Letavernier and Ozouf, 1987; Matsuoka, 1990) in which frost-

induced spalling and/or expansion occurs. Unfortunately, most experiments to date lack sufficient control over the thermal and moisture regimes involved and are not precise enough as regards the exact magnitude, timing and location of the frost-induced deterioration. For example, numerous laboratory experiments have involved periodic measurements of weight loss following repeated and varied freezing and thawing of different rock types (e.g. Williams and Robinson, 1981; Lautridou and Ozouf, 1982; Lautridou, 1988; Matsuoka, 1990). The weakness of these studies is that there is relatively little information on the exact time and the temperature range under which actual breakdown occurred. Also, the spatial distribution of the weight loss and any growth in microcracks or fractures are not usually recorded. Thus, the ice segregation model is largely untested at present and requires further study. Table 4.3 compares aspects of the two frost weathering models.

4.7.3 Cryogenic weathering of unconsolidated deposits

Frost weathering may be regarded as one component of the more poorly understood complex of processes generally referred to as cryogenic weathering.

A number of field and experimental studies in the FSU have shown that one of the main effects of cold-climate weathering is the production of silty particles with grain sizes of between 0.05 and 0.01 mm in diameter. Loess-like sediments are extremely common and widespread in the zones of both present-day and Pleistocene permafrost. Analysis of this material indicates that it consists mainly of primary minerals such as quartz, feldspars, amphibolites and pyroxenes (Konishchev, 1982; Konishchev and Rogov, 1993).

Russian scientists argue that frost weathering occurs within the layer of unfrozen water adsorbed on the surfaces of these particles and the susceptibility of these particles to weathering depends not so much on their mechanical strength as on the thickness and properties of this unfrozen water film. According to Konishchev (1982), the protective role of the stable film of unfrozen water is highest with silicates, such as biotite and muscovite, and lowest with quartz. Cryogenic disintegration occurs when the thickness of the protective unfrozen water film becomes less than the dimensions of the microfractures and defects that characterize the surface of mineral particles.

In a series of laboratory experiments in which minerals were subject to repeated freeze–thaw it was established that 0.05–0.01 mm grain sizes are the limit for the cryogenic disintegration of quartz, amphiboles and pyroxenes, 0.1–0.5 mm for feldspars and 0.25–0.1 mm for biotite. Quartz grains, in all the size fractions investigated, proved to be less resistant as compared with corresponding grain sizes of unchanged feldspars (Fig. 4.8). These relationships are opposite to the behaviour of these minerals under temperate or warm climates. The yield of heavy minerals is also unusual in that the 0.05–0.01 mm fraction is lower than that in the 0.05–0.1 mm fraction.

The relatively high degree of instability of quartz under cold-climate conditions has also been confirmed by other studies (e.g. Minervin, 1982; Rogov, 1987; Table 4.4). According to Minervin (1982), the mechanism of cryogenic disintegration is based on the wedging effect when ice forms in microcracks and produces volume widening following repeated freeze–thaw while Rogov (1987) states that the freezing of gas–liquid inclusions, commonly containing salts, is the specific cause of the widening.

Konishchev and Rogov (1985) have also been able to characterize unconsolidated surficial sediments taken from many parts of Siberia on the basis of a coefficient of cryogenic contrast (CCC), defined as:

$$\mathrm{CCC} = \frac{Q_1/F_1}{Q_2/F_2}$$

where Q_1 = quartz content (per cent) in the fraction 0.05–0.01 mm, F_1 = feldspar content (per cent) in fraction 0.05–0.01 mm, Q_2 = quartz content (per cent) in fraction 0.1–0.05 mm, F_2 = feldspar content (per cent) in fraction 0.1–0.05 mm. Using sediments of different ages in northern Yakutia and the Kolyma Lowlands, it was possible to determine that deposits affected by cryogenic weathering have CCC values typically in excess of 1.5.

Additional experimental studies concerning the stability of minerals under negative temperatures are required before the significance of these Russian results can be assessed.

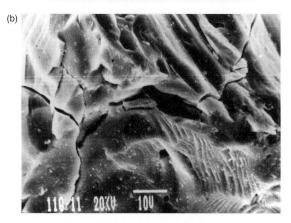

(a)

(b)

Figure 4.8 Cracks in quartz particles, formed as a result of freezing in gas-liquid inclusions:
(a) magnification × 400
(b) magnification × 1800 (Photos courtesy of V. Konishchev)

Table 4.4 Experimental data which demonstrate the instability of quartz particles under cryogenic weathering

Condition of Experiment		Mineral	Content of Grain Size (%)				
			Diameter of Grain (mm)				
			0.25–0.1	0.1–0.05	0.05–0.01	0.01–0.005	0.005–0.001
1. Before experiment		Quartz	100	–	–	–	–
		Feldspar	100	–	–	–	–
		Calcite	100	–	–	–	–
		Biotite	100	–	–	–	–
2. Freezing–thawing water-saturated	(–10 °C) (+15 °C)	Quartz	11	20	68	1	–
		Feldspar	7	44	48	1	1
		Calcite	6	1	20	30	29
		Biotite	98	–	1	–	1
3. Freezing–heating dry	(–10 °C) (+50 °C)	Quartz	98.5	1	0.5	–	–
		Feldspar	98	1.5	0.5	–	–
		Calcite	93.5	5	1	0.5	–
		Biotite	100	–	–	–	–
4. Watering–drying in laboratory condition	(+18 to +20 °C)	Quartz	100	–	–	–	–
		Feldspar	100	–	–	–	–
		Calcite	100	–	–	–	–
		Biotite	100	–	–	–	–

Source: from Konishchev and Rogov (1993)

4.7.4 Physico-chemical weathering

Even more poorly understood are the physico-chemical changes which occur under negative temperatures. For example, one special problem is the behaviour of the fine-grained (clay) fraction. Several complex processes appear to operate. In early experiments, Konishchev *et al.* (1976) and others found that the particle sizes of kaolin and montmorillonite decreased while the crystalline lattice and interparcel distances generally increased after 200 freeze–thaw cycles. In later experiments described by Ershov (1984) particle disintegration dominated in the early stages of cryogenic transformation but then, after 10–100 freeze–thaw cycles, aggregation and coagulation occurred together with marked changes in pH and the ion exchange complex. Several other Russian experimental studies, summarized in Konishchev and Rogov (1993), indicate the complexity of physico-chemical changes that occur in fine-grained sediments subject to cold conditions. One set of such results is presented in Table 4.5. However, until more is understood about these physico-chemical processes that take place at negative temperatures, it seems impossible to interpret these data or to assess the nature of cryogenic weathering in fine-grained soils. In all probability, transformations take place not only during freeze–thaw cycles, when temperature transitions cross 0 °C, but also within negative temperature fluctuations.

4.8 Salt weathering

An important mechanism of frost weathering is the crystallization pressures generated by growing ice crystals that feed off migrating pore water, as explained earlier in section 4.7.2. Commonly, however, the water and ice are not necessarily pure. This leads to a number of solute effects which can range from the relatively simple pressures generated by salt crystallization itself to the complexities of physico-chemical weathering, as explained in section 4.7.4.

Laboratory experiments have shown that some rock types normally resistant to frost weathering become highly susceptible once they have been immersed in salt solution (e.g. Williams and Robinson, 1981). At the same time the damage caused by the combination of salt and frost to building materials, bridges and highway construction in general, are well known in countries which experience seasonal frost such as Canada, the United States and Sweden. For example, a considerable literature exists upon the durability of cement and concrete in frost-dominated climates (e.g. Rösli and Harnik, 1980).

Table 4.5 Chemical changes observed following repeated freezing and thawing of clay minerals

Mineral	Number of Freeze–Thaw Cycles	Content (mmol/100 g)		
		Na^+	K^+	Ca^{2+}
Kaolinite	0	0.08	0.19	13.86
	100	0.20	–	11.65
Bentonite	0	8.26	6.00	44.22
	100	15.66	0.38	47.53
Polymineral clay	0	0.16	0.13	57.42
	100	6.00	0.64	75.25

Source: data from Datsko and Rogov (1988)

Geomorphological studies into salt and frost weathering have concentrated upon their effects upon limestone and dolomite terrains (e.g. St-Onge, 1959; Goudie, 1974; Dredge, 1992), along coastal platforms (e.g. Trenhaile and Rudakas, 1981), and how different freezing regimes and varying strengths of salt solutions influence rock types (e.g. Fahey, 1985; Jerwood *et al.*, 1990a, 1990b). In addition, several descriptive studies document exfoliation, honeycomb weathering and granular disintegration, all partially or wholly attributed to a combination of salt and frost weathering (e.g. Calkin and Cailleux, 1962; Cailleux and Calkin, 1963; Czeppe, 1964; Selby, 1971a; Watts, 1983).

Williams and Robinson (1991) summarize the various explanations that have been suggested as to why salts often accelerate frost weathering. The more important are described here. First, salts can accumulate in the outer layers of rocks as a result of surface evaporation. This tends to block the pores and seal the surface, often leading to surface hardening. As a result, water cannot escape by extrusion through freezing, thus increasing the stresses within the rock. Second, salts may intensify frost weathering because the rock is subject to both ordinary frost action (i.e. volume expansion and/or ice crystallization) and salt crystallization. In theory, however, it is only at temperatures below the depressed freezing point that weathering can be due to the combined pressures. Therefore, this simple explanation does not account for the enhanced frost weathering in combination with salt, which is known to occur at temperatures above this. Third, frost damage may result from the expansion and contraction of adsorbed water on clay particles. This is sometimes referred to as 'hydration shattering' (White, 1976). If salts are present, freezing of such adsorbed water is delayed and they can continue to expand, as freezing progresses, causing enhanced rock disintegration. This explanation does not account for frost and salt weathering of non-sorption-sensitive rocks such as sandstones. Fourth, the enhanced damage associated with salt and rock weathering may partly be the result of the slower rates of freezing associated with dilute salt concentrations. Thus, the resulting ice crystals will be larger than normal. In this case, experimental studies have yet to demonstrate that slower rates of freezing cause more frost disintegration than faster rates.

It is clear that much is not understood about the relationship between frost action and salt weathering. On the other hand, there is an obvious relationship between salt weathering and certain landforms that is best illustrated in the very cold, arid environments of the world. In the ice-free areas of Antarctica for example, such as the Dry Valleys, honeycomb or cavernous weathering forms, often termed 'taffoni', and granular disintegration in granites and gneisses are common (Fig. 4.9, Table 4.6). Under these extremely cold conditions, the number of freeze–thaw cycles is exceptionally small since temperatures frequently remain below 0 °C throughout the year. The amount of ice present in the soil is also small. Several arguments suggest that salt crystallization is the dominant process responsible for these distinct weathering forms. First, the weathered particles are composed of angular granules and flakes which show no signs of chemical alteration. Second, weathering occurs not only on exposed bedrock but also beneath and inside boulders, forming hollows and irregular undercut niches. This precludes direct wind action but suggests that salts are picked up by wind from the surface of sea ice and soil and carried in snow where it accumulates around and beneath boulders.

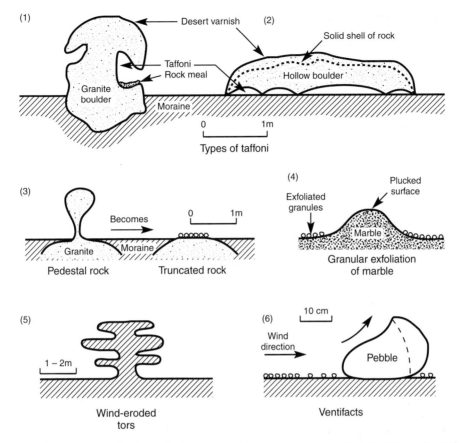

Figure 4.9 Types of cavernous weathering, taffoni structures and wind erosional features occurring in Antarctica (modified from Selby, 1971a).

Then, as the snow sublimates, salts gradually accumulate. Thus, salt weathering in Antarctica is a form of mechanical weathering, and probably influenced by wind. Similar features occur in northeast Greenland and interior Yukon.

4.9 Solution and karstification

The downslope percolation of rainwater and snowmelt may effect considerable denudation by solution if the underlying sediments are of a calcareous nature. This is on account of the solubility of calcium carbonate ($CaCO_3$) in water. In areas underlain by relatively pure limestones, this process assumes particular importance. Furthermore, since the solubility of $CaCO_3$ in water increases with a decrease in temperature, it has been suggested that

solution in periglacial and polar regions is considerably greater than in other regions. In his study of denudation in northern Sweden, Rapp (1960a) concluded that solutional loss was by far the most important agent of denudation. However, other studies in different periglacial environments suggest that solutional activity is no greater under periglacial conditions than under other conditions. For example, using data obtained from the central Canadian Arctic, Smith (1972) has shown that (a) solution rates are actually smaller than in low latitudes, (b) carbonate concentrations in standing water bodies are of the same order of magnitude as those of temperate regions, and (c) that concentrations of carbon dioxide in snowbanks do not necessarily exist. Some typical limestone solution values and rates of denudation are listed in Table 4.7. It would appear that a wide range of solutional values occur in periglacial environments and other

Table 4.6 Reports of honeycomb weathering in Antarctica

Location	Rock Type	Reference
Antarctica:		
West coast, Antarctic Peninsula	Gabbro	Muscoe (1982, table 1)
Queen Maud Land	Granite, gneiss	Muscoe (1982, table 1)
Sor Rondane Mountains	Not specified	Sekyra (1969)
South Victoria Island:		
Cape Evans	Granite, gneiss, dolerite	Muscoe (1982, table 1)
Cape Royds	Alkaline lavas	Muscoe (1982, table 1)
Taylor Valley, McMurdo Oasis	Gneiss	Selby (1971a); Muscoe (1982, table 1)
Victoria Valley	Granite, gneiss	Calkin and Cailleux (1962); Cailleux and Calkin (1963)
Wilkes Land:		
Bunger Oasis, Schirmacher Oasis	Granite, gneiss, schist	Sekyra (1969); Muscoe (1982, table 1)
Bunger and Freedom Hills:		
Freedom Archipelago	Dolerite, granite, quartz, pegmatite	Muscoe (1982, table 1)

factors being equal, precipitation controls the solution rate. Therefore, the generally low rates of limestone denudation which characterize the polar and continental localities reflect the relative aridity of these areas.

The significance of limestone solution is usually considered within the context of limestone or 'karstic' relief. In periglacial environments, the presence of permafrost in many areas and the inability of water to percolate downwards suggests that limestone solution is incapable of producing a karst-like relief similar to that which is found in other environments. Thus, St-Onge (1959) remarked upon the absence of solutional effects in terrain developed in gypsum of Ellef Ringnes Island, and Bird (1967, pp. 257–270), in a detailed account of the limestone scenery of the central Canadian Arctic, concluded that typical solutional effects are weakly developed. However, recent studies now suggest that a 'subcutaneous karst' model, first proposed by Ciry (1962), is applicable to limestone permafrost terrain (Ford, 1984). This model asserts that groundwater circulation and solution are limited to the seasonally active zone, favouring the development of spreads of

Table 4.7 Some typical rates of limestone solution under periglacial and non-periglacial conditions

Location	Mean Annual Precipitation (mm)	Net Rate of Denudation (mm/1000 years)	Total Carbonate Hardness (ppm)	
			$CaCO_3$	$MgCO_3$
Periglacial				
Somerset Island, NWT, Canada	130	2	84	22
Northern Yukon, Canada	215	n.d.	80	106
Spitsbergen	300	27		
Tanana River, central Alaska	450	40		
Svartisen, northern Norway	740–4000	400		
Non-periglacial				
Western Ireland	1000–1250	51–63	66	11
Southern Algeria	60	6		
Indonesia	200–300	83		

Source: data from Jennings (1971, Table 6); Sweeting (1972, Tables X and XI); Smith (1972); Thibaudeau *et al.* (1988)

(a)

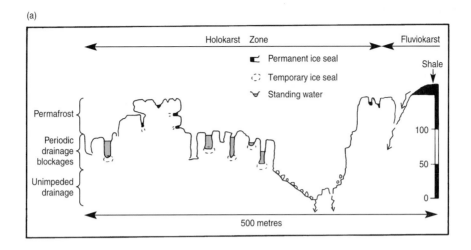

(b)

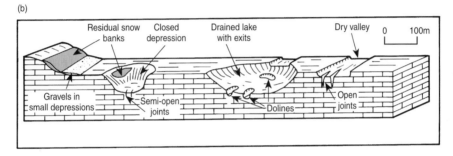

Figure 4.10 Karst morphologies associated with discontinuous permafrost terrain:
(a) Nahanni karst, NWT (from Ford, 1987); (b) Akpatok Island, NWT
(from Lauriol and Gray, 1990).

shallow karren (i.e. solutionally pitted) ground at the expense of sinkhole and cavern topography.

The relationship between karst and glaciation has been considered by Ford (1984, 1987) for northern Canada under several categories. The first category is the high Arctic islands where continuous permafrost exists. Here, the bedrock remained frozen both beneath Pleistocene ice and during deglaciation. Thus, karst development is postglacial in age and restricted to the active layer, especially along the edges of scarps where the active layer is deepest and where drainage is most effective. Today, widespread but minor solutional forms (karren) on exposed bedrock surfaces in these regions accelerate rock disintegration by other weathering processes. A second category is the southern Arctic islands and northern mainland where limestone terrain is characterized by reticulate patterns of large 'corridor' troughs. Ford (1984) hypothesizes that these were created by melt-

water beneath weakly erosive basal ice of the ice cap interior. A third type of karst results from the hydrological conditions associated with warm-based marginal ice, or from sustained thaw during the postglacial. This occurs in the subarctic, in the zone of widespread discontinuous permafrost. Here, large fluvio-karst systems have formed, as in the Great Bear Lake region (van Everdingen, 1981), the central Yukon Mts (Harris *et al.*, 1983) and Akpatok Island (Lauriol and Gray, 1990). Large closed depressions, powerful karst springs and ephemeral lakes are characteristic. In all probability, these karst systems antedate the last glaciation and were either sustained beneath the ice or re-established during the deglacial phase. Finally, the case of the Nahanni karst, located close to the southern limit of widespread permafrost, must be mentioned. Here, the last glaciation is thought to have occurred more than 300 000 years ago (Brook and Ford, 1978, 1982). Thus, an extensive period of cold non-glacial conditions has allowed the development of 'the most accidented cold regions karst that is known' (Ford, 1987, p. 520), possessing impressive canyons, gorges, caves, springs and subterranean drainage.

Two models for karstification (Fig. 4.10) within the discontinuous permafrost zone of northern Canada summarize the major relief features associated with cold karst. Karstic terrain known to exist on Svalbard (Salvigsen and Elgersma, 1985) and in Siberia (Popov *et al.*, 1972) suggests that these karst models are of wide applicability.

study using acoustic emissions. *Permafrost and Periglacial Processes*, **2**, 283–300.

Konishchev, N.V. and V.V. Rogov (1993) Investigations of cryogenic weathering in Europe and Northern Asia. *Permafrost and Periglacial Processes*, **4**, 49–64.

Matsuoka, N. (1991) A model of the rate of frost shattering: application to field data from Japan, Svalbard and Antarctica. *Permafrost and Periglacial Processes*, **2**, 271–281.

Williams, P.J. and M.J. Smith (1989) *The frozen earth. Fundamentals of geocryology*. Cambridge University Press, pp. 1–26, 83–121.

Further reading

Ford, D. (1987) Effects of glaciations and permafrost upon the development of karst in Canada. *Earth Surface Processes and Landforms*, **12**, 507–521.

Hallet, B., J.S. Walder and C.W. Stubbs (1991) Weathering by segregation ice growth in microcracks at sustained subzero temperatures: verification from an experimental

Discussion topics

1. How do ice segregation and frost heave of the ground take place?
2. Compare the volumetric expansion model and the segregation ice model of frost weathering.
3. What processes constitute cryogenic weathering?
4. How effective is freeze–thaw weathering in promoting rock disintegration?

CHAPTER 5

Permafrost

More than 20 per cent of the world's land area is underlain by permafrost. The Former Soviet Union (FSU) possesses the largest extent of permafrost, $c.$ 49 per cent of its territory (11×10^6 km²). Canada is second with $c.$ 50 per cent (5.7×10^6 km²) underlain by permafrost. The People's Republic of China ranks third, with $c.$ 22 per cent (2.1×10^6 km²) underlain by permafrost. Elsewhere, more than 80 per cent of Alaska possesses permafrost, bodies of alpine permafrost with areas greater than 100 000 km² occur in the contiguous western part of the United States, and other permafrost bodies occur in Scandinavia, Greenland, Antarctica and the various high mountains of the world.

The distribution of permafrost is controlled by a number of variables, the most important being climate. Permafrost gives rise to unique terrain conditions and landforms. Many are the result of the aggradation and degradation of ground ice. The groundwater hydrology of permafrost terrain differs from that of non-permafrost terrain in a number of ways, and also promotes unique landform features.

In many periglacial regions, a consequence of the long period of winter cold and the relatively short period of summer thaw is the formation of a layer of frozen ground that does not completely thaw during the summer. This perennially frozen ground is termed permafrost.

5.1 Historical perspective

Despite the numerous reports of frozen ground made by early eighteenth and nineteenth century travellers and explorers, our understanding of permafrost has developed only recently. Russian scientists have traditionally been more advanced than their North American counterparts in this field, primarily because of the earlier history of settlement of Siberia. The earliest known scientific investigations of permafrost were carried out at Yakutsk in eastern Siberia by the Russian scientist A. F. von Middendorf in 1844–46. He studied the temperature regime of Shergin's Well, a shaft 116 m deep, which was dug for a wealthy merchant in a vain quest for underground water. Von Middendorf found that not only did the temperature of the permafrost increase with depth but that the seasonal fluctuations of temperature did not extend beneath 20 m. Subsequently, other Russian scientists developed the study of permafrost and by the late nineteenth century attempts were being made to plot permafrost boundaries in Russia. Today the Siberian Division of the Russian Academy of Sciences maintains a large Permafrost Institute at Yakutsk, employing several hundred people.

In North America, the importance of permafrost was only realized when attention focused on Alaska and other northern regions during the Second World War. The building of the Alaskan Highway in 1942 and the construction of the Canol pipeline in 1943 were major engineering undertakings on permafrost

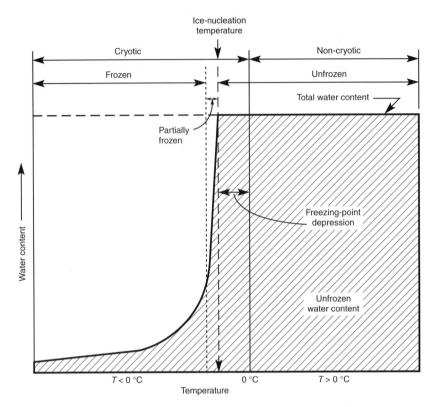

Figure 5.1 Terms used to describe the state of the water relative to ground temperature in soil materials subjected to freezing temperatures (modified from van Everdingen, 1985).

which highlighted the inadequacies of traditional methods of construction. In addition, the difficulties of water and sewage provision, and the limitations placed on agriculture and mining by permafrost meant that large-scale permanent settlement of Arctic North America was unrealistic until permafrost problems were understood. Referring specifically to Alaska, S. W. Muller, of the US Army Corps of Engineers, wrote in 1945

> The destructive action of permafrost phenomena has materially impeded the colonization and development of extensive and potentially rich areas in the north. Roads, railways, bridges, houses and factories have suffered deformation, at times beyond repair, because the condition of permafrost ground was not examined beforehand, and because the behaviour of frozen ground was little, if at all, understood. (Muller, 1945, pp. 1–2)

The past 50 years have seen significant advances in permafrost research.

5.2 Moisture in permafrost

Traditionally, permafrost has been defined on the basis of temperature: that is, ground (i.e. soil and/or rock) that remains at or below 0 °C for at least two consecutive years. However, permafrost may not necessarily be frozen since the freezing point of included water may be depressed several degrees below 0 °C. Moisture, in the form of either water or ice, may or may not be present. Therefore, to differentiate between the temperature and state (i.e. frozen or unfrozen) conditions of permafrost, the terms 'cryotic' and 'non-cryotic' have been proposed. These terms refer solely to the temperature of the material independent of its water/ice content (ACGR, 1988). Perennially cryotic ground is, therefore, synonymous with permafrost, and permafrost may be 'unfrozen', 'partially frozen' or 'frozen', depending upon the state of the ice/water content (Figs 5.1 and 5.2(a)).

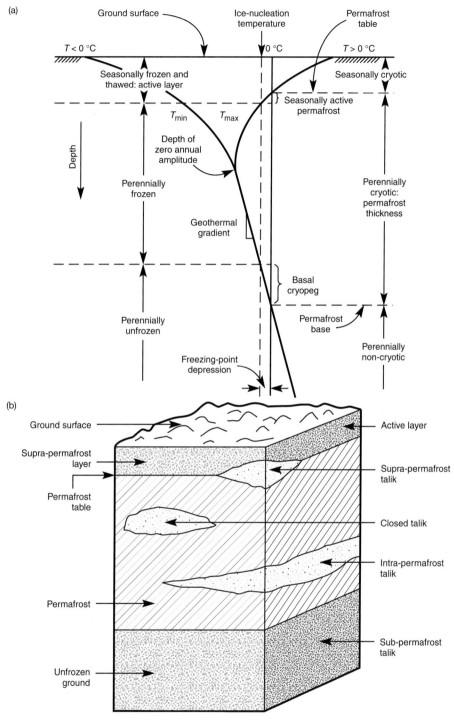

Figure 5.2 Permafrost terminology: (a) terms used to describe the ground temperature relative to 0 °C, and the state of the water, versus depth (modified from van Everdingen, 1985; from ACGR, 1988); (b) relationship between permafrost, the permafrost table, the active layer and supra, intra- and sub-permafrost taliks (modified from Ferrians *et al.*, 1969).

Several other terms need immediate definition. The permafrost table is the upper surface of the permafrost, and the ground above the permafrost table is called the supra-permafrost layer (Fig. 5.2 (b)). The active layer is that part of the supra-permafrost layer that freezes in the winter and thaws during the summer, that is, it is seasonally frozen ground. Although the seasonal frost usually penetrates to the permafrost table in most areas, in some areas it does not and an unfrozen zone exists between the bottom of the seasonal frost and the permafrost table. This unfrozen zone is called a talik. Unfrozen zones within and below the permafrost are also termed taliks.

The terminological subtleties described above are more than mere semantics. Many of the important problems posed by permafrost are related, either directly or indirectly, to the water and/or ice content of permafrost. These may be summarized under three main categories.

First, the freezing of water in the active layer at the beginning of winter each year results in ice lensing and segregation as explained in Chapter 4. The magnitude of heave varies according to the amount and availability of moisture present in the active layer. Poorly drained silty soils usually possess some of the highest ice or water contents and are termed 'frost-susceptible'.

Long-continued secondary heaving may also occur at temperatures below 0 °C, as unfrozen water progressively freezes. Field experiments have demonstrated that moisture migrates through permafrost in response to a temperature gradient, and this causes an ice-rich zone to form in the upper few metres of permafrost (e.g. Cheng, 1983; Mackay, 1983; Smith, 1985b). The annual cost of rectifying seasonal frost damage to roads, utility foundations and buildings in areas of deep seasonal frost such in Canada, Sweden and northern Japan is often considerable.

Second, ground ice is a major component of permafrost, particularly in unconsolidated sediments (e.g. Harry, 1988). Frequently, the amount of ice held within the ground in a frozen state exceeds the natural water content of that sediment in its thawed state. If the permafrost thaws therefore, subsidence of the ground results. Thaw consolidation may also occur as the thawed sediments compact and settle under their own weight. In addition, high pore water pressures generated in the process may favour soil instability and mass movement. These various processes associated with permafrost degradation are generally termed thermokarst. This is discussed more fully in Chapter 6; a related problem is that the physical properties of frozen ground, in which the soil particles are cemented together by pore ice, may be considerably greater than if the same material is in an unfrozen state (Tsytovich, 1973). In unconsolidated and/or soft sediments there is often a significant loss of bearing strength upon thawing.

Third, the hydrological and groundwater characteristics of permafrost terrain are different from those of non-permafrost terrain (Hopkins *et al.*, 1955; van Everdingen, 1990). For example, the presence of both perennially and seasonally frozen ground prevents the infiltration of water into the ground or, at best, confines it to the active layer. At the same time, subsurface flow is restricted to unfrozen zones or taliks. A high degree of mineralization in subsurface permafrost waters is often typical, caused by the restricted circulation imposed by the permafrost and the concentration of dissolved solids in the taliks.

5.3 Geothermal regimes of permafrost

The growth of permafrost reflects a negative heat balance at the surface of the Earth in which the complete thawing of ground frozen during the previous winter does not take place. The minimum limit therefore, for the duration of permafrost is two years. Thus, if the ground freezes one winter to a depth of 60 cm and thaws in the following summer to a depth of only 55 cm, 5 cm of permafrost comes into existence in the second year. If the climatic conditions are repeated in following years, the layer of permafrost will thicken and grow downwards from the base of the seasonal frost. Ultimately, permafrost several hundreds of metres in thickness can be formed.

The thickness to which permafrost develops is determined by a balance between the internal heat gain with depth and the heat loss from the surface. According to Lachenbruch (1968), heat flow from the Earth's interior normally results in a temperature increase of approximately 1 °C per 30–60 m increase in depth. This is known as the geothermal gradient. Thus, the lower limit of permafrost occurs at that depth at which the temperature increase due to internal earth heat (i.e. the geothermal gradient) just offsets the amount by which the freezing point exceeds the mean surface temperature. If there is a change in the climatic conditions at the ground surface, the thickness of the permafrost will change appropriately. For example, an increase in mean surface temperature will result in a decrease in

Table 5.1 Permafrost depths and mean annual air temperatures at selected localities in the northern hemisphere

Locality	Latitude	Permafrost Zone	Mean Air Temperature (°C)	Permafrost Thickness (m)
Canada[1]				
Resolute, NWT	74°N	Continuous	−12	390–400
Inuvik, NWT	69°N	Continuous	−9	100
Dawson City, YT	64°N	Discontinuous	−5	60
Yellowknife, NWT	62°N	Discontinuous	−6	60–100
Schefferville, PQ	54°N	Discontinuous	−4	80
Thompson, Man.	55°N	Discontinuous	−4	15
Alaska[2]				
Barrow	71°N	Continuous	−12	304–405
Umiat	69°N	Continuous	−10	322
Fairbanks	64°N	Discontinuous	−3	30–120
Bethel	60°N	Discontinuous	−1	13–184
Nome	64°N	Discontinuous	−4	37
USSR (FSU)[3]				
Nord'vik	72°N	Continuous	−12	610
Ust'Port	69°N	Continuous	−10	455
Yakutsk	62°N	Continuous	−10	195–250
Qinghai-Xizang (Tibet) Plateau[4]				
Fenghuo Shan	34°N	Widespread	−6	110
Wudaoliang	35°N	Widespread	−5	40

[1] Brown (1970), Table 1
[2] Ferrians (1965) and Brown and Péwé (1973), Fig. 2
[3] Quoted in Washburn (1979)
[4] Wang and French (1994)

permafrost thickness, while a decrease in surface temperature will give the reverse.

Above the permafrost is a layer of ground subject to annual thawing and freezing (see Fig. 5.2 (a)). This is called the active layer. Its thickness varies from year to year, depending on such factors as ambient air temperature, vegetation, drainage, soil or rock type, water content, snow cover and degree and orientation of slope. Some Canadian permafrost scientists propose that the active layer includes the uppermost part of the permafrost whenever either the salinity or clay content of the permafrost allows it to thaw and refreeze annually, even though the material remains cryotic (below 0°C) (ACGR, 1988; see Fig. 5.2 (a)). Others argue that this definition of the active layer, in terms of its frozen or unfrozen nature, is inconsistent with the basic thermal definition of permafrost. Ignoring these complications for the present, the bottom of the active layer (i.e. usually the top of the permafrost in the continuous permafrost zone, see below) is that depth at which the maximum mean annual temperature is 0°C.

In some areas, especially in the discontinuous permafrost zone, the active layer does not reach the permafrost table. This often occurs when permafrost is relict; in this case the active layer is separated from the permafrost by a residual thaw layer, that is, by a thawed and non-cryotic (i.e. above 0°C) layer of ground.

Assuming a constant geothermal gradient of 1°C/50 m (Gold *et al.*, 1972) and stable surface temperatures, it is possible to predict the approximate thickness of permafrost at any locality, given the mean annual temperature. This is done by multiplying the negative of the mean annual air temperature by the geothermal gradient. For example, a locality with a mean annual air temperature of −10°C might be expected to have a permafrost thickness of 500 m. However, when known permafrost thicknesses are tabulated against annual air temperatures (Table 5.1), it is clear that this rule of thumb is of only limited use, since there are significant variations in permafrost thicknesses. At least four additional factors must be considered.

Table 5.2 Global distribution of permafrost according to I. Ya. Baranov (1959) and Shi (1988)

Northern Hemisphere (million km²)		Southern Hemisphere (million km²)	
USSR (Former Soviet Union)	11.0	Antarctica	13.5
Mongolian People's Republic	0.8		
China	2.1		
North American continent (a) Alaska	1.5		
(b) Canada	5.7		
Greenland	1.6		
Total	22.7		13.5
Total for both hemispheres	36.2 million km²		
Total land area for both hemispheres	149.0 million km²		
Area occupied by permafrost	24 per cent		

First, as Lachenbruch (1957) has demonstrated, large bodies of water exert a distinct warming effect upon adjacent landmasses. Permafrost is generally absent from beneath the oceans and many of the larger water bodies. This probably explains why permafrost thicknesses at coastal locations are usually less than predicted. Second, the effects of past climatic changes must be considered. For example, even where present-day mean annual surface temperatures exceed –15 °C, permafrost thicknesses may be so great (in excess of 800 m in theory) that they must reflect little-known climatic changes that occurred during the early Pleistocene. Third, the assumption of climatic stability is questionable. For example, in parts of Siberia, permafrost extends to great depths (1600 m) and varying geothermal gradients at varying depths indicate definite past climatic fluctuations. It seems reasonable to assume therefore that much permafrost is relict and unrelated to present climatic conditions. The fourth factor, especially appropriate in the case of the Tibet Plateau, is that thermal discontinuities related to faults, sand dunes, lakes and hot springs combine with normal altitudinal variations in the mean annual air temperature (MAAT) to produce a situation where it is difficult to generalize about the distribution of permafrost.

5.4 Distribution of permafrost

Permafrost occurs in two contrasting and overlapping geographical regions, namely, high latitudes and high altitudes (Harris, 1988). Accordingly, permafrost can be classified into one of the following categories: (a) polar (or latitudinal) permafrost, i.e. permafrost in arctic regions, (b) alpine permafrost, i.e. permafrost in mountainous regions, (c) plateau permafrost, i.e. extensive permafrost at high elevation, such as on the Tibet (Qinghai-Xizang) Plateau of China and (d) subsea permafrost, i.e. on the continental shelves of the Laptev, Siberian and Beaufort Seas.

The importance of permafrost is best appreciated when it is realized that approximately 25 per cent of the Earth's land surface is underlain by permafrost (Table 5.2). The majority occurs in the northern hemisphere. Excluding those areas of frozen ground lying beneath glaciers and ice sheets, the Former Soviet Union (primarily Russia) possesses the largest area of permafrost, followed by Canada and then China. Permafrost may vary in thickness from a few centimetres to several hundreds of metres. In parts of Siberia and interior Alaska, permafrost has existed for several hundred thousand years; in other areas, such as the modern Mackenzie Delta, permafrost is young and currently forming under the existing cold climate.

Permafrost is usually classified as being either continuous or discontinuous in nature. In areas of continuous permafrost, frozen ground is present at all localities except for localized thawed zones, or taliks, existing beneath lakes and river channels. In discontinuous permafrost, bodies of frozen ground are separated by areas of unfrozen ground. At the southern limit of this zone permafrost becomes restricted to isolated 'islands', typically occurring beneath peaty organic sediments.

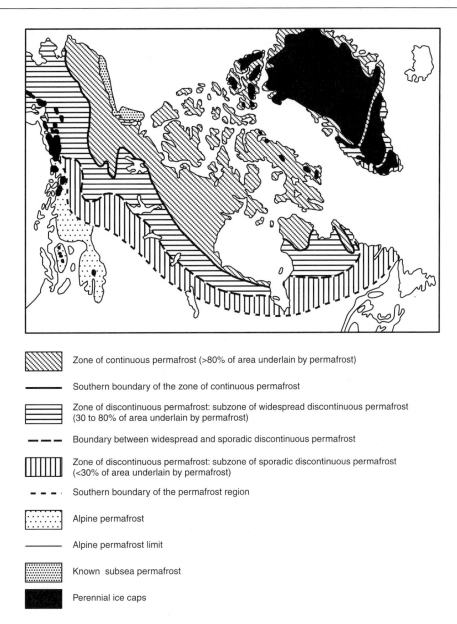

Zone of continuous permafrost (>80% of area underlain by permafrost)

——— Southern boundary of the zone of continuous permafrost

Zone of discontinuous permafrost: subzone of widespread discontinuous permafrost (30 to 80% of area underlain by permafrost)

– – – Boundary between widespread and sporadic discontinuous permafrost

Zone of discontinuous permafrost: subzone of sporadic discontinuous permafrost (<30% of area underlain by permafrost)

– – – Southern boundary of the permafrost region

Alpine permafrost

——— Alpine permafrost limit

Known subsea permafrost

Perennial ice caps

Figure 5.3 Distribution of permafrost in Canada, with extension into Alaska and Greenland (from ACGR, 1988).

In the following discussion emphasis will be placed upon the permafrost conditions in Arctic North America, Russia (Siberia) and China, and the broad climatic conditions over its distribution. The comparison of permafrost conditions between these three areas provides an introduction to mountain (alpine) permafrost, subsea permafrost and relict (Pleistocene) permafrost.

5.4.1 Canada and Alaska

In North America, the broad outline of permafrost distribution is well known. A number of permafrost maps are available for both Alaska (e.g. Ferrians, 1965) and Canada (e.g. Heginbottom and Radburn, 1993; Natural Resources Canada, 1995). In Canada,

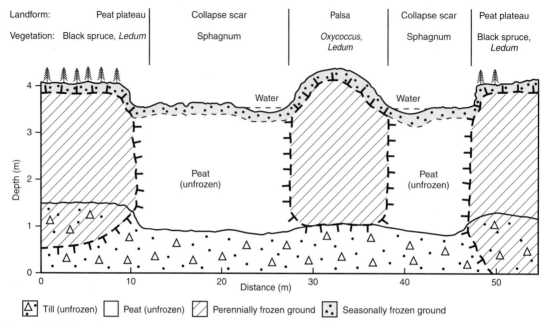

Landform:	Peat plateau	Collapse scar	Palsa	Collapse scar	Peat plateau
Vegetation:	Black spruce, *Ledum*	Sphagnum	*Oxycoccus, Ledum*	Sphagnum	Black spruce, *Ledum*

△• Till (unfrozen)   ☐ Peat (unfrozen)   ⧄ Perennially frozen ground   ⦙• Seasonally frozen ground

Figure 5.4 Schematic representation of the relationship between permafrost, landforms and vegetation in the discontinuous zone of Canada. The diagram illustrates a cross section through a peat-plateau – collapse scar with a young palsa in summer (modified from Tarnocai, 1973).

nearly one-half of the country is affected, while in Alaska, 80 per cent of the land surface is underlain by various types of permafrost (Fig. 5.3).

The distribution of both continuous and discontinuous permafrost is broadly governed by climate. Observations indicate a general relation between the mean annual air and ground temperatures in permafrost regions. As a result of the complex energy exchange system at the ground surface, the mean annual ground temperature measured at the depth of zero annual amplitude is usually several degrees warmer than the mean annual air temperature. According to Brown (1966) a difference of 3–4 °C is typical.

Field observations in both Alaska and Canada indicate that the southern limit of continuous permafrost coincides with the general position of the –6 to –8 °C mean annual air temperature isotherm (Brown, 1960, 1967a; Péwé, 1966b). This relates to the –5 °C isotherm of mean annual ground temperature measured just below the zone of annual variation. This –5 °C ground temperature isotherm was first selected by Russian scientists and subsequently adopted by North Americans after numerous field observations indicated that discontinuities began to appear in the permafrost south of this isotherm.

In North America, the southern boundary of the continuous permafrost zone extends from the Seward Peninsula in Alaska, north through the Brooks Range foothills, and then southwards through Canada in a broad curve north of the Slave Lakes. Continuous permafrost reaches its most southerly extent at latitude 55 °N where it fringes the southern shore of Hudson Bay. East of Hudson Bay, continuous permafrost reappears in the northern part of the Ungava Peninsula at latitude 60 °N. The reason for this latitudinal jump in the vicinity of Hudson Bay is because the greater snow accumulation in the autumn to the east of Hudson Bay keeps ground temperatures relatively high.

In the continuous zone, permafrost occurs everywhere beneath the ground surface, except in newly deposited sediments and beneath large lakes and deep bodies of standing water. It is probable, however, that unfrozen ground exists beneath the channels of the larger rivers such as the Mackenzie and Yukon. The known thickness of permafrost varies from 60–90 m at the southern limit of the continuous zone to depths of over 500 m in the Canadian Arctic Archipelago and northern Alaska. A maximum of 610 m has been reported from Prudhoe Bay in Alaska and

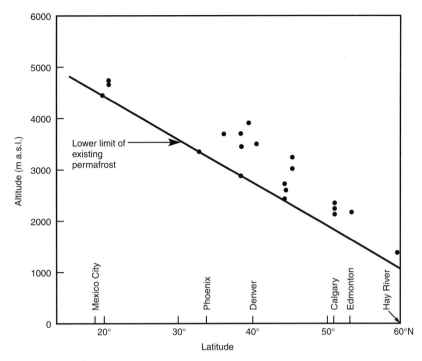

Figure 5.5 Graph showing relationship between latitude and altitude of reported localities of existing mountain permafrost in the cordillera of North America. Points indicate localities where permafrost has either been measured by ground temperatures, or inferred from local micro-climatic data or from geomorphic phenomena (ice-cemented rock glaciers, blockfields; from Péwé, 1983a).

557 m from Melville Island in Canada. Probably much greater thicknesses occur in the interior of the Arctic islands and thicknesses in excess of 1000 m may exist at high elevations on parts of Baffin and Ellesmere islands (Brown, 1972).

The discontinuous zone lies to the south of the continuous zone. Here, unfrozen and frozen bodies exist together. According to Brown (1967a), the southern limit of discontinuous permafrost in Canada roughly coincides with the –1 °C mean annual air temperature isotherm. Southwards of this isotherm, the climate is generally too warm for permafrost to form. Between the –1 °C and –4 °C mean annual air isotherms, permafrost is restricted to drier areas of peatlands, or to north-facing slopes or shady river banks. The delicate balance that exists between permafrost, terrain, drainage and vegetation in the discontinuous zone is schematically illustrated in Fig. 5.4. From the –4 °C air isotherm northwards, permafrost becomes increasingly widespread and thicker until the southern limit of the continuous permafrost, as defined above, is reached.

In the North American cordillera, the distribution of permafrost varies both with altitude and with latitude. Field observations suggest that the lower altitudinal limit of permafrost rises progressively from approximately 1000 m a.s.l. at 60 °N to over 3000 m a.s.l. in Colorado and New Mexico at latitudes 39 °N to 33 °N. In Central Mexico, isolated occurrences of frozen ground have been either reported or inferred from the summits of volcanic peaks at elevations of 4500–4800 m a.s.l. (Fig. 5.5).

5.4.2   Russia and Siberia (the Former Soviet Union (FSU))

The extent and thickness of permafrost in the area of the FSU is illustrated in Fig. 5.6. According to Baranov (1959; see Table 5.2), permafrost occupies over 11 000 000 km² or 49.7 per cent of the total area of the FSU. Most of it lies in the forest zone east of the Yenesei River. As a generalization, the permafrost is thicker than in North America (Kudryavtsev,

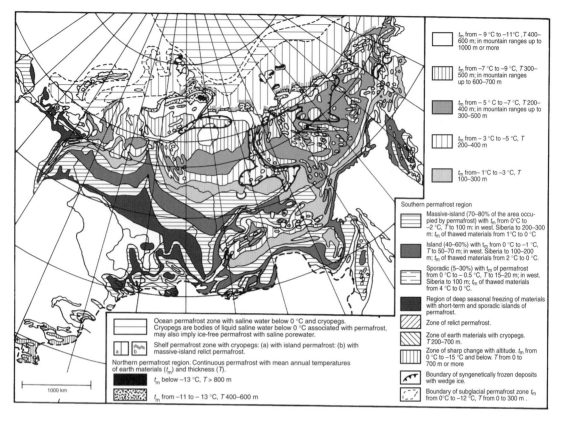

Figure 5.6 Permafrost in the FSU (after Kudryavtsev *et al.*, 1978.)

1965). In the continuous zone the permafrost increases northwards from 300 m at the southern limit to over 600 m along the Arctic coastal plain. Thicknesses in excess of 500 m also occur in central Yakutia while in other areas such as the Taimyr Peninsula, permafrost reaches 400 m in thickness (Baranov, 1959, pp. 15–19). The thickest known permafrost exists in northern Yakutia to depths of 1600 m, probably caused by the deep penetration of supercooled brine (Katasonov, in Brown, 1967b, p. 742).

Discontinuous permafrost is encountered in limited areas in the Kola Peninsula and in the tundra and boreal forest zone between the White Sea and the Ural Mountains. East of the Urals, a broad zone of discontinuous permafrost exists in western and eastern Siberia. Here, the transition from discontinuous to continuous permafrost coincides with the northern boundary of the boreal forest (taiga) and is accompanied by a sharp increase in the thickness of permafrost. For example, within the boreal forest (taiga) discontinuous zone, average thicknesses of

25–30 m are typical, as compared with 300 m in the forest tundra and 400 m in the tundra. Thus, the continuous–discontinuous permafrost boundary is rather easier to identify in the FSU than in North America.

Given similar mean annual temperatures at the depth of zero annual amplitude, the Siberian permafrost is colder than the North American. This can be illustrated by the geothermal gradient. In Yakutia, values of the geothermal gradient range from 40 to 178 m/°C in permafrost and from 30 to 135 m/°C in non-frozen rock (Melnikov, in Brown, 1967b, p. 742). Observations in North America indicate values ranging from 20 m/°C at stations adjacent to large rivers or oceans to 55 m/°C at interior locations, all of which indicate considerably steeper gradients than in the FSU.

The greater extent, thickness and coldness of the permafrost in Siberia reflect a number of factors. Probably the most important is the difference in the history of continental glaciations of North America and Siberia. During the Pleistocene, ice sheets covered much of Arctic North America. In Siberia, however, localized ice sheets formed only in the principal mountain belts, leaving the lowland plains largely free of ice. An additional factor is that the retreat of the latest (Wisconsinan) ice sheet in North America was accompanied by the development of extensive postglacial lakes and marine inundations. The presence of these large water bodies limited the extent of terrain exposed to extremely low air temperatures. This has far-reaching ramifications as regards the development of Pleistocene periglacial phenomena in southern Canada and the United States (see Part 3). When combined with the late glacial amelioration of climate and the rapid northward advance of the treeline, conditions were not conducive for the development of an extensive or long-lasting 'periglacial zone'. In contrast, ice-free areas occurred widely in Siberia throughout the Pleistocene and deep and continuous permafrost developed in response to the very low air temperatures to which the ground was exposed (Gerasimov and Markov, 1968). The reason for the lack of extensive glaciation in Siberia seems best explained by the lower snowfall amounts which that area receives, since high mountain belts and the vastness of the landmass effectively prevent the penetration of moisture-laden winds from either the Pacific or the Atlantic oceans.

The importance of the glacial limits as regards permafrost distribution and thickness can be demonstrated with reference to known permafrost thicknesses in glaciated and unglaciated terrain currently experiencing similar mean annual air temperatures. For example, 60 m of permafrost exist at Dawson City, in the unglaciated part of the Yukon Territory of Canada. The mean annual air temperature is –5 °C. Approximately similar permafrost depths occur in southeast Siberia at Chita and Bomnak which also experience mean annual air temperatures of –5 °C (Brown, 1967b, p. 746). However, at Fort Simpson, NWT, and Thompson, Manitoba, where air temperatures are similar to the other stations but which are located in recently glaciated terrain, the permafrost is only about 15 m thick (Brown, 1970, p. 10).

5.4.3 China

The permafrost areas of China occur in two distinct and separate regions (Fig. 5.7). First, there is the occurrence of permafrost in northeast China, the distribution of which is similar to that previously described for the FSU and North America. As a consequence, this is sometimes termed 'high latitude' permafrost, or simply 'latitudinal' permafrost (Shi, 1988). This is because it can be mapped as being either continuous, discontinuous or isolated (island) in nature, and the climatic controls vary in broad agreement with latitude.

Second, permafrost occurs in western China, on the Qinghai-Xizang (Tibet) Plateau, and in the various mountain ranges of the Tian Shan and Quilian Shan. Here, the controls over permafrost are quite different from those of latitudinal permafrost and, as such, demand more detailed description and explanation. On the Qinghai-Xizang Plateau, the permafrost is sometimes referred to as 'Plateau Permafrost', to distinguish it from traditional, alpine permafrost.

Permafrost on the Tibet Plateau is mapped as being either 'predominantly continuous' (with 70–80 per cent of the area underlain by permafrost) or 'isolated' (less than 40–60 per cent of the area underlain by permafrost) by Chinese scientists (Shi, 1988). These terms are inconsistent with terms used elsewhere (e.g. ACGR, 1988; Harris, 1988). Equivalent terms in the North American literature are the 'widespread zone' and 'sporadic zone'. It is important to note that no continuous permafrost zone, according to the North American definition, exists on the Tibet Plateau. Equally, the differentiation between plateau permafrost and alpine permafrost is important because areas of alpine permafrost are characterized by steep slopes and extensive bedrock. In contrast, the Tibet Plateau surface has relatively low relief between the mountain ranges and in places it is underlain by unconsolidated sediments that may exceed 1000 m in thickness (Guo *et al.*, 1982). Therefore, the term 'plateau permafrost' is reserved exclusively for permafrost on the Tibet Plateau. Recently, however, the term 'mountain permafrost' has been used to include both alpine and plateau permafrost (Cheng and Dramis, 1992).

Plateau permafrost ranges from a few metres to 130 m in thickness. The mean annual ground temperature (at the depth of zero annual amplitude) is from a fraction of a degree below 0 °C to –3.5 °C.

Some studies have reported that the thickness of the Tibet Plateau permafrost increases at a rate of between 10 and 30 m for each increase of one latitudinal degree (e.g. Tong and Li, 1983). This is not supported by ground temperature measurements,

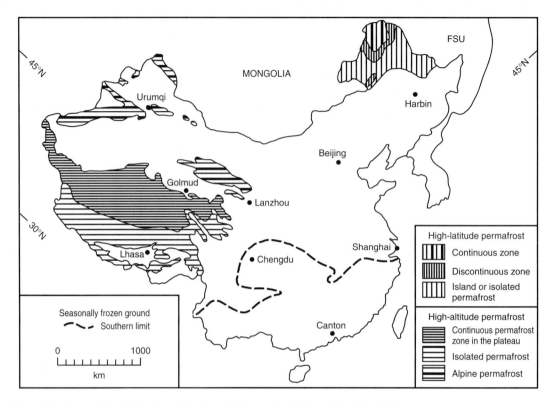

Figure 5.7 Permafrost distribution in the People's Republic of China (after Shi, 1988).

because the air temperature varies irregularly with latitude. Permafrost thickens with increasing altitude at a rate of 15–20 m for each 100 m increase in elevation (Shang, 1982; Zhou and Guo, 1982; Tong and Li, 1983). A unique characteristic of plateau permafrost is the change in lower altitudinal limit (i.e. the zone above which permafrost occurs) from the north (4200 m a.s.l.) to the south (4800 m a.s.l.), at a rate of about 110 m per latitudinal degree. The lower altitudinal limit of permafrost on the Plateau is usually 800–1100 m lower than the snowline (Zhou and Guo, 1982). The mean annual air temperature at the lower limit is in the range of –2.5 °C to –3.6 °C (Tong and Li, 1983), considerably lower than that of the Rocky Mountains in North America (0 to –1 °C) (Péwé, 1983a) and that of the southern boundary of high latitude permafrost in Canada (about –1.1 °C) (Brown, 1969; Brown and Péwé, 1973). The average geothermal gradient on the Plateau is 22 m/ °C in permafrost, and 16 m/ °C below permafrost. This is much higher than elsewhere, and is almost certainly due to the high geothermal heat flux associated with the recent geological uplift of the Tibet Plateau.

The regional distribution of permafrost on the Plateau is complicated by a number of site-specific factors, the most important of which is faulting. Others include lakes and springs, and highly mobile sand dunes. The effect of snow cover is negligible since snow accumulation on the surface is slight (<7 cm). Figure 5.8 generalizes the distribution and thickness of permafrost, together with air and ground temperatures, in a N–S transect along the Trans-Plateau Highway.

5.4.4 Mountain permafrost

Permafrost existing at high altitudes in middle and low latitudes is traditionally referred to as 'alpine' permafrost (e.g. ACGR, 1988; Péwé, 1983a), to form an alpine periglacial zone (e.g. Harris, 1988) in the Lozinski sense (see Chapter 1). However, since mountains exist in polar regions and some temperate latitude mountain chains extend into polar regions for considerable distances (e.g. cordillera of North America, Ural Mountains in Russia), it is difficult to

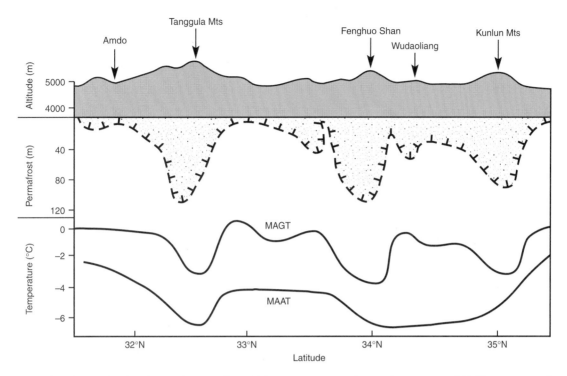

Figure 5.8 Graph showing changes in permafrost thickness, mean annual ground temperature (MAGT), mean annual air temperature (MAAT), and topography across the northern part of the Tibet Plateau (from Wang and French, 1995c).

distinguish between alpine and polar (high latitude) permafrost. The term 'mountain permafrost' is increasingly being used to refer to both alpine permafrost, as defined above, and polar mountain permafrost, which has not conventionally been regarded as alpine permafrost (e.g. Cheng and Dramis, 1992).

Mountain permafrost is not to be confused with plateau permafrost, a term reserved exclusively for the permafrost on the Tibet Plateau (see above). This is because many of the controls over the latter are quite different from those over mountain (alpine) permafrost, and because mountain permafrost implicitly involves steep slopes, aspect and snow. Clearly, the most important control over mountain permafrost is climate; this depends on the geographical location of the mountain in question (latitude, altitude, distance from ocean). Zonation of mountain permafrost is not unlike that of high-latitude (polar) permafrost; namely a zone of continuous permafrost below the snow (firn) limit is replaced by a zone of discontinuous permafrost at lower elevations, and this in turn by a zone of sporadic permafrost.

Difficulties arise in determining the lower altitudinal limit of mountain permafrost. While the basis of the zonation is the lapse rate of temperature decreasing with elevation, the occurrence of cold air drainage, or temperature inversions (e.g. Harris, 1983) and ice-caves (Harris, 1979), complicate the situation. Surface features, such as rock glaciers, are often used to infer the lower limit of mountain permafrost, but this can be controversial. Some rock glaciers may be inactive and not ice-cemented (i.e. permafrost) in origin but ice-covered (i.e. glacial) in origin (Barsch, 1988). The problem of rock glaciers is discussed in more detail later in this chapter.

The relationship between the lower altitudinal limit of mountain permafrost and latitude can be expressed by a Gaussian curve (Fig. 5.9 (a)) (Cheng, 1983; Corte, 1988) which resembles, in broad outline, the 0 °C isotherm, the snow line, the alpine cold desert zone and the treeline plotted against latitude (Fig. 5.9 (b)). More regional controls over mountain permafrost can be illustrated by the example of central Scandinavia (Fig. 5.9 (c)). There, the increasing continentality as one moves inland from the

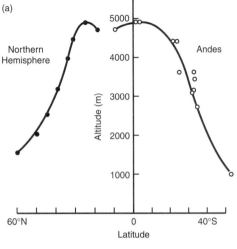

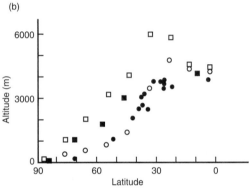

- ● Treeline
- ○ Lowest snowline
- □ Highest snowline
- ■ Height of cold desert soil

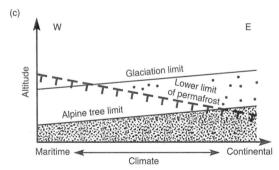

Figure 5.9   The lower limit of mountain permafrost:
(a) permafrost lower limit in the Andes
compared with the average for the Northern
Hemisphere; (b) altitude of some geographical
boundaries plotted against latitude;
(c) relations between lower limit of permafrost,
treeline and glaciation in Central Scandinavia.
(Source: (a) and (b) modified from Cheng and
Dramis, 1992; (c) from King, 1986).

Norwegian coast results in the snowline or glacial limit rising, the lower limit of permafrost falling and the treeline rising in elevation. Similar W–E changes occur in the cordillera of North America with greater snowfall in the Coastal Ranges causing the lower limit of permafrost formation to decrease eastwards. Thus, permafrost is present at Plateau Mountain, southeast Alberta (2494 m a.s.l., latitude 50°N) but absent from the Coast Range in British Columbia at similar latitude and elevation (Harris and Brown, 1978, 1982).

Attempts to predict the occurrence of mountain permafrost on the basis of mean annual air temperatures, and freezing and thawing indices, or by the use of landform features, such as rock glaciers, have met with only limited success. One method which appears to work in the maritime mountains of mid-latitudes is the bottom temperature of the winter snow cover. This is called the BTS method. Haeberli (1973, 1978) and others (e.g. King, 1983) have demonstrated that permafrost is usually present in the Alps and in Scandanavia if the BTS during February and March is less than –2 °C beneath at least a 1.0 m cover of snow. The distribution and zonation of mountain permafrost in the more arid mountain ranges of interior Asia, such as the Tian Shan (Gorbunov, 1988) is less easy to predict and requires further field verification.

5.4.5   Subsea permafrost

Since permafrost is defined exclusively upon the basis of temperature, permafrost may occur on the seafloor wherever mean annual sea bottom temperatures are below 0 °C. A complicating factor is that because of the lower freezing point which exists under saline conditions, the sediments are not necessarily frozen.

The major area of subsea permafrost occurs beneath the waters of the Laptev and East Siberian seas (Baranov, 1959). Extensive areas of subsea permafrost also occur beneath the southern Beaufort Sea in the western Arctic (Shearer *et al.*, 1971; Mackay, 1972b). Those areas of subsea permafrost which are known to exist have been identified either by drilling, or by acoustic geophysical surveys. The latter approach only recognizes ice-bonded permafrost; that is, permafrost which is cemented together by ice crystals, and therefore, underestimates the existence of unfrozen, saline permafrost bodies (Hunter *et al.*, 1976).

According to Mackay (1972b), subsea permafrost can be in either thermal equilibrium or disequilibrium with sea bottom temperatures and the geothermal heat flow. In areas where sea bottom temperature is negative, and has remained so over a considerable time period, shallow (<150 m thick) equilibrium permafrost may exist. The thickness of the permafrost will depend upon such variables as the mean sea bottom temperature, soil properties, the geothermal heat flux and sedimentation rates. Where subsea permafrost is not in thermal equilibrium with a negative sea bottom temperature, the permafrost is in disequilibrium. Most of this category of subsea permafrost is probably relict degrading permafrost. It probably developed during the colder periods of the Quaternary when eustatic sea level fluctuations exposed areas of the present sea floor to cold, sub-aerial conditions for many thousands of years.

Subsea permafrost can also originate in a number of other ways. Extensive and rapid coastal retreat will result in permafrost existing in nearshore areas, irrespective of whether water temperatures are positive or negative. The progressive burial of permafrost by coastal sedimentation is a second method. Both mechanisms, however, are of only local importance and eustatic sea level changes are more relevant to the majority of subsea permafrost.

5.4.6 Relict permafrost

Much terrestrial permafrost is relict and unrelated to present climatic conditions. At Cape Thompson, Alaska, for example, a permafrost thickness of over 360 m is found despite the fact that the mean annual air temperature is –5 °C. Assuming a constant geothermal gradient of 1 °C/50 m, the present-day air temperature indicates that permafrost should only be approximately 250 m thick. By inference, therefore, surface temperatures have been approximately 2–3 °C colder in the past for the permafrost at Cape Thompson to have developed to its present thickness (Lachenbruch et al., 1966).

More striking examples of relict permafrost are to be found at the southern limits of permafrost in both Alaska and Siberia. Permafrost thicknesses of over 180 m have been recorded from the coastal plain of the Kuskokwim River valley in Alaska where mean annual air temperatures are between 0 and 2 °C. In such a situation, it is probable that the permafrost is degrading and that the geothermal gradient is isothermal. At the southern limit of permafrost in Canada, however, the known thicknesses of permafrost seem to be in a reasonable equilibrium with the present climate (Brown, 1970; Brown and Péwé, 1973), although even here, there is evidence of recent degradation of permafrost (e.g. Zoltai, 1971).

Some permafrost may be early Wisconsinan or late Pleistocene in age. In the western Arctic of Canada, glacially deformed ground ice and icy sediments exist in areas beyond the maximum limits of assumed late Wisconsinan ice (Mackay et al., 1972). The icy sediments have never undergone thawing and refreezing since thawing would have obliterated the primary sedimentary structures. [14]C dates and geomorphic evidence indicate the Arctic coastal plain was not glaciated during the last 40 000 years. It follows, therefore, that the permafrost is early Wisconsinan or older in age and that it existed prior to the glacier-ice thrusting. Evidence from Siberia also suggests that much permafrost originated during the Pleistocene (Gerasimov and Markov, 1968). The most incontrovertible evidence is the presence of limbs of Pleistocene woolly mammoths and other animals preserved in permafrost (e.g. see Chapter 13). Finally, in many areas of southern Siberia and southern Alaska, the upper surfaces of many permafrost bodies lie at depths not reached by present winter freezing. These residual thaw layers are proof that the permafrost is unrelated to present climatic conditions.

Pleistocene permafrost, and its implications for Pleistocene periglacial environments, are discussed in more detail in Chapter 13.

5.5 Permafrost and terrain conditions

Although the broad controls over permafrost formation and distribution are climatic in nature, local variations in permafrost conditions are determined by a variety of terrain and other factors (Brown, 1973a, 1973b). Of widespread importance are the effects of relief and aspect, and the nature of the physical properties of soil and rock. More complex are the controls exerted by vegetation, snow cover, water bodies, drainage and fire.

In the following discussion emphasis will be placed upon the latitudinal permafrost of North America and Siberia.

Generally speaking, in the discontinuous permafrost zones of high latitudes, variations in terrain conditions are primarily responsible for the patchy

Table 5.3 Some typical values of thermal conductivity of various materials

Material	Thermal Conductivity (k) (W/m K)
Air	0.024
Water	0.605
Ice (at 0 °C)	2.23
Snow	
Loose, new	0.086
On ground	0.121
Dense	0.340
Organic material	
Peat, dry	0.05
Peat, saturated unfrozen	0.50
Peat, saturated frozen	2.00
Rocks	
Shale	1.5
Granite	1.7–4.0
Building materials	
Concrete	1.3–1.7
Steel	35–52
Wood	0.12–0.16
Asbestos	0.07
Polystyrene	0.033

Sources: Johnston (1981); Williams and Smith (1989)

occurrence of permafrost, the size of the permafrost islands and the thickness of the active layer. In the continuous permafrost zone, however, the thermal properties of the ground as a whole, together with the climate, are more important. In many ways, the most complex of permafrost–terrain relationships occur in the discontinuous permafrost zones.

Relief influences the amount of solar radiation received by the ground surface and the accumulation of snow. Slope orientation also influences the amount of solar radiation received. The effects of differential insolation are particularly clear in mountainous regions such as northern British Columbia and the Yukon Territory where permafrost may occur on north-facing valley slopes and not upon adjacent south-facing slopes. Similarly, in the continuous zone, the active layer is usually thinner on north-facing slopes, but in certain instances, exposure to local weather conditions assumes greater importance. For example, on the Beaufort Plain of northwest Banks Island the active layer is thinnest on southwest-facing slopes (French, 1970). This is

attributed to the influence of the dominant southwest winds in this part of the Arctic which promote evaporation and latent heat loss from exposed slopes during the summer months.

Variations in the nature of rock and soil express themselves in differing albedo and thermal conductivity values. For example, the thermal conductivity of silt is only one-half that of coarse-grained sediments and several times less than that of crystalline rock. This, and the albedo factor, attain their greatest significance in the continuous permafrost zone, where the climate is sufficiently cool to produce permafrost regardless of the type of terrain. Average albedo values for bare rock and soil can vary between 10 and 40 per cent. Thus, significant variations in active layer thicknesses and permafrost thermal regimes are to be expected in different rock and soil types. Table 5.3 provides typical thermal conductivity values for various materials. An important point to note is that the thermal conductivity of ice is much higher than for water. Hence, frozen soils, especially if they are ice-rich, have higher thermal conductivities than unfrozen soils. Another important observation is that loose fresh snow has an extremely low thermal conductivity and, hence, is a good insulator of the ground.

Probably the most complex terrain factor is vegetation. It affects permafrost in a variety of ways and is significant in all areas of discontinuous and continuous permafrost with the exception of the vegetation-free polar deserts. The most fundamental influence of vegetation is to shield the underlying permafrost from solar heat. This insulating property is probably the single most important factor in determining the thickness of the active layer. Numerous observations from a wide variety of permafrost environments indicate not only a broad climatic relationship but also that the thickness of the active layer is thinnest beneath poorly drained and vegetated areas, and thickest beneath well-drained bare soil or rock.

The presence of peaty organic materials at the ground surface is particularly effective in protecting permafrost from atmospheric heat. This is most clearly demonstrated in the southern part of the discontinuous zone where permafrost only occurs in peatlands and not in other adjacent terrain types. The preservation of permafrost in peatlands is due to the unique thermal properties of peat. Dry sphagnum has thermal conductivity values approximately one order of magnitude less than the lowest value for mineral soil. During the summer, therefore, when the surface layer of peat becomes dry by evaporation, warming of the underlying soil is limited. As a result, the depth of seasonal thawing in peatlands is considerably less than in other types of terrain. During the autumn and early winter, however, the peat becomes saturated with moisture as evaporation rates fall off. When the peat freezes, many of the interstices are filled with ice and the thermal conductivity of the peat increases considerably. Thus, the peat offers less resistance to the cooling of the underlying soil in winter than to the warming of it in summer. This leads to lower mean annual ground temperatures under peat than in adjacent areas without peat. If the mean annual ground temperature beneath the peat remains below 0 °C throughout the year, permafrost results.

In addition to ground cover, trees are important controls over local permafrost conditions. Much permafrost terrain is forested, particularly in the FSU where the treeline extends in an east–west direction not far south of the Arctic coastline. In North America, the treeline extends south of Hudson Bay almost as far as the discontinuous permafrost zone, and a greater percentage of permafrost terrain is in the tundra and polar desert environments. The presence of trees shades the ground from solar radiation and intercepts some of the snowfall in winter. Thus, the winter cold penetrates more deeply into the ground beneath trees than in areas of thick snow cover, and summer solar radiation is restricted. Actual vegetation differences further complicate local permafrost conditions. For example, the Siberian taiga is composed predominantly of pine (*Pinus silvestris*) and tamarack (*Larix dahurica*), whereas the spruce (*Picea glauca* and *Picea mariana*) is more common in North America. Since the spruce forest is more shady, a surface moss cover is widely developed and this tends to favour a thinner active layer in the boreal forest than in the taiga. In those areas where the treeline and the southern boundary of continuous permafrost are in close proximity, as is the case for much of North America, the presence or absence of trees can assume a critical importance as regards permafrost occurrence. In Alaska, for example, Viereck (1965) has shown how even isolated white spruce may influence the energy exchange at the ground surface sufficiently for a small permafrost body to exist.

Snow cover is a further factor influencing local permafrost variations since it insulates the underlying ground from the extremes of winter cold (see Table 5.3). The snowfall regime and the length of time the snow lies on the ground are the critical fac-tors. In general terms, a heavy snowfall in the autumn or early winter will inhibit frost penetration, while a winter of low snowfall will do the reverse. Also, if snow persists late into the spring, ground thawing will be delayed. In detail, variations in snow cover at any one locality are controlled by site characteristics such as micro-relief and vegetation and their relation to the dominant snow-bearing winds.

In the continuous permafrost regions north of the treeline, snowfall amounts are limited and the effects of snow cover are less important than in areas further south. However, subtle differences in active layer conditions are to be found in the tundra and polar desert regions of high latitudes. It is not uncommon for upland surfaces and interfluves to be swept clear of snow for much of the winter while extensive snowbanks accumulate in gullies and on lee slopes. Deeper frost penetration may occur on the uplands and interfluves, therefore, than in the depressions and on lee slopes. On the other hand, ground thawing at snowbank localities may be delayed until late summer when the snowbank finally disappears. As a consequence, the active layer is often thinner at snowbank localities than on uplands. South of the treeline, in the discontinuous permafrost zone, snow cover assumes greater importance. Studies at Schefferville in northern Quebec indicate that the pattern of accumulation of the seasonal snowcover is the controlling factor in the distribution of permafrost in that area (Granberg, 1973; Nicholson and Thom, 1973). Since mean annual air temperature in the Schefferville region is −4.5 °C, widespread permafrost could be expected. However, permafrost occurs only in the upland areas where the absence of trees allows snow to be blown clear and deep winter frost penetration to take place. In the adjacent lowlands, where thick snow covers accumulate, permafrost is generally absent. It appears that a winter snow depth of 65–70 cm is sufficient to prevent the development of permafrost in the Schefferville region (Nicholson and Granberg, 1973).

To illustrate the complexity of climate–terrain–vegetation interactions, Table 5.4 provides ground temperature data from near Churchill, Manitoba (latitude 58 °N), where permafrost occurs in three adjacent boreholes but not in a fourth. All are located within a 2 km^2 area. Churchill is at the junction between continuous and discontinuous permafrost and is located a few kilometres north of the treeline. The mean annual air temperature is −7.3 °C and the average permafrost thickness, where present, is between 40 and 60 m. It can be

Table 5.4 Ground temperature conditions at four adjacent sites near Churchill, Manitoba (lat. 59 °N), 1974–76

Location	Average Hole Temperature (°C)	Active Layer Thickness (cm)	Organic Layer (cm)	Snow Depth (1974/75/76) (cm)	Average Snow Densities (1974/75/76)	Permafrost Yes\No
1. Quartzite bedrock	−2.9	~ 750	–	61/51/20	0.23/0.32/0.26	Yes
2. Marine deposits overlying till	−2.6	75–90	23	46/36/33	0.27/0.31/0.34	Yes
3. Palsa	−0.9	50	40	56/53/38	0.22/0.33/0.22	Yes
4. Depression	+0.4	75 (seasonal frost)	150	69/102/58	0.23/0.24/0.19	No

Source: Brown (1973b, 1978)

demonstrated that the increase in mean annual temperatures at 20 m depths at sites 2, 3 and 4 corresponds to an increase in peat thickness and snow cover, and a decrease in snow density. The absence of permafrost at site 4, a depression adjacent to site 3 (a palsa), is probably caused by waterlogging, enhanced by the thick snow cover in the depression.

Similar subtle differences in terrain conditions occur widely in the discontinuous permafrost zones and it is often extremely difficult to predict permafrost conditions without detailed and costly site investigations.

Water is another factor which influences permafrost formation and distribution. This is because of the high specific heat possessed by a water body. In the discontinuous zone, drainage is usually linked to vegetation, snow cover and other terrain factors, and is of secondary importance. In places, however, such as in the fenlands at the southern fringes of the discontinuous permafrost, or near Churchill, Manitoba, as described above, drainage conditions assume great importance in determining the presence or absence of permafrost (e.g. Zoltai, 1973; Brown, 1973b).

In the continuous permafrost zone, the effects of water upon permafrost are especially clear. Numerous observations indicate an unfrozen layer or talik often exists beneath water bodies that do not freeze to their bottoms in winter. The extent and nature of these taliks vary with the area and depth of the water body, the water temperature, the thickness of the winter ice and snow cover, and the nature and compaction of the bottom sediments (e.g. Johnston and Brown, 1964).

The geothermal disturbance which result from the presence of water bodies of varying dimensions is suitable to numerical simulation based on heat conduction theory (Smith, 1977; Smith and Huang, 1973). Several models are available. One that calculates the thermal contribution of a lake to the ground temperature field at a point is illustrated by application to the Sachs River lowlands of southern Banks Island (Fig. 5.10). Given a mean annual air temperature of approximately −12 °C, the model predicts maximum permafrost thickness to be 450–500 m beneath land and 50–60 m in the immediate offshore. However, the permafrost thickness varies greatly because of the influence of numerous water bodies. Beneath lakes approximately 50 m in radius (for example, lakes A and C in Fig. 5.10), the thermal disturbance extends downwards for 100–150 m and only shallow taliks develop. Beneath lake B, which has a radius of approximately 250 m, the upper permafrost boundary is depressed to form a 40 m deep talik. The thermal influence of this lake is also sufficient to raise the lower permafrost boundary. Finally, the large lakes greater than 1.0 km in radius (for example, lakes D and E in Fig. 5.10) are predicted to possess through-going taliks. Mackay (1979a, p. 30) suggests, as a first approximation for the Mackenzie Delta, that lakes with minimum widths of twice the permafrost thickness will always be underlain by through-going taliks, and all lakes >2.0 m deep will possess some sort of talik.

Numerical models are limited by their inability to predict disequilibrium permafrost conditions. As outlined earlier, permafrost temperatures may be related to past climatic conditions. The downward penetration of a thermal wave is such that a lag develops progressively with respect to surface temperatures. One estimate is that a thaw period of 10 000–20 000 years is required to form a through-going talik in 500 m of permafrost with a mean surface temperature of −10 °C (Mackay, 1979a, p. 30).

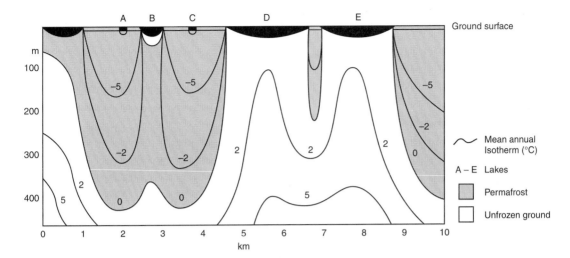

Figure 5.10 Numerical simulation of geothermal disturbances resulting from water bodies in the Sachs River lowlands, southwest Banks Island, Canada. Simulation performed by D. G. Harry in 1982.

A final terrain factor which may influence permafrost conditions is the effect of fire. Many forest fires start by lightning each year, particularly in the discontinuous zone. Many, if not all, of these regions have been burned over at least once and the boreal forest is, in many ways, a fire climax. Fires in the tundra zone are rare, although not unknown, on account of the relative absence of woody materials and the lower summer temperatures. The effects of a fire upon the permafrost will depend upon the nature and dampness of the vegetation, and the speed at which the fire passes through the area. If the fire passes rapidly, and if the surface cover is of peat, mosses or lichens, only the trees may burn and the ground beneath 2–3 cm may remain untouched. In this case, little change will occur to the permafrost conditions. If the surface vegetation is exceptionally dry, however, and if the fire moves slowly, considerable change in permafrost conditions may result. At Inuvik, NWT, for example, the effects of a 1968 forest fire have been documented by Heginbottom (1973). The destruction of much of the ground vegetation in addition to the trees resulted in the thawing of ice-rich sediments, rapid gullying and thermal erosion, and numerous earthflows. The more long-term effect has been an increase in the thickness of the active layer in the burned-over area (see Table 7.1(b)).

5.6 Surface features of permafrost

A number of important surface features are either the direct or indirect result of the presence of permafrost, and their identification, either from air photographs or in the field, is a valuable indicator of permafrost conditions. Although the majority of these features are examined in detail in the following chapters, it is appropriate to identify them at this point.

In broad terms, permafrost-related features can be divided into either (a) those associated with the aggradation of permafrost or (b) those associated with the degradation of permafrost (Brown, 1974). In each case, the landforms are often associated with the build-up or degradation of ground ice. Features associated with the growth of permafrost include ice-wedge polygons and frost mounds. Many of these are treated in Chapter 6. Those features associated with the degradation of permafrost and the melting of ground ice bodies are examined in Chapter 7.

A number of other surface features are commonly associated with permafrost. These include the many varieties of patterned ground and the various forms of solifluction. It must be emphasized, however, that although these features attain their best development in permafrost regions, particularly the continuous zone, these features are not restricted to permafrost regions, and may equally be the result of other, non-permafrost factors. Patterned ground is examined in Chapter 8, solifluction and mass wasting processes in Chapter 9.

Figure 5.11   Mature palsas on the Varanger Peninsula, Northern Norway. The palsa is 4–5 m high and undergoing block collapse around its edges.

5.6.1 Palsas and peat plateaux

Palsas and their associated peat plateaux find no easy place in the treatment given to frost mounds in Chapter 6. But since palsas are regarded as one of the few reliable surface indicators of permafrost in the discontinuous zone, they merit attention at this point.

Palsas are peaty permafrost mounds possessing a core of alternating layers of segregated ice and peat or mineral soil material (Fig. 5.11). They are typically 1.0–7.0 m in height and less than 100 m in diameter. Usually, they occur in bogs and protrude as low hills or knolls. The term is of Fennoscandian origin, originally meaning 'a hummock rising out of a bog with a core of ice' (Seppälä, 1972b). Implicit in this definition are their constructional nature, their origin in wetlands (fens or peat bogs) and that ice segregation in mineral soil beneath peat is the process responsible for growth. As such, palsas are quite distinct from seasonal frost mounds. The somewhat contradictory term 'mineral palsa' is occasionally used to refer to an ice segregation mound not covered with peat (e.g. Pissart and Gangloff, 1984).

Peat plateaux are flat-topped expanses of peat, elevated above the general surface of a peatland, and containing segregated ice that may or may not extend downwards into the underlying mineral soil. The latter is probably the main difference, genetically, between palsas and peat plateaux, since some argue that peat plateaux result from the growth and coalescence of adjacent palsas. However, it seems best to regard peat plateaux as being the simple result of the freezing of peat with the formation of segregated ice lenses and the consequent uplift of the peaty surface (Zoltai, 1972; Zoltai and Tarnocai, 1975). Peat plateaux may be several square kilometres in extent.

The initial growth of a palsa is problematic. One hypothesis is that palsa formation is triggered when wind turbulence causes a thinning of the snow cover on certain parts of a bog, so that frost is able to pene-

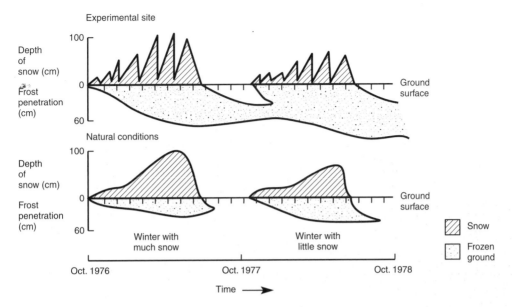

Figure 5.12 The influence of repeated snow clearance on the development of ground freezing during two winters in Finnish Lappland is compared with an uncleared control plot. The maximum depth of frost produced in the experimental site was about 110 cm (after Seppälä, 1982).

trate deeply causing initial heave of the surface. Once formed, the knoll tends to become snowfree each winter and thus, permafrost continues to aggrade. This hypothesis was tested over a three-year period in Finnish Lappland (Seppälä, 1982) when snow was systematically removed from an experimental plot a number of times each winter. The result was the formation of permafrost (Fig. 5.12) and the growth of a small artificial palsa some 30 cm high. Subsequently, Seppälä (1988) proposed a cycle of palsa evolution. The youthful stage is as described above. Then when the freezing of the palsa core reaches mineral soil at the base of the bog, the mature stage of palsa growth commences. Degradation then commences as peat blocks from the edge of the palsa collapse. In old age, palsas are partially destroyed by thermokarst and become scarred by pits and collapse forms. 'Dead' palsas are unfrozen remnants, either low circular rim ridges or rounded open ponds, or open peat surfaces without vegetation.

The most frequent occurrence of palsas is at the southern fringes of the discontinuous permafrost zone. They have been described most frequently from the subarctic regions of Canada, Iceland, Sweden and Russia but can also occur in alpine regions where suitable bog terrain is present (e.g. Kershaw and Gill, 1979). Towards the northern limit of the

discontinuous permafrost zone, peat plateaux become increasingly more common. In Manitoba and Saskatchewan, Zoltai (1971) has mapped the southern limit of palsas and peat plateaux to coincide with the 0 °C mean annual air temperature isotherm. This is south of the limit of sporadic discontinuous permafrost. A characteristic of many palsas and peat plateaux in this zone is that they often show signs of either past or present collapse. This may be the result of natural vegetation changes or forest fires. Equally, the thawing of peat landforms may be the first sign of current climatic warming.

5.6.2 Rock glaciers

Rock glaciers also do not fit easily within the organization of this chapter yet they are regarded as diagnostic features of mountain (alpine) permafrost (Barsch, 1978; Haeberli, 1985). Rock glaciers are lobate or tongue-shaped bodies of frozen debris with interstitial ice and ice lenses, which move downslope or downvalley by deformation of the ice contained within them (Fig. 5.13). Rock glaciers occur in the periglacial zone of most major mountain systems. In some ways, they are the mountain permafrost equivalent of palsas in that they can be used to indicate

Figure 5.13   Talus rock glacier, Ogilvie Mountains, North Klondike Valley, Yukon, Canada. The feature is largely inactive.

the lower altitudinal limit of discontinuous mountain permafrost, just as palsas often indicate the southern latitudinal limit of high-latitude permafrost.

There has been much debate as to the significance of rock glaciers. Some investigators regard rock glaciers as simple debris-covered glaciers (e.g. Potter, 1972; Johnson, 1974), others regard rock glaciers as pure periglacial features (e.g. Barsch, 1978, 1988; Haeberli, 1985). The key to their origin lies in their internal structure. This is often difficult to ascertain without costly and sometimes impossible drilling. As a result, geophysical (seismic) methods are frequently used. Referring specifically to the Galena Creek rock glacier described by Potter (1972), Barsch (1988) comments that this rock glacier is probably composed of a mixture of debris and ice since P-wave velocities of 2400–4000 m/s are typical, whereas a core of pure glacier ice should have P-wave velocities of about 3600 m/s. Observations such as these, and those made by co-workers elsewhere (e.g. King, 1986), lead Barsch to conclude that 'the evidence to

date fails to support the views that rock glaciers are debris-covered glaciers' (Barsch, 1988, p. 79). Furthermore, if rock glaciers are periglacial features unrelated to the glacial morpho-climatic system, it is preferable to refer to them as rockglaciers (i.e. one word, e.g. Barsch, 1992). This terminology, however, has yet to receive widespread acceptance and is not used in this text.

According to Barsch (1988) there are two types of periglacial rock glaciers (a) those occurring below talus slopes, 'talus rockglaciers', and (b) those occurring below glaciers, 'debris rockglaciers' (Fig. 5.14). Active rock glaciers are best developed in continental and semi-arid climates since, under these conditions, the extent of the mountain periglacial zone is greatest (i.e. the snowline is highest). Rock glaciers form where permafrost is possible and where there is an adequate supply of debris. Two supply mechanisms are common: first, from talus slopes and their associated mechanical weathering, and second, from adjacent moraines where the moraine forms the

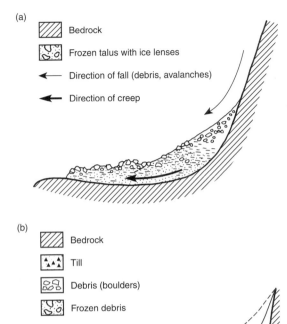

(a)

⧄ Bedrock

⬚ Frozen talus with ice lenses

⬅ Direction of fall (debris, avalanches)

⬅ Direction of creep

(b)

⧄ Bedrock

▲ Till

⬚ Debris (boulders)

⬚ Frozen debris

⬅ Direction of creep

Glacier ~ 1850

Glacier ~ 1970

Figure 5.14   Types of rock glaciers, acording to Barsch (1988). (a) Talus rock glaciers are formed below talus slopes; they are built up by frozen talus. Their ice content is derived from snow meltwater as well as from avalanches. (b) Debris rock glaciers are formed below glaciers. During times of glacier growth the glacier advances onto the upper end of the rock glacier, and adds new material. This is subsequently incorporated (as debris) into the rock glacier.

debris supply. Given an adequate accumulation of coarse clastic debris, percolating snowmelt infiltrates and freezes to form an ice-debris matrix which then deforms. Typical movement rates vary from several centimetres/year to several metres/year and a typical surface relief consists of arcuate ridges and furrows aligned, in general, perpendicular to the flow direction. Rock glaciers are reported from many localities including the Alps, the Himalayas, the Tian Shan, the Kunlun Shan and the American cordillera (e.g. White, 1971; Corte, 1978; Ciu Zhijui, 1983; Haeberli, 1985; Jakob, 1992). In high latitudes, talus rock glaciers have been described from Svalbard (Sollid and

Sorbel, 1992) while inactive or relict rock glaciers have been described from numerous locations including the northern Yukon (Vernon and Hughes, 1966; Harris *et al.*, 1983, p. 69), the Italian Alps (Carton *et al.*, 1988), the central Apennines (Dramis and Kotarba, 1992), the Pyrennees (Chueca, 1992) and the southern Carpathians (Urdea, 1992).

Rock glaciers, like palsas, are unique permafrost forms.

5.7 Permafrost hydrology

It is generally assumed that groundwater movement in permafrost is restricted by the presence of both perennially and seasonally frozen ground. This is because permafrost, containing water in the solid state, acts as a confining layer. This assumption is only partly true, however, since it is not uncommon for unfrozen zones or taliks to exist in which normal groundwater movement may occur.

5.7.1 Aquifers

The groundwater hydrology of permafrost regions is unlike that of non-permafrost regions since permafrost acts as an impermeable layer. Under these conditions the movement of groundwater is restricted to various thawed zones or taliks (Fig. 5.15). These may be of three types. First, a supra-permafrost talik may exist immediately above the permafrost table but below the depth of seasonal frost. In the continuous permafrost zone, supra-permafrost taliks are rare but in the discontinuous permafrost zone the depth of seasonal frost frequently fails to reach the top of the permafrost since the latter is often relict. In these areas, the supra-permafrost taliks are a residual thaw layer which may be several metres or more thick. Second, intra-permafrost taliks are thawed zones confined within the permafrost. Third, sub-permafrost taliks refer to the thawed zones beneath the permafrost.

Taliks may also be distinguished by the nature of the mechanism responsible for their unfrozen condition (Table 5.5). It is important to remember that taliks may be either cryotic (i.e. below 0 °C) or non-cryotic (i.e. above 0 °C) in nature. Taliks may be either open or closed depending upon whether the talik is completely enclosed by permafrost or whether it reaches to the seasonally thawed zone. Open taliks are common features even within the

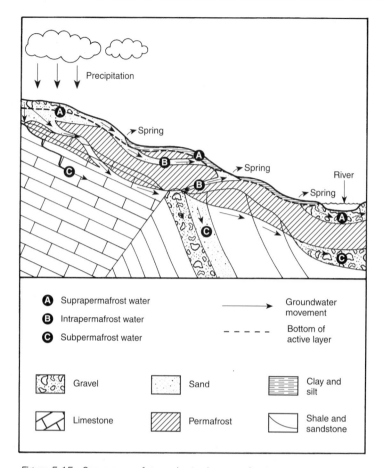

Figure 5.15 Occurrence of groundwater in permafrost areas

continuous permafrost zone. The majority result from local heat sources such as lakes, river channels and other standing water bodies. Closed taliks usually result from a change in the thermal regime of permafrost, such as might occur following lake drainage and the downward encroachment of permafrost. Where closed taliks occur at depth in thick permafrost bodies, they probably reflect long-past fluctuations in regional climate. In the discontinuous zone where the thickness of permafrost progressively decreases, unfrozen zones may perforate the permafrost layer and form 'through taliks' linking the unfrozen ground above and below the permafrost.

5.7.2 Hydrochemistry

The low ground temperatures associated with permafrost regions mean that reaction and dissolu-

tion rates are reduced. At the same time, because of the increased solubility of carbon dioxide at low temperature, the solubilities of calcites, dolomites and gypsum are increased.

The chemical composition of intra- and sub-permafrost waters will depend largely upon the residence time of the water in the subsurface and on the mineral composition of the aquifer. Low-dissolved solids contents are usually associated with rapidly moving groundwaters, as might be found in karst terrain or in fractured non-soluble rock. Sub-permafrost waters range from being freshwater of the $Ca(mg)-HCO_3$ type, to saline, to calcium/sodium brines. Needless to say, the latter may often be at temperatures below $0°C$, emerging from cryotic taliks. On the other hand, in some places, such as Engineers Creek on the Dempster Highway, northern Yukon, exceptionally iron-rich, sulphurous and acidic springs occur, with pH values as low as

Table 5.5 Various types of taliks occuring in permafrost regions

Closed talik – a non-cryotic talik occupying a depression in the permafrost table below a lake or river (also called 'lake talik' and 'river talik'): its temperature remains above 0 °C because of the heat storage effect of the surface water.

Hydrochemical talik – a cryotic talik in which freezing is prevented by mineralized groundwater flowing through the talik.

Hydrothermal talik – a non-cryotic talik, the temperature of which is maintained above 0 °C by the heat supplied by groundwater flowing through the talik.

Isolated talik – a talik entirely surrounded by perennially frozen ground; usually cryotic but may be non-cryotic (see transient talik).

Lateral talik – a talik overlain and underlain by perennially frozen ground; can be non-cryotic or cryotic.

Open talik – a talik that penetrates the permafrost competely, connecting supra-permafrost and sub-permafrost water (e.g. below large rivers and lakes). It may be non-cryotic (see hydrothermal talik) or cryotic (see hydrochemical talik).

Thermal talik – a non-cryotic talik, temperature of which is above 0 °C owing to the general thermal regime. It includes the seasonally thawed ground in the active layer.

Transient talik – a talik that is gradually being eliminated by freezing, e.g. the initially non-cryotic closed talik below a small lake which, upon draining of the lake, is turned into a transient isolated talik by permafrost aggradation.

Source: from ACGR (1988); van Everdingen (1990, pp. 77–86)

2.8, a temperature of +9 °C and dissolved solids as high as 1080 mg/l (Harris *et al.*, 1983, pp. 75–79). In the same general vicinity, at Castle's Hill in the Ogilvie River gorge, powerful freshwater springs discharge at a rate of 1.4 m³/s, with a temperature of +4 °C and a dissolved-solids content of only 362 mg/l. Data such as these illustrate the importance of local geological conditions upon the specific hydrochemistry and water quality of permafrost waters.

If permafrost degrades it is not uncommon for the water immediately below the permafrost to be unusually low in dissolved solids. This results not only from the contribution of relatively fresh water following the thawing of ice-rich permafrost but is also the result of the low solution rates at low temperatures and, in the absence of CO_2, the low solubility of carbonates. The latter inhibits the re-dissolution of carbonates and sulphates that had been precipitated out during the initial formation of the permafrost. As a result, certain perennial springs in permafrost regions, especially in central Yakutia, are renowned for their excellent drinking quality.

5.7.3 Surface-water hydrology

The presence of permafrost and a seasonally frozen active layer usually restricts the infiltration of water and its recharge to groundwater systems. Hence, a very high percentage of rainfall and snowmelt in permafrost regions tends to contribute to surface runoff. This condition in turn leads to extreme differences between seasonal maximum and minimum streamflow rates.

The chemistry of river-water also shows extreme seasonal variations because of the great differences between seasonal maximum and minimum flow rates in individual rivers. Dissolved solids concentrations, which may be as low as 25 mg/l during high-rate snowmelt runoff, rise during the summer owing to increasing contributions from active-layer aquifers. These concentrations may reach values in excess of 500 mg/l in the same river during the winter, when most or all of the limited runoff is supplied by discharge of more mineralized water from intra-permafrost or sub-permafrost aquifers.

Winter baseflow in rivers generally ranges from 1.0 to 5.0 l/s/km² in the zone of discontinuous permafrost. It approaches zero with increasing latitude, because a rapidly increasing percentage of the discharge is stored as icings. The latter are sheetlike masses of ice which form at the surface in winter where water issues from the ground (Carey, 1970). They are also known as *aufeis* (e.g. Washburn, 1979, p. 44) or '*nalyedi*' (Brown, 1967b, pp. 74–79). Sometimes, the water source is of a sub- or intra-permafrost nature in which case the spring is usually a perennial one. Therefore, it is often useful to make the distinction between groundwater icings and river icings. Most commonly, groundwater icings are the

(a)

(b)

Figure 5.16 Icings and related phenomena. (a) The Babbage River Icing, Barn Mts, northern Yukon. This annual groundwater icing is associated with perennial discharge through Triassic-age sandstones and limestones. The icing shown is 3–4 m thick. Photo taken July 1979. (b) An icing mound on the Big River, central Banks Island. Photo: April 1979. This feature formed in a braided river channel in mid-winter. The mound is about 2.5 m high. Photo courtesy of David Nasagaloak, Sachs Harbour.

result of supra-permafrost waters. If the seasonal frost extends to the top of the permafrost table, flow may cease in mid-winter but if there is a sub-permafrost talik, flow can be perennial. The majority of groundwater icings are small, usually less than 1.0 m in thickness and less than 0.5 km^2 in extent. Groundwater icings which are associated with perennial springs, however, may assume considerable dimensions. In the Momskaya Depression of northeast Yakutia, complex icings as large as 62 km^2 are known to occur (Nekrasov and Gordeyev, 1973, pp. 37–40). In Alaska, an icing over 10 m thick and more than 1 km wide and 2 km long formed in the St John River valley in 1969 (Ferrians *et al.*, 1969, p. 346). The Babbage River icing, northern Yukon (Fig. 5.16 (a)), is a favourite gathering place for caribou to escape the heat and mosquitoes in the summer.

River icings develop at localities where rivers freeze to the bottom and water is forced out of the bed. Where high hydraulic potentials develop, usually associated with restricted hydraulic conductivities in open sub-channel taliks beneath braided stream channels, small mounds can form (Fig. 5.16 (b)).

Some of the earliest studies of large groundwater icings were undertaken in central Yakutia by the Permafrost Institute of the Siberian Division of the USSR Academy of Science (Anisimova *et al.*, 1973, pp. 37–47). There, although icings start to form as soon as streams are frozen, the major period of icing growth is in the mid-winter to early spring period. The small monthly accretions of icing volumes during the early winter are explained by discharge continuing either in the channels or through the sub-river taliks which freeze only in late winter. Maximum ice accretions involve sub- or intra-permafrost waters and occur in February and March when the ground is fully frozen and before the spring rise in air temperatures which lead to ablation of the icing. During the early summer months, icings usually melt away completely, leaving a grassy, largely treeless area in the taiga forest. Sometimes, the thickness of the icing can be inferred from scars on the barks of trees adjacent to the icing location.

Similar icing accretion patterns occur throughout the subarctic of northern Alaska and Canada (e.g. van Everdingen, 1982, 1990). The amount of discharge stored in icings can be considerable and the release of this water in the ablation period may significantly alter the stream flow characteristics of the watershed concerned. For example, the annual water stored in the icings of the Caribou–Porcupine watersheds near Fairbanks, Alaska, is equivalent to 4 per cent of total runoff and 40 per cent of total winter stream flow. This is concentrated into the four weeks following ablation of the snowpack and provides a flow augmentation of

0.28 m^3/s. In other areas of Alaska, it has been calculated that the melt of icings over the ablation period may increase stream flow by as much as 20 m^3/s.

Thus, icings provide an important seasonal redistribution of surface-water resources; their melt produces additional runoff during spring and summer at rates that may be 1.5 to 4 times higher than the rates of groundwater discharge that contributed to their formation.

Icings are discussed further in Chapters 11 and 16.

5.7.4 Seasonal and perennial frost mounds

Where freezing of the active layer restricts perennial discharge from intra-permafrost or sub-permafrost aquifers, a variety of seasonal and perennial frost mounds (frost blisters, open system pingos) can develop at the site of groundwater discharge. It must be emphasized, however, that such features are not necessarily restricted to permafrost regions since they can also form under conditions of deep seasonal frost and impermeable, but fractured, bedrock.

Seasonal frost mounds are usually between 1.0 and 4.0 m high. They form through the doming of seasonally frozen ground by a subsurface accumulation of water under high hydraulic potential during progressive freezing of the active layer. Figure 5.17 illustrates the formation of frost blisters, one of the most common types of seasonal frost mounds.

Seasonal frost mounds should not be confused with palsas. The latter form by ice segregation while seasonal frost mounds form by ice injection from free water under high hydraulic potentials. Thus, the interior of a frost blister is characterized by a core of pure ice with ice crystals aligned in a vertical columnar fashion to reflect the freezing of free water (e.g. Pollard and French, 1984, 1985).

Some seasonal frost mounds are destroyed completely by thawing and slumping of the active layer and melt of the ice during the first summer after their formation. Others may be preserved through one or more summers, depending on the insulating quality of their soil cover. Seasonal frost mounds have been described from a wide range of localities, including Alaska, Scandinavia, the Tibet Plateau, China, and northern Canada (Yukon) (Fig. 5.18).

The continued development of frost mounds at the same locality is probably the origin of perennial (open system) pingos. Unlike closed system pingos (see Chapter 6), open system pingos are perennial ice-cored mounds, usually partially collapsed, which develop at sites where groundwater, under artesian

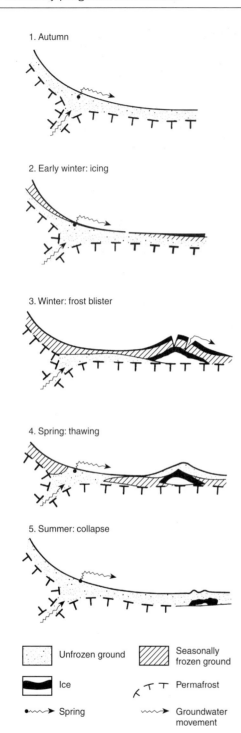

1. Autumn

2. Early winter: icing

3. Winter: frost blister

4. Spring: thawing

5. Summer: collapse

Unfrozen ground

Seasonally frozen ground

Ice

Permafrost

Spring

Groundwater movement

Figure 5.17 Sequence of events in the formation and decay of frost blisters (modified from van Everdingen, 1978)

pressure, ruptures the overlying permafrost. The role of the permafrost is to act as an impermeable and confining layer for sub-permafrost waters; where the permafrost is thin and/or discontinuous, the artesian pressures may exceed the overburden pressure and rupture ensues. Commonly, the emergence of water under an artesian head occurs at the downslope limit of permafrost bodies, usually in the central and lower parts of slopes. If the groundwater temperature is close to 0 °C and if air temperatures are below 0 °C, the water freezes as it rises through the permafrost zone or enters the seasonally frozen zone.

Open system pingos were first described from Spitsbergen (e.g. Müller, 1959). However, by far the largest concentration of open system pingos occurs in the Yukon–Tanana uplands in central Alaska (Holmes *et al.*, 1968) and in Yukon, Canada (Hughes, 1969). They are found in narrow upland valleys particularly on the lower parts of south- and southeast-facing slopes but are not found on the north-facing slopes or in the broader river valleys. This is probably because there are more opportunities for surface water to enter the ground in the permafrost-free areas of the upper sections of south-facing slopes than on north-facing slopes which are totally frozen (Brown and Péwé, 1973, p. 80). A second requirement for the formation of open system pingos is restricted groundwater flow since too large a flow rate would prevent freezing of the water supply. A third requirement is that the subsurface temperature be close to 0 °C in order to provide the minimum tensile strength of frozen ground and prevent premature freezing of the groundwater. However, theoretical calculations by Holmes *et al.* (1968) suggest that the total force required both to maintain a pingo 30 m high and to overcome the tensile strength of ground and force it upwards is considerably greater than the highest artesian pressure yet measured in Alaska. This may explain why the majority of open system pingos never attain a fully domed state but persist as doughnut-shaped, semicircular or circular ramparts. Open system pingos are discussed more fully in Chapter 6.

Further reading

Academia Sinica (1975) *Permafrost*. Research Institute of Glaciology, Cryopedology and Desert Research, Lanzhou, China. (National Research Council of Canada Ottawa, Technical Translation No. 2006, 1981, 224 pp.)

Associate Committee on Geotechnical Research (1988) *Glossary of permafrost and related ground ice terms*. Permafrost Subcommittee, National Research Council of Canada, Technical Memorandum 142.

Figure 5.18   Remnants of a seasonal frost mound, North Fork Pass, Ogilvie Mts, interior Yukon, Canada (August 1983).

Ferrians, O.J., R. Kachadoorian and G.W. Greene (1969). *Permafrost and related engineering problems in Alaska*. US Geological Survey Professional Paper 678, 37 pp.

Haeberli, W. (1985) *Creep of mountains permafrost; internal structure and flow of alpine rock glaciers*. Mitteilungen der Versuchsanstalt fur Wasserbau, Hydrologie und Glaziologie, No. 77, 142 pp.

Johnston, G.H. (ed.) (1981) *Permafrost: engineering design and construction*. New York: Wiley and Sons, 340 pp.

Kudryavtsev, V.A. (1965) Temperature, thickness and discontinuity of permafrost. In: *Principles of geocryology (permafrost studies), Part 1, General geocryology*, Ch. VIII. USSR Academy of Sciences, Moscow, 1959, pp. 219–273. (National Research Council of Canada, Ottawa, Technical Translation 1187.)

Muller, S.W. (1945) *Permafrost or permanently frozen ground and related engineering problems*. United States Engineers Office, Strategic Engineering Study, Special Report No. 62, 136 pp. (Reprinted in 1947, J.W. Edwards, Ann Arbor, Michigan, 231 pp.)

Péwé, T.L. (1983) Alpine permafrost in the contiguous United States: A review. *Arctic and Alpine Research*, **15**, 145–156.

Péwé, T.L. (1991) Permafrost. In: G.A. Kiersch (ed.) *The heritage of engineering geology: the first hundred years*. Boulder, Colorado: Geological Society of America Centennial Special Volume 3, pp. 277–298.

Sloan, C.E. and R.O. van Everdingen (1988) Region 28, Permafrost region. In: W. Back, J. G. Rosenshein and P.R. Seaber (eds) *Hydrology. The geology of North America*, Volume 0–2, Boulder, Colorado: Geological Society of America, pp. 263–270.

Discussion topics

1. What are the controls over the distribution of permafrost?

2. What are the unique hydrological characteristics of permafrost?

3. What surface features are typical of permafrost terrain?

CHAPTER 6

Ground ice

The nature and extent of ground ice is of great significance to our understanding of periglacial environments. First, the thaw of ice-rich permafrost terrain is of geotechnical importance. The processes associated with the degradation of permafrost (thermokarst) are dealt with in Chapter 7. Second, the stratigraphic analysis of ground ice bodies and the cryotextures of their enclosing sediments are important tools in reconstructing Quaternary environmental history. Third, within regions beyond the present permafrost limits, the recognition of certain ground ice pseudomorphs or casts provides evidence of the former existence of permafrost.

6.1 Ground ice description

Ground ice is a general term used to refer to all types of ice formed in freezing and frozen ground. Ground ice occurs in the pores, cavities, voids or other openings in soil or rock and includes massive ice (ACGR, 1988, p. 46). Although traditional North American usage of the term has generally excluded buried surface ice (e.g. Mackay, 1972a), a recent trend is to consider such ice (i.e. buried glacier, lake, river and snowbank ice) as one type of ground ice, as is the case in Russia (e.g. Shumskiy and Vtyurin, 1966).

Two quantitative parameters are used to describe ground ice conditions. First, the 'ice content' of a soil is defined as the weight of ice to dry soil, and is expressed as a percentage. For example, if a soil sample weighed 100 g when frozen and 40 g when oven dried, then the weight of ice (i.e. moisture) in that sample was 60 g. Therefore, the ice content would be 150 per cent. To be really meaningful, a number of ice content determinations should be made at different depths and the moisture content of the seasonally thawed zone should also be determined. Low ice content soils are generally regarded as those having ice contents less than 40–50 per cent. Soils with high ice contents are usually fine grained and have ice content values which commonly range between 50 and 150 per cent.

In certain instances, it is important to determine the Atterberg Limits for the sediment content of the permafrost. It is not uncommon for the natural water (ice) content of frozen soils to exceed their liquid limits. If this were the case, the ground will pass upon thawing from a solid state possessing considerable strength to a considerably lower liquid state strength. In this case, buildings may subside and the thawed sediments will become relatively mobile, capable of flowing on very slight inclines.

The amount of 'excess ice' is a second parameter commonly used in the description of ground ice. Excess ice refers to the volume of supernatant water present if a vertical column of frozen sediment were thawed. In this case, the sample is allowed to thaw and the relative volumes of supersaturated sediments and standing water (i.e. excess ice) are noted. The volume of supernatant water is then expressed as a percentage of the total volume of sediment and water. For example, if upon thawing the relative volumes of supersaturated sediments and supernatant water were 300 and 500 cm respectively, then the excess ice value would be 62.5 per cent. The advantage of this index is that it provides some indication of the potential morphological change, or volumetric ground loss, consequent upon thaw of permafrost.

Visual estimates of excess ice are deceptive since sediment may not necessarily contain excess ice even though it may contain visible ice lenses, because the sediment between the lenses may not be saturated with ice and, upon melting, all water is retained in the voids. Sediments that contain excess ice are often referred to as 'ice-rich' or 'icy sediments'. In unconsolidated materials, excess ice values of between 15 and 50 per cent are reasonably common although exceptionally icy sediments may have values as great as 70–80 per cent. Frozen sediments containing excess ice are 'thaw-sensitive' (van Everdingen, 1979) and may be contrasted with 'thaw-stable' materials. The latter contain no excess ice and are not subject to thaw settlement and retain much of their mechanical strength when thawed.

The terms 'massive ice' or 'massive icy bodies' are usually reserved for relatively pure ground ice whose ice content averages at least 250 per cent for thicknesses of several metres.

6.1.1 Cryostructures, cryotextures and cryofacies

Ice within perennially frozen sediments imparts structures distinct from those found in other sedimentary environments. These are termed cryostructures. They are determined by the amount and distribution of ice within pores (often termed pore or cement ice), and by lenses of segregated ice. Depending upon the ini-

tial water content and the extent of water migration during freezing will be the type and arrangement of the ice within the frozen material. Figure 6.1 (a) illustrates a cryostructure formed in frozen lacustrine clay near Mayo, Yukon.

Cryostructures must be distinguished from cryotextures. The latter refers to the grain and/or ice crystal size and shape, and the nature of the contacts between grains and ice crystals in frozen earth materials. Both cryostructures and cryotextures are useful in determining the nature of the freezing process and the conditions under which the sediments have accumulated.

The first to identify and use cryotextures and cryostructures systematically were Soviet permafrost scientists (e.g. Katasonov, 1969, 1975; Melnikov and Tolstikhin, 1974; Kudryavtsev, 1978). However, besides being complex, their classifications tended to blur the distinction, made above, between texture (i.e. grain size) and structure (i.e. aggregate shape). Traditionally, Russian scientists use the term texture to describe what North Americans denote as structure (see comment, ACGR, 1988, p. 24). This confusion was perpetuated in one of the only English language translations of Russian literature on this subject (Demek, 1978, pp. 139–153). Russian and Soviet geocryologists recognize at least ten 'cryogenic textures' (i.e. cryostructures); these are termed massive, massive-porous, basal, basal-layered, crust-like, massive agglomerate-lens-type, lattice type, layered and lattice-block type (Kudryavtsev, 1978, pp. 301–304). This classification of 'cryotextures' is primarily one of cryostructures (Murton and French, 1994).

(a)

(b)

Figure 6.1   Examples of cryostructures in frozen ground: (a) inclined ice lenses, 30–80 cm long and 5–10 cm thick, formed by subaqueous syngenetic freezing of glaciolacustrine silty clay near Mayo, Yukon Territory; (b) fine reticulate network of ice veins formed in silty clay diamicton, Pelly Island, Pleistocene Mackenzie Delta, NWT. Photo courtesy of D.G. Harry.

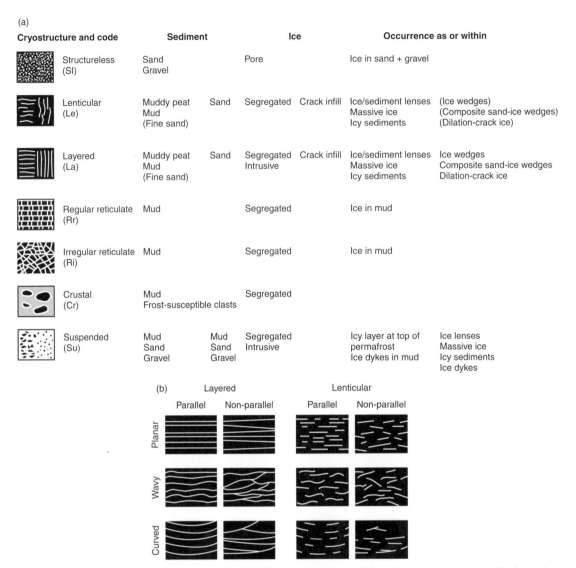

Figure 6.2 Classification of cryostructures. (a) Ice is shown in white and sediment in grey or black. In lenticular and layered cryostructures, lenses and layers may comprise either ice or sediment. (b) Terms describing layered and lenticular cryostructures (from Murton and French, 1994).

One of the most common cryostructures observed in silty and/or clayey permafrost is the reticulate ice vein network (Fig. 6.1 (b)). Mackay (1974c) suggested that these ice veins grow in vertical and horizontal shrinkage cracks, with the water being derived from the adjacent clay in a semi-closed freezing system, rather than the upward migration of water in a closed system. Subsequently, McRoberts and Nixon (1975) proposed hydraulic fracturing in unfrozen soil ahead of the advancing freezing front

as the mechanism for the cracks, and inferred that the cracks are filled by expelled pore water.

Problems with the various Russian cryostructural classifications primarily result from their complex and unwieldy nature. For example, Katasonov's (1969) classification involves 18 different cryostructures and Popov *et al.*'s (1985b) classification has 14, excluding those that are composite. A second limitation is that these classifications apply primarily to permafrost containing little excess ice, detailing the distribution

(a)

(b)

(c)

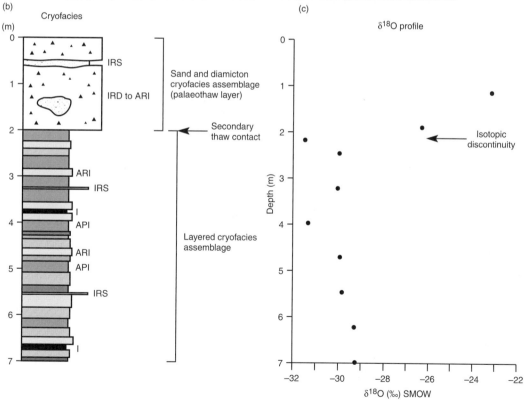

Figure 6.3 Cryostratigraphy at Crumbling Point, Pleistocene Mackenzie Delta, Canada. (a) Sand wedge penetrating both a layered and a sand and diamicton cryofacies assemblage. Arrows mark the contact between the assemblages. Person is 1.8 m. (b) Generalized cryofacies log. (c) $\delta^{18}O$ profile of ground ice within both cryofacies assemblages. At their contact is an isotopic discontinuity. SMOW, standard mean ocean water (from Murton and French, 1994).

Table 6.1 Cryofacies types applicable to ice-rich sediments in the Pleistocene Mackenzie Delta

Cryofacies type	Volumetric Ice Content (%)	Cryofacies	Code	Cryostructures[1]
Pure ice	100	Pure ice	I	Le, Le
Sediment-poor ice	>75	Sand-poor ice	SPI	Le, La, Su
		Aggregate-poor ice	API	
Sediment-rich ice	>50 to ≤75	Sand-rich ice	SRI	
		Aggregate-rich ice	ARI	Le, La, Su
Ice-rich sediment	>25 to ≤50	Ice-rich sand	IRS	Sl, Le, La
		Ice-rich mud	IRM	Le, La, Rr, Ri, Cr
		Ice-rich diamicton	IRD	
Ice-poor sediment	≤25	Ice-poor mud	IPM	Sl; various non-ice
		Ice-poor sand	IPS	sedimentary structures
		Ice-poor gravel	IPG	
		Ice-poor diamicton	IPD	
		Ice-poor peat	IPP	

[1]See Fig. 6.2

Source: from Murton and French (1994)

of ice within sediment and neglecting that of sediment within ice. Thus, Kudryavtsev's (1978) classification contains seven cryostructural terms describing frozen ground whose ice content is ≤ 50 per cent by volume and only one term (basal layered: ataxitic or breccia-like, e.g. Cheng, 1983; Shur, 1988) describing permafrost that is very ice-rich.

A recent attempt at a cryostructural classification that is simple to apply and encompasses the range of ice contents found within permafrost is illustrated in Fig. 6.2 (Murton and French, 1994). Several Russian terms are transliterated but all six cryostructures proposed can be recognized by the naked ice. The structureless cryostructure refers to frozen sediments in which ice is not visible and consequently lacks a cryostructure. Lenticular cryostructures, by comparison, can be of several types (see Fig. 6.3 (b)); they are described by inclination, thickness, length, shape and relationship to each other. For example, the dominant cryostructure illustrated in Fig. 6.1 (a) is best described as 'lenticular, parallel, curved' according to this classification. In the case of lenticular cryostructures, the orientation of ice lenses reflects the orientation of freezing fronts and/or the structural properties of the sediment (e.g. bedding; Smith and Williams, 1990). Layered cryostructures are continuous bands of ice, sediment or a combination of both. They occur in both massive ice and icy sediments (see Fig. 6.3) and in ice wedges (see Fig. 6.8). The reticulate category, already described, is a three-dimensional net-like structure of ice veins surrounding mud-rich blocks. The best known, but probably least common, cryostructure is that of an ice crust or

rim around a rock clast. This is termed crustal; it occurs commonly just beneath the permafrost table where ice crusts up to a few centimetres thick may envelop pebbles and wood fragments, typically within silt-rich facies. Crustal cryostructures most likely form by localized ice segregation around frost-susceptible clasts. The suspended category refers to grains, aggregates and rock clasts suspended in ice and, by definition, refers to icy sediments and massive icy bodies. The aggregates are typically mud (silt), and range in diameter or length from ≤ 1 mm to several centimetres or more. Suspended sediment aggregates occur in a range of ice types, including segregated, intrusive, crack-infill and glacier ice. In segregated ice, angular mud aggregates are abundant in the ice-rich layer commonly observed at the top of permafrost (e.g. Mackay, 1972a; Cheng, 1983; Burn, 1988; Shur, 1988). Rounded mud aggregates have been reported from debris-rich glacier ice (Boulton, 1970; Lawson, 1979; French and Harry, 1988).

Many cryostructures are composite or transitional, either merging into adjacent categories or mixing two categories. They may also be hierarchical, although such hierarchies do not necessarily imply genesis.

The concept of cryofacies needs also to be considered. Cryofacies in frozen sediments can be defined according to volumetric ice content and ice crystal size, and then subdivided according to cryostructure. One such system of cryofacies is illustrated in Table 6.1 where five types of cryofacies are distinguished according to arbitrarily defined volumetric ice content. Although this classification was developed specifically for the ice-rich sediments of the Mackenzie Delta, it can be modified to meet other conditions.

Cryofacies can be divided according to cryostructures. Where a number of associated cryofacies form a distinctive cryostratigraphic unit, these are termed a cryofacies assemblage. An example of the use of this cryostratigraphic classification is given in Fig. 6.3 which describes a 6 m high exposure of massive ice overlain by 2 m of sand and diamicton.

6.1.2 Thaw unconformities

The presence of ground ice can be used to detect discontinuities in freezing history and thus to deduce past permafrost conditions. A thaw unconformity, similar in concept to a geological unconformity, represents a period of thaw. During that time, ice bodies or cryostructures above the unconformity would have been destroyed and vertical and/or large ice bodies, such as ice wedges or veins, would have been truncated at the depth of the thaw unconformity (Fig. 6.4(b)). At this point in time, a residual thaw layer would be present above the thaw unconformity and below a surface zone of seasonal frost penetration. If this were then followed by a renewed period of climatic cooling, permafrost would reform and aggrade downwards, ultimately to join the relict permafrost below. In so doing, new cryostructures would be formed and the initial thaw unconformity would be characterized by a transition between different cryotextures and ice contents. It then becomes a secondary thaw unconformity since the primary thaw unconformity now becomes the base of the active layer (Fig. 6.4(c)). A secondary thaw unconformity is illustrated in Fig. 6.5.

Besides the truncation of ice bodies and differences in ice contents, a thaw unconformity might be recognized by differences in stable isotope contents (e.g. see Fig. 6.3(c)), heavy mineral and pollen assemblages above and below the unconformity (e.g. Burn et al., 1986), and horizons of enhanced micro-organisms (e.g. Gilichinsky and Wagener, 1995). The recognition of thaw unconformities is a valuable line of evidence in reconstructing past permafrost histories. In currently unfrozen Pleistocene sediments of middle-latitudes, thaw unconformities are sometimes inferred from the recognition of certain soil microfabrics and structures (e.g. van Vliet-Lanoë, 1988; Derbyshire et al., 1985).

6.1.3 Ice crystallography

The petrofabric analysis of ground ice is not only useful for descriptive purposes but, like the study of cryostructures, may help to infer growth processes and conditions. This is because the crystal size, shape, boundary characteristics and c-axis orientation are directly related to the direction and speed of the freezing process; ice crystals normally grow at right angles to the direction of freezing and crystal size varies inversely with the rate of freezing. In recent

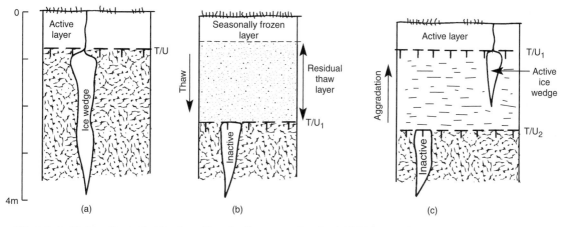

Figure 6.4 Diagram illustrating the formation of a thaw unconformity: (a) initial permafrost conditions with ice wedges and reticulate cryostructures; (b) degradation of permafrost, formation of primary thaw unconformity (T/U$_1$) and residual thaw layer; (c) aggradation of permafrost, formation of lenticular cryostructures. The thaw unconformity becomes a secondary thaw unconformity (T/U$_2$) marked by the ice wedge truncation and a change in cryostructures.

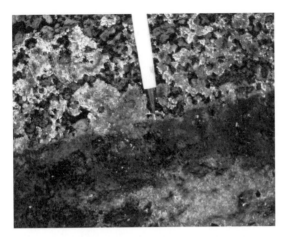

Figure 6.5 Cryostructural discontinuity between aggregate-rich ice that has melted out from underlying aggregate-poor ice. The contact is a secondary thaw unconformity.

years, petrofabric analyses of ground ice bodies have become standard procedures (e.g. Solomatin, 1986; French and Pollard, 1986; Pollard, 1990). The techniques and procedures used follow closely those developed for glacier ice (e.g. Ostrem, 1963).

Although Pollard (1990) suggests that different ice types display a characteristic range of fabric and texture patterns, the reality is that a wide range of fabrics exists. Without good cryostratigraphic control the fabrics do not permit unambiguous identification of ice types. However, according to Pollard (1990), segregated ice tends to be composed of large equigranular anhydral crystals whose c-axes form a loose girdle oriented normal to the plane of the ice layer. By contrast, buried snowbank ice is composed of small anhedral equigranular crystals with a high concentration of vertically oriented intercrystalline bubble trains and tubular bubbles. The petrography of intrusive ice reflects the groundwater transfer mechanism and freezing conditions; for example, in seasonal frost mounds, the ice mass is composed of large tabular crystals oriented normal to the freezing direction with c-axes forming a horizontal girdle normal to the long axes of the crystals (Pollard and French, 1985).

6.1.4   Ice geochemistry

Standard chemical analyses, including conductivity and cations (Ca, Na, Mg and K), can be undertaken to characterize ground ice (water). Although such determinations usually reflect local geological and/or hydrological conditions, they are useful for comparison purposes and for differentiating between ice bodies.

More inferential is the use of isotopic data (e.g. ^{18}O, deuterium and tritium) and these techniques demand brief explanation. For example, when water freezes, $\delta^{18}O$ is preferentially incorporated into the ice which becomes isotopically heavier. Usually isotopic values are compared to standard mean ocean water (SMOW) values and expressed in ‰. There is also a positive linear relationship between temperature and $\delta^{18}O$, as demonstrated from ice cores from Greenland. Finally, there is also a relationship between $\delta^{18}O$ and $\delta^{16}O$: the colder the climate, the lower the $\delta^{18}O$: $\delta^{16}O$ ratio becomes. It follows that the isotopic analysis of ground ice is not only a useful descriptive tool but one can also infer, first, the approximate temperature of the water prior to freezing and second, by comparing the isotopic signatures with those from adjacent groundwaters, the source of the water.

A simple example of the effects of freezing upon the oxygen isotope composition of groundwater is provided by data in Table 6.2. Two sites, one a large drained lake where growing permafrost is 20–35 m in thickness, the other a more recently drained lake where permafrost is currently only 15–20 m thick, are compared. It is assumed that the initial groundwater conditions are similar. The ice (water) sample from within newly formed permafrost is –16‰ while the sub-permafrost waters range from –27‰ to –29‰, thus indicating that significant fractionation has occurred during freezing. The values for surface water compare favourably with annual SMOW values.

Tritium (^3H) is a radioactive isotope of modern age with a short half-life (12.43 years). Its detection in the upper layers of permafrost, in the active layer, and in seasonal ice bodies is useful in determining recent water migration into permafrost (e.g. Michel and Fritz, 1982; Burn and Michel, 1988), the age of seasonal frost mounds (e.g. Pollard and French, 1984) or recent ice-wedge growth (e.g. Lewkowicz, 1994).

It is clear, therefore, that isotopic compositional differences in groundwater can assist in the interpretation of the history and stability of permafrost, such as whether permafrost grew in open or closed systems, in the recognition of thaw unconformities (see above, and Fig. 6.4), in understanding certain geomorphic processes and in the characterization of massive icy bodies.

Table 6.2 Isotopic and geochemical composition of water (ice) at two drained lake sites in the Mackenzie Delta region, Canada: Site 1 Lake drained about 150 years ago: permafrost is 20–35 m thick; Site 2 Lake drained between 1935 and 1950; permafrost is 15–20 m thick

	Site 1			Site 2	
	Surface Water (Residual Lake)	Permafrost (at 20.5 m)	Sub-permafrost Water (at 21.5 m)	Surface Water	Sub-permafrost Water (at 17 m)
$\delta H_2^{18}O$ (in ‰)	−21.6	−16.2 (at 14.5 m)	−28.8	−19.7	−27.7
Specific conductance (μmho/cm)	188	190	1224	134	1714
Chloride	16	–	106	18	141
Magnesium	7	2.3	49	4	148
Potassium	2.4	2	5.6	1.5	7.3
Calcium	14	17	93	10	54
Sodium	12	4	83	9	92

Source: data from Mackay and Lavkulich (1974)

6.2 Type and amounts of ground ice

6.2.1 Classification

Several attempts have been made to classify ground ice. In general terms, ground ice may be either 'epigenetic' (i.e. develops inside the enclosing rock and after the latter has formed) or 'syngenetic' (i.e. forms at, or almost at, the same time as the enclosing sediments are deposited and usually associated, therefore, with surface aggradation). The distinction between epigenetic and syngenetic becomes especially important when understanding ice wedges.

A commonly used classification developed by Mackay (1972a) is based upon (a) the source of water immediately prior to freezing, and (b) the principal transfer process which moves water to the freezing plane. The various types of buried ice (e.g. glacier ice; sea, lake or river ice; snowbanks; river ice) are excluded from this classification which results in ten mutually exclusive ground ice forms (Fig. 6.6).

In addition to its clarity, an advantage of this classification is that it emphasizes the variety and complexity of the transfer process, recognizing at least six basic mechanisms. Moreover, although the theoretical principles behind these transfer processes are beyond the scope of this book, the classification has

the added advantage that it focuses attention upon three broad types of ground ice: (1) wedge ice, categories 2, 3 and 4; (2) segregated ice, categories 6 and 7; (3) intrusive ice, categories 8 and 9. These three types of ground ice are particularly important from a geomorphological viewpoint since their localized occurrence gives rise to distinctive periglacial landforms and terrain, such as ice-wedge polygons, frost mounds and various types of ice-cored topography. In addition, pore ice (category 10) and segregated ice (categories 6 and 7) are the major determinants of cryotextures and frost heave (see earlier).

The more important types of ice and their characteristics require brief description. Pore ice is the bonding cement that holds soil grains together. The distinction between pore ice and segregated ice is related to the water content of the soil. It is best determined by thawing the soil and noting the presence or absence of excess ice or supernatant water. If supernatant water is present, this indicates that the frozen soil was supersaturated and that segregated ice was present.

Segregated ice is a broad term for soil with a high ice content. The mechanism of formation of segregated ice has already been discussed in some detail in Chapter 4. Usually, the ice lenses are visible to the naked eye but in certain soils, particularly those that are fine-grained, lensing may be minimal. Segregated

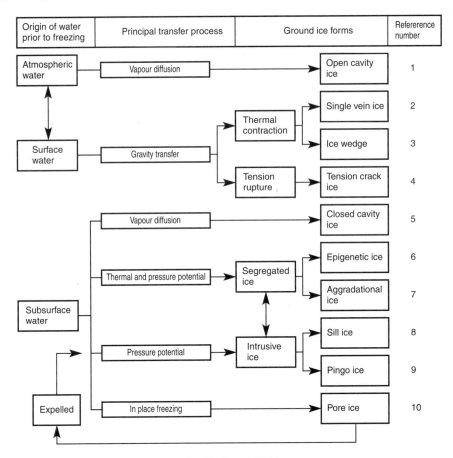

Figure 6.6 A genetic classification of ground ice (after Mackay, 1972b).

ice lenses vary in thickness from layers a few centimetres thick to massive ice bodies, sometimes tens of metres thick (see Figs 6.3 and 6.17). In theory, segregated ice may be distinguished from intrusive ice on account of the relative purity of the latter and the stratification and presence of soil particles and air bubbles oriented normal to the freezing plane in the former. However, when dealing with massive icy bodies, this distinction is often difficult to make.

Vein ice is formed by the penetration of water into open fissures developed at the ground surface. In contrast to segregated ice, therefore, the origin of the water prior to its freezing is of a surface nature, usually snowmeltwater and summer rain. Vein ice can be distinguished from segregation ice on account of its vertical foliation and structures. Single vein ice develops in small fissures usually formed in the upper 60 cm of permafrost, probably by thermal contraction. The majority are very thin, less than 0.2 cm in

thickness. In silty/clayey material reticulate ice veins are common (see earlier). Repeated vein ice is a specific variety of single vein ice and is the result of successive ice formation in frost fissures periodically forming in the same place for many years. The result is the formation of vertical or near-vertical sheets of ice which, because of their form, are termed ice wedges. Since these are important features of permafrost environments, they are dealt with separately in section 6.3.

Intrusive ice is formed by water intrusion, usually under pressure, into the seasonally or perennially frozen zone. Sill and pingo ice are the two types of intrusive ice which are usually identified. The former grows when water is intruded into a confining material and freezes in a tabular mass along the base of the active layer and parallel to the permafrost surface. In many instances, small frost mounds can results (e.g. Lewis, 1962; Pollard and French, 1983; Sharp, 1942a).

Table 6.3 Ground ice volumes in upper 5 m of permafrost in selected areas, western Canadian Arctic

Area	Pore/segregated ice (%)		Wedge ice (%)		Total ice (%)	
King Point, Yukon	43.5	(79.2)	11.4	(20.8)	54.9	(100)
Richards Island, NWT	28.3	(79.3)	7.5	(21.0)	35.7	(100)
Southwest Banks Island, NWT	38.7	(66.2)	19.8	(33.8)	58.5	(100)

Note: Values in parentheses indicate percentage contribution of ground ice to total ice volume
Sources: King Point, Harry *et al.* (1985); Richards Island, Pollard and French (1980); Banks Island, French and Harry (1983)

6.2.2 Amount

The amount of ground ice present within permafrost can vary from negligible, as in certain igneous and metamorphic rocks, to considerable, as in the case of unconsolidated, fine-grained Quaternary-age rocks. For example, Table 6.3 lists the typically high ground ice volumes which exist in the upper 5.0 m of permafrost at three localities underlain by unconsolidated Quaternary-age sediments in the western Canadian Arctic. The total volumetric ice content varies between 35 and 60 per cent, of which by far the majority (66–80 per cent) is either segregated or pore ice. Clearly, in such regions ground ice is an extremely important component of permafrost. Elsewhere, typical ground ice contents vary from 1–2 per cent to 10–15 per cent by volume.

6.2.3 Distribution with depth

The majority of ground ice is concentrated in the upper 1–3 m of permafrost, in a zone immediately below the permafrost table (Fig. 6.7). One of the first to highlight this was the German geomorphologist J. Büdel, following observations of shattered ice-rich bedrock below stream channels on Spitsbergen. As a consequence, he formulated the 'ice-rind' concept in which this near-surface ice-rich layer favoured rock shattering and, thus, stream incision (Büdel, 1982, pp. 103–105).

The 'ice-rind' concept is not particularly satisfactory in explaining what Büdel termed the 'excessive valley deepening' in zones of permafrost. This generalization is obviously not correct for many tundra regions and, instead, valley incision on Spitsbergen is best explained by recent deglaciation combined with isostatic uplift. On the other hand, his observations upon the ice-rich nature of near-surface permafrost have been confirmed by many others (e.g. P.J. Williams, 1968; Mackay, 1981; Stangl *et al.*, 1982).

Our current understanding of moisture migration within freezing and frozen soils now permits a better explanation for this ice-rich zone near the top of permafrost. In Chapter 4, it was explained that unfrozen water in frozen ground can move in the direction along which the ground temperature decreases in response to an imposed thermal gradient. Later, in Chapter 8, it will be explained how the ice content in the active layer increases when a positive ground temperature gradient exists in winter (i.e. when the ground is warmer than the air). Using similar reasoning, water migrates downwards into the upper part of permafrost in winter. Thus, an ice-rich zone comes to characterize the zone of seasonal ground temperature variation. The highest amounts occur at the boundary between the base of the active layer and the perennially frozen permafrost.

6.3 Ice wedges

Their widespread occurrence and distinctive surface manifestation make ice wedges (Fig. 6.8) one of the most characteristic features of the periglacial landscape. By definition, they require permafrost for their existence. There are numerous references to ice wedges in the literature and the polygonal surface patterns which they form have been called tundra polygons, fissure polygons, ice-wedge polygons and Taimyr polygons. Most wedges are epigenetic in nature; that is, they are younger than the enclosing sediments and are usually related to a stable ground surface. Syngenetic wedges are less common and relate to changing surface conditions.

6.3.1 Size

The size of ice wedges varies considerably from locality to locality, depending largely upon the availability of water and the age of the ice wedge. The

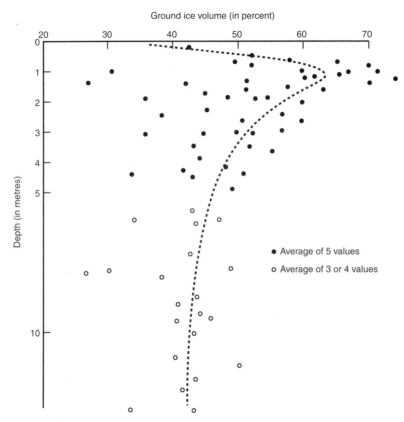

Figure 6.7 Typical distribution of ground ice with depth, Richards Island, Pleistocene Mackenzie Delta, Canada. Note: curve represents a visual best fit line (from Pollard and French, 1980).

majority of epigenetic wedges are probably no more than 1.0–1.5 m wide near the surface, and extend into the ground for 3.0–4.0 m as somewhat irregular wedge-like ice masses. In parts of northern Siberia and in the lowlands of the western Arctic, ice wedges may attain considerable dimensions, often 3.0–4.0 m wide near the surface and extending downwards for 5.0–10.0 m. Although some Russian authorities regard wedge ice as the dominant type of underground massive ice in certain localities (e.g. Popov, 1962; Shumskiy and Vtyurin, 1966; Dostovalov and Popov, 1966), Table 6.3 suggests that in other areas wedge ice constitutes only 20–30 per cent of the ground ice present in the upper 5.0 m of permafrost.

The most favourable conditions for development of ice wedges are to be found in the relatively poorly drained tundra lowlands within the continuous permafrost zone. In the more arid polar desert regions, such as the high Arctic islands and in Antarctica,

and on the Qinghai-Xizang (Tibet) Plateau, ice wedges are not well developed. Undoubtedly this reflects the lack of moisture and/or an absence of fine-grained silt and colluvium. Many of the large ice wedges known to exist in the boreal and taiga forest of southern Alaska, northern Canada and Siberia are probably largely relict features formed under colder conditions in the past (Péwé, 1966b).

In northern Siberia, ice wedges reach their greatest thickness and vertical dimensions on ancient alluvial surfaces or river terraces. In many cases, their growth appears to have paralleled the slow accumulation of sediments. Such ice wedges are termed 'syngenetic' (Dostovalov and Popov, 1966). A characteristic of such wedges, when examined in the field, is that their internal near-vertical foliations (see below) are truncated along the sides of the wedges. In addition, the edge of a syngenetic ice wedge is typically 'serrated' and the wedge may vary in width. However, limited observations in North America (e.g. French *et al.*,

Figure 6.8 Large epigenetic ice wedge formed in silty diamicton, Pleistocene Mackenzie Delta, Canada.

1982) suggest that syngenetic wedges are much smaller than the Soviet literature suggests (Fig. 6.9). This is also the case of Pleistocene pseudomorphs of syngenetic wedges (e.g. French and Gozdzik, 1988). Epigenetic ice wedges have foliations which extend the length of the ice wedge.

Anti-syngenetic wedges have been described by Mackay (1990a; 1995b). These are associated with eroding or retreating surfaces, in which the wedge 'burrows' downwards to keep pace with surface denudation. According to Mackay, they are probably widespread, although not reported in the literature.

6.3.2 Origin

Undoubtedly the most comprehensive and systematic series of field investigations into the growth of ice wedges have been undertaken by J.R. Mackay in the Mackenzie Delta region, Canada (e.g. Mackay, 1974b, 1978a, 1986d, 1992, 1993a, 1993b). A variety of sophisticated and innovative measurement techniques have been employed over a 30-year period of field observation (Fig. 6.10). Breaking cables and electronic crack detectors have established the timing, frequency and direction of cracking. The initiation of cracking has been monitored on the floor of Illisarvik, an artificially drained lake in which permafrost is currently aggrading. The speed and sound of cracking have been investigated, as have the relationships between ice-wedge cracking, snow cover, air and ground temperatures, and the creep of frozen ground. In many ways the data obtained contradict many previously held assumptions about the formation and growth of ice wedges. For this reason, detailed discussion is warranted.

Figure 6.9 An example of a small relict syngenetic ice wedge (vein), Sachs Harbour lowlands, Banks Island, Canada.

Figure 6.10 Typical terrain and instrumentation at the ice-wedge monitoring site of J. R. Mackay at Garry Island in the Mackenzie Delta region.

In the western Canadian Arctic, it appears that cracking is concentrated between mid-January and mid-March and is not necessarily related simply to a rapid drop in air temperatures in early winter, as first suggested by Lachenbruch (1962) and others. The best correlation between air temperature drops and ice-wedge cracking occurs in localities of thin snow cover. The favoured duration and rate of a temperature drop that results in cracking is about four days, at a rate of about 1.8 °C/day (Mackay, 1993b). Where snow cover is thicker, the snow insulates the ground from the extremes of temperature change. It follows that the tensions which cause cracking originate at the top of permafrost or in the frozen active layer, rather than at greater depth in permafrost, since these short-duration air temperature fluctuations do not penetrate deeply into the ground. Proof of this can be seen by the repeated cracking which has been monitored by Mackay beneath a shallow pond of standing water, and beneath water in the trough commonly formed at the surface above the ice wedge (Fig. 6.11). In both cases, neither the water above the ice wedge (Fig. 6.11, case 1) nor the semi-liquid active layer (Fig. 6.11, case 2) possesses a 'memory' which would permit cracking to occur in exactly the same location the following year. Thus, cracking has to commence

in the frozen ground beneath and propagate both upwards and downwards.

Observations also indicate that probably less than half of the wedges in any given area crack annually (Mackay, 1975, 1989b; Harry *et al.*, 1985). The size of an ice wedge therefore, should not be used to infer age (see Black, 1973) without other supporting evidence. Moreover, whether an ice vein will form or not will depend largely upon the ability of meltwater to penetrate the crack before the crack closes in the early spring. The frequency of cracking and the formation of ice veins is also site specific; for example, observations at Garry Island indicate that one part of an ice wedge may crack nearly every year whereas the same wedge several metres away may crack only once in every 10 years or so. Moreover, a year of exceptionally heavy snowfall will inhibit cracking totally; along the western Arctic coast, Mackay concludes that an average snowdepth of 60 cm or more across a polygon will prevent cracking.

In spite of, and also probably because of, these detailed field observations, much still remains unclear about the mechanism of thermal contraction cracking and ice-wedge formation. For example, the early stages of ice-wedge growth at Illisarvik were characterized by unusually large (wide) thermal

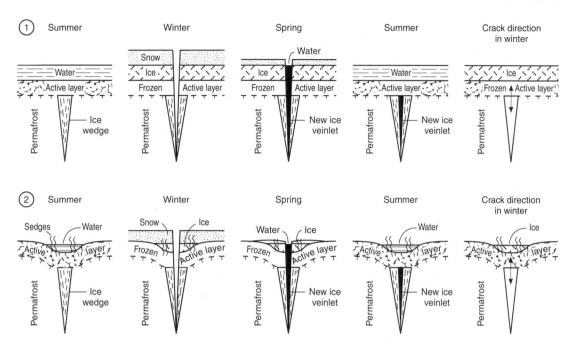

Figure 6.11 Diagram illustrating the growth of ice wedges and how crack initiation must commence in wedge ice at the top of permafrost and then propagate upwards and downwards. It is argued that neither water above an ice wedge (1 above), nor a semi-liquid active layer (2 above) can memorize the location of the previous years crack (from Mackay, 1989b).

contraction cracks (Mackay, 1986d), the cause of which is unclear. Another complication is the role played by the creep of frozen ground, especially in the active layer, and the cause of the typical ridges which can form on either side of the crack. They may be related to differential movement between the active layer and the top of permafrost (Mackay, 1980a). The differences between high-centred and low-centred polygons, and the influence which such topography exerts upon snow distribution, ground temperature regimes and the cracking process, also need further clarification. Finally, the development of the polygonal net itself is still not fully understood; observations show that cracks propagate laterally as well as downwards. However, the lateral propagation is short, often unconnected and frequently offset. Few cracks extend horizontally for more than 5 m. These observations throw doubt upon the adequacy of the traditional hypotheses which explain the development of the polygonal net (see below).

Few data sets exist with which to compare the observations of Mackay. Black (1974) reported upon observations at Barrow, Alaska for 1949–52 which indicated crack frequencies ranged from 37 to 64 per cent. Harry *et al.* (1985) found that only 38 per cent of ice wedges examined showed signs of growth during the previous winter (1983–84) at King Point on the Yukon coast. At Ust' Port, Siberia, Podbornyi (1978) used breaking cables to monitor cracking for the 1975–77 period, and found general agreement with the data of Mackay.

In reflecting upon his data, Mackay (1992, p. 244) points out that the various theoretical discussions of thermal contraction cracking (e.g. Lachenbruch, 1962; Grechishchev, 1970) dealt with simple uniform conditions. The reality, however, is that as ice wedges grow, their growth generates complexity because of changes in relief, material, polygon development, vegetation and snow cover. It may be that cracking is to be regarded as a random process and requires a probabilistic approach (Podbornyi, 1978). Mackay (1992) refers to 'chaos' theory, and to the complexity which follows growth, to explain the discrepancies between these theoretical considerations and the reality of the field situation.

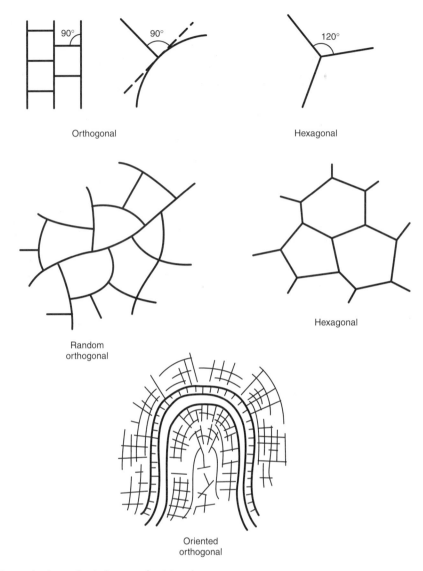

Figure 6.12 Types of polygonal nets in permafrost terrain.

6.3.3 Development of the polygon net and ice-wedge relief

Ice wedges join predominantly at right angles and form polygonal, chiefly tetragonal, nets of patterned ground that cover extensive areas of the Arctic and subarctic. Commonly, the average dimensions of the polygons range from 15 to 40 m.

The development of the polygonal pattern was theoretically examined first by Lachenbruch (1962, 1966) and then by Grechishchev (1970). Lachen-

bruch concluded that the angular intersection of a polygonal network of frost cracks will exhibit a preferred tendency towards an orthogonal (i.e. right angle) pattern (Fig. 6.12). However, this conclusion contrasts with the many descriptions of polygonal ground in which hexagonal or angular junctions dominate (e.g. Leffingwell, 1919; Black, 1952). The implications of the hexagonal pattern and angular intersections of 120° are that the frost cracks develop at a series of points and that each crack develops more or less simultaneously. On the other hand, the

Figure 6.13 Oblique air view of oriented orthogonal ice-wedge pattern in an abandoned channel, Mackenzie Delta region, Canada. As the water progressively shrunk in the channel, ice wedges developed normal to the retreating water line, to be followed by ice wedges parallel to the water line.

orthogonal pattern is thought to infer an evolutionary sequence in which primary frost cracks develop in an essentially random pattern. These are then followed by secondary frost cracks which progressively divide up the area and which have a tendency for an orthogonal intersection pattern. Lachenbruch (1966) classifies the resultant crude polygonal network as a 'random orthogonal system' in contrast to an 'oriented orthogonal system' (Fig. 6.13) which develops in the vicinity of large bodies of water. In the case of 'oriented orthogonal systems', one set of cracks develops normal to the water body and the other at right angles. The apparent dichotomy between the theoretical tendency towards an orthogonal pattern and existence of hexagonal patterns is difficult to explain. One suggestion is that the hexagonal pattern is best developed in homogeneous materials subject to uniform cooling, while the orthogonal pattern develops in heterogeneous materials.

According to Dostovalov and Popov (1966) the size of the polygonal net reflects the severity of the climate. When temperatures are relatively warm, large rectangular polygons are formed by primary and secondary fissures. However, with increasingly severe winter temperatures, these rectangles are successively broken up by fissures of consecutively higher orders into smaller and smaller bodies (Fig. 6.14 (a)). However, detailed field measurements by Mackay on the lateral propagation of cracking which developed on a newly exposed lake floor at Illisarvik do not support the concept of a simple fissure hierarchy (Fig. 6.14 (b)). As Mackay (1986d, p. 1784) points out, the continued development of the system illustrated in Fig. 6.14 (b) was limited by the influx of vegetation to the site in subsequent years and the trapping of snow such that, with 60 cm of snow cover, the main and lateral crack systems became inactive after the fourth winter.

Typical of many ice-wedge polygon systems is a distinct rim or raised rampart on either side of the fissure. Sometimes the rampart may be as much as 0.5–1.0 m high and, if a trough exists above the ice-wedge, relative relief of 1.0–1.5 m may be generated. Even in newly forming permafrost, as on a recently drained lake floor, a shallow raised ridge some centimetres high forms adjacent to the frost cracks during the first winter (Mackay, 1980a, p. 291).

A commonly held view is that these polygon ramparts are related to the growth of the ice wedges; as the latter grow in size, frozen material from within the polygon is deformed upwards to form the raised rim. The typical upturning of frozen sediment

(a)

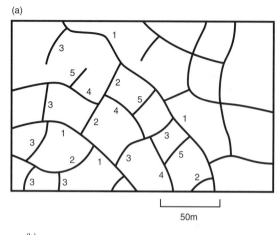

50m

(b)

Crack pattern

⌐ 13 March 1979

------ 19 June 1979

Old shoreline

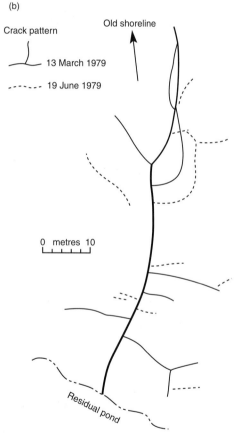

0 metres 10

Residual pond

Figure 6.14 The growth of the polygonal net: (a) according to Dostovalov, there is a successive growth of fissures of higher orders; (b) a newly born ice-wedge system at Illisarvik, in Year 1 (1979) after drainage, does not support the simple hierarchical growth model (from Mackay, 1986d).

adjacent to large ice wedges is often mentioned in this context. However, measurements by Mackay of the movement of steel tubes inserted into permafrost on either side of an ice wedge and across the adjacent polygons casts doubts upon this mechanism (Fig. 6.15). Contrary to what might be expected, most distances between steel tubes on either side of an ice-wedge trough progressively decreased, even though the ice wedges cracked and continued to grow. Mackay (1980a) concludes that thermally induced mass transport in the active layer results in the accumulation of material at the periphery of the polygon. This movement, reflecting summer warming and expansion of the active layer, is generally radially outwards from the middle of the low-centre polygon. A rate of 0.25 cm/year was estimated for one polygon, implying a coefficient of thermal expansion of about $1.7 \times 10^{-5}/°C$. By contrast, the upper part of permafrost adjacent to a growing ice wedge may move inward in the opposite direction to that of the active layer. It follows, therefore, that some shearing occurs at the active layer/permafrost interface. If these movements are real, the probability of appreciable thermally induced slope movement must be considered in any interpretation of creep and/or solifluction data (see Chapter 8).

6.3.4 Climatic significance

The formation of ice wedges is of climatic and palaeoclimatic significance: (a) they require the presence of permafrost and (b) they can only form when air temperatures drop well below 0 °C. Based upon the distribution of active ice wedges in Alaska and elsewhere, Péwé (1966b) concluded that ice wedges only form in areas where the mean annual air temperature is –6 °C or colder. Active ice wedges only occur in the zone of continuous permafrost; those found in the zone of discontinuous permafrost are generally inactive.

Since it has been demonstrated (see above) that ice-wedge cracking is sensitive to a number of climatic factors, winter snowfall being particularly critical, it follows that long-term monitoring of ice-wedge cracking is a useful method of studying global climate change. Although this topic is dealt with in Chapter 17, some brief comments are necessary at this point.

In the western Arctic there is a body of anecdotal evidence related to ice-wedge cracking (Mackay, 1993a). For example, the sound of ice-wedge cracking

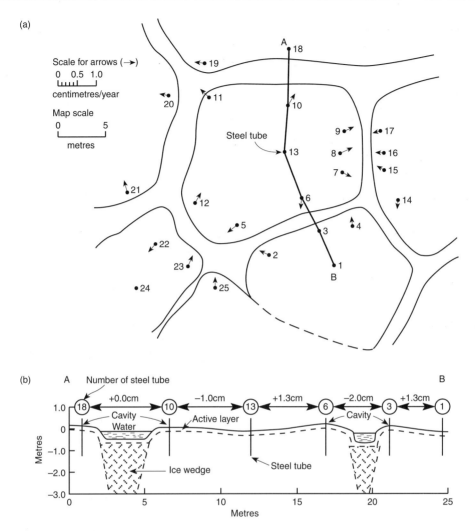

Figure 6.15   Data on polygon deformation, Garry Island, Mackenzie Delta region (Mackay, 1980a): (a) plan of experimental site indicating locations of steel tubes and 1966–78 rate and direction of movement of active layer; (b) cross-section between tubes 1 and 18 indicating changes in distances between tubes, 1966–78.

was reported in early literature (e.g. Leffingwell, 1915, pp. 638–639) from along the northern Alaska coast. Today, audible cracking is only reported from the high Arctic islands and Mackay, at his field station on Garry Island, has never experienced ground tremors resulting from cracking or heard audible cracking. Equally, at Inuvik, 150 km to the south, no ice-wedge cracking has been observed in the 1980–88 observation period, yet both Inuvik and Garry Island have similar winter temperatures. However, the critical factor is that Garry Island has less than half the winter snowfall of Inuvik. The presence of inactive ice wedges

at Inuvik and the absence of audible cracking along the mainland Arctic coast today suggest, therefore, that there have been significant increases in winter snowfall amounts, and probably higher winter temperatures, in the last hundred years.

The climatic significance of ice wedges is further complicated by the nature of the substrate in which cracking occurs. For example, Romanovskii (1985) has shown how, in Siberia, the formation of either an ice wedge or a soil wedge may depend on the different mean annual ground temperature (Fig. 6.16). In general, ground temperatures are lower in clay than

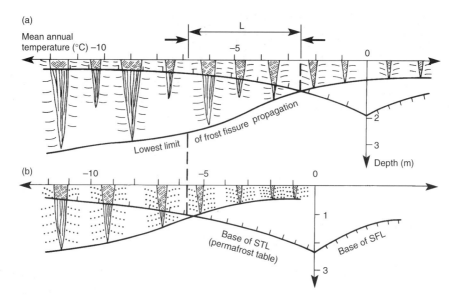

Figure 6.16 The relationship between mean annual ground temperature, the formation of ice and soil wedges, and the nature of the substrate: (a) clay; (b) sand and gravel. SFL seasonally frozen layer; STL seasonally thawed layer (permafrost table); L is the distance between boundaries of ice wedges in loam and ice wedges in sand and gravel (from Romanovskii, 1985).

in sand and gravel. As a result, ice wedges can occur in clay with mean annual temperatures as high as –2 °C, while in gravel, the minimum temperature required is –6 °C.

These considerations mean that the use of ice-wedge casts to infer Pleistocene air temperature depressions is fraught with difficulty. Additional caution is provided by Burn (1990) with data from central Yukon where the mean annual air temperature is –4 °C. There, elevated tritium concentrations in ice veins exposed near Mayo indicate that these features have experienced cracking during the past 30 years. In all probability, cracking at Mayo is related to below normal winter temperatures, possible associated with cold air drainage. It follows that any palaeo-climatic interpretation of ice-wedge casts must focus upon winter air temperatures, local site conditions and winter snowfall amounts. The problems of Pleistocene palaeogeographical and palaeoclimatic reconstruction are dealt with in Chapters 13 and 14.

6.4 Massive ice and massive icy bodies

Thick, often bedded and sometimes deformed layers of massive ground ice and icy sediments, often tens

of metres thick, are the most spectacular of ground ice forms (Fig. 6.17). They are important not only because of their origin, and the light this may throw upon permafrost histories, but also because of the thaw settlement properties of terrain underlain by such material.

6.4.1 Nature and extent

Massive ground ice and massive icy bodies are known to exist in parts of western Siberia (e.g. Astakhov and Isayeva, 1988; Kaplanskaya and Tarnogradskiy, 1986), northern Alaska (e.g. Lawson, 1983) and the western Canadian Arctic (e.g. Mackay, 1971, 1973b; French and Harry, 1988, 1990; Mackay and Dallimore, 1992). The two main theories usually suggested for their origin are (a) segregated ice which, with increasing importance of water injection processes, grades into intrusive ice and (b) buried glacier ice, without a clear distinction being made between glacier ice derived from snow and subglacier regelation ice which, in essence, is segregated ice. Other theories which have been advanced include buried lake, river or sea ice, and buried snowbank ice. A general classification of massive ground ice is illustrated in Fig. 6.18 where

Figure 6.17   Deformed massive ground ice near Nicholson Island, Pleistocene Mackenzie Delta, Canada.

the two main theories mentioned above are grouped within the two categories of 'buried' or 'intrasedimental' ice.

Natural exposures of massive ground ice are rare and usually short-lived. The best-known in Canada are those that occur along the coasts of the western Arctic, especially in the vicinity of Tuktoyaktuk. Drillhole data from both Canada (Mackay, 1973b) and the FSU (Dubikov, 1982) indicate two salient facts about the occurrence of these massive ice bodies; first, in the vast majority of instances where massive ice is encountered, the ice is overlain by clay-grade sediment and underlain by sand-grade sediment; second, a significant number of drillholes encounter massive ice at depths in excess of 30 m, sometimes at depths of 100–200 m. In some holes two or more layers of massive ice, usually separated by sand, are penetrated by the same drillhole. It can reasonably be argued that these observations support a segregation or segregation–injection origin. They fit a model of ice growth with fine-grained sediment

underlain by coarse-grained sediment which provide a permeable zone and reservoir for pore water expulsion, probably in association with injection of free water. However, these observations do not eliminate the buried glacier ice hypothesis. The latter has been suggested by Russian permafrost scientists and Quaternary geologists (e.g. Kaplanskaya and Tarnogradskiy, 1986; Astakhov and Isayeva, 1988). In this respect, it should be pointed out that, in the vast majority of instances in both the western Canadian Arctic and in western Siberia, massive ground ice occurs in regions which have been glaciated. In the western Canadian Arctic, for example, much of the massive ice and/or icy bodies reported in the literature come from areas towards the outer limits of known Wisconsinan ice (e.g. French and Harry, 1988, 1990). The same situation occurs in western Siberia on the Yamal and Gydan Peninsulas; both are near the southern limit of the Kara Sea Ice sheet of the last glaciation (Astakhov, 1992).

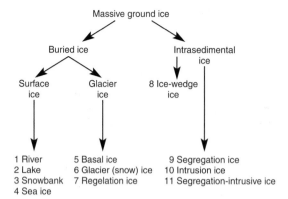

Figure 6.18 A classification of massive ground ice proposed by J. R. Mackay at a GSC Workshop in 1989.

6.4.2 Differentiating criteria

Any field differentiation between massive segregated ice and buried glacier ice is complicated by the fact that the two may appear very similar. For example, in common with segregated ice, which is frequently interbedded with sediment layers, basal glacier ice may also contain considerable quantities of sediment, again frequently stratified (see, e.g., Klassen and Shilts, 1987, pp. 15–22). Moreover, basal glacier ice which has experienced regelation is essentially segregation ice. As such, it may be difficult, if not impossible, to distinguish between the two ice types if one were to consider only the ice characteristics. A further complication arises because, in both cases, the ice may have been buried beneath an overburden of variable thickness for several thousands of years. As a consequence the ice may have experienced major post-formational or post-burial alteration (e.g. moisture migration, thermal and geochemical changes, and loading/unloading).

Mackay (1989a) has summarized a number of field criteria which can be used to differentiate between different types of massive ice (Fig. 6.19). The nature of the contact between the ice and the overlying or underlying sediments is fundamental; the ice contacts can be gradational or sharp, conformable or unconformable, and thaw or erosional in nature.

Gradational contacts (Fig. 6.19 (a)) should rarely exist with buried ice, and, in the case of intrusive ice, suspended fragments might occur just below the contact (Fig. 6.19 (b)). Conformable contacts in segregated ice commonly show bubbles extending downwards from the soil–ice interface (Fig. 6.19 (c)).

If water has been intruded along bedding planes or fractures, contacts may be both conformable or unconformable. In the case of lake or river ice buried by sedimentation, the lower contact should be unconformable while the upper could be either conformable or unconformable. In the case of buried glacier ice, the contacts should both be unconformable.

Thaw and erosional contacts are a second line of evidence. If the contact between the overlying material and the underlying ice is of a thaw or erosional nature, this indicates that the ice predates burial and must be buried. In theory, an erosional or thaw contact will have bubbles within the ice just below the contact infilled with sediment from above (Fig. 6.19 (d)). Several features suggestive of ice origin may also be found within the ice itself, For example, matched soil fragments (Fig. 6.19 (e)) indicate segregated and/or intrusive ice, ice coatings beneath clasts within the ice indicate segregation (Fig. 6.19 (f)), striated clasts and pods of diamicton within the ice suggest glacier ice, and lumps of clear ice frozen (i.e. suspended) within silty bubbly ice suggest regelation. Finally, ice dykes formed from water intruded upwards under pressure into permafrost along fissures are to expected with segregated and/or segregated-intrusive ice (see Mackay, 1989a; Mackay and Dallimore, 1992).

6.4.3 Intrasedimental ice

Since the process of ice segregation can be accompanied by intrusion, a segregation-intrusive mechanism is probably the most likely explanation for many massive ground ice bodies in western Arctic Canada (Mackay and Dallimore, 1992). Perhaps the best-known exposure is at Peninsula Point, 5.5 km southwest of Tuktoyaktuk, NWT. This tabular body of nearly pure ice has a maximum thickness in excess of 20 m and is overlain by diamicton and underlain by sand. Following extensive and numerous investigations, Mackay and Dallimore (1992) conclude that this ice is of an intrasedimental nature with the ice growing during the downward aggradation of permafrost as cold, probably glacier, meltwaters moved upwards through the unfrozen sand. Ice dykes which penetrate the overlying diamicton are proof of the high water pressures involved and possess isotopic signatures similar to the massive ice. The contact between the massive ice and the overlying diamicton is conformable and the continuity of $\delta^{18}O$ and δD profiles from the top of the massive ice downwards into the underlying sand indicates a common water source for the massive ice and

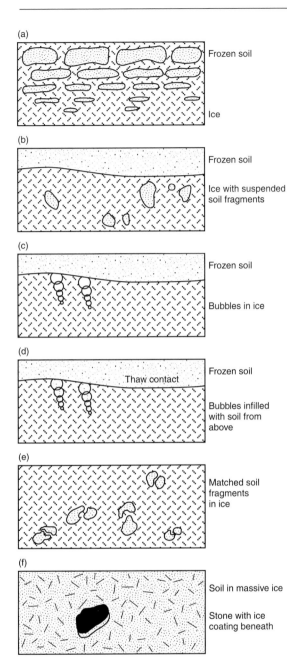

(a) Frozen soil / Ice

(b) Frozen soil / Ice with suspended soil fragments

(c) Frozen soil / Bubbles in ice

(d) Frozen soil / Thaw contact / Bubbles infilled with soil from above

(e) Matched soil fragments in ice

(f) Soil in massive ice / Stone with ice coating beneath

Figure 6.19 Features commonly seen in detailed observation of massive ice (from Mackay, 1989a).

the interstitial ice in the underlying sand. A network of reticulate ice veins in the overlying diamicton and bubble trains which originate at the upper ice–sediment contact are further evidence of downward freezing.

6.4.4 Other mechanisms

Many Russian geologists believe that the massive ice and icy bodies of western Siberia are of buried glacier origin (e.g. Astakhov and Isayeva, 1988; Astakhov, 1992; Kaplanskaya and Tarnogradskiy, 1986; Solomatin, 1986). Terms such as 'ice/sediment complex', 'sheet-ice complex', and 'deposit-forming ice' are often used to describe icy sediments which are interpreted as being the remnants of basal layers of Pleistocene ice sheets. They are the product of incomplete or 'arrested' deglaciation, and are protected from melting by covers of till, fluvioglacial sand and/or solifluction deposits.

Several studies in the western Canadian Arctic suggest that at least some of the massive ice and icy bodies may be buried basal glacier ice (e.g. Lorrain and Demeur, 1985; Dallimore and Wolfe, 1988; French and Harry, 1988, 1990). Several lines of evidence support the buried-glacier ice mechanism: (a) some deformation structures are typical of glacier ice – in some exposures there are folds of varying dimensions and intensities; (b) in places sediment-rich layers resemble shear planes (e.g. Rampton and Walcott, 1974); (c) there is a range of grain and clast sizes contained within the massive ice and icy bodies, from clay to pebbles to striated boulders; and (d) the overlying soil–ice contact is often unconformable.

In addition to the two main hypotheses discussed above, several others have also been proposed. For example, Fujino *et al.* (1983, 1988) conclude that the massive ground ice at Peninsula Point is 'superimposed' ice, an undefined form of surface ice formed by congelation. In the unglaciated Klondike, interior Yukon, a buried snowbank origin is considered to be one possible origin for massive icy bodies occurring in valley bottoms (e.g. French and Pollard, 1986). Since tabular massive ice bodies are known to exist elsewhere, such as in the Arctic islands (e.g. Pollard, 1990) and in northern Alaska (e.g. Lawson, 1983), it is possible that there are additional mechanisms.

6.5 Ice-cored mounds and pingos

Various types of frost mounds occur in permafrost regions. They can be distinguished on the basis of their structure and duration, and by the character of the ice contained in them. Fig. 6.20 summarizes the various types of frost mounds in terms of their uplift

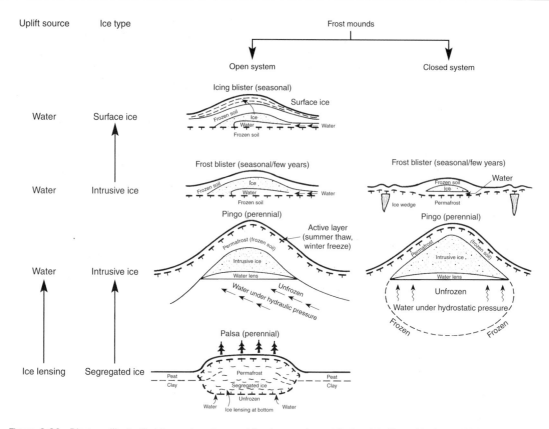

Figure 6.20 Diagram illustrating the various types of frost mounds and their origin (from Mackay, 1986c).

source and ice type. Palsas and the various types of seasonal frost mounds have already been treated in Chapter 5. Here, the highly distinctive perennial ice-cored features known as pingos are discussed together with various small ice-cored mounds or hydrolaccoliths.

The term pingo, first proposed by Porsild (1938), is a local Inuit word used for an ice-cored conical hill in the Mackenzie Delta. In Siberia, the term 'bulgan-nyakh' is commonly used.

6.5.1 Open system pingos

These have already been examined in Chapter 5 and so only a few additional comments are necessary at this point. Essentially, open system pingos are hydrological phenomena, the result of high hydraulical potential due to water originating in upland areas. The biggest concentration occurs in the northern interior Yukon (Hughes, 1969) and central Alaska

(Holmes *et al.*, 1968), but they also occur on Spitsbergen (Müller, 1959), northern Alaska (Hamilton and Curtis, 1982), and central Yakutia (Soloviev, 1973a, 1973b).

The fact that nearly all open system pingos lie in unglaciated terrain is an aspect of their distribution which is not clearly understood. In North America, they are extremely rare in areas glaciated within the last 25 000 years; none is known in Alaska and only two are known in Yukon Territory (Hughes, 1969). Differences in the extent and thickness of permafrost in glaciated and unglaciated terrain may be a factor.

In general, open system pingos occur as isolated features, or as small groups within the same locality. It is not uncommon for a new pingo to develop inside the crater, or on the flank of an older one. Many are oval or oblong in form, and a high proportion of open system pingos are ruptured to varying degrees.

Hydrological conditions and the role of artesian pressures in the formation of open system pingos need to be stressed. So also does the existence of thin and/or discontinuous permafrost. Since the role of artesian pressure is not to force the overlying sediments upwards but merely to ensure a steady but slow supply of groundwater, it follows that the development of open system pingos by 'injection' with the core of the pingo being composed solely of 'injection ice' (Müller, 1959) is not necessarily the only growth mechanism. Mackay (1973a, p. 1000) has argued that pingo growth from injection ice, which requires a constantly replenished pool of water beneath the ice core, would represent a very unstable condition. If water were injected faster than it could freeze, pressure would rise until the pingo ruptured and water flowed from the ground as a spring. Equally, if water were injected slower than it could freeze, the unfrozen water pool would freeze and cease to exist. In fact, an unlikely long-term balance would be required between three independent variables: water pressure which is determined by conditions external to the pingo, the overburden strength which would vary with time of year, and the rate of freezing which would depend upon temperature. Since all three may change independent of the others, this balance will rarely be maintained for the total growth lifetime of a pingo. This implies that the growth of an open system pingo probably requires a certain amount of segregated as well as injection ice. In Yakutia, for example, where both 'flat' bulgannyakhs (dome-like elevations 2–5 m high) and upstanding large bulgannyakhs (hills 10–50 m high) exist in close juxtaposition (Fig. 6.21), it is thought that the ice core is of several origins, produced both by injection from groundwater under pressure below and by segregation (Soloviev, 1973b, pp. 148–51). According to Soloviev, the flat bulgannyakhs are primarily of a segregated (i.e. closed system) nature, composed of icy sediments, while the larger forms possess massive ice cores 5–10 m thick formed through the repeated injections of water (i.e. open system). The evolution of Yakutian bulgannyakhs is directly related to the development of alas thermokarst relief discussed in Chapter 7.

6.5.2 Closed system pingos

Closed system pingos form by doming of frozen ground due to freezing of injected water. The latter is supplied by the expulsion of pore water during aggradation of permafrost, typically in a closed talik under a former water body.

Closed system pingos occur almost exclusively in areas of continuous permafrost, often in alluvial lowlands with little vertical relief. For the most part, they occur in specific geomorphic situations. The largest concentration (over 1350) of closed system pingos occurs on the Pleistocene coastal plain of the Mackenzie Delta, Canada (Mackay, 1962). Others occur in the modern Mackenzie Delta, the Yukon coastal plain, western Victoria Island, and on Banks Island. Isolated pingos, or small groups, have also been reported from the District of Keewatin, Baffin Island and other areas. Conical mounds discovered on the floor of the Beaufort Sea have also been interpreted as submarine pingos, possibly of a closed system origin.

Closed system pingos vary from a few metres to over 60 m in height and up to 300 m in diameter. They possess a variety of forms ranging from symmetrical conical features, to asymmetric and elongate features. It cannot be assumed that all pingos have a recognizable and typical form. Their one common characteristic, however, usually concealed by 1.0–10.0 m of overburden, is the core of massive ice or icy sediments. This may be remarkably pure and with an absence of internal structures, or it may be layers of icy sediments. Fractures and faults are sometimes seen within the pingo core. Frequently, the pingo is ruptured at the top to form a small star-like crater. This is the first stage in the progressive decay of a pingo, the melt of the ice core, the collapse of the updomed sediments and the ultimate formation of a shallow rimmed depression (Fig. 6.22).

Within a periglacial landscape of low relief dominated by mass wasting, a well-developed pingo is a striking geomorphic form. It is probably because of this that the closed system pingo has received so much attention in the literature, and why open system pingos which occur within more hilly environments have not received comparable attention. On the other hand, although they represent a classic periglacial phenomenon, pingos, of whatever kind, should not be regarded as common features of all periglacial regions. In fact, their existence and development are usually the result of a number of distinctive and limiting geomorphic and hydrologic conditions.

In the Mackenzie Delta region, closed system pingos typically occur within small shallow lakes or former lake beds. They usually occur singly and not in groups, although some drained lake beds are known in which three or four small pingos are growing (see Mackay, 1973a, 1979a).

Figure 6.21   Large bulgannyakh (pingo) in Olong Erien alas, central Yakutia, Siberia. A 'flat' bulgannyakh is just visible in near left of the photograph.

The most detailed, and unparalleled, studies upon their growth mechanisms have been undertaken by J.R. Mackay in the Mackenzie Delta, Canada (e.g. Mackay, 1962, 1973a, 1979a, 1986b, 1988, 1990b). He has used precise levelling techniques, air-photographs, drilling, geochemical analyses of pingo ice and waters, and anecdotal and historical evidence. A wealth of knowledge is now available following these unique studies.

It is now generally agreed that closed system pingos are the result of high pore water pressure, the result of pore water expulsion. This causes the updoming of the overlying sediments. The most common site for their growth is a recently drained lake basin or abandoned drainage channel where both upward and downward permafrost growth occurs in the previously unfrozen sediments which constituted the sub-lake or subchannel talik (Fig. 6.23). Saturated sands are especially conducive to pingo formation.

Of the numerous pingos studied by Mackay, the birth and growth of a small pingo called Porsild Pingo (Mackay, 1988) is representative of more than 2000 closed system pingos of the western Canadian Arctic and adjacent Alaska. This pingo has grown in a lake which drained catastrophically around 1900. Birth probably took place between 1920 and 1930 when the newly aggrading permafrost ruptured and there was intrusion of water into the unfrozen part of the active layer, to form small frost mounds. One such mound, approximately 3.7 m high, was photographed by the Arctic botanist A. Porsild in May 1935 and subsequently described as part of a paper on 'earth mounds' (Porsild, 1938, p. 53). Since then, Porsild Pingo grew steadily until 1976 at a growth rate approximately linear with height. After 1976, the growth rate has decreased but there is every indication that it will continue to grow for a few centuries. Elsewhere in the Mackenzie Delta region Mackay has monitored the growth of other small pingos in a lake

Figure 6.22 Collapsed closed system pingo occurring in Sachs River Lowlands, southern Banks Island, Canada.

(Tuk 3) which drained by coastal erosion between 1935 and 1950, approximately 20 km to the west of Tuktoyaktuk (Mackay, 1973a, 1979a, pp. 14–18). In all cases, growth was rapid in the initial years, often as much as 1.5 m/year. With increasing age, however, the growth rate decreased such that some of the largest pingos in the Mackenzie Delta, such as Ibyuk Pingo, are over a thousand years old and growing at a rate of only 2.3 cm/yr (Mackay, 1986b). As a rough estimate, Mackay suggests that possibly 15 pingos may commence growth in a century in the Mackenzie Delta region, and there are probably only approximately 50 actively growing. Similar conclusions have been reached by Russian investigators in Siberia, although quantitative observations on bulgannyakh (i.e. pingo) growth are lacking. In central Yakutia, for example, some of the open system bulgannyakhs are known to have developed in recently drained alas depressions in the last 50 years. Eyewitness accounts indicate growth rates in the beginning stages to be of the same order of magnitude, approximately 0.5–2.0 m/year (Soloviev, 1973a).

Significant advances have also been made in understanding the growth mechanism of closed system pingos (see Fig. 6.23). The ice in a pingo core was traditionally thought to be 'injection ice', frozen from a pool of water injected under pressure. It is now believed that the majority of pingo growth is by ice segregation although, in the early growth stages, injection ice may dominate. However, the condition of injection ice is unstable and unlikely to be maintained for the duration of pingo growth. More likely, the long-term source of water and the associated positive pore water pressures necessary for ice segregation result from permafrost aggradation and pore water expulsion ahead of the freezing plane. Therefore, at different stages of pingo growth, different types of ice formation may assume greater or lesser importance.

For example, Mackay (1973a) has illustrated theoretically how, for a constant overburden pressure which is a function of pingo height, an increase in pore water pressure from a low to high value can cause a change from the freezing of pore ice, through segregated ice, to injection ice, and finally rupture of the pingo. It follows that several stages of pingo growth can be recognized. In the pore ice stage the ice core does not form. Instead, as the pore ice freezes, the entire lake bottom

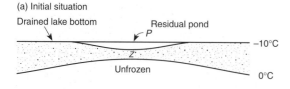

(a) Initial situation

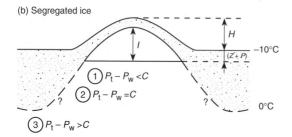

(b) Segregated ice

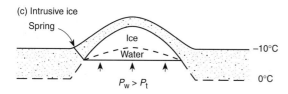

(c) Intrusive ice

Figure 6.23 Illustration of the growth of a closed-system pingo (modified from Mackay, 1979a). (a) The initial condition: the residual pond has a depth P in the centre, the overburden thickness of the permafrost is Z; permafrost is thinnest beneath the centre of the residual pond. (b) The growth of segregated ice: P_t is the total resistance to heaving and includes lithostatic pressure and resistance to bending of the overburden; P_w is the pore water pressure; and C is the soil constant. Ice lensing is favoured at location 1 beneath the growing pingo; ice lenses and pore ice develop at location 2 beneath the margin of the pingo; and pore water expulsion occurs at locality 3. The values of P_t and P_w change from location 1 to location 3. H and I denote the height of the pingo and the thickness of the ice body, respectively. (c) The formation of a subpingo water lens and the accumulation of intrusive ice: as the pore water pressure exceeds P_t (the total resistance to uplift), a subpingo water lens accumulates and intrusive ice forms by freezing of bulk water. Peripheral failure may result in spring flow.

heaves slowly upwards. When the pore water pressure equals or exceeds the overburden pressure, segregated ice tends to form and pingo growth commences. This is

a segregated ice stage. As pore water pressures continue to increase, the overburden will eventually yield and water will be injected faster than it can freeze. This is a third or injected ice stage. Finally, if water continues to be injected faster than it can freeze, the pingo will rupture. It follows that all types of ice may be present in a pingo core, and that it need not be pure ice; at depth, soil and ice lenses may be intermixed. It is also clear that pingo growth is merely one example, although a dramatic one, of frost heaving of the ground.

Drilling has also indicated that large sub-pingo water lenses are present beneath growing pingos (Mackay, 1978b). Moreover, these pressures build up, only to be released as water escapes to the surface at points of weakness, usually at the periphery of the pingo where the overburden strength (i.e. permafrost thickness) is least (see Fig. 6.23). Seasonal frost mounds are common adjacent to growing pingos (e.g. Mackay, 1979a, pp. 18–24) which exhibit pulsating patterns of growth responding to the rate of accumulation and loss of water beneath them (Mackay, 1977). If penetrated, these sub-pingo water lenses can cause temporary artesian flow and geysers several metres high.

Study of the ice cores within pingos is difficult because natural exposures are rare and usually short-lived. According to Mackay (1985) all pingos contain pore ice and varying proportions of intrusive ice, segregated ice, dilation crack ice and ice-wedge ice. The intrusive ice is associated with the sub-pingo water lenses. At one pingo ice exposure, Mackay (1990b) has described how seasonal growth bands, consisting of alternating clear and bubble-rich bands, may form in the ice (Fig. 6.24). The propagation of asymmetric temperature waves resulting from differences in the summer and winter thermal properties of the ground surface are thought to cause the gradual transition from the clear to bubble-rich ice (i.e. change from winter to summer) and the abrupt transition from bubble-rich to clear ice (i.e. change from summer to winter).

6.5.3 Other pingos and hydrolaccoliths

In addition to the open and closed system pingos as described above, it is possible that several other types of ice-cored mounds may exist.

In one category are groups of pingos which have been described from the Canadian high Arctic, on Prince Patrick Island (Pissart, 1967a) and Amund Ringnes Island (Balkwill *et al.*, 1974). On Prince Patrick Island, the features occur in a broad north–

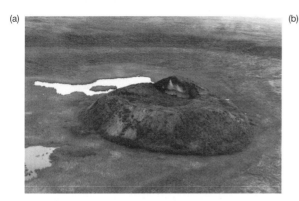

Figure 6.24 Seasonal growth bands in pingo ice, observed in Pingo 20, Tuktoyaktuk Peninsula, Pleistocene Mackenzie Delta (see Mackay, 1990b): (a) general view of the pingo showing partial collapse and exposure of the ice core; (b) seasonal ice banding in the ice core. Both photos taken in August 1988.

south zone along the summit of the island. They are far from any lakes or other surface water bodies. Generally, the mounds have an approximately circular plan and are of relatively small dimensions, varying in height from around 1 to 13 m, and with average dimensions of about 60 m. None appear to be growing and their location suggests that they are probably related to faults in the underlying bedrock. In the absence of detailed geophysical research, the exact mechanism of their formation is unclear. Since the permafrost is probably 300–400 m thick, their formation by injection requires that sub-permafrost water was able to move through the permafrost by way of the faults without freezing *en route*. This is unlikely unless the pingos are very old and/or formed at a time when the permafrost was much thinner. In Tibet, the large pingo in the Kunlun Shan Pass is also thought to have formed by groundwater rising to the surface along a fault or faults (see Wang and French, 1995c). In this case, the permafrost is younger, thinner and warmer, and the explanation suggested is more credible.

In a second category are a number of elongate and partially collapsed pingos on Banks Island (French, 1975b; Pissart and French, 1976). These features, rarely exceeding 15 m in height, occur on low fluvial terraces of the major rivers in the interior lowlands. Pissart and French (1976) hypothesize that the majority of these features grew, in an unstable fashion, through the freezing of local taliks which developed beneath the deeper parts of old river channels.

In a third category are smaller mounds with either ice cores or ice lenses within them which occur in the tundra and polar deserts of high latitudes. They are not regarded as pingos, mainly on account of their size and their location primarily within the active layer. The variety of features suggests that they are not all the same. As a generalization, they have been little studied. In the Russian literature the term '*bugor*' has been used to describe small gently rising and oval-shaped mounds which occur in the subarctic and tundra regions of Siberia (Dostovalov and Kudryavtsev, 1967). They occur in groups or scattered, ranging in height from 1.0 to 5.0 m. Analogous features occur in the North American Arctic. For example, Porsild (1955), Pissart (1967b), French (1971a, 1976a) and Washburn (1983) all describe low circular mounds, rarely exceeding 2 m in height, and usually between 1.5 and 5.0 m in diameter, on many of the high Arctic islands. They are frequently used as owl perches and stand out as relatively dry sites, cut by tundra polygons and with a lichen and/or grass surface cover.

The origin of these *bugor*-like features is not clear since they show no apparent relationship to topography. According to both Porsild and Washburn, these mounds are probably the result of localized ice segregation or injection which occurs within the active layer in response to subtle thermal differences in earth materials. French suggests that the raised rims of low-centred polygons create a closed system during freezing. Even smaller hydrolaccoliths are almost certainly of a segregational origin. Bird (1967, p. 203) has described mounds of clear ice covered with vegetation or peat, less than 4 m in diameter and 1 m high, which occur on Southampton Island, and Sigafoos (1951) has described slightly larger features from the Seward Peninsula of

Alaska. In both cases, the peaty soils favour the development of clear ice lenses immediately beneath the vegetation mat.

Further reading

Associate Committee on Geotechnical Research (1988) *Glossary of permafrost and related ground ice terms.* Permafrost Subcommittee, National Research Council of Canada, Ottawa, Technical Memorandum 142.

Mackay, J.R. (1979) Pingos of the Tuktoyaktuk Peninsula area, Northwest Territories. *Géographie physique et quaternaire*, **33**, 3–61.

Mackay, J.R. (1990) Seasonal growth bands in pingo ice. *Canadian Journal of Earth Sciences*, **27**, 1115–1125.

Mackay, J.R. (1993) Air temperature, snow cover, creep of frozen ground, and the time of ice-wedge cracking, western Arctic coast. *Canadian Journal of Earth Sciences*, **30**, 1720–1729.

Mackay, J.R. and S.R. Dallimore (1992) Massive ice of the Tuktoyaktuk area, western Arctic coast, Canada. *Canadian Journal of Earth Sciences*, **29**, 1235–1249.

Murton, J.B. and H.M. French (1994) Cryostructures in permafrost, Tuktoyaktuk coastlands, western Arctic, Canada. *Canadian Journal of Earth Sciences*, **31**, 737–747.

Discussion topics

1. How can we describe ice within permafrost?

2. What are the growth conditions for (a) ice wedges and/or (b) pingos?

3. Differentiate between the various forms of frost mounds.

4. What is the origin of massive ground ice?

5. Can ice wedges and pingos be used to make palaeoclimatic and palaeoenvironmental inferences?

CHAPTER 7

Thermokarst

Thermokarst processes are some of the most important processes fashioning the periglacial landscape. They achieve their greatest activity in lowlands such as the western Arctic and northern Siberia where alluvial sediments with high ice contents are widespread. Some types of thermokarst are probably the most rapid erosional agents presently operating in the tundra and Arctic regions. In alpine regions, and other areas underlain by consolidated and resistant rocks, soils with high ice contents are relatively rare. In such regions, thermokarst development is less important in landscape development.

The term thermokarst was first proposed by the Russian, M. M. Ermolaev in 1932 to describe irregular, hummocky terrain due to the melting of ground ice. Subsequently, the term has been applied specifically to the process of ground ice melt accompanied by local collapse or subsidence of the ground surface. Although Dylik (1968) argued initially to reserve the term for the melting of underground ice as opposed to buried glacier or surface ice, it is now accepted that the word 'thermokarst' applies to the melting process of all ground ice bodies, irrespective of origin. Moreover, the meaning of the word has rapidly enlarged to include not only the process of subsidence and collapse, but also a large number of more complex activities. For example, thermal abrasion, thermal erosion and thermo-erosional wash are all considered to be thermokarst-controlled processes (Kachurin, 1962, p. 52; Dylik, 1971, 1972). In fact, thermokarst encompasses the whole range of geomorphic effects resulting from subsurface water on landforms in permafrost regions (e.g. Higgens et al., 1990).

Despite the apparent similarity of topography, it should be made quite clear that thermokarst is *not* a variety of karst. The latter is a term which is applicable to limestone areas where the dominant process, solution, is a chemical one. Underlying the development of thermokarst, however, is a physical, i.e.

thermal, process, that of ground ice melting, which is peculiar to regions underlain by permafrost.

Thermokarst phenomena have been reported from many parts of the FSU ranging from the subarctic and Arctic regions of northern Siberia in the north to the mountainous areas of the central Tian-Shan in the south (e.g. Grave and Nekrasov, 1961). In parts of central Yakutia and eastern Siberia, it is thought that over 40 per cent of the land surface has been affected, at some time or another, by thermokarst processes (Czudek and Demek, 1970). In the periglacial regions of North America, the past 30 years has seen an increase in awareness of thermokarst (e.g. Brown, 1974; Rampton, 1974) but its importance may still be underestimated in certain areas (Harry et al., 1988). In the interpretation of Pleistocene periglacial features, Dylik (1964b) stressed that thermokarst processes do not seem to have been fully considered, a comment still valid today (see Chapter 14).

7.1 Causes of thermokarst

The development of thermokarst is due primarily to the disruption of the thermal equilibrium of the

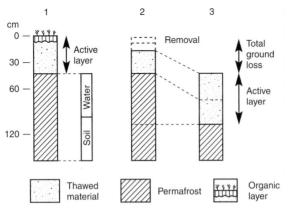

Figure 7.1 Diagram illustrating how terrain disturbance of an ice-rich tundra soil can lead to thermokarst subsidence (*Source*: Mackay, 1970).

permafrost and an increase in the depth of the active layer. Thermokarst subsidence is then a function of the new equilibrium depth of the active layer and the supersaturation of the degrading permafrost. This can be illustrated with a simple example (Fig. 7.1). Consider a well-vegetated tundra soil with an active layer of 45 cm underlain by supersaturated permafrost which yields upon thawing, on a volumetric basis, 50 per cent excess ice (water) and 50 per cent saturated soil. If the top 15 cm of soil is removed, the thermal insulating role played by the organic mat disappears. Under the bareground conditions that result, the depth of seasonal thaw might increase to 60 cm. Since only 30 cm of the original active layer remains, a further 60 cm of the permafrost must thaw in order to increase the active layer thickness to 60 cm since 30 cm of supernatant water will be released. Thus, in addition to the original 15 cm of material loss from the surface, the terrain subsides a further 30 cm before a new thermal equilibrium is reached.

There are many reasons why thermal disequilibrium and permafrost degradation may take place. These are summarized in Fig. 7.2. On a large scale, regional climatic conditions might change, while on a small scale, there are an infinite number of local conditions. With respect to regional climatic changes, thermokarst development should be most intense when: (a) associated with a rise in the mean annual temperature of the soil, i.e. an amelioration of climate, and (b) associated with an increase in amplitude of temperature, i.e. an increase in continentality. A combination of these two conditions should lead to maximum increase in the depth of the

seasonally thawed layer. In reality, however, an increase in mean annual temperatures would probably lead to a diminution of heat exchange in the soil and a lower summer soil temperature, since it would most likely be associated with an increase in precipitation and cloud cover. As a result, there would be a decrease in the depth of thaw, which is the exact opposite to what is required for thermokarst development. Therefore, the simplest condition for the onset of thermokarst would be a progressive increase in continentality of climate resulting in a greater range of soil temperatures and summer thaw depths. However, recent global warming scenarios suggest that increases in winter temperatures and snowfall amounts will be the greatest in the high latitudes. As a result, the predicted permafrost response to global climate change is not simple. This topic in discussed in detail in Chapter 17.

In central Siberia, where thermokarst appears to have occurred on a regional scale, it probably reflects a long-term regional climatic amelioration. In the western Arctic of North America, however, active thermokarst is largely the result of local, non-climatic factors. Here, palynological evidence suggests climatic conditions progressively ameliorated during the period 11000–8500 BP, and between 8500 and 4000 BP, the climate may have been significantly warmer than today. This induced a period of regional thermokarst development. After 4000 BP, however, the climate has cooled and current thermokarst activity due to regional climatic change is limited.

Under stable climatic conditions, thermokarst develops in response to a variety of geomorphic and/or vegetational conditions. These may be either natural or human-induced. One widespread natural cause is the presence of polygonal ice-wedge systems. In summer, water accumulation occurs in the central trough above the thermal contraction crack, or at the junction of ice wedges, or within low-centred polygons. These shallow bodies of standing water invariably favour more intensive thawing during summer and impede the winter freeze-up. The concentration of water also has a chemical effect upon the underlying ice vein since the water is often extremely pure. Once initiated, the concentrations of water in summer and snow in winter increase. The depression grows larger, thus promoting further thaw of the ground without any supplementary agents. This phenomenon has been called 'self-developing thermokarst' (Aleshinskaya *et al.*, 1972). As such, it can occur within stable but exceptionally severe periglacial and arctic climates. For example, the

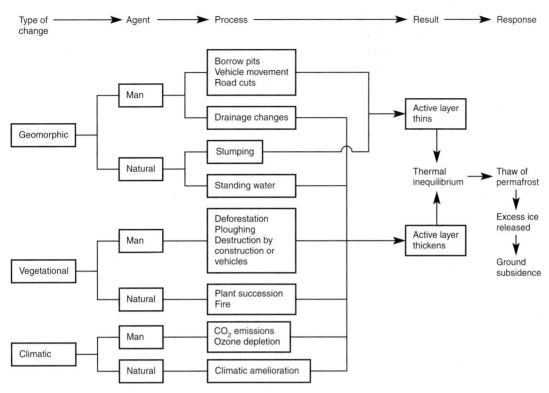

Figure 7.2 Diagram illustrating how geomorphic, vegetational and climatic changes may lead to permafrost degradation (modified from French, 1987c).

thickness of the active layer in the Indigirka lowlands of Siberia, where the permafrost temperature is −9 °C or less, is twice as great beneath 20–25 cm of water than in adjacent ground (Table 7.1(a)).

Another natural cause of thermokarst development is associated with lateral stream erosion developing a thermo-erosional niche (Walker and Arnborg, 1966) which causes the undermining and slumping of the overlying material. The thermal regime of the terrain is disrupted as a consequence. Often, this process is associated with asymmetrical valley development. For example, on eastern Banks Island, retrogressive semi-circular ground ice slumps occur predominantly upon the steeper west and southwest facing slopes of asymmetrical valleys. They appear to be triggered initially by the lateral migration of the stream to the base of that slope (French and Egginton, 1973).

A third natural cause of thermokarst development in the boreal forest zone is forest fire; for example, in part of the Siberian taiga, the active layer increased from 40 to 80 cm in 12 years following a fire in 1953 (Czudek and Demek, 1970), and at Inuvik, in the Northwest Territories of Canada, where a forest fire

occurred in 1968, Heginbottom (1973) observed an increase in the depth of the active layer in the burned-over area of approximately 40 per cent in four years. The more long-term changes are complex, depending on site conditions and year-to-year climatic fluctuations (Table 7.1(b)).

Other local causes for various types of thermokarst include ice-push and scour along coastlines, cyclical changes in vegetation, local slope instability, and deforestation or disruption of the surface vegetation by humans.

The amount or extent of morphological change associated with the thermokarst process depends upon (a) the magnitude of the increase in depth of the active layer, (b) the ice content in the soil, and (c) the tectonic regime of the region. Factor (a) has already been dealt with in the previous paragraph. With respect to factors (b) and (c), two points need to be stressed. First, thermokarst forms develop best in lowland areas experiencing stable tectonic histories since, in subsiding regions, thermokarst forms are quickly infilled with sediment. Second, although the amount of morphological change depends largely upon the amount of

Table 7.1 Active layer thickness under different terrain conditions: (a) depth of the active layer in ice-wedge polygon terrain in the Yana-Indigirka lowlands of northern Siberia, illustrating thermal effects of standing water bodies (b) increase in active layer depth, thickness of permafrost thawed and ground subsidence at the site of the 1968 forest fire at Inuvik, NWT, Canada

(a) [1]Moisture Conditions in Central Part of Polygon	Depth of Active Layer (cm)	
	Latitude 70°N	Latitude 71°N
Relatively dry	30–34	23–25
Moist	38–41	31–33
Water layer, 7–10 cm deep in polygon centre	52–56	39–42
Water layer, 20–25 cm deep in polygon centre	62–69	51–53
Lake, 30 × 40 m with depth 25 cm or more	75+	

(b) Site	Mean increase in active layer depth (approx.)	Mean thickness of permafrost thawed (cm) (approx.)	Mean ground[3] subsidence (cm) (approx.)
1 Unburned (mean of 9 stakes)	From 42 cm in 1968 to 52 cm in 1979	15	5
2 Burned (mean of 10 stakes)	From 35 cm in 1968 to 72 cm in 1973	55	18
3 Burned			
Ridges (mean of 4 stakes)	From 60 cm in 1968 to 137 cm in 1988	116	39
Depressions (mean of 4 stakes)		117	39
4 Unburned			
Hummocks (mean of 5 stakes)	From 115 cm in 1968 to 132 cm in 1981	26	9
Depressions (mean of 10 stakes)	From 76 cm in 1968 to 108 cm in 1981	48	16
5 Burned			
Hummocks (mean of 5 stakes)	From 116 cm in 1968 to 136 cm in 1979	30	10
Depressions (mean of 10 stakes)	From 68 cm in 1968 to 102 cm in 1979	51	17

[1]Data from Czudek and Demek (1970) [2]Data from Mackay (1995a) [3]Assumes 33% thaw settlement

excess ice present, the distribution of ground ice determines, to a large extent, the pattern and nature of ground subsidence. For example, ice-wedge ice, which is distributed vertically throughout the soil in polygonal systems, will lead to mound-like thermokarst forms. By contrast, segregated and pore ice, being distributed relatively uniformly in the horizontal plane, lead to widespread surface subsidence.

It is difficult to generalize about the distribution of thermokarst phenomena since the climatic, permafrost and ground ice controls vary not only with latitude but also between each other. In general, however, thermokarst processes are favoured in the tundra and forest regions, and in particular, along the southern margins of the permafrost zone. In the subarctic regions of Canada, for example, permafrost degradation is not uncommon (e.g. Zoltai, 1971; Thie, 1974; Séguin and Allard, 1984). Moreover, in these regions the surface vegetation has an important control over subsurface temperatures and thaw depths, and if disturbed for any reason will radically alter the thermal regime. In general, the more luxurious the vegetation, the less is the depth of thaw. Thus, in such areas, the potential for human-induced thermokarst, induced by the modification or destruction of the surface vegetation, will be extremely high. North of the treeline and in the high Arctic, the situation is slightly different. In some respects, thermokarst becomes less important in the far north because the active layer is shallow, and the period of summer thaw is increasingly restricted. The absence of vegetation further reduces the complexity of the thermal regime of the soil, and the potential for human-induced thermokarst is reduced. On the other hand, natural thermokarst processes, particularly ground ice slumping and self-developing thermokarst, may assume greater relative importance (e.g. French, 1974b; Lewkowicz, 1987), especially in ice-cored terrain or where near-surface ground ice amounts are high.

7.2 Thermokarst subsidence and thermal erosion

Of the various processes included within the term 'thermokarst', a basic distinction should be made between *thermokarst subsidence* and *thermal erosion*.

Thermal erosion is a dynamic process involving the 'wearing away' by thermal means, i.e. the melting of ice. The easily identifiable characteristics of thermal erosion are flowing water, a slope and ice which can be melted. By contrast, thermokarst subsidence is 'thermal solution' or more precisely 'thermal melting'. The loss of water then results in subsidence. Thermal melting depends upon heat conduction, for example, from a pool of water directly overlying icy soil, or from conduction through an intervening layer of unfrozen soil. Therefore, quite unlike thermal erosion, no flowing water or surface gradient is required. Thermokarst subsidence can operate just as efficiently upon a flat and well-drained area as in a poorly drained valley bottom.

From a geomorphic point of view, thermal erosion generally results in lateral permafrost degradation or backwearing while thermokarst subsidence results in permafrost degradation from above or downwearing. This distinction, proposed by Czudek and Demek (1970) to describe the thermokarst features of Siberia, is useful and enables one to identify a number of distinct and separate thermokarst phenomena. In essence, lateral permafrost degradation takes place as the result of cliff retreat, lateral river erosion, and marine or lacustrine abrasion. Ground ice slumps, thermo-erosional niches and thermokarst (thaw) lakes are some of the more distinctive features developed in this way. Permafrost degradation from above mainly occurs on flat terrain, and is a process of subsidence and collapse of the ground surface. Where it operates over extensive areas, the end result is the destruction of the original surface relief and the creation of a new thermokarst relief at a lower elevation. The development of closed depressions, collapse features and hummocky irregular terrain are typical of this process. In the mature stages of thermokarst development, it is not uncommon to have both thermokarst subsidence and thermal erosion operating together.

7.3 Alas thermokarst relief

The simplest downwearing thermokarst process is that of straightforward subsidence of the ground, the amount of ground loss being a function of the new equilibrium depth of the active layer and the amount of water (ice) lost from the soil (see earlier).

The most distinct thermokarst forms develop in areas of considerable ground ice, particularly where well developed ice wedges and ice-wedge polygons are present. In central Siberia, Soloviev (1973a, 1973b)

and other Russian scientists believe thermokarst phenomena can develop in a predictable and sequential fashion. The type area where this occurs is upon terraces of the Lena and Aldan rivers in central Yakutia.

7.3.1 Central Yakutia

As with most 'type areas', a number of relatively unique factors aid in the development of the distinct topography. In central Yakutia, one may distinguish at least three controlling factors. First, the terraces are underlain by considerable thicknesses of alluvial silty loams in which segregated ice lenses may constitute up to 50–80 per cent of the soil. In addition, thick syngenetic ice wedges, reported to exceed 50–60 m in vertical extent in some areas, underlie between 30 and 60 per cent of the surface of the terraces. In terms of ground ice conditions, therefore, the area is exceptionally well suited for thermokarst development. Second, the geomorphic history which enabled such conditions to occur is rather uncommon. The central Yakutian lowland appears to have remained unglaciated for much, if not all, of the Quaternary. It acted as a stable aggradational environment in which alluvial sediments were deposited under cold-climate conditions over a long period of time. Third, the present climatic conditions are continental and among the most extreme in the world. For example, the annual temperature range at Yakutsk (latitude 62°N) is 62°C (see Chapter 3, Table 3.1(a)). As a result, active layer depths in excess of 2.0 m are not uncommon in Yakutia where air temperatures in August often reach 30°C. In general terms, therefore, one must regard the thermokarst terrain of central Yakutia as being unique, and it is unlikely that exactly similar conditions will be found elsewhere.

Bearing these considerations in mind, it is instructive to examine the nature and development of the various thermokarst relief forms found in Yakutia. The sequence of alas thermokarst relief, as suggested by Soloviev, is outlined in Fig. 7.3. In the first stage following the increase in the depth of thaw, a polygonal system of ice wedges begins to thaw. High-centred polygons or 'degradation polygons' (Katasonov and Ivanov, 1973) begin to develop with trough-like depressions along the ice wedges. An undulating, convex surface quickly develops but the vegetation cover is not destroyed. However, as soon as the preferential thawing and subsidence along the line of the ice wedges exceeds 1–2 m in depth, slumping starts, the vegetation cover is broken and the polygon centres become distinct conical mounds.

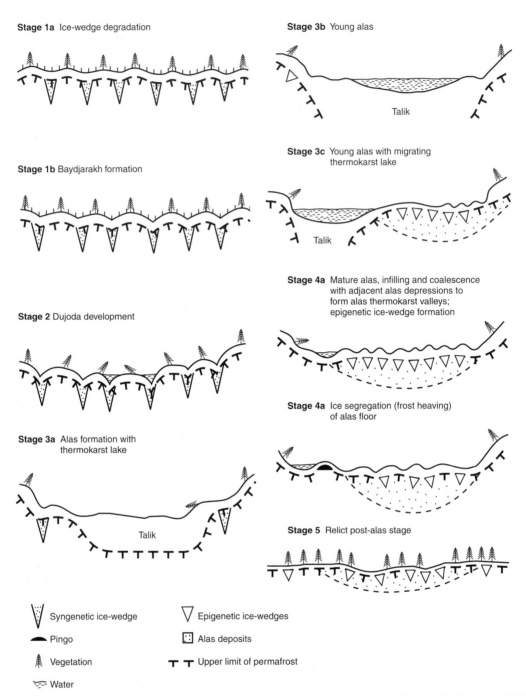

Stage 1a Ice-wedge degradation

Stage 1b Baydjarakh formation

Stage 2 Dujoda development

Stage 3a Alas formation with thermokarst lake

Talik

Stage 3b Young alas

Talik

Stage 3c Young alas with migrating thermokarst lake

Talik

Stage 4a Mature alas, infilling and coalescence with adjacent alas depressions to form alas thermokarst valleys; epigenetic ice-wedge formation

Stage 4a Ice segregation (frost heaving) of alas floor

Stage 5 Relict post-alas stage

▽ Syngenetic ice-wedge

▽ Epigenetic ice-wedges

Pingo

Alas deposits

Vegetation

⊤ ⊤ Upper limit of permafrost

Water

Figure 7.3 The sequence of development of alas thermokarst relief in central Yakutia, according to P. A. Soloviev (1973b).

These mounds are called '*baydjarakhs*', a Yakutian term used to describe silty or peaty mounds. They are commonly between 3 and 4 m high, 3 and 15 m wide and up to 20 m long. As such, they closely resemble the dimensions of the polygons from which they have developed. Young baydjarakhs have a

Figure 7.4 A small man-induced alas depression which has developed in historic time near Maya village, central Yakutia. Deforestation was probably the cause of thermokarst.

clearly truncated conical form but old baydjarakhs have a more convex form. From the air, baydjarakhs resemble a cobblestoned surface, distributed in a checkerboard or rectilinear pattern. Similar features occur in the Taimyr Peninsula, near Dickson, and in other parts of Siberia adjacent to the Laptev Sea. In the discontinuous permafrost zones where the active layer is at its thickest, or in areas where the ice wedges have almost disappeared, those features are called 'graveyard mounds' (Popov *et al.*, 1966).

The second stage of thermokarst downwearing is characterized by the progressive collapse and decay of the baydjarakhs as a depression develops in the centre of the baydjarakh field, often with a central hollow or sinkhole. With the linkage of these sinkholes, continuous depressions form with steep slopes and uneven bottoms which are called 'dujodas' in Yakutia.

By stage 3, a distinct depression with steep sides and a flat bottom has developed through the continued collapse of the baydjarakhs on the sides of the dujodas. This depression is called an 'alas' in Yakutia, denoting a circular or oval depression with steep sides and a flat floor with no trees but with a thermokarst (thaw) lake (Fig. 7.4). The latter, upon obtaining a minimum depth at which it does not freeze to the bottom during the winter, promotes the development of a talik. Thus, as the ground melts and the sediments beneath the lake consolidate, the thaw lake deepens and sub-surface thawing is further enhanced. Ultimately, alas development proceeds to the complete thawing of the permafrost or to the formation of a stabilized open talik. In the fourth stage, the alas

lake disappears either by infilling with alas (thermokarst) deposits (see section 7.8) or by draining to a lower alas level or to a river valley. Permafrost aggradation takes place as the talik progressively freezes. Ice segregation results in heaving of the alas floor and new epigenetic ice wedges begin to develop. Sometimes, bulgannyakhs (pingos) form either by the intrusion of water under pressure into the frozen ground (open system) or by the freezing of local taliks (closed system). The majority of the larger bulgannyakhs in the major alasses are probably of the open system type since the permafrost beneath the alas floor is often thin or discontinuous. The end result of this sequence of alas relief is the development of a depression with gentle slopes and an undulating floor.

In central Siberia, alas formation has greatly modified the lowland areas. In one region near to Yakutsk nearly 40 per cent of the initial land surface has been destroyed by alas formation (Fig. 7.5). The coalescence of adjacent alasses has led to the formation of large depressions often in excess of 25 km² and to the development of complex thermokarst valleys. The latter are irregular in plan consisting of wide sections (alas depressions) connected by narrow sections cutting through the intervening watersheds. Other characteristics of these valleys are right angle turns, blind spurs and a general misfit relationship with the overall topography and drainage. The long profiles are also irregular owing to the differential thaw settlement within the various alas depressions. With time, the deeper alasses are infilled and the higher floors are lowered as erosion progresses along thermokarst gullies originating above epigenetic ice wedges.

The rate of alas formation varies considerably since there are reports that some alasses have developed within historic time, while others are obviously very old features. Kachurin (1962) regards the beginning of thermokarst development in Siberia to coincide with the warmer climate of the Atlantic Period (8200–5300 years BP in Western Europe). Subsequently, thermokarst was inhibited in the Sub-Atlantic Period when temperatures dropped. In recent years, it has recommenced under the present climatic regime. Many of the alasses of the Yakutia region developed during the Holocene climatic optimum which, in that region, was approximately 4000–5000 years BP. Soloviev (1973a) concluded that many of the thermokarst forms are not active today; in fact, probably only 10 per cent of the terrain in the vicinity of Yakutsk is undergoing active thermokarst modification.

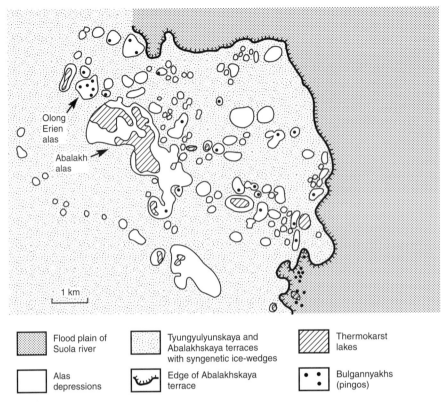

Olong
Erien
alas

Abalakh
alas

1 km

| | Flood plain of Suola river | | Tyungyulyunskaya and Abalakhskaya terraces with syngenetic ice-wedges | | Thermokarst lakes |
| Alas depressions | | Edge of Abalakhskaya terrace | | Bulgannyakhs (pingos) |

Figure 7.5 Map showing extent of alas thermokarst terrain in the vicinity of the Abalakh settlement, central Yakutia, FSU. The depressions give the appearance of pitted outwash (kettle) topography, yet the area has not been glaciated (from Soloviev, 1973a)

7.3.2 Arctic North America

In North America, the full range of alas thermokarst features has not been identified. Given the rather different geomorphic history and the less continental climatic conditions of much of arctic North America, it is unlikely that similar relief exists. On the other hand, certain aspects of the alas thermokarst relief find striking analogies with certain North American terrain conditions.

In Alaska for example, Rockie (1942) first drew attention to the settling of ground caused by the thawing of ice wedges in recently cleared field systems near Fairbanks. Péwé (1954) and others have subsequently referred to the hummocks as 'thermokarst mounds'. In many respects, these features are analogous to the baydjarakhs or 'graveyard mounds' of Yakutia. The 'dujoda' stage also has analogies in Alaska with the thaw sinks, funnels and 'cave-in' lakes reported from the Seward Peninsula and other

areas (e.g. Wallace, 1948; Péwé, 1948; Hopkins, 1949). However, the circular alas depression, and in particular with bulgannyakh or pingo growth within the depression, has not been reported. The closest comparable features are the thermokarst depressions and lakes of the Mackenzie Delta in which closed system pingos form (see earlier). In general though, few of the thermokarst depressions of the Mackenzie Delta region have the same striking relief as the Yakutian alasses and they are more the result of lateral growth than subsidence. Probably the most analogous terrain to the alas thermokarst relief is the ice-cored topography described by Mackay (1963), Rampton (1974) and Harry *et al.* (1988) from parts of the lowlands of the western Canadian Arctic coastal plain. In the Tuktoyaktuk Peninsula, thermokarst development along small creeks has produced 'macro-beaded' drainage systems where a series of depressions, partly lake-filled, are connected to each other by narrower sections or shallow interfluves. Elsewhere, the ice-cored topography and 'involuted hills' to the east of Tuktoyaktuk (Mackay, 1963) are a type of thermokarst topography. The hills have relatively flat tops and steep sides and rise 15–50 m above the surrounding terrain. They can vary in size from 0.5 to 2.0 km². A unique characteristic is their surface appearance which '. . . resembles, on air photographs, the wrinkled skin of a well dried prune' (Mackay, 1963, p. 138). The involuted nature is the result of 'curving to branching ridges, ranging up to several hundreds of yards in length, several score of yards in width, and 20 feet in height' (Mackay, 1963, p. 138). According to Rampton (1974), 4.0–5.0 m of reworked clayey till or diamicton commonly overlies the massive ice that forms the core of the upland, and sand and gravel generally lies beneath. Creep and deformation of the massive ice, in conjunction with thermokarst, is the most likely explanation for this distinctive terrain.

Much of the lowland terrain of the Yukon Coastal Plain may also be essentially thermokarst in nature. Harry *et al.* (1988) explain areas of ice-cored terrain near Sabine Point as being remnants of an initial upland surface, greatly modified by thermokarst processes. Widespread massive ice and icy sediments formed as permafrost aggraded following ice retreat from the maximum (Buckland) glacial limit. Then, multiple episodes of regional, climatically-induced thermokarst occurred during the period 14 000–8000 years BP. These resulted in thaw settlement of both Buckland and post-Buckland age sediments, and in surface subsidence within a series of coalescent and polycyclic thaw lake basins. Thaw mobilization of sediments resulted in the transport of mudflow sediments from upland areas into adjacent basins and to the progressive isolation of areas of ice-cored terrain. Similar terrain analogues exist in northern Alaska and, in more general terms, there is correspondence with the cycle of alas relief suggested for central Yakutia. An important point is that all these sequences of thermokarst development highlight the importance of thaw mobilization and redistribution of sediments. The distinctive nature of thermokarst sediments are considered later in this chapter and also in the context of Pleistocene conditions (Chapter 14).

7.4 Ice-wedge thermokarst terrain

Although ice wedges and ice-wedge polygon relief have been studied in some detail (e.g. Carson and Hussey, 1962; Hussey and Michelson, 1966; Mackay,

1963), the genetic relationship between the various polygon relief forms and the thermokarst process has not been emphasized. Two types of tundra ice-wedge polygon relief forms are commonly recognized: a high-centred type and a low-centred type (Fig. 7.6). Since the high-centred type invariably appears to develop through the low-centred type, the latter must be examined first.

7.4.1 High- and low-centred polygons

Low-centred polygons are characteristic of low marshy areas and commonly possess upstanding rims, often in excess of 50 cm in height, and a low wet centre composed of sedges and tussock grass (see Fig. 7.6). The raised rims are probably the result of thermal expansion and contraction within the active layer, as explained earlier (see Chapter 6). In exceptionally poorly drained areas, the centre of the polygon together with the central trough running along the line of the ice wedge is filled with standing water in summer. Low-centred tundra polygons are well suited, therefore, for the initiation of self-developing thermokarst. The most favoured location for thaw of the underlying wedge is at the junction of two or more wedges and small irregularly shaped ponds often persist in such localities throughout the summer. If integrated drainage occurs in such terrain, it can assume a 'beaded' pattern.

The change from low-centred to high-centred polygons is probably brought about by an improvement in drainage conditions. As a result, the depth of seasonal thaw increases and there is preferential thaw settlement above the ice wedges. As a consequence, a deep trough develops which accentuates the better drainage of the polygon centre. At the same time, the polygon rims begin to widen, probably by vegetation growth, and the central sedge and tussock area progressively disappears. An elevated peaty polygon finally emerges surrounded by troughs along the underlying ice wedges (Fig. 7.6).

In a few localities, exceptionally well-developed low-centred polygons form in which the polygon rims create near-vertical walls, 1.0–1.5 m high, enclosing a flat relatively dry centre. Mackay terms these 'fortress polygons' (see Root, 1975). Their exact origin is not fully understood but they appear to form in ice-rich areas that have had recent lowering of the drainage base level. Exceptionally deep troughs develop above the underlying ice wedges

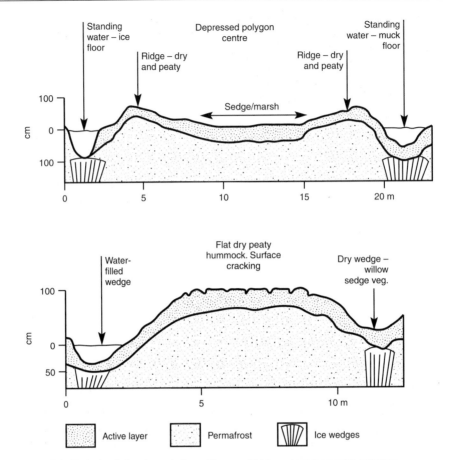

Figure 7.6 Typical relief and vegetation of low- and high-centred ice-wedge polygons.

while thermokarst subsidence in the centre of the polygon probably accentuates the existence of the raised rim. Clearly, there must be a complex relationship between the ice wedge, drainage improvement, and the sediment : ice ratio for such terrain to form.

Once high-centred polygon terrain has developed, it inevitably concentrates surface water and thermal erosion along the lines of the underlying ice wedges. Shumskiy and Vtyurin (1966) have summarized this process in a number of stages. In the initial destruction stage, the polygons (i.e. degradation polygons) may be either plane, with raised edges, or with a convex form. Then, in the mature destruction stage, the polygon form develops to be either convex with deep thawing furrows or to assume a domed, 'graveyard mound' type of appearance (Fig. 7.7). Ultimately, it may proceed to a thermokarst depression or alas.

7.4.2 Badland thermokarst relief

Dramatic badland-type relief can develop as the result of thermal melting and erosion operating preferentially along large ice wedges in ice-rich sediments. The result is striking baydjarakh-like terrain. For example, in one area drained by two small streams on eastern Banks Island a large amphitheatre-like hollow has been eroded nearly 0.5 km in diameter, and several hectares in area (Fig. 7.8). Drilling to depths of 6 m revealed the underlying silts to possess 20–30 per cent excess ice on average, and to contain ice wedges exceeding 6 m in depth (French, 1974b, pp. 791–793). Fluvial erosion is operating preferentially along the ice wedges to isolate sharp conical mounds on the floor of the depression, and to give a serrated edge to the amphitheatre. The presence of shallow lakes together with a number of localized 'active layer failures' (see

Figure 7.7 Oblique air view of degradation polygons or 'graveyard mounds' occurring on sloping terrain, eastern Banks Island, Canada. The relative relief of the mounds is 2–3 m; the size of the polygons is indicated by the tents.

Chapter 9) within the amphitheatre suggest development has proceeded in two stages: (a) fluvio-thermal erosion along ice wedges and the development of the baydjarakh-like mounds, and (b) subsequent degrada-

tion of the mounds brought about by the high ice content of the silts, and their exposure to thawing from all sides. Since the natural water (ice) content of the silts exceeds their liquid limits, the silts are extremely mobile upon thawing.

7.5 Retrogressive thaw slumps

Retrogressive thaw slumps (Fig. 7.9) result from the thaw of ice-rich permafrost. They attain their largest dimensions and most frequent occurrence in areas underlain by massive icy bodies, or silts of high ice content. They are known to occur in forested (Czudek and Demek, 1970; Zoltai and Pettapiece, 1973; McRoberts and Morgenstern, 1974), tundra (Mackay, 1966; Lewkowicz, 1985) and high Arctic (Lamothe and St-Onge, 1961; French, 1974b; Lewkowicz, 1987) environments. In general, they are short-lived but rapidly developing features, the majority of which become stabilized within 30–50 summers after their initiation. They are important in

Figure 7.8 Oblique air view from 50 m elevation of terrain undergoing rapid thermal melting and erosion operating preferentially along ice wedges, eastern Banks Island, Canada. The conical mounds are over 8 m high. Remnants of the original polygon surface can be seen in both the foreground and mid-distance.

Figure 7.9 A retrogressive thaw slump, eastern Banks Island, Canada. Ground ice is exposed in the headwall and there is active slumping and sliding of material across the face.

that they represent one of the most rapid erosive processes currently operating in present-day periglacial environments.

Retrogressive thaw slumps resemble the earthflows of more temperate regions but because there is no surface of rupture, features characteristic of rotational slides are largely absent. The crown has no lunate tension cracks paralleling the main scarp but, instead, there are minor cracks in the active layer along hummocks, created as the hummocks become detached and fall down the face. The term 'thermocirque', proposed by Czudek and Demek (1970) to describe these features in Siberia, is graphic but is not used in the North American literature because it fails to identify the nature of the processes involved.

Mackay (1966) has identified three main processes involved in scarp retreat: (a) free fall or sliding of the active layer, (b) erosion, both thermal or mechanical, on the exposed and frozen scarp face, and (c) slumping of thawed debris from above the frozen scarp face. The third process is the most significant in terms of material removed and involves the progressive thawing of the scarp face, with negligible movement, until the overburden is 1–2 m thick. Then, rapid slippage along the frozen surface exposes a surface of failure not unlike that of a rotational landslide. The rate of retreat of the slump scar depends primarily upon the ice content of the underlying materials. Mackay (1966, pp. 70–71) demonstrated how, if the ice content is at least 200–300 per cent, a scarp face of up to 6 m in height may be able to retreat with little transport of thawed

soil beyond the foot of the scarp. In the Mackenzie Delta region average annual retreat rates are probably between 2 and 5 m (Mackay, 1966). However, rates in excess of this have been observed, especially in localities where wave action removes material from the base of the slump (Lewkowicz, 1985).

The size of retrogressive thaw slumps may vary considerably. In the Mackenzie Delta region, an average sized feature may be 50–100 m in diameter and possess a scarp face of between 2 and 7 m in height. Many slumps, however, are polycyclic features and several hectares in extent. In the high Arctic, the slumps are exceedingly broad and shallow, since the height of the headwall including the ice exposure rarely exceeds 2 m, while the maximum horizontal dimensions may often exceed 200 m (French, 1974b; Lamothe and St-Onge, 1961). Thus, they are usually shallower than those that occur in the tundra and forest tundra zones, and reflect differences in the annual rate, depth and duration of thaw in high Arctic regions. Ground ice slumps appear to be widespread throughout the high Arctic, and occur wherever unconsolidated ice-rich sediments are found.

On the silty morainal terrain of eastern Banks Island, retrogressive thaw slumps attain a regional density of 0.5/km² (French and Egginton, 1973). Both active and stabilized features can be recognized. Maximum rates of headwall retreat of between 6.0 and 8.0 m year appear typical (French, 1974b). Since the maximum size of the slumps as revealed on air photographs does not usually exceed 200–300 m in diameter, French and Egginton (1973) conclude that the majority of slumps become stabilized within 30–50 summers of their initiation. On the Sandhills moraine of southern Banks Island, similar mean headwall retreat rates have been measured (Lewkowicz, 1987) although a maximum of 15.5 m/year was recorded for one slump in 1983–84. On average, slumps in this area were active for a much shorter period, approximately 12–15 years, and slumps, either active or inactive, have affected over 15 per cent of the terrain adjacent to the coast. From these and other studies it is possible to identify some of the common trigger mechanisms. For example, many slumps on eastern Banks Island occur on the steeper slopes of asymmetrical valleys and have been triggered by lateral stream erosion undercutting the west-facing bank. Others are found adjacent to lakes or to the coast, as in the Sandhills, and probably owe their initiation to wave action or ice pushing (see Chapter 11). Finally, some slumps, unrelated to any obvious trigger mechanism and occurring randomly, may have developed initially from simple active layer slope failures. Such failures are not uncommon in permafrost regions, and have been widely reported from the high Arctic (e.g. Bird, 1967, pp. 217–20; Lewkowicz, 1992b). In such regions, where over 50 per cent of the total precipitation falls as summer rain, the development of high pore water pressures is not uncommon after prolonged summer rain or drizzle. Similar conditions are favoured in years of exceptionally high winter snowfall and/or rapid and late thawing (see Chapter 9).

The ultimate stabilization of the headwall is related to the balance between the rate at which debris is supplied to, and removed from, the base of the headwall. This will be a function of the relative height of the icy sediments in relation to the base of the headwall. Assuming that the icy sediments occur as a body parallel to the regional slope of the ground, as the ground slope gradually decreases towards the top of the slope, less of the icy sediments are exposed above the base of the headwall. Ultimately, when the icy sediments are lower than the base of the headwall, the feature becomes inactive. Given the generally subdued relief of many slopes developed in unconsolidated ice-rich sediments, it is possible for extensive headwall retreat to occur and for entire slopes to be consumed by regressive slumping. Thermokarst slope modification is discussed more fully in Chapter 9.

7.6 Thaw lakes and depressions

Perhaps the most common thermokarst phenomena which occur in the lowland periglacial environments are shallow rounded depressions, often with semicircular or circular ponds or lakes within them (Fig. 7.10). In the North American literature, they have variously been called thaw lakes, thaw depressions, thermokarst lakes and tundra ponds (Black, 1969). They have attracted considerable attention particularly in Alaska (e.g. Wallace, 1948; Hopkins, 1949; Black and Barksdale, 1949; Sellman et al., 1975) and in the Mackenzie Delta area (Mackay, 1963). Similar features have been reported widely from the Russian and Siberian Arctic coastal plains (e.g. Dostovalov and Kudryavtsev, 1967). In fact, they are ubiquitous in flat lowland areas wherever silty-clay alluviums with high ice contents are present (e.g. Burn and Smith, 1988). Fluviatile terraces, outwash plains, coastal areas and drained lake bottoms are favoured localities.

7.6.1 Morphology and growth

The initial cause of the thaw lake or depression may be the quite random melting of ground ice, the subsidence of the ground, and the accumulation of water in the depression. For example, in the Seward Peninsula of Alaska, in the boundary zone between the discontinuous and continuous permafrost, Hopkins (1949) has described thaw depressions and some of the small lakes that occupy these depressions. The depressions appear to have been initiated by locally deep thawing, the result of (a) disruption of vegetation cover by frost heave, (b) accelerated thaw beneath pools occupying intersections of ice-wedge polygons, and (c) accelerated thaw beneath pools in small streams. In some instances, where the permafrost is particularly thin, the lakes have pierced or thawed the permafrost and subterranean drainage into underlying thawed sediments has occurred. This creates 'cave-in' lakes and thaw 'sinks' (Wallace, 1948). In areas of thicker permafrost, however, the lakes often originate in poorly drained areas characterized by low-centred ice-wedge polygons. In such areas, the depressed polygon centre promotes standing water bodies which, in turn, promote differential thawing. Through coalescence of adjacent polygon lakes, small tundra ponds are created.

Thaw lakes vary considerably in size, frequency of occurrence and shape. Some attain diameters of 1–2 km but the majority are smaller features rarely exceeding 300 m in diameter. They are also extremely shallow, in all cases less than 3–4 m deep, and often less than 0.3 m deep in the littoral margins.

The development and growth of thaw lakes is thought to proceed in a distinctive manner. To begin with, the lake may be irregular in shape; however, it rapidly assumes a circular and smooth form through thaw of the permafrost combined with undercutting of the vegetation, causing collapse and retreat of the bank. As such, thaw ponds are dynamic features of the tundra landscape. In Alaska, average annual rates of bank retreat vary from 15 to 20 cm per year according to Wallace (1948), depending upon the strength and persistence of wave (wind) action, and the temperature of the water, among others. Hopkins (1949) outlined an idealized growth cycle from youth to old age. In essence, the thaw lakes grow in size to begin with, coalescing with adjacent lakes. As the thaw lake migrates, the old lake bed emerges as a shallow depression. Tundra vegetation begins to develop upon the newly exposed and silty lake floor and organic matter begins to accumulate. At the same time the lake itself slowly begins to infill with

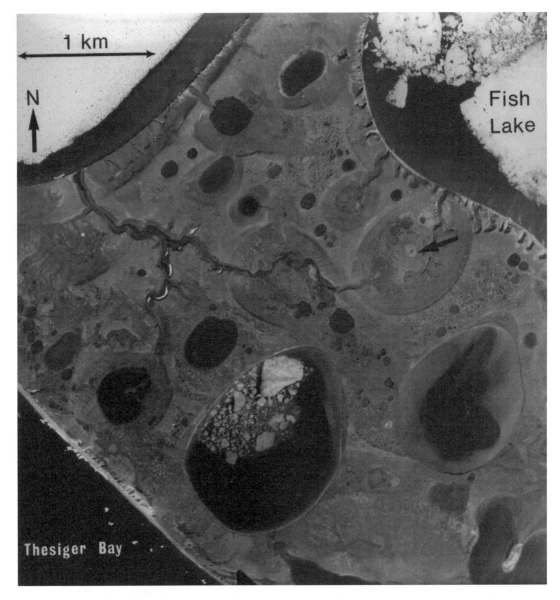

Figure 7.10   Vertical air photo of part of the Sachs River lowlands showing thaw lake terrain. Note the elliptical, D-shaped orientation of many of the lakes, and the drained lake basins, one of which possesses a small pingo (arrow). (Air photograph A 15980–25, National Air Photo Library, Natural Resources, Canada, Ottawa.)

silt and organic matter. Alternatively, the lake basin can be emptied catastrophically by the expansion of an adjacent depression. Often, tapping occurs through erosion along ice-wedge systems (Walker, 1978). Subsequently, ice segregation and heave takes place on the floor of the depression, and solifluction and mass-wasting takes place upon the banks,

moving material into the depression. Ultimately, the depression and all traces of the former lake and lake basin may be obliterated from the landscape.

The growth, drainage and rebirth of small thaw lakes and depressions as described above is thought to complete itself within 2000 to 3000 years. In the Barrow region of Alaska, ^{14}C dating of organic matter in two drained lake basins suggests ages of several thousand years (Black, 1969). In the Umiat region, Tedrow (1969) has dated material from a level within a thaw depression at approximately 4500 years old and to be some 4000 years younger than the initial surface in which the thaw depression first developed. These dates give some idea as to the relative magnitude and rapidity of the thaw lake cycle.

7.6.2 Oriented thaw lakes

One of the more perplexing aspects of thaw lakes is that they are often elongate in shape, with a common and systematic orientation of the long axis (e.g. Fig. 7.10). The thaw lakes of the Point Barrow region are exceptionally good examples of this phenomenon and possess long axis orientations approximately N9W–N21W (Carson and Hussey, 1963). Other oriented lakes have been described along the Arctic coastal plain (e.g. Black and Barksdale, 1949; Mackay, 1963) as well as in the interior Yukon (Price, 1968), southwest Banks Island (Harry and French, 1983), and in other parts of Arctic Canada (e.g. Dunbar and Greenaway, 1956, pp. 132–134; Bird, 1967, pp. 212–216). They also occur on the alluvial lowlands of northern Siberia (Tomirdiaro and Ryabchun, 1978).

A variety of oriented forms can be recognized. For example, in northern Alaska, the lakes are commonly elliptical or rectangular in shape, ranging in size from small ponds to large lakes 15 km long and 6 km wide (Black and Barksdale, 1949). In Alaska the ratio of length to breadth varies from 1 : 1 to 1 : 5. The depths of the lakes suggest two varieties: (a) with a shallow shelf surrounding a deeper central part, which may be 6–10 m deep, and (b) with a uniform saucer-shaped cross profile with depths of less than 2 m. In the Tuktoyaktuk Peninsula of the Mackenzie Delta, there are numerous very similar oriented lakes (Mackay, 1963). Their shape has been classified as being either lemniscate, oval, triangular or elliptical. On southwest Banks Island, the lakes assume a D-shape (Harry and French, 1983). In western Baffin Island, however, in the eastern Arctic, on the Great Plain of Koukdjuak, many thaw lakes are clam-shaped with one straight edge and with length:breadth ratios varying between 1.5:2.5 and 1.5:1 (Bird, 1967, p. 215).

The cause of the orientation of thaw lakes has attracted considerable controversy. In most cases, the long axes of the lakes are at right angles to the present-day prevailing winds, and some relationship between the two variables is clearly apparent.

However, the problem is not simple since oriented lakes are not solely a feature of the periglacial environment. Many are found in other morpho-climatic regions (e.g. Price, 1968). At the same time, it is clear that oriented lakes are of a contemporary nature and are forming today under present periglacial climatic conditions, because they are sometimes found upon plains and terraces that have only recently emerged from beneath the sea. Mackay (1963) has concluded, in a general fashion, that the oriented lakes of the Mackenzie Delta area represent an equilibrium condition in response to the processes currently operating. Likewise, French and Harry (1983) talk of quasi-equilibrium. Others have focused attention upon the role of wind which either produces wave current systems which scour at right angles or deposits sediment on the east and west shores, insulating them from further thaw (e.g. Carson and Hussey, 1962). One suggestion is that wind-induced littoral drift reaches a maximum at the corner ends of lakes, and that the eroded materials are then distributed uniformly along the long axis shorelines. This explanation does not account for either the orientation of very small lakes where such circulation systems are not so well developed or for the lack of erosive currents at the ends until after the basin is elongate. Equally limiting are other explanations. For example, French and Harry (1983) conclude simply that a strong relationship exists between lake morphology and the storm wind regime during the summer period of open water conditions, and go no further in explanation, thus implicitly supporting the ideas of Carson and Hussey (1962) and others. Clearly, it is difficult to distinguish between cause and effect in the circulation pattern of oriented thaw lakes. More detailed studies are required concerning wave and current effects upon thaw versus transportation of sediment.

The question of thaw lake drainage is another interesting aspect of the thaw lake problem. Many thaw lakes are either partially or completely drained (e.g. see Fig. 7.10). Two contrasting modes of lake drainage have been suggested: either gradual infilling and sedimentation, or catastrophic outflow following lake tapping or truncation by coastal retreat (e.g. Mackay, 1979a, p. 31; Walker, 1978; Weller and Derksen, 1979). The latter is a specific permafrost-related process. Tapping usually occurs by headward erosion of streams along ice wedges, or by coastal retreat and truncation in certain instances. Once flow is initiated through the new outlet, drainage may be extremely rapid, resulting in the formation of box-canyon outlet channels characterized by steep lateral bluffs and flat floors. Under certain circumstances ground ice bodies may provide subsurface outlets for lake drainage. For example, one lake on southwest Banks Island experienced catastrophic subterranean drainage in the winter of 1987 (French and Harry, 1988). While this may be common in areas of thin or discontinuous permafrost, resulting in the formation of thaw sinks, it is rarely reported from areas of thick permafrost. In this case, lake drainage may have been initiated by thermal contraction cracking, allowing water to escape into an ice cave in underlying massive ice.

The concept of the thaw lake cycle, consisting of sequential stages of initiation, expansion and drainage is well established (e.g. Britton, 1967; Tedrow, 1969; Billings and Peterson, 1980; Everett, 1981). While it may be appropriate for northern Alaska where topography, climate and geology are reasonably uniform, this model is by no means universally applicable. It has also been suggested that the processes responsible for thaw lake orientation may also result in migration of the lake basins across the tundra surface (e.g. Tedrow, 1969; Tomirdiaro and Ryabchun, 1978). However, no geomorphic or stratigraphic evidence of this can be found in many areas of oriented thaw lakes and it seems best to conclude, following Mackay (1963), that thaw lakes are quasi-equilibrium landscape elements in most permafrost regions.

Figure 7.11   A thermo-erosional niche developed in sand and gravel, Ballast Brook, northwest Banks Island, Canada. The niche extends inwards for over 4 m. There is sloughing of material from the face and the building of a ridge of material at the foot which will ultimately cover and protect the niche.

7.7 Fluvio-thermal erosion

A rather specific type of lateral or backwearing thermokarst process occurs along river banks, large lakes and coasts. It combines both the thermal and fluvial erosive capacities of running water and is termed 'fluvio-thermal' erosion.

An important characteristic of the fluvial regime of many periglacial areas is the marked peak of surface runoff which occurs in the early weeks of summer (see Chapter 10). It reflects the rapid snowmelt at that time. A consequence is that floodwaters are capable of eroding river banks not only by normal, mechanical or abrasive means, but also by the thermal melting of the permafrost. In unconsolidated sediments, the result is the development of a 'thermo-erosional niche' at the flood water level (Fig. 7.11), which may extend beneath the banks for upwards of 10 m. Similar, if not larger, niches develop along coastal bluffs following high tides or storms. Subsequently, the undercut frozen sediments may collapse along a line of weakness, often an ice wedge, destroying the thermo-erosional niche. This process is common in many present-day periglacial regions and has been described by Péwé (1948) along the lower Yukon River near Galena in Alaska, by Walker and Arnborg (1966) in the Colville River Delta of northern Alaska, and by Czudek and Demek (1970) who give several illustrations of how this process operates along some of the major rivers in Siberia (Fig. 7.12). Even in Pleistocene periglacial environments, where, in all probability, the fluvial regime was rather different, fossil thermo-erosional niches and collapsed blocks have been identified (Dylik, 1969a). The development of a thermo-erosional niche and subsequent block collapse is an important mechanism of coastal erosion in many permafrost regions underlain by ice-rich unconsolidated sediments. For example, Are (1972) has described thermo-abrasion niches some 3 m high and 20 m deep occurring at the base of sea cliffs along the Laptev Sea and other areas of northern Siberia. In northern Alaska and in the Mackenzie Delta region of Canada a number of coastal erosion studies have also emphasized this process (e.g. Hume *et al.*, 1972; McDonald and Lewis, 1973; Harry *et al.*, 1983; Mackay, 1986a).

Two types of river bank modification were recognized by Walker and Arnborg (1966). The first, river bank sloughing, is the less important. In the first few weeks after the recession of the floodwaters, air temperatures rise and there is a thawing and sloughing from an oversteepened bank face. Sediment accumulates, therefore, in front of the niche, and may seal it until the following year. According to Walker and

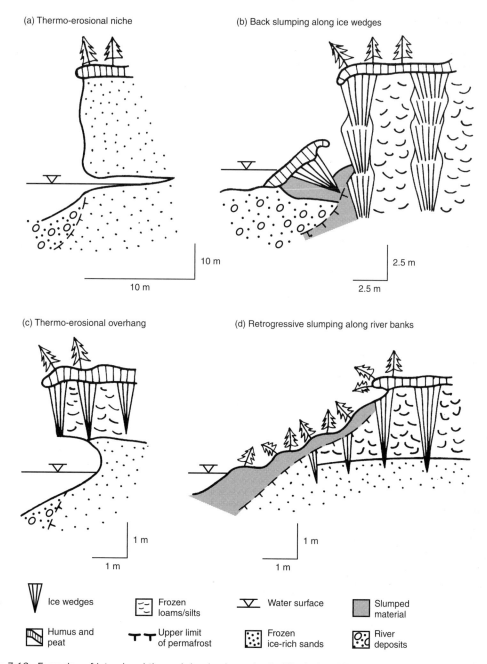

(a) Thermo-erosional niche

(b) Back slumping along ice wedges

10 m

10 m

2.5 m

2.5 m

(c) Thermo-erosional overhang

(d) Retrogressive slumping along river banks

1 m

1 m

1 m

1 m

| | Ice wedges | | Frozen loams/silts | | Water surface | | Slumped material |
| | Humus and peat | | Upper limit of permafrost | | Frozen ice-rich sands | | River deposits |

Figure 7.12 Examples of lateral and thermal river-bank erosion in Siberia (modified from Czudek and Demek, 1970).

Arnborg, bank sloughing does not account for more than 1 m of bank recession per year. By contrast, very rapid and drastic morphological change can result from the collapse of the overlying frozen sediments along the line of ice wedges which may parallel the river. In one instance, total bank retreat of over 10 m was observed in a two-day period.

Any discussion of thermal erosion within the periglacial environment should not restrict itself solely to the relationship of the thermo-erosional niche to coastal and river bank undercutting. Thermal erosion is but one aspect of fluvial erosion in general, and this topic is dealt with in Chapter 11. Also, thermal erosion is a factor influencing the nature of periglacial slopewash ('*ruissellement*'). The nature of slopes is discussed in Chapter 9. In fact, thermal erosion is intimately linked to the whole question of slope and valley development in periglacial environments. Finally, fluvio-thermal erosion is important in the rapid coastal retreat of unconsolidated ice-rich sediments (see Chapter 12).

7.8 Thermokarst involutions

During the degradation of ice-rich permafrost, thermokarst involutions may form. Typically, they take the form of load casts, pseudo-nodules, ball-and-pillow structures and diapirs. They form by a number of mechanisms, the most important being loading, buoyancy and water-escape. In dimensions, they vary from a few to 90 cm in width and from a few centimetres to several metres in depth. Murton and French (1993c) stress that there is nothing sedimentologically unusual about these involutions, similar structures having been observed in other depositional environments throughout the geological record.

To form thermokarst involutions, ice-rich permafrost must thaw, drainage conditions must be poor and sediments must vary in texture or composition. In addition, the sediments should be susceptible to fluidization, liquefaction or hydroplastic deformation. Those formed by loading and buoyancy require a reversed density gradient; those formed by fluidization require open-system groundwater conditions or associated water-saturated sediments susceptible to liquefaction.

Relatively few studies have described these phenomena from present permafrost environments, with the notable exceptions of French (1986) and Murton and French (1993c) from the western Canadian Arctic. On Banks Island, French (1986) refers to these features as 'periglacial involutions', formed by loading and liquefaction in the active layer in late summer with the underlying permafrost acting as a confining layer. By contrast, Murton and French (1993c) describe features occurring in a palaeo-thaw layer in the Pleistocene Mackenzie Delta.

Undoubtedly, some of the most detailed descriptions of thermokarst involutions are to be found in the Pleistocene periglacial literature, especially from northern Germany (e.g. Eissmann, 1978, 1994).

There, the occurrence of thick lignite beds meant that large ice lenses must have formed during permafrost conditions. When degradation occurred, extensive deformations resulted from water-escape and loading. These Pleistocene thermokarst structures are discussed more fully in Chapter 14, where the distinction is made between involutions (i.e. frost-disturbed soils and structures; section 14.3.5), and thermokarst soft-sediment deformations (section 14.7.2). These structures should also not be confused with those caused by cryoturbation; these are discussed in Chapter 8.

Further readings

Carson, C.E. and K.M. Hussey (1962) The oriented lakes of Arctic Alaska. *Journal of Geology*, **70**, 417–439.

Czudek, T. and J. Demek (1970) Thermokarst in Siberia and its influence on the development of lowland relief. *Quaternary Research*, **1**, 103–120.

French, H.M. (1974b) Active thermokarst processes, eastern Banks Island, Western Canadian Arctic. *Canadian Journal of Earth Sciences*, **11**, 785–794.

Harry, D.G. (1988) Ground ice and permafrost. In M.J. Clark (ed.), *Advances in periglacial geomorphology*, Chapter 6. Chichester: J. Wiley and Sons Ltd, pp. 113–149.

Mackay, J.R. (1970) Disturbances to the tundra and forest tundra environment of the western arctic. *Canadian Geotechnical Journal*, **7**, 420–432.

Murton J.B. and H.M. French (1993c) Thermokarst involutions, Summer Island, Pleistocene Mackenzie Delta, western Canadian Arctic. *Permafrost and Periglacial Processes*, **4**, 217–229.

Rampton, V.N. (1974) The influence of ground ice and thermokarst upon the geomorphology of the Mackenzie–Beaufort region. In: B.D. Fahey and R.D. Thompson (eds), *Research in Polar and Alpine Geomorphology*, Proceedings, 3rd Guelph Symposium on Geomorphology. Norwich: Geo Abstracts, pp. 45–59.

Discussion topics

1. What are the most common causes of thermokarst?

2. What happens when ice-rich permafrost degrades?

3. Discuss the origin of oriented thaw lakes.

4. Explain why thermokarst processes are some of the most important processes fashioning the lowland periglacial landscape.

CHAPTER 8

The active layer

The fact that the ground surface in permafrost regions is subject to annual thaw was well known to the early inhabitants and explorers of northern regions. Often, they preferred to travel overland during winter when the ground was frozen rather than in summer when the ground was soft and wet. Until relatively recently, however, the processes relating to the thermal and physico-mechanical properties of the active layer, in both its thawed and frozen states, were little known. In the past 15 years, the necessity to plan, design and construct major engineering structures, in both North America and the FSU (Former Soviet Union), has led to significant advances in our understanding of the permafrost active layer.

8.1 Definition

The active layer refers to the layer of ground in areas underlain by permafrost which is subject to annual freezing and thawing. As a rule, it is thinnest in polar regions (as little as 15 cm) and becomes thicker in sub-arctic regions (as much as 1.0 m or more). In the zone of continuous permafrost, it generally reaches the permafrost table. In the zone of discontinuous permafrost, it may be separated from the permafrost by a talik, or residual thaw layer. The thickness of the active layer may vary from year to year depending on the interaction of such factors as the ambient air temperature, degree and orientation of slope, vegetation, drainage, snow cover, soil and/or rock type, and water content.

The active layer includes the uppermost part of the permafrost wherever either the salinity or clay content of the permafrost allows it to thaw and refreeze annually, even though the material remains cryotic (i.e. below 0 °C). The term 'depth to permafrost' as a synonym for the thickness of the active layer is misleading, especially in areas where the active layer is separated from the permafrost by a thawed or non-cryotic (i.e. above 0 °C) layer of ground.

8.2 Thermal regime of the active layer

The freezing and thawing of the active layer occurs either on a diurnal basis, as in many temperate and subtropical regions, or on a seasonal basis, as in high latitudes. The depth of frost penetration depends mainly upon the intensity of cold, its duration, the thermal and physical properties of the soil and rock, the overlying vegetation and snowcover (if any).

In the field, the frost table can be located by probing with a metal rod to a resistant layer which is assumed to be the frost table. A simple but more permanent field device is the frost tube, developed by Mackay (1974a), in which a flexible inner tube is inserted within a more rigid PVC (poly(vinyl chloride)) outer tube installed in the permafrost. The inner tube is then filled with water and allowed to freeze, at which time marker objects (pebbles and sand) are dropped into the tube to rest upon the ice. As the active layer subsequently thaws, the objects descend in the tube, ultimately to mark the level of maximum thaw. Then, as upfreezing commences from the permafrost table, the sand particles are uplifted. Upon inspection the following year, both

Table 8.1 Typical values of soil diffusivity

	Thermal diffusivity (α) ($\times 10^{-6}$ m²/s)
(a) **Soil constituents**	
Quartz	4.14
Clay minerals	1.22
Organic matter	0.10
Water (0 °C)	0.13
Ice (0 °C)	1.16
(b) **Unfrozen soils** (40% porosity, water content 0.2 m³/m³)	
Sandy soil	0.85
Clay soil	0.53

Source: Johnston (1981); Williams and Smith (1989)

the maximum thaw depth and the amount of upfreezing can be determined.

The depth of seasonal freezing and thawing can be predicted by several indirect methods which use values of thermal conductivity for frozen soil and latent heat of water in the soil (Washburn, 1979, pp. 18–19). Gold and Lachenbruch (1973) provide an approximation of the active layer thickness, x (cm), with the following:

$$x = \sqrt{\alpha \, P/\pi \log e \mid A_0/T_0 \mid}$$ (8.1)

where α = soil thermal diffusivity, P = period of the temperature cycle, A_0 = surface temperature amplitude and T_0 = mean annual surface temperature. Typical values of soil diffusivity (m²/s) are listed in Table 8.1.

From a geomorphic viewpoint, the nature and rate of both the spring thaw and the autumn freezeback are of interest. The former influences the nature of spring runoff while the latter controls the nature of frost heaving and ice segregation in the soil. Usually, the spring thaw occurs quickly, and over three-quarters of the soil thaws during the first four or five weeks in which air temperatures are above 0 °C. It is important to note that thawing is one-sided, from the surface downwards.

Autumn freeze-back is a more complex process because in regions underlain by continuous permafrost, the freezing is two-sided, occurring both downwards from the surface and upwards from the perennially frozen ground beneath. Moreover, the freezing period is much longer and may persist for six to eight weeks. At Inuvik, NWT, for example, freezing begins in late September and only finishes in mid-December (e.g. Heginbottom, 1973; Mackay and MacKay, 1976). During the majority of this time the

soil remains in a near-isothermal condition, sometimes referred to as the 'zero curtain'. This phenomenon results from the release of latent heat upon freezing, thereby retarding the drop in temperature. Initially, freezing progresses at a slow rate from the surface downwards, but then dramatically speeds up at depth. This is because of (a) the occurrence of upward freezing from the permafrost beneath (Mackay 1973c, 1974a) and (b) the fact that moisture decreases with depth since soil water is initially drawn upwards to the freezing plane, thereby preferentially increasing the latent heat effects in the surface layers.

Ground thermal regimes are also closely related to snow thickness and density. This has been illustrated earlier with data from Churchill, Manitoba (see Chapter 4) and is now illustrated with further data from the vicinity of Thompson, Manitoba, located in the discontinuous permafrost zone of Canada (Brown and Williams, 1972; Goodrich, 1982) (Fig. 8.1). In summary, years of heavy snowfall retard thaw yet prevent extremes of ground freezing. Also, extremely subtle terrain differences can have an important influence upon the ground temperature regime. At Thompson, for example, only two of the four sites monitored in 1968 were underlain by permafrost, despite apparently similar terrain and vegetation conditions. By the third year of monitoring (1971) the permafrost at one site had degraded, probably in response to snowmelt seepage along the daily track followed by the technician.

The actual formation and growth of an active layer has been monitored at the Illisarvik experimental drained lake site in the Mackenzie Delta region, Canada (Mackay, 1982). Following drainage in 1978, permafrost commenced to grow downwards in the first winter on the exposed lake bottom. Contrary to

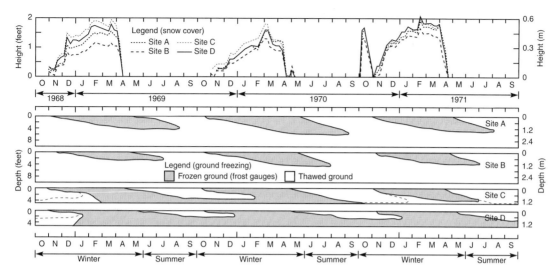

Figure 8.1 Ground thermal regimes in the active layer at four closely spaced sites near Thompson, Manitoba, 1968–71. Only two sites are underlain by permafrost. Note that at site C the permafrost degraded during the period of measurement (data from Brown and Williams, 1972).

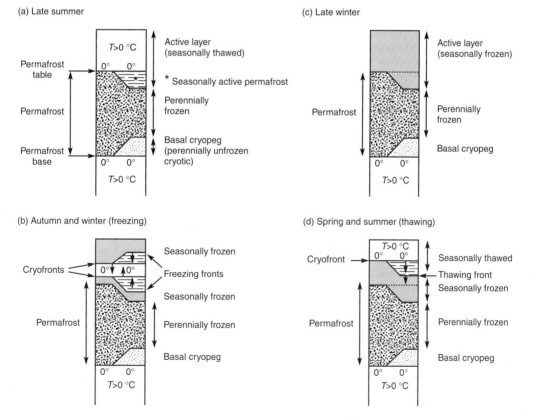

Figure 8.2 Seasonal changes (a–d) in the active layer. The temperature relative to 0 °C and the state of water are also indicated (*source*: ACGR, 1988).

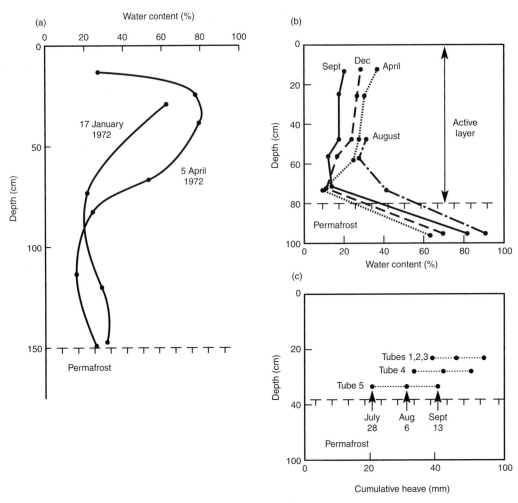

Figure 8.3 Seasonal changes in moisture content in the active layer, as reported from China, Siberia and North America: (a) changes in water content in winter 1972 in No. 2 experimental embankment at Reshui Qiliar Shan, People's Republic of China (from Cheng, 1983); (b) seasonal changes in water content for the active layer and top of permafrost, Siberia (from Parmuzina, 1978); (c) 1978 summer movement of active layer heavemeters installed at Garry Island, Mackenzie Delta region, Canada (from Mackay, 1983).

what might have been anticipated, the active layer depth showed no decrease in response to the growth of permafrost in the first three years. The absence of a thinning trend is attributed to warm (i.e. −1.5 to −3.0 °C) subjacent permafrost temperatures which result from two heat sources – the active layer above and the former sub-lake-bottom talik, whether frozen or unfrozen. However, further data upon active layer growth from year 'one' for a number of environments are required before a more complete understanding can be obtained.

8.3 Unfrozen water in freezing and frozen soils

A complicating factor in our understanding of the active layer relates to the presence of moisture within the active layer (see Chapter 4). Not all water freezes at 0 °C and, in certain frost-susceptible soils, as much as 40 per cent of the water content may remain unfrozen at −1.0 °C (e.g. Williams, 1976, 1977).

In the context of the active layer, one must differentiate, therefore, between the seasonally thawed layer possessing a temperature > 0 °C (i.e. seasonally

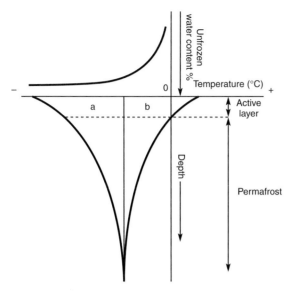

Figure 8.4 Relationship between ground temperature envelopes and curves of unfrozen water content versus temperature of frozen soil: (a) region of positive ground temperature gradient; (b) region of negative ground temperature gradient (from Cheng, 1983).

cryotic) and the upper layer of permafrost which thaws seasonally but remains below 0 °C (i.e. seasonally active permafrost). Equally, it is useful to distinguish between the *freezing front* (the boundary between frozen and unfrozen soil) and the *cryofront* (the 0 °C boundary) when considering the freezing of the active layer in the fall and winter. In the case of spring and summer thaw, the distinction must be between the *cryofront* and the *thawing front* (the boundary between seasonally frozen and seasonally thawed soil). The seasonal dynamics of the active layer are illustrated in Fig. 8.2 where use of these terms is indicated.

It is also known that unfrozen water in frozen ground can move in the direction along which the ground temperature decreases in response to an imposed thermal gradient (see Chapter 4). This has important implications for the ice distribution within the active layer when frozen, and for water migration when the active layer is in its thawed, or thawing, state. For example, the ice content in the upper part of the active layer will increase when a positive ground temperature gradient occurs in winter (i.e. the ground is warmer than the air). Field data presented by Parmuzina (1978), Cheng (1983) and Mackay (1983) provide convincing proof that significant changes in water (ice) content occur in the active layer in the winter months

(Fig. 8.3). For the same reasons, in summer, under a negative ground temperature gradient, unfrozen water will migrate downwards, and the ice content in the upper part of permafrost will increase. Late summer heaving of the active layer also occurs (Mackay, 1983). These observations explain the well-known facts that the highest ground ice amounts usually occur in the top 1–5 m of permafrost (see Chapter 6), and that an ice-rich zone often characterizes the boundary between the base of the active layer (the seasonally active permafrost) and the perennially frozen permafrost (e.g. Vtyurina, 1974; Ershov, 1979; Ershov *et al.*, 1980; Mackay, 1981; Shur, 1988). As illustrated in Fig. 8.4, the upward and downward movements of unfrozen water in the active layer in any one year are not equal. The upward migration of unfrozen pore water takes place in the time period when there is a low unfrozen pore water content (i.e. in winter, Region A, Fig. 8.4). By contrast, the amount of downward migration of unfrozen pore water caused by the negative ground temperature gradient (i.e. in summer, Region B, Fig. 8.4) is greater. The net result is that more water migrates downward to the permafrost in the thaw cycle than migrates upward in the freezing cycle.

8.4 Frost heave

Intimately associated with the freezing of the active layer is the phenomenon of frost heave. This occurs wherever moisture is present and where sediments are frost-susceptible. Annual ground displacements of several centimetres (Table 8.2) with cyclic differential ground pressures of many kilopascals per square centimetre are common. Engineering hazards due to these displacements and pressures, together with the adverse effects of accumulations of segregated ice in freezing soil, are widespread and costly. Frost heave problems are often encountered in the construction and maintenance of roads, buildings and pipelines in cold environments. These aspects are considered in Part 4.

8.4.1 Primary and secondary heave

Based upon theoretical considerations and detailed field measurements, two types of frost heave can be recognized. These are primary (i.e. capillary) and secondary heave (Miller, 1972; Smith, 1985a). In primary heave, the critical conditions for the growth of segregated ice are:

Table 8.2 Some typical frost heave values recorded in a number of different localities

Location	Climatic Type	Year of Record	Site Characteristics		Total Heave, per year (cm)
Mesters Vig, Greenland,[1] 72°N	High Arctic	1958–64	Slopes (a) 'Wet' (b) 'Dry'	Depth 10 cm 20 cm 10 cm 20 cm	0.0–1.0 1.5–5.8 0.5–0.7 0.8–1.4
Signy Island, South Orkney Islands,[2] 61°S	Low-temperature range	1964	Sorted circle, highly frost-susceptible (a) Surface (b) Buried (c) On stones (d) At edge		4.0 0.4 3.6 2.0
Colorado Front Range, USA,[3] 39°N	Alpine	1969–70	Frost boil; highly frost-susceptible. Surface		25.0–29.5
Cape Thompson, Alaska,[4] 70°N	High Arctic		Frost boil; highly frost-susceptible		32.5
Inuvik, Mackenzie Delta,[5] 69°S	High Arctic	1976–78	Mud hummocks (a) Undisturbed (b) Disturbed		10.3 14.0
Mackenzie Delta[6]	High Arctic	1983–84	Silty clay mud hummocks	Depth 0.20 cm 20–40 cm 40–60 cm 60–80 cm	1.4–1.6 0.9–1.0 0.8–1.6 −0.2–+0.2
Mackenzie Delta[7]	High Arctic	1987–88	Lake bottom sediments		9.4–20.5
Sor-Rondane Mountains,[8] Antarctica, 72°S	High Arctic	1987	Ridge site	Diurnal heave > 0.2 mm <1.8 mm occurred 12 times	
Alberta Rockies,[9] 50°N	Alpine	1980–82	Sloping terrain; non-sorted circle		2.0–4.5
Qinghai-Xizang (Tibet) Plateau[10]	n/a	1991–92	Sloping terrain (4 sites)		4.3–7.7

Sources: (1) Washburn (1969); (2) Chambers (1967); (3) Fahey (1974); (4) Everett (1965); (5) Mackay *et al.* (1979); (6) Smith (1985b); (7) Burn (1989); (8) Matsuoka *et al.* (1988); (9) Smith (1987); (10) Wang and French (1995a).

$$P_1 - P_w = \frac{2\sigma}{r_{1w}} < \frac{2\sigma}{r} \qquad (8.2)$$

where P_1 is pressure of ice, P_w is pressure of water, σ is the surface tension between ice and water, r_{1w} is the radius of the ice–water interface, and r is the radius of the largest continuous pore openings. Primary heave occurs predominantly in the autumn freeze-back period and is related to the volumetric expansion of water as it freezes combined with the growth of segregational ice lenses.

Secondary heave is not so clearly understood, but occurs at temperatures below 0 °C and at same distance behind the freezing front. Secondary heave is associated with unstable conditions in a cryogenic zone immediately adjacent to the frost line which Miller (1972) terms 'the frozen fringe'. It also refers to water redistribution within existing frozen ground. Figure 8.5 schematically

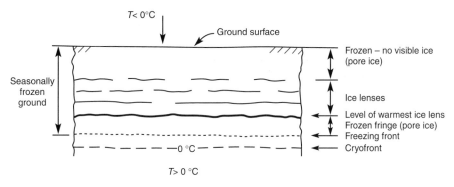

Figure 8.5 Diagram showing the relative positions of the frozen fringe, the freezing front and the cryofront during freezing of a fine-grained, frost-susceptible soil (*Source*: ACGR, 1988).

illustrates the position of the frozen fringe, the freezing front, and the cryofront during the freezing of a fine-grained frost-susceptible soil. It follows that, while primary heave is, by definition, largely associated with the active layer (or seasonally freezing ground), secondary heave occurs not only in the (frozen) active layer but also in the underlying permafrost.

Telescoping tubes, termed heavemeters, are commonly used to measure primary frost heave in the field. Since the tubes are inserted to different depths, differential heave can be measured. When temperatures are also measured, it is then possible to relate the heave to the time of freezing, and to temperature. For example, in the Mackenzie Delta region, several field studies using heavemeters have demonstrated conclusively that heave occurs not only during the autumn freeze-back (i.e. primary heave), but also during winter when ground temperatures are below 0 °C (e.g. Mackay *et al.*, 1979; Smith, 1985b).

The actual measurement of frost heave within frozen ground can be achieved using a magnet probe to measure the separation distances between a series of magnets placed adjacent to an access tube and firmly embedded in permafrost (Mackay and Leslie, 1987). For example, at Illisavik, Mackay's experimental drained lake site in the Mackenzie Delta region, two magnets were installed at depths of 40 and 58 cm in an earth hummock. Between 8 April and 30 May, 1984, when the ground was still frozen, the separation of the two magnets increased by 1.25 cm. Under certain circumstances, therefore, the *in situ* heave of frozen soil is considerable.

8.4.2 Bedrock heave

The frost heaving of coherent bedrock is a widespread process in permafrost regions. Depending upon the pre-existing fracture characteristics of the bedrock, the geomorphic expression of bedrock heave can vary from single ejected blocks (Fig. 8.6) to dome-shaped accumulations up to several metres in diameter. According to L.S. Dyke (1984) yearly movements may be as much as 5 cm, horizontally and vertically. As such, even compact sedimentary strata or igneous bedrock may experience deformation sufficient to damage structures preferentially located upon these (assumed) firm foundations.

The interaction between the bedrock and groundwater controls the nature of bedrock heave (Fig. 8.7). Usually, the upward displacement is the result of excess water pressures created in the zone between the permafrost table and downward freezing. Where the saturated zone in the active layer becomes confined by the downward-advancing freezing front, the attempted expulsion of water supplies the heaving force. This is usually relieved along joints and bedding planes. Bedrock heave is particularly favoured where the water table lies close to the surface in massive granites, gneisses and quartzites, such as the Canadian Shield and similar areas. In such terrain, it is not uncommon for the active layer to be several metres in thickness.

The main resistance to heave is offered by the weight and the shear resistance of the overlying ice-bonded rock mass. Also, the behaviour of frost-heaved bedrock blocks is influenced by the ice-filling material, such that deformation is of a plastic nature. Laboratory experiments (Michaud and Dyke, 1990) suggest that the vertical displacement of bedrock blocks is characterized by a progressive (increase through time) and relatively slow movement (up to months). Thus, bedrock heave is different from the normal frost heave in soils discussed in the preceding section.

Figure 8.6 Bedrock heave in Palaeozoic greywacke, near Churchill, Manitoba.

Bedrock heave can also be discussed within the context of frost weathering. For example, the varying rates of frost rupturing and dislocation of bedrock on different morphostratigraphic units on Baffins Island has been considered by A.S. Dyke (1978). There, it appears that 5000–10 000 years are required to produce relatively minor disruptions of gneissic bedrock terrain. However, where such terrain has been exposed to subaerial weathering for 20 000 to 40 000 years bedrock blocks are commonly heaved in excess of 1.0 m and the bedrock surface is mantled with felsenmeer. It follows that while bedrock terrain much disrupted by bedrock heave may reflect its enhanced susceptibility to such a process, it may equally reflect a very much older stage of landscape evolution.

8.4.3 Upfreezing of stones and objects

In addition to the general heaving of the mineral soil consequent upon ice segregation, the progressive upward movement of stone and objects is a further characteristic of frost heaving. This process is called upfreezing, and appears to be common in sediments which possess coarser particles in association with an appreciable content of fines.

The mechanics of upfreezing are still not completely understood. However, at least two different hypotheses have been suggested. The 'frost-pull' hypothesis involves the assumption that, as the ground freezes from the top downwards, the top of a pebble or coarser particle is gripped by the advancing freezing plane and raised in conjunction with the overall heave that is associated with the freezing of the overlying sediments. Upon thawing, the pebble is not able to return to its initial position because (a) lateral frost

heaving (frost thrusting) during the freezing process would have compressed the hollow originally occupied by the pebble, and (b) during thawing, material would have slumped into the hollow.

Partial support for this process is provided from field experiments by Chambers (1967, pp. 18–19). In one location, a series of stakes was inserted vertically to depths of 10–100 cm in a large sorted circle. At each depth, two stakes were inserted, one with a sharpened end and one with a blunt end. All pairs of stakes showed identical uplift, indicating that the force which uplifted the stakes came from the sides. On the other hand, the frost-pull hypothesis is not completely adequate to explain the mean annual movement with depth as shown in Table 8.3. Theoretically, the stakes should be gripped by the fines at the extreme surface when freezing first started so that the stakes should be drawn upwards as the surface was lifted. The amount of uplift of any stake should be related to the depth of insertion in the ground; as the freezing plane reached the base of each stake, differential movement would cease and both fines and stakes would have been uplifted together. The deepest stakes should, therefore, be uplifted the greatest. The results indicate, however, that the maximum uplift occurred at depths of 15–20 cm and that movement at depths below 20 cm actually decreased.

A second explanation for the upfreezing of objects has been termed the 'frost-push' hypothesis. According to this theory, upfreezing is the result of the greater thermal conductivity of stones resulting in the formation of ice around and beneath the stones. This ice forces the pebble upwards. Upon thawing, as in the frost-pull hypothesis, the infill of fines beneath the pebble prevents its return to its original position. Experimental work has shown that this process is viable, especially in instances of numerous freeze–thaw cycles and rapid upfreezing (Corte, 1966).

Both the 'frost-pull' and 'frost-push' hypotheses are based on the assumption that ice lenses grow on the cold (freezing) side of the object with water migration from the warm (unfrozen) side. However, the recognition of two-sided freezing of the active layer, whereby the active layer freezes not only from the surface downwards but also from the late summer frost table upwards means that these conventional theories cannot be directly applied to upward freezing. This is because the vertical direction of thaw and gravity cannot be reversed. In addition, the possibility of downward water movement in summer from the thawed active layer into

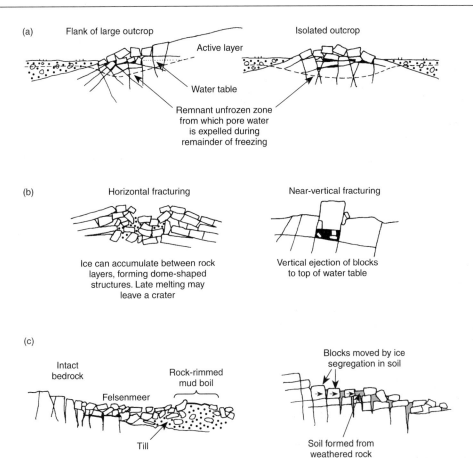

Figure 8.7 Examples of bedrock heave (from Dyke, 1984). Schematic diagram illustrating frost heaving of bedrock: (a) water expulsion mechanism in well-indurated rock with relatively thick active layer (mainland Canadian Shield); (b) influence of fracture fabric on heaving style; (c) ice-segregation mechanism displaces rock either by freeze–thaw creep of rock transported to a soil surface or by direct application of pressure applied by ice segregation in weathering products.

the lower portion of the frozen active layer, where refreezing and associated ice lensing and heaving may occur, complicates the process. Mackay (1984) concludes that the unfreezing of objects must be considered within the context of several variables which include (a) the direction of freezing, either upwards or downwards, (b) the degree of frost susceptibility of the enclosing soil and (c) the degree of frost-susceptibility of the object concerned.

A common surface microfeature of many areas subject to frost action is the presence of tilted stones, often standing on end (Fig. 8.8 (a)). This phenomenon is the result of differential frost heave at the top and bottom of the stone resulting in a rotation and tilting of the

axis. The probable mechanism is illustrated in Fig. 8.8(b). As the ground freezes from the surface downwards, the top of a stone at or near the ground surface is gripped by the freezing layer and subject to frost heave (i.e. 'frost-pull'). The lower part of the stone remains within the unfrozen zone and is not subject to heave. Thus the stone experiences differential movement with the greatest vertical movement near the surface. Depending upon the viscosity and other strength parameters of the unfrozen material, the axis of the stone undergoes rotation and there will be some readjustment of the object at depth. When all of the stone is totally within the frozen layer, there will no longer be any differential heave and rotation, and tilt-

Table 8.3 Values of upfreezing of wooden stakes and stones inserted to various depths

Depth (cm)	Upward Movement, 1962 (cm)	Upward Movement, 1963 (cm)	Mean Movement (cm/year)
Stones			
10–15	–	5.0	5.0
Stakes			
10	4.0	5.0	4.5
15	5.0	6.0	5.5
50	5.0	6.0	5.5
25	2.0	4.0	3.0
50	1.0	3.0	2.0
100	1.0	2.0	1.5

Source: data from Chambers (1967)

(a)

Figure 8.8 Stone tilting: (a) uptilted siltstone and sandstone slabs of Weatherall Formation (late Devonian age), near Rea Point, Eastern Melville Island; (b) diagrammatic illustration of the mechanism by which a stone becomes tilted through frost heaving of the ground (from Pissart, 1970).

(b)

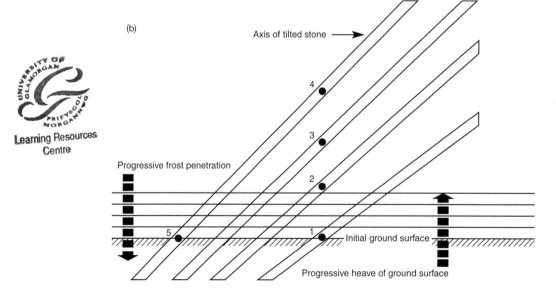

ing will cease, although frost heave and upward movement of the soil in general may continue as the frost penetrates deeper. Upon thawing of the ground, again from the surface downwards, the stone is prevented from returning to its original inclination by the settling of thawed sediments. Thus, with repeated cycles of freezing and thawing, there is a progressive increase in the angle of the axis of many stones towards the vertical, as well as a progressive upward movement of the stones in general.

It follows that the upward tilting of pebbles is a characteristic of cold-climate slope deposits. Angles of between 25° and 45° from the horizontal are most common since higher angles are prevented by gravity-influenced mass wasting process, mainly solifluction, in the seasonally thawed layer. The fabric of many periglacial slope deposits is distinctive therefore, in that (a) the long axes of clasts are oriented downslope and (b) the clasts are tilted upwards towards the surface at their downslope end (see Fig. 9.4).

An interesting, but small-scale, heave (upfreezing) phenomenon produced by diurnal one-sided freezing at or just beneath the ground surface is the formation of needle ice. Delicate vertical ice crystals grow upwards in the direction of heat loss and can range in length from a few millimetres to several centimetres. Occasionally, they may lift small pebbles or, more commonly, soil particles. Needle ice formation is particularly common wherever wet, silty frost-susceptible soils are present. The thawing and collapse of needle ice is thought significant in frost sorting, frost creep, the differential downslope movement of fine and coarse material, and the origin of certain micro-patterned ground forms (e.g. Pissart, 1977). The importance of needle ice as a disruptive agent in the soil has probably been underestimated, especially in exposing soils to wind action, deflation and cryoturbation activity. In some areas, it may be responsible for damage to plants when freezing causes vertical mechanical stresses within the root zone (e.g. Brink *et al.*, 1967). In the coast range of British Columbia, needle ice occurs in oriented stripes (Mackay and Mathews, 1974), and both wind direction and solar radiation have been suggested as explanations. However, it is not clear whether oriented needle ice is primarily a shadow effect, developed by thawing, or a freezing effect.

8.4.4 Frost sorting

Frost sorting is a complex process by which migrating particles are sorted into uniform particle sizes.

Often, a number of other frost-related processes, such as needle ice and frost heaving, contribute to the sorting process. The complexity of the sorting process is probably best illustrated by the varieties of patterned ground that exist. These are discussed later in this chapter.

Several laboratory experiments have examined the frost sorting process particularly as it relates to freeze–thaw. Some of the earliest were by Corte (1966). He concluded that the movement of particles depends on the amount of moisture present, the rate of freezing, the particle size distribution and the orientation of the freeze–thaw plane. Three types of sorting mechanisms can be simulated under laboratory conditions:

1. Sorting by uplift (i.e. frost heaving), when freezing and thawing occurs from the top. The larger particles move upwards, the smaller move downwards. This is called vertical sorting and gives horizontally bedded layers of different particle size.

2. Sorting by migration in front of a moving freezing plane, when freezing and thawing occurs from either the top or the sides. Under such conditions the finer particles migrate away from the advancing freezing plane, and the coarser particles are left nearest the cooling side. This is called lateral sorting. If the freezing takes place from the sides it can produce vertical layers of different particle sizes.

3. Mechanical sorting occurs when mounds and frost-heaved structures are produced. The coarser particles migrate under gravitational influences to form borders of coarser material surrounding finer sediment.

Vertical sorting has already been discussed under frost heaving and upfreezing, and needs little further explanation. Likewise, mechanical sorting is an easily understood concept. However, neither process is able to explain the variety of sorting phenomena observed in periglacial regions, and attention must focus, therefore, upon lateral sorting. Experiments have shown that fine particles migrate under a wider range of freezing rates than coarser particles. Below a certain freezing rate, finer particles travel more than coarser ones. This means that a heterogeneous material inevitably becomes sorted by freezing. Corte (1971) has also demonstrated how side freezing can change vertical sorting of material into lateral sorting. In one series of experiments vertical sorting was simulated in shallow trays by placing layers of different particle sizes on top of each other. In one experiment, three types of

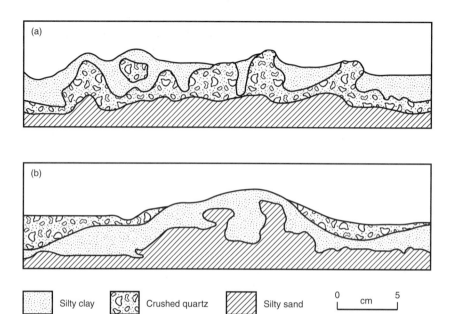

Silty clay   Crushed quartz   Silty sand

0   cm   5

Figure 8.9 Section through extrusion features developed after repeated freezing and thawing in a tray of layered sediments. (a) crushed quartz was the middle layer; (b) silt was the middle layer (from Corte, 1971).

sediment were used; two, a silty clay and a silty sand, were frost-susceptible, while the third, a crushed quartz of sandy silt size, was less so. The samples were placed in the trays with different vertical arrangements. Where the crushed quartz was the middle layer, a hummocky topography progressively developed after 28 freeze–thaw cycles and by cycle 57 sand particles were extruded to the surface of some of the mounds from the lower layers (Fig. 8.9). In another experiment where the quartz was the surface layer, a single dome developed after 57 cycles by extrusion from the finer layers below. The coarser surface sediments moved to the sides, thus forming a simple sorted circle.

More recent experiments by van Vliet-Lanoë (1988, 1991) emphasize the importance of negative frost-susceptibility gradients in producing differential frost heave and sorting. In van Vliet-Lanoë's experiments, small mounds formed where the surface soils were less frost-susceptible than the underlying soils (i.e. under a negative frost-susceptibility gradient). The underlying materials heaved more and were injected upwards, exploiting mechanical weaknesses, to burst to the surface to form mud boils or coalescing sorted circles. Field observations upon hummocks on Svalbard are thought to conform with this model.

From these and similar experiments conducted elsewhere, a number of conclusions can be drawn as regards the mechanism of frost sorting.

1. Sorting decreases as the moisture supply decreases.

2. Sorting develops best under conditions of slow freezing rates and saturated soils. Heterogeneous sediments subject to fast freezing rates will produce little sorting in comparison to the same sediment subject to very slow freezing.

3. Fine particles can be sorted under a wider range of freezing rates than coarser particles.

4. By changing the orientation of the freeze–thaw plane, it is possible to change vertical sorting (i.e. horizontally bedded and sorted layers) into lateral sorting (i.e. vertically sorted layers).

5. Horizontal layers of fine particles produced by vertical sorting can become dome-shaped when subject to a vertical freeze–thaw plane (i.e. when freezing takes place from the sides.

These conclusions should be treated with caution since there may be other processes of sorting which have not been examined. Moreover, the role of frost sorting in the formation of patterned ground requires continued laboratory experimentation and detailed field investigation.

8.5 Thaw consolidation

An important cause of instability in the active layer is associated with the time-dependent compression of frozen ground which results from thawing of the ground and the subsequent drainage of pore water. This process, which occurs annually in the active layer, is termed thaw consolidation (Morgenstern and Nixon, 1971). Many geotechnical engineers working in permafrost regions (e.g. McRoberts and Morgenstern, 1974) or upon slope stability problems of strata previously frozen (e.g. Hutchinson, 1974; Hutchinson and Gostelow, 1976) regard gelifluction as one form of thaw consolidation. In all probability, a process continuum exists between slow mass wasting and certain rapid mass movements (see Chapter 9) with thaw consolidation being the central, common mechanism.

The significance of thaw consolidation has yet to be fully appreciated by many geomorphologists working in permafrost regions and some additional words of explanation are appropriate. During thaw the flow of water from a thawing soil can be unimpeded. In this situation the variation of settlement with time is controlled solely by the position of the thawing front. However, if a thawed soil is not sufficiently coarse grained, and flow is impeded, the rate of settlement with time is controlled by the compressibility and permeability of the thawed ground. In the case of thawing fine-grained soils, if the rate of thaw is sufficiently fast, water is released at a rate exceeding that at which it can flow from the soil. This increases the pore water pressures which in turn may cause instability on slopes.

The excess pore pressures required and the degree of consolidation in thawing soils depend principally on the thaw consolidation ratio (Morgenstern and Nixon, 1971; Nixon and McRoberts, 1973). This is a measure of the relative rates of generation and expulsion of excess pore fluids during thaw. According to Morgenstern and Nixon (1971), a value of the ratio greater than unity predicts the danger of sustained substantial pore pressure at the thawing front, and hence the possibility of instability due to reduction of shear strength at that plane. Certain rapid mass movements, common to many tundra regions, can probably be explained within the context of thaw

consolidation, especially when they occur on very low-angled slopes. Under such conditions, the permafrost table acts as a lubricated slip plane and controls the depth of the failure plane. Such failures, termed 'skin flows' (e.g. Capps, 1919), or 'active layer detachment failures' (e.g. Hughes, 1972a), are attributed either (a) to local conditions of soil moisture saturation following summer precipitation or (b) to high pore water pressures which develop following exceptionally rapid or deep thaw. In all cases the active layer and its vegetation mat detaches from the underlying permafrost surface (Fig. 8.10). In some instances, failure takes the form of a mudflow; in others, a distinct slump scar or hollow is formed. In several of the Arctic islands, where the active layer is very thin and fine grained, ice-rich sediments are widespread, active layer failures are common and difficult to predict (e.g. Hodgson, 1982; Stangl et al., 1982; Lewkowicz, 1990). They also occur in the boreal forest zone of the Mackenzie Valley lowlands especially along river banks and on ice-rich colluvial slopes. It is not uncommon for failures to develop following the destruction of vegetation by forest fire (e.g. Zoltai and Pettapiece, 1973). Where substantial bodies of ground ice are exposed in the slump, the failure may be the trigger mechanism for retrogressive thaw slumps (e.g. French, 1974b).

8.6 Thermally induced mass displacements

If frozen ground contracts as temperature drops below zero, it follows that it subsequently expands as temperature rises. The same is true for soil in the active layer during the summer, although little is known about such thermally induced movements.

Thermally induced mass displacements in the active layer have been inferred from direct field measurement. At Garry Island for example, Mackay (1980a) observed how cavities formed preferentially on one side of rigid steel tubes inserted into the permafrost to monitor ice-wedge growth (see Chapter 6). The cavities were restricted to the active layer and decreased in size from the surface downwards. It is clear that they were not caused by heating or cooling to the ground by the tubes because they were not related to orientation, nor were they preferentially located on the upslope side of the tube and the result of either slumping or gelifluction. At the specific site examined by Mackay, the movement appeared to be radially outwards from polygon centres.

(a)

(b)

Figure 8.10   Examples of rapid mass movements occurring in summer and confined to the active layer, western Canadian Arctic. (a) detachment failure occurring on very low-angled slope, eastern Melville Island, NWT; (b) skin flows and multiple mudflows, Masik Valley, southern Banks Island, NWT.

The cavities indicate considerable mass transport of the active layer during the summer months since the cavities did not form in the underlying permafrost. The average net movement of the top of the active layer past the tubes, over a 13-year period of measurement, was 0.25 cm/year. Using this value, an approximation of the coefficient of thermal expansion (α) can be estimated:

$$\alpha = \frac{\delta}{L\,\Delta T} \qquad (8.3)$$

where δ is the observed expansion, L is the length over which the expansion occurs and ΔT is the tem-

perature change from the mean. Mackay (1980a) concludes that the calculated value for α ($1.7 \times 10^{-5}/\,^{\circ}C$) is of the correct order of magnitude.

Thus, limited evidence suggests that lateral movement of the active layer occurs in polygon flats and could be the result of summer warming. In theory, such movement should be widespread throughout the tundra and polar regions of the world; indeed, on hillslopes it would contribute significantly to downslope movement such as gelifluction. However, until more data are available, it seems best to regard thermally induced mass displacement as a potential, but largely unproven, cause of slow deformation in the active layer.

8.7   Cryoturbation and patterned ground

Most patterned ground phenomena occur within the active layer. But it must be emphasized that patterned ground may form in seasonally frozen ground also.

Patterned ground attracted much attention from the early explorers and scientists of the tundra and Arctic regions, who travelled on foot or by dog team. They had ample opportunity to obtain first hand acquaintance with such phenomena. The lack of vegetation made the various patternings of the ground particularly distinctive, and early botanical explorers quickly identified the intimate relationships existing between patterned ground and vegetation habitats. This early emphasis upon rather descriptive studies of patterned ground was unfortunate in that interest was directed away from the more fundamental aspects of the landscape such as slopes and rivers. A second reason for this early emphasis upon patterned ground studies was the recognition of active miniature forms in alpine locations in middle latitudes and the desire to make comparisons.

Although a voluminous literature describes patterned ground phenomena, the processes responsible for its formation still remain largely unproven. But there is certainly no lack of hypotheses; for example, in his classic review paper, Washburn (1956) listed no less that 19 hypotheses for patterned ground development.

After a seemingly long period in which relatively little progress was made in our understanding of patterned ground phenomena, the last 15 years has seen a range of new ideas, many based upon detailed field experiments, which now hint at several universal explanations (e.g. Mackay, 1980b; Krantz *et al.*, 1988; Gleason *et al.*, 1986; Hallett *et al.*, 1988; Hallet, 1990;

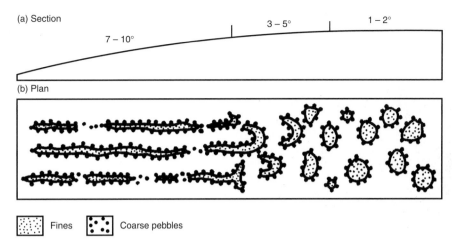

(a) Section

7 – 10°   3 – 5°   1 – 2°

(b) Plan

▨ Fines   ⊡ Coarse pebbles

Figure 8.11 Diagram illustrating the change from circles to stripes as slope angle increases, according to J. Büdel (1960).

Werner and Hallet, 1993). These important contributions are summarized later in this chapter.

The term cryoturbation is often used to explain patterned ground phenomena. Yet it commonly causes confusion since it has two meanings. The first (singular) uses cryoturbation as a collective term to describe all soil movements due to frost action. The second (plural) uses cryoturbation as a term to refer to irregular structures formed in soils by deep frost penetration and frost action processes. It is the first meaning (cryoturbation, singular) which is relevant here in the context of patterned ground. Cryoturbation includes frost heave, thaw settlement/consolidation, and all differential movements including contraction and expansion due to temperature changes and the growth and disappearance of (segregated) ice bodies. According to ACGR (1988), the water–ice phase change is necessary for cryoturbation and this distinguishes cryoturbation from other soil movement processes.

8.7.1 Description

The terminology proposed by Washburn to describe patterned ground is widely accepted since it is both simple and unambiguous. Patterned ground is classified on the basis of (a) its geometric form and (b) the presence or absence of sorting. The main geometric forms recognized are circles, polygons, stripes, nets and steps, all of which may be sorted and unsorted, thus giving ten principal categories of patterned ground. Circles, polygons and stripes are self-explanatory. A net refers to a mesh which is intermediate between a polygon and a circle in plan. A step is a bench-like feature with a downslope border of vegetation or stones embanking an area of relatively bare ground upslope. The relation between these various forms and angle of slope is illustrated in Fig. 8.11. Circles, polygons and nets usually occur on flat or nearly flat surfaces. As slope angle increases to 2–3°, however, these forms become elongated due to mass wasting and, depending upon local conditions, may change to stripes further down the slope. Steps are the transitional form in this sequence.

In detail, the main features of circles, polygons and stripes can be readily identified. Sorted circles are defined as features 'whose mash is dominantly circular and which have a sorted appearance commonly due to a border of stones surrounding fine materials' (Washburn, 1956, p. 827). They may occur singly or in groups, and commonly vary from 0.5 to 3.0 m in diameter. All varieties of sorted circles exist. For example, on steep, rubble-covered slopes concentrations of fine material may appear amid blocks and boulders. These are called 'debris islands'. Non-sorted circles are essentially similar to sorted circles except that they lack a border of stones. They are usually bounded by vegetation and give the appearance that the fine material of the central area has been intruded from below. A particularly striking non-sorted circle is illustrated in Fig. 8.12 (a). Here, the unvegetated central area of fines is completely surrounded by a closed rim of tussock grass. More

(a)

(b)

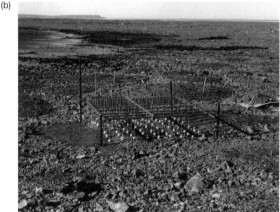

Figure 8.12 Examples of patterned ground:
(a) non-sorted circle surrounded by tussock
rim, Eastern Banks Island, NWT; (b) sorted
circles, Resolute Bay, NWT, site of
experimental studies by A. L. Washburn.
Vertical displacements within the circle at
varying depths are being measured by
free-moving rods (see Washburn, 1989).

typical are the sorted circles developed on silty grav-elly terrain shown in Fig. 8.12 (b).

Polygonal forms can be distinguished from circular ones. Non-sorted polygons lack a border of stones. They can be categorized into small forms (diameter less than 1.0 m) and large forms (diameter greater than 1.0–2.0 m). The large polygons, which often possess ice wedges along their borders, form the ice-wedge poly-gons (tundra or Taimyr polygons) which have been discussed at length in Chapter 6. The smaller non-sorted polygons commonly form meshes or nets over wide areas. They are delineated by furrows and cracks to give a hummocky micro-relief of between 0.1 and

0.3 m. North of the treeline, many of the polygons may be as small as 5 cm but more often are 20–50 cm in diameter. Often, *Dryas* clumps develop on the drier and more elevated polygon centres, while mosses and lichens occupy the damper depressions. Terms such as 'tundra hummocks', 'earth hummocks', 'slope hum-mocks' and 'thufurs' have been used to describe these features (e.g. Beschel, 1966; Raup, 1966; Corte, 1971; Schunke, 1977; Lewkowicz, 1992c), although they are probably not all of the same origin.

Stripes occur only on sloping terrain. Non-sorted stripes are defined as 'patterned ground possessing a . . . striped pattern and a non-sorted appearance due to par-allel lines of vegetation covered ground and intervening stripes of relatively bare ground oriented from the steep-est slope available' (Washburn, 1956, p. 837). Both large and small forms occur. Large non-sorted stripes are commonly 0.3–1.0 m wide (Fig. 8.13 (a)). The interven-ing stripes of vegetation occupy shallow hollows between the stripes of non-vegetated ground and may be of equal width as the stripe. In areas of fine-grained sediment, many of the stripes show a well-developed dentritic pattern which suggests that surface rill-wash is the cause of the patterning. Sorted stripes show a well-marked differentiation between lines of stones and intervening stripes of finer material oriented parallel to the gradient (Fig. 8.13 (b)). They seldom occur on slopes of less than 3° and are most common on slopes of 5–15° in angle. The coarse stripes are usually nar-rower than the fine stripes, and vary from 0.3 to 1.5 m in width. Stones and boulders are commonly on edge with their long axes parallel to the line of movement.

8.7.2 Origins

There are many suggested origins for patterned ground and in this section no attempt is made to cover all possible interpretations. The interested reader is referred to Washburn (1979) for a more detailed sum-mary of the various hypotheses. Today, most investigators generally agree with Washburn that (a) much patterned ground is polygenetic and (b) that similar forms can be created by different processes. Washburn (1970) has attempted a comprehensive genetic classification of patterned ground (Table 8.4). This classification is not restricted to periglacial phe-nomena. From a periglacial perspective, the major feature of the classification is the twofold division of the processes responsible for patterned ground: (a) those in which cracking is essential and (b) those in which cracking is non-essential.

(a)

(b)

Figure 8.13   Examples of stripes: (a) non-sorted, central Banks Island; (b) sorted, eastern Prince Patrick Island, NWT, Canada.

Cracking is important in the development of most polygonal forms, and relatively unimportant in the development of most circular forms. In the periglacial context, three types of cracking processes occur: desiccation cracking, thermal contraction cracking and seasonal frost cracking. The last two have already been discussed in Chapter 4 and need no further comment. Desiccation cracking, however, is unrelated to either frost action or the presence of permafrost. In theory, desiccation can occur for a number of reasons: wind action may promote evaporation from exposed surfaces or the terrain may be subjected to a change in drainage conditions. Desiccation may occur in association with freezing and ice segregation. In reality, most investigators conclude that wind desiccation is the most likely cause of the extensively developed and regular non-sorted poly-

gons of small sizes which characterize many upland tundra sites (e.g. Tricart, 1970, p. 91; Washburn, 1979). Where they develop considerable micro-relief and become distinct hummocks, it is likely that additional processes such as differential frost heave and snowmelt erosion are also important processes.

Circular forms of patterned ground are most likely the result of cryoturbation. As defined earlier, this term refers to the lateral and vertical displacement of soil which accompanies seasonal and/or diurnal freezing and thawing. Undoubtedly, the most common circular form of patterned ground is the non-sorted circle or 'hummock' (Washburn, 1979). These features are ubiquitous wherever fine-grained sediments are present (Fig. 8.14). Typically, hummocks are composed of fine-grained frost-susceptible soils and are 1–2 m in diameter and as much as 30–50 cm high. Beneath the hummock, the late summer frost table is bowl-shaped, and the hummocks grade from those that are completely vegetated (earth hummocks) to those with bare centres (mud hummocks).

The mound form was traditionally attributed to an upward displacement of material resulting from cryostatic (i.e. freezeback) pressures generated in a confined, wet unfrozen pocket in the active layer. However, the existence of substantial cryostatic pressures in the field has not been convincingly demonstrated (e.g. Mackay and MacKay, 1976). On more general grounds, it can be argued that the presence of voids in the soil, the occurrence of frost cracks in the winter and the weakness of the confining soil layers lying above prevent pressures of any magnitude from forming. Moreover, on theoretical grounds, cryostatic pressures should not develop in a frost-susceptible hummock soil because ice lensing at the top and/or bottom of the active layer will desiccate the last unfrozen pocket so that the pore water is under tension, not under pressure. Mackay (1979b, 1980b) concludes that the upward displacement of material is caused by the freeze and thaw of ice lenses at the top and bottom of the active layer, with a gravity-induced, cell-like movement. An equilibrium model is proposed in which the cell-like movement occurs because the top and bottom of the freeze–thaw zones have opposite curvatures (Fig. 8.14 (c)). Evidence of cell-like circulation is deduced from the grain size distribution of the hummocky soils, radiocarbon dating of organic materials intruded into the hummock centres from the sides, and from upturning tongues of saturated soil observable in late summer (e.g. Zoltai and Tarnocai, 1974; Zoltai *et al.*, 1978).

Table 8.4 A genetic classification of patterned ground

	Cracking essential						Cracking non-essential						
				Thermal cracking									
			Salt Cracking	Frost cracking									
	Desiccation Cracking	Dilation Cracking	Salt Cracking	Seasonal Frost Cracking	Permafrost Cracking	Frost Action Along Bedrock Joints	Primary Frost Sorting	Mass Displacement	Differential Frost Heaving	Salt heaving	Differential Thawing and Eluviation	Differential Mass Wasting	Rillwork
Circles Non-sorted								Mass displacement circles	Frost-heave circles	Salt-heave circles			
Sorted						Joint-crack circles (at crack inter-sections)	Primary frost-sorted circles, incl.? Debris islands	Mass displacement circles, incl. Debris islands	Frost-heave circles	Salt-heave circles			
Polygons Non-sorted	Desiccation polygons	Dilation polygons	Salt-crack polygons	Seasonal frost-crack polygons	Permafrost-crack polygons, incl. ice-wedge polygons,	Joint-crack polygons?	Primary frost-sorted polygons?	Mass displacement polygons?	Frost heave polygon?	Salt-heave polygons?			
Sorted	Desiccation polygons	Dilation polygons	Salt-crack polygons	Seasonal frost-crack polygons	Permafrost-crack polygons	Joint-crack polygons	Primary frost-sorted polygons?	Mass displacement polygons?	Frost heave polygons?	Salt-heave polygons?	Thaw polygons?		
Nets Non-sorted	Desiccation nets incl.? Earth hummocks	Dilation nets		Seasonal frost-crack nets incl.? Earth hummocks	Permafrost-crack nets, incl. ice-wedge and? sand-wedge nets			Mass displacement nets	Frost-heave nets	Salt-heave nets			
Sorted	Desiccation nets	Dilation nets		Seasonal frost-crack nets	Permafrost-crack nets		Primary frost-sorted nets	Mass displacement nets	Frost-heave nets	Salt-heave nets	Thaw nets		
Steps Non-sorted								Mass displacement steps	Frost-heave steps?	Salt-heave steps?		Mass wasting steps	
Sorted							Primary frost-sorted steps	Mass displacement	Frost-heave steps?	Salt-heave steps	Thaw steps?	Mass wasting steps	
Stripes Non-sorted	Desiccation stripes	Dilation stripes?		Seasonal frost-crack stripes?	Permafrost-crack stripes?	Joint crack-stripes?		Mass displacement stripes	Frost-heave stripes	Salt-heave stripes		Mass-wasting stripes?	Rillwork stripes?
Sorted	Dessication stripes	Dilation stripes		Seasonal frost-crack stripes?	Permafrost-crack stripes?	Joint crack-stripes	Primary frost-sorted stripes	Mass displacement stripes	Frost-heave stripes	Salt-heave stripes	Thaw stripes	Mass-wasting stripes	Rillwork stripes

Source: Washburn (1970)

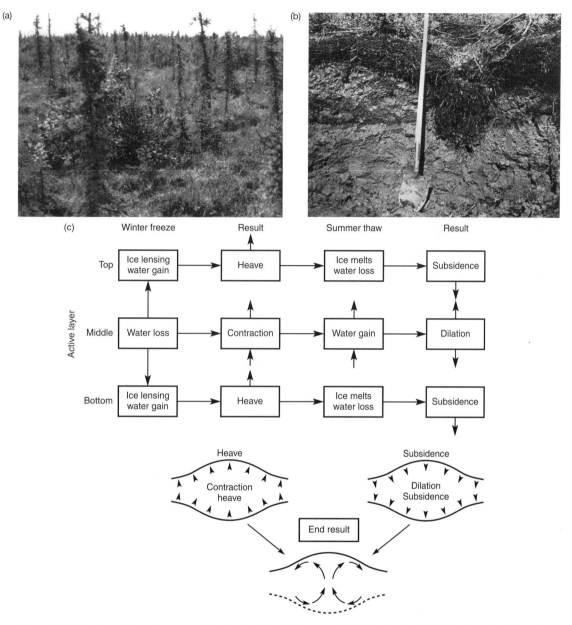

Figure 8.14 The formation of non-sorted circles (mud/earth hummocks) in the Mackenzie Valley, Canada: (a) mud hummock in the boreal forest (*Picea mariana*) near Inuvik, NWT; (b) section through earth hummock showing cryoturbated organic material in centre, Hume River region, near Fort Good Hope, NWT (photo courtesy of S. C. Zoltai); (c) equilibrium model of hummock growth (from Mackay 1980b).

More recent field experiments add support to the idea of a cell-like soil circulation in the formation of circular patterned ground. For example, at Resolute Bay in the high Arctic, movement of dowels indicates radial-outward soil displacements in the order of millimetres per year in the fine-grained central areas of sorted circles. These increase to a maximum near the stony borders (Washburn, 1989). On western Spitsbergen, a progressive circulatory motion of the soil has been measured, with periods of activity in the summer separated by long quiescent periods (Hallet and Prestrud, 1986; Hallet *et al.*, 1988) (Fig. 8.15). Finally, percolative pore water convection through thawed soil has been suggested as a mechanism for displacement (e.g. Ray *et al.*, 1983; Gleason *et al.*, 1986). This process might operate during summer when temperature is a few degrees above zero near the ground surface but approximately zero at the base of the layer of thawed soil. It is argued that the density difference of water between 0 and 4 °C may be sufficient to induce free convection of water which moves through the soil–pore network. This would lead to spatially non-uniform thawing at the top of frozen ground caused by convective heat transfer. Such a process may explain the concave upward curvature of the frost table beneath circles, a phenomenon not adequately explained in Mackay's (1980b) equilibrium model.

Even though soil circulation can be demonstrated, it still does not completely explain the origin of all circular forms. For example, Washburn (1989, pp. 953–954) suggests that the circulation pattern may have evolved subsequent to a protoform, such as a diapir, which has reached a stage of development conducive to initiation of soil circulation. In this context, mudboils are known to form by diapirism resulting from hydrostatic or artesian pore pressures (see below). Elsewhere, there is still debate as to the process(es) involved. For example, the traditional concepts of differential heave and ice segregation have been combined recently with density instability in thawed soils to explain hummocks and cryoturbation structures in Spitsbergen and, by extension, to the hummocks of the Mackenzie Delta region studied by Mackay (e.g. van Vliet-Lanoë, 1988, 1991).

8.7.3 Palaeoclimatic significance

The environmental significance of patterned ground phenomena is not clear in view of the variety of origins that may be possible, and our limited understanding of cryoturbation. It is complicated by the fact that most patterned ground forms are not unique to periglacial regions.

On empirical grounds, the southern limit of active patterned ground of a periglacial nature has been suggested by Williams (1961) to correspond with a mean annual air temperature of +3 °C.

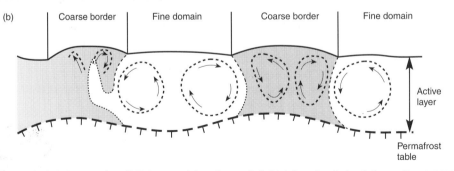

Figure 8.15 Non-sorted circles, western Spitsbergen: (a) surface relief; (b) inferred soil circulation patterns according to Hallett *et al.* (1988).

(a)

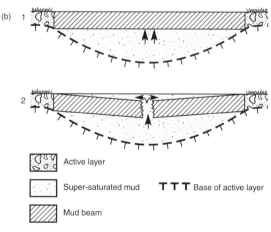

In terms of the relatively large-scale polygonal patterned ground forms discussed in Chapter 6, however, this limit is too far south, and Bird (1967, p. 197) suggests that in northern Canada the southern limit of such phenomena is more closely linked with the −4 °C isotherm. On the other hand, Williams's proposed boundary relates well to the distribution of the various miniature patterns that have long been recognized as occurring in less severe climatic zones where the larger forms are absent, such as the Alps, the Pyrenees, and the uplands of northwest Europe.

Until our understanding of the various patterned ground processes is more complete, it seems unwise to attach any more specific significance than that of cold-climate conditions.

8.8 Active layer hydraulics and mud boils

In many respects, the groundwater hydrology of the active layer is not unlike that of regions with deep seasonal frost. Discharge, in the form of surface and subsurface wash (e.g. Lewkowicz and French, 1982a, 1982b; Lewkowicz, 1983; Woo and Steer, 1982, 1983) is closely linked to snowmelt runoff, with the underlying frozen ground acting as an impermeable layer. These processes are discussed in Chapter 9.

Under certain circumstances, locally high hydraulic potentials may result from water confinement between the underlying permafrost and an overlying semi-rigid carapace. The carapace is usually produced by desiccation and hardening of the surface soil layers, usually silty-clay sediments, in late summer. Hydrostatic or artesian pressures on slopes, and excess pore water pressures created by rain, are usually the causes of the high hydraulic potentials.

Possibly the most dramatic features which result from these hydraulic processes are seasonal frost mounds. These have been described in Chapter 6. Less dramatic but much more common are patterned ground phenomena generally termed 'mudboils'. These are described below.

Mudboils consist of round to elongate, 1–3 m in diameter, bare soil patches (Fig. 8.16 (a)). They differ from earth hummocks since not only is their process of formation different, but they also develop in poorly sorted sediments (muds) with significant silt and/or clay content. Mudboils of this type are ubiquitous over extensive areas of Keewatin and northern Canada and, together with earth hummocks (nonsorted circles; see earlier), are undoubtedly the most

Figure 8.16 Formation of mudboils: (a) mudboils formed on lower slopes near Rea Point, in silty sandy sediment, eastern Melville Island, NWT; (b) schematic evolution of a mudboil with rupture of a surface carapace according to Egginton (1986).

common patterned ground forms in most periglacial regions. In Keewatin, where they have been studied extensively (e.g. Egginton and Shilts, 1978; Shilts, 1978; Dyke and Zoltai, 1980; Egginton and Dyke, 1982), the natural moisture contents of the sediments are very near the liquid limits so the muds liquefy and flow readily in response to slight changes in moisture content or slight internal or external stresses. When the stresses cannot be relieved by downslope movement, mud may burst through the semi-rigid surface layer to create the mudboil (Fig. 8.16 (b)). The process occurs primarily in late summer when the active layer thickness is greatest. It is often associated with excess pore water pressures created by summer rain and/or the thawing of the ice-rich layers at the top of the permafrost in years of exceptionally deep thaw. Sometimes, mudbursts produce small-scale mudflows which extend downslope for several metres.

8.9 Conclusions

Our understanding of geocryological processes operating in the active layer has increased dramatically in the past 15 years. Some of these advances can be summarized as follows:

1. In regions underlain by continuous permafrost, the concept of two-sided freezing must now be recognized.

2. The migration of unfrozen water within the active layer, both upwards and downwards, and the recognition of primary and secondary frost heave and ice segregation are important concepts for engineering design and construction in permafrost regions.

3. The concept of thaw consolidation explains the occurrence of:
   (a) rapid mass movements which are confined to the active layer;
   (b) the existence of instability conditions on very low-angled slopes which, by conventional geotechnical analysis, would be regarded as stable.

4. There is evidence to indicate that thermally induced deformation of the active layer is widespread, although its contribution to other processes operating in the active layer is unclear at present and its relationship to permafrost creep and frozen soil creep is uncertain.

5. Most patterned ground phenomena originate in, and are confined to, the active layer. The most

common are the non-sorted circles, described either as earth hummocks or mudboils. Process mechanisms for these phenomena are now available in the form of either cryoturbation, or active layer hydraulics. Sorted forms, which are less common, are usually related to frost-susceptible materials and differential one-sided freezing processes, such as frost creep and needle ice activity.

Further reading

Dyke, L.S. (1984) Frost heaving of bedrock in permafrost regions. *Bulletin, Association of Engineering Geologists*, **21** (4), 389–405.

French, H.M. (1988) Active layer processes. In: M.J. Clark (ed.), *Advances in periglacial geomorphology*. Chichester: John Wiley and Sons Ltd, 151–177.

Gleason, K.J., W.B. Krantz, N. Caine, J.H. George and R.D. Gunn (1986) Geometrical aspects of sorted patterned ground in recurrently frozen soil. *Science*, **232**, 216–220.

Hallet, B., S.P. Anderson, C.W. Stubbs and E.C. Gregory (1988) Surface soil displacements in sorted circles, Western Spitzbergen. In: *Proceedings, 5th International Conference on Permafrost*, vol. 1. Trondheim: Tapir Publishers, pp. 770–775.

Mackay, J.R. (1980b) The origin of hummocks, western Arctic coast. *Canadian Journal of Earth Sciences*, **17**, 996–1006.

Mackay, J.R. (1983) Downward water movement into frozen ground, western Arctic coast, Canada. *Canadian Journal of Earth Sciences*, **20**, 120–134.

Morgenstern, N.R. and J.F. Nixon (1971) One-dimensional consolidation of thawing soils. *Canadian Geotechnical Journal*, **8**, 555–565.

Ray, R.J., W.B. Krantz, T.N. Caine and R.D. Gunn (1983). A model for sorted patterned ground regularity. *Journal of Glaciology*, **29**, 317–337.

Shilts, W.W. (1978) Nature and genesis of mudboils, Central Keewatin, Canada. *Canadian Journal of Earth Sciences*, **15**, 1053–1068.

Discussion topics

1. Explain the moisture redistribution that occurs annually in the active layer.
2. What phenomena result from frost heave?
3. What processes produce patterned ground?

CHAPTER 9

Hillslope processes

Hillslopes constitute that part of the landscape which occurs between the summits of hills and interfluves and their drainage channels. The geometry of the drainage basin determines the basic length and height parameters of the slope.

Slopes evolve under cold-climate conditions primarily by mass wasting processes. These may be of either a flow, slip or fall nature. Flow includes permafrost creep, soil (frost) creep, gelifluction, slopewash, debris flow and slushflow; slip involves active layer failures and ground ice slumps; fall involves avalanches and rockfalls. Superimposed upon these various processes is the control exerted by the presence of frozen or thawing substrate.

There are several reasons why our understanding of slope development in periglacial environments is limited. First, many slope changes through time are poorly documented because of their general slowness. Second, as argued in Chapter 2, most landscapes in periglacial regions are in disequilibrium with many of the cold-climate processes currently operating. There is, therefore, the inevitable problem of distinguishing between the effects of past and present processes and climates. Third, although significant advances have been made in our understanding of certain slope processes in recent years, the link between hillslope form and process is still unclear.

9.1 Mass wasting

Mass wasting is the term applied to the downslope movement of debris under the influence of gravity. It is a process which is not unique to periglacial environments. On the other hand, mass wasting processes probably reach their greatest intensity and efficacy under periglacial conditions. There are several reasons for this. First, intense frost action in certain periglacial regions accelerates surface movement through the frost creep mechanism (see below). Second, the high moisture content, often typical of the thawing active layer, is particularly favourable for the operation of gelifluction (see below). Third, permafrost directly aids mass wasting by limiting the downwards infiltration of water into the ground, thereby inducing high pore water pressures. Also, the permafrost surface itself acts as a water-lubricated slip plane for movement of the overlying active layer. Fourth, in many periglacial regions, a striking legacy of recent glaciation is the presence of oversteepened slopes and loose glacial debris, both of which are conducive to the active development of slopes.

A number of processes which operate either separately or in association are usually included within the term mass wasting. It is not unreasonable to assume that in any one area a specific process or group of processes will dominate, depending upon such factors as climate, lithology and local topography.

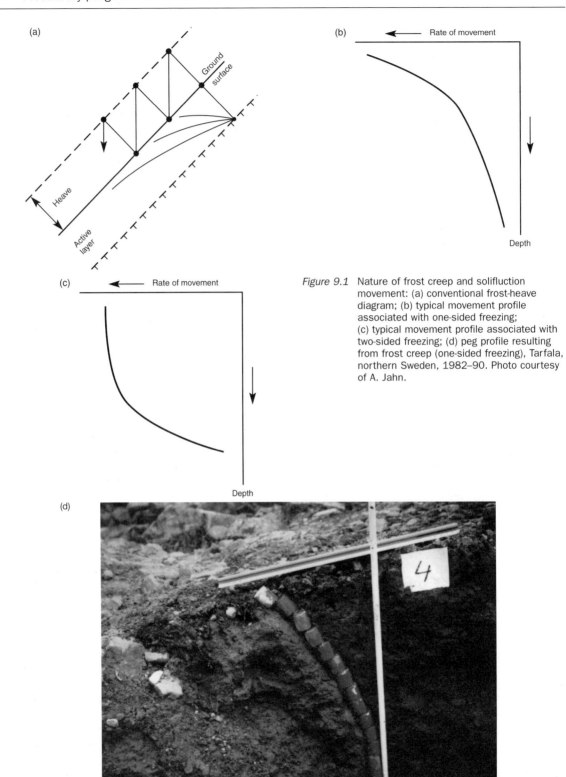

(a)

(b)

(c)

(d)

Figure 9.1 Nature of frost creep and solifluction movement: (a) conventional frost-heave diagram; (b) typical movement profile associated with one-sided freezing; (c) typical movement profile associated with two-sided freezing; (d) peg profile resulting from frost creep (one-sided freezing), Tarfala, northern Sweden, 1982–90. Photo courtesy of A. Jahn.

9.2 Solifluction

Solifluction is regarded as one of the most widespread processes of soil movement in periglacial regions. The term was first used by J. G. Andersson to describe the 'slow flowing from higher to lower ground of masses of waste saturated with water' which he observed in the Falkland Islands (Andersson, 1906, p. 95). Since solifluction, so defined, is not necessarily confined to cold climates, the term 'gelifluction' has been proposed to describe solifluction associated with frozen ground (e.g. Washburn, 1979). Intimately associated with solifluction is frost creep. This has been described as 'the net downward displacement that occurs when the soil, during a freeze–thaw cycle, expands normal to the surface and settles in a more nearly vertical direction' (Benedict, 1970, p. 170). When operating together, the two processes of gelifluction and frost creep constitute the movement which is generally termed solifluction in the modern sense.

Both gelifluction and frost creep result from the thaw consolidation of ice-rich soils. Suitable conditions for gelifluction occur wherever the downward percolation of water through the soil is limited, or where the melting of segregated ice lenses in the thawing soil provides excess water which reduces internal friction and cohesion. Significant gelifluction occurs usually when moisture values approach or exceed the Atterberg liquid limits.

To avoid confusion concerning use of the terms gelifluction and solifluction, it is necessary to consider whether the ground is seasonally or perennially frozen; that is, whether the ground is subject to one-sided or two-side freezing. Under one-sided freezing, solifluction consists of only two components: (a) frost creep, usually in the autumn or in association with repeated diurnal frost throughout the year, and (b) gelifluction, occurring in the spring as the seasonally frozen ground thaws from the surface downwards. Under two-sided freezing, solifluction comprises not only frost creep and gelifluction but also a movement which occurs in late summer when the thawed active layer is capable of sliding, *en masse*, across the lubricated slip plane provided by the ice-rich zone at the top of permafrost. This is termed 'plug-like' flow (Mackay, 1981).

The relative importance of each component of movement will vary from locality to locality, depending upon site factors such as moisture availability or regional factors such as the seasonal rhythm. For example, in alpine regions with strong diurnal and seasonal rhythms, such as the Colorado Front Range, USA, frost creep is the dominant process operating for much of the year (Benedict, 1970). Only in certain micro-environments such as the axial positions of wet gelifluction lobes, do the effects of gelifluction exceed the effects of frost creep. On the other hand, observations from a high latitude environment, such as East Greenland (Washburn, 1967), indicate that either process may dominate in any given year, and in different sectors of the same slope depending upon moisture conditions. Likewise, Egginton and French (1985) have observed marked variability of movement across the same slope on Banks Island, NWT. According to Washburn (1967), frost creep tended to exceed gelifluction by not more than 3 : 1 in most years, and frost creep commonly resulted in 30–50 per cent of the total movement. In East Greenland, it would appear that frost creep due to the annual cycle is more important than creep due to short-term cycles. Finally, in areas of ice-rich silty permafrost, such as the western Canadian Arctic, an end-of-summer 'plug-flow' movement appears to be the dominant mechanism (Mackay, 1981; Egginton and French, 1985).

9.2.1 Frost creep

Frost creep is defined as the ratchet-like downslope movement of particles as the result of the frost heaving of the ground and the subsequent settling upon thawing, the heaving being predominantly normal to the slope and the settling more nearly vertical (Jahn, 1975; French, 1976a; Washburn, 1979). This movement can be associated with either one-sided or two-sided freezing (Fig. 9.1). The traditional concept of one-sided frost creep involves movement decreasing from the surface downwards (Fig. 9.1(d)). It depends upon the frequency of freeze–thaw cycles, angle of slope, moisture available for heave, and the frost susceptibility of the soil. Thus, if the slope angle is σ, the heave normal to the ground surface is h, and the soil settles vertically upon thaw, the potential frost creep (Δl) parallel to the surface is:

$$\Delta l = h \tan \sigma \qquad (9.1)$$

In the case of two-sided freezing, which is the situation when dealing with permafrost regions, the actual frost creep may exceed the amount calculated from equation 9.1. In particular, it can be argued that the growth of ice lenses at the top of permafrost during freeze-back means that the potential frost creep (Δl) varies from a maximum in the thickest part of the ice lens to zero at the periphery. Furthermore, towards the end of the thaw period, a residual ice lens in a soupy matrix may make a larger contribution to total movement than that of Δl due to vertical settlement. According to Mackay (1981) this causes the plug-like flow observed in mud hummocks, with the hummocks sliding over the water-saturated sediment lying immediately above the permafrost table. In a similar fashion, ice veins within the seasonally frozen layer may induce significant frost creep as thawing occurs. This may explain why Benedict (1970) measured more frost creep at one of his sites than could be explained by his actual measurements of frost heave.

9.2.2 Gelifluction

Gelifluction is the form of solifluction associated with either seasonal or perennially frozen ground. Conditions suitable for gelifluction occur in areas where downward percolation of water through the soil is limited by the frozen ground and where the melt of segregated ice lenses provides excess water which reduces internal friction and cohesion in the soil. Gelifluction is essentially a process operating mainly during the thaw period. Locations of abundant moisture, such as below late-lying or perennial snowbanks, are especially favoured.

Most investigations indicate that gelifluction movement is laminar in nature. This can be loosely regarded as 'classic' solifluction. Usually, movement is restricted to the uppermost 50 cm of the active layer. Slope angle appears to be of little importance in influencing such movement, although there is certainly a significant difference in movement between slopes of less than 5° and those over 15°. It is difficult to generalize about rates, but average rates of surface movement of between 0.5 and 10.0 cm/year are typical. On very low-angle slopes, rates in excess of 2.0–2.5 cm/year are probably unusual; equally, rates is excess of 6.0–10.0 cm/year probably involve some other gravity-controlled process in addition to gelifluction and are usually only encountered on steep slopes. It is perhaps significant that some of the highest rates of movement are from recently deglaciated areas such as Svalbard and parts of Scandinavia where slopes are commonly oversteepened and loose glacial debris is widespread.

Under laminar flow, the decrease of movement with depth is usually of a linear nature. If one assumes an average surface movement rate of between 0.5 and 5.0 cm/year, and that movement in the upper 50 cm is on average one-quarter of this amount, it can be estimated that gelifluction transports between approximately 6.0 and 60.0 cm³/cm/year of material (cf. French, 1974a, 1976b). Long-term field data from relatively gentle, tundra-covered slopes in the Mackenzie Delta support this gross approximation (Table 9.1).

'Plug-like' flow should be distinguished from gelifluction. Plug-like flow was first described by Mackay (1981) from Garry Island, NWT, following the observation of semi-flexible plastic tubes inserted vertically into clay hummocks. The vertical velocity

Table 9.1 Slope movement data for hummocks at two sites, Garry Island, NWT, Canada

Tube No.	Measurement Period	Slope (deg. approx.)	Surface Movement (cm/year)	Heave (h) for Frost Creep (cm)	Approx. Active Layer Thickness (cm)	Volumetric Transport (cm³/cm/year)
Site 1						
1	1964–1977	3	0.40	8	75	20
2	1964–1977	5	0.80	9	55	31
3	1964–1977	7	0.60	6	55	23
4	1964–1977	7	1.00	8	55	38
Site 2						
8	1965–1976	3	0.20	4	50	7
9	1965–1977	1	0.20	11	45	–
10	1965–1976	3	0.30	6	60	13
11	1965–1977	7	1.00	8	75	52
12	1965–1977	1	0.25	14	40	–

Source: data from Mackay (1981)

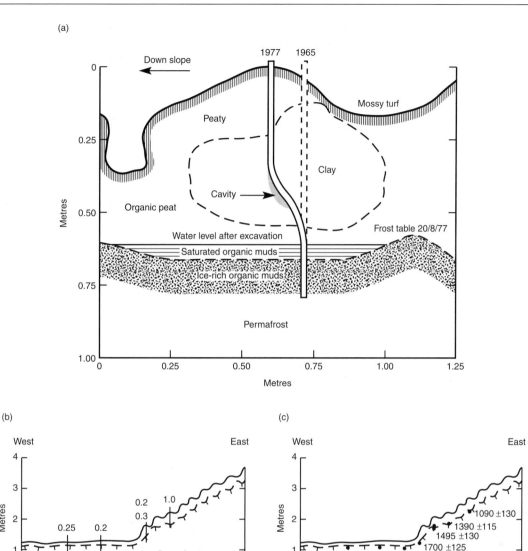

(a)

Figure 9.2 Gelifluction movement, Garry Island, NWT (data from Mackay, 1981); (a) vertical velocity profile, illustrating plug-like flow; (b) site 2 slope profile and mean annual movement (1965–76) (see Table 9.1); (c) ^{14}C dates for organic material along the bottom of late summer active layer at site 2.

profile was found to be convex downwards (Fig. 9.2 (a)), quite the reverse to normal gelifluction. Also, movement occurred in late summer. Typically, a cavity developed on the downslope side of the plastic tube and the movement progressively buried inter-hummock peat to form a buried organic layer. Rates of hummock movement of between 0.2 and 1.0 cm/ year were recorded over a 10–13 year period; they indicate volumetric transport of between 7 and 52 cm³/cm/year (Table 9.1 and Fig. 9.2 (b) and (c)). Mackay attributes plug-like flow to frost creep by thaw of the ice-rich layer at the bottom of the active layer. The ice-rich layer forms by upfreezing in winter and the ice content is augmented by ice lensing in the

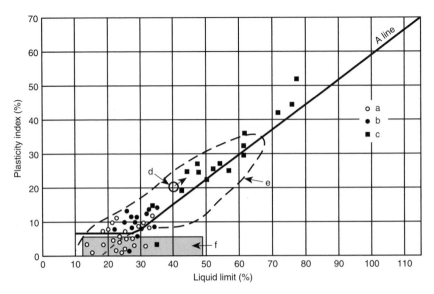

Figure 9.3 Typical plasticity values for solifluction sediments (from Harris, 1987). (a) Active solifluction sediments, Banks Island (French, 1974a), Greenland (Everett, 1967; Washburn, 1967) and Norway (Harris, 1977). (b) Fossil solifluction sediments, England (Mottershead, 1971; Harris and Wright, 1980; Wilson, 1981). (c) Fossil planar slides in clay, England (Chandler, 1970a, 1970b; Chandler *et al.*, 1976). (d) Minimum plasticity and liquid limit from Garry Island, NWT, Canada (Mackay, 1981). (e) Range of values reported for near-surface sediments, District of Keewatin, NWT, Canada (Shilts, 1974). (f) Range of values reported for solifluction lobes in the Swiss Alps (Furrer *et al.*, 1971).

summer thaw period. Plug-like flow results from two-sided freezing and only occurs in areas underlain by perennially frozen ground.

Possibly related to plug-like flow are small mud-bursts and mudflows which have been described from eastern Banks Island by Egginton and French (1985). On slopes experiencing plug-like flow, surface materials episodically liquefy and flow for some distance downslope before losing moisture and consolidating. The snouts of these mud bursts, which have a characteristic transversely ribbed surface, can often be traced 1–2 m upslope to where they originate. The mud surface may or may not revegetate before burial by another mudflow. In this way a series of parallel to subparallel sheets or lobes up to 30 cm thick are produced. Mudbursts usually occur on the upper to mid parts of slopes, near the base of snowbanks, and where more permeable materials underlie a surface veneer of silty colluvium. Liquefaction of the mud results from positive differential pore water pressures which are released along shearing zones associated with the plug-like movement. The phenomena may also be linked to the mudboils described in Chapter 8.

Whatever the precise mechanism, this type of movement is rapid and, like plug-flow, is quite distinct from classic solifluction. As the muds originate at depth within the active layer, the movement must be a mid-to-late-summer phenomenon.

In all probability, solifluction processes constitute a continuum from the very slow to the very fast, and evidence of classic solifluction (gelifluction), plug-like flow and mudburst and mudflow activity might all be found on any one slope. Thaw consolidation (see below) may be a unifying concept in our understanding of solifluction and related processes in permafrost regions.

Gelifluction deposits are heterogenous in nature and include coarse talus, alluvial silt and clay, and diamictons of glacial or periglacial origin. The diamictons are usually matrix-supported, the matrix commonly consisting of clay, silt, or silty sand. Such sediments generally have low liquid limits and plasticity indices (Fig. 9.3). Where plug-like flow occurs, the clay size fraction may exceed 25–30 per cent (Mackay, 1981). A second characteristic of gelifluction deposits is that the larger clasts tend to become

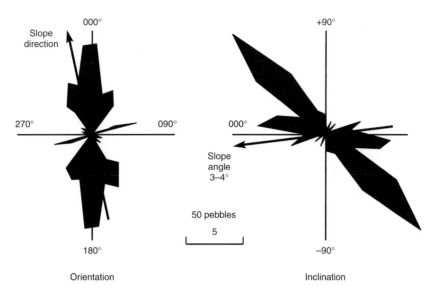

Figure 9.4 Typical fabric diagram of gelifluction (colluvium) deposit on the gentle slope of an asymmetrical valley, Beaufort Plain, northwest Banks Island, Canada (from French, 1971b).

oriented with the longer axis becoming parallel to the direction of gelifluction movement (e.g. Harris, 1981, 1987). The clasts also show low-angled dips. Referring specifically to solifluction deposits on Baffin Island, NWT, Cailleux and Taylor (1954) suggest that at least two-thirds of all elongate clasts in such deposits lie parallel to the slope direction. A typical fabric diagram for gelifluction deposits on Banks Island is illustrated in Fig. 9.4.

Certain soil and micromorphological characteristics are also typical of solifluction deposits. For example, where plug-like flow has occurred, soil pods may have slickensided surfaces due to small-scale shears as observed in the Brooks Range, Alaska (Reanier and Ugolini, 1983), and lateral displacement has been observed along small slip planes associated with the thawing of ice lenses in the active layer in Spitsbergen (van Vliet-Lanoë et al., 1984). Platy microfabrics are typical of frozen silty sediments containing segregated ice lenses and these promote localized slip during thaw (e.g. Harris, 1985), thus providing a further characteristic of solifluction deposits.

9.2.3 Rates of solifluction movement

Numerous studies have investigated the magnitude and rate of movement of solifluction by direct field measurement. Surface movement is usually monitored by marked stones and pegs placed on the surface or protruding through the surface (e.g. Pissart, 1964; Washburn, 1967; Akerman, 1993), while variations of movement with depth have been studied by the insertion of plastic cylinders which subsequently deform (Rudberg, 1962; Harris, 1972; Mackay, 1981), by rectangular tin foil markers (French, 1974a; Egginton and French, 1985; Akerman, 1993), by probes attached to strain gauges (Williams, 1962; Price, 1973), and by linear motion transducers (Everett, 1967). Some of the various rates recorded and published in the literature are summarized in Table 9.2.

Vegetation has a marked influence upon movement rates since, by restricting surface movement, it may lead to greater subsurface movement. An illustration of this is provided by the work of Price (1973), who investigated solifluction movement on slopes of different aspect in the Ruby Range, Yukon Territory. There, certain sites showed a convex profile of subsurface movement (i.e. greater subsurface movement) while others showed the normal decrease in movement with depth. Movement also varied with aspect and micro-climate. On the north- and east-facing slopes for example, where vegetation was poorly developed, the greatest rates of movement occurred (2.4–2.7 cm/year); lower values were recorded on southeast-facing slopes (1.6 cm/year),

Table 9.2 Some recorded rates of solifluction movement

Locality	Reference	Gradient (degrees)	Rate (cm/year)
Spitsbergen	Jahn (1960)	3–4	1.0–3.0
Spitsbergen	Jahn (1961)	7–15	5.0–12.0
Kärkevagge, Sweden	Rapp (1960a)	15	4.0
Tarna area, Sweden	Rudberg (1962)	5	0.9–1.8
Norra Storfjell, Sweden	Rudberg (1964)	5	0.9–3.8
French Alps	Pissart (1964)		1.0
East Greenland	Washburn (1967)		
		'Wet' sites	3.7
		'Dry' sites	0.9
Colorado Rockies	Benedict (1970)		0.4–4.3
Okstindan, Norway	Harris (1972)	5–17	1.0–6.0
Ruby Range, YT, Canada	Price (1973)	14–18	0.6–3.5
Sachs Harbour, Banks Island, NWT, Canada	French (1974a)	3	1.5–2.0
Garry Island, NWT, Canada	Mackay (1981)	1–7	0.4–1.0
Swiss Alps	Gamper (1983)		0.02–0.1
Eastern Banks Island, NWT, Canada	Egginton and French (1985)	<10	0.6
Svalbard	Akerman (1993)	2–25	
		Stripes	1.4–2.0
		Steps	0.9–2.2
		Lobes	3.3
		Sheets	4.3

where the vegetation cover was well developed. Movement was least (0.7 cm/year) on southwest-facing slopes which, exposed to the prevailing winds, were drier than the other three slopes. With respect to subsurface movement, only the southeast-facing slope showed greater subsurface movement than surface movement. According to Price, this reflected the inhibiting influence of a thick organic turf layer combined with a shallow active layer and abundant moisture just beneath the surface.

9.2.4 Solifluction phenomena

Geomorphic features produced by frost creep and gelifluction include uniform sheets of locally derived surficial materials and tongue-shaped lobes. Perhaps the least studied but most widespread feature is the solifluction sheet. Usually the result of extensive gelifluction and frost creep, solifluction sheets produce uniform expanses of smooth terrain, often at angles as low as 1–3° (Fig. 9.5). The downslope edge of such sheets is usually characterized by numerous small lobate forms with *Dryas*-banked risers, often only a few centimetres high. Not only are these solifluction sheets capable of movement on extremely low-angled slopes but they are capable of transporting large erratic boulders. The latter, referred to as 'ploughing blocks' or braking blocks, are rafted on

the surface, their undersides resting at or near the permafrost table. Sometimes, they leave a shallow trough upslope indicating the path of their movement. Ploughing blocks have also been reported from alpine environments (e.g. Lewkowicz, 1988) and mid-latitude uplands (Tufnell, 1972). Solifluction sheets are probably best developed in high Arctic regions where the absence of vegetation enables solifluction to operate uniformly. In the lowland tundra and the forest-tundra further south, vegetation hinders the sheet-like extension of solifluction and, instead, favours more localized lobate movement.

Lobes are relatively well known solifluction phenomena. They have been reported to occur in most periglacial environments, but are probably best developed in alpine regions or areas of significant local relative relief. The lobes commonly give rise to a stepped, tread-like slope which may range in angle from 3–5° upwards to 15–20°. The micro-relief of such slopes varies from vertical turf risers in excess of 2–3 m in height, down to small *Dryas*-backed risers only a few centimetres high. Each riser is separated by treads of low angle and varying extent. Both creep and gelifluction contribute significantly to the movement of lobes, with gelifluction being more important in the wetter, axial parts and creep more important in the drier, peripheral parts. Obviously, for lobes to develop, the gelifluction

Figure 9.5 Solifluction sheet, northwest Banks Island, NWT, Canada.

movement must be greater than frost creep and must be concentrated in well-defined linear paths. Particularly favoured locations for the development of lobes are immediately below snowpatches and on the lower parts of valley slopes. Given time, solifluction lobes will advance downslope, progressively burying other solifluction lobes developed at lower elevations.

Some lobes are marked by a concentration of large stones or boulders at their downslope ends. These have been variously called 'stone garlands', 'block-banked terraces' or 'boulder steps'. The stones are commonly tilted upwards and appear to be 'emerging' from the terrace or lobe. Their existence is usually interpreted as indicating that subsurface movement is greater than surface movement. Turf-banked features, on the other hand, indicate surface movement to be greater and pebbles at the downslope ends of these features often possess a more horizontal or even a 'submerged' character (i.e. downslope inclination).

9.3 Slopewash

Slopewash is an azonal process and therefore not unique to the periglacial environment. It is particularly well known in the non-periglacial regions of the world. The literature indicates a number of different processes contribute to slopewash. Erosion may be by (a) rainsplash impact, (b) unconcentrated surface wash, commonly termed sheetwash, (c) concentrated surface wash, commonly termed rillwash, and (d) subsurface wash, in which particles are transported through the soil pores. In the case of the surface wash processes, particles are carried along in an overland flow. Where the flow is thin, individual particles are removed from the surface without any marked concentration of erosion to give uniform denudation. If the flow varies in thickness, or if it is turbulent, flow becomes progressively concentrated into smaller channels of higher intensities of erosion to give differential denudation. It has also been found that vegetation is the major influence upon the rate of transport of sediment. Vegetation intercepts precipitation, breaks the impact of raindrops, improves soil structure and infiltration around roots, binds the soil and subdivides overland flow around plant stems and litter. According to Carson and Kirkby (1972, p. 219), rates of surface soil transport are greatest in arid and semi-arid areas of the world which receive less than 1000 mm of precipitation a year and least in humid temperate areas with continuous vegetation. For example, in the UK several hundreds of measurements for a variety of sites give a median value of only 0.09 $cm^3/cm/year$. On the other hand, studies in the arid and sparsely vegetated regions of the western United States have recorded values ranging from 200 to over 1000 $cm^3/cm/year$ (e.g. Schumm, 1964; Leopold *et al.*, 1966; Carson and Kirkby, 1972, p. 209).

Since many periglacial regions are arid or semi-arid, and since vegetation is often sparse or totally lacking, relatively high rates of surface soil transport might be expected. But where vegetation is present, as in the boreal or taiga forest zones and on tundra lowlands, surface wash is probably much less significant. One might assume that slopewash progressively increases in importance northwards from the tree-line, and bears an inverse relationship to the percentage of ground covered by vegetation.

Over and above these general considerations, there are additional reasons why slopewash may be particularly effective in periglacial regions. First, the presence of permafrost prevents infiltration and favours surface runoff even on very low-angled slopes. Second, periglacial areas have a high effectiveness of runoff since evaporation rates are low and runoff is concentrated in the short summer season. Third, moisture for slopewash in non-periglacial regions is usually considered to be derived from rainfall. In many periglacial regions, however, the most important source is the spring melting of the seasonal snow cover combined with the melt of ice lenses as the active layer thaws.

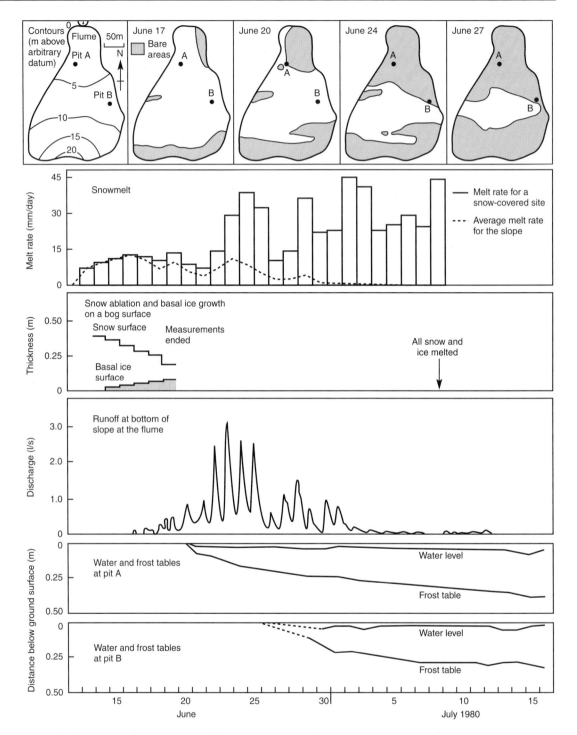

Figure 9.6 Typical pattern of snow ablation and associated runoff and active layer conditions near Resolute, high Arctic, Canada (from Woo and Steer, 1983).

9.3.1 Nivation

Slopewash in periglacial regions has often been linked to the concept of nivation. Since the latter has been the cause of some confusion in the periglacial literature, brief mention must be made here. However, modern use of the term nivation is not recommended (see Thorn, 1988) and it is not included in the Canadian glossary of permafrost and related ground ice terms (see ACGR, 1988).

Nivation was the term given to the combined action of frost shattering, gelifluction and slopewash processes thought to operate in the vicinity of snowbanks. It was seen as an erosive process involving localized and intense physical weathering, the result of an abundant moisture supply percolating into the rock beneath and around the snowbank. In its simplest form, nivation processes were thought to erode shallow hollows or cirque-like basins which form on slopes and upland surfaces (Cook and Raiche, 1962). Debris was removed from the hollows by sheetwash, rillwash and gelifluction. The hollows were categorized as being either transverse (i.e. linear), with the major axis lying transverse to the drainage, longitudinal (i.e. elongated downslope), or circular (a transition between the other two types). The end result was a variety of erosional landforms (e.g. St-Onge, 1969).

This causal relationship between snowbanks and landforms, via the nivation process, does not stand up to rigorous analysis. Detailed field studies upon the geomorphic effects of snow, and the lack of effective freeze–thaw cycles beneath snowbanks, led Thorn and others to question the concept (e.g. Thorn, 1976, 1979, 1988; Thorn and Hall, 1980). The abandonment of the nivation concept now allows a clearer understanding of slopewash processes since the mechanical (i.e. weathering) aspects of nivation can be ignored in favour of the transportational and denudational aspects of running water.

Snowbank hydrology is an essential first step in understanding the nature and significance of slopewash in periglacial regions.

9.3.2 Snowbank hydrology

The distribution of snow is largely controlled by prevailing winds and topography. North of the treeline and above the timberline snow is often blown clear from exposed surfaces and accumulates in lee-slope positions, hollows and other topographic irregularities. Thus, at the time of snowmelt in the spring, the snow cover is quite uneven in its distribution. In the boreal forest zones, the snow distribution is not so simple, and often depends on the type of forest and forest-shrub that is present.

Although the pattern of snow melt varies from year to year and locality to locality, a few generalizations can be made. For example, Fig. 9.6 illustrates the pattern of snowcover melt from a small drainage basin near Resolute, in the Canadian Arctic, over a three-week period commencing in early June. By the end of this period, the entire winter snow cover had disappeared. Usually, in high latitudes snowmelt is extremely rapid because of the continuous solar insolation; in mid-latitudes and low latitudes, the melt is less rapid and may persist throughout the summer, often with diurnal discharge peaks. In general, therefore, one can assume that the primary control over snowmelt is insolation.

As the snowpack melts water percolates downwards through the pack and refreezes as ice layers at the base. Multiple freezing and melting of the water in basal ice layers complicates the snowmelt–runoff relationship by delaying initial runoff and prolonging the end of the snowmelt season. In addition, by protecting the channel bed (in the case of small stream valleys) or the ground surface (in the case of hillslopes), it both increases flow velocity and the capacity for sediment transport while reducing the opportunities for erosion.

Figure 9.6 also illustrates the relationship between snow ablation and runoff, as recorded by a stage recorder and weir at the base of the slope. Even at this high latitude, there is a marked diurnal fluctuation in runoff, related to solar radiation inputs. As the snowbank ablates and shrinks in size, the exposed ground surface progressively starts to thaw. At the same time the thickness of the snowbank decreases until it consists almost entirely of basal ice. The latent heat released by the refreezing process accelerates the warming of the active layer beneath the ice such that upon final exposure, thawing quickly commences.

Depending upon the volume and rapidity of thaw of the snow, and the nature of the substate, runoff can be both overland (surface) and subsurface in nature. Both are concentrated at the downslope edge of the basal ice layer.

9.3.3 Surface and subsurface wash

One of the earliest quantitative measurements of slopewash is provided by Jahn (1961) from Spitsbergen. Using simple sediment trays, he concluded that approximately 12–18 g/m^2 year of sediment was being washed downslope beneath large perennial snowbanks. This corresponds, however, to a surface denudation rate of only approximately 7 mm/1000 years, a value considerably lower than comparable rates from non-permafrost regions (Young, 1974).

Since then, studies by Lewkowicz (1983; Lewkowicz and French, 1982a, 1982b) and Woo and Steer (1982, 1983) in the Canadian Arctic have attempted to provide more detailed information. Figure 9.7 shows the typical instrumentation used by Lewkowicz to monitor slopewash beneath a large snowbank on Banks Island. A portable weir complete with water level recorder enabled wash volumes to be monitored. The analysis of samples for suspended sediment and solute concentrations, for both surface and subsurface flow (the latter by means of pipes inserted at varying levels into the active layer the previous summer) enabled the calculation of both material removed from the slope and average denudation rates.

Lewkowicz and French (1982a), like Jahn (1961), found that most surface wash was derived primarily from snowmelt. Rainfall produced overland flow only once in the three-year period of study. Suspended sediment concentrations were low and field simulation experiments, with surface wash discharges as much as three times greater than observed in nature, failed to induce significant erosion. Surface denudation due to suspended sediment removal varied from only 0.4 mm/1000 years to 2.6 mm/1000 years. By contrast, solute removal was 8–30 times greater (2.0–74.1 mm/1000 years), thereby supporting Rapp's (1960a) conclusion regarding the dominance of solute transport on slopes (see Table 9.4). Lewkowicz (1983) concluded that, while surface wash erosion probably reaches its maximum in the polar deserts, rapid landscape modification by this process is unlikely.

Relatively little is known about subsurface wash and the role of seepage in slope modification. Some Russian literature suggests that 'thermo-erosional wash' exists, in which small mineral particles are liberated by the melting of frozen ground. This contributes to a process termed 'thermo-planation' (Kachurin, 1962; Dylik, 1972). Recent field studies have yet to confirm this. Likewise, if throughflow (subsurface flow) is concentrated at any one locality, and if litho-

Figure 9.7 Snowbank runoff plot and portable weir with water level recorder used to monitor surface wash, Thomsen River area, north central Banks Island, Canada.

logical conditions are favourable, local collapse hollows may be formed by subsurface erosion and the transport of fines. This process, termed 'suffosion', is well known in parts of central Yakutia where springs, emerging from the foot of terraces and fed by supra- and sub-permafrost waters, excavate large amounts of fine sand (Anisimova *et al.*, 1973). However, this process must be regarded as a local condition.

Probably more typical are the conclusions of Lewkowicz (1983) with respect to the importance of subsurface wash in periglacial environments. On Banks Island, for example, subsurface wash was found to transport sediment primarily in the form of solution. Solute concentrations were relatively low during snowmelt but increased later in the summer in response to a higher residence time and progressive desaturation of the active layer. Denudation rates varied from 3.5 to 29.0 mm/1000 years, indicating that solution equalled or exceeded total erosion by surface wash. Indeed, the ratio of denudation due to solution to denudation due to suspended sediment transport in surface wash varied between 22:1 and 200:1, further confirming the overall importance of solution as a slope denudational process. A more detailed discussion of solution weathering in cold regions has been given in Chapter 4.

9.3.4 Slopewash phenomena

Very few phenomena can be attributed directly to the action of slopewash. However, in the gravel terrains of many polar desert regions, small subtle features may be associated with seepage of supra-permafrost ground water or subsurface flow (Woo and Xia, 1995). With both large hydraulic conductivities to facilitate water flow and a shallow frost table to prevent deep percolation, there are numerous localities where the topography intersects the water table. On concave slopes, such seepage produces local saturated zones ('wet' spots) and where seepage is concentrated, wetlands, ponds and small seepage lines or depressions are maintained. These slight but real elements of the polar desert landscape indicate the presence of slopewash and seepage processes.

The typical slopewash deposits currently being formed in high latitudes are the colluvium and other fine unconsolidated sediment that accumulates at the foot of slopes and below snowbanks. Mention must also be made of the belief that slopewash and intense freeze–thaw activity during the Pleistocene resulted in the deposition of rhythmically bedded slope deposits (Dylik,1960). Such deposits have been termed '*grèzes litées*' (see Chapter 14). However, similar deposits have not been widely reported from high latitudes and it is probable that high latitudes do not experience the repeated freeze–thaw oscillations that favour the frost shattering and slurrying which the stratification of '*grèzes litées*' suggests.

Until more data are available, it seems best to regard surface wash as being a minor denuding agent in high latitudes. By contrast, subsurface wash, in the form of solution, is a major contributor to landscape evolution, albeit at a slow pace, and seepage, especially in gravelly terrain, gives rise to a number of localized surface conditions which promote plant growth, and generally provide diversity to otherwise barren terrain. Other aspects of the hydrology of the active layer have been discussed in Chapter 8.

9.4 Rapid mass movement

The final category of mass wasting processes is that involving the relatively rapid or even catastrophic movement of material downslope. Slope failures of various sorts, rockfalls, debris flows and avalanches are the more important of these processes. All are more localized and/or periodic processes than the mass wasting processes previously described.

9.4.1 Active layer failures

Localized and small-scale slope failures which are confined to the active layer are relatively common in regions underlain by perennially frozen and ice-rich unconsolidated sediments. In recent years systematic study of these features has been undertaken in certain high Arctic regions because they can present a hazard to northern development. They are usually restricted to the middle or upper parts of slopes, with the entrance and exit of the failure plane well within the slope (see Fig. 8.10). These rapid mass movements have been variously described as skin-flows, detachment failures, active layer glides or, more generally, as active layer failures (ACGR, 1988). In all cases, the failure involves the thawed or thawing active layer, together with the overlying vegetation mat, becoming detached from the underlying frozen material. Where the failure exposes massive ice or icy sediments, the failures can develop into retrogressive thaw slumps (see Chapter 7).

The cause of such failures is attributed to local conditions of soil moisture saturation with resulting high pore water pressures. At some point the shear strength is exceeded and the slope becomes unstable. The permafrost table acts as a lubricated slip plane for movement and controls the depth of the failure plane. Thus, active layer failures are usually shallow, the slump scar or hollow often being no more than 1 m deep. In particularly fine-grained sediments possessing high liquid limits, failure can take the form of a mudflow which may extend downslope for distances in excess of 100 m in certain cases (see Fig. 8.10 (b)). If icy sediments are exposed at the permafrost table, these melt and the slump scar develops in a regressive manner. The extreme case of regressive slumping is that of ground ice slumping (see Chapter 7).

On certain of the Canadian Arctic islands, active layer failures are especially frequent (e.g. Stangl *et al.*, 1982; French, 1988, pp. 167–68; Lewkowicz, 1990, 1992b). On eastern Melville Island and on Banks Island, terrain underlain by the ice-rich and unconsolidated shales of the Christopher Formation is especially vulnerable to this type of failure; on the Fosheim Peninsula of Ellesmere Island, poorly lithified shales and siltstones of the Deer Bay Formation are involved. In all cases, the liquid limits are frequently exceeded during rapid spring thaw and/or following periods of summer precipitation.

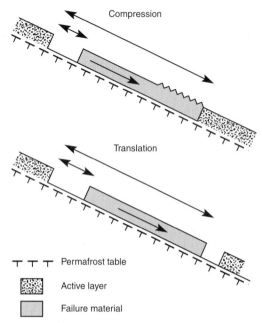

Figure 9.8 Different mechanisms of active layer failures (from Lewkowicz, 1990). In both cases, failure occurs in late summer.

Lewkowicz (1990) has calculated volumes of material involved in such failures, and the transportation rates. Both compression and translation of the soil mass is involved (Fig. 9.8), with most failures involving elements of both. In one valley, approximately 5.3 km² in extent was affected by an average of 3.5 failures per year during the period 1950–90 and 75 failures were initiated during the unusually warm summer of July and August 1988. Table 9.3 summarizes the volumes of sediment moved and the frequency and rates of transport involved in three failures.

Favourable conditions for active layer failures also occur when the spring thaw follows a winter of above average snowfall, or when the spring thaw is late and therefore rapid. In both cases, high pore water pressures develop at a time when the active layer is not fully developed.

Similar slope failures are known to occur in the boreal forest zone of the Mackenzie Valley lowlands where they have been termed 'detachment failures' (Hughes *et al.*, 1973; Chatwin and Rutter, 1978). They are common along river banks and on ice-rich colluvial slopes developed on shales, fine-grained tills and glacio-lacustrine sediments. In some areas active layer failures may develop following the destruction of the surface vegetation by forest fire (e.g. Zoltai

and Pettapiece, 1973) or following man-induced terrain disturbance (e.g. Heginbottom, 1973). In both instances, the destruction of vegetation results in a greater penetration of rainwater into the active layer, a deepening of the active layer and the thawing of ground ice.

9.4.2 Debris flows and avalanches

In periglacial areas characterized by abundant snowfall and high mountain relief, rapid mass movement may occur through various types of snow and debris avalanches. Such activity is favoured where glacially oversteepened slopes have developed. Most avalanches start as snow avalanches which then pick up varying amounts of rock debris en route, ultimately becoming debris avalanches or slides. These are sometimes termed 'dirty avalanches' (Rapp, 1960a, p. 127) or 'mixed avalanches' (Washburn, 1979, p. 193). More liquid forms such as slush avalanches and mudflows may also occur where excessively wet (ripe) snow is subject to rapid thaw.

Debris flows are rapid movements of masses of rock and/or debris, gliding on one or several slide planes on the substratum and causing considerable friction erosion (Rapp, 1985). They are characterized by a distinct slide scar, and an eroded slide track terminating in a slide tongue or lobe. Many debris slides become heavily saturated with water, usually from melting snow, and quickly become viscous debris flows creating lateral debris flow levées and terminating in outspread debris fans (Fig. 9.9).

The importance of debris flows and avalanches as opposed to the other mass wasting processes will obviously depend upon such factors as relief, climate and lithology. One of the earliest studies to distinguish quantitatively between the various processes was that of A. Rapp, working in the Kärkevagge Valley, a formerly glaciated trough valley in northern Lappland (Rapp, 1960a). The most important conclusion was that solution loss, or the transport of dissolved salts, was the largest transporter of material but that rapid mass movements, in the form of debris flows and slides, were the most important in terms of specific denudation (Table 9.4). Surprisingly, solifluction was of only minor significance.

It would be unwise to assume that the denudation measured in the Kärkevagge Valley is typical of all mountainous, snowy periglacial environments. Much of the activity reported by Rapp resulted from a series of extreme events which occurred in October

Table 9.3 Summary data on three active layer failures, Fosheim Peninsula, Ellesmere Island, NWT, Canada

	Black Top Creek		Big Slide Creek		Hot Weather Creek	
Area mapped (km²)	5.3		11.5		1.6	
Assumed failure mechanism[1]	C	T	C	T	C	T
Slide volume ($\times 10^3$ m³)	307	195	161	71	30	14
Downslope mass transfer ($\times 10^6$ Mg m)[2]	24.3	28.5	24.3	19.5	0.9	0.8
Vertical mass transfer component ($\times 10^6$ Mg m)[3]	5.1	5.9	5.1	4.2	0.3	0.2
Horizontal mass transfer component ($\times 10^6$ Mg m)[3]	23.9	27.9	23.7	18.9	0.8	0.8
Recurrence interval (years)	50	100	50	100	50	100
Mean downslope movement (mm/year)[4]	122–143	61–72	45–56	23–28	13–14	6–7
Number of active-layer detachment slides[4]	35		4		24	
Slide volume[4]	44–47		2–3		35–36	
Downslope mass transfer[3]	68–72		<1		39–40	
Downslope movement (mm)[5]	4420–4910		11–12		250–280	

[1] Volumes and distances moved calculated assuming compression (C) or translation (T).
[2] Bulk density of soil materials assumed to be 1.5 Mg/m³.
[3] Rates calculated as an average movement for the top 0.5 m of soil material over the period shown; range of values produced assuming pure compression or pure translation during failure.
[4] % total in 1989.
[5] Calculated as an average movement for the top 0.5 m of soil materials; range of values produced assuming pure compression or pure translation during failure.
Source: data from Lewkowicz (1990)

1959. These were regarded as 'a centennial or probably even millennium maximum' (Rapp, 1960a, p. 185). It is important, therefore, to consider the frequency and magnitude of occurrence of episodic events when assessing their overall importance.

Assuming a recurrence interval of 200 years for such major events, Rapp (1985) extrapolated rates of rock denudation from a number of documented debris slides and flows which occurred in Scandinavia and Spitsbergen over the previous three

Table 9.4 Ranked list of major slope processes in Kärkevagge, Lappland, 1952–60

Process	Tonnes/ km/year	Denudation (mm/year)	Mass transfers (tonne–metres)	Remarks
1. Transport of solutes by running water	26	0.010	136 500	
2. Debris slides and flows	49.4	0.019	96 300	Extreme event, October 1959
3. Slush avalanches, rock debris transport	14	0.005	20 000	Extreme events, 1956 and 1958
4. Rockfalls	8.7	0.003	19 600	Seasonal events of high frequency
5. Solifluction	5.4	0.002	5300–19 800	Based on 9 km of soliflucted slope length; material density of 1.8
6. Talus creep	1.5	0.001	2700–4700	Based on 6 km of talus slope length; material density of 1.8

Source: modified from Rapp (1960a, p. 185)

(a)

(b)

Figure 9.9 (a) Debris flow tracks on talus slopes, Sleepy Mountain, northern interior Yukon, Canada. (b) Debris flows, Longyeardalen, Spitsbergen.

decades (Table 9.5). This analysis demonstrated that the activity recorded at Kärkevagge is at the low end of the high-magnitude scale, and that catastrophic debris slides and flows can be an important landscape modifier in mountainous regions.

In some instances avalanche activity has been shown to be more important than debris flow activity. For example, studies by Luckman (1988) at Surprise Valley in the Canadian Rockies over the 1969–81 period indicate mean debris accumulation rates of 5 mm/year. In detail, however, these values were strongly influenced by the magnitude and frequency of snow avalanche activity, while debris flows were relatively unimportant. In a second study, in northwest Spitsbergen, André (1993) documented the frequency of occurrence and spatial extent of avalanches, and the amount of debris deposited at the foot of avalanche paths. By correlating these volumes with rock wall surfaces, average rates of denudation of 0.007 mm/year in massive gneiss and 0.08 mm/year in fractured mica schist were obtained (Table 9.6). These values are considerably higher then the comparable values obtained by Rapp from Kärkevagge.

Slush avalanches are a particular type of snow avalanche that occurs along steep watercourses or small valleys. They are relatively poorly documented and one of the few comprehensive accounts is for northern Swedish Lappland (Nyberg, 1985). Slush avalanches consist of large masses of very wet and heavy snow, ice blocks, water and variable quantities

Table 9.5 Cases of alpine debris slides and flows in Scandinavia and Spitsbergen and estimated indices of their denudation impact

Locality	Date	Catchment area (km²)	Rock Type	Volume of debris (m³)	Denudation		
					Debris (mm)	Rock (mm)	Extrapolated rock[1] (mm)
Nissunvagge, N. Sweden	23.6.79	5.5	Amphibolite	85 000	15.5	10.8	54
Tarfala, N. Sweden	6.7.72	11	Amphibolite	55 000	5	3.5	18
Kärkevagge, N. Sweden	6.10.59	15	Mica-schists	4 600	0.3	0.2	1
Longyearbyen, Spitsbergen	11.7.72	4.5	Schists, sandstones	5 000	1	0.7	3.5
Ulvådal, W. Norway	26.6.60	7	Granite	300 000	43	30.1	150

[1] Extrapolated rates of rock denudation are given in mm per 1000 years assuming that the recurrence intervals is 200 years.
Source: from Rapp (1985)

Table 9.6 Tentative rates of denudation due to avalanche activity in glacial cirques from Spitsbergen

Avalanche Activity	Annual mean 1983–85			
	Number (%)	Surface (m²)	Weight (kg)	Volume (m³)
(a) Steep cirque wall in massive gneisses. Area: 145 000 m²				
Debris-free avalanches	21 (65%)	5 800	0	0
Slightly dirty avalanches	9 (26%)	1 300	390	0.12
Moderately dirty avalanches	2 (6%)	310	1 530	0.5
Highly dirty avalanches	1 (3%)	50	1 030	0.4
Total	33 (100%)	7 460	2 950	1.0
(b) Cirque wall in densely fractured mica schists. Area: 135 000 m²				
Debris-free avalanches	8 (14%)	1 400	0	0
Slightly dirty avalanches	26 (48%)	4 200	1 250	0.4
Moderately dirty avalanches	16 (29%)	2 600	13 000	4.8
Highly dirty avalanches	5 (9%)	760	15 200	5.6
Total	55 (100%)	8 960	29 450	10.8
Rate of denudation in massive gneisses: 0.007 mm/year				
Rate of denudation in fractured mica schists: 0.08 mm/year				

Source: from André (1993)

of eroded soil and bedrock. Usually, they occur in the spring in years of exceptionally rapid melt. According to Nyberg (1985, p. 147) slush avalanches probably have recurrence intervals varying between 2 and 10 years, and, depending upon magnitude, can transport anywhere between 50 and 200 m³ of rock debris.

The data presented in this section suggest that it is still difficult to assess the relative importance of debris flow and avalanche activity. A general perspective is that debris flows range from events of major geomorphic importance, with recurrence intervals of several hundreds of years, to smaller 'spot' events occurring every two or three years within limited areas. Slush avalanches, by contrast, are confined to smaller valleys where they occur in years of catastrophic spring breakup. As regards avalanches, the clear relationship between winter snowfall and spring temperatures is critical and recent investigations suggest that avalanches are, in themselves, an important denudation process in snowy mountainous regions. With all three processes, frequency and magnitude concepts are fundamental to any interpretation of their geomorphic significance.

9.4.3 Rockfalls

Where resistant rocks outcrop in the form of vertical or near-vertical free faces, rockfalls assume local importance and extensive scree slopes may build up below the free-face. Theoretically, if the scree is not renewed, the free-face will be progressively eliminated by the accumulation and upward growth of the scree slope. Often, as in parts of Spitsbergen, Scandinavia and the eastern Canadian Arctic, extensive and imposing rock faces have been inherited from the previous glacial period; in other areas, these slope forms occur in association with specific geological structures, with sea cliffs, or with deeply incised stream valleys. The weathering and recession of these free-faces occur primarily through the melting of interstitial ice and the loosening of rock particles by frost wedging in the small joints and fractures that are inevitably present. Eventually, the shear strength of the material is reduced below the level at which it is capable of countering the stresses imposed by gravity.

Like debris flows and avalanches, the rockfall process is episodic and may vary in magnitude from year to year, as well as spatially across the free-face. Again, it is difficult to establish rates of debris production and rockwall retreat without extensive and long-term observations. It can be hypothesized that rockfalls occur most frequently in the spring and autumn when air temperatures fluctuate around the freezing level. Rockfalls may also be accelerated by undercutting at the base of the slope, such as in the case of marine cliffs, or by gullying below the resistant rock outcrop if softer rock lies immediately beneath.

A number of studies have attempted to measure the rate of rockwall retreat under periglacial conditions. The values recorded are listed in Table 9.7. The rates, which range from 0.003 to 2.50 mm/year, should be treated with caution since all are gross

Table 9.7 Some rates of cliff recession under periglacial and non-periglacial conditions

Location	Lithology	Recession (mm/year)	Source
Periglacial			
Mt Templet, Spitsbergen	Limestones and sandstones	0.34–0.50	Rapp (1960b)
Mt Langtunafjell, Spitsbergen	Limestones and sandstones	0.05–0.50	Rapp (1960b)
Longyeardalen, Spitsbergen		0.3	Jahn (1976)
Spitsbergen, Kongsfjord	Massive gneiss Fractured mica-schist	0.007 0.08	André (1993)
Spitsbergen, Wijdefjord	Amphibolites	0.03–0.11	André (1993)
Spitsbergen, Ossian Sarsfjellet	Quartzites	0.1–1.5	André (1993)
Northern Lappland, Karkevagge	Schists	0.04–0.15	Rapp (1960a)
Ellesmere Island, NWT, Canada	Dolomitic limestones	(1) 0.30–0.80 (2) 0.50–1.30	P. Souchez; personal communication (1971)
Yukon, Canada	Syenite, diabase	0.003–0.019	Gray (1973)
Austrian Alps	Gneiss, schists	0.7–1.0	Poser, in Rapp (1960a)
Swiss Alps		2.5	Barsch (1977)
Canadian Rockies	Limestone	0.06–0.26	Luckman (1972)
Non-periglacial			
Mt St Hilaire, PQ, Canada	Gabbro, breccias	0.02–0.04	Pearce and Elson (1973)
Brazil	Granite	2.0	Quoted in Young (1972)
South Africa	Granite	1.5	Quoted in Young (1972)
Southwest USA	Shale	2–13	Quoted in Young (1972)

approximations. For example, R. Souchez computed the volume of scree material lying downslope of a raised beach dated at approximately 8000 years BP to arrive at his figures. This involved assumptions concerning the shape of the scree, its thickness, and the particle size and porosity (i.e. pore space) within the scree. His computed volumes may be too large, therefore, and his retreat rates might need to be reduced in magnitude. On the other hand, Rapp (1960a) estimated the volume of material in fresh rockfalls and then averaged that amount over the whole area of the vertical rockwall in the Kärkevagge Valley. This probably led to an underestimate of retreat values since rockfalls do not necessarily occur uniformly over the whole of the free-face.

The methods used to arrive at mean recession rates (mm/year) also vary considerably in reliability, precision and nature. For example, the values obtained by André (1993) from the Kongsfjord region were derived from debris arriving at the foot of snow avalanches (see earlier) while those from Wijdefjord and Ossian Sarsfjellet were computed using standard growth curves for the *Rhizocarpon* lichen.

Bearing these considerations in mind, the available evidence suggests that maximum rates of rockwall retreat of between 0.3 and 0.6 mm/year are probably typical for most lithologies. If correct, there is little support for the conventional view that weathering and slope retreat is appreciably faster in periglacial climates than in non-periglacial climates. In fact, there is evidence that exactly the reverse may be the case, especially in those periglacial environments where extreme aridity and intense cold prevent effective frost wedging. For example, Souchez (1967b) has commented upon the scarcity of scree material and the general geomorphic inertness of slopes in the Sor-Rondane and Victoria Mountains of Antarctica. Furthermore, when the rates of recession as listed in Table 9.8 are compared with recession rates in humid temperate and subtropical semi-arid regions, it is clear that retreat rates in periglacial regions are, in general, at least one order of magnitude less.

Table 9.8 Permafrost creep data from a number of localities

Locality	Mean Annual Ground Temperature (°C)	Slope Angle	Movement Rate (cm/year)	Source
Cold permafrost Rea Point, Eastern Melville Island, NWT	–16.0	5°	0.03–0.05	Bennett and French (1988, 1990)
Warm permafrost Great Bear River Valley, Mackenzie Valley, NWT	–2.0	15–31°	0.0–0.3	Savigny and Morgenstern (1986a, 1986b, 1986c)
Fenghuo Shan, Qinghai-Xizang (Tibet) Plateau	–3.0	9–25°	0.44 (1.6 m depth) 0.16 (2.8 m depth)	Wang and French (1995b)

9.5 Frozen slopes

The frozen nature of much periglacial terrain introduces at least two complications when one considers the nature of slope processes and slope evolution. These relate to the creep of frozen ground and the thawing of permafrost.

9.5.1 Permafrost creep

Permafrost creep is the long-term deformation of frozen ground under the influence of gravity. Deformation is due mainly to the creep of pore ice and the migration of unfrozen pore water. In frozen soils with large unfrozen water contents (e.g. clays) slow deformation due to thaw consolidation (see Chapter 8) may also occur. Although frozen soil creep can occur in seasonally frozen ground, it is in permafrost that frozen soil creep is most important.

A priori reasoning suggests that permafrost creep will be most effective in ice-rich soils on steep slopes in areas of warm permafrost. The unfrozen water at these temperatures and the increasingly plastic nature of the ice would promote deformation. Ground temperatures and ground ice amounts are obvious controlling variables; the warmer the permafrost and the greater the amount of ground ice, the greater will be the deformation.

Permafrost creep must be considered in any study of permafrost landscape evolution. Specifically, permafrost creep has been stated to result in the downslope curvature of ice wedges (Bozhinskiy and Konishchev, 1982) and it complicates the thermal contracting cracking of the ground (Mackay, 1993b). Lewkowicz (1988) concludes that permafrost creep is a potentially important denudational process in permafrost regions where ground temperatures are near 0 °C. Based on data supplied by Morgenstern (1981), Lewkowicz computes that downslope volumetric transport rates of 800–1000 cm³/cm/year are possible.

Relatively few attempts have been made to monitor *in situ* permafrost creep. One of the first, by Thompson and Sayles (1972), describes the *in situ* creep in the CRREL permafrost tunnel near Fairbanks, Alaska. Another short-term study, by Ladanyi and Johnston (1973), investigated *in situ* creep at a permafrost site near Thompson, Manitoba. In the Swiss Alps, studies by Haeberli (1985), Wagner (1992) and others have measured the *in situ* creep of rock glaciers using photogrammetric, geodetic and slope indicator techniques.

In terms of slope evolution three recent field studies document permafrost creep and permit some generalizations to be made (Table 9.8). In relatively warm permafrost, such as in the Mackenzie Valley and in Tibet, annual rates of deformation of 0.1–0.4 cm/year appear typical for slopes of moderate angle. By contrast, in the cold permafrost of the high Arctic, and on low-angled slopes, movement is one order of magnitude less, in the vicinity of 0.03–0.05 cm/year.

9.5.2 Stability of thawing slopes

In addition to the slow creep deformation of frozen ground described above, certain frozen slopes may experience failure, often at angles considerably lower than the equilibrium angle predicted by standard

Table 9.9   Summary data of reported failures in thawing soils

Locality	Lithology	Soil Residual Strength ϕ (degrees)	Predicted Angle (degrees)	Failed Angle (degrees)	Source
Active slope failures					
Northern Norway	Fine silty sand, some gravel	29–33	15.5–18	5–17	Harris (1972)
Spitsbergen	Sandy clayey silt	36	20	6–12	Chandler (1972)
Mackenzie Valley, NWT	Clay	23	12.5	3–9	McRoberts and Morgenstern (1974)
Pleistocene slope failures					
England	Soliflucted Weald, Gault, and London Clay	12.4–15.5	6.8–8.1	3–7	Weeks (1969)
England	Sandy clay	23	12.0	6.8	Chandler (1970a)
	Sandy clayey silt	16	8.8	4.0	Chandler (1970b)

geotechnical analysis. Table 9.9 lists a number of localities where frozen slopes have failed at angles below their predicted equilibrium angle. It is no coincidence that all are from localities where the frozen ground is relatively warm. Several studies of Pleistocene slope stability have also concluded that failures have occurred on unusually low-angled slopes (see Table 9.9). Frozen ground has been invoked as the cause.

In the Mackenzie Valley, NWT, Canada, investigations by McRoberts and Morgenstern (1974) demonstrated that failure occurred through frozen soil with the base of the slide in unfrozen clay (Fig. 9.10). The permafrost temperatures were between –2 and –4 °C. High pore water pressures controlled the available shear strength in the unfrozen clay and the long-term strength of the permafrost soil was governed by a frictional resistance

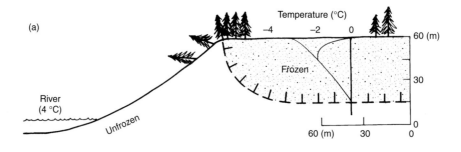

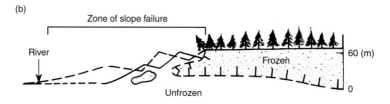

Figure 9.10   Failures of frozen slopes: (a) schematic diagram illustrating permafrost conditions on Mackenzie River banks, NWT; (b) Typical method of slope failure; example of Mountain River site (from McRoberts and Morgenstern, 1974).

factor. Since a considerable amount of unfrozen water was present in the relatively warm permafrost, the frictional resistance of the frozen clay was significantly reduced and failure occurred.

In environments of colder permafrost and/or more coherent stata similar failures have not been reported. However, with predicted global climate warming, it must be anticipated that such failures will become more frequent as ground temperatures rise and permafrost degrades. For example, it seems certain that many Pleistocene low-angle slope failures (see also Fig. 9.3) have occurred in association with the degradation of ice-rich clayey permafrost. Equally, various non-diastrophic Pleistocene structures, such as cambering and valley bulging (e.g. Kellaway, 1972), probably reflects the increased creep deformation experienced by degrading permafrost. These features are discussed more fully in Chapter 14.

K.S. Richards (eds), *Slope stability*. Chichester: J. Wiley and Sons Ltd, pp. 531–559.

Lewkowicz, A.G. (1988) Slope processes. In: M.J. Clark (ed.), *Advances in periglacial geomorphology*. Chichester: J. Wiley and Sons Ltd, pp. 325–368.

Mackay, J.R. (1981) Active layer slope movement in a continuous permafrost environment, Garry Island, Northwest Territories, Canada. *Canadian Journal of Earth Sciences*, **18**, 1666–1680.

McRoberts, E.C. (1978) Slope stability in cold regions. In: O.B. Andersland, and D.M. Anderson (eds), *Geotechnical engineering for cold regions*. New York: McGraw-Hill, pp. 363–404.

Nixon, J.F. and B. Ladanyi (1978) Thaw consolidation. In: O.B. Andersland, and D.M. Anderson (eds), *Geotechnical engineering for cold regions*. New York: McGraw-Hill, pp. 164–215.

Rapp, A. (1960) Recent development of mountain slopes in Kärkevagge and surroundings, northern Scandinavia. *Geografiska Annaler*, **42**, 65–200.

Further reading

Benedict, J.B. (1970) Downslope soil movement in a Colorado alpine region: rates, processes and climatic significance. *Arctic and Alpine Research*, **2**, 165–226.

Harris, C. (1987) Mechanisms of mass movement in periglacial environments. In: M.G. Anderson and

Discussion topics

1. What are the mass wasting processes which operate on slopes in periglacial environments?
2. How does the presence of frozen or thawing substrate influence slope processes?

CHAPTER 10

Slope morphology

Slope evolution under cold-climate conditions is central to our understanding of periglacial landscapes. It is clear that a variety of slope forms exist in periglacial regions and that none is exclusively 'periglacial' in nature.

Periglacial slope forms exhibit many similarities with those found in other arid and semi-arid regions of the world. Slope evolution involves a progressive and sequential reduction of relief with the passage of time. This is effected by slope replacement from below, with the formation of Richter denudation slopes that are ultimately replaced by low-angle pediments.

There is no one slope form or assemblage of slope forms which may be regarded as unique to the periglacial environment. All the available evidence suggests that all kinds of hillslopes are to be found in all kinds of climates. This led Leopold *et al.* (1964, p. 383) to conclude that '. . . the similarities of form in diverse climatic regions and the differences of form in similar climatic environments emphasises the need not of classification but of understanding the interrelation of climate, lithology, and process'. In this section, an attempt is made to follow such an approach. As a starting point, a number of slope form assemblages, identified largely on the basis of the writer's personal experience, are recognized (Fig. 10.1). All gradations between all types of slope forms exist, and the classification adopted here is purely one of convenience of presentation.

10.1 The free-face model

Probably the most well-known slope form of periglacial regions is one composed of a vertical or near-vertical rockwall below which is, first, a talus or scree slope and, second, a basal or footslope complex. According to Jahn (1960), four distinct zones can be recognized on slopes of this type in Spitsbergen: (a) the rock wall, (b) the talus slope, (c) a zone of solifluction activity and (d) a wash slope. As such, this sort of hillslope is very similar to the 'standard' hillslope of L.C. King (1953) in which there is a crest (waxing slope), a scarp (free-face), a debris slope (constant slope) and a pediment (waning slope). It is no coincidence that this slope form is well developed in those periglacial regions that have experienced recent glaciation and oversteepening of valley-side walls (e.g. Spitsbergen). However, the pediment and inselberg-like slope assemblages of certain non-glaciated regions, as illustrated by the Barn Mountains (see Chapter 2), may also be interpreted in this framework (see Fig. 9.9 (a)).

The free-face usually stands at angles in excess of 40° and is subject to weathering and cliff recession through frost wedging and rockfalls. The scree slope below is at the angle of repose of the coarser material, usually between 30° and 40°, and is progressively built up by rock falling from the free-face. The junction between the scree slope and the zone of solifluction is

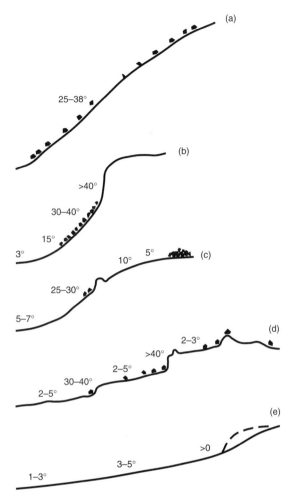

Figure 10.1   Typical slope forms found in present-day
periglacial regions: (a) the rectilinear
debris-mantled (Richter) slope;
(b) the free-face and debris slope profile;
(c) smooth convexo-concavo debris-mantled
slopes; (d) stepped profiles;
(e) pediment-like forms.

These slope forms can be found in many cold
regions. They are particularly common in formerly
glaciated areas where the oversteepening of valley
side slopes produced rockwalls in excess of the angle
of repose. In this sense, therefore, this particular
slope form assemblage can be regarded as an inherited, glacial form, which is being progressively
modified by periglacial processes. In formerly
unglaciated areas, this slope form is less pronounced
except where some form of basal undercutting prevents the free-face from being consumed by the talus
slope, such as adjacent to laterally eroding rivers, or
along sea cliffs.

Some of the most detailed studies of this slope
form have been undertaken on Spitsbergen, first by
Rapp (1960b) at Tempelfjorden, then by Jahn (1976)
at Longyeardalen, and more recently by André
(1993) at Kings Bay. Jahn (1976) concluded that the
processes operating fell into three groups: (a) debris
flows and gullying, the result of meltwater and rainwater on the slopes, (b) rockfall and debris cone
(apron) accumulations, the result of mechanical
weathering of free-faces and (c) solifluction. Of greatest geomorphological importance, in terms of the
rapidity of profile change, was debris flow activity. In
particular, significant slope changes which occurred
following an unusually heavy rainstorm in 1972 are
described. The role of snow avalanches, first highlighted by Rapp (1960b), was the focus of study by
André at Kings Bay where it seems likely that this is
also an important process. A logical conclusion is
that a combination of such processes characterizes
the free-face and debris slope assemblage.

At Kärkevagge in northern Sweden, the free-face
and debris slope assemblage is the typical slope form
(Rapp, 1960a). However, no extensive wash slopes
were reported to occur beneath the solifluction zone.
This contrasts with the extensive development of
wash slopes in Spitsbergen, as reported by Jahn
(1960). In spite of approximately similar precipitation
amounts, the apparent greater efficacy of slopewash
on Spitsbergen than at Kärkevagge might be
explained by (a) the sparser vegetation cover on
Spitsbergen, and (b) the greater susceptibility of
sandstones and shales on Spitsbergen to produce
sandy and silty particles upon weathering than the
granites and gneisses at Kärkevagge.

The scree or talus slope lying beneath the free-face
has been the subject of much investigation. The
visual impression of great thickness is misleading
since, except for talus cones or aprons, the scree is
usually less than 5 m in thickness and mantles a

usually marked by an abrupt junction, although in
places the two zones merge to produce a smooth concave profile. The solifluction zone varies in angle from
25° to 10° and sometimes extends to as low as 3°. It is
characterized by a micro-relief of solifluction lobes,
terraces and block streams. Downslope, the solifluction zone merges into a low-angled slope with
inclinations of between 2° and 5° in which the effects
of solifluction are much reduced and presumably
slopewash processes are more important. This is a
zone of net accumulation of sediment.

bedrock surface. Scree profiles are usually concave and not rectilinear as is often thought, with the steeper section of the scree occurring towards the top of the slope.

The coarse stratification of the talus is probably related primarily to debris flows, similar in nature to either the frost-coated clast flows described by Hétu (1995) from the Gaspésie, or the dry debris flows described by van Steijn *et al.* (1995). Although these deposits have sometimes been used as Arctic analogues for the distinct stratified deposits of northwest Europe (e.g. the *grèzes litées* of Guillien, 1951), this is not appropriate since the latter are better stratified, finer, occur on lower slope angles, and appear intimately linked to the local outcropping of frost-susceptible limestones and sandstones.

Movement of material down scree slopes may also result from talus shift. The latter is an azonal process not restricted to cold environments; it refers to the slow downslope movement of rock fragments initiated by the melt of ice binding the surface particles to those beneath, and the slippage of overlying particles on the moistened surface. Talus shift may also be locally initiated by the impact of falling rock and movement of one part of the scree is often transmitted by gravity through the scree. Movement by talus shift is, by nature, extremely variable across and down the slope. Greatest movement usually occurs in mid afternoons and/or during periods of strong solar insolation and surface heating.

10.2 Rectilinear debris-mantled slopes

Less well known but equally characteristic of many high latitudes are extensive, straight (rectilinear) slopes. Typically, the slopes are at the angle of repose, varying from 25 to 35–38°, and are covered with coarse angular and gravelly debris. They are a kind of Richter denudation-slope (Young, 1972, p. 107) in which debris supply and debris removal are in some form of equilibrium.

Such slopes have been described from the McMurdo ice-free valleys of Antarctica (Selby, 1971b, 1974) and from the Sor Rondane Mountains of East Antarctica (Iwata, 1987). Variants also exist in the mountains of the unglaciated northern Yukon. Selby (1971b, 1974) concluded that the debris on the slopes was supplied from backwalls as the backwalls retreated and that salt weathering, enhanced probably by frost action, is balanced by wind removal. In these arid environments, the slopes have little snow cover and the balance between weathering supply and removal results in the rectilinear sections at repose angles. An essentially similar explanation is proposed by Iwata (1987).

There is little reason to doubt that the existence of these slopes is related to the arid and ice-free nature of these regions. The pre-existing slope forms have changed to rectilinear debris-mantled slope by the slow prolonged retreat of the backwalls throughout much, if not all, of the Quaternary. Figure 10.2(a) illustrates the theoretical development of slopes, as proposed by Selby (1974). If the rate of weathering exceeds the rate of debris removal (b), then talus cones or aprons will accumulate. A more complex situation is illustrated in (c) where a glacier disappears to expose the lower part of a slope. A talus quickly forms to cover that part of the slope as the result of blockfalls associated with stress release. Then, as the cliff retreats, the rate of debris supply is progressively reduced since the size of the headwall is decreasing. Ultimately a Richter denudation-slope extends upslope.

If one believes the slope sequence hypothesized by Selby, it is tempting to suggest that the free-face debris slope assemblages described earlier from Spitsbergen, Scandinavia and other recently deglaciated regions are the early stages of Richter slope development.

10.3 Convexo-concavo debris-mantled slopes

A third type of slope form is characterized by a relatively smooth profile with no abrupt breaks of slope. There is a continuous or near-continuous veneer of frost-shattered and solifluction debris but no widely developed free-face or bedrock outcrop. Maximum slope angles are highly variable, ranging from 10° to as high as 25–30°, depending upon lithology. Under certain conditions, and in areas of relatively resistant rock, valley-side tors may be present in the upper sections and indistinct mounds of coarser, less weathered debris may constitute the summits of rounded interfluves (Fig. 10.3 (a)). In form, the slope profiles extend over the complete range of convexo-concavo forms, from dominantly convex (Fig. 10.3 (b)) to dominantly concave .

Although the presence of convex and concave slopes is implicit in the periglacial cycle of erosion as proposed by Peltier (1950), they have not been widely reported from present-day periglacial regions. This is

(a)

(b)

(c)

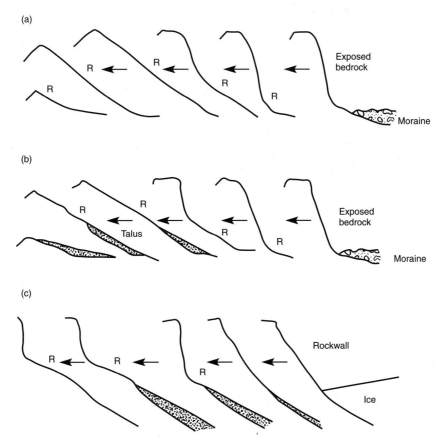

Figure 10.2 Theoretical development of slopes proposed for the McMurdo dry valleys, Antarctica. In (a) the rate of weathering is less than or equal to the removal of debris; hence the Richter denudation-slope (R) extends headwards. In (b) the weathering rate exceeds the rate of removal and talus accumulates. Once the free face is eliminated, weathering breaks down debris to finer sizes, and progressive slope flattening and development of an increasingly large basal concave slope will occur. In (c) the disappearance of a glacier allows block fall through stress release to occur over the whole cliff face, but especially at the cliff base where a talus is formed. As the cliff retreats and the talus extends upwards the rate of debris supply is reduced. The talus becomes finer in texture and much is removed by wind, until the bedrock is exposed and graded to the angle of rest of the talus material. Thereafter a Richter denudation-slope extends in the manner of (a) (from Selby, 1974).

in contrast to the numerous reports of convexo-concavo slopes in temperate regions which have been interpreted as being relict Pleistocene periglacial forms (e.g. Dylik, 1956). Although these slope forms have only been reported from certain localities on Spitsbergen (e.g. Büdel, 1960; Jahn, 1975, pp. 163–165), and from the western high Arctic (Rudberg, 1963; Pissart, 1966b), convex and concave slopes are probably more widespread than is thought. Certainly, on central and western Banks Island, where the underlying sediments are sand and gravel of the Beaufort Formation or Cretaceous shale and sand overlain by a thin veneer of glacial sediments, smooth convexo-concavo slopes are very common.

Our understanding of these slope forms is limited and the lack of detailed observations makes their interpretation difficult. It would appear that convex and concave slopes develop in areas of predominantly soft or unconsolidated rocks, usually Cretaceous or Tertiary in age, or in surficial

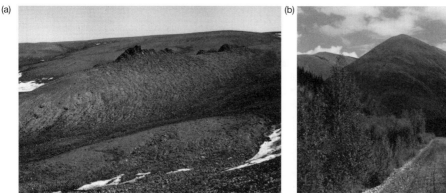

Figure 10.3 Examples of convexo-concavo debris-mantled slopes: (a) smooth convexo-concavo debris-mantled slope with bedrock outcrop (summit tor), Prince Patrick Island, NWT; (b) smooth, predominantly convex debris-manted slopes, Ogilvie Mountains, northern Yukon, Canada.

Quaternary-age deposits. For the most part, these are lowland, as opposed to upland, areas. On such terrain, solifluction and slopewash processes appear to be the dominant agents of landscape sculpture. According to Büdel (1960), the convexities and concavities reflect these processes while the steeper middle section of the slope is a backwearing debris slope subject to weathering and gravitational processes. The maximum slope angle, which may range from 10° to 25–30°, is essentially one of repose and reflects lithological factors. Thus, it can be regarded as a modified Richter slope. The lower concavity is generally dominated by slopewash and solifluction processes. The slopewash zone lies immediately downslope of the debris slope and is the result not only of the progressive downslope increase in wash but also of the accumulation of snowpatches at that position on the slope. In these locations, the depth of thaw is restricted and vegetation growth is limited because of the lateness of the thaw. As the vegetation progressively increases lower down the concavity and as the active layer assumes normal thicknesses, solifluction activity increases at the expense of sheetwash. The solifluction movement is commonly in the form of lobes. According to Pissart (1966b), slopes with inclinations of 5–7° appear to be the lower limit for the development of such lobes. Below this angle solifluction continues to operate but predominantly in sheets. The lower concavity represents, therefore, the minimum slope across which material brought from upslope is transported, first by sheetwash and then by solifluction.

The interpretation of the summit convexity is equally conjectural. Most probably the convexity relates to the dominance of slopewash, the volume of which increases downslope from the crest leading to an increase in the power of detachment of particles and of transport. If correct, the convexity is also a denudation slope subject to control by removal.

Two further characteristics of this particular slope form need to be mentioned. First, many convexo-concavo slopes have an abrupt break of slope at the junction between the debris slope and the lower concavity. This phenomenon is reminiscent of the pediment junction of hot arid regions and has been frequently commented upon (e.g. Rudberg, 1963; Pissart, 1966b). A probable explanation is that snowpatches remain longest in depressions and at the foot of lee slopes. Thus, in relation to the total slope profile, there is a sharp increase in the intensity of slopewash below the snowpatch. In particular, the slow but continuous action of sheetwash may lead to the progressive removal of fine particles. This in turn leads to the development of the knickpoint and the steepening of the debris slope above.

A second characteristic is the occasional presence of rock stacks or tors. These features stand out from the debris-covered slope, and are usually angular, frost-shattered rock protuberances bounded by sets of near-vertical joints. Tors occur widely in many periglacial regions underlain by suitably resistant rocks. For example, hillslope tors developed on sandstone and dolerite have been described from Victoria Land, Antarctica (Derbyshire, 1972), on limestone, sandstone and gneiss on the Boothia Peninsula, Canadian Arctic (Dyke, 1976), on Cretaceous shale on Prince Patrick Island, Canadian Arctic, and on highly resistant quartzite in the Klondike Plateau (Fig. 10.4).

(a)

(b)

Figure 10.4 Examples of hillslope tors associated with debris-mantled slopes; (a) hillslope tor developed in Upper Jurassic-age sandstone, surrounded by frost shattered angular debris, Prince Patrick Island, NWT; (b) hillslope tor in quartzite, unglaciated Klondike Plateau, Yukon Territory.

In view of the complexity of their origin, and their climatic significance (see Chapter 14), it is useful to distinguish between hillslope tors and summit tors. Hillslope tors are located in valley-side locations and are surrounded by debris-covered slopes commonly between 20° and 30° in angle, depending upon lithology. Summit tors, located on interfluves or points of high elevation relative to the surrounding terrain, are surrounded by slopes of much lower angle, often less than 5–7°. The latter are examined in the following sections dealing with pediments and cryoplanation. The majority of hillslope tors apparently develop through slope retreat and frost wedging and are

structurally controlled. They are surrounded by coarse angular debris. The latter usually rests at the angle of repose and moves downslope under gravity processes. Local site differences, affecting microclimate, are also important. For example, in Victoria Land, angular hillslope tors are only developed on west- and northwest-facing slopes, the result of relatively intense solar radiation received by these slopes. Rock temperatures may exceed 30 °C at times, and thawing of snow lying on dark surfaces has been observed when air temperature is –20 °C. However, mechanical (i.e. frost) weathering may not be the only process responsible for hillslope tors. On Ellef Ringnes Island, in the Canadian Arctic, St-Onge (1965) has interpreted tor-like features ('relief ruinifore') occurring on slopes developed in sandstone as the result of wind erosion.

10.4 Pediment-like forms

The existence of extensive low-angled surfaces has been reported from many continental and high-latitude periglacial regions. These include unglaciated central Siberia (e.g. Demek, 1972a; Czudek and Demek, 1973), and unglaciated northern Yukon (Hughes, 1972b; Priesnitz and Schunke, 1983; Priesnitz, 1988; French and Harry, 1992). Mention is also made from Svalbard (e.g. Büdel, 1982, pp. 18–80) and the Canadian Arctic islands (Pissart, 1968). Cold-climate pediments are also reported to exist, as Pleistocene relicts, in certain mid-latitude environments (e.g. Dylik, 1957; French, 1972a; Karrasch, 1972; Castleden, 1977; Czudek, 1985; Beck, 1989).

These distinctive surfaces are sometimes termed cryopediments, '. . . gently inclined erosion surface developed at the foot of valley sides or marginal slopes of geomorphological units developed by cryogenic processes in periglacial conditions' (Czudek and Demek, 1970, p. 101). Dylik (1957) concluded that these forms were analogous with the pediments of tropical and sub-tropical regions, and that they developed during the colder periods of the Quaternary.

The dominant characteristics of cryopediments are (a) their low angles of inclination, (b) their extremely shallow concave, nearly rectilinear, profile and (c) their geomorphic location at the foot of valley-side slopes. In form, cryopediments vary in angle from as much as 8–10° in their upper sections to as low as 1° in their lower sections (Fig. 10.5). The

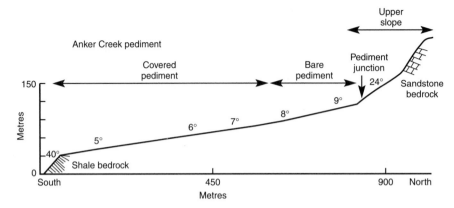

Figure 10.5   Topographic profile of a pediment in the Barn Mountains, unglaciated Northern Yukon (from French and Harry, 1992).

upper limit of the cryopediment is commonly marked by an abrupt break of slope or knickpoint, and the pediment may encroach upon the inter-valley area in the form of embayments. Since cryopediments are slopes of transportation, only a thin veneer of surficial material mantles the slope. According to Priesnitz (1981, p. 149), the main processes operating on pediments in cold regions are frost wedging and rillwash of the upper, steeper slope and solifluction and sheetwash/snowmelt activity on the pediment surface itself.

Pediments in hot arid regions have been the subject of considerable controversy in the geological and geomorphic literature; they are generally believed to be rock-cut transportation surfaces which truncate geologic boundaries. Some workers regard pediments as part of the semi-arid landscape evolution model proposed by L. C. King (1953) and earlier authors (e.g. Johnson, 1932). Others regard such surfaces as being essentially basal weathering surfaces or 'etch-plains' (e.g. Büdel, 1970).

The cause of the planation is not easy to understand but most workers in hot semi-arid regions generally agree that pediments are developed by the action of rills, gullying, rainwash and sheetflooding coupled with the backwearing of steep upper slopes (Leopold *et al.*, 1964, pp. 496–498). A slightly divergent opinion is expressed by Twidale (1987) who concludes that 'pediments are shaped by streams in flood, in brief high energy flows' (p. 72). The problem is whether these explanations apply to cold regions.

In periglacial regions our understanding of pediments is limited by a lack of field observations upon processes currently active on the pediment surfaces.

The traditional interpretation of cryopediments relies upon the assumed activity of cryogenic processes (e.g. Czudek and Demek, 1970, 1973; Priesnitz, 1981) whereby frost action extends the pediment upslope by a process of scarp retreat.

Several recent investigations question this interpretation. In particular, the low efficacy of mechanical (frost) weathering in regions which lack low-magnitude, high-frequency freeze–thaw events and abundant moisture availability (e.g. Matsuoka, 1990) does not support a frost-action interpretation. In the cold, semi-arid periglacial regions, it seems prudent to downplay the role attributed to frost wedging in landscape evolution even given the considerable period of time available for pediment formation. Instead, it seems more reasonable to assume that cold-climate processes, both physico-chemical and transportational, have acted within the constraints imposed by a pre-existing pediment morphology. This suggests Büdel's concept of 'traditional development' (Büdel, 1982, pp. 181–183).

Referring specifically to some of the northern Yukon pediment surfaces, French and Harry (1992) hypothesize that pediments in cold semi-arid regions are effective slopes of transportation of waste material only under certain conditions (Fig. 10.6); they are active during periods of intense frost wedging and high sediment removal, and are inactive whenever moisture levels fall below a critical level. This combination of temperature and humidity probably restricts activity to the transitory periods marking the beginning and end of cold-climate fluctuations.

Both Czudek and Demek (1973) and French and Harry (1992) comment upon the nature of the

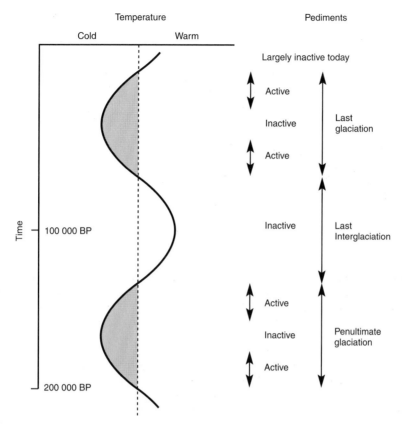

Figure 10.6 Schematic diagram illustrating possible relationship between Pleistocene climatic fluctuations and enhanced pediment activity in the Barn Mountains (from French and Harry, 1992).

processes currently operating on cold region pediments. In eastern Siberia, the majority of pediment surfaces are overgrown with taiga (*Larix dahurica*), many of which are inclined or tilted, forming what are termed 'drunken forests'. While this phenomenon may reflect subsurface wash and/or suffusion processes (see earlier), the tilting of trees may also reflect merely cryoturbation activity.

In the Barn Mountains, for example, current geomorphic activity on the pediments is limited to cryoturbation and earth hummock formation in the seasonally thawed silty materials which veneer the pediment surface (French and Harry, 1992). Elongate hummock ridges suggest plug-flow but there is little or no evidence for sheetwash activity. Two other lines of evidence suggest that the Barn Mountain pediments are largely inert under present climatic conditions. First, the lichen-covered nature of rock rubble, where exposed at the surface, suggests the

regolith is largely inactive. Second, the fact that the sediments which veneer the pediment surfaces have not encroached upon fluvial terraces cut in bedrock demonstrates that the last period of sediment transport on the pediments pre-dates terrace incision.

10.5 Stepped profiles

Closely related to the pediment-like surfaces previously described are large terraces or steps carved in bedrock and occupying upper hillslope positions (Fig. 10.7). Terms used to describe these features include 'goletz' terraces, altiplanation terraces, nivation terraces and equiplanation terraces. All are now generally referred to as cryoplanation terraces (e.g. Demek, 1969b; Priesnitz, 1988, Table 3.2). Such features occur mainly in unglaciated northern Yukon and Alaska (e.g. Reger

Figure 10.7 Bedrock (i.e. cryoplanation) terrace at a high elevation in the Buckland Hills, Yukon Territory, on argillite and chert of the Neruokpik Formation (Precambrian).

and Péwé, 1976; Hughes, 1982; Lauriol and Godbout, 1988; Lauriol, 1990), and in Siberia (e.g. Boch and Krasnov, 1943; Demek, 1969a, 1969b).

Cryoplanation terraces are of varying size and form depending upon lithological conditions and geomorphic location. In form, the terraces may be sickle-like in shape, or elongate and relatively narrow. Their dimensions vary widely; the smallest are often less than 50 m in maximum dimensions while others may be 400–600 m in length and 150–200 m in width. Some cryoplanation terraces in Siberia reach even greater dimensions, being over 1 km in width and several kilometres in length. Summit cryoplanation flats are also of considerable size; the summit flat on the top of the Turku Hill in the Kular Range of Siberia is more than 400 m wide (Demek, 1969a, p. 42). The height of the frost-riven scarps, limiting the cryoplanation terraces, varies not only with the resistance of the rock and the degree to which the riser (free-face) is preserved, but also with the inclination of the original slope. On flat summits and on gentle slopes underlain by unconsolidated sediments

the height of the risers may only be between 1 and 2 m but in other areas with greater relief and overall dimensions of the terraces, the height of the frost-riven scarps may be as much as 10–20 m. The angle of the terrace flat varies between 1° and 12°; usually the larger the flat and the lower the inclination of the original slope, the smaller is the gradient. Occasionally, polygonal patterned ground, block streams and solifluction stripes develop on the terrace flat.

Several stages in the development of cryoplanation terraces have been recognized (Fig. 10.8) by Demek (1969b). The intensity and importance of processes are thought to change at each stage. In the beginning, cryoplanation terraces develop in relation to snowbanks which, in the low precipitation regions of the Arctic and Siberia, concentrate physical weathering. As a rule, therefore, cryoplanation terraces are thought to develop on lee slopes, or below structural benches or slope irregularities, all of which allow the accumulation of snowbanks. In this initial stage, frost-shattered debris is removed by sheetwash and gelifluction. The second stage is the formation of the

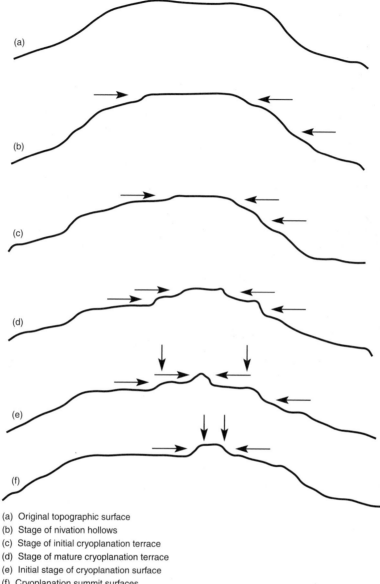

(a) Original topographic surface
(b) Stage of nivation hollows
(c) Stage of initial cryoplanation terrace
(d) Stage of mature cryoplanation terrace
(e) Initial stage of cryoplanation surface
(f) Cryoplanation summit surfaces
➜ Direction of surface modification

Figure 10.8   Stages in the development of cryoplanation terraces in resistant rock, according to J. Demek (1969b).

tread (flat) and riser (free-face). Frost action on the riser results in its steepening and retreat. On the terrace below, a combination of solifluction and wash transports material away from the frost-riven scarp. The third stage is the development of a summit flat or surface, as the frost-riven scarp is ultimately con-sumed through intersection with an adjacent terrace. In coarse-grained and resistant rocks, tors or bedrock outcrops may rise above the surrounding surface. In the final stages, downwearing is thought to become the dominant mode of evolution and frost action leads to sorting and patterned ground development.

Lithology is thought to play an important role in the development of the various forms of cryoplanation. For example, on Ellef Ringnes Island, Canadian Arctic, St-Onge (1969) has described the different forms which develop in gabbro, sandstone and shale. In gabbro, the evolution of the terraces is slow in comparison to their formation in other rocks since gabbro is a hard, compact rock with a low porosity, and frost shattering takes place only under the most favourable of circumstances. The terrace flats are usually between 10 and 15 m in width and the risers, with slopes of between 25° and 35°, are between 2 and 5 m in height. The terrace flats form giant, near-horizontal steps which reflect the predominantly coarse boulders and the few fines which result from the disintegration of gabbro. Since the finer particles are quickly removed by water percolating through the boulders, the terrace is bounded by an apron of coarse, angular debris. On adjacent sandstones the terraces are more subdued in form. The sandstones weather to silt, sand and sandstone aggregates, all of which are more easily moved by gelifluction and sheetwash. Thus, the terrace flat becomes an inclined surface of 6–8°. Finally, in shale and siltstone, a variety of features develop ranging from large amphitheatre-like hemicircles to smaller hollows and ledges. These features reflect the ease with which weathering reduces the soft shale to fine sand and silt, and the effectiveness of wash in removing such material.

The significance of cryoplanation terraces is highly debatable, although the existence of these steps is not in question. The steps are almost certainly erosional in nature; at Boundary, for example, on the Alaska–Yukon border, the features cross dip directions and attitudes (e.g. see Reger and Péwé, 1976; French *et al.*, 1983, pp. 61–63). At the same time, most appear to be inactive or relict and their age is uncertain. Cryoplanation is thought to require conditions of intense frost wedging combined with sufficient snow fall for snowbanks to accumulate, yet not too much snow such that the bedrock is insulated from freeze–thaw activity. According to Demek (1969a), cryoplanation terraces best develop in continental semi-arid periglacial environments and Reger and Péwé (1976) believe that cryoplanation terraces require permafrost for their formation. Yet no quantitative process study to date has demonstrated the active development of these steps and the process(es) involved.

10.6 Slope evolution

Problems of slope evolution usually centre around the manner and rapidity of profile change with time. In spite of a considerable literature upon slope evolution in general, relatively little deals directly with such changes and even less is concerned with present day, as opposed to Pleistocene, periglacial environments.

Souchez (1966) developed one of the few process–response models of slope evolution specifically related to periglacial environments. The model dealt with slopes developing in coherent rock under the action of slow mass movement of the surface mantle and emphasized the role of plastic deformation and shearing failure. Under conditions of plastic flow, downslope regolith movement was assumed to be at a rate proportional to the angle of slope, and ground loss proportional to convex curvature. The resulting model is one in which slopes decline but remain predominantly convex at all stages. Although such slopes do exist in periglacial regions (e.g. Büdel, 1960) there are several reasons why this model is of only limited applicability. First, the model does not account for the presence of erosional concave slopes (e.g. (cryo)pediments). Second, the model does not apply to slopes developed in unconsolidated sediments. Third, the assumption that solifluction follows the laws of plastic flow is not necessarily true since there are instances where movement is plug-like and, of course, an important component of solifluction is frost creep, which is unrelated to plastic flow.

There is a further consideration which, in general terms, complicates the development of any process–response model. Only in a few regions is it likely that periglacial slope evolution has managed to run its full course. Two such regions have been described in Chapter 2. In many other regions, slope forms have been inherited from the previous glacial period, and are, therefore, in varying stages of disequilibrium. Only in areas which either (a) have experienced long and uninterrupted cold-climate conditions or (b) are underlain by soft, unresistant rocks can one assume with any confidence that the slope forms represent a reasonably close adjustment with process. In reality, the only areas of significant extent in the northern hemisphere in which periglacial slope development may have proceeded to its equilibrium condition are the unglaciated regions of northern and eastern Siberia, some Canadian Arctic islands and certain parts of interior Yukon Territory and central Alaska.

10.6.1 Cryoplanation

The periglacial literature contains numerous references to cryoplanation as a cryogenic process promoting the low-angled slopes and level bedrock surfaces typical of many periglacial regions (e.g. see Dylik, 1957; Demek, 1972a, pp. 148–149; French, 1976a, pp. 155–165; Washburn, 1979, pp. 237–243). Suffosion, 'thermo-planation' and slopewash are some of the possible processes suggested (e.g. Kachurin, 1962; Soloviev, 1973a; Dylik, 1972). However, this literature must be treated with caution since most descriptions are of cryoplanation terraces rather than cryopediments. Moreover, many are of relict rather than active features (e.g. Péwé, 1970) and, notwithstanding the work of J. Demek (1969a, 1969b; Czudek and Demek, 1973), and earlier mention of 'goletz' terraces and 'mountain planation' (e.g. Jorré, 1933; Boch and Krasnov, 1943; Richter et al., 1963), recent Soviet geocryological texts rarely mention cryopediments or cryoplanation in northern Siberia (e.g. see Kudryavtsev, 1978; Romanovskii, 1980; Popov et al., 1985b). There is the real possibility that many features previously identified as cryoplanation terraces are lithologic and/or structural benches.

Thus, special attention should be given to the opinion of Büdel (1982, p. 78) who concludes that, in today's periglacial environments, there is not '. . . the slightest evidence of any etchplain creation such as the cryoplanation or altiplanation proposed by some authors.' Moreover, the importance attached to nivation in promoting rock weathering must also be critically re-examined (Washburn, 1985, pp. 186–187; Thorn, 1988), although it must be admitted that the pediment junction, if formed by frost action, is often the site of frequent snowbank accumulation. Finally, several workers (e.g. Dylik, 1957; Rudberg, 1963; Pissart, 1968) have drawn attention to the similarity between slope forms in the hot and cold semi-arid regions of the world, and much of the available data suggest that the nature and rate of slope evolution under periglacial conditions is no faster than that of non-periglacial regions. Collectively, these comments suggest that any differentiation between pediments and cryopediments is artificial. It follows that the pediment 'problem', which is central to understanding landscape evolution in the hot arid regions of the world, is also central to the cold non-glacial regions. The pediment problem is still unresolved.

Notwithstanding these problems, the cryoplanation concept is useful and needs discussion. It was first summarized by Peltier (1950) in his periglacial 'cycle of erosion'. Peltier envisaged an existing landscape formed under non-periglacial conditions being subject to intense frost action ('congelifraction') and solifluction ('congeliturbation'). The initial stage (Fig. 10.9) saw the downslope movement of soil and rock-rubble by congeliturbation which exposed bedrock on the upper slopes. This bedrock was then subject to frost shattering, rockfall and retreat, with the accumulation of a talus or 'congeliturbate mantled' slope beneath. On upland surfaces, congelifraction produced extensive areas of angular frost-shattered debris, forming blockfields. With time, the continued retreat of the frost-riven scarp consumed the cliff leaving only residual tor-like features at the summit. At this stage 'maturity' was reached in which the pre-existing landscape had disappeared and the landscape was covered with a mantle of frost-shattered and solifluced material. Then, in 'old age', solifluction continued to degrade and flatten the summits while adjacent valleys and lowlands were progressively 'plugged' by the accumulation of the frost-shattered and solifluced debris.

In terms of slope evolution, Peltier's idealized cycle represented an intuitive synthesis of field observations since it emphasizes many of the typical slope forms described earlier in this chapter. It is too general, however, to provide anything but an overall framework within which to view slope evolution. For example, no quantitative parameters are given for the landscape changes which are thought to occur, and there is no realistic discussion of the manner in which frost shattering and mass movement influence slope form. Finally, the lack of attention paid to other processes, particularly running water, is a fundamental weakness.

10.6.2 Slope replacement and Richter denudation-slopes

In tropical semi-arid and arid areas, where free-face and talus slopes assemblages are well developed, slopes evolve by replacement, with scree slopes replacing cliffs and these in turn being replaced by low-angled, concave, transportational slopes. If weathering and removal of fine material from the scree occurs in addition to cliff retreat, an equilibrium condition may be achieved in which the cliff

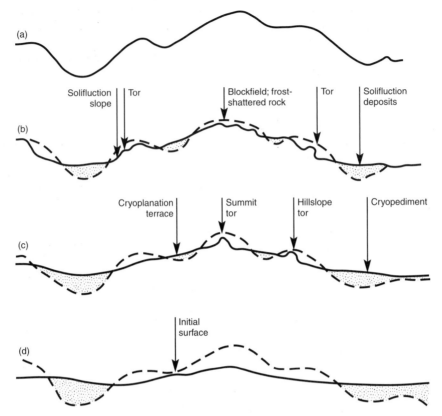

Figure 10.9 Schematic illustration of the cycle of periglacial landscape modification suggested by Peltier (1950); (a) pre-existing relief; (b) onset of periglacial conditions; (c) maturity; and (d) cryoplanation.

and the scree retain the same slope proportions during retreat (Carson and Kirkby, 1972, pp. 353–355). As the cliff and scree slopes are reduced in height, the gradient of the low-angled basal slope would become lower to compensate for the reduction in debris carried. This sort of development is illustrated graphically in Fig. 10.10 for conditions of a broad plateau and a fixed base level (i.e. stream) which exports debris from the concavity.

This model may be applicable to the arid periglacial environments in continental and polar locations, where the similarity of certain slope forms with those of tropical semi-arid regions has already been mentioned. The cryopediments and the angular, pediment-like junctions may develop in this manner, with successive erosional regrading of the pediment surface. The difference between periglacial and tropical semi-arid slope forms may merely be one of degree.

The concept of Richter denudation-slopes fits well in the context of slope replacement (see Fig. 10.2).

Where the rate of weathering of the free-face and the debris at its base is less than or equal to the ability of transportational processes to remove weathered debris, a Richter denudation-slope forms below the free-face. Since weathering rates are assumed to be uniform over Richter slopes, they will decline at a

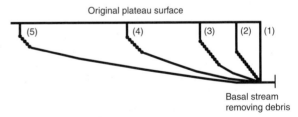

Figure 10.10 The evolution of a free face and talus slope under conditions of basal removal from a fixed point (from Carson and Kirkby, 1972).

constant and inherited angle (Selby, 1971b). Over time, Richter slopes will gradually be replaced by concave pediments as relief is reduced.

This model incorporates many of the slope forms described earlier. Moreover, it can certainly be applied to the Barn Mountains landscape and, to a lesser degree, to the Beaufort Plain of northwest Banks Island (see Chapter 2). If these localities are classical periglacial landscapes, *senso stricto*, then slope replacement and Richter denudation-slopes are unifying concepts in our understanding of periglacial slope evolution.

10.6.3 Rapidity of profile change

It is often assumed that slopes evolve more rapidly under periglacial conditions than under non-periglacial conditions (e.g. Tricart, 1970, p. 112). This remains unproven, since what little data that are available suggest that weathering and slope processes do not operate at a significantly faster rate in periglacial, as opposed to non-periglacial, climates. For example, the rate of rockwall retreat under periglacial conditions appears to be less than in rain-forest, humid temperate and tropical semi-arid conditions (Table 9.7), and limestone solutional activity is no greater in Arctic regions than in other arid or semi-arid areas (Table 4.7). The assumption of rapid slope evolution probably results from the widespread assumption of the importance of frost shattering in periglacial climates, which, as has been demonstrated earlier (Chapter 4), is not necessarily true.

When considering rates of slope evolution, it is necessary to consider (a) the regional and micro-climates, (b) the lithology and (c) the dominant weathering process. For example, cliff retreat is clearly faster on rocks which enable water penetration into and along joints and bedding planes than on coarse-grained and massive rocks with few joints or bedding planes. Equally, frost-wedging is less effective and slope retreat less rapid in areas of extreme aridity than in areas of greater humidity. Even within areas of uniform climate and lithology, micro-climatic differences on slopes of different orientations may induce the more rapid weathering of some slopes than of others. The best example is the formation of asymmetrical valleys (see Chapter 11). For reasons such as these, it is probably unwise to assume that slope evolution is faster under periglacial conditions than non-periglacial conditions. Indeed, although the impression gained from most cold-climate slope studies is one of relatively dynamic evolution, it must be remembered that this merely reflects the fact that the majority of such studies have been undertaken in recently deglaciated regions. The few studies from the arid, cold and never-glaciated regions of the world suggest a more subdued model of landscape evolution.

10.7 General reflections

It is clear from Chapters 9 and 10 that our understanding of slopes in periglacial environments is still highly speculative. Further study of slope form, together with detailed investigations of the link between form and process, is urgently required. Bearing this in mind, a number of points summarize the preceding discussion.

First, slopes evolve in periglacial environments primarily through the combined action of mass movement and running water, and not through 'unique' periglacial processes.

Second, a variety of slope forms exist in periglacial regions. Probably none is limited to periglacial regions. Slope form is primarily influenced by the lithological characteristics of the underlying rock. The presence or absence of moisture, in determining the type and rate of weathering and weathering removal, is of prime importance.

Third, periglacial slope forms exhibit many similarities with slope forms found in the arid and semi-arid regions of the world. The difference may only be one of emphasis.

Fourth, many slopes are best interpreted as having been inherited from a previous glacial period, and are, therefore, in disequilibrium with the present climatic environment.

Fifth, periglacial slope evolution probably involves a progressive and sequential reduction of relief with the passage of time. Limited evidence suggests that this takes place by slope replacement from below, with the formation of Richter denudation-slopes which ultimately, are replaced by pediments.

Sixth, there is no evidence to assume that slopes evolve more rapidly under periglacial conditions than under non-periglacial conditions.

Further reading

French, H.M. and D.G. Harry (1992) Pediments and cold-climate conditions, Barn Mountains, unglaciated Northern Yukon, Canada. *Geografiska Annaler*, **74A**, 145–157.

Jahn, A. (1976) Contemporaneous geomorphological processes in Longyeardalen Vestspitsbergen (Svalbard). *Biuletyn Peryglacjalny*, **26**, 253–268.

McRoberts, E.C. and N.R. Morgenstern (1974) The stability of thawing slopes. *Canadian Geotechnical Journal*, **11**, 447–469.

Priesnitz, K. (1988) Cryoplanation. In: M.J. Clark (ed.), *Advances in periglacial geomorphology*. Chichester: J. Wiley and Sons Ltd, pp. 49–67.

Rapp, A. (1960) Talus slopes and mountain walls in Tempelfjorden, Spitsbergen. *Norsk Polarinstitutt Skrifter*, **119**, 96 pp.

Selby, M.J. (1974) Slope evolution in an Antarctic oasis. *New Zealand Geographer*, **30**, 18–34.

Souchez, R. (1966) Réflexions sur l'évolution des versants sous climat froid. *Revue de Géographie Physique et de Géologie Dynamique*, **VIII**, 317–334.

Discussion topics

1. How similar are the slope forms found in the hot and cold semi-arid regions of the world?
2. How do slopes evolve under cold non-glacial conditions?
3. Is there a distinct periglacial cycle of landscape evolution?

CHAPTER 11

Fluvial processes and landforms

Fluvial processes are a major element in fashioning the periglacial landscape. Both large and small rivers exist, all dominated to a varying extent by a spring snowmelt-induced (nival) peak discharge. Freeze-up and breakup are also distinct cold-climate characteristics, together with fluvio-thermal erosion. Although all types of channel morphology can be found in periglacial regions, braided channels are the most common. The asymmetry of many small stream valleys reflects the complex interaction between slope and channel processes.

11.1 Introduction

The large-scale organization of periglacial terrain is not unlike that of other regions. A well-developed drainage network exists, even in those areas which have recently emerged from beneath Wisconsinan or late Pleistocene ice. This fluvial network is most striking within the high Arctic landscape where, because of the lack of vegetation, the intricacies of the network are clearly visible.

The fluvial network is essentially composed of two types of rivers. First, a number of very large rivers and their tributaries, such as the Mackenzie and Yukon rivers in North America, and the Ob, Yenesei, Kolyma and Lena rivers in Siberia, originate from non-periglacial regions or from deep springs in the discontinuous permafrost zone. These are some of the largest rivers in the world, flowing for several thousands of kilometres from their headwaters to the Arctic Ocean. To some extent, their discharge and sediment characteristics are independent of the terrain and climatic regions through which they flow. Second, there are the innumerable smaller rivers of varying sizes which constitute the overwhelming majority of the fluvial network. The drainage of these streams originates totally within periglacial regions and their discharge and sediment characteristics more truly reflect the environment in which they flow.

Since the geomorphic activity of the very large rivers reflects non-periglacial as well as periglacial conditions, most of the following comments are directed primarily towards those fluvial networks that originate within periglacial regions. Moreover, since there is an extensive geomorphological and hydrological literature available for both temperate (e.g. Gregory and Walling, 1973) and cold environments (e.g. Woo, 1986; Clark, 1988), emphasis is further directed toward the distinct or cold-climate aspects of these fluvial regimes.

Many Arctic rivers flow only during the few summer months when temperatures rise above freezing. For most of the year there is little surface or subsurface water movement. Because of this, it was originally thought that running water was of minor significance in fashioning the periglacial landscape (e.g. Peltier, 1950). This is not the case. It is now abundantly clear that flowing water in periglacial regions is capable of significant denudation and transportation activity especially when compared with other geomorphological agents. The spring snowmelt is very rapid indeed, usually occurring over a period of two or three weeks, and gives rise to a prominent freshet, or flood. Thus, although the precipitation in many regions is slight and is spread throughout the year, between 25 and 75 per cent of total runoff is concentrated in a few days. Furthermore, in certain of the extremely arid regions, the majority of precipitation falls as summer rain and not as snow, during a few periods of prolonged rain. Because the ground is relatively bare of vegetation, and because permafrost inhibits the penetration of such rain into the ground, a high proportion of summer rain runs off directly on the surface. In other areas, the presence of permanent snowfields or glaciers provides a near-constant source of summer runoff, which varies with the local weather conditions.

11.2 Major rivers

Before proceeding any further, it is appropriate to briefly consider the nature of the very large northern rivers which extend across the continental periglacial domains of North America and Siberia. These rivers serve as vital communications networks and their channel hydrology has a significant impact upon transportation, shipping and adjacent settlements. The Mackenzie River, northern Canada, is typical of these rivers (Fig. 11.1(a)). The simplicity of the flow hydrograph masks the complexity of tributary sources and the different effects of both mountain and northern hydrology. In Fig. 11.1(b) are shown the 1986 daily hydrographs of the Mackenzie River above its junction with Arctic Red River and of several of the other major tributaries.

The Hay River (drainage area 47 900 km²) drains the northern lowlands and has the normal attributes of winter low flow, brief spring-snowmelt high flow, and summer recession interrupted by rainstorms. The Liard River (drainage area 33 000 km²), typical of cordilleran rivers, also has low winter flow, but high runoff is sustained for a longer period by snowmelt from a range of elevations. Large runoff per unit area is another feature of this mountainous basin. By contrast, the Camsell River (drainage area 30 900 km²) drains the Canadian Shield, where low precipitation is impounded by a myriad of lakes; lake storage evens out the flow over the year so that snowmelt runoff is withheld and a moderate level of winter flow is maintained. Although these sub-basins have distinct hydrological regimes of either nival or mountain character, the Mackenzie's annual flow is the sum total of these tributary contributions combined with regulation of flow provided by dammed and natural lakes.

The Mackenzie is navigable through its length from Hay River on the south shore of Great Slave Lake to Tuktoyatuk on the coast of the Beaufort Sea. The river plays a vital role in the annual resupply of settlements in the western Canadian Arctic. During the navigation season (Table 11.1), barges frequent the waterway. However, the season is short: breakup begins in May just north of the Liard River junction and progressively moves downriver, while freeze-up begins during early October in the Mackenzie Delta. In Siberia, similar roles are played by the Lena, Ob, Yenesei, Kolyma and Indigirka Rivers with the added advantage of a northern sea route along the Siberian coast from Kolymsk in the east to Archangel'sk in the west.

These large rivers usually retain water under the ice all winter. Also, the channels are often surprisingly deep. Breakup usually begins with flows of local meltwater over the ice surface. Then, the ice rises as flow increases underneath and shore leads develop. Break-up is usually rapid, often accompanied by flooding. Ice jams are a frequent occurrence and can accentuate flooding problems causing serious damage to bridges and other structures (e.g. Gerard, 1990). Figure 11.2 schematically illustrates a typical ice jam while Table 11.2 lists the direct costs associated with ice jams on the Mackenzie and Yukon River systems in recent years.

Comparable data for the large Siberian rivers are not easily available but it is reasonable to assume that similar hydrograph patterns and freeze-up/breakup conditions prevail.

11.3 Channel hydrology

We must distinguish between stream channels that are fed by both surface runoff and by groundwater and those that are fed almost entirely by surface runoff. The latter occur in areas of continuous permafrost while the former occur in subarctic locations where discontinuous permafrost permits springs to emerge from taliks and subpermafrost aquifers. In both types of stream channel the intense winter cold and the abundance of snow and/or ice in the channels intensifies the freeze-up and breakup processes.

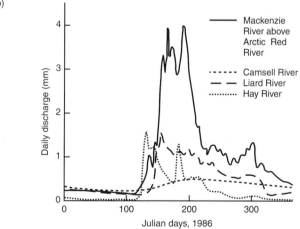

Figure 11.1 The Mackenzie River, northern Canada; (a) extent of drainage, with major tributaries; (b) daily discharge, 1986, above Arctic Red River, and, of Camsell, Liard and Hay River tributaries.

Table 11.1 Mean freeze-up and breakup dates, Mackenzie River, NWT, 1946–55

Location	Distance from Great Slave Lake (km)	Freeze-up	Breakup
Fort Providence	80	24 Nov.	18 May
Fort Simpson			
Mackenzie above Fort Simpson	335	27 Nov.	15 May
Mackenzie below Fort Simpson	351		11 May
Fort Norman	825	15 Nov.	14 May
Norman Wells	909	10 Nov.	15 May
Fort Good Hope			
Ramparts	1094	5 Nov.[1]	22 May
Settlement	1101	12 Nov.	15 May
Arctic Red River Settlement			
Arctic Red River	1445	8 Oct.	25 May
Mackenzie River	1445	1 Nov.	24 May
Lang Trading Post	1561	9 Oct.[2]	26 May
Aklavik	1607	9 Oct.[2]	28 May
Reindeer Station	1615	18 Oct.	27 May

[1] Seven years of record
[2] Nine years of record
Source: quoted in French and Slaymaker (1993)

11.3.1 Freeze-up

The processes of river ice formation are well described in the geotechnical literature (e.g. Gerard, 1990) and need relatively brief explanation here. In the initial stages, the turbulence generated by flow is sufficient to produce supercooled water and the first ice to form is sheet ice over the quiet waters of the ponds or shallows along the banks. Elsewhere, 'frazil' ice forms (floating ice crystals) and where this comes in contact with the bed, as in shallow reaches, it forms 'anchor ice'. As freezing continues, the frazil particles form slush, which in turn agglomerates into frazil pans. At the same time border ice grows out from shore and eventually the frazil pans will lodge between the border ice. As more frazil pans arrive from upstream, the initial pack grows in the upstream direction. At this point, water levels begin to rise in response to the increasing resistance to flow beneath the ice and the necessity for the channelway to carry the discharge with increased resistance. This depth increase is typically greater than 30 per cent of the mean depth of the open water situation. The situation is further aggravated by the fact that the ice cover or pack floats with more than 90 per cent of its thickness submerged; this necessitates a further rise in water level. River geometry and weather conditions then influence the final stages of freeze-up. If the river is gentle, the flow is slow and the cold is intense during formation of the pack, the pack will be thin and frazil production high. In this case, the pack forms as one pan and progression upstream is rapid. If the river is steep and fast, and the air temperatures are mild during formation, the initial pack will be thick and the rate of frazil-pan production will be slow. In this case the increase in water level will be large but pack progression will be slow.

River icing formation (*naledi*, in the Russian literature) is another phenomenon which occurs during late freeze-up at certain locations on subarctic rivers. River icings are usually attributed either to a reduction in the cross-sectional area of the ice-covered flow conduit as freezing advances (Wankiewicz, 1984), or to an increase in snow load on an initial ice cover thus raising the hydrostatic head beneath the ice to an elevation higher than the ice surface. Because the water cannot escape from the banks because of freezing of

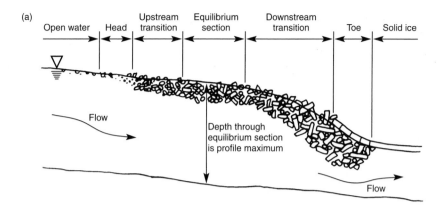

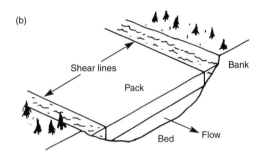

Figure 11.2 Cross-section through a typical ice jam on a large northern river in Canada: (a) longitudinal; (b) channel cross-section (*source*: Gerard, (1990).

the active layer, fractures in the ice allow water to escape over the ice cover, for it subsequently to freeze as an icing. In shallow braided streams, distinct icing mounds, 1–3 m high, may develop in response to localized restrictions of flow by ice freezing to the bed of the braid bars. These river icing mounds are analogous to the seasonal frost mounds discussed in Chapter 5. The river freeze-up processes described above are illustrated diagrammatically in Fig. 11.3.

11.3.2 Breakup

Breakup of the rivers in subarctic regions occurs rapidly, often with considerable flooding. The problem is accentuated in rivers that have headwaters in the south where snowmelt and icemelt begin earlier. This supply of water accelerates and intensifies the breakup process.

Ice jams frequently occur, as described earlier for the Mackenzie River, with significant economic impact. On smaller rivers, where the ice has often frozen to the bed, breakup often involves diversion of flow around the ice obstacle and significant bank erosion may occur.

In high Arctic regions, where river ice and icings are rarer, the valleys are usually unfilled with snow at the time of breakup. The snow has accumulated by wind drifting throughout the winter months. The associated breakup sequence has been described by both Pissart (1967b) and Woo and Sauriol (1980). To begin with, the snow reaches saturation point through the arrival of runoff from the adjacent, thawing, slopes. As ripening of the pack continues, a slushflow is briefly initiated, followed by flow which rapidly carves unstable channels or tunnels in the snow. In places, large snow drifts can dam sections of valleys to impound water upvalley, only for this to be released when the snow jam breaks (Woo and

Table 11.2 Ice-jam damage events on Yukon and Mackenzie Rivers, Canada, 1960–85

	Year	Cost of flooding (Can. $)
Yukon		
Yukon River, Dawson City	1979	2 910 136.00
Stewart River, Mayo	1973	23 041.00
Ross River, Ross River	1973	45 824.00
Stewart River, Mayo	1972	14 890.00
Yukon River, Dawson City	1967	182 912.00
Stewart River, Mayo	1965	103 833.00
Yukon River, Dawson City	1965	158 573.00
Yukon River, Dawson City	1963	27 994.00
Northwest Territories		
Mackenzie River System[1]		
Hay River, Hay River	1985	695 736.00
Hay River, Hay River	1963	3 953 374.00
Liard River, Fort Simpson	1963	3 294 479.00

[1] Other known sites include: Aklavik, Arctic Red, Fort Good Hope, Fort Liard, Fort McPherson, Fort Norman and Nahanni Butte
Source: from Van der Vinne *et al.* (1991)

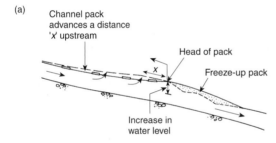

(a)

Channel pack advances a distance '*x*' upstream

Head of pack

Freeze-up pack

x

Increase in water level

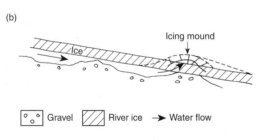

(b)

Icing mound

Ice

Gravel   River ice   Water flow

Figure 11.3   River freeze-up processes: (a) growth of ice cover at freeze-up and associated water level changes (from Gerard, 1990); (b) formation of river icings (*naledi*) in shallow sections of multiple-channel systems.

Sauriol, 1980). According to Woo and Sauriol, the drainage network along small valleys often opens up in segments and, until all the segments are linked, the basin is incapable of the coherent transport of melt-water runoff (Woo, 1986).

11.4 Basin hydrology

Because permafrost restricts downward percolation, the runoff in basins underlain by permafrost responds quickly to snowmelt and rainfall events. Vegetation also influences the runoff regime since a good vegetation cover promotes a longer recession period, especially in wetlands with extensive standing water.

One of the first quantitative studies on basin hydrology in the high Arctic of North America was by Cook (1967) who measured the flow of the Mecham River on Cornwallis Island, NWT. This was followed by more detailed studies by McCann *et al.* (1972), and on Baffin Island by Church (1972). Subsequently, Church (1974) summarized the different hydrological regimes of northern rivers, and his classification (Fig. 11.4) has now gained widespread acceptance (e.g. Woo, 1986, 1991).

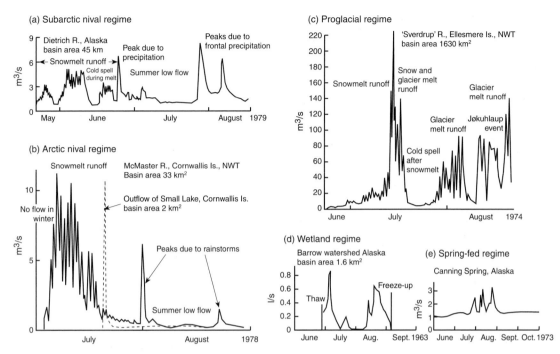

Figure 11.4 Hydrographs representing typical streamflow regimes in periglacial areas: (a) subarctic-nival regime; (b) arctic-nival regime, also shown is outflow from an arctic lake; (c) proglacial regime; (d) wetland regime; (e) spring-fed regime (from Woo, 1986, 1990b).

11.4.1 Stream flow regimes

Hydrographs representing typical stream flow regimes in periglacial regions are presented in Fig. 11.4. To varying extents, all the runoff regimes are dominated by the rapid melting of snow and ice in the short winter–summer transition period. In the Canadian Arctic, for example, this occurs in late June or early July. Then, during the rest of the summer, the runoff steadily decreases as less and less snow remains to be melted. This progressive decrease in runoff is periodically interrupted by subsidiary runoff peaks related to summer storms and direct surface runoff. Such a runoff regime is termed 'nival', and may be subarctic or arctic in nature depending upon whether flow is maintained throughout the winter or not. A second type of river regime occurs in those watersheds where permanent snow or icefields exist. Here, renewed melting occurs throughout the summer whenever warm and overcast conditions develop. Peak runoff under these conditions is often delayed until late July or early August, and the nival freshet is not so important a component of the runoff

regime. This is called a proglacial regime. A third regime is the wetland type. Because of the water-retaining capacity of muskeg or lowland grassy tundra, and the high resistance to runoff presented by it, flood flows are attenuated in such drainage basins. A final category is the spring-fed regime, often associated with basins underlain by carbonate rocks in the discontinuous permafrost zone. These streams have relatively stable discharges because the primary source of water supply is from groundwater.

The Arctic runoff season can be divided into four seasons; breakup, the snowmelt period (the 'nival flood'), late summer and freeze-back. In detail, however, each season is determined by the pattern of local summer weather for each year. Usually, breakup begins in early June, when air temperatures are still below 0 °C, through local snowmelt brought about by direct solar radiation. The meltwater percolates to the base of the snowpack and into snow-choked stream courses, where it refreezes. It is not until two or three weeks later that sufficient melt has occurred for flowage of saturated snow to occur. The river channels turn to slush and runoff begins over the snow and ice in the stream bed. Usually after two or three days of intensive runoff, the winter ice on the stream bottom has melted and runoff continues on the stream bed proper. There is usually a trigger which initiates the runoff; this is commonly a period of warm weather or a heavy storm which flushes an appreciable length of the stream channel.

In nival watersheds the majority of snowmelt occurs in the spring period. Runoff subsequently decreases from the nival flood and comes to be dominated by storm runoff, either after heavy cyclonic activity or following periods of prolonged overcast and drizzly conditions. The hydrological response is rapid, illustrating the importance of the presence of permafrost and the absence of vegetation. Superimposed upon these short-term storm-controlled fluctuations are diurnal fluctuations, which are well developed in midsummer. Discharges usually increase in late afternoons and early evenings, or following periods of uninterrupted solar radiation.

During late summer, many of the smaller streams are virtually without flow, and by the freeze-back period at the end of the summer there is very little melt for runoff. That stream flow which does exist is maintained almost entirely by recession flow from the groundwater discharge. Since the active layer is thin, flow is low. Figure 11.5 illustrates the difference in runoff conditions in a small stream on eastern Banks Island in late June and mid-August of the same year.

In proglacial watersheds, the importance of the nival flood is much reduced and peak flow is usually delayed until late July or early August. According to Church (1972, p. 32), this indicates that (a) the early season heat deficit near the glacier surface has been overcome, (b) the albedo of the glacier surface has been lowered by melt of seasonal snow and exposure of darkened glacier ice, and (c) a drainage network has extended over the entire glacier watershed. During the melt, the daily runoff closely reflects daily heat inputs. The most extreme daily ranges of flow occur during fine weather conditions when there is a strong diurnal control on glacier melt. By contrast, damp, stormy weather reduces the diurnal range of discharge.

In proglacial streams, an interesting extreme event is the occurrence of jokulhlaups. These are localized flood surges caused by the bursting of ice dams along the margins of the ice. In nival watersheds, true jokulhlaups do not occur. However, Church (1972, p. 38) described a small-scale event on Baffin Island in which the discharge curve possessed all the characteristics of a jokulhlaup. It was caused, however, by a combination of very heavy rain and rapid melting occurring together. This was not, therefore, an abnormal event, but merely appears so in the short term. St-Onge (1965, Fig. 13), following observations on a small stream on Ellef Ringnes Island, makes the same point.

It is difficult to generalize about the magnitude and frequency of flow events in the more typical nival and proglacial basins, since there is a lack of long-term hydrological data. However, in the last decade, several studies, with a minimum of eight years of record, have been undertaken in northern Canada, mostly by governmental and other regulatory bodies. Woo (1986) has drawn much of this material together (Table 11.3) which allows preliminary analysis of the longer-term flow characteristics. The mean and standard durations of flow, standardized into discharges per unit area, together with the

(a)

(b)

Figure 11.5   (a) A small stream in eastern Banks Island, NWT, Canada, towards the end of spring snowmelt in late June. (b) The same stream in mid August.

Table 11.3 Mean annual discharge $(\overline{Q})$ and standard deviation of flow (S) of selected rivers in northern Canada

River	Drainage Area (km²)	$\overline{Q}$	S	CV	Years of Record	Environment
Kluane	4 950	0.0148	0.0027	18.5	30	Mountainous, glacierized, discontinuous permafrost (below lake outlet)
Klondike	7 800	0.0078	0.0016	20.1	18	Mountainous, discontinuous permafrost
Kakisa	14 900	0.0026	0.0010	39.4	19	Interior plain, discontinuous permafrost (below lake outlet)
Thoa	9 630	0.0037	0.0010	27.4	15	Canadian Shield, discontinuous permafrost
Dubwant	67 600	0.0049	0.0008	16.2	15	Canadian Shield, continuous permafrost (below lake outlet)
Freshwater	1 490	0.0050	0.0013	25.9	8	Arctic Islands, continuous permafrost

$\overline{Q}$ and S are mean and standard deviation of flow in m³/s/km².
CV is coefficient of variation (in %)
Source: from Woo (1986)

coefficients of variation, indicate that specific discharges are largest for basins with glacier input, next largest for mountainous basins without such input and least for the rivers of the northern interior plains. It is highly probable that similar relationships exist for the discharges of the rivers of northern Siberia. As might be expected, annual peak flows are highest for mountain rivers fed by glaciers followed by rivers in the continuous permafrost zone, while the presence of lakes and extensive wetlands reduces the variability of the annual peaks.

It is unfortunate that most periglacial regions, unlike temperate regions, lack the long-term and relatively widespread data sets that would allow more explicit analysis.

11.4.2   Water balance studies

Long-term flow measurements in northern basins are sometimes accompanied by observations upon precipitation, snow cover and evaporation. Together, these data are usually analysed within a water balance context in which the various water gains and losses within the basin are examined.

The simplest water balance relationship is:

$$Q = P - E + \Delta S \qquad (11.1)$$

where Q = runoff (discharge), P = precipitation, E = evaporation and ΔS is the change in basin storage. Several water balance studies have been made in the permafrost regions of North America. A typical illustration is by Woo *et al.* (1983) for the McMaster River basin, Cornwallis Island, NWT, between 1975 and 1981. Summary data are presented in Fig. 11.6. According to Woo (1990b, p. 70) water balance studies in non-glacial permafrost basins indicate that (a) snowfall constitutes the bulk of annual precipitation and is crucial in determining the total basin snow storage; (b) most annual runoff in the Arctic is fed by snowmelt but the importance of snow declines southwards where rainfall contributes larger portions of the precipitation; then the fluvial run-off regime dominates; and (c) runoff consumes much of the precipitation; runoff ratios (R/P) may be as high as 0.7–0.8 for most basins except wetlands. Although the active layer does afford some limited storage capacity, year-to-year changes in basin storage may be as high as 10 per cent of total annual precipitation. Woo was cautious, therefore, that one should not assume that basin storage change from year to year is minimal. One problem in these sorts of studies

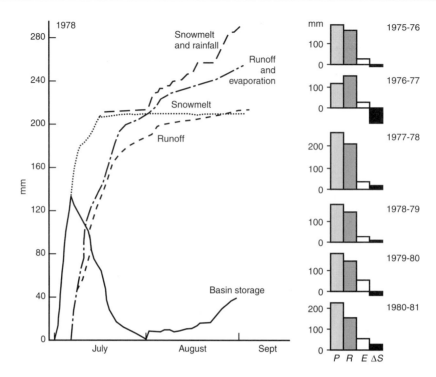

Figure 11.6   Daily water balance for McMaster River basin, Cornwallis Island, NWT, during the summer of 1978 and the annual water balance for 1975–1978 (data from Woo, 1990b). *P* = precipitation; *R* = runoff; *E* = evaporation; Δ*S* = change in storage.

is that relatively little is known about the rate of snow sublimation especially in winter when the air humidity is very low. The available data suggest it is low, about 10–20 per cent of total precipitation, leaving approximately 80 per cent to generate runoff.

11.5   Sediment flow, surface transport and denudation

Sediment movement occurs through a combination of solution, suspension and bedload transport. In periglacial regions there are several sources of sediment for such transport. Material is moved off slopes to the stream channel by rockfall, solifluction and slopewash processes. Many areas, furthermore, possess an abundance of unconsolidated surficial sediments inherited from the previous glacial period. These are easily picked up by streams through undercutting and erosion of river banks. Finally, frost weathering provides rock particles suitable in size for transport.

One of the few comprehensive studies of sediment movement in periglacial streams was undertaken in the Canadian Arctic by Church (1972). Values of total sediment discharge, by solution, suspension and bedload transport, for three rivers on Baffin Island are summarized in Table 11.4. The solution and suspended sediment values were derived by traditional methods of field sampling while the bedload values were computed as values of 'potential sediment transport' at full supply. Thus, they may be higher than the actual bedload transport achieved. Bearing this in mind, the data nevertheless show the dominance of bedload sediment transport. At Ekalugad River in 1967, bedload accounted for over 90 per cent of the load, while at Lewis River, over a three-year period, bedload accounted for 79 per cent of the total load. By contrast, the amount of movement in solution was insignificant, being less than 1 per cent each year, and suspended sediment made up the balance, varying between 5 and 25 per cent.

It is unwise to accept these values uncritically as being typical of all fluvial networks in periglacial areas. Church points out that much of the present

Table 11.4 Sediment movement in some Baffin Island streams

(a) Total sediment movement

River	Total Sediment Transport (tonnes)	Sediment Yield (tonne/km² of watershed)	Volume Removed (m³)	Equivalent Surface Lowering of Watershed (mm/1000 years)
Lewis River 1963–65 (mean)	151 021	735	56 989	277
Middle River Ekalugad Valley, 1967	64 461	609	24 325	230
Upper South River, Ekalugad Valley, 1967	104 851	1 168	39 566	441

(b) Proportional distribution of sediment load

	Solution	Suspension	Bedload
Lewis River, 1963	0.004	0.181	0.816
Lewis River, 1964	0.008	0.222	0.770
Lewis River, 1965	0.005	0.207	0.788
Middle Ekalugad, 1967	0.004	0.060	0.936
Upper South Ekalugad, 1967	0.004	0.042	0.954

Source: from Church (1972)

sediment yield is derived from the removal of unconsolidated glacial sediments and, hence, sediment yield bears no relationship to present rates of sediment production in these watersheds (Church, 1972, p. 63). Baffin Island, as with most other recently deglaciated parts of Arctic Canada, is currently going through a 'relaxation' process or disequilibrium phase in which streams are actively redistributing a mass of detrital materials laid down at the various ice marginal positions. On the other hand, it appears that the dominance of bedload transport is a characteristic of many periglacial rivers, even in areas unaffected by recent glacierization. In northern Alaska for example, Arnborg *et al.* (1967) found that over 80 per cent of the sediment transfer in the Colville River was of either a bedload or suspended nature. This dominance of bedload movement may explain the distinctive flat-bottomed form of some periglacial stream valleys. These are discussed later in this chapter. In most rivers in other environments, bedload transport is thought to be relatively minor, and even mountain streams in alpine situations apparently move little bedload (see Church, 1972, p. 61).

The difficulties involved in generalizing about sediment transport in periglacial regions is further illustrated when one considers total annual sediment yield. A number of comparable data sets exist for many parts of the world. A wide range of yields are

found in Arctic regions. For example, when compared with a suggested North American mean yield of 130 tonnes/km²/year (Gregory and Walling, 1973), these data sets suggest that periglacial yields are not markedly different from those of other environments (Table 11.5). Furthermore, although suspended sediment transport peaks range widely from hundreds to several thousands of mg/l, Clark (1988, p. 433) concludes that 'few values actually exceed 50 mg l⁻¹ and a more representative value might be taken as 5 mg l⁻¹'. A similar variability is found in the case of solute transport. In spite of Rapp's (1960a) conclusion that solute transport was the dominant type of sediment transport in the Kärkevagge Valley of northern Sweden, no consensus has emerged. Much solute transport is of the same order of magnitude as suspended sediment transport (Table 11.6). Furthermore, other data suggest that the dissolved organic carbon transport for the major northern rivers is little different from, or less than, the other major river systems of the world (Table 11.7), again leading one to question the assumption of solute dominance in cold regions.

Some insights into the significance of fluvial processes in fashioning the periglacial landscape are also provided by the data in Tables 11.4 to 11.7. Computations involving the total amount of material transported from the various watersheds studied by

Table 11.5 Some selected values of total sediment yield from periglacial catchments

Location	Measure (tonne/km²/year)
Sweden	0.8–4.7 (ton/km²/year)
Yenisei, USSR	5
Ob, USSR	7
Mecham River, NWT	22.1 (ton/km²/year)
Four large USSR Rivers	3–25
Kärkevagge, Sweden	53
Colville River, Alaska	80–85 (ton/km²/year)
Baffin Island, NWT	400–790
North America average	130

Source: data quoted in Clark (1988)

Church (1974) indicate average ground surface lowering of the order of 200–450 mm/1000 years (Table 11.4). However, as noted earlier, it is probable that normal sediment production, and therefore, average ground lowering, is at least one order of magnitude lower than the present yield rate. Thus, the rate of 52 mm/1000 years, measured by Arnborg *et al.* (1967) on the Colville River in northern Alaska, is probably more typical of unglaciated periglacial areas or those that have completed their relaxation process.

Table 11.6 Typical volumes of suspended and solute sediment transport in periglacial regions

(a) Suspended sediment transport

Location	Measure
Mackenzie/Yukon (catchments < 10 000 km²)	0.2–11.5 t/km²/year
Mackenzie/Yukon (catchments > 10 000 km²)	36–126 t/km²/year
Yukon coast	5–300 mg/l
Finnish Lappland	Typically 5–50 mg/l
Hoffellsjökull, Iceland	Mean 1337 mg/l (glacier-fed); 776 mg/l (non-glacial)

(b) Solute transport

Location	Total Dissolved Solids (mg/l)
Baffin Island	5–50
Swedish Lappland	CaCO 25–55
Queen Elizabeth Islands	30–50 increasing to 70–100
Devon Island	CaCO peaked at 102
Banks Island slope plots	44–252
Hoffellsjökull, Iceland	Mean 271 (glacier-fed); 52 (non-glacial)

Source: data quoted in Clark (1988)

Table 11.7 Dissolved organic carbon transport for periglacial and non-periglacial rivers

River	Discharge (km³/year)	Area (10³ km²)	Runoff (mm/year)	Concentration Range (mg/l)	(t/km²/year)
Periglacial					
Yukon	210	840	250		3.0
Mackenzie	249	1810	138	3–6	0.7
Lena	533	2430	219		2.1
Ob	419	2550	164		1.5
Yenesei	562	2580	218		1.6
Non-periglacial					
Amazon	5520	6300	876	3–5	3.2
Orinoco	1135	950	996	2–5	6.1
Mississippi	439	3267	154	2–8	1.1
Ganges	366	975	375	1–9	1.7
Niger	152	1125	171	2–6	0.5
Yangtsekiang	883	1950	453	5–23	6.1

Source: data from Goudie (1995, p. 60)

From a geomorphic point of view, it is of interest to know when, and under what conditions, the majority of the sediment was transported. This usually bears some relationship to discharge. In the Canadian Arctic, Robitaille (1960) first drew attention to the importance of the nival flood in transporting material on Cornwallis Island, and this was subsequently confirmed by stream flow measurements by Cook (1967) on the Mecham River. On the other hand, in the more arid areas of the western high Arctic, both Rudberg (1963) and Pissart (1967b) have stressed the fact that the nival flood does not necessarily give rise to extensive transport of material. Not only is the actual discharge associated with the nival freshet rather small, on account of the small amount of snow present in such regions, but the majority of the flood is completed by water flowing over the winter ice in the stream bed, effecting little or no stream erosion.

Data from the Lewis and Ekalugad Rivers, Baffin Island, Canada, illustrate the variability of sediment transport with discharge in the nival and proglacial environments. Table 11.8 lists the proportion of total seasonal runoff and sediment transport of each type listed cumulatively on the highest five days of flow/transport for the years 1963–65 (Lewis River) and 1967 (Ekalugad River). The data clearly indicate the very high concentration of sediment movement

events achieved by streams dominated by nival and storm events. For example, over 75 per cent of total sediment movement of the South Ekalugad River in 1967 occurred in less than 8 per cent of the runoff time of record. If typical, one must conclude that a major proportion of total sediment transport is accomplished in a very restricted period of time in periglacial environments.

11.6 Fluvial-thermal erosion

One of the more distinctive aspects of fluvial activity in periglacial regions is linked to the thermal effects of running water. In addition to the normal mechanical or abrasive effects, running water possesses the ability to thaw permafrost. This phenomenon has already been discussed in an earlier chapter (see Chapter 6), and needs little amplification. In summary, thermal erosion operates predominantly laterally, by undercutting river banks and sea cliffs, to produce thermo-erosional niches. This process is important for at least three reasons: (a) the subsequent collapse of river banks provides material for bedload transport and deposition downvalley, and is also instrumental in the rapid coastal retreat which occurs in certain areas (see Chapter 12); (b) it is one

Table 11.8 Proportional distribution of discharge and sediment transport for the highest flow events in nival and proglacial streams, Baffin Island, Canada

River	Days of Record		Cumulative Proportional Discharge/ Transport During Highest Flow Days				
			1	2	3	4	5
(a) Nival type	66	Q	0.103	0.155	0.200	0.245	0.288
South Ekalugad, 1967		Q_c	0.059	0.099	0.135	0.171	0.207
		Q_s	0.407	0.471	0.530	0.575	0.612
		Q_b	0.477	0.579	0.653	0.724	0.793
		Q_t	0.466	0.562	0.635	0.702	0.767
(b) Proglacial type	206	Q	0.032	0.059	0.081	0.102	0.122
Lewis River, 1963–65		Q_c	0.015	0.029	0.042	0.054	0.066
		Q_s	0.074	0.121	0.161	0.200	0.232
		Q_b	0.080	0.139	0.184	0.226	0.262
		Q_t	0.078	0.135	0.179	0.220	0.255

Q discharge; Q_c solution; Q_s suspended; Q_b bedload; Q_t total movement
Source: data from Church (1972)

factor aiding the development of the flat and braided valley bottoms which are characteristic of many permafrost areas; and (c) it helps explain the relative efficiency of lateral stream corrosion and subsequent stream migration in permafrost areas.

11.7 Channel morphology

River channels may be either single or multiple, straight or meandering, and large or small. In periglacial regions, all types of channel patterns exist but undoubtedly the most distinctive and common is the multiple, or braided, channelway.

11.7.1 Braided channels

The dominance of braided channelways necessitates a brief consideration of the controls over braiding. We may identify several factors as being significant. First, the majority of braided channels occur in high-energy streams flowing in non-cohesive sediments and carrying heavy sediment loads. Bank erodibility is clearly a factor since excessive lateral erosion in weak sediments will lead not only to very wide channels in which shoaling occurs on central bars and thus, to the development of multiple channels, but also to the entrainment of large quantities of debris. Braiding is also related to rapid and large variations in runoff. In

terms of hydraulics, an appreciable bedload transport appears to be the essential factor for braiding (Fahnestock, 1963). Once such a situation is present, any decrease in the competence of the stream will result in bar development and multiple channels. This decrease in competence may be caused by a variety of factors such as slope variations, discharge fluctuations and variations in channel width and depth.

All the factors which determine braiding are present, to varying degrees, in periglacial regions. First, thermal erosion is a particularly effective agent of lateral bank erosion. The large-scale collapse of river banks adds sediment to the river as well as broadening the channel. Second, in recently deglacierized areas, the current redistribution of glacigenic sediments means a further source of material for transport, and in unglaciated regions where unconsolidated sediments outcrop widely, such as the western Canadian Arctic, a similar source of abundant sediment is present. Finally, the discharge of both nival and proglacial streams is subject to rapid and extreme fluctuation, as outlined earlier.

As a result, the floors of many stream valleys in the Canadian Arctic are essentially flat. Such a floor is dissected by shallow braiding channels which are cut in alluvial sediments ranging from coarse gravel to medium sand. The banks of the channels are abrupt, giving a shallow box-like profile to the valley bottom (Fig. 11.7). At times of flood, the entire valley floor becomes covered with a layer of turbulent water, in which bedload transport dominates and the whole

Figure 11.7 Oblique air view from 150 m elevation of small box-shaped valley with braided stream incised within fluviatile terrace, eastern Prince Patrick Island, Canada.

river becomes a moving mass of debris. Undercutting of the bank also occurs at this stage. As discharge decreases and as competence drops, the coarser material is redeposited, and the river once again assumes a new braided pattern. Sometimes, the major channel may be relocated on the far side of the valley floor opposite to its position the previous year. Thus, given time and repeated adjustments to the braided channel pattern, all parts of the valley floor experience both flood conditions and braided stream activity. The channel floor is constantly being reworked.

11.7.2 Straight and meandering channels

Straight channels are rare and meandering channels localized in the meso-scale fluvial networks of most periglacial and northern rivers.

The importance of abundant bedload sediment in producing braided stream channels is illustrated by the absence of well-developed braided stream channels in those areas where bank erodibility is limited

and where debris suitable for transport is limited. For example, on Banks and Prince Patrick Islands, a number of large rivers flow west and northwest across the interior lowlands of the islands. For the most part the drainage dissects redeposited glacial materials and/or late Tertiary (Beaufort Formation) sand and gravel. As such, there is no lack of coarse bedload sediment for transport and all of these rivers possess well-developed braided channels. Since the hydrological regimes are distinctly nival, the fluctuations of discharge and associated variations in competence best explain the braided channel patterns. In certain places, however, braided streams often change to meandering ones for limited distances. This is related to exposures of underlying fine sand of the Eureka Sound Formation in the river banks. The relative absence of coarse sediments at this point results in the stream becoming overcompetent and, to compensate and equalize energy, the streams adopt a meandering course.

It is instructive briefly to consider the Thomsen River on Banks Island, the largest river in the

Figure 11.8 The Ballast Brook, northwest Banks Island, Canada; an example of a large braided channel with periglacial valley sandur.

Canadian Arctic islands. It flows northwards for approximately 120 km from its headwaters in the eastern morainal belt to the north coast. For the majority of its length, the channel is a single, somewhat sinuous one, with only occasional braiding. As such, it is in stark contrast with the other northeast- and westward-flowing braided rivers, such as the Bernard, Big, Storkerson and Kellett systems. The explanation is that the Thomsen river flows within a shallow incised trough in which relatively consolidated Cretaceous-age shale and sand is exposed in the channel banks. Thus, bedload transport is less than in the west-flowing streams and, as a consequence, braiding is less apparent.

At the macro scale, the very large northern rivers, such as the Mackenzie, Lena and others, usually possess single and well-defined channelways which permit navigation in summer. Despite the fact that these rivers freeze over during the winter months, flow beneath the ice cover is maintained throughout the year. Thus, discharge fluctuations are not so extreme as in smaller rivers. In addition, the thermal influence

of the water promotes sub-river taliks, and an abrupt shelving of the permafrost table. All these factors favour the development of steeply inclined channel sides and a deep, well-defined channel. Braiding only develops on a large scale where tributaries meet or where these rivers exit into the sea or into large water bodies. In such deltaic situations, the energy available to the river rapidly diminishes and multiple channels develop. The Mackenzie Delta is the classic example of such conditions (Mackay, 1963) and other deltaic environments exist elsewhere along the northern Arctic coasts of Alaska and Siberia.

11.7.3 Periglacial sandar

A sandur (plural: 'sandar') is an Icelandic term used to refer to alluvial surfaces formed by rivers carrying meltwater away from the fronts of glaciers (Krigstrom, 1962). Two types of sandur are recognized: valley sandur ('*dalsandur*') and plain sandur ('*Slattlands-sandur*') which identify their topographic

Table 11.9 Some characteristics of valley asymmetry in northern regions

Source	Locality	Valley Alignment	Orientation of Steeper Slope
East Greenland			
Poser[1]	Wollston–Vorland	E–W	N
Malaurie (1952)[3]	Disko	E–W	N
West Spitsbergen			
Dege[1]	Andreeland	E–W	S
Dege[1]	Conwayland	N–S	W
Klimaszewski[1]	Kaffioya–Ebene	E–W	S
Klimaszewski[1]	Brogger–Halbinsel	N–S	E
Siberia			
Shostakovitch (1927)	Yakutia	E–W	N
Presniakow (1955)[3]	Yakutia	E–W	N
Gravis (1969)	Yakutia	E–W	N
Northern Canada			
Bronhofer (1957)[2]	Southampton Island	E–W	N
French (1971b)	Banks Island	NW–SE	SW
Kennedy and Melton (1972)[3]	Caribou Hills, NWT	E–W	N, S
Alaska			
Hopkins and Taber (1962)[3]	Central Alaska	E–W	N
Currey (1964)	Northwest Alaska	E–W	N

[1] Quoted in Karrasch (1970, p. 205)
[2] Quoted in Bird (1967, p. 250)
[3] Quoted in French (1976a, p. 179)

locations within large valleys, or as outwash plains in proglacial positions. Sandar are characteristic of rapid aggradation and are crossed by braided streams that are continually shifting their pattern, as described earlier. Sandar surfaces developed extensively along the margins of the Pleistocene ice sheets in both North America and Eurasia. Most of the valley sandar developing today are in recently glacierized valleys, such as in Baffin Island (e.g. Church, 1972), the western cordillera (e.g. Fahnestock, 1963), and Iceland (e.g. Price, 1969).

In certain periglacial environments, far removed from present-day glacial activity, extensive but shallow valley fill deposits exist of a coarse clastic nature. In places, they cover many square kilometres and form some of the most prominent physiographical features of the landscape (Fig. 11.8). To all intents and purposes, these depositional surfaces are plain sandar. To avoid confusion, however, the descriptive term 'periglacial sandur' is used in this text. It refers not only to the braided stream but also to the materials and the channel morphology. Periglacial sandar can be distinguished from classical alluvial flood plains, since the latter include layers of finer sediments which are deposited by a river. Furthermore,

braided streams characterize active sandar surfaces, and channel scars on older deposits indicate a similar channel pattern in the past. By contrast, alluvial flood plains develop thaw ponds and lakes and well-developed ice-wedge polygons.

Periglacial sandar are particularly well developed in the coastal lowlands which drain towards the Beaufort Sea in the western high Arctic. According to Church (1972), three factors are necessary for the deposition of coarse gravelly valley fill. First, an abundance of coarse detrital material; second, the stream gradient should be sufficient to move the material in the water course; and third, the hydraulic regime should be characterized by relatively frequent and high floods, enabling large quantities of material to be moved. These characteristics are present in possibly four environments: semi-arid, periglacial, high mountain and proglacial. All are characterized by frequent flooding which, in the periglacial (i.e. nival) context, is the result of the spring melt. The unique feature of the western Arctic coastal lowlands for sandur development is undoubtedly the abundance of coarse sediment available for transport, originating from the underlying Tertiary-age bedrock formations.

Figure 11.9　Asymmetrical valleys on the Beaufort Plain, northwest Banks Island, Canada.

11.8　Valley asymmetry

Although stream valleys are frequently mentioned in the periglacial literature it is somewhat surprising that there is a lack of quantitative information on valley cross-sections. In fact, most studies of valley forms have been made within the context of slope asymmetry. To judge by the literature on valley forms in periglacial regions, one might conclude that asymmetrical valleys are the only type present. This, of course, is not the case, since the lack of asymmetry does not attract the same attention.

The presence of asymmetrical valleys in areas currently underlain by permafrost was first noticed by Shostakovitch (1927) in Siberia, where the steeper slopes commonly face north. To judge from the literature (Table 11.9), this appears to be the 'normal' for higher latitudes. Steeper north-facing slopes have been reported from Disko, Greenland, from northwest and central Alaska, from Southampton Island in the central Canadian Arctic, from the Mackenzie District of the NWT, and from northern Siberia. However, in extreme high Arctic localities, such as Spitsbergen (latitude 78°N) and northwest Banks Island (latitude 74°N), no such regularity exists, and

instead, steeper slopes have been reported to face either southwest, west, south or east.

The most probable explanation for the 'normal' asymmetry, with steeper north-facing slopes, involves greater solifluction activity on south-facing slopes and asymmetric lateral stream corrasion (e.g. Currey, 1964; Gravis, 1969). Since none of the reported examples of this type of asymmetry lies appreciably north of latitude 70°N, these regions experience a distinct change in the inclination of the sun throughout the polar day. Greatest insolation is received on slopes oriented south and southwest, and these slopes often possess deeper active layers. Where valleys are aligned approximately east–west, unequal debris arrival at the base of slopes is most pronounced. Thus, the stream migrates to the foot of the slope producing least debris, which is then undercut and steepened.

A variant of this model has been used by the writer to explain the striking asymmetrical valleys which exist on the Beaufort Plain of northwest Banks Island, Canada (French, 1971b). There, the steeper slopes bear no relationship to geological structure and are typically oriented towards the west and southwest (Fig. 11.9), clearly anomalous to the 'normal' asymmetry of high latitudes. The reason for the asymmetry appears connected to the dominant westerly winds in summer in this part of the Arctic. During winter, snow is blown off the upland surface of the plain and deposited in gullies and lee slope positions. In the summer, the strong westerly winds promote evaporation and latent heat loss from exposed westerly slopes which become both drier and cooler than east-facing slopes (French, 1970). At the same time, the melt of snowpatches on east-facing slopes provides additional moisture for that slope throughout the summer. It also develops a deeper active layer because it is not subject to the same degree of evaporation and heat loss as the opposite slope. Thus, solifluction processes are particularly active upon the east-facing slope. Consequently, the stream moves laterally to the slope producing the least colluvium, and the southwest-facing slope is then undercut and steepened through fluvio-thermal erosion processes. An asymmetry of the valleys is subsequently produced in which the two slopes are constantly adjusting to each other and to the basal stream channel. The asymmetry is regarded as a quasi-equilibrium form which is closely related to the climatic and geomorphic environment of the area.

Further reading

Church, M.A. (1972) *Baffin Island sandurs: a study of Arctic fluvial processes.* Geological Survey of Canada, Bulletin 216, 208 pp.

Church, M.A. (1974) Hydrology and permafrost with reference to northern North America. In: *Permafrost Hydrology, Proceedings of Workshop Seminar*, Canadian National Committee, International Hydrological Decade, Environment Canada, Ottawa, pp. 7–20.

Clark, M.J. (1988) Periglacial hydrology. In: M.J. Clark (ed.), *Advances in periglacial geomorphology*. Chichester: J. Wiley and Sons Ltd, pp. 415–468.

Gerard, R. (1990) Hydrology of floating ice. In: T.O. Prowse and C.S.L. Ommanney (eds), *Northern hydrology, Canadian perspectives*. National Hydrology Research Institute (NHRI) Science Report No. 1, pp. 103–134.

Woo, M.K. (1986) Permafrost hydrology in North America. *Atmosphere–Ocean*, **24**, 201–234.

Woo, M.K. (1990) Permafrost hydrology. In: T.D. Prowse and C.S.L. Ommanney (eds), *Northern hydrology, Canadian perspectives*. National Hydrology Research Institute (NHRI) Science Report No. 1, pp. 63–76.

Discussion topics

1. Explain the different stream flow regimes which occur in periglacial environments.
2. What are the unique characteristics of cold-climate rivers and streams?
3. What is the importance of fluvial processes in fashioning the landscape of periglacial regions?
4. How similar are channel and valley forms in periglacial and non-periglacial regions?

CHAPTER 12

Wind action and coastal processes

The majority of processes operating within the periglacial environments are not unique to such environments. On the other hand, the activity of certain processes is either enhanced or inhibited by the climatic conditions of these areas. This is the case for wind action and coastal processes and justifies their treatment in a separate chapter. It is not the intention, however, to present a systematic treatment of these topics. Instead, the approach highlights those aspects of wind action and coastal processes which are peculiar to, and achieve their greatest importance in, cold regions.

12.1 The role of wind

It is widely believed that wind action played a dominant role in both erosion and transportation in the mid-latitudes during the Pleistocene (see Chapter 15). Evidence includes the presence of wind-modified pebbles and blocks ('ventifacts'), stone pavements, frosted sand grains, and extensive loess and aeolian deposits. The factors thought to have favoured intense wind action included the absence of vegetation, extensive deposits of fine-grained sediments laid down at the margins of the ice sheets, the large amounts of comminuted debris produced by intense frost action, and higher wind and pressure gradients on account of the continental ice sheets.

While this general conclusion may very well be correct for Pleistocene environments, it should not be assumed that a similar situation is true for the present-day periglacial environments of polar and continental locations. In most regions, it seems best to regard the direct action of the wind as being of relatively minor importance, giving rise to relatively small-scale and localized weathering effects, niveo-aeolian deposits, and certain patterned ground phenomena (Pissart, 1966a; Bird, 1967, pp. 237–241; Washburn, 1969). In a few regions, however,

extensive late Pleistocene sand deposits occur and the formation of dunes is a dynamic process (e.g. the Great Kobuk sand dunes of northwestern Alaska, e.g. Dijkmans et al., 1986; Hamilton et al., 1988; Dijkmans and Koster, 1990). Elsewhere, as on Banks Island, NWT, aeolian processes are especially active on alluvial and outwash plains adjacent to the large rivers and wherever sandy Mesozoic and Tertiary deposits are subject to deflation (e.g. Pissart et al., 1977). Likewise, on the Qinghai-Xizang (Tibet) Plateau active sand dunes are related to local sandstone source areas (Wang and French, 1995c). Numerous other examples could be cited in which wind action has a direct, but local, impact.

The indirect effects of wind action are more important and certainly more widespread than thought previously. For example, wind plays a primary role in snow redistribution, from exposed locations into gullies and lee slopes during the winter months. It influences, therefore, the operation of solifluction (see Chapter 9) and runoff processes (see Chapter 11). In summer, wind action results in significant evaporation and latent heat loss from exposed slopes, which in turn can influence the depth of the active layer. This may lead to slope and valley asymmetry (see Chapter 11). A further example of the indirect effect of the wind is to be found in the oriented nature of many thaw lakes in alluvial tundra lowlands (see Chapter 7). Finally, the wind is important to the movement of sea ice and in wave generation. It is clear, therefore, that the wind operates in a number of indirect ways to influence landforms. Since these indirect effects of wind action are dealt with in the appropriate sections, the following discussion centres around the direct role of wind in periglacial environments.

12.1.1 Wind erosion

If wind is to carry out significant erosion, there must be a source of abrasive material suitable for transportation by the wind. Silt and fine sand particles, picked up from the ground surface during the summer months, are one source of abrasive material. However, in the forest and tundra zones, there is a general lack of exposed surfaces from which it can be picked up, and only the vegetation-free polar desert zone is well suited to the pick-up of abrasive material. The time duration for such erosion is also short, being limited to one or two months in middle and late summer, and the ease of detachment of surface particles is often limited by the presence of a salt crust or hard pan at the ground surface. For these reasons, wind erosion is probably less effective in the summer months.

Instead, the majority of wind erosion in high latitudes is probably carried out during the six to ten months of winter by wind-driven snow particles. It is well known that the hardness of ice increases as the temperature drops, such that at −50 °C ice has a Moh hardness of about 6 (Bird, 1967, p. 237). It is also during the winter months that winds are strongest and most constant in direction since well-developed high-pressure systems become established over the polar landmasses. Widespread wind erosion on the Qinghai-Xizang (Tibet) Plateau, however, is attributed to strong diurnal winds associated with night-time cooling of uplands. As such, it is a year-round process transporting predominantly fine silt and sand since snow cover is thin and discontinuous.

A variety of wind-erosional features have been described from periglacial and polar regions. For example, ventifacts form when a pebble or boulder projects from the ground surface and is exposed to strong wind transporting abrasive material. As a result, the pebble assumes a fluted, faceted or grooved appearance on its exposed side. An absence of vegetation to protect the pebble, an exposed location, a suitable supply of abrasive material, and dry conditions during part of the year are essential requirements.

In the polar deserts of the northern hemisphere, ventifacts and wind-erosional features have been reported from ice-free Peary Land in northeast Greenland (e.g. Fristrup, 1952/53) and from northern Siberia (e.g. Sverdrup, 1938). In the Canadian Arctic, however, ventifacts are relatively rare (Pissart, 1966a) and in general, there is an absence of wind-erosional features in northern Canada (Bird, 1967). Significant wind-eroded landforms in the form of badland topography are limited to soft sandstone or silt (e.g. St-Onge, 1965).

The greatest variety and frequency of occurrence of wind-erosional features occurs in the ice-free areas of Antarctica (e.g. Nichols, 1966, pp. 35–36; Sekyra, 1969, p. 282). According to Sekyra, conspicuous aeolian corrasion in the form of wind troughs and mushroom-like forms occurs in the inland oases and on old Pleistocene morainic accumulations in mountain areas. In some instances, chemical weathering processes associated with wind action combine with mechanical disintegration through the growth and expansion of salt crystals to produce a number of weathering-induced honeycomb structures. These are called 'taffoni' and are best developed in coarse-grained crystalline bedrock and morainic boulders (e.g. Selby, 1971a). Case hardening, for example, is a particular process by which the exterior of a boulder or rock is made more resistant to weathering by the evaporation of mineral-bearing solution from the rock surface leaving a thin cementation layer. When combined with cavernous weathering beneath, case hardening may produce very striking shell-like structures (see Fig. 4.9). Instances of case hardening and cavernous weathering have also been reported from Greenland (e.g. Washburn, 1969, p. 32). The origin of taffoni structures is complex and the role played by wind not clearly understood. Many areas of taffoni show a preferred orientation which may, or may not, relate to present-day wind patterns. At McMurdo Sound, for example, Cailleux and Calkin (1963) have noted that the preferred orientation of taffoni in that region is not consistent with present-day wind direction and may be unrelated to wind action.

Many questions remain unanswered with respect to wind erosion in present-day periglacial regions. The apparently greater frequency of wind-erosional features in Antarctica than in Arctic North America and Eurasia is not readily explainable. It may be that the winds are stronger and more constant in direc-

(a)

(b)

Figure 12.1 Examples of wind erosion and deposition: (a) niveo-aeolian deposits on melting snowbank, central Banks Island, Canada; (b) blow-out adjacent to Qinghai-Xizang Highway, China. Note the exposed small-diameter pipeline.

tion in the Antarctic. A second possibility is that the ice-free areas of Antarctica have experienced a longer period of stable and uninterrupted cold-climate conditions.

12.1.2 Deflation

Deflation, the second aspect of wind activity, is the winnowing out of fine particles and their transportation by the wind. Since plant cover is one of the major controlling factors, deflation probably reaches its greatest intensity in the unvegetated and ice-free areas of the polar deserts, and not in the tundra and forest zones. In the tundra zones, deflation is limited to sparsely vegetated areas such as valley sandar, recent deltas and terrace deposits.

The most obvious indicator of deflation in the polar deserts is the widespread presence of a lag gravel or desert pavement at the surface. Deflation may also produce shallow vegetation-free depressions or blow-outs, usually only a few centimetres deep and 1–3 m wide. As with wind erosion, the majority of deflation activity occurs during the winter months on exposed, snow-free surfaces. Evidence for this is to be found in the nature of the snowbanks which accumulate in the gullies and depressions during the winter. They are often composed of layers of snow separated by fine dirt bands. These deposits are termed 'niveo-aeolian' (e.g. Cailleux, 1974; Koster and Dijkmans, 1988) and may result in a significant concentration of water-lain silt-size particles in snowbank locations. In mid and late summer, as the snowbanks melt, it is not uncommon for the surface of the snowbank to assume a grey, almost black colour, and a pitted, small-scale thermokarst-like relief similar to glacier and other snow surfaces (Fig. 12.1 (a)). Intense deflation may also occur in late summer with localized dust storms brought on by surface heating and instability. Dust clouds may rise several hundreds of metres into the air, and blanket the surrounding terrain with a thin cover of fine sand particles. Areas of sandy sediments exposed on valley sandar and along the flood plains of the major rivers are particularly suited to this aeolian activity. In the Pleistocene literature, the term 'cover sand' (e.g. Maarleveld, 1960) is used to describe similar fine sands of aeolian origin.

Where deflation is concentrated, shallow basins or depressions ('blow-outs') may form (Fig. 12.1 (b)). In Finnish Lappland, Seppälä (1974) measured sand transport of 0.15 g/cm/h during a four-month period in a blow-out approximately 75 m wide. This translates into 3.2 tonnes of sand moving through this 'gateway', certainly sufficient to prevent vegetation stabilizing the surface. In other areas a discontinuous vegetation cover protects the ground beneath from erosion to form deflation mounds. These are well described by Pissart *et al.* (1977) from the Sachs River lowlands of southern Banks Island, where clumps of willow (*salix*) have led to the preservation of sand mounds 1.3 m high, separated by deflation troughs.

12.2 Loess-like silt

Aeolian silt, sometimes referred to as 'loess', is the most widespread product of periglacial action. It is a buff or grey coloured, unstratified and relatively well-

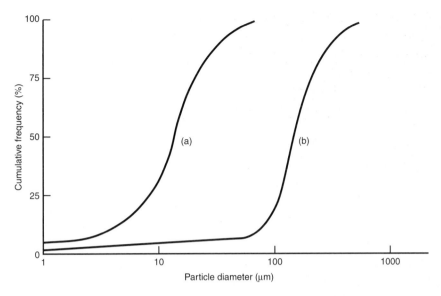

Figure 12.2 Typical grain size distribution for loess (a) and cover sand (b).

sorted deposit. Not all loess-like silt is related to periglacial conditions, however, since it occurs widely in and around the margins of most warm deserts. Presumably, in periglacial environments the silt is picked up from unvegetated floodplains, glacial outwash plains, till plains and lake shores. Wind-blown silt has been described in detail from Alaska (e.g. Péwé, 1955, 1975), where it is called 'upland silt', central Siberia (Péwé and Journaux, 1983) and Tibet (Péwé et al., 1995). It is clearly analogous to the loess of mid-latitudes (see Chapter 15).

In detail, wind-blown silts are well-sorted, homogeneous and unstratified. Loosely coherent grains of between 0.01 and 0.05 mm in diameter form the 'loess fraction'; this often exceeds 50–60 per cent of the deposit. The typical grain size distributions of wind-blown silt (loess) and cover sand are illustrated in Fig. 12.2.

Silt entrainment requires a dry soil surface. This probably explains the occurrence of loess-like silt in continental periglacial regions. In such environments, suitable conditions occur both during the hot summers through evaporation from the ground surface and during the cold winters through sublimation.

In North America, thick deposits of Holocene loess-like silt occur in central Alaska and parts of the Yukon Territory of Canada. In the Fairbanks region, Alaska, there is evidence of deposition from the middle Quaternary onwards through to the present day. The silt mantles the upland surfaces and originated from the outwash plains to the south of Fairbanks and the flood plain of the Tanana River (Péwé, 1955). Subsequently, it has been retransported to the valley bottoms by solifluction and incorporated with organic debris and now constitutes between 1 and 60 m of perennially frozen ground.

Pleistocene loess deposits are discussed more fully in Chapter 15.

12.3 Sand dunes and sand sheets

In certain periglacial environments, cold-climate sand dunes and sand sheets are actively forming. For the most part, the dunes are either of the transverse type or crescentic in nature (i.e. *barchanoid* with horns pointing in the direction of movement, or *parabolic*, with horns pointing away from the direction of movement). Occasionally, linear forms are superimposed on dune fields consisting mainly of transverse types. Sand bodies lacking a dune relief, i.e. without slip faces, are referred to as sand sheets.

Outside northern Alaska, parts of the Canadian Arctic, and northern Finland and Sweden (Table 12.1), dune fields are rare and sand sheets not extensive. This contrasts with their extent and thickness in the mid-latitudes of both North America and Europe (Koster, 1988) where they are largely of Pleistocene age (see Chapter 15).

Table 12.1 Major cold-climate dune fields in Arctic Canada, Alaska and northern Scandinavia

Location	Aeolian Forms	Age	Wind Direction	Comments	Source
Arctic Canada					
Yukon Territory	Sand sheets		S–SW	Discontinuous, active	Nickling (1978)
Banks Island	Sand sheets	Mid-Holocene	SE	Continuous, active, niveo- and fluvio-aeolian	Pissart *et al.* (1977); Good and Bryant (1985)
Southeast Baffin Island	Dunes, sand sheets		N–ESE	Scattered, partly active	McKenna-Neuman and Gilbert (1986)
Alaska					
Big Delta; Yukon Flats	Dunes: parabolic, sand sheets	Illinoian (?) – Wisconsin	N	Scattered	Péwé (1975)
Tanana River Valley	Dunes: parabolic, longitudinal Dunes: parabolic	Illinoian (?) – Wisconsin	NE	Scattered, extent >10 000 km² scattered	
Kuskokwim River Valley	Dunes: parabolic	Illinoian (?) – Wisconsin		Scattered	
Koyukuk Valley	Dunes: parabolic, transverse, longitudinal sand sheets	Late Wisconsin – Holocene	NE	Scattered, partly active discontinuous	Koster (1988)
Kobuk Valley	Dunes: parabolic, transverse, longitudinal, barchanoid sand sheets	Late Illinoian (?) – Late Wisconsin – Recent	NE–SE	Scattered, partly active megadunes up to 50 m high	Péwé (1975)
Arctic Coastal Plain	Dunes: parabolic, longitudinal	Late Wisconsin – Recent	(SW–W) – NE–E	Scattered, partly stabilized	Carter (1981)
Finland					
Finnish Lappland	Dunes: parabolic	Late Wisconsin – Holocene	NW	Partly stable	Seppälä (1971)
Sweden					
Northern Sweden	Dunes: parabolic	Late Wisconsin – Holocene	NW	Partly stable	Seppälä (1972a)

Koster (1988) outlines a number of characteristics which indicate the cold-climate origin for these aeolian sands. They include (a) interfingering or conformable relations with glacial and/or fluvioglacial deposits, (b) evidence for snow meltwater activity or 'denivation' forms (i.e. features due to melting or sublimation of snow from niveo-aeolian sediments), (c) inclusion of plant, pollen or insect remains indicative of cold environments and (d) structures or forms of permafrost or seasonal frost origin (e.g. thermal contraction cracks). Here, discussion focuses upon the role of snow meltwater and aeolian deposition, commonly referred to as 'niveo-aeolian'.

12.3.1 (Niveo-)aeolian processes

The combination of wind-driven sand and snow as an important transporting and depositional process has been described from many Arctic and subarctic regions (e.g. Fristrup, 1952/53; Pissart, 1966b; Cailleux, 1974, 1978; McKenna-Neuman and Gilbert, 1986; Koster and Dijkmans, 1988), and also from mid-latitude uplands (e.g. Ballantyne and Whittington, 1987). The term 'denivation' is used to refer to the various sedimentological and morphological disturbances that result when the sand-covered snow lenses on dune slip faces melt. These include tension cracks, compressional features and irregular layerings.

Cold semi-arid conditions rather than snow-rich climates favour niveo-aeolian transport. It is also clear that the unvegetated parts of modern periglacial river systems supply most of the aeolian sediments. Autumn and winter transport is dominant, especially on plains associated with proglacial discharge regimes (e.g. McKenna-Neuman and Gilbert, 1986), although a continuous snow cover can effectively prevent aeolian transport. By contrast, on the flood plains of rivers with nival discharges sediment supplied by the peak spring discharge is then subject to aeolian transport at the time of low discharge in the late summer. This is certainly the case for the Sach River on southwest Banks Island (e.g. Good and Bryant, 1985), and for the Kobak River in northwestern Alaska (e.g. Fernald, 1964).

Facies analyses of niveo-aeolian sand deposits in Arctic and subarctic regions are relatively few (e.g. Koster and Dijkmans, 1988) and do not compare in detail with the in-depth studies undertaken in Europe on Weichselian periglacial sand dunes and sheets (e.g. Ruegg, 1983; Schwan, 1986, 1987). Thus the processes by which aeolian sediments are reworked by snow and meltwaters are still poorly understood, yet clearly relevant to the interpretation of Pleistocene 'cover-sand' and other aeolian sediment (see Chapter 15). Further investigations are required of the interactions between permafrost, moisture (snow) and aeolian transport (sediment) in present periglacial environments.

12.4 Coastal processes

The extent of coastlines currently experiencing periglacial conditions is considerable. For example, in the northern hemisphere, the Arctic Ocean is almost completely land-locked. Extensive ice-free coastlines occur in Alaska, northern Canada, Greenland and along the whole of the Russian mainland from the Kola Peninsula in the west to the Chuckchi Sea in the east. In addition, there are the various island groups such as the Canadian Arctic archipelago, Spitsbergen, Franz Josef Land, Novaya Zembyla, the North Land, the New Siberian Islands and Wrangel Island. Although the majority of the Antarctic coastline is composed of ice shelves, there are also significant ice-free stretches of coastlines in the Grahamland Peninsula, and the South Shetland and South Orkney Islands.

It is not surprising, therefore, that there are significant differences in environmental conditions along periglacial coastlines as regards ice cover, wave climate and tidal range, not to mention structural and lithological variations. Nevertheless, there are several characteristics of all of these coastal areas which, in varying degrees, reflect the periglacial environment in which they occur. These characteristics may be summarized under three broad headings: first, the presence of sea ice and its effect upon wave generation; second, the effects of ice upon the beach regime, and third, the influence of permafrost and ground ice upon coastal development. In a final section, the nature of cold-climate river deltas is briefly summarized.

12.4.1 Sea ice and wave generation

The major characteristic of the majority of the above-mentioned coastlines is the long season when they are ice-bound, and the very short open water season during which coastal processes operate. In certain sheltered areas, such as the various islands located in the middle of the Canadian Archipelago, wave action is restricted to as little as eight to ten weeks a year (Owens and McCann, 1970). In other areas, open water conditions may exist for several months, such as in northern Alaska from Point Barrow southwards to Cape Thompson (Hume and Schalk, 1964, 1967) and along the Siberian coast. At the other extreme of the spectrum, the warm North Atlantic Drift enables certain parts of the coasts of Greenland and Spitsbergen to be virtually ice-free for most of the year. A second factor to consider is that, even when there is open water, the nearby presence of the permanent pack ice drastically reduces the distance of fetch and, thus, the magnitude of wave action. Moreover, the movement of sea ice during the open water season may further reduce the distance of maximum fetch in any one situation. A third restraint upon the effectiveness of wave action is the presence of a narrow strip of ice which may be frozen to the shore and unaffected by tidal movements. This land-fast ice is called an 'ice foot' and is a common feature on many Arctic beaches (e.g. McCann and Carlisle, 1972). It is important from a geomorphic viewpoint in that it further protects the beach from the limited wave action that does occur, and decreases the effective duration of the open water season. As a result of all these factors, Arctic beaches are essentially low-energy environments in which normal wave action and coastal processes are limited.

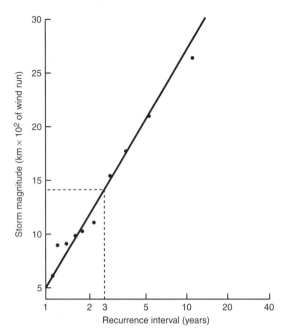

Figure 12.3 Recurrence interval of annual maximum onshore storm events during open water conditions at Sachs Harbour, 1971–80. The frequency of storms with RI ≤ 3 years is apparent (from Harry *et al.*, 1983).

In this context, the magnitude and frequency of periods of significant wave action assume great importance. It would appear that the majority of beach reworking and sediment transport occurs during the few major events which have a frequency of occurrence of two or three times a year. For example, Harry *et al.* (1983) identified the annual maximum summer storm for each year at Sachs Harbour, southwest Banks Island, from 1971 to 1980 on the basis of duration and kilometres of wind run, the latter providing an indication of storm magnitude. These data were used to generate a storm frequency curve (Fig. 12.3) from which the recurrence intervals and thus geomorphic significance of storm events observed between 1979 and 1981 were determined.

Periods of maximum wave generation are likely to occur during storm events which coincide with the existence of ice-free fetch. At Sachs Harbour in the period 1971–77, no storms acted over a fetch greater than 100 km and the long-term probability of such an event is less than 0.1 per cent. Of the 47 storm events with ice-free fetch in the same period, less than 40 per cent had predicted significant wave heights greater than 2.0 m (Harry *et al.*, 1983). Data such as

these demonstrate not only that sea ice is an important constraint upon wave generation and significant storm erosion, but also that traditional methods of coastal analysis are useful, even in ice-infested waters.

Similar observations emphasizing the role of major but low-frequency storms in effecting shoreline change have been made by Owens and McCann (1970) and McCann (1972) for the Resolute Bay area of the high Arctic. Using wind data and calculations of fetch distances from published ice survey maps, they concluded that in the years 1961, 1962 and 1963, there were only three, five and two periods respectively when waves of over 0.5 m in height could possibly have been generated. This conclusion was substantiated by field observations between 1968 and 1970 when only one major storm occurred which produced waves capable of significant action on the beach (McCann, 1972). During this one storm, the whole of the beach was combed down and the profile lowered by 0.3–0.6 m in the mid- to high-tide zone. Other observations have been made by Hume and Schalk (1967) and Hume *et al.* (1972) for the Point Barrow area of Alaska. There, the period of open water is greater than at Resolute Bay. Variations in coastal cliff retreat between 1948 and 1968 appear to have been related to the frequency of west-wind storms per year which changed from approximately two per year in the years 1948–62 to one per year in the years 1962–68. It would appear that a 50 per cent decrease in west-wind storms during the open water season resulted in a decrease in cliff retreat from approximately 4 m/year to 1 m/year.

There are certain problems inherent in isolating and defining the geomorphic effectiveness of single, major events. At Point Barrow, for example, unusually high cliff retreat rates for 1961–62 were largely attributed to beach borrow associated with construction needs (Hume and Schalk, 1964). Under these conditions, the effectiveness of a storm of a given magnitude would increase. Likewise, on Devon Island, the effectiveness of the single storm observed by McCann was accentuated by a preceding period in which large waves had broken up the remaining beach-fast ice which normally protects the beach.

As a direct result of the relatively limited wave action on many Arctic beaches, beach processes and the transport and redistribution of material are thought to operate at a slow rate. In general, beaches are poorly developed and narrow, often composed primarily of coarse sand and cobbles. Beach sediments are poorly sorted and possess low roundness values as compared with other beach environments

Table 12.2 Some roundness values for beach materials in various periglacial and non-periglacial regions

Locality	Beach Environment	Rock Type	Cailleux Roundness Values
Periglacial			
Devon Island, NWT, Canada	Sheltered	Limestone	25–267
Hall Beach, NWT, Canada	Sheltered	Limestone	216
Jacobshaven, west Greenland	Sheltered	Quartz	90–105
Kuggsa Dessa, west Greenland	Exposed	Quartz	135–160
Godthaab, west Greenland	Exposed	Quartz	270–388
Non-periglacial			
Western Mediterranean (various sites)	Enclosed sea	Limestone	355
Lake Ontario, Canada	Enclosed sea	Gneiss	388
Finistère, northwest France	Exposed	Quartz	250–270 400–460

Source: data taken from McCann and Owens (1969)

(Table 12.2). However, there is abundant evidence that considerable long-shore transport of material does take place on certain Arctic beaches. This is particularly true of the western Arctic where coastlines have developed in unconsolidated, often ice-rich sediments, with relatively long open water periods. Numerous large and often complex depositional spits and offshore bars have developed. Two of the largest, and most classic, are the Point Barrow spit, Alaska, and the Cape Kellett spit on southwest Banks Island, the latter extending for a total distance in excess of 12 km. Along the northern coast of Alaska, Hume and Schalk (1967) report approximately 10 000 m^3 of net sediment transport as being typical. At Sachs Harbour, Clark *et al.* (1984) conclude that the annual sediment gain over a 29-year period is approximately 57 000 m^3 and that a 1.6 km long spit at the mouth of the harbour could have grown in a period estimated at between 70 and 230 years (Fig. 12.4). Clearly, while the predominance of ice-limited fetch conditions leads many to characterize Arctic shorelines as low-energy environments, in the western Arctic of Alaska and Canada, and along parts of the Siberian coast, rapid erosion and dynamic growth of depositional features is also typical.

12.4.2 The effects of ice on the beach

The ice-foot plays an important role in limiting beach changes. It develops in the upper part of the intertidal zone and often extends well below the high-water mark. It forms in the autumn freeze-up period when swash or spray from breaking waves freezes on contact with the beach. Once a layer of ice has formed on the surface of the beach, wave-induced movement of beach material will cease. Likewise, in the spring, considerable amounts of ice may remain frozen to the beach after the sea ice breaks up and may prevent the direct action of waves for several weeks. The presence of ice on the beach before the development of the winter sea ice and after the spring breakup means that conventional freeze-up and breakup dates do not necessarily apply to the Arctic beach zone (Owens and McCann, 1970). The size and extent of the ice-foot vary from year to year depending primarily upon the sea conditions the previous autumn; moderate to strong wave action is an optimum for ice-foot accretion. The tidal range and beach slope are other factors that influence ice-foot widths and thicknesses. The greater the tidal range, the greater is the zone of spray and swash accretion, while the steeper the beach profile, the smaller is the width and thickness of the ice-foot. Usually, the ice-foot ablates during the early part of the open water season. Initially, a shore lead develops some 5–15 m offshore to isolate the sea ice proper from the ice-foot. Then the ice-foot is breached by water draining seawards from the melting snow in the backshore zone.

The more direct effects of ice on the beach occur when iceflows or the sea ice pack are forced, by strong onshore winds, to impinge upon the shoreline (Fig. 12.5). Commonly, the impinging ice pushes and scours beach material to form irregular lobate ridges and scour depressions in and above the high tide

(a)

Figure 12.5   Sea ice pushed onshore in July 1984 at Thesiger Bay, southern Banks Island, NWT, Canada.

(b)

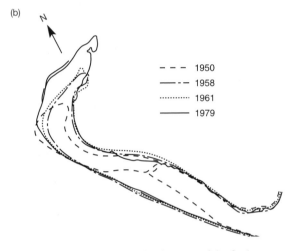

– – – 1950
——·— 1958
············ 1961
———— 1979

Figure 12.4   Sequential development of the Sachs Harbour spit, 1950–1979 (from Clark *et al.*, 1984; Harry *et al.*, 1983). (a) oblique air view of spit in July 1972. Note the pack ice offshore. (b) change derived from air photo coverage, 1950, 1958, 1961 and ground survey, 1979.

zone (Hume and Schalk, 1964; Owens and McCann, 1970). These ridges may be as much as 1.0–2.0 m in height. Where ice becomes buried by beach materials, its eventual melt produces enclosed depressions and highly irregular topography.

Ice-push features also occur around the shores of the larger inland water bodies. However, because of the absence of a tidal range, there is no protection by a well-developed ice foot, and the ice push ridges are formed at the same elevation each year. As a result, these features are often more regular in plan and form. In general, beach ridges are not long-term features of periglacial shorelines since they are systematically reworked every few years.

12.4.3   The influence of permafrost and ground ice

Where coasts are developed in permafrost terrain composed of unconsolidated and ice-rich sediments, rapid and dramatic coastal retreat may be associated with the melting and release of the excess ice. This is accomplished in at least two ways. First, in those areas where the frozen sediments are sand and gravel, beaches can form which protect the bluff from direct wave action. In these situations, retreat of the bluff is relatively slow, occurring through the subaerial melting of the permafrost and the transport of the thawed material to the beach by solifluction and rainwash. The finer particles are then removed and transported in suspension along the coast, leaving the coarser pebbles and cobbles as a beach gravel. Second, in areas where the frozen sediments are silt and clay, beaches do not form and the bluff is exposed to direct wave action. Since fine-grained sediments are usually associated with high ice contents, storm waves result in either the exposure of the ice bodies or the undercutting and formation of thermo-erosional niches at high-tide level (Fig. 12.6 (a)). The former induces rapid melting and slumping of the ice face while the latter may lead to collapse of the bluff, often in blocks delineated by ice wedges (Fig. 12.6 (b)). In both cases, the sediment within the permafrost is released and carried away in suspension.

The shorelines developed around the Beaufort Sea in the western Arctic are probably the best example of rapid coastal retreat. For example, in the vicinity of Barrow, Alaska, average retreat rates of between

(a)

(b)

Figure 12.6 Cliff erosion in unconsolidated ice-rich sediments: (a) thermo-erosional niche formed at base of cliffs, 5.0 m deep, Sachs Harbour, Banks Island, Canada; (b) cliff failure by block detachment along ice wedge oriented parallel to the cliffline, Maitland Bluffs, Mackenzie Delta region, NWT, Canada.

2 and 4 m a year appear typical (Hume *et al.*, 1972) for sections with no protecting beach gravels. Where beach gravels are present, annual retreat is less. It is also debatable how much erosion is due to exceptional storm events or to excessive beach borrow to maintain the townsite and facilities (Walker, 1991). Along the Yukon coast and in the Mackenzie District of Canada, a similar pattern of rapid coastal retreat can also be observed (Mackay, 1963; McDonald and Lewis, 1973). Measurements at the Yukon–Alaska border indicate the coast there has retreated 43 m since 1912, while the southeast side of Herschel Island has probably undergone 1–2 km of retreat in postglacial times. In the vicinity of Tuktoyaktuk, coastal retreat of over 150 m has occurred since 1935 (Mackay, 1986a). In one locality this has caused the

draining of a lake and the growth of a number of pingos in the drained lake bottom (see Chapter 6).

The rates of coastal retreat observed around the Beaufort Sea of the western Arctic are clearly exceptional, being the result more of thermal erosion than true coastal erosion. For the most part, wave action and coastal processes play a subsidiary role in transport of thawed sediments away from 'source' areas towards 'sinks' or zones of deposition. Similar conditions with respect to permafrost, ground ice and open water conditions exist in Siberia along the Laptev Sea, where retreat rates of between 4 and 6 m per year are not uncommon (Are, 1972). Barr (1976) cites historical evidence for the complete disappearance of certain islands in the Laptev Sea and attributes this to rapid coastal retreat.

Retreat rates in ice-rich permafrost terrain can be compared to retreat rates in unconsolidated sediments in non-permafrost environments and where wave action is year-round. For example, in England, cliffs developed in boulder clay at Holderness have receded 3 km since Roman times (i.e. nearly 2 m per year), while those developed in Tertiary-age sand at Barton-on-Sea, Hampshire, are retreating at approximately 1 m per year (Small, 1970, p. 442).

Finally, it must be stressed that ground ice and unconsolidated sediments, and the associated rapidity of coastal change, are not typical of all coastlines in periglacial environments. Large extents of coastline in the central and eastern Arctic, Greenland, Spitsbergen and Antarctica are developed in relatively resistant and coherent rock in which retreat rates are slow. The absence of fine-grained sediments limits depositional features. Abrupt coastal cliffs and raised shoreline platforms are probably the most typical forms (e.g. John and Sugden, 1975). Within this context, the coastal conditions of the ice-rich and unconsolidated sediments of the Siberian and western Arctic lowlands are unusual.

12.5 Cold-climate deltas

Deltas form wherever rivers carrying high sediment loads enter the marine environment. The largest that concern us include those of the Mackenzie, Colville and Yukon Rivers in North America and the Ob, Yenesie, Lena, Indigirka and Kolyma in Siberia.

The unusual aspect of these deltas is that sedimentation takes place under cold-climate conditions.

Permafrost growth is often syngenetic with corresponding cryostructures and wedges (see Chapter 6). Because of the abundance of silty materials and surface water, ice wedges, pingos and other permafrost aggradational forms are also characteristic. One of the most comprehensive monographs dealing with cold-climate deltas, that of the Mackenzie Delta, NWT, is by Mackay (1963) and detailed study of the Colville River delta, Alaska, has been undertaken by H. J. Walker (e.g. Walker, 1974, 1978, 1983).

More relevant here are the innumerable smaller meso-scale deltas which dot the periglacial coastlines. One such delta is that of the modern Horton River following its breakthrough to the sea in about AD 1640 (Mackay and Slaymaker, 1989). This delta illustrates the relative roles of river and sea ice. The major process affecting surface morphology is the annual break-up of the Horton River since an ice jam commonly forms on the seaward side of the coastal bluff through which the river has broken through. The river ice bulldozes, scrapes and flutes the surface, upon which there are individual large boulders. These are the result of the ice action and are similar in origin to the ice-rafted boulders which occur along the estuary of the St Laurence (Dionne, 1972), Hudson Bay and northern Quebec-Labrador (e.g. Lauriol and Gray, 1980). A further characteristic is that the delta surface lacks typical levées. This is largely because much of the delta is already flooded when high water occurs at breakup because of the ice jamming. In the autumn, sea ice prevents wave action on the delta for at least six months. A similar pattern of geomorphic change probably characterizes other meso-scale deltas in cold regions.

Further reading

Harry, D.G., H.M. French and M.J. Clark (1983) Coastal conditions and processes, Sachs Harbour, Banks Island, western Canadian Arctic. *Zeitschift für Geomorphologie, Supplementband*, **47**, 1–26.

John, B.S. and D.E. Sugden (1975) Coastal geomorphology of high latitudes. *Progress in Geography*, **7**, 53–132.

Koster, E.A. (1988) Ancient and modern cold-climate aeolian sand deposition: a review. *Journal of Quaternary Science*, **3**, 69–83.

Koster, E.A. and J.W.A. Dijkmans (1988) Niveo-aeolian deposits and denivation forms, with special reference to the Great Kobuk Sand Dunes, northwestern Alaska. *Earth Surface Processes and Landforms*, **13**, 153–170.

Mackay, J.R. (1985) Fifty years (1935 to 1985) of coastal retreat west of Tuktoyaktuk, District of Mackenzie. Geological Survey of Canada, Paper 86-1A, pp. 727–735.

Owens, E.H. and S.B. McCann (1970) The role of ice in the Arctic beach environment with special reference to Cape Ricketts, southwest Devon Island, NWT, Canada. *American Journal of Science*, **268**, 397–414.

Péwé, T.L. (1955) Origin of the upland silt near Fairbanks Alaska. *Geological Society of America, Bulletin*, **66**, 699–724.

Péwé, T.L., L. Tungscheng, R.M. Slatt, and L. Bingyuan (1995) *Origin and character of loesslike silt in the southern Qinghai-Xizang (Tibet) Plateau, China.* US Geological Survey Professional Paper 1549, 55 pp.

Pissart, A., J.-S. Vincent and S. Edlund (1977) Dépôts et phénomênes éoliens sur l'île de Banks, Territoires du Nord-Ouest, Canada. *Canadian Journal of Earth Sciences*, **14**, 2462–2480.

Discussion topics

1. What is the importance of wind in landscape evolution in present-day periglacial regions?
2. How does wind influence the efficacy of other geomorphic processes in periglacial regions?
3. What are the unique aspects of coastal processes in cold non-glacial environments?

PART 3 Pleistocene periglacial environments

13 Pleistocene periglacial conditions

14 Relict periglacial phenomena

15 Pleistocene wind action, tundra rivers and periglacial landscape modification

CHAPTER 13

Pleistocene periglacial conditions

Part 3 describes the periglacial conditions which occurred in mid-latitudes during the Pleistocene. The roles played by permafrost and the various frost-action processes in the development of mid-latitude landscapes are examined within the context of our understanding of present periglacial environments, as previously summarized in Part 2.

This particular chapter reviews the time scales involved and the duration of the cold-climate fluctuations. It then generalizes about the nature of Pleistocene periglacial climates and considers the specific problems of palaeo-reconstruction. Finally, the extent of Pleistocene periglacial conditions is briefly summarized.

13.1 Introduction

By necessity, emphasis is upon late Pleistocene periglacial conditions in Europe and North America, because these are best understood and there is most evidence for them. Since mid-latitudes are now temperate and periglacial conditions no longer prevail, the approach must be through the identification of relict periglacial features, sediments and structures. These can be described in terms of their morphology and distribution. Their interpretation, however, necessitates palaeoclimatic reconstructions and an understanding of the nature of periglacial processes. Both identification and interpretation can be difficult and certainly ambiguous. In particular, attempts at Quaternary climatic reconstructions are complex and rely heavily upon detailed stratigraphic and biological investigations together with considerations of Quaternary vegetation and fauna successions. Since these are the fields of Quaternary geologists and biologists, involvement in such detail is kept to a minimum, although such information is extremely relevant. Here, the approach adopted concentrates primarily upon morphology and secondarily upon sediments and sedimentary structures.

13.2 The time scale and climatic fluctuations

Some comments on terminology and the time scale involved need to preface any discussion of late Pleistocene conditions. In broad outline, the various glacial and interglacial stages are known for both North America and Europe. Our knowledge is based upon a combination of methods using a variety of techniques. One of the most useful is the variation in isotopic composition of ocean waters over time. This is revealed by the changing ratios of $^{18}O/^{16}O$ in carbonate shells and skeletons of small organisms (e.g. Foraminifera) found in deep sea sediments. There is convincing evidence that the ratios of $^{18}O/^{16}O$ in ocean waters varied in a quasi-cyclic fashion with the glacial and interglacial periods. The same is true for snow trapped in the Greenland and Antarctic ice sheets. When compared to standard mean ocean water (SMOW), ice sheets

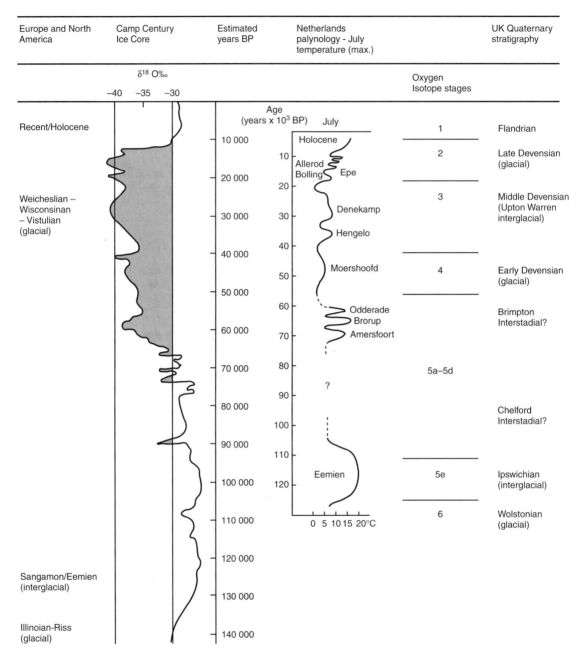

Figure 13.1   Climatic variations in the last 150 000 years expressed as changing $\delta^{18}O/^{16}O$ ratios, and July temperatures, together with generalized late Quaternary stratigraphies for Europe, North America and the UK. Colder temperatures are indicated by decreasing $\delta^{18}O$ values (shaded areas) (modified from West, 1977, Fig. 10.10; Lowe and Walker, 1984; Ballantyne and Harris, 1994, Table 2.1; Vandenberghe and Pissart, 1993, Fig. 6.5).

contain relatively large quantities of ^{16}O, leaving the oceans relatively enriched in ^{18}O (i.e. isotopically more positive). One such curve based upon the per mile (‰)

deviation of $^{18}O/^{16}O$ ratios in Greenland ice samples from that of SMOW for the last 150 000 years is illustrated in Fig. 13.1. A second useful approach is

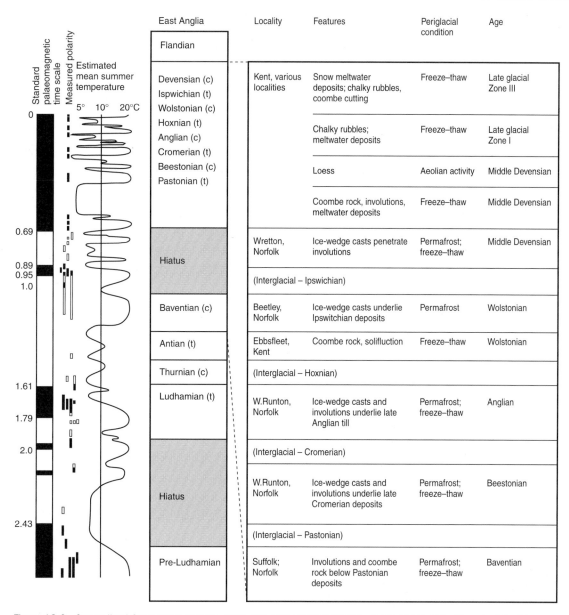

Figure 13.2   Generalized Quaternary climatic curve, the palaeo-magnetic time scale, the East Anglian stratigraphic record, and the occurrence of various periglacial phenomena in south and east England; c, cold; t, temperate (data from West, 1977).

through palynology, where maximum July air temperatures are inferred from plant pollens found in terrestrial stratigraphic cores. One curve for the Netherlands is also illustrated in Fig. 13.1. Other lines of evidence which are used include the analysis of tree rings (dendrochronology), the identification of insect remains such as specific Coleoptera (beetle)

species which have narrow temperative tolerance limits, amino acid dating, and various age-equivalent stratigraphic markers (e.g. palaeomagnetism and tephrachronology).

On the longer time scale of the entire Quaternary period (a period of approximately 2.5 million years) it is believed that periglacial conditions roughly coin-

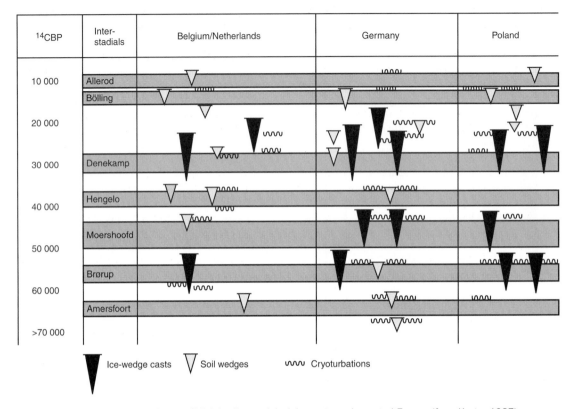

Figure 13.3 Stratigraphic positions of Weichselian periglacial structures in central Europe (from Karte, 1987).

cided in time with the various advances and retreats of the ice sheets, as indicated by the temperature curve fluctuations. For example, the stratigraphic positions of frost-fissure casts, involutions and various solifluction deposits in south and east England certainly suggest a number of periods during which either permafrost or cold-climate (frost action) conditions were present (Fig. 13.2). In Central Europe, Karte (1987) has demonstrated the same stratigraphic relationship for the middle and late Pleistocene (Fig. 13.3).

From a practical point of view, we need only be concerned with the cold conditions associated with the last two glacial stages. Surface periglacial features formed in earlier cold periods are unlikely to have survived to the present day without having been modified beyond recognition by the later cold stages or by the intervening interglacial periods of more temperate conditions. In both Europe and North America, the penultimate cold stage occurred some time prior to 150 000 BP. The last interglacial period is generally believed to have lasted until approximately 120 000 BP after which the climate deteriorated. The final cold

stage lasted until approximately 10 000 years ago. For simplicity, the more general terms Weichselian and Wisconsinan are used in preference to the more local terms frequently used in Europe (including the British Isles) and North America to describe this last major cold period.

During the last glacial stage, environmental conditions fluctuated considerably, both in time and space, with the onset of the climatic deterioration, and the growth, advance and retreat of the ice sheets. Various small-scale climatic oscillations gave periods of relatively more temperate, or interstadial, conditions (e.g. the Brimpton and Chelford Interstadials in the UK). In addition, there were periods of climatic transition before and after the glacial stages which were also more temperate. These fluctuations meant that periglacial conditions varied in intensity and were by no means continuous throughout the whole of the last glacial stage. In northwest Europe for example, where our understanding of these events is furthest advanced, the various Weichselian climatic fluctuations resulted in arctic and subarctic conditions for only about

25 000–30 000 years during the last 60 000–70 000 years. At least two major ice advances are believed to have occurred, one in the early/middle Weichselian time, the other in late Weichselian time, separated by a definite period of relatively warmer conditions. There is evidence to believe that broadly similar fluctuations occurred in North America. For example, in the western Arctic, one can identify both early and late Wisconsinan ice advances. The latter attained its maximum extent approximately 25 000–16 000 years BP, and corresponds to the second Weichselian period of cold conditions. It seems reasonable to assume that severe periglacial conditions only developed at the height of these cold stages, and that the interstadial periods saw repeated fluctuations between periglacial and non-periglacial conditions.

The late Glacial transition from cold to temperate conditions well illustrates the oscillating nature of cold-climate conditions during the Pleistocene. In Europe, the late and Postglacial stages of the last glaciation can be divided into pollen zones, indicating the dominance of different vegetation sequences (Table 13.1). For example, fluctuations in the arboreal and non-arboreal pollen ratio indicate that during deglaciation, two periods of relatively warmer conditions occurred, the Bolling and Allerod interstadials, at which time the tundra vegetation was replaced temporarily by shrub tundra (dwarf birch) and birch forest. Then, in the Postglacial times, the climate rose to a peak of warmth and dryness between 5000 and 3000 years BP. In all probability, therefore, strict periglacial conditions were only present during zones I and III, since by zone IV a forest cover had become well established.

In North America, detailed pollen stratigraphies are for localities scattered over a larger geographic area. Thus, the vegetational sequences available for late and Postglacial times are more general (Table 13.1). However, they suggest a strong synchroneity of climatic events with Europe. For example, the vegetational fluctuations in the 'cooler' portion of the sequences have apparent correlations with Bolling (zone IB) and Allerod (zone II) fluctuations in Europe. The pollen record suggests, however, that the tundra belt beyond the receding ice margin was much narrower and moister than in Europe, and was intermixed with forested areas. Since the climatic amelioration was accentuated by the development of large proglacial water bodies such as the Champlain Sea, the tundra belt was quickly replaced by spruce-fir and then by pine. Only upland areas retained an open tundra environment for any length of time. It seems

reasonable to assume, therefore, that the late Wisconsinan periglacial environment of North America was neither so extensive nor so severe as in Europe.

A more detailed description of late Pleistocene climatic and vegetational conditions is beyond the scope of the book. There is an abundant literature available, and the interested reader is referred to the works of Lowe and Walker (1984) and West (1977). Regional texts are also available for both North America (e.g. Wright and Porter 1983; Fulton, 1989) and Europe; in the UK, for example, volumes by Jones and Keen (1993) and Ballantyne and Harris (1994) contain useful summaries.

In conclusion, it is clear that (a) periglacial conditions occurred many times during the Pleistocene, each occurrence being of varying duration and intensity, and (b) the most recent periods of periglacial conditions occurred during the middle and late Wisconsinan/Weichselian cold stage.

13.3 Geomorphic considerations

From a geomorphic point of view, there are a number of important differences between the Pleistocene periglacial environments of mid-latitudes and those of present-day high latitudes.

The major difference is undoubtedly one of solar conditions. While both middle and high latitudes experience both summer and winter, the contrast between the two seasons and the rapidity of the change from one to the other is not as marked in middle as in high latitudes. In middle latitudes there is no equivalent of the 'arctic night' or 'arctic day', each of which lasts for periods of several months without interruption. Instead, the daily rhythm of daytime and night-time is the dominant condition. During the Pleistocene, therefore, this diurnal solar radiation regime was far more important in mid-latitudes than it is today in high latitudes. It probably led to a considerably greater frequency of freeze–thaw cycles of shallow depth and of short duration. An average frequency of between 50 and 100 cycles per year might be a realistic figure, bearing in mind the number of freeze–thaw cycles currently occurring in alpine mid-latitude environments (see Chapter 4). If correct, frost shattering and frost creep processes, including needle ice, were probably several times more intense than in high latitudes today, and contributed greatly to the mechanical breakdown of rock and the downslope transport of frost-shattered debris.

Table 13.1 Generalized sequence of Late Glacial and Postglacial (Flandrian/Holocene) vegetational successions in the British Isles, New England and southwestern Québec

British Isles (West, 1977)					Eastern North America	
Stage	Period	Date	Pollen zone	General characteristics of vegetation (dominants)	New England (Peteet et al., 1994)	Southwest Québec (Richard, 1994)
Postglacial (Flandrian) (Holocene)	Sub-Atlantic		VIII-modern	Afforestation	North American mixed forest (boreal-broadleaf) ←	
		AD 1000 AD/BC	VIII	Alder, oak, birch, beech, ash		
		1000 BC 2000 3000	VIIb	Alder, oak, lime – deforestation Elm decline		
	Atlantic	4000 5000	VI	Alder, oak, elm, lime		
	Boreal	6000	VI	Hazel, pine (a) Oak, elm, lime (b) Oak, elm (c) Hazel, elm	Mixed white pine oak forest	Maple; pine
		7000	V	Hazel, pine, birch	White pine forest	
	Pre-Boreal	8000	IV	Birch, pine	Boreal forest	
Late Glacial (Weichselian) (Wisconsinan)	Younger Dryas	9000	III	Shrub tundra (dwarf birch)		Birch, pine
	Allerod	10 000	II	Birch with shrubs; tundra	Woodland (Picea, Betula)	
	Older Dryas	11 000	Ic	Shrub tundra/tundra	Poplar, spruce	Champlain Sea
	Bolling		Ib		Tundra	Dwarf birch; herb tundra
	Early Dryas	12 000	Ia			Ice

The effect of orientation, with respect to solar radiation inputs, was also more marked than in high latitudes today. The fact that the sun disappeared below the horizon at the end of each mid-latitude day meant that in the northern hemisphere the north- and northwest-facing slopes were exposed to very low angles of inclination of the sun. Other things being equal, this would favour lower air and ground temperatures on such slopes and deeper frost penetration. If permafrost had formed, it would also imply a thinner active layer. The effect of orientation is not that simple, however, since the various climatic fluctuations would promote a space–time change in the micro-climatic conditions on any one slope. For example, with the deterioration of climate from an interglacial or interstadial period, the north- and east-facing slopes would have begun to experience freeze–thaw conditions first. But during the period of maximum severity of periglacial conditions, the south- and west-facing slopes would probably experience the greatest frequency of freeze–thaw cycles, while the colder slope would remain frozen for a longer period of time. Then, as the climate progressively ameliorated, frost-action processes would linger longest on the cooler slope. It is possible, therefore, that depending upon the severity of the temperature drop, frost-action processes would be favoured either on south- and west-facing slopes (being 'warmer' slopes with greater solar radiation enabling ground temperature to rise temporarily above $0\,°C$) or on north- and east-facing slopes (being 'colder' slopes with temperatures falling temporarily below $0\,°C$). In all probability, the frost shattering and creep occurring on south-facing slopes repeatedly rising above freezing during the summer months would be the more potent geomorphic situation. This is because the south-facing slope would be in a near-constant frozen state, with moisture being available at each occasion of thaw, either from the annual melt of segregated ice lenses in the active layer or from the melt (degradation) of permafrost.

Related to solar radiation inputs is the question of permafrost. In high latitudes the long arctic night enables intense cooling of the ground surface and the formation of permafrost. However, the relatively short duration of the mid-latitude winter and the fact that even in winter temperatures followed a diurnal pattern, probably meant that the extremes of winter temperatures, as experienced by polar and continental environments today, did not exist. This would have been particularly true of the oceanic periglacial environments. On the other hand, in continental areas radiation cooling during the winter nights would have created temperature inversions which might have persisted through the daylight hours. It has been suggested that temperature depressions as great as $10–12\,°C$ might have existed in the central European lowlands. In areas under such climatic conditions, permafrost would certainly have formed but in the more oceanic locations, it is unreasonable to envisage the formation of thick permafrost.

Snow cover would have been an important factor inhibiting the formation of any permafrost. In western Europe in particular, permafrost was probably thin and discontinuous, and less than $10–30$ m in thickness at most times. In all likelihood, it was a transitory phenomenon, typical of only the coldest periods of the cold-climate oscillations. Deep seasonal frost, rather than permafrost, was probably a more typical condition for a large duration of the cold periods. The evidence concerning the nature and extent of Pleistocene permafrost is examined in more detail in the next chapter.

The closest present-day analogues, in terms of solar radiation conditions, are probably to be found in the subarctic interior Yukon of northwest Canada and the Qinghai-Xizang (Tibet) Plateau of China. Neither is satisfactory, however, since they are at latitudes $60–65°$ and $30–35°N$ respectively, and not in the critical mid-latitude range of $40–55°N$. Moreover, the continental location of interior Yukon and the high altitude of Tibet complicate assessment of the effects of solar radiation.

A second major difference between the mid-latitudes during the Pleistocene and the high latitudes of today arises from the fact that global atmospheric circulation patterns were very different during glacial times when large ice sheets extended into mid-latitudes. This is in addition to the normal, latitudinal, differences that are expected when comparing mid- and high-latitude climates. In all probability, there was an increased intensity of the climatic gradients equatorwards away from the ice margins. The mid-latitude westerlies, while being displaced latitudinally would also have been stronger because of this. At the same time, intense anticyclonic conditions probably developed over the ice sheets and in ice-free continental locations. In Europe, for example, the development of strong high-pressure systems, especially in winter, may have led to the 'blocking' of travelling disturbances in the westerlies. These would have been diverted either northwards towards Iceland and Spitsbergen or southwards towards the Mediterranean Sea. If this were correct, central and eastern Europe would have experienced below average precipitation amounts while the western fringes of France, south-west England and southern Ireland would have experienced above average amounts for that time.

Several reasons suggest a greater importance of wind action in middle latitudes during the Pleistocene than in high latitudes today. First, as already mentioned, wind gradients were strong at the southern margins of the ice sheets owing to the contraction in space of the various climatic zones. Second, anticyclonic conditions which developed over the ice sheets led to strong local winds blowing off them. Third, the periglacial zone developed in an ice-marginal position, where extensive outwash and till plains had been exposed as the ice sheets retreated. Abundant sources of fine-grained and unconsolidated sediments were available, therefore, for transport and use as abrasive materials. Fourth, the effectiveness of wind action in middle latitudes was further enhanced by the general decrease in precipitation resulting from the colder conditions of glacial times and the anticyclonic blocking of travelling disturbances in the westerlies.

On a more specific level, the nature of fluvial processes in Pleistocene mid-latitude environments needs a brief mention. In all probability, fluvial activity was greater than is conventionally imagined. Moreover, it was different in nature from the fluvial activity currently experienced by high latitudes. In particular, the absence of a long and continuous arctic night in which temperatures dropped well below 0 °C meant that running water was an important characteristic of the periglacial landscape for more than just two or three months, as is the case in high latitudes today. In addition, there would not have been the same dramatic spring flood as occurs in high latitudes. Some of the winter snowfall would have melted and entered the drainage system during the winter daytime periods. If permafrost were absent, or discontinuous, there would have been infiltration of water to the groundwater table, and there would have been less direct runoff from either summer storms or spring snowmelt. For these reasons, fluvial activity involving both slopewash and channel flow would have been of a more year-round importance, particularly so in the milder maritime environments, and the nival flood, while important, would have been less pronounced.

In summary, we might speculate that the periglacial environments of middle latitudes during the Pleistocene were different from those of polar and continental high latitudes in the following ways. First, the solar radiation pattern was dominated by a daily,

as opposed to a seasonal, rhythm. This led to a greater intensity of frost action processes, notably frost shattering and frost creep. Second, the effects of orientation and local micro-climatic differences with respect to geomorphic processes were more obvious. Third, atmospheric conditions were different as a result of the large Pleistocene ice sheets. In particular, wind gradients were strong on account of (a) intense high-pressure systems developing over the ice sheets and (b) the concentration of the various climatic zones. Fourth, wind action, as both an erosive and transporting agent, assumed great importance on the extensive outwash and till plains adjacent to the ice margins. Fifth, permafrost may not have been such an important element of the mid-latitude periglacial landscape and, except in continental locations, was relatively thin and/or discontinuous. Deep seasonal frost was probably a more typical condition for extensive periods. Sixth, the extremes of winter temperatures, as currently experienced in high latitudes, were probably never reached. Seventh, the fluvial regime was different in that streams may have flowed for much of the year, and there was not the same concentration of fluvial activity in a short period of time as there is in the high latitudes today. Finally, it seems reasonable to argue that there were significant variations in Pleistocene periglacial climates, both in a spatial and temporal sense, in the same way that there are marked variations in present-day periglacial climates.

13.4 Problems of reconstruction

The spatial extent of the periglacial conditions which existed during the Pleistocene is difficult to assess for a number of reasons. These are summarized as being either geomorphic or climatic.

From the geomorphic point of view, the major problem is related to the lack of reliable indicators of cold conditions. Most attention has been concentrated upon the identification of 'relict' frost action phenomena and/or the previous existence of permafrost. At first, a wide range of features was thought to be diagnostic of periglacial climates; Smith (1949), for example, listed 13 types of features as being of climatic significance. Many, however, such as landslides, superficial folds, earth mounds, stabilized talus, dry valleys and asymmetric valleys, can demonstrably be shown to occur under non-periglacial conditions as well, and their usefulness, therefore, is limited. Others, such as patterned ground phenomena, solifluction deposits, involutions and blockfields, are more reliable indicators of frost action (Wright, 1961). But these features are still open to interpretation since some do not require permafrost for their formation, and others require different degrees of cold climates for their development. Probably, the only reliable indicator of past periglacial conditions is that of ice- and sand-wedge casts or pseudomorphs, since only they unambiguously demand permafrost for their formation. However, in Chapter 6 the importance of the nature of the enclosing sediments was stressed when discussing the critical ground and air temperatures required for cracking and both Harry and Gozdzik (1988) and Burn (1990) warn against the uncritical use of frost-fissure pseudomorphs in inferring palaeotemperatures. It must be remembered that thermal contraction cracking can occur when the mean annual ground temperature is significantly warmer than –6 °C. Frost cracking has also been observed to occur in regions of deep seasonal frost rather than permafrost (see Chapter 4).

It has also been demonstrated in Chapter 6 that winter ground temperatures rather than mean annual ground temperatures are the more critical, and these are influenced by a variety of local, site-specific factors such as snow cover and localized air temperature inversions.

Thermokarst forms have also been suggested as valid indicators of past permafrost conditions, but with the possible exception of pingo remnants, their identification in the landscapes of now temperate latitudes is extremely difficult indeed. Even when the previous existence of permafrost has been established, there is still no simple relationship between permafrost and air temperatures. Permafrost may be relict, inherited from an earlier cold period, and, if it is discontinuous, numerous local factors in addition to air temperatures can influence the presence or absence of permafrost at any one locality. As has been demonstrated in Chapter 5, the prediction of permafrost distribution and thickness in the discontinuous permafrost zones of North America, Eurasia and Tibet is especially difficult. Equally, when the rather broader category of frost action phenomena (blockfields, involution, etc.) is used as the diagnostic criterion, the relationship between the inferred frost structures and air temperatures is also not clear. Local lithological, moisture, site and vegetation conditions influence the effectiveness of frost action at any one locality.

From the climatological point of view, a number of problems hinder attempts to calculate possible temperature depressions during the Pleistocene, and hence, to give quantitative parameters to the cold conditions. Usually, temperature depressions have been calculated on the basis of modern lapse rates and present snowlines in alpine regions. For example, assuming a lapse rate of 0.5 °C/100 m, a mean annual temperature at the snowline of 0 °C, and an elevation difference between the present snowline and the inferred Pleistocene snowline of approximately 1000 m, it has been calculated that there was a probable temperature depression of between 4 and 6 °C in Europe during the last glacial period (Wright, 1961, pp. 966–970). This sort of analysis masks the considerable variability of modern lapse rates which occurs in mountainous regions. Moreover, there is no guarantee that lapse rate conditions were similar during the Pleistocene to those of today and, furthermore, that the European alpine conditions are representative of the lowland periglacial zone lying between the Alps and the continental ice sheets. In fact, within the lowland periglacial zone, marked temperature inversions were probably very common up to 1500 m in elevation on account of the very low ground surface temperatures brought on by anticyclonic conditions, terrestrial radiation and a negative heat balance. As a result, a mean annual air temperature 10–12 °C lower than today is probably more realistic for the European lowlands during the last cold stage (e.g. Shotton, 1960).

Estimates of the drop in elevation of the Pleistocene snowline are also difficult to make because (a) the Pleistocene snowline is usually identified upon morphological evidence, such as cirque heights or nivation hollows, which themselves may be of considerable amplitude or variability with respect to elevation, (b) the modern snowline is not necessarily at 0 °C as is often assumed, but generally lower, and (c) in certain areas, such as southern Africa, a hypothetical snowline has to be assumed.

Finally, there is little evidence from which to make deductions concerning precipitation amounts. In general, the colder conditions and the blocking of travelling disturbances in the westerlies would have led to an overall decrease in precipitation. Based upon the absence of cirques from southern Britain, Manley (1959) has suggested that the uplands of western Britain received only 80 per cent of today's amounts. If such areas were above average for Europe, then one might expect only 40 per cent of today's amount to

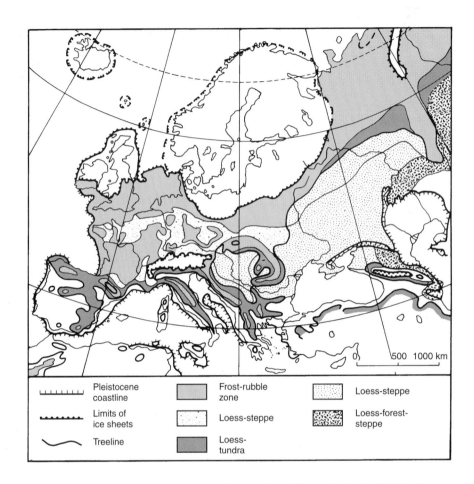

Figure 13.4 Climatic reconstruction and regionalization of Europe during the Weichselian
stage, according to Büdel (1951, 1953).

have fallen in parts of central and eastern Europe. In
Poland for example, where current precipitation
amounts are approximately 400–500 mm/year, this
would mean less than 200 mm year, an amount comparable to many high Arctic regions today.

13.5 Extent of late Pleistocene periglacial conditions

Perhaps the most reliable criterion for the extent of
the periglacial climates during the late Pleistocene is
the distribution of plants, and the extent of the different eco-zones. In terms of periglacial climate
identification, this means the analysis of the past
migration and extent of the tundra, steppe tundra
and forest tundra zones. As stated earlier, palynological studies have been particularly helpful in outlining
late and postglacial vegetational successions in both
middle and high latitudes. In addition, the study of
Pleistocene steppe and tundra faunal remains, such
as land Mollusca and insects, has helped determine
environmental conditions and absolute chronology.
Unfortunately, the number of such studies is limited,
even in Europe, and the accurate delineation of Pleistocene periglacial climatic zones is far from complete.
In many cases, heavy reliance is placed upon morphological evidence, some of which is open to
differing interpretations.

For Europe, where most information upon late
Pleistocene climatic and vegetational changes is avail-

able, one of the earliest attempts at morpho-climatic reconstruction was by Büdel (1951). This reconstruction is illustrated in Fig. 13.4. It should be treated with extreme caution, however, since in spite of its claims, there is no evidence that palaeobotanical evidence was used in either the distribution or classification of the forested areas. Instead, it should be regarded as an intuitive synthesis which, in broad terms, is probably representative of conditions at the maximum advance of the Weichselian ice sheets in Europe. Büdel identified three vegetation zones which, together, may well have represented the extent of the periglacial domain at that time.

First, a frost-rubble tundra zone ('*frostschuttzone*') lay to the south of the continental ice sheets. It was characterized by intense frost action and strong winds, and the spread of subarctic and arctic plants and animals. This zone covered much of southern England, France and the north European plain extending eastwards through Poland into European Russia. A further characteristic, designated by Büdel as a distinct eco-zone, was a loess–tundra belt extending from western France eastwards into Poland. Frost action is recorded by ice-wedge casts, involutions and solifluction/head deposits. Wind action is recorded by loess deposits, frosted sand grains and ventifacts. The absence of a forest cover, the presence of large unvegetated outwash plains and extensive areas of comminuted frost debris and exposed till sheets, all accentuated the effects of the wind. Continuous or discontinuous permafrost underlay this zone.

Second, a forest–tundra zone, generally more restricted in extent, lay to the south of the polar treeline and the frost-rubble tundra zone. Parts of southern France, the Iberian Peninsula, northern Italy and the areas between the Adriatic and Black Seas were included within this eco-zone. Because of the tree cover, the effectiveness of wind action was reduced while permafrost was discontinuous or absent. In upland areas, local frost-rubble tundra zones probably occurred at elevations below the Pleistocene snowline.

Third, a steppe zone of open parkland vegetation lay to the east of the polar treeline, and extended over large areas of eastern Europe and European Russia as far as the Ural Mountains in the east and the northern shores of the Black Sea in the south. Drier, more continental conditions were probably the control over this particular eco-zone, and the sheltered Carpathian Basin represented the most westerly limit to this zone. Büdel subdivided the zone into (a) loess–steppe, representing the eastern extension of the loess–tundra zone, and (b) loess–forest steppe, which was a transition from forest–tundra and loess–steppe conditions.

If one agrees with this reconstruction, one is led to conclude that much, if not most, of Europe to the south of the continental ice sheets was affected by periglacial conditions at the height of the last glacial advance. According to Büdel, only the southern parts of the Iberian Peninsula and coastal areas bordering the Mediterranean escaped.

A more specific indicator of the former extent of Pleistocene periglacial conditions is the former extent of Pleistocene permafrost. This can be inferred from the recognition of frost fissure pseudomorphs and casts, and other structures indicating the former existence of ground ice. Although the latter are difficult to identify since the nature of the thermokarst is a self-destroying process (see Chapter 7), numerous ice-wedge pseudomorphs and sand-wedge casts provide reasonably reliable evidence for the former existence of frozen ground. Other phenomena have also been used (see Chapter 14) but their palaeoclimatic significance is debatable and these results are not emphasized here. Bearing these considerations in mind, it is instructive to reconstruct the southern permafrost limits in Europe (Fig. 13.5). It can be seen that at the Weichselian glacial maximum, permafrost is thought to have been present in a wide zone south of the ice limit in eastern, central and northwestern Europe. In France, there is no consensus and the situation in southwestern England is also unclear. However, there is no doubt concerning the widespread existence of a periglacial belt, approximately 500 km wide in central and western Europe extending into East Anglia and the Central Midlands of England. The difficult, unresolved problems relate to (a) the severity of the periglacial climate, especially the mean January air and ground temperatures, (b) the thickness and distribution of the permafrost and whether discontinuous permafrost or deep seasonal frost was widespread, and (c) the temporal duration of these conditions.

In North America, an early attempt to map the various eco-zones which existed in mid-latitudes at the height of the Wisconsinan glaciation was made by Brunschweiller (1962). More recent syntheses now permit a more definite reconstruction (Fig. 13.6). Several considerations suggest that this map over-emphasizes the extent of the tundra and steppe eco-zones. First, the pollen record for many parts of the United States and southern Canada does not sug-

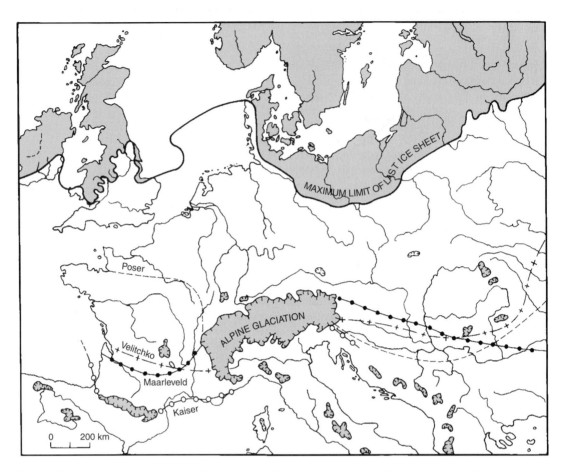

Figure 13.5 Map of western and central Europe showing the southern permafrost limits as proposed by
Poser (1948), Kaiser (1960), Maarleveld (1976) and Velichko (1982), according to the distribution of
periglacial phenomena dated from the last cold maximum.

gest a widespread frost-rubble tundra zone, and
instead, indicates that forest zones intermingled with
loess–steppe zones. Second, the southern extent of the
Wisconsinan ice sheets was further south than that of
the Weichselian in Europe; as a consequence, the zone
of most severe periglacial conditions was probably
more restricted than in Europe owing to the tighter
alignment of the displaced climatic zones. Third, the
retreat of the Wisconsinan ice sheet was accompanied
by the development of extensive proglacial lakes along
its southern margin, brought about by isostatic
depression and the ponding of meltwaters or the
influx of marine waters. These water bodies exerted
modifying influences upon the regional climate, and
restricted the amount of land surface exposed to subaerial conditions. Furthermore, by the time of their

retreat, either hundreds of several thousands of years
later, the climate had ameliorated sufficiently to allow
forest growth to re-establish itself.

The most convincing evidence for Pleistocene permafrost comes from frost fissure pseudomorphs found
in the north central United States (Wisconsin) and the
interior and western plains (Iowa, Nebraska,
Wyoming). Presumably, more continental and drier
environments occurred in these regions while in eastern
North America, especially in the Appalachian region
and New England, the evidence for extensive frost
debris (see Chapter 14) rather than permafrost suggests
milder conditions and more frequent freeze–thaw. As
in western Europe, one must also envisage a time-
transgressive shift of the periglacial zone northwards
as the Wisconsinan ice sheet progressively withdrew.

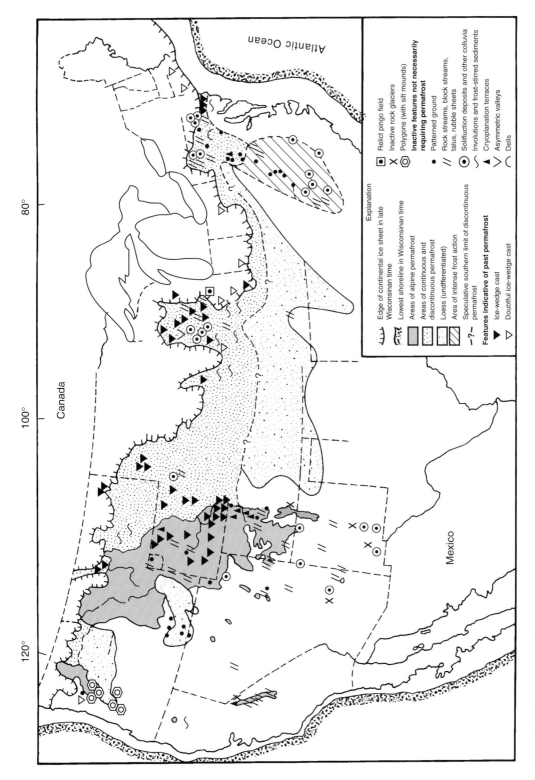

Figure 13.6 Tentative reconstruction of the maximum extent of Late Wisconsinan periglacial conditions in the USA south of the ice sheet limits. Based upon Péwé (1983), Clarke and Ciolkosz (1988), Braun (1989) and Washburn (1979).

Attempts at palaeo-reconstruction in other parts of the world are considerably less advanced, with the possible exception of the FSU. There, several detailed maps have been produced for Russia and elsewhere (e.g. Popov, 1961; Popov *et al.*, 1985a, 1990) but their small scale and somewhat uncritical reliance upon previously published literature limit their credibility. However, there is general agreement as to the changes in the extent of permafrost during the late Quaternary (e.g. Velichko, 1975; Kondratjeva *et al.*, 1993). During the Zyriansk (50 000–60 000 BP) and Sartansk (15 000–27 000 BP) cold periods permafrost reached its maximum thickness and extent (48–49 °N) on the Russian Plain. An interesting difference between the relict permafrost of the glaciated areas, such as western Siberia and the European northeast, and the unglaciated areas of central and eastern Siberia is that in the former, relict early Pleistocene permafrost is separated at depth from late Pleistocene permafrost by a thin unfrozen layer, while in the latter the permafrost is continuous and thick. In general, one must envisage thick and cold permafrost in never-glaciated terrain and thinner or non-existent permafrost existing beneath the ice sheets. Schematic illustrations of the relationships between permafrost thickness adjacent to Pleistocene ice sheets and following climatic fluctuations are illustrated in Fig. 13.7.

From other regions of the world there is also evidence for the existence of Pleistocene periglacial conditions in now-temperate mid-latitudes. In northern China, for example, the southern limit of late Pleistocene permafrost has been mapped as far south as 40 °N, based primarily upon ice-wedge casts and sand wedges (Fig. 13.8).

Because of the wide-ranging nature of much evidence, it is somewhat difficult to evaluate the importance of the various observations without personal acquaintance with the terrain. Of note, however, are the claims for Pleistocene frost-action phenomena in the southern hemisphere, particularly southern Argentina (e.g. Grosso and Corte, 1991), Tasmania (e.g. Derbyshire, 1973), New Zealand (e.g. Soons and Price, 1990), and southern Africa (e.g. Boelhouwers, 1991).

It should also be stressed that although Pleistocene frost-action conditions apparently existed in the southern hemisphere, evidence for the previous existence of widespread permafrost is not always convincing. For example, none of the periglacial phenomena described from Tasmania (e.g. talus, solifluction debris, blockstreams, nivation cirques and bedded screes) necessarily require permafrost. The only diagnostic feature which has been convinc-

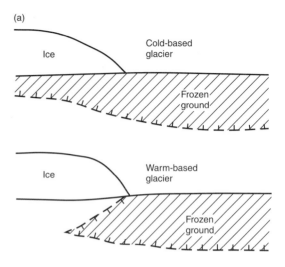

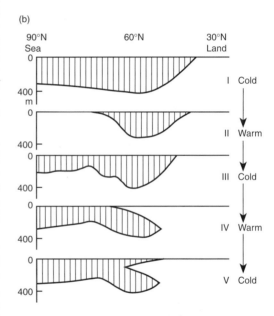

Figure 13.7 Simplified relation between growth and decay of permafrost and (a) cold/warm-based ice-sheets and (b) climatic fluctuations (from Romanovskii, 1993; Dostovalov and Kudryavtsev, 1967).

ingly recognized so far (ice-wedge casts) relate to Patagonia, southern Argentina (Grosso and Corte, 1989). This suggests that the periglacial environments of the southern hemisphere did not experience the same magnitude of temperature depressions as did the periglacial environments of the northern hemisphere. For example, Derbyshire (1973) suggests a

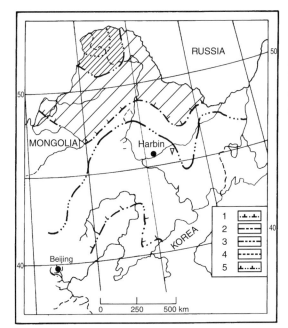

Figure 13.8 Changes in permafrost distribution since the Pleistocene in northern China (from Qiu and Cheng, 1995: 1, present southern limit of discontinuous permafrost; 2, present southern limit of continous permafrost; 3, southern limit of permafrost in Little Ice Age; 4, southern limit of permafrost in Holocene Hysithermal; 5, southern limit of late Pleistocene permafrost.

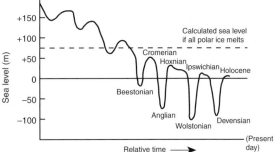

Figure 13.9 Quaternary sea-level changes.

depression of only 6.5 °C for the last cold period in Tasmania. Presumably, the much milder periglacial conditions of mid-latitudes in the southern hemisphere reflects their more oceanic surroundings.

Pleistocene periglacial coasts are usually discussed in the context of isostatic rebound and raised shorelines (e.g. West, 1977, pp. 151–179; Sissons, 1981; Synge, 1981). Rarely are Pleistocene coastal processes discussed in the periglacial literature, a notable exception being that of Dawson (1980, 1986). Undoubtedly, this is because most late Pleistocene periglacial shorelines are now submerged or have been destroyed by the Holocene rise in sea level. Moreover, if one accepts the 'staircase' theory of Quaternary sea-level change (Fig. 13.9), only shorelines of Hoxnian or older age presently lie above sea level. In theory, the combination of frost action and marine (salt) waters would have been an effective agent of mechanical weathering during the cold peri-

ods. It is unlikely, however, that remnants of any of these shorelines are recognizable in the landscape today. Even in the relatively well-known late glacial (i.e. periglacial) marine environment of the Champlain Sea of eastern North America, discussion of cold-climate beach processes is strangely absent.

Estimates as to the global extent of late Pleistocene periglacial conditions is extremely difficult. The periglacial climates varied in time and space. Some were characterized by both intense frost action and permafrost; others, by intense frost action only. The two areas for which there is sufficient information of reliable quality to allow one to make estimates are Europe and, possibly, North America. If it is assumed that these areas, together with southern Siberia, were the major areas of late Pleistocene periglacial conditions, a conservative guess would be that as much as 20 per cent of the Earth's surface has experienced cold-climate, non-glacial conditions in the past.

Further reading

Qiu Guoqing and Cheng Guodong (1995) Permafrost in China: past and present. *Permafrost and Periglacial Processes*, **6**, 3–14.

Kondratjeva, K.A., S.F. Krutsky and N.N. Romanovsky (1993) Changes in the extent of permafrost during the Late Quaternary Period in the territory of the Former Soviet Union. *Permafrost and Periglacial Processes*, **4**, 113–119.

Lowe, J.J. and M.J.C. Walker (1984) *Reconstructing Quaternary environments*. Harlow: Longman, 389 pp.

Péwé, T.L. (1983) The periglacial environment in North America during Wisconsinan time. In: S.C. Porter (ed.),

The Late Pleistocene. Late Quaternary environments of the United States, Vol. 1. Minneapolis, Minnesota: University of Minnesota Press, pp. 157–189.

Vandenberghe, J. and A. Pissart (1993) Permafrost changes in Europe during the last glacial. *Permafrost and Periglacial Processes*, **4**, 121–135.

West, R.G. (1977) *Pleistocene geology and biology*, Second Edition. Harlow: Longman, 440 pp.

Wright, H.E. (1961) Late Pleistocene climate of Europe: a review. *Geological Society of America, Bulletin*, **72**, 933–984.

Discussion topics

1. How extensive, in time and space, were the Pleistocene periglacial environments in mid-latitudes?
2. What are the problems of palaeo-reconstruction of Pleistocene cold climates?

CHAPTER 14 Relict periglacial phenomena

On the basis of the information in Chapter 13, the Pleistocene periglacial environments were characterized by (a) intense frost action and (b) frozen ground.

The evidence from which we can deduce the previous existence of frozen ground is reasonably unambiguous, although the distinction between permafrost and deep seasonal frost can be obscure. There is increasing evidence for Pleistocene thermokarst. The evidence in favour of intense frost action, while widespread, is less reliable in terms of palaeo-reconstruction.

14.1 Introduction

This chapter reviews the geomorphological evidence thought diagnostic of the periglacial conditions which existed in mid-latitudes during the Pleistocene. Because biological evidence is equally as important, a few other comments are appropriate as a preface.

For our purposes, faunal and insect remains, pollen taxa and even the drawings of ancient cave men provide the most convincing and dramatic evidence. Certain insects, such as beetles (Coleoptera) and land snails (non-marine Mollusca) survive only under somewhat limiting temperature and moisture ranges. Many living species are only found today in subarctic and arctic environments. Both beetles and landsnails have been used successfully in palaeo-reconstructions (e.g. Kerney, 1963; Sher *et al.*, 1979; Morgan and Morgan, 1980; Morgan *et al.*, 1983) since they live at or near the ground surface. As such, they provide good indications of surface, soil and ground temperatures. The same is true for pollen with regards to July air temperatures (e.g. Kolstrup, 1980). The larger mammals, with their greater mobility, have less rigid environmental controls, but even here the evidence is clear. For example, in caves in the Dordogne region of southern France, occupied by *Homo sapiens* 20 000–30 000 years ago at the height of the maximum extension of the Weichselian ice sheet to the north, crude wall drawings depict a variety of now-extinct animals including woolly mammoths, bears, woolly rhinoceros and reindeer (Fig. 14.1). Likewise, in the mid-latitude prairies of North America, the Middle and Late Quaternary stratigraphic records reveal mammal bones from a variety of animals either now extinct or which live today in subarctic and arctic environments (e.g. Stalker and Churcher, 1982; Stalker, 1984).

It must also be emphasized that Pleistocene periglacial conditions were not restricted to middle latitudes. Extensive subarctic areas of central and eastern Siberia, central Alaska and the northwest Canadian Arctic were ice-free for much, if not all, of the Quaternary. These areas acted as northern refugia for Pleistocene plants and animals at the height of the glacial periods. Most explicit evidence is provided by the frozen carcasses of woolly mammoths and other mammals found within permafrost in northern Siberia, Alaska and Canada (Fig. 14.2). More common, however, is a wide range of Pleistocene flora and fauna remains contained within silty surficial

(a)

(b)

Figure 14.1   Cave drawings in the Dordogne region,
southern France, indicate that cold-climate
fauna, now extinct, once lived in the
Pleistocene periglacial zone:
(a) woolly mammoth, Cave of Les
Combarelles; (b) woolly rhinoceros, Cave
of Font de Gaume (from Sutcliffe, 1985).

materials. These organic-rich frozen deposits are
commonly termed 'muck' in Alaska and Yukon; in
Siberia similar deposits are classified as 'Yedoma
Suite' or 'ice-complex'. In all probability, the Pleistocene periglacial environments of high latitudes
were just as extensive as their middle latitude counterparts. However, these environments are not the
object of our study here and are more properly
treated within the context of regional Arctic and
subarctic Quaternary geology.

In conclusion, when discussing the geomorphology
of mid-latitude Pleistocene periglacial environments
we must remember (a) the importance of a wide
range of biological evidence and (b) that Pleistocene
periglacial environments also existed in many northern latitudes at the same time.

14.2 Perennial or seasonal frost?

In the Pleistocene context, it is important to distinguish between perennially frozen and seasonally
frozen ground. In all probability, permafrost only
developed during the maximum severity of the cold
periods and immediately adjacent to the ice margins
where cold winds coming off the ice sheets would
have kept ground temperatures low. For extensive
periods of time, and certainly towards the southern
limits of the periglacial zones, deep seasonal frost
rather than permafrost would have characterized the
majority of the ice-free mid-latitudes during the
Pleistocene.

This distinction is a useful one. For example, with
frost fissures it is necessary to distinguish between
seasonal frost cracks, or ground veins ('soil wedges'
in the Russian literature), and perennial frost cracks.
The former are limited to deep seasonal frost, the
latter penetrate permafrost. A second illustration is
that of frost mounds; it is necessary to distinguish
between seasonal and perennial features since only
the latter are unambiguous indicators of permafrost.

In theory, it should be possible to identify the
former permafrost table (i.e. the boundary between
the base of former seasonal frost penetration and the
top of former permafrost) by a number of methods,
but, surprisingly, few studies have attempted this with
any conviction. For example, Maarleveld (1976) used
the depth to which involutions occur to infer the
depth of the active layer but, as outlined later in this
chapter, this approach assumes much about the origin
of such deformations. It should also be possible to
infer the permafrost table by a change in mineral
weathering characteristics above and below the permafrost, since the base of the active layer is a thaw
unconformity. In present-day permafrost regions, few
studies have attempted to identify secondary thaw
unconformities by mineralogical and cryostructural
changes above and below the unconformity (e.g. Xing
et al., 1980). In now-unfrozen terrain, studies by Van
Vliet-Lanoë (1982, 1985) and Harris (1985), among
others, have used soil micromorphology to deduce the
previous existence of frozen ground. The problem
with these interpretations is that the degree of differentiation between perennially frozen and seasonally
frozen sediment will depend largely upon the time
over which the permafrost existed, and the specific
lithological and mineralogical (weathering) complexes
involved. These considerations often mean that it is
difficult to generalize.

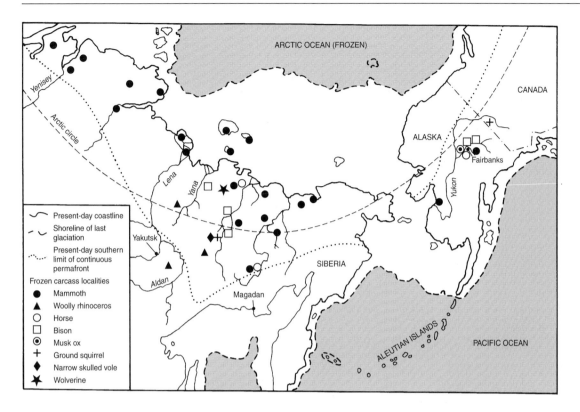

Figure 14.2 Distribution of frozen Pleistocene mammalian carcasses and parts of carcasses in Siberia, Alaska and Canada. From Sutcliffe (1985).

A more qualitative approach is the degree to which bedrock appears to have undergone frost weathering and disintegration. For example, in Chalk cliffs along the south coast of England (e.g. Kerney, 1963) it is common for the upper 3–5 m to be intensely fissured and for involuted structures to occur in the near-surface horizon. It is tempting to interpret the boundary between the frost disturbed soils and the *in situ* fissured bedrock within the context of the 'ice-rind' concept of Büdel (1982) (see Chapter 6).

14.3 Evidence for frost action

It should be expected that frost-action phenomena from the last cold period are especially well developed and widespread. However, their recognition and interpretation is sometimes difficult. To begin with, the effects of present-day frost-action processes must be correctly assessed before a feature can be attributed to past, more intense, frost action. Even when it is clear that present frost activity is not responsible for the feature concerned, its 'relict significance' depends upon an evaluation of the lithological susceptibility of the rock in question to frost action, and the moisture, vegetation and local site conditions which existed during the period of colder conditions. A second problem arises from the fact that certain features, such as tors, can be produced under both periglacial and non-periglacial conditions. Finally, the effects of humans in clearing and ploughing the land must be considered since soil structures may be modified or even obliterated. Under certain conditions, for example, it is easy to mistake a series of old plough furrows for a sequence of shallow involuted structures.

For these reasons, the recognition of relict frost-action phenomena requires caution. Few provide unequivocal proof of periglacial conditions and only where several different features occur together or in association is one justified in assuming a frost-action environment.

14.3.1 Blockfields and frost-weathered bedrock

A mid-latitude feature commonly interpreted as reflecting intense frost wedging of exposed rock surfaces is the presence of extensive accumulations of angular boulders and coarse debris. These rock and rubble accumulations are termed 'blockfields' or '*felsenmeer*' and are clearly analogous to the debris-mantled upland surfaces or *kurums* of Arctic regions. They are particularly common in areas of hard, relatively well-bedded rocks such as shales and sandstones which are susceptible to frost wedging along major joints and bedding planes and which weather into coarse debris and angular boulders. More localized block accumulations which occur on slopes and in valley bottoms are variously termed boulder fields, or 'stone streams' (*coulées pierreuses*) and clearly demand some additional form of mass movement. Scree slopes are localized boulder fields developed beneath vertical or near-vertical rock faces. Pro-talus ramparts, sometimes linked to boulder fields, are ridge-like accumulations of coarse angular blocks which develop some distance from the base of the steep slope from which they are derived.

In Europe blockfields and related forms are known to occur in most of the upland massifs and low mountain ranges (e.g. Pissart, 1953; Dylik, 1956). In North America, numerous blockfields occur south of the glacial limits, especially in the central interior uplands and the Appalachian plateaus (e.g. Smith, 1962). In parts of Asia (Japan, Korea) and in the southern hemisphere, blockfields, talus and frost-shattered debris are the most widespread of the periglacial phenomena reported (e.g. Derbyshire, 1973; Kwon, 1978, 1979; Lewis, 1988, 1994).

Blockfields and related forms are of limited use in Pleistocene periglacial reconstruction. To begin with, it must be proven that these deposits are not being formed under present-day climatic conditions, or, if they are, that the current rate of weathering is insufficient to explain them. For example, scree slopes in the English Lake District have been compared to similar forms in subarctic Labrador-Ungava (Andrews, 1961). According to Andrews, these screes formed under periglacial conditions in relatively recent (i.e. Postglacial) times. Further study (Caine, 1963) indicated, however, that the scree slopes are

still very active. The same problem occurs in the case of blockfields; in the Appalachian Mountains of the United States for example, both actively forming and relict blockfields are thought to exist (e.g. Hack and Goodlett, 1960, pp. 31–3; Rapp, 1967). Thus, there is no proof that blockfields form only under periglacial conditions, and they cannot be regarded as diagnostic of such a climate.

A second problem is that many of the *kurums* and boulder fields reported from present-day cold regions, such as the Transbaikal Mountains (Tyurin *et al.*, 1982; Romanovskii, 1985), the northern Urals (Perov, 1969) and the northern Yukon (French, 1987b), appear to be largely inactive and may have taken many millennia to form.

A third problem is the uncertainty as to whether blockfields can form under glacial, as opposed to periglacial, conditions. In the Narvik Mountains of Norway, for example, it is not clear whether blockfields formed since the last glaciation or whether they developed during a much longer period of time, either in a nunatak position or beneath an inactive and protective ice sheet (e.g. Dahl, 1966; Ives, 1966). Recently, the idea that blockfields, and entire periglacial landscapes, can be preserved beneath the late Weichselian ice sheets has been proposed by Kleman and Borgström (1990) for parts of central Sweden. A final problem, stressed in the introduction to this chapter, and also in Chapter 4, is that different lithological properties and moisture conditions determine the effectiveness of frost weathering.

14.3.2 Tors and croplanation terraces

The existence of hillslope and summit tors in many mid-latitude regions (Fig. 14.3) has attracted considerable attention, but their climatic significance is also the subject of dispute. Tors are well-known phenomena in many of the uplands of central and western Europe, notably the Sudetes Mountains (e.g. Jahn, 1962), the Bohemian Massif (e.g. Czudek, 1964; Demek, 1964), the Pennines of northern England (e.g. Palmer and Radley, 1961; Linton, 1964), and the Dartmoor Massif of southwest England (e.g. Linton, 1955; Te Punga, 1956; Palmer and Nielson, 1962). Tors are also known to exist in many mid-latitude areas of the southern hemisphere (e.g. Caine, 1967; Fahey, 1981; Wood, 1969) .

(a)

(b)

Figure 14.3 Frost-weathered bedrock features, southwest England (a) hillslope tor, 10 m high, near Lynton, N. Devon; (b) frost-riven scarp, 4–5 m high, on Cox Tor, Dartmoor, N. Devon, developed in metadolorite. Both photographs courtesy of D. N. Mottershead.

One school of thought interprets mid-latitude tors as essentially angular landforms produced by frost shattering under Pleistocene periglacial conditions. They are interpreted, therefore, as being 'palaeo-arctic' (e.g. Palmer and Radley, 1961). Such an interpretation may be classified as a one-stage hypothesis involving weathering and simultaneous removal of the regolith. It assumes that formation of tors is intimately linked to the evolution of slopes through cryoplanation. Under such a hypothesis, the tors reflect the remnants of a frost-riven bedrock outcrop surrounded by a low-angled pediment across which frost-shattered debris is transported by solifluction and mass wasting processes. A second school of thought argues that tors are prepared by deep weathering principally along bedrock joints to produce subsurface rounding of corestones ('woolsacks')

under warm temperate or tropical conditions in late Tertiary times. Subsequently they are exhumed by solifluction and mass wasting, and sharpened by frost action during the Pleistocene (e.g. Linton, 1955, 1964). In this context, tors are interpreted as being 'palaeo-tropical', analogous, but on a smaller scale, to the larger inselbergs and castle koppies of central Africa and other tropical regions.

It is unlikely that there is one single hypothesis of tor formation. Instead, a variety of processes and environmental conditions may produce essentially the same landform, and periglacial conditions merely represent one set. In parts of the Polish Sudetes, for example, there is convincing evidence that summit tors were formed by deep weathering of granite, chiefly during warm interglacials, and by exhumation under periglacial conditions during the glacial periods (Jahn, 1962). On the other hand, in the adjacent Hruby Jesenik Mountains of Czechoslovakia, Demek (1964) has described how tors and castle koppies of both a deep weathered (i.e. two-cycle) origin and a frost shattering or periglacial (i.e. one-cycle) origin exist in the same area. According to Demek, exhumation of the deep weathered tors had already begun at the end of the Tertiary, and continued during the Pleistocene, at which time the parallel retreat of frost-riven cliffs caused the isolation of other tors and the formation of cryoplanation terraces.

A similar explanation may reconcile the apparently conflicting interpretations of the Dartmoor tors in southwest England (Linton, 1955; Palmer and Nielson, 1962). Decomposed granite, or 'growan', usually attributed to chemical rather than mechanical weathering (e.g. Eden and Green, 1971), is encountered in a number of localities in or near the main river valleys. In general, the majority of tors are also located in such positions and are peripheral, therefore, to the planation surfaces of supposed Tertiary age which occupy the higher interfluves. While these facts support Linton's (1955) two-cycle hypothesis of tor formation, they also suggest the localization of the deep weathering process. Thus, the existence on the higher summits (e.g. Cox Tor) of one-cycle tors surrounded by bedrock terraces covered with a veneer of frost-shattered rubble (Fig. 14.3) is not contradictory. Both exhumation and modification of two-cycle tors and the formation of one-cycle tors could have occurred contemporaneously in different parts of Dartmoor depending upon the localization of the deep weathering process.

Hillslope tors, occurring on the upper parts of slopes and in areas where there is little evidence for deep weathering, such as northern England (e.g. Palmer and Radley, 1961) and Bohemia (e.g. Czudek, 1964), are less ambiguous. They seem best explained by a one-stage development of slope retreat caused by frost action, with mass movement, nivation and wind action as subsidiary transporting and erosive processes.

It is also unwise to assume uncritically that tors reflect intense frost action since, in current periglacial environments, frost shattering is not the only process capable of forming tors. In Antarctica, for example, both rounded and angular forms develop side by side in dolerite (Derbyshire, 1972). The angular forms occur in depressions where snowpatches permit effective frost shattering. The rounded tors, on the other hand, occur in more exposed locations where snowpatches are absent and where long and slow chemical weathering and exfoliation has been experienced. In the Canadian high Arctic, on Ellef Ringnes Island, St-Onge (1965) has described tor-like features developed in sandstone ('relief ruinifore') which he attributes to wind abrasion. Clearly, therefore, tors cannot be used as diagnostic indicators of Pleistocene frost action without careful field investigation of the morphology and weathering patterns of the associated terrain.

Cryoplanation terraces are also ambiguous phenomena, as stressed in Chapter 10. Although they have been described by many workers from Alaska, Yukon and Siberia (e.g. Demek, 1969a, 1968b; Reger and Péwé, 1976; Lauriol and Godbout, 1988) no process studies have yet demonstrated that they form under prevailing cold-climate conditions. Moreover, certain features initially interpreted as cryoplanation, or altiplanation, forms have been shown to be elevated marine benches (on Spitsbergen; Waters, 1962; Péwé *et al.*, 1982, pp. 25–30). Finally, there are arguments to suggest that the distinction between cryopediments and pediments is largely artificial (see Chapter 10). Thus, it seems more appropriate to stress the role of mass wasting rather than frost action in the periglacial interpretation of tors and their associated bedrock surfaces.

14.3.3 Stratified slope deposits and *grèzes litées*

Intense frost action together with periglacial slopewash is generally believed to result in rhythmically stratified slope waste deposits (Dylik, 1960). These have been termed '*grèzes litées*' or '*éboulis ordonnés*'

in the French literature (e.g. Guillien, 1951; Malaurie and Guillien, 1953). The sediments involved are essentially frost-shattered debris, the nature of which depends upon the bedrock. Such deposits can be distinguished from those of solifluction since they possess coarse bedding and a certain amount of sorting. Occasionally, stratified deposits interdigitate with solifluction and other deposits. In the Charente region of France, the type region for *grèzes litées*, the stratified sediments occur on relatively steep slopes and are composed of small angular limestone particles, up to 2–3 cm in diameter, together with finer fractions (Fig. 14.4). At Walewice in central Poland, rhythmically stratified slope deposits attain thicknesses of over 10 m and are composed of alternating sand and silt (Dylik, 1969b). The calcareous meltwater muds which mantle the foot of the Chalk escarpments of southern England (e.g. Kerney *et al.*, 1964) are a form of stratified slope deposit. Bedded or stratified scree, composed of alternating stratified angular to sub-angular coarse talus, with stratification parallel to the slope, is another form of *grèzes litées* found in upland areas (e.g. Derbyshire, 1973; Boardman, 1978; Karte, 1983).

The formation of stratified slope deposits is understood in only general terms. A useful review is provided by DeWolf (1988). The typically angular particles and the finer matrix within which they are incorporated, are thought to reflect frequent, probably diurnal, oscillations of freezing and thawing. The sorting and bedding, and eluviation and deposition of finer particles downslope, is usually attributed to slopewash operating on vegetation-free slopes below snowpatches, and to the melting of pore ice.

Interpretation is not helped by the apparent absence of stratified slope deposits from high latitudes, although they have been reported from west Greenland (Malaurie and Guillien, 1953). Probably, high latitudes do not experience the repeated freeze–thaw oscillations thought favourable for their development. A second problem is the complexity of terms used in France to describe stratified slope deposits (e.g. '*grèzes*', '*groizes*', '*graveluche*', *éboulis ordonnés*) and the desire to identify generic morphological characteristics of such deposits.

In recent years it has become clear that *grèzes litées* are a localized form of stratified slope deposit occurring only in the Charente region of southwest France. Also, stratified slope deposits can possess a wide range of textural characteristics related to local bedrock conditions. Thus, their frost-action significance is very imprecise. The closest present-day

Figure 14.4 *Grèzes litées* near Sonneville, Charente region, southwest France.

process analogue is possibly the stratified scree and the frost-coated debris flow mechanism described by Hétu (1995) and Hétu *et al.* (1994) from the Gaspésie region of eastern Canada. There, stratification is achieved by the sliding of icy block fragments over scree slopes aided by niveo-aeolian processes. Another analogous process is suggested by Francou (1988, 1990) following fieldwork on steep scree slopes in the Andes of Peru and the French Alps. Stratification is thought to be achieved by a combination of differential solifluction and mudflow/elluviation following snowmelt and thaw of the active layer. Finally, stratified slope deposits can be formed by other processes such as dry grain flows, and debris flows (e.g. Hétu *et al.*, 1995). These can be unrelated to periglacial conditions. The various sedimentological models are reviewed by van Steijn *et al.* (1995).

14.3.4 'Head' and solifluction deposits

In present-day periglacial environments, frost heaving of the ground surface leads to the downslope move-ment of material by frost creep. This process, as described in Chapter 8, is one component of solifluc-tion. In areas where there are relatively high frequencies of freeze–thaw cycles, frost creep is thought to be the most important component of solifluction (e.g. Benedict, 1970). Given the probable importance of freeze–thaw activity in middle latitudes, one should expect to find evidence for the widespread existence of solifluction deposits, frost creep and gelifluction movements. Accordingly, many of the unstratified and heterogeneous 'drift' or superficial deposits which mantle the lower parts of valley side slopes are regarded as indicative of Pleistocene solifluction, and frost creep in particular.

In Europe, these deposits were first reported from southwest England where they were termed 'head' since they formed a capping to many coastal cliff sections (De La Beche, 1839). Later, Reid (1887) described the Coombe Rock which infilled the valleys and mantled the foot of the steeper slopes of many of the chalk regions of southern England, and Prest-wich (1892) documented the raised beach and overlying 'head' or 'rubble drift' deposits of southern

England. Subsequently, the mapping of 'head' deposits in England became standard practice by both the Geological Survey and the Soil Survey (e.g. Dines *et al.*, 1940; Avery, 1964). On the European Continent too, the significance of 'pseudo-glacial' sediments was appreciated at an early date and the recognition of frost-derived sediments in the lowlands of western and central Europe became commonplace (e.g. Troll, 1944; Büdel, 1944). In North America, the mapping of 'surficial' materials has been standard practice for several decades, although much is clearly glacial rather than periglacial in origin.

The variety of solifluction and 'head' deposits is considerable. All gradations exist between 'head' and river deposits and it is sometimes difficult to draw the line between the two. However, two general characteristics need to be emphasized. First, 'head' deposits are composed of predominantly poorly sorted angular debris of local derivation. Stratification is poorly developed and often absent. Where present, the stratification at the top and the bottom of the deposit is not horizontal. Often pebbles are aligned in a downslope direction and tilted upwards. Second, some of the 'head' deposits contain faunal remains indicative of cold-climate conditions at the time of deposition. Today, downwash and soil creep account for the various types of 'head' being formed in temperate mid-latitudes.

As general indicators of cold-climate conditions, solifluction and 'head' deposits represent an important line of evidence. However, as with the evidence already discussed, their direct interpretation in terms of frost action is not always easy. A fundamental problem lies in our inability, even in present-day periglacial environments, to differentiate between a solifluction deposit primarily the result of frost creep and retrograde movement, and one primarily the result of gelifluction. The former implies seasonal frost and the latter implies the presence of permafrost. This distinction is also important in terms of either one-sided or two-sided freezing, and the possible occurrence, and significance, of any patterned ground phenomena.

A second problem is that not all deposits contain readily identifiable cold-climate faunal remains, and a third is that many deposits are often difficult to distinguish from tills. In the latter situation, the distribution and surface morphology (e.g. lobes, stripes, etc.) of the deposit are often clues, but where landforms have been considerably modified since deposition, or where the deposit is derived from a glacial deposit and thus contains its erratics, it may be impossible to distinguish till from solifluction.

14.3.5 Frost-disturbed soils and structures (involutions)

Disturbed, distorted and deformed structures occurring in Quaternary sediments have been described frequently from middle-latitudes. In the European literature, these structures are usually referred to as 'cryoturbations' following Edelman *et al.* (1936), or '*brodelböden*' following K. Gripp (1926, quoted in Jahn, 1975) and Troll (1944). In the North American literature the term 'involution' is used (Denny, 1936; Sharp, 1942b).

Differing usage of the term cryoturbation in the European and North American literature has led to some confusion. While cryoturbation in the European sense refers primarily to structures, cryoturbation in the North American sense refers to the process of frost churning in soil brought about by repeated frost heaving and ice segregation within the seasonally frozen layer (ACGR, 1988). In present-day permafrost regions, cryoturbation is responsible for the widespread occurrence of non-sorted circles, or earth hummocks (see Chapter 8). Associated with these phenomena are deformed, irregular structures or mass displacements (see Chapter 8). These should not be confused with involutions as discussed here in a Pleistocene context.

In many instances, Pleistocene involuted structures have been interpreted to indicate the former existence of permafrost and/or deep seasonal frost (e.g. Dylikowa, 1961; Johnsson, 1962; Gozdzik, 1973; Vandenberghe and Van den Broek, 1982). Not only do they have a regularity in form and occurrence, but they appear to terminate at a horizontal level stratigraphically below an inferred palaeo-surface (e.g. Williams, 1975; Gullentops and Paulissen, 1978) (Fig. 14.5). However, this interpretation may be incorrect since it can be demonstrated that certain structures can be explained by azonal processes, chiefly related to either gravity and/or liquefaction (e.g. Butrym *et al.*, 1964; Anketell *et al.*, 1970). Moreover, involuted structures were originally thought to reflect cryostatic, or freezing-induced, processes which would have been generated in unfrozen pockets of soil trapped between the downward advancing freezing plane and the frozen ground (either seasonal or perennial) beneath. As described in Chapter 8, field studies have failed to measure significant cryostatic pressures and it can be

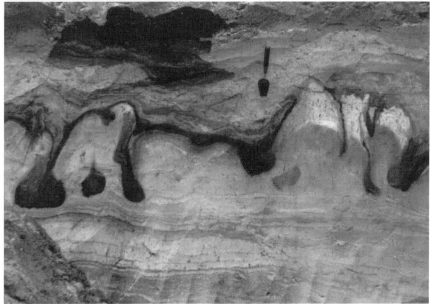

Figure 14.5 Pleistocene frost-disturbed structures: (a) cryoturbated surface layer in Chalk, Pays de Caux, northern France, resulting from intense frost action within the seasonally frozen layer. (b) 'Bird-foot' involutions in fluvial silt and sand with organic layers, northern Belgium. These structures are related to loading and density differences in water-saturated sediments, probably during the degradation of ice-rich permafrost.

demonstrated that during the freeze-back of the active layer, the middle section becomes desiccated and over-consolidated by water loss both upwards and downwards. The concept of two-sided freezing suggests that the middle section is not a viscous semi-fluid mass capable of deformation.

For both reasons, the use of involutions to infer intense frost action and/or to predict the depth of an active layer is unwise without careful consideration of all other possible explanations. Thus, Vandenberghe (1988) makes the useful distinction between the larger involutions which probably form during degradation of permafrost (type 2) and smaller features which do not require permafrost for their formation (type 3).

Many of the irregular structures and deformations found in unconsolidated Quaternary deposits are best interpreted as soft-sediment deformations which can occur under depositional conditions not necessarily unique to the cold regions of the world. This is not to deny, however, that a water-saturated active layer in mid-summer is highly suitable to such deformations. For example, the author has described deformed sediments on a river terrace in southern Banks Island which appear to have resulted from a liquefaction process leading to a loss of intergranular contact in silty sand (French, 1986). The most likely cause of such liquefaction was the creation of high pore water pressures in the active layer in late summer, following heavy summer precipitation.

It is relevant, therefore, to distinguish between (a) 'periglacial' involutions formed by repeated frost action (cryoturbation) within the seasonally frozen layer and (b) those due to gravity (loading), and intimately related to thermokarst degradation (Fig. 14.5). Many of the more irregular, complex and thick deformations described from Pleistocene sediments are probably related to the thaw of ice-rich permafrost. In the lowlands of eastern Germany, Eissmann (1978, 1994) has described dramatic diapiric upturning of lignite and other sediment deformations in this context (Fig. 14.6). Ice-wedge casts and pseudomorphs in adjacent sediments provide evidence of the former existence of permafrost and many deformations are thought to have resulted from the consistency changes brought about by the thaw of massive segregated ice layers associated with the lignite bodies. As described by Murton and French (1993c), thermokarst involutions take various forms including ball-and-pillow, dish and flame structures. It seems reasonable to assume that many Pleistocene deformed sediments, especially if they are more than 1.0–2.0 m in vertical extent, are thermokarst involutions.

In summary, only small, regularly spaced involutions, formed within a seasonally frozen zone beneath an inferred ground surface, can be used to deduce intense frost action (cryoturbation). Similar structures can result from soft-sediment deformations which may, or may not, be associated with cold-climate conditions. Finally, structures at depth and with vertical dimensions in excess of 2.0 m can only be interpreted as periglacial if there is additional evidence for the previous existence of permafrost, in which case they are probably thermokarst involutions associated with the degradation of ice-rich permafrost.

14.4 Evidence for frozen ground

The evidence in favour of the previous existence of frozen ground in mid-latitudes is less ambiguous than that of frost action. Certain features demand permafrost for their growth and development and, upon thawing of permafrost, leave morphological and/or stratigraphic evidence as proof of their previous existence. This is the case of (1) thermal contraction cracks (frost fissures) and (2) frost mounds (e.g. pingos) and other ice segregation features. Here, the problem is not primarily one of their palaeo-significance; rather, it is their recognition in the landscape as casts, pseudomorphs and remnants, and their differentiation from similar features or structures of different origin. A third category of evidence is provided by thermokarst, but the self-destroying nature of thermokarst and the range of processes involved mean that recognition is not straightforward. Climatic inferences are also unwise since it must be proven that the cause of thermokarst is indeed a regional climatic amelioration and not a local, site-specific one. Moreover, thermokarst merely indicates that ground temperatures were >0 °C. In a final category are non-diastrophic structures which suggest the previous occurrence of permafrost-related processes, such as permafrost creep, and the altered groundwater hydrology which would have characterized permafrost terrain.

As in the case of frost action, one must always refer back to what is known about all these processes and phenomena from present-day permafrost regions. Chapters 5–9 are especially relevant.

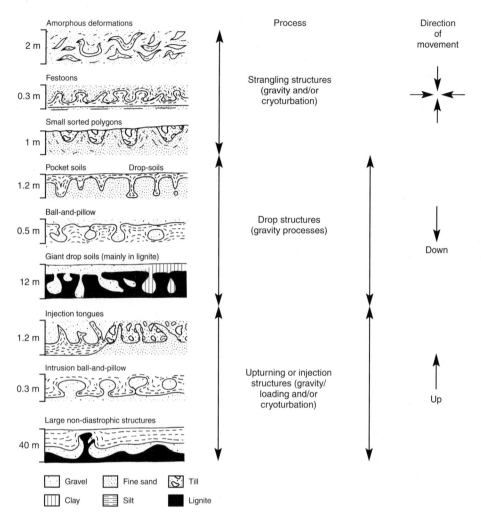

Figure 14.6 The most frequent deformation structures in Pleistocene seasonally frozen or active layers (according to L. Eissmann, 1994).

14.5 Pleistocene frost fissures

The existence of wedge-shaped structures interpreted as casts or pseudomorphs of thermal contraction cracks has frequently been reported from mid-latitudes. Their recognition is particularly important since such cracks required permafrost for their development. Moreover, it is commonly believed that the top surface of the ground must cool significantly, and rapidly, to temperatures as low as –15 to –20 °C. In high latitudes today this commonly means a mean annual air temperature of –6 to –8 °C.

The climatic thresholds and other variables influencing thermal contraction cracking (see Chapter 6) now enable us to suggest that the palaeo-temperature significance of Pleistocene frost cracking is less obvious. The lithology involved, and the duration and thickness of the snow cover are particularly important variables. In addition, the occurrence of seasonal frost cracks is a complication. Finally, there is a need to distinguish thermal contraction cracks from other fissure structures such as (a) fissures originating during the upheaving of frost mounds, (b) sand dykes generally formed through injection into overlying deposits (e.g. Butrym *et al.*, 1964) and (c) water escape structures (e.g. Burbridge *et al.*, 1988).

Figure 14.7 Oblique air photograph showing Weichselian ice-wedge polygons as revealed by differential crop markings. The pattern is a crude random orthogonal one, with some incompleteness to the pattern. Stäme, Swedish west coast. Photo courtesy of H. Svensson.

The outline of the frost fissure polygons can sometimes be seen by differential crop ripening on air photographs (Fig. 14.7). In Europe, areas from which such patterns have been reported include Sweden (e.g. Svensson, 1988) and southern England (e.g. Morgan, 1971). In North America, polygonal patterns have been observed in the north and central United States (e.g. Johnsson, 1990; Wayne, 1991; Walters, 1994), and parts of southern Ontario (e.g. Morgan,1972). However, only the most recent features are usually identified and older polygon nets are often concealed by overlying younger deposits.

It is useful at this point to relate the terms used to describe Pleistocene features with those used to describe analogous features in current permafrost regions. As discussed in Chapters 4 and 6, the wedges formed by thermal contraction cracking can be either active or inactive. The latter refers to wedges which exist in relict permafrost, as in central Alaska, or to

wedges which no longer crack, as at Inuvik, NWT. The former refers to wedges which currently crack, as at Garry Island, NWT.

When we discuss the nature of Pleistocene wedges in non-frozen sediments a slightly different terminology must be used to take into account the complex changes that occur as permafrost degrades (e.g. Harry and Gozdzik, 1988; Murton and French, 1993b). Obviously, all Pleistocene structures are inactive. Depending upon the degree of deformation during thaw, the feature is either a *cast* (i.e. bears some resemblance to the original form) or a *pseudomorph* (i.e. bears little resemblance to the original form). The degree of deformation largely depends upon the nature of the enclosing sediments and the amount of ice originally contained within them, upon the rapidity of thaw, and upon the importance of running (surface) water in eroding along the wedge. It is perhaps not surprising that most ice-

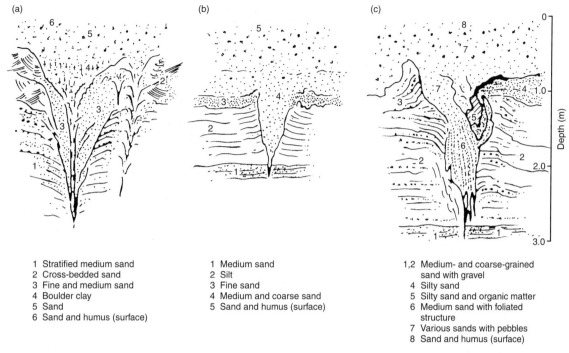

(a)

(b)

(c)

1 Stratified medium sand
2 Cross-bedded sand
3 Fine and medium sand
4 Boulder clay
5 Sand
6 Sand and humus (surface)

1 Medium sand
2 Silt
3 Fine sand
4 Medium and coarse sand
5 Sand and humus (surface)

1,2 Medium- and coarse-grained
   sand with gravel
4 Silty sand
5 Silty sand and organic matter
6 Medium sand with foliated
   structure
7 Various sands with pebbles
8 Sand and humus (surface)

Figure 14.8 Examples of different types of Pleistocene frost fissures, Łódź region, central Poland. (a) wedge of secondary infilling (i.e. old ice wedge); (b) wedge of primary infilling (i.e. old sand wedge); (c) composite wedge (from Gozdzik, 1973; Harry and Gozdzik, 1988).

wedge pseudomorphs or casts are found in sand and gravel since these sediments were usually ice-poor, while few ice-wedge pseudomorphs are recognized in silt and clay. Thus, thaw modification results in the selective preservation of pseudomorphs and casts. Sand wedges are more likely to be preserved than are ice-wedge casts pseudomorphs or composite-wedge pseudomorphs, because only those sand wedges that penetrate massive ice or icy sediments are prone to thaw modification. Furthermore, whereas ice wedges preferentially develop in ice-rich, fine-grained sediments (thaw-sensitive), their pseudomorphs appear to be selectively preserved in ice-poor, coarse-grained sediments (thaw-stable).

Once a cast or pseudomorph has been recognized, the nature of the infill needs description. Here the terminology of Gozdzik (1973) is useful. The infill is either of a primary nature (e.g. the initial sand/mineral soil, as in a sand wedge) or of a secondary nature (e.g. as the original, icy infill thaws, the void space so created is infilled by material from above or from the sides). Where there is evidence of both primary and secondary infill, the cast or pseudomorph

is composite in nature. Detailed drawings of Pleistocene wedges of primary, secondary and composite infilling are illustrated in Fig. 14.8.

14.5.1 Ice-wedge pseudomorphs

Ice-wedge pseudomorphs represent irregular fissures or, more rarely, wedge casts of structures of secondary infilling. They form when the ice wedge slowly melts, usually as permafrost degrades. As this happens, there is a general collapse of sediment into the trough. In arctic regions today, a range of processes may be involved, including thermal erosion, collapse, subsidence, refreezing, loading, buoyancy, spreading, folding and shearing (Murton and French, 1993b). A typical pseudomorph above a partially-thawed ice wedge in the Mackenzie Delta region is illustrated in Fig. 14.9. Of particular note is the bent, U-shaped involution (60–70 cm deep and ≤ 20 cm wide) above the ice wedge. Such structures appear characteristic of the thaw transformation stage (e.g. see Harry and Gozdzik, 1988, Fig. 5).

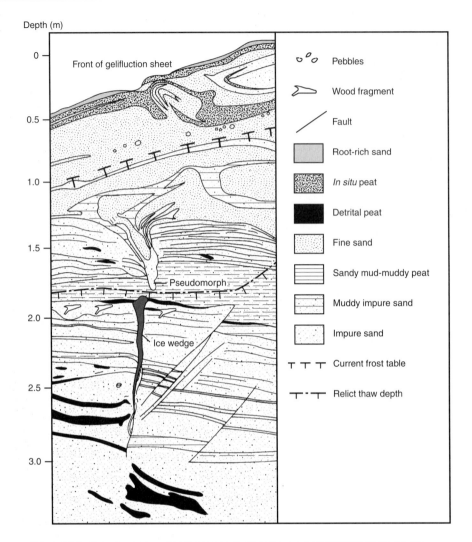

Figure 14.9 Pseudomorph and U-shaped involution above a partially thawed ice wedge, North Head, Richards Island, Pleistocene Mackenzie Delta, NWT, Canada (from Murton and French, 1993b).

A fully developed ice-wedge pseudomorph is characterized by the penetration of material into the fissure from above and from the sides, the downward inflection of layers if the enclosing sediments are stratified, and various systems of miniature faults. An example of an ice-wedge pseudomorph (cast) developed in sand and silt is illustrated in Fig. 14.10. The majority of ice-wedge pseudomorphs are probably much more complex than this however, since it must be stressed that the melting of the ice and the release of excess water from the surrounding sediments may result in considerable deformation of the structure, and a shape far removed from a simple wedge form. The irregular form of many pseudomorphs is a major problem in their identification.

14.5.2 Sand-wedge casts

Sand-wedge casts represent fissures or wedge structures of primary infilling. In contrast to ice-wedge pseudomorphs, these wedges contain an infilling of

Sand-wedge casts are sometimes interpreted to indicate colder, drier conditions than ice-wedge casts or pseudomorphs. This is not necessarily the case since (a) both sand and ice wedges can form in the same climatic environment, as can be witnessed in numerous localities in Arctic Canada today and (b) observations in western Jutland, Denmark, indicate that ice-wedge pseudomorphs, composite wedge-casts and wedges of primary mineral infilling (i.e. sand-wedge casts) all exist in the same area (Kolstrup, 1987). Local site differences and the availability of water to infill the crack appear to be the reason for the differentiation rather than any marked climatic difference over a relatively small geographical area.

Figure 14.10 Ice-wedge pseudomorph, or wedge of secondary infilling, Belchatow, Poland. Note the infilling from above and the faulting of adjacent strata.

Figure 14.11 Composite wedge developed beneath fossil soil within loess, Miechow Plateau, Southern Poland. The upper, inner wedge is formed by primary infilling; the lower wedge shows evidence of secondary infilling.

sandy, relatively well-sorted sediments, which is markedly different from the enclosing sediment. The sands are often highly aeolianized. In many cases, sand-wedge casts possess a more truly wedge shape, being relatively wider in cross-section than ice-wedge pseudomorphs, with a clear junction between the wedge and the enclosing material. The lack of water, consequent upon the thawing of the permafrost and the non-icy infilling material, does not lead to the same amount of intermixing of the infilling material as occurs in ice-wedges. In sand-wedge casts, there is no necessity for downturning of adjacent beds since the wedge does not need to be infilled after thawing. A further characteristic of sand-wedge casts, as observed in central Poland, is that the distance between casts is often much less than that between ice-wedge pseudomorphs (Gozdzik, 1973).

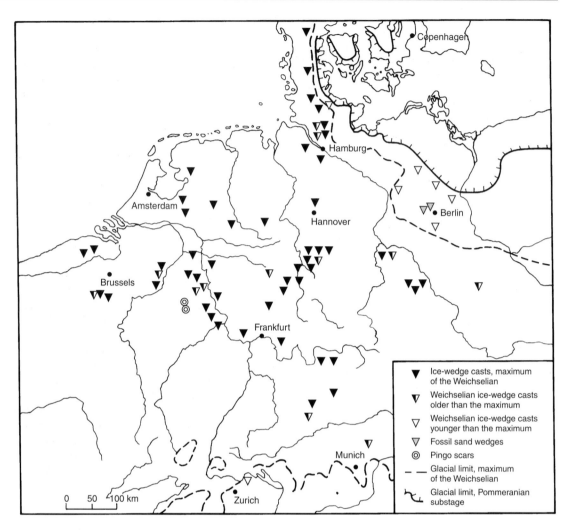

Figure 14.12   Distribution of Pleistocene frost fissures and other evidence of permafrost at the maximum of the last glaciation in Central Europe (from Karte, 1987).

14.5.3 Composite wedge casts

The variety of frost fissure casts and the difficulty of distinguishing between sand- and ice-wedge casts is further illustrated by composite wedges (e.g. Gozdzik, 1973). These are features which show evidence of both primary and secondary infilling (Fig. 14.11). Sometimes, two wedges are visible, one inside the other. The inner wedge is of primary infilling while the outer wedge has signs of secondary infilling. In some composite wedges, the infilling sand may have almost the same structure and texture as the sand in typical fissures of primary infilling. However, there may also be the inclusion of material from the fissure walls and some inflection of the adjacent sediments bordering the wedge. In cases such as these, it seems that the fissures were alternately filled with sand and ice. Melting of the ice contained in the sand occurred at such a slow rate that the foliated structure was not destroyed. The volumetric loss of water within the wedge, however, caused a downwards development of the adjacent sediments and a degree of infilling of the upper parts of the wedge.

14.5.4 Distribution

In Europe, the distribution of ice- and sand-wedge casts and pseudomorphs has been mapped by numerous workers (Fig. 14.12). Poser (1948) was the first to observe that the depth and width of the various wedge casts which lay to the south of the limits of the last ice sheet tended to increase to a maximum in central Europe. While such characteristics may reflect the greater age of wedges in locations where the duration of periglacial conditions may have been longer, Poser chose to interpret these dimensions as indicating a more severe periglacial climate in central Europe and a gradual amelioration of conditions westwards and southwards. Since wedge casts are also recognized from other areas south of the maximum limit of the last ice sheet in France, southern Germany and southern England, it seems reasonable to assume that permafrost was quite widespread in Europe during the last glacial stage. Probably, it was thickest in central and eastern Europe where it may have been continuous, while in the milder environments of western Europe, it was probably discontinuous and/or restricted to the upland plateaux. Wedge casts are also known to occur in areas within the limits of the Weichselian ice sheet, as in the English Midlands (Morgan, 1971) and in parts of Scandinavia (e.g. Johnsson, 1959). Their occurrence indicates that, as the ice sheet withdrew, a periglacial zone underlain by permafrost developed peripheral to the ice margin.

The distribution of ice- and sand-wedge casts in temperate latitude North America (Fig. 14.13) suggests that a similar permafrost zone formed in a belt, approximately 80–250 km in extent, adjacent to the retreating Wisconsinan ice sheet. A number of wedges, reported from beyond the maximum limit of the Wisconsinan ice sheet, in a broad zone extending through Montana (Schafer, 1949), Nebraska (Wayne, 1991), Wisconsin (Black, 1964), Iowa (Walters, 1994) and Illinois (Wayne, 1967; Johnsson, 1990), are believed to be between 15 000 and 20 000 years old. As the Wisconsinan ice sheet retreated northwards, ice and sand wedges were able to develop north of the Wisconsinan glacial border, in southern Ontario (Morgan, 1972), southern Québec (Dionne, 1971), and the Maritime Provinces (Borns, 1965; Brooks, 1971), and in the drier parts of the Canadian prairies (Berg, 1969). Although a number of tentative ice-wedge pseudomorphs have been reported from New

England, the climate there was probably too mild for wedge formation.

Compared with Europe, the Wisconsinan permafrost zone of North America, as indicated by ice- and sand-wedge casts and pseudomorphs, was much narrower. This probably reflected the more southerly limit of the ice sheet in North America, and the steeper climatic gradient to the south. In some areas, the treeline was very close to the ice margin. Another difference between Europe and North America was that the time duration of the late glacial permafrost conditions in North America was short on account of the development of extensive proglacial water bodies. For example, Morgan (1972) attributes the 'incompleteness' of the polygonal network in the Kitchener area of southern Ontario to the short-lived permafrost regime; in that area, suitable cold-climate conditions existed only between approximately 14 000 and 13 000 years BP, immediately after the retreat of the late Wisconsinan ice and immediately prior to the formation of Glacial Lake Whittlesey. This time period was not sufficient to allow either the development of a thick permafrost body or the wedges to propagate laterally in order to intersect fully and provide a complete polygon pattern. Similar proglacial water bodies existed in many parts of Canada following the retreat of the Wisconsinan ice sheet, especially in the St Lawrence Lowlands and the central prairies. They undoubtedly restricted the land area exposed to periglacial conditions and certainly ameliorated the climate of adjacent terrain.

14.6 Frost mounds

The remnants (scars) of certain kinds of frost mounds ('*buttes cryogènes*') provide convincing evidence for the previous existence of permafrost. In terms of morphology, one might expect frost mound remnants to possess a raised rim or rampart formed by the movement of material down their sides by solifluction and creep, and a central depression in which the ice cores had developed and from which the overburden had moved towards the rim. The rampart is the most significant feature since it enables one to distinguish frost mound depressions from those of a simple thermokarst origin. The height of the ramparts will vary considerably,

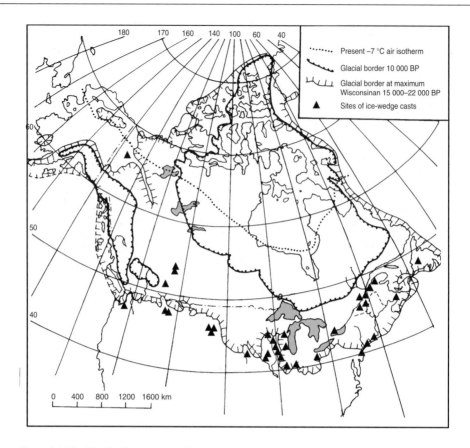

Figure 14.13 Distribution and age of ice-wedge casts in North America (exclusive of Alaska) in relation to position of Wisconsinan glacial ice fronts (*source*: Péwé, 1973, and others).

depending upon the size of the initial mound. If modern pingos and pingo remnants are a guide, the ramparts can vary from as little as 0.5 m to over 5.0 m in height, and the diameter of the depressions within the ramparts may be as great as 200–300 m. One group of hollows and ramparts thought to be remnants of frost mounds in eastern England is illustrated in Fig. 14.14.

As our understanding of modern frost mounds in present permafrost regions increases, their recognition and interpretation in mid-latitudes becomes relatively easier. The variety of forms and shapes in present periglacial environments implies that a similar diversity existed in Pleistocene environments, and many features initially regarded as not 'typical' of frost mounds can now be reconciled with an ice-cored origin.

The basic problem still remains, however, of distinguishing between the remnants of seasonal and perennial types, since only the latter unambiguously require permafrost for their formation. It is important to remember that seasonal frost mounds require cold-climate conditions but not necessarily permafrost and that deep seasonal frost with an underlying impermeable layer is an equally suitable condition. Moreover, it must be stressed that frost mounds are hydrological phenomena. As such, any credible interpretation of Pleistocene remnants must consider the hydrological implications.

In addition to these problems, there still remains the necessity of eliminating alternative, non-periglacial, explanations for mid-latitude features. On the Chalk of southern England and northern France, for example, the presence of marl pits (e.g. Prince,

Figure 14.14   Oblique air view of part of Walton Common, Norfolk, England, showing ramparts and enclosed depressions associated with the formation of frost mounds, probably seasonal in nature. Photo by permission of University of Cambridge.

1961) and of Chalk solutional forms (e.g. Sparks *et al.*, 1972, pp. 333–334) may also produce enclosed depressions similar at first sight to frost mound depressions. In glaciated terrain, a kettle origin has to be considered.

The possibility that some depressions may be the remnants of palsas or mineral palsas has also to be taken into account. However, palsas merely reflect the presence of icy permafrost bodies beneath localized peaty bodies. Moreover, their degradation does not take place through a collapsing of the summit, as is the case with pingos, but through a caving and slipping process at the base of the palsa. Thus, no ramparts should develop and, in the absence of a large ice core, there would be no central depression upon thawing. The problems of pingo remnant recognition and their utility in Pleistocene palaeo-reconstruction are usefully summarized by Flemal (1976), de Gans (1988) and Pissart (1987).

Features interpreted as the remnants of Pleistocene frost mounds have been identified from localities both within and outside the glacial limits in both eastern North America and Western Europe (e.g. Maarleveld and Van de Toorn, 1955; Pissart, 1963; Weigand, 1965; Watson, 1971; Sparks *et al.*, 1972; Flemal *et al.*, 1973; Paris *et al.*, 1979; de Gans and

Sohl, 1981; Coxon, 1986; de Groot *et al.*, 1987; Marsh, 1987). Surprisingly few frost mound remnants have been reported from Poland, eastern Europe and the western United States.

The form and distribution of many frost mound remnants in western Europe suggest that the original mounds were of the open system type. For example, the majority of remnants occur in clusters (Figs 14.14 and 14.15). The ramparts are often irregular in plan and 'mutually interfering', thus giving a complex alignment and distribution. Only a minority of the ramparts are clear-cut circular or oval forms. Many are semicircular and open in an upslope direction while others are elongate in the direction of slope. In terms of morphology, these characteristics are typical of open system features in which new generations are repeatedly born at the site of older ones by the continual movement of water to the surface. In terms of their distribution, many of the remnants occur in typical open system localities, such as on lower valley-side slopes, as at Llangurig in Wales (Watson, 1971), or at spring line locations, as at Walton Common, Norfolk (Fig. 14.14).

Features which have attracted considerable attention over the years are the circular, rampart-surrounded depressions known as the '*viviers*' (fish

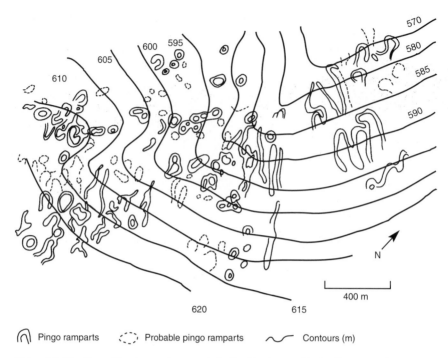

570
580
600 595
585
605
590
610

N

400 m

620   615

⌂ Pingo ramparts   ⌂ Probable pingo ramparts   ⌒ Contours (m)

Figure 14.15 Plan of frost mound ramparts in the Brackvenn, Hautes Fagnes region, Belgium, as identified by A. Pissart (1965).

ponds) of the Hautes Fagnes of Belgium. First described and interpreted by Pissart (1956) as pingo remnants, they have subsequently been reinterpreted as remnants of mineral palsas (Pissart and Juvigné, 1980; Pissart, 1987). According to Pissart, the closest present-day analogues are the frost mounds occurring in northern Québec (Pissart and Gangloff, 1984) and Swedish Lappland (Akerman and Malmström, 1986), where mean annual temperatures are less than –4 °C.

The age of Pleistocene frost mounds in Europe has been investigated by detailed stratigraphic and palynologic studies of the infilling material within the central depressions. These depressions were natural collecting grounds for pollen and organic sediments since they constituted small ponds during the decay stage of the mound. In Belgium, the material infilling the Hautes Fagnes features is commonly stratified clay, gyttja mud and peat (Mullenders and Gullentops, 1969). Pollen analyses suggest that the mounds formed during the late Dryas (10 500–11 000 years BP). In East Anglia, Sparks *et al.* (1972) have concluded that Zone III of the late Glacial was the most likely phase of cold conditions for the Walton Common features, while in Wales, the basal peat in one of the Llangurig

depressions has been assigned to a Zone III/IV transition (Watson, 1971). In general, therefore, it would appear that many of the frost mound remnants of western Europe formed in late Glacial times and represent the most recent period of periglacial conditions. During the full glacial, temperatures would have been colder and prevented the ground-water flow necessary to feed the open system features.

The significance of an open system interpretation lies in the fact that this explanation requires thin or discontinuous permafrost.

There appears to be little regularity to the overall distribution of Pleistocene frost mounds in western Europe. This may be explained in terms of the rather demanding hydrological conditions for open system growth. Water flowing beneath or within the permafrost must be small in amount and close to 0 °C. If the volume is too large it will not freeze, while if the temperature is considerably in excess of 0 °C, it will form a perennial spring, not a frost mound. Also, if the water temperature drops significantly below 0 °C, the conduit will be sealed and the mound will cease to form. The palaeo-groundwater hydrology of the site is crucial, therefore, for the formation of open system frost mounds, of either the seasonal or perennial type. One must also consider the possibility that icings and related features formed at the site, yet direct morphological and stratigraphic evidence for such occurrence is difficult to find.

Frost mound remnants, consisting of the typical circular ramparts and central depressions filled with pond and vegetation debris, have not been reported from the temperate areas of North America with the same frequency as western Europe. The reason for this is not clear. One of the few examples is from central Pennsylvania, in the Ridge and Valley province located beyond the limit of Pleistocene glaciation (Marsh, 1987). There, elliptical basins, 20–50 m in diameter and 3–4 m in depth, are bounded by low ramparts. They are interpreted as open system pingos. Radiocarbon analysis of the basin infill indicates a late Glacial age (12 800 years BP) and, on morphological grounds, suggests that discontinuous permafrost bodies, up to 5 m thick, had formed at that time. More puzzling are the DeKalb Mounds of north-central Illinois (Flemal et al., 1973). Their singular characteristic is an excess of material that appears to have moved to the mound from the surroundings. The majority are circular or elliptical, rising 1–5 m above the ground surface, and flat-topped with slightly depressed centres. The mounds are composed of lacustrine silt and clay surrounded by a sandy rim 30–100 m in diameter. It has been speculated that the sediments formed within the lakes of pingo craters and, as such, the mounds are the remnants of a large pingo field of mid-Wisconsinan age (22 000–12 500 years BP). Other features interpreted as Pleistocene frost mound remnants include the 'prairie mounds' of southern Alberta (Bik, 1969). However, these possess few characteristics of other Pleistocene pingo remains and until further evidence is forthcoming, it seems best to regard them as a type of ablation till phenomenon (e.g. Stalker, 1960).

14.7 Thermokarst forms and structures

Other features which permit an understanding of the former distribution of permafrost include the presence of various thermokarst and related phenomena. However, their recognition in temperate latitudes is particularly difficult. Thermokarst forms assume a variety of shapes and sizes, all of which suffer modification, particularly infilling from the sides, during their formation and subsequently. Furthermore, there are few distinct structures associated with thermokarst. Finally, as permafrost degrades, the features or structures cease to exist or, at best, become less apparent in the landscape.

Enclosed and shallow depressions which lack surrounding ramparts are sometimes given a thermokarst interpretation. Present-day analogues are, presumably, the thaw lakes and depressions of the tundra regions. In northwest Europe, inferred thermokarst depressions have been referred to as 'mares', 'mardelles' or 'solle' (Cailleux, 1956; Troll, 1962). They occur most frequently in the lowlands of northern France, especially in the Beauce and Brie areas where their density may reach 35 per km^2 (Cailleux, 1956). Although Pissart (1958, 1960) has explicitly interpreted these depressions to be thermokarstic in origin, a human origin is also possible. For example, some of the pits, ponds and other shallow depressions in eastern England and northern France are certainly marl pits dug by humans (e.g. Prince, 1961) in which the underlying Chalk was brought to the surface to be mixed with the overlying till deposits. However, old marl pits are generally deeper and smaller in dimensions than many of the enclosed depressions, and the frequency of depressions, often exceeding one per field, argues against a human origin for all of the hollows. A thermokarst origin has been given to essentially similar features occurring in Denmark (Cailleux, 1957), where a kettle moraine origin is also ruled out. The possibility that the Breckland Meres of eastern England may also be of a thaw lake origin has been raised, but not proven (Sparks et al., 1972). In North America, a number of enclosed depressions in New Jersey (Wolfe, 1953) may also be of a periglacial nature. Generally speaking, however, the separation of thermokarst depressions from the multitude of enclosed depressions of all sizes and shapes of other origins which may exist in a temperate latitude landscape seems almost impossible.

14.7.1 Palaeo-thaw layers

Past thermokarst activity may be recognized in the stratigraphic record by the existence of a palaeo-thaw layer (i.e. a horizon corresponding to the depth to which previous thawing of permafrost had proceeded). In present permafrost regions, palaeo-thaw

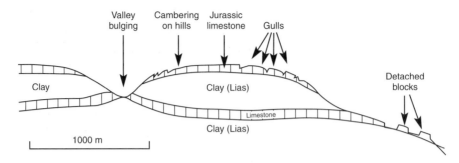

Figure 14.16　Types of non-diastrophic structures associated with Pleistocene permafrost in central England (after Hollingworth *et al.*, 1944; Dury, 1959).

layers often correspond to secondary thaw unconformities. These are frequently characterized by truncated ice bodies and cryostructures, and differences in clay mineralogy and geochemistry above and below the boundary (see section 6.1.2).

Weichselian palaeo-thaw layers in now-unfrozen sediments have been described from the southern Netherlands and northern Belgium (Vandenberghe and Krook, 1981; Vandenberghe, 1983). These, and similar horizons elsewhere in Europe, have been interpreted as either former active layers associated with stable permafrost conditions (e.g. Williams, 1975), or deepening thaw layers formed during permafrost degradation (e.g. Eissman, 1978; Maarleveld, 1981; Vandenberghe and van den Broek, 1982). The latter are of particular relevance here.

There are several characteristics of a palaeo-thaw layer: (a) it may underlie an inferred palaeo-ground surface (e.g. desert pavement, Vandenberghe, 1983), (b) its thickness can correspond with involuted (cryoturbated) horizons (e.g. Vandenberghe and Krook, 1981; Kolstrup, 1987), and (c) it is sometimes characterized by large soft-sediment deformation structures interpreted as either water-escape structures (Eissman, 1978) or 'thermokarst involutions' (Murton and French, 1993c), in which case its thickness far exceeds any possible active layer thickness. Murton and French (1993c), in discussing palaeo-thaw layers in the Mackenzie Delta, Canada, stress the importance of involuted structures as the diagnostic feature. It is not unreasonable to assume that similar structures characterized degrading ice-rich permafrost during the Pleistocene.

14.7.2　Soft sediment deformations

As Pleistocene ice-rich permafrost degraded, various structures would have formed at depth, either by gravitational (i.e. dropping) processes or loading (i.e. upturning or injection) or by water escape. All can be classified as plastic, or soft sediment, deformations.

In the unconsolidated Quaternary deposits of northern and western Europe, such plastic deformation structures occur widely and many have been interpreted within a degrading permafrost context (e.g. Eissman, 1978, 1994; Murton *et al.*, 1995). For example, Fig. 14.6 illustrates the variety of plastic deformation structures which occur in the Saale-Elbe region of central Germany. Amorphous deformations, small polygons, festoons, pocket and drop soils, ball-and-pillow structures and injection/ intrusion phenomena are all identified. Figure 14.5 (b) illustrates a typical plastic deformation structure of the 'drop-soil' or 'bird-foot' type. If correctly interpreted, all these structures provide indirect evidence for the previous existence of perennially frozen ice-rich sediments. However, there is often considerable debate as to the role played by thawing ground, and site-specific sedimentological considerations need to be fully understood. Therefore, it is with caution and experience that these structures need to be examined.

14.7.3　Non-diastrophic structures

At a larger scale than the soft sediment deformations described above are various non-diastrophic struc-

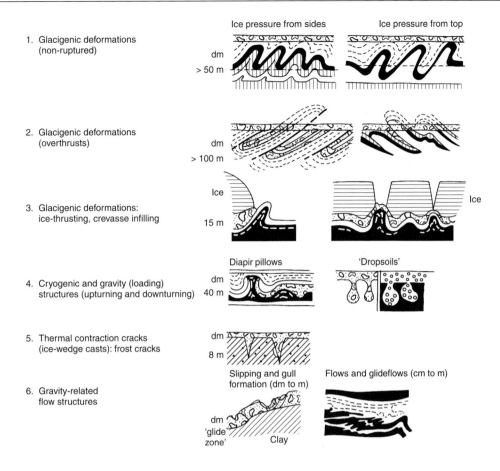

1. Glacigenic deformations (non-ruptured)
   dm
   > 50 m

   Ice pressure from sides   Ice pressure from top

2. Glacigenic deformations (overthrusts)
   dm
   > 100 m

3. Glacigenic deformations: ice-thrusting, crevasse infilling
   Ice
   15 m
   Ice

4. Cryogenic and gravity (loading) structures (upturning and downturning)
   dm
   40 m

   Diapir pillows   'Dropsoils'

5. Thermal contraction cracks (ice-wedge casts): frost cracks
   dm
   8 m

6. Gravity-related flow structures
   Slipping and gull formation (dm to m)   Flows and glideflows (cm to m)
   dm
   'glide zone'   Clay

Figure 14.17   Non-diastrophic structures in unconsolidated sediments (according to L. Eissmann, 1994, following observations in Central Germany).

tures which occur in both unconsolidated and consolidated strata in mid-latitudes, especially central Europe and Great Britain. These are given a Pleistocene periglacial significance by certain geologists (e.g. Kellaway, 1972; Eissman, 1978).

In central and southern England, these structures are well developed in Jurassic and Cretaceous sediments which contain thick, often overconsolidated argillaceous sequences (e.g. Hollingworth *et al.*, 1944; Dury, 1959, pp. 179–181; Horswill and Horton, 1976; Hawkins and Privett, 1981; Whiteman and Kemp, 1990). They take the form of gently dipping strata adjacent to valleys (cambering), uparching of strata in valley bottoms (valley bulging), and the formation of expanded joints (gulls) in coherent bedrock that

appears to have preferentially moved across plastically deforming softer sediment beneath (Fig. 14.16). An attractive explanation for all these phenomena is that they developed as ice-rich permafrost degraded at various times during the Pleistocene, and when permafrost creep accelerated as ground temperatures approached 0 °C.

In unconsolidated sediments, a wider range of structures occurred. In central Germany for example, Eissman (1994) has classified the various non-diastrophic structures which occur in unconsolidated sediments (Fig. 14.17). Many are glacigenic in nature but others, such as gravity-related flow structures, and cryogenic and gravity (loading) structures (discussed above in section 14.7.2) are relevant here.

Our understanding of the significance of these non-diastrophic structures is still limited and, to some degree, they have been overlooked by many workers involved in Pleistocene periglacial reconstruction. However, as our understanding of present-day permafrost degradation improves, there is increasing evidence to support the view that these structures relate to the Pleistocene thawing of perennially frozen, often ice-rich, strata. Many of the glacigenic structures suggest deformation in a frozen but plastic state, as might exist when permafrost temperatures were approaching 0 °C and unfrozen water contents would have been high.

Further reading

Black, R.F. (1976) Periglacial features indicative of permafrost: ice and soil wedges. *Quaternary Research*, **6**, 3–26.

French, H.M. and J.S. Gozdzik (1988) Pleistocene epigenetic and syngenetic frost fissures, Belchatow, Poland. *Canadian Journal of Earth Sciences*, **25**, 2017–2027.

De Gans, W. (1988) Pingo scars and their identification. In: M.J. Clark (ed.), *Advances in periglacial geomorphology*. Chichester: J. Wiley and Sons Ltd, pp. 299–322.

DeWolf, Y. (1988) Stratified slope deposits. In: M.J. Clark (ed.), *Advances in periglacial geomorphology*. Chichester: J. Wiley and Sons Ltd, pp. 91–110.

Karte, J. (1987) Pleistocene periglacial conditions and geomorphology in north central Europe. In: J. Boardman, (ed.), *Periglacial processes and landforms in Britain and Ireland*. Cambridge: Cambridge University Press, pp. 67–75.

Kellaway, G.A. (1972) Development of non-diastrophic Pleistocene structures in relation to climate and physical relief. In: *Report, International Geological Congress, 24th Session, Montreal*, Vol. 12, pp. 120–146.

Pissart, A. (1987) Weichesian periglacial structures and their environmental significance: Belgium, the Netherlands and northern France. In: J. Boardman, (ed.), *Periglacial processes and landforms in Britain and Ireland*. Cambridge: Cambridge University Press, pp. 77–83.

Washburn, A.L. (1980) Permafrost features as evidence of climatic change. *Earth Science Reviews*, **15**, 327–402.

Discussion topics

1. How reliable is morphological and stratigraphic evidence in inferring either (a) Pleistocene frost action or (b) the previous existence of frozen ground?

2. Why is the distinction between seasonal and perennial frost important in Pleistocene periglacial reconstruction?

3. What were the physical and structural changes that occurred when Pleistocene permafrost degraded?

CHAPTER 15

Pleistocene wind action, tundra rivers and periglacial landscape modification

The Pleistocene periglacial environments were characterized by particularly intense wind action. Fine sediment (loess), derived from vegetation-free outwash plains adjacent to the ice margins, was picked up, transported and redeposited, often to blanket and flatten the landscape. This material was then reworked to form cover sand by rain and snow. Large tundra rivers crossed the periglacial zone, and ice-marginal channels (pradolinas) paralleled the ice margins. Landscape modification was by solifluction and mass wasting on slopes, the asymmetrical modification of some valleys and the infilling of others, localized weathering and intense erosion, and shallow fluvial dissection into either seasonally or perennially frozen ground.

15.1 Wind action

In 1942, A. Cailleux published the results of a study of the wind-modified form of over 3000 sand samples collected from across Europe. Sand grains that have undergone transportation and saltation are rounded and possess a matt or 'frosted' appearance (Fig. 15.1), while those that have not are subangular and shiny. Cailleux found that frosted grains occurred widely in a broad belt extending eastwards from European Russia through the lowlands of central Europe into northern France. Moreover, he found that the percentage of frosted grains increased eastwards and reached nearly 100 per cent in eastern Europe in areas to the south of the glacial limits (Fig. 15.2). He advanced the idea, therefore, that periglacial conditions were most severe, and wind action most intense, in these areas. Further west, as the percentage of frosted grains decreased, so did the intensity of wind action.

Since then, the importance of wind action within the Pleistocene periglacial environment has become widely accepted. Other features and deposits which

are the result of periglacial wind action, include dunes, wind-abraded pebbles (ventifacts), windblown or aeolian sands (cover sands) and windblown silts (loess). It must immediately be stated, however, that a periglacial origin for all of these phenomena is not always the case, since they can form in other climatic environments besides the periglacial. In all cases, the assignment of a periglacial origin must be made individually, in the light of all available local evidence.

15.1.1 Loess

Pleistocene periglacial loess is thought have to have been derived from the frost-comminuted glacially derived outwash deposits laid down at the margins of the retreating ice sheets (e.g. Troll, 1944). During the middle and late summer months, as these outwash plains dried out, strong winds winnowed out the finer silt particles forming dust clouds probably similar to those observed today in Arctic regions on valley sandar and outwash plains. Eventually, the sediments were deposited at some distance from the

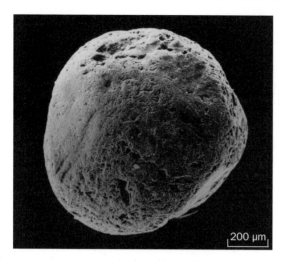

Figure 15.1   Rounded mat grain caused by wind action
from Pleistocene dunes, Belchatow, Poland
(photo courtesy of J. Gozdzik).

ice margin where tundra vegetation was able to trap
and stabilize the silt particles.

The nature of loess provides useful, but general,
information as to the climatic conditions at the time
of its formation. First, it is agreed that loess formed
in essentially dry environments. This is indicated by
the fact that if wetted, the loess experiences shrinkage
and compaction, proving that it was not soaked by
water or deposited by it. Also, unweathered loess is
calcareous; calcium carbonate segregates into nodules, indicating no leaching of any significance.
Second, loess often contains large quantities of
faunal remains, especially land snails suited to open
vegetation conditions as found today in cold
steppe/tundra regions. It is generally accepted, therefore, that loess formed in glacial rather than
interglacial times.

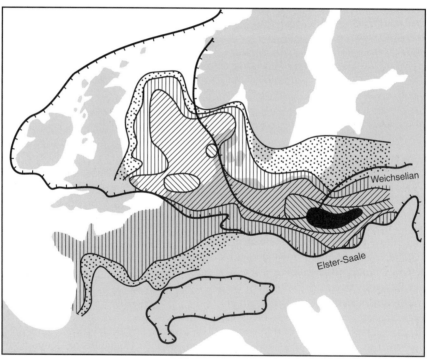

Figure 15.2   The distribution and frequency of occurrence of wind-modified sand grains
(04–0.1 mm) in Europe (from Cailleux, 1942).

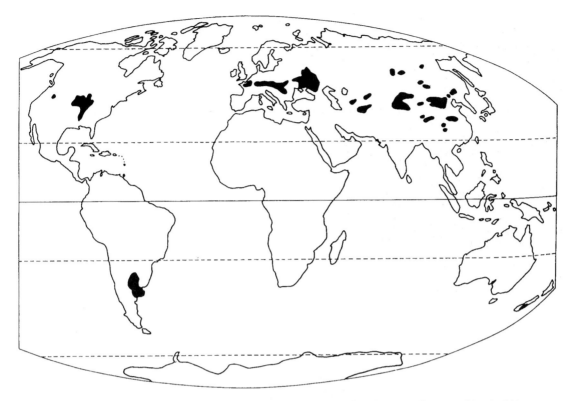

Figure 15.3 Global distribution of major loess occurrences (after Pye, 1984). The loess-like silts of Alaska/Yukon, central Yakutia and the southern Qinghai-Xizang Plateau are not included.

Loess is largely a northern hemisphere phenomenon (Fig. 15.3) and usually confined to the middle latitudes. The extensive Loess Plateau of western China, where thicknesses exceed 200–300 m in places, is unusual and has attracted much study by both Chinese and western scientists. Recent ideas suggest that the proximity to the Gobi deserts of central Asia and the uplift of the Tibet Plateau in Quaternary times may explain this concentration of sediment, but a complete understanding of its origin is still lacking. Most other loess deposits in Europe and North America, however, are more clearly linked to the onset of periglacial conditions along the equatorward limit of the Pleistocene ice sheets.

Not included in Fig. 15.3 is the loess-like silt which mantles extensive areas of Alaska, south central Yakutia, the Qinghai-Xizang Plateau and other cold non-glaciated regions today (e.g. Péwé *et al.*, 1995; Péwé and Jounaux, 1983; Péwé, 1955). These have been discussed earlier in Chapter 12.

In Europe, the loess is thickest in central and eastern regions where it mantles extensive areas of both upland plateaux and lowland plains. In places, it attains a thickness in excess of 30 m. From a stratigraphic point of view, the loess of eastern Europe is of considerable importance. In southern Poland for example, at least five late Pleistocene fossil soils and several different horizons of periglacial structures are preserved within the loess deposits (Jersak, 1973, 1977). They provide evidence of cyclic environmental changes throughout much of the late Pleistocene. Further west, in Germany, northern France, and Belgium loess deposits are not so thick but still provide a good stratigraphic record (e.g. Haesaerts and van Vliet-Lanoë, 1981; Haesaerts, 1983). Thermo-luminescence (TL) dating provides additional information (e.g. Balescu *et al.*, 1988). The source area for the loess deposits of western Europe was probably the exposed floor of the North Sea and the English Channel during the glacial low water levels. In southern England, true loess is rare, but many of the older drift deposits which mantle the Chalk uplands, such as the Plateau Drift (e.g. Loveday, 1962), and some of the lowland valley infill deposits, such as the brickearths, clearly possess a loess fraction. Loess is even reported from the head deposits of southwest England (e.g. Mottershead, 1977; Roberts, 1985). In all probability, successive episodes of loess deposition left a veneer of silty sediments throughout much of western Europe and southern, central and southwestern England. Subsequently, these have been either incorporated into underlying materials through frost action and solifluction, or reworked by meltwater and redeposited on valley-side slopes and in valley bottoms.

In North America, extensive loess deposits occur in the north-central United States, mainly in the Ohio–Missouri–Mississippi drainage basins (Smith, 1964). They attain thicknesses of over 35 m and extend over a zone several hundreds of kilometres south of the glacial border. There is convincing evidence that the loess was derived mainly from large proglacial streams which, in late summer, exposed broad areas of alluvial sediments on the higher bars between the major channels. In many areas, the loess is thickest near the main valleys and progressively decreases with distance from the valleys. According to Leonard and Frye (1954), the greater thicknesses of loess near to the valleys is the result of a forested belt which existed on the moister and more sheltered locations adjacent to the rivers, while on the uplands, a grassland vegetation with only occasional trees developed. Thus, the forested belt reduced wind velocities and trapped windblown sediments. In some areas, the source for the loess comprised till as well as stream outwash sediments. As in Europe, various episodes of loess deposition are recognized; loess sheets of Kansan, Illinoian and Wisconsinan age are now correlated to the advance and retreat of the continental ice sheets (e.g. Ruhe, 1983). In general terms, there is also evidence to suggest that the most recent loess in central North America was deposited under slightly moister conditions than in eastern Europe. For example, the Peoria loess of Iowa, of Wisconsinan age, contains faunal remains which indicate moister conditions than today. A forest grassland vegetation cover is to be inferred for central North America, as opposed to a predominantly tundra cover for Europe during the last glacial stage.

15.1.2 Cover sand and dunes

Aeolian sands are usually in the size range 0.06–1.00 mm in diameter. They commonly form an irregular formless mantle deposit, or 'cover sand', but in some places they also form dunes. Ventifacts may be found with aeolian sands and in certain instances, silt may also be incorporated. Occasionally, cover sand shows a certain degree of stratification, involving alternating loamy and sandy layers. Cover sand is usually interpreted as being niveo-aeolian in origin, the result of sheetwash and solifluction. In northern France similar sediments, termed '*limons-a-doublets*' (Lautridou and Giresse, 1981) are better explained by the migration of clay and iron within the loess following an initial loss of carbonate. Thus, the formation of '*limons-a-doublets*' imply a moister periglacial environment than typical loess with short periods of climatic amelioration. In general, cover sand can be related to a nearby source of sediment. Its widespread development in the Netherlands for example (e.g. Maarleveld, 1960), may reflect the proximity of the exposed delta of the Rhine River during glacial times when sea level was lowered and the continental shelf of Europe was more extensive.

The distribution of cold-climate dunefields and sand sheets in Europe and North America, and their relationship to the glacial limits, are illustrated in Fig. 15.4. It is clear that all were located immediately beyond the Pleistocene ice margins. According to Koster (1988), the sands were typically derived from unvegetated flood plains, glacial outwash plains, till plains and lake shores. Parabolic and transverse dunes are common, similar to those which form in warm semi-arid regions today. Detailed facies analyses of the sand sheets in northwestern Europe (e.g. Ruegg, 1983; Schwan, 1986) indicates a complex interaction between fluviatile, lacustrine and aeolian processes in their formation and distribution.

Under favourable conditions, wind direction can be inferred from dune morphology and orientation, the dip of the forset beds and the relation of dunes to known sediment source areas (Koster, 1988). For example, Maarleveld (1960) concluded that wind directions in the Netherlands in late Glacial times were predominantly northwesterly in the early Dryas period but changed to southwest and west in the late Dryas.

(a)

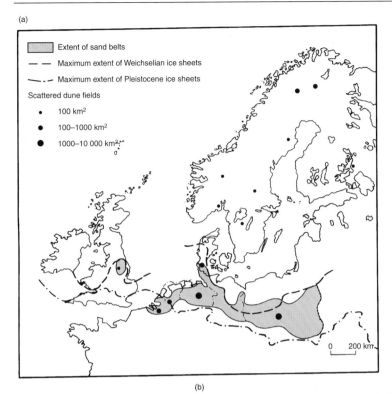

(b)

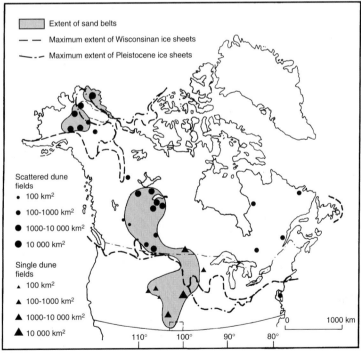

Figure 15.4 Distribution of Pleistocene cold-climate dune fields and sand sheets in (a) Europe and (b) North America, together with glacial limits (from Koster, 1988).

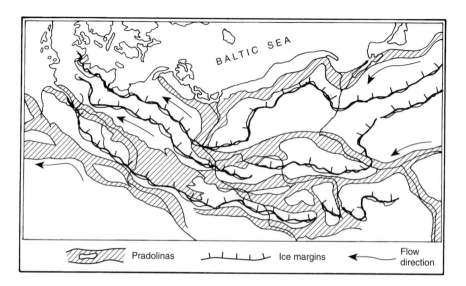

Figure 15.5 The pradolinas (*Urstromtaler*) of the North European Plain together with ice- marginal limits (from Jahn, 1976).

15.1.3 Ventifacts

Pleistocene ventifacts are particularly numerous in the mid-latitude regions of North America and Europe, particularly in those areas which experienced continental and dry conditions such as eastern Europe (e.g. Dylik, 1956), southern Scandinavia (e.g. Svensson, 1983) and the north-central United States (e.g. Sharp, 1949). In more maritime locations, ventifacts are not so common. In most cases, ventifacts are found in association with aeolian sand and silt. They are often buried by younger windblown sediments and, where *in situ*, may form a layer of coarser pebbles from which the finer particles have been winnowed out. The present-day analogue is the 'desert pavement' of the polar deserts. In special instances, ventifacts can provide valuable evidence of Pleistocene wind directions. Grooving and fluting of a constant orientation is the best criteria but is rarely found. More important is that the ventifact needs to be *in situ* (i.e. it has not moved). Usually, however, during the period of periglacial conditions, the pebble has been moved by either frost heave or solifluction. Thus, only very large sand-blasted boulders are reliable for wind direction inferences.

15.2 Tundra rivers

The large Pleistocene rivers which drained the periglacial (proglacial) zone were of two types. First, there were wide, shallow, meltwater channels adjacent to the ice margins, and often running in the latitudinal direction. These channels are especially well developed on the North European Plain where they are termed 'pradolinas' or '*Urstromtaler*' (Fig. 15.5). There is evidence that pradolinas experienced repeated use during the Pleistocene.

The second category of Pleistocene rivers consists of those that flowed outwards, away from the ice margins. Rather then being flat-floored, erosive channels, these were broad outwash (i.e. aggradational) plains characterized by numerous braided channels, low terraces and both diurnal and seasonal flow regimes. In northwest Europe, the Pleistocene Rhine River flowed northwestwards across a broad tundra lowland now occupied by the North Sea. In southern England, the proto-Thames also drained eastwards towards the North Sea, probably joining the proto-Rhine. In North America, the ancient Mississippi drained the continental ice margin in a broad zone from the foot of the Rockies in the west to the

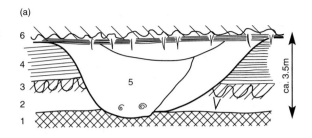

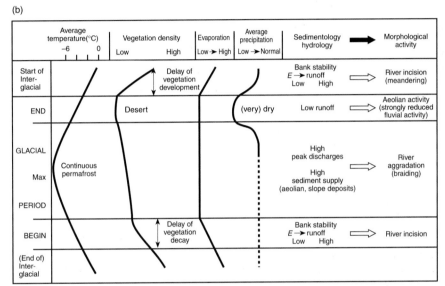

Figure 15.6 The Pleistocene periglacial fluvial cycle. (a) Late Weichselian incision and infilling sequence, Maastricht, southern Netherlands: 1, Eemian soil; 2, Early Weichselian silt loam; 3, Cryoturbations; 4, Middle Weichselian silt loam; 5, Late Weichselian gully infilling; 6, Late Weichselian horizon of cryoturbations and frost cracks. (b) The generalised fluvial cycle during a glacial (cold) period (from Vandenberghe, 1993).

Appalachians in the east (Baker, 1983). Today, evidence of these broad tundra river systems is to be found in flights of terraces, the best known being those of the Thames (e.g. Gibbard, 1988), the lower Rhine and Maas (e.g. van Huissteden and Vandenberghe, 1988; van Huissteden, 1990), and the central Mississippi (e.g. Brakenridge, 1981).

The presence of frost-fissure pseudomorphs, involutions and faunal remains within the terrace sediments indicate that aggradation took place under cold-climate conditions. There was probably a cyclic pattern of river incision and subsequent infilling (Vandenberghe, 1993), corresponding to the start and end of each periglacial period (Fig. 15.6 (a)). In theory, fluvial erosion would have been favoured at the beginning of the cold stages because slope and riverbank stability would have been maintained by the degrading vegetation cover relative to a decline in evapotranspiration and an increase in runoff. At the cold period maximum, sediment supply and discharge (Q) would probably have peaked and aggrading, braided channel systems would have been characteristic. Then, during the transition back to the warmer interstadial or interglacial conditions, there would have been incision due to the reduction in sediment load. Although somewhat speculative, this model is supported by stratigraphic observations. For example, Fig. 15.6 (a) shows a typical channel fill sequence from a Maas river terrace in southern Netherlands. From their analyses of palaeo-fluvial systems in the Dutch and Polish lowlands, Vandenberghe *et al.* (1994) conclude that there were frequent transitions between braided and high-sinuosity meandering systems.

Pollen spectra from late Pleistocene cold stage floodplain sequences in East Anglia support this general fluvial model (West and Pettit, 1993). The assemblages are generally poor and of low diversity, consisting mostly of *Salix*, Graminae and Cyperaceae pollen. They indicate rapid deposition at times of low pollen production. Assemblages from more organic abandoned channel fillings on the floodplains yield a richer assemblage but still an absence of arboreal (tree) and heath pollens. Leaf-rich beds in gravels, however, suggest the falling stages of nival regimes with overlying fines reflecting summer-flow conditions.

In summary, some of the Pleistocene periglacial rivers were unique in that ice-marginal channels of the magnitude in question are rare in the present-day periglacial zones of high latitudes. Others, however, which drained away from the ice margins, appeared to have been somewhat similar to those of the present-day tundra.

15.3 Asymmetrical valleys

The presence of asymmetrical valleys in mid-latitudes has frequently attracted attention. In many cases, the asymmetry is thought significant in terms of either past frost action, permafrost or wind action, or combinations of these conditions. Before a periglacial interpretation can be accepted, however, there is the necessity to eliminate a variety of non-periglacial causes of asymmetry. For example, asymmetry can result from structural controls, from differences in local slope erosional environments, or from different micro-climatic conditions existing under present temperate conditions (e.g. Hack and Goodlett, 1960).

Asymmetrical valleys attributed to a periglacial origin occur widely throughout Europe (Table 15.1), and in parts of North America (e.g. Smith, 1949) and Asia (e.g. Iwata, 1977). In western Europe, the steeper slope commonly faces towards the west or southwest, and this is regarded as the 'normal' for western Europe. In North America, the steeper slopes frequently face towards the north. The most popular periglacial explanation involves differential insolation and freeze–thaw processes operating on exposed south- and west-facing slopes while the 'colder' north- and northeast-facing slopes remained frozen and geomorphologically inert (e.g. Ollier and Thomasson, 1957). A second group of explanations involve the differential deposition of either snow or loess on leeward slopes, resulting in greater solifluction on those slopes (e.g. Taillefer, 1944; Büdel, 1944). A third interpretation involves a combination of differential insolation and freeze–thaw on exposed south- and west-facing slopes, and snow- or loess-induced solifluction on the leeward slopes together with a migrating stream in the valley bottom (e.g. Geukens, 1947; Edelman and Maarleveld, 1949).

The 'normal' asymmetry of western Europe can be compared to the asymmetry currently developing in present periglacial environments (see Table 11.9). The most striking difference is that in high latitudes the steeper slope, irrespective of orientation, is usually the colder slope (e.g. Currey, 1964; French, 1971b) while in western Europe, the steeper slope is usually the warmer (e.g. Geukens, 1947; Ollier and Thomasson, 1957). Presumably, mid-latitude freeze–thaw processes were dominant on the 'warmer' slopes, leading to their steepening. In high latitudes by contrast, the 'warmer' slopes give rise to thicker active layers and greater solifluction movement rather than greater freeze–thaw frequencies.

The presence of asymmetrical valleys in temperate latitudes is not necessarily a reliable indicator of past periglacial conditions. It must be remembered that there are a number of non-periglacial causes of asymmetry. If of a periglacial origin, however, asymmetrical valleys in mid-latitudes provide circumstantial evidence as to the importance of (a) freeze– thaw activity, (b) differential insolation, snow distribution and solifluction activity, and (c) fluvial activity. They provide little or no direct evidence for the previous existence of permafrost.

15.4 Periglacial landscape modification

Since periglacial conditions existed in mid-latitudes at several times during the late Pleistocene, one must ask how much of the present landscape reflects this periglacial legacy. Unfortunately, there is no easy answer. Not only did periglacial conditions vary in intensity and duration in different areas, but different rock types would have reacted differently.

To give some perspective to this problem, this section briefly describes the nature and extent of periglacial landscape modification in two areas of Europe, the Chalklands of southern England and the lowlands of central Poland.

Table 15.1 Some examples of slope asymmetry attributed to Pleistocene periglacial conditions in Europe

Location	Reference	Orientation of Steeper Slope	Processes Involved[1]					Mechanism Involved[1]	
			(1) Differential Insolation and Freeze–Thaw	(2) Differential Solifluction	(3) Wind and Snow	(4) Wind and Loess	(5) Lateral Stream Erosion	Decline of N- and E-facing Slope	Steepening of S- and W-facing Slope
United Kingdom									
Chiltern Hills	Ollier and Thomasson (1957)	W/SW	X	x			x		x
Hertfordshire	Thomasson (1961)	W	X	x			x		x
Chalk, southern England	French (1972a, 1973)	W/SW	X	x	x		x		x
France									
Gascony	Taillefer (1944)	W		x	X		x	x	x
Gascony	Faucher (1931)	W				x	x	x	x
North France	Gloriad and Tricart (1952)	W	x	X			x		x
Netherlands and Belgium									
Haspengouw	Geukens (1947)	W	X	x	x		x	x	x
Veluwe	Edelman and Maarleveld (1949)	W/SW		x	X		x	x	x
Hesbaye	Grimberbieux (1955)	W	X		x		x		x
Ardennes	Alexandre (1958)	W		X			x	x	x
Germany									
South Germany	Büdel (1944, 1953)	W/SW		x	X	X	x	x	x
Muschelkalk	Helbig (1965)	W		X			x		x
Czechoslovakia									
Bohemia	Czudek (1964)			X			x		
Poland									
Łódź plateau	Klatkowa (1965)	W	X	x	x		x	x	x

[1]X dominant process; x secondary process

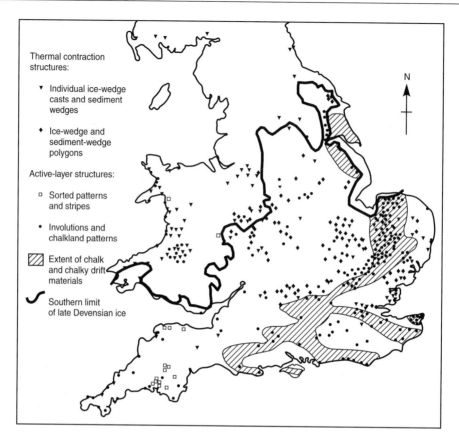

Figure 15.7   Extent of Chalk outcrops and Chalky Drift materials in southern England and the maximum extent of the last glaciation. Also shown are locations of various periglacial phenomena reported in the literature (*source*: Rose *et al.*, 1985a).

15.4.1 The Chalk landscapes of southern England

Chalk and Chalky Drift materials make up a large area of southern and eastern England, ranging in topography from upland plateaus and escarpments rising to over 200 m in elevation to undulating lowland plains. The extent of the Chalk outcrops and Chalky Drift materials and the limits of the last glaciation are indicated on Fig. 15.7.

For a number of reasons, the Chalk terrain is well suited for the preservation of relict periglacial phenomena. First, Chalk and Chalky Drift materials are highly frost-susceptible. Second, the desiccation of the Chalk plateaux has meant that Holocene fluvial modification has been limited, and the probability of the preservation of relict forms is greatly increased over other lithologies. Third, nearly all of the Chalk and Chalky Drift outcrops lay to the south of the maximum limit of the Weichselian/Devensian ice sheet. They were exposed, therefore, to periglacial climatic conditions for the duration of the last cold stage.

Periglacial deposits

Much of the Chalk is covered with a veneer of periglacial deposits which, on faunal and stratigraphic grounds, can be assigned to the middle and late stages of the last, Weichselian (late Devensian), glaciation (e.g. Kerney, 1963; Evans, 1968). In most cases, these deposits have been derived through frost shattering from the Chalk. In many of the larger valleys in southern England, fluvial gravels and river sediments often contain remains of cold-climate fauna (e.g. Green *et al.*, 1983), or possess sedimentological characteristics that suggest cold-climate deposition (e.g. Bryant, 1983).

At least three types of deposits can be recognized. First, solifluction debris, or 'coombe rock', consists of a heterogeneous material composed of coarse angular nodules of Chalk held within a fine calcareous matrix. It is widespread on lower valley-side slopes and in valley bottoms where it may attain thicknesses of several metres. A second deposit consists of sorted or stratified muds and solifluction gravels. In that they are stratified, they resemble fluvial deposits but in some, the presence of a terrestrial fauna of land Mollusca indicates a subaerial origin. It is thought that the muds resulted from the frost shattering of the Chalk in association with the release of meltwater from beneath snowpatches and the melting of frozen ground each spring (e.g. Kerney *et al.*, 1964; Preece *et al.*, 1995). The gravels probably originated from the solifluction of earlier till deposits, notably of the penultimate ice advance. The third category of periglacial deposits are those of a loessic nature. These veneer exposed upland surfaces and testify to drier conditions than either of the previous two types of deposit. Where present in valleys, the loess has usually been reworked by either solifluction or meltwaters and is termed 'brick-earth'. For convenience flinty loams are included in this category, although they are not derived from the Chalk, and their parent materials are various Tertiary sediments. The latter, notably 'clay-with-flints', have undergone movement through solifluction while loessic materials have been incorporated through frost action.

The solifluction and coombe deposits mainly relate to the cold and damp conditions during the middle Devensian, or earlier. The formation of the gravels of East Anglia probably date from the end of the Saale glaciation or the beginning of the Weichselian (Devensian). The brickearths, flinty loams and loessic deposits relate to a late–middle Devensian period of relatively drier conditions but which were still sufficiently moist for their deposition in valley bottoms and on slopes by solifluction and meltwater. The Chalky muds are primarily of a late Devensian age and reflect the higher temperatures that occurred at that time.

These deposits can be related to a number of landform modifications which took place during the last glacial stage. It is not unreasonable to assume that similar episodes of periglacial modification took place earlier in the Pleistocene.

Asymmetrical valley development

Many of the dry valleys which dissect the Chalk plateaux and dipslopes of southern England are asymmetrical in cross-profile, with the steeper slope commonly facing west or southwest (e.g. Ollier and Thomasson, 1957). In addition to their slope asymmetry, these valleys also possess an asymmetrical pattern of soils, deposits and tributary patterns. Similar valleys are known to occur on the Chalk plateaux of northern France (e.g. Gloriad and Tricart, 1952), Belgium (e.g. Grimberbieux, 1955) and northern Germany (e.g. Helbig, 1965).

The most likely explanation for the asymmetry of the Chalk valleys is that it developed during the various cold periods, when the Chalk was able to support a transitory surface drainage on account of a frozen subsoil. This is not to admit that all Chalk valleys were formed in a periglacial fashion, by higher surface runoff and meltwater at a time when the Chalk was frozen and impermeable, as suggested by Reid (1887) and Bull (1940). Many are undoubtedly polycyclic since their long profiles show evidence of successive rejuvenations, and it is inconceivable that the Chalk possessed no valleys before the onset of periglacial conditions. In all probability, the major Chalk valleys developed through normal stream action at a time of higher water table. Then, as the water table gradually fell throughout the Pleistocene, the smaller valleys became successively drier from their upper parts downwards. If this were so, the downvalley sections may have been active while the upvalley sections were dry and fossilized. During periglacial periods, therefore, this normal sequence of progressive desiccation was reversed, as the upper sections were reactivated by increased surface runoff over the impermeable (i.e. frozen) substratum.

If this general assessment of Chalk morphology is correct, the asymmetrical development of the valleys provides illustration of the nature of periglacial landscape modification. In essence, one must envisage (a) perennially or seasonally frozen ground on colder, east-facing slopes, (b) intense physical weathering and erosion occurring through repeated freeze–thaw activity on the west-facing slopes as the result of greater insolation, and (c) running water in valley bottoms for at least part of the year.

No absolute age for the asymmetrical modification of the Chalk valleys can yet be given. However, the asymmetry appears intimately related to the chalky rubbles and coombe rock which mantle the foot of the steeper slopes. The middle Devensian was probably the last period of asymmetrical modification; the probability is high that the asymmetry reflects more than one period of periglacial conditions.

Figure 15.8 The sarsen 'rock stream' in the Valley of Stones, near Blackdown, Dorset, southern England.

The 'rock streams' of Wiltshire and Dorset

A number of more specific features of the Chalk landscape indicate periglacial modification during the middle Devensian, or earlier, times. The most striking are the periglacial 'rock streams' or 'sarsen streams' which occur within certain of the Chalk valleys of Wiltshire and Dorset (e.g. R.B.G. Williams, 1968; Small *et al.*, 1970). The sarsen stones themselves are large blocks of silicified sand and flint conglomerate, usually regarded as being of early Tertiary age. Presumably, they originated on the upland surfaces of the Chalk as a form of 'duricrust' or silcrete. Being extremely resistant, they have managed to survive the Pleistocene epoch.

Many of the sarsens have moved considerable distances from their initial positions on summits and interfluves, first downslope and then downvalley in the form of 'stone streams' (Fig. 15.8). In the Marlborough area for example, some may have moved as much as 4 000 m on an average gradient of between 1° and 3°. An explanation involving their movement by early humans is not generally accepted. It is more likely that the stones, often weighing several tonnes, were rafted downslope by solifluction as a form of 'ploughing block'.

The evolution and age of the 'rock streams' has been considered by both R.B.G. Williams (1968) and Small *et al.* (1970). At Clatford Bottom, Wiltshire,

the valley bottom infill exceeds 3 m and consists of flinty loam and coombe rock. No late glacial sediments were found and the infill is assigned to an early or main Weichselian period. Although Small *et al.* (1970) envisage one episode of solifluction and sarsen movement (Fig. 15.9) it is more likely that there were several episodes of movement during the Pleistocene during which the sarsens became progressively concentrated in the valley bottoms. The 'rock streams' of Wiltshire and Dorset provide convincing proof of the operation of solifluction processes in central southern England, especially during the last cold stage. In terms of landscape modifications, they indicate denudation from upland surfaces and the transport and deposition of debris in valley bottoms.

Patterned ground features of the East Anglian Chalk

Large polygons and stripes occur widely on the very gentle terrain of the East Anglian Chalky Drift. They are sometimes referred to as 'Breckland' polygons and stripes (e.g. Williams, 1964). Their origin is not known with certainty; they are given a periglacial significance simply because of the lack of an adequate alternative explanation and second, in East Anglia, there is evidence of other cold-climate phenomena.

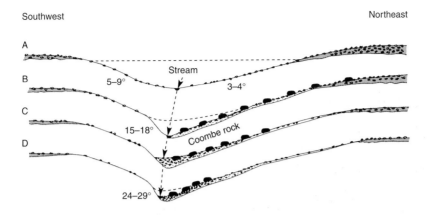

Southwest

Northeast

A

5–9°   Stream

B   3–4°

C

15–18°   *Coombe rock*

D

24–29°

A Initial valley incised through hill top surface of sarsens and Tertiary deposits

B Downcutting and beginning of sarsen/solifluction movement

C Main period of sarsen movement downslope and downvalley

D Period of fluvial reworking

Figure 15.9 Possible development of Clatford Bottom, Wiltshire, according to Small
et al., (1970).

In terms of the polygons and stripes described from high latitudes (see Chapters 8 and 9), the East Anglian features are large, the average distance between polygon centres being approximately 10 m and that between stripes being approximately 7.5 m (Williams, 1964). Typically, the polygons form on flat terrain while the stripes develop on gentle slopes, 1–3° in angle. A significant fact is that when the stripes reach level terrain, the patterns either disappear or turn to polygons once again. This suggests that solifluction is not the only process involved. Also significant is the departure of some of the stripes from the line of maximum slope, and the meandering, bifurcation and joining by cross-partition of others. This suggests surface wash to have been important. In cross-section, the polygons and stripes form broad troughs infilled with sandy materials overlying the Chalk or Chalky Drift. As the stripes disappear downslope, thin waste mantles of partly stratified but still largely unsorted sand and sandy gravel veneer the lower slopes. These deposits sometimes grade into extensive unsorted and stratified gravels which form low fluvial terraces.

The East Anglian patterns are puzzling since no exact analogues are known from present Arctic regions. The most similar features known to the writer occur on the undulating morainic terrain of eastern Banks Island. There the stripes and patterns are similar but much smaller, usually less than 2–3 m

in width and slope angles are higher, between 3° and 5°. The Banks Island features undoubtedly reflect linear zones of concentrated surface and subsurface wash, with lichen and moss identifying the lines of greater moisture. In general, therefore, there is support for R.B.G. Williams's (1968) interpretation of the East Anglian patterns as reflecting a stage of relative landscape stability, or 'maturity', in which sheetwash processes assumed dominance on slopes of low angle. Probably, the patterns developed on low-angled slopes where solifluction had practically ceased. The very small amounts of chalky debris incorporated into the slope deposits suggests that surface wash, and not solifluction, was the main transporting process. The poorly stratified and weakly sorted sand which infills the patterns and which mantles the lower slopes also indicates wash.

It follows that the glacial legacy in East Anglia, which gave a subdued relief to much of the Chalk north of the Chiltern Hills, was very important with respect to subsequent periglacial modification. During the last cold stage at least, the low and undulating terrain was quickly reduced to slopes of extremely low angle. Despite the intensity of cold which eastern England experienced, drastic landscape modification did not take place. Instead, rillwash and sheetwash dominated on the low-angled slopes and merely led to a further flattening and levelling of the landscape.

Periglacial valleys (dells)

Although the majority of dipslope valleys probably existed prior to their asymmetrical modification, there are valleys, both on the dip and scarp slopes of the Chalk outcrops, which are true periglacial valleys (dells) in the sense that they originated under periglacial conditions. Typically, these valleys are small, being less than 1–2 km in length with no apparent integration into the larger valley networks.

The most striking are deeply incised escarpment valleys or 'coombes', possessing steep, almost recti-linear, slopes, commonly 30–35° in angle, and abrupt headwalls. The angular course of some, such as Rake Bottom, in Hampshire, probably reflects their head-ward extension along major joint lines in the Chalk. In others, there is evidence that their formation was associated with intense physical weathering in combination with meltwater movement over seasonally frozen ground. One such group of these periglacial escarpment valleys occurs on the south-facing escarpment of the North Downs near Brook, Kent (e.g. Kerney et al., 1964) and a second group occurs on the Chiltern escarpment near Ivinghoe, in Buckinghamshire (Brown, 1969). At Brook, the largest, the Devil's Kneadingtrough, possesses a flat floor and an elongate triangular ground plan with a steep but smooth head-wall. The valley infill, which forms the flat bottom, is composed primarily of calcareous chalk rubbles and muds which, on faunal and stratigraphic grounds, are assigned to a late Devensian (Zone III) age. These deposits extend, in the form of a large apron, over the lowlands at the foot of the escarpment. Since the muds are well sorted and often stratified, and since they have been transported over slopes of very low angle at the foot of the escarpment, they must have been associated with considerable meltwater activity. It is thought that the majority of the erosion of the valleys at Brook took place during a relatively short period of time, approximately 500 years, when the climatic deterioration of Zone III resulted in a specific combination of humidity and repeated freeze–thaw action. Probably, groundwater seepage, as indicated by springs today, was the factor that localized the frost shattering. The Chalk debris would have been moved into the widening and deepening valley partly by solifluction and partly by water released from melting snowbanks on the escarpment summit and flowing over seasonally frozen ground. Transportation out of the valley was probably accomplished by surface meltwaters and also by flow from scarp foot springs.

Periglacial valleys of a slightly different nature exist on the dipslopes of the Chalk. They occur on gentle valley-side slopes, particularly the gentler slopes of asymmetrical valleys, as shallow, paddle-shaped or bowl-like depressions, 100–200 m in diameter (French, 1972a). In all probability, these depressions developed through wash processes beneath and below snowpatches when the subsoil was either perennially or seasonally frozen. If wind directions during the colder periods were not substantially different from those of today, and westerly winds dominated, this would account for their preferential development on east- and northeast-facing slopes. In size, frequency of occurrence and distribution, they appear unrelated to the larger dry valley network and a periglacial origin is the most likely.

The periglacial legacy in southern England

There is no doubt that much of southern England experienced periglacial conditions several times during the Pleistocene, a thesis first proposed in a systematic fashion by Te Punga (1957). One of the earliest periods is now documented by recognition of the early Anglian Barham Soil of eastern England (Rose et al., 1985b). This is a buried palaeosol occurring beneath glacial and glaciofluvial deposits of the Anglian glaciation. It is characterized by involutions, ice-wedge pseudomorphs, sand-wedge casts, platey and banded microfabrics and wind-polished pebbles. Evidence of the most recent period of periglacial conditions, the Devensian, is most obvious today on the Chalk. Here, landscape modification took the form of wash and solifluction, valley infilling and slope flattening, asymmetrical slope modification, and localized intense erosion of the Chalk by freeze–thaw and niveo-fluvial action.

The evidence for periglacial activity elsewhere in southern England on non-chalk lithologies is less clear. The Chalk, by virtue of its desiccation, has been 'fossilized' and protected from the postglacial fluvial modification which has occurred elsewhere. Nevertheless, periglacial slope deposits have been described from a variety of non-Chalk localities in southern England; they include Norfolk (West et al., 1974), Dorset (Keen, 1985) and Essex (Whiteman and Kemp, 1990). In Hertfordshire and north Middlesex asymmetrical valleys essentially similar to those of the Chalk terrain occur on drift materials overlying London Clay (Thomasson, 1961). North and west of the Chalk outcrops, there is abundant evidence for permafrost conditions during the last cold stage, as indicated by the presence of ice-

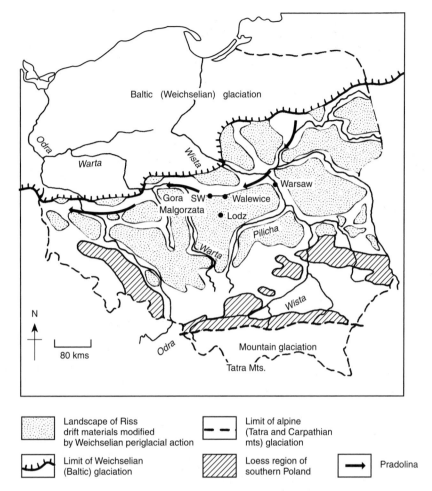

Figure 15.10   Map showing the limits of the last glaciation and the periglacial zone of central Poland.

and sand-wedge casts and non-diastrophic structures in the lowlands of the English Midlands (e.g. Hollingworth *et al.*, 1944; Shotton, 1960; Kellaway, 1972; Morgan, 1973). If frozen ground conditions existed there, they must also have existed on the adjacent Chalk uplands. However, the absence of wedge casts reported from the Chalk is not surprising, in view of the permeable and fissured nature of the Chalk. Instead of regular thermal contraction cracking, the intense cold probably saw the opening up of joints and fissures in the Chalk. These widened joints can be seen today in the Chalk cliffs of Kent and Sussex. Equally predictable is the absence of thermokarst phenomena from the Chalk uplands since widespread ice segregation would have been unlikely in view of the permeability of the Chalk and the low level of the water table.

In the west of England beyond the limits of the Chalk outcrops, there is also evidence of the previous operation of periglacial conditions, although not necessarily of permafrost. For example, the small sarsen stream at Corscombe, northwest of the high hill mass of Beaminster Down in northwest Dorset, indicates previous solifluction activity, and head deposits and frost debris occur widely throughout the southwest peninsula (e.g. Mottershead, 1977).

15.4.2 The landscape of central Poland

The classic example of relict Pleistocene periglacial terrain has long been regarded as central Poland, following the pioneer periglacial studies of J. Dylik and colleagues at Lódź (e.g. Dylik, 1953, 1956). Initially, it was concluded that virtually the entire landscape of central Poland had been fashioned by periglacial processes. More recently, the impact of fluvial and glacial influences upon the landscape have been better appreciated (e.g. Klatkowa, 1994) and a less extreme interpretation of the landscape has become accepted. Needless to say, approximately half of the central Polish landscape is of Saalian, or older age, and as much as one third is of Weichselian (Vistulian) age. The landscape provides numerous examples of Pleistocene periglacial modification. Three examples are described from the Lódź Plateau and the adjacent lowland terrain of the Warsaw–Berlin pradolina.

Geographical situation

Typically, the relief of central Poland consists of extremely flat or gently undulating lowland terrain developed in drift materials of middle Polish (Riss) age. During the last cold stage, central Poland lay beyond the limits of the Baltic (Weichselian) ice sheet (Fig. 15.10). Thus, an extensive periglacial zone developed in the area between the ice sheet to the north and the mountain glaciation of the Carpathian (Tatra) Mountains to the south. In places, this periglacial zone was over 300 km wide.

The Lódź Plateau is an undulating low plateau, 200–300 m in elevation, lying to the north of the loess terrain of southern Poland and south of the recent (Weichselian) glacial terrain of northern Poland. It is dissected by a number of broad shallow valleys which drain to the Pilicha and Warta rivers. Slopes are long and gentle, usually less than 5–7° in angle. The plateau is underlain by a thick cover of Quaternary sediments which rest upon a shallow platform of Jurassic and Cretaceous bedrock. The surface sediments are sand, gravel and boulder clay of the Middle Polish (Riss) glaciation. The northern part of the Lódź Plateau descends to the main Warsaw–Berlin pradolina through a series of broad levels, each separated by a zone of steeper slopes.

The Warsaw–Berlin pradolina is a large, east–west trending depression, between 15 and 20 km wide, which lies to the north of the Lódź Plateau. During the last (Weichselian) glaciation, the maximum limit of the ice lay 35–40 km to the north and the depression acted as a channel for the evacuation of meltwater from the ice front. A number of low terraces within the pradolina indicate that it operated on a number of occasions.

The dry valleys of the Lódź Plateau

The northern half of the Lódź Plateau, and in particular, the steeper slopes along its northern edge, are

Figure 15.11 Periglacial dells, northern edge of the Lódź Plateau near Swardzew, central Poland

dissected by numerous shallow depressions and small valleys (dells) which are now dry (Fig. 15.11). They occur in groups or as isolated features. On morphological grounds, they can be divided into two groups. Many are less than 300 m in length, and straight in plan (Klatkowa, 1965). They are clearly analogous to the paddle-shaped or bowl-like depressions which occur on the Chalk terrain of southern England. The second type is longer, between 300 and 1500 m in length, and both deeper and broader in dimensions. These valleys are more irregular in plan, are best developed on slopes of between 2 and 4° in angle, and correspond, in a general sense, to the dry valleys of the Chalklands. Some are asymmetrical in cross-profile, with the steeper slope facing west or northwest.

Detailed geomorphological studies indicate that the smaller depressions formed through concentrated slopewash during the early and middle stages of the last cold stage, probably at snowbank sites when the subsoil was frozen. The larger valleys are the result of more than one period of periglacial conditions. According to Klatkowa (1965), the valleys were initiated during the late stages of the penultimate (Riss) glaciation, then deepened by normal fluvial activity during the following interglacial period, and were further modified during the last cold stage. Their asymmetrical modification occurred during the latter stage. Finally, with the thawing of ground at the end of the last cold stage and the increase in infiltration which resulted, the drainage network contracted, leaving the dells and valleys dry.

Gora Sw Malgorzata

The isolated hill of Gora Sw Malgorzata is situated in the axial part of the Warsaw–Berlin pradolina, and rises 20 m above the flat bottom of the broad depression. The hill possesses smooth concave slopes, grading from 25–35° in angle in their upper parts to 10° in their lower parts. The hill, composed of glacifluvial sand, silt and gravel which overlie till, is interpreted as a kame which originated during deglaciation of the penultimate ice sheet (Riss) of the Warta stage (Dylik,1963).

Periglacial slope deposits mantle the foot of the hill and enable reconstruction of the slope modifications which took place during the last (Weichselian) cold stage (Fig. 15.12). The lowermost deposits are fine, cross-bedded, fluvial sands indicating the previous existence of a braided stream at the foot of the slope. Overlying and obliterating the relief of these channel deposits are 5–10 m of solifluction debris and rhyth-

mically stratified sediments, all clearly derived from the glacifluvial sediments which make up the hill. Lobe-like solifluction structures constitute the lower section of the deposits. The change to rhythmically bedded sediments indicates a change to sheet solifluction combined with slopewash on progressively lower-angled slopes. A second series of lobate deformations occur in an upper layer of stratified sand. Overlying all these sediments, and extending to the foot of the present hillslope, is a layer of cross-bedded sand and gravel with numerous stone and boulder beds.

These slope deposits indicate a progressive change in the form of Gora Sw Malgorzata. In the earliest phase of periglacial conditions, probably at the beginning of the Weichselian, solifluction and then slopewash obliterated the old braided channel. As a result, the slope became longer and gentler. Then, lobate solifluction on the steep slope infilled the channel depressions and gave a step-like profile to the slope. As the slope gradient decreased, slopewash and stratified sheet-like deposition occurred, and slope assumed a smoother profile. Ultimately, the old channel deposits and relief were completely obliterated by a gentle depositional slope of 2–4° in angle. During the latter stages of the last cold period, the slope experienced a further phase of solifluction activity, but slope evolution was terminated by the deposition of bedded gravels which covered all the preceding deposits and rose to the foot of the present-day hill. This suggests that the pradolina came into operation once again.

Thus, the slopes of Gora Sw Malgorzata are thought to have experienced active periglacial modification throughout the last cold stage. As climatic conditions deteriorated, solifluction and then sheetwash processes progressively reduced the lower slope in angle and extended it in length, while the upper part suffered erosion and retreat. Ultimately, a near-stable slope was attained. Then, in the climatic amelioration which followed, a second phase of solifluction was initiated before the lower slope was buried beneath the fluvial sediments of the pradolina drainage.

Walewice

A more complex example of periglacial slope modification has been described by Dylik (1969a, 1969b) in which mass wasting processes operated in conjunction with thermal erosion and the presence of frost fissures. The locality was a long and extremely gentle slope extending away from the edge of the 10–20 m

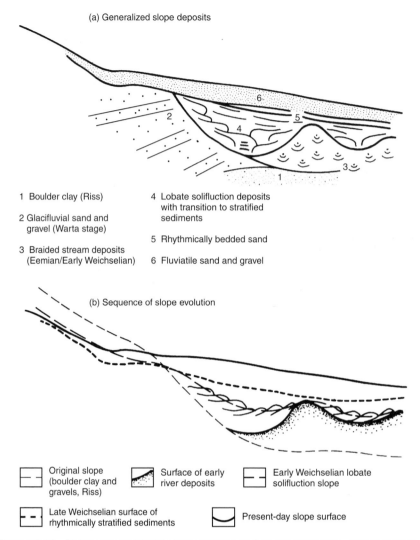

(a) Generalized slope deposits

1 Boulder clay (Riss)

2 Glacifluvial sand and
   gravel (Warta stage)

3 Braided stream deposits
   (Eemian/Early Weichselian)

4 Lobate solifluction deposits
   with transition to stratified
   sediments

5 Rhythmically bedded sand

6 Fluviatile sand and gravel

(b) Sequence of slope evolution

Original slope
(boulder clay and
gravels, Riss)

Surface of early
river deposits

Early Weichselian lobate
solifluction slope

Late Weichselian surface of
rhythmically stratified sediments

Present-day slope surface

Figure 15.12   Pleistocene periglacial slope evolution at Gora Sw Malgorzata, central Poland.
(from Dylik, 1963, 1969a)

terrace of the Warsaw–Berlin pradolina near the village of Walewice. The top of the terrace is mantled with a layer of boulder clay derived from the Middle Polish (Riss) glaciation. As at Gora Sw Malgorzata, the last glaciation did not extend to this area. Therefore, the modifications of the terrace edge took place during the last cold phase.

The sediments which form the slope are rhythmically bedded silt and sand (Fig. 5.13). They appear to have buried two older and steeper slopes. The older slope represents the original terrace edge, first covered with a veneer of boulder clay which had moved

down the slope from the terrace edge and which had then been buried by stratified sediments. Further downslope the stratified sediments are truncated by a younger, fossil slope, at the foot of which is a block of sediment apparently upturned and buried by non-stratified earth-slide deposits. The block appears to have fallen in a frozen state and to have been quickly buried since, if it had thawed, it would not have been preserved. The most likely explanation is that it formed when a stream undercut and temporarily steepened the slope. The development of a thermo-erosional niche probably caused the collapse of the

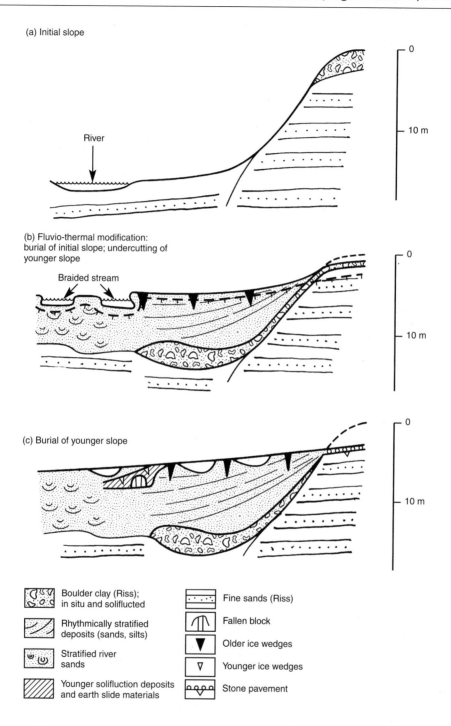

(a) Initial slope

River

0

10 m

(b) Fluvio-thermal modification:
burial of initial slope; undercutting of
younger slope

Braided stream

0

10 m

(c) Burial of younger slope

0

10 m

Boulder clay (Riss);
in situ and soliflucted

Rhythmically stratified
deposits (sands, silts)

Stratified river
sands

Younger solifluction deposits
and earth slide materials

Fine sands (Riss)

Fallen block

Older ice wedges

Younger ice wedges

Stone pavement

Figure 15.13   Pleistocene periglacial slope evolution at Walewice, central Poland
(from Dylik, 1969b).

block along the line of weakness presented by a frost fissure. Sloughing-off of the new bank then led to its rapid burial. In excavations, at least two generations of frost fissures could be identified: an older set associated with the collapse of the block and a younger set developed in the material which fossilized the fallen block. They prove that permafrost was present throughout this period of slope modification. The older fossil slope was cut probably during the last (Eemiam) interglacial or during one of the older Wurm interstadials. The burial of the original terrace edge by solifluction and slopewash deposits, and the steepening, undercutting and burial of the younger fossil slope all took place during the climax of the last cold stage.

Thus, periglacial landscape modification at Walewice saw the elimination of the terrace edge and the development of a smooth, low-angled slope. Slope angles declined from 20–25° along the original terrace edge to 3–4° on the depositional surface, and there was a progressive reduction in relative relief through the movement of material into the pradolina bottom.

15.5 Summary

Pleistocene periglacial landscape modification took place in an environment of strong wind action, in which aeolian transport and deposition was widespread. Reworking of dunes and loess by meltwater and solifluction occurred. Large tundra rivers and ice-marginal channels removed water from the ice margins. As valley incision occurred, so did valley infilling, in a cyclic fashion.

There are similarities in the landscape modification that occurred in central Poland and southern England.

The 'rock streams' and solifluction deposits of southern England and the evolution of slopes at Gora Sw Malgorzata and Walewice illustrate how mass wasting of upper slopes led to a general flattening of landscapes and the production of smooth, gently concave slopes of low angle. These erosional slopes merged into depositional surfaces formed by the infilling of original valleys and depressions. In both East Anglia and the lowlands of central Poland the already undulating drift terrain and the unconsolidated nature of the surficial deposits quickly led to relief reduction. As slopes attained gentle gradients, slopewash processes assumed dominance.

Streams were also effective both as transporting and eroding agents. These shallow, braided streams were characterized by high sediment loads and variable (nival) discharges. In certain situations, such as the Lódź Plateau and the Chalk escarpments, intense physical weathering on climatically favoured south- and west-facing slopes saw asymmetrical modification and further deepening of existing valleys. Elsewhere, numerous small depressions and valleys were initiated on the seasonally or perennially frozen subsoils.

Further reading

Baker, V.R. (1983) Late Pleistocene fluvial systems. In: S.C. Porter (ed.) *Late Quaternary Environments of the United States*, Volume 1. Minneapolis: University of Minnesota Press, pp. 115–128.

Dylik, J. (1969a) Slope development under periglacial conditions in Lodz region. *Biuletyn Peryglacjalny*, **18**, 381–410.

Dylik, J. (1969b) Slope development affected by frost fissures and thermal erosion. In: T.L. Péwé (ed.), *The periglacial environment*. Montreal: McGill–Queen's Press, pp. 365–386.

Jahn, A. (1976) Thermoerosion and the problems of ice-marginal valleys (pradolinas) in the European lowlands. In: *Problems of the periglacial zone*, Chapter 12. Warsaw: PWN-Polish Scientific Publishers, pp. 113–126.

Koster, E.A. (1988) Ancient and modern cold-climate aeolian sand deposition: a review. *Journal of Quaternary Science*, **3**, 69-83.

Klatkowa, H. (1995) Evaluation du role de l'agent périglaciaire en Pologne central. *Biuletyn Peryglacjalny*, **33**, 79–106.

Ollier, C.D. and A.J. Thomasson (1957) Asymmetrical valleys of the Chiltern Hills. *Geographical Journal*, **123**, 71–80.

Ruhe, R.V. (1983) Depositional environment of late Wisconsinan loess in the mid continental United States. In: S.C. Porter (ed.) *Late Quaternary environments of the United States*, Volume 1. Minneapolis: University of Minnesota Press, pp. 130–137.

Sharp, R.P. (1949) Pleistocene ventifacts east of the Big Horn Mountains, Wyoming. *Journal of Geology*, **57**, 175–195.

Small R.J., M.J. Clark and J. Lewin (1970) The periglacial rock stream at Clatford Bottom, Malborough Downs, Wiltshire. *Proceedings, Geologist's Association*, **81**, 87–98.

Discussion topics

1. Describe the typical landscape modifications that occurred under periglacial conditions in mid-latitudes during the Pleistocene.

2. Discuss the roles of wind, rain, snow and aspect as regards landscape modification during the cold periods of the Pleistocene.

3. What are the causes of asymmetrical valleys and what do they tell us about Pleistocene periglacial conditions?

4. What was the role of fluvial processes in fashioning the Pleistocene periglacial landscape?

PART 4 Applied periglacial geomorphology

16 Geotechnical and engineering aspects
17 Global change and periglacial environments

CHAPTER 16

Geotechnical and engineering aspects

Permafrost and intense frost action affect virtually every aspect of man's existence in periglacial regions. Geotechnical and engineering problems are caused primarily by frost heave and thaw settlement. The provision of housing, municipal services, water supply, roads, bridges, railways, airstrips and pipelines all require that the peculiarities of cold-climate terrain be taken into account. The extra cost is often significant.

16.1 Introduction

Many important geotechnical and engineering problems result from the occurrence of permafrost (Johnston, 1981). For the most part they relate to the water and/or ice content of permafrost. These are summarized below.

First, pure water freezes at 0 °C and in so doing expands by approximately 9 per cent of its volume. The most obvious result of soil freezing is frost heaving. This has considerable practical significance since it causes the displacement of buildings, foundations and road surfaces (e.g. Ferrians *et al.*, 1969). The annual cost of rectifying such damage in areas of permafrost and deep seasonal frost, such as in Canada, Alaska, Sweden and northern Japan, is considerable.

Second, ground ice is a major component of permafrost. Following the thaw of ice-rich permafrost, thermokarst and ground subsidence can result. Moreover, thaw consolidation may occur as the thawed sediments compact and settle under their own weight and the high pore water pressures generated may favour soil instability. A related problem is that the physical properties of frozen ground, in which soil particles are cemented together by pore ice, may be considerably different from those of the same material in an unfrozen state. For example, in unconsolidated and/or soft sediments there is often a significant loss of bearing strength upon thawing. Beneath heated buildings, therefore, it is often essential to maintain the frozen state of the underlying material.

Third, the hydrological and groundwater characteristics of permafrost terrain are different from those of non-permafrost terrain. For example, the presence of both perennially and seasonally frozen ground prevents the infiltration of water into the ground or, at best, confines it to the active layer. At the same time, subsurface flow is restricted to taliks. A high degree of mineralization in subsurface permafrost is often typical, caused by the restricted circulation imposed by permafrost and the concentration of dissolved solids in the taliks. Thus, frozen ground eliminates many shallow depth aquifers, reduces the volume of unconsolidated deposits or bedrock in which water is stored, influences the quality of groundwater supply and necessitates that wells be drilled deeper than in non-permafrost regions.

16.2 Human-induced thermokarst and terrain disturbance

Permafrost terrain is generally regarded as highly 'sensitive' to thermal disturbance. The necessity of maintaining the thermal regime is widely recognized

Table 16.1 Some examples of the effects of man-induced vegetational changes upon permafrost conditions in Siberia, according to P. I. Koloskov (1925)

(a) Increase in average July soil temperature at 40 cm depth after ploughing, Yenesie region

Soil	Previous Vegetation Cover	Temperature Increase (°C)
Semi-bog	Forest	+14
Peat-bog	Grass	+12
Semi-bog	Grass	+9
Light sod, gravelly	Grass	+3

(b) Soil temperature changes as a result of deforestation, Amur Province

Depth of Measurement (m)	Thickness of Snow (cm)	Soil Temperature Changes within One Year (°C)
0.2	20	+0.5
	10	−1.6
0.3	20	+0.7
	10	−1.2
0.4	20	+0.6
	10	−0.6

Source: quoted in Tyrtikov (1964)

and measures to prevent thermal change are now widely adopted. In spite of this, numerous examples of man-induced thermokarst have occurred, and still do.

The FSU, by virtue of its long history of northern exploration and settlement, has by far the greatest experience in this respect. As early as 1925, for example, experiments were being undertaken to determine the effects of vegetation changes on the underlying permafrost, brought about either by deforestation or by ploughing (Table 16.1).

Figure 16.1 Man-induced thermokarst in borrow pits adjacent to the Sachs Harbour airstrip, Banks Island, Canada (see French, 1975a).

In Alaska, similar experimental studies have been undertaken. One of the earliest was in the Fairbanks region and involved the cutting and/or stripping of the surface vegetation by the US Army Corps of Engineers in 1946. In the stripped area, the active layer increased from 1 m to more than 3 m in thickness over a ten-year period. Subsequently, numerous other studies have emphasized the thermal role played by the surface organic layer and/or forest cover (e.g. Brown *et al.*, 1969; Kallio and Reiger, 1969; Haugen and Brown, 1970; Babb and Bliss, 1974). It must be emphasized that even very small disturbances to the surface may be sufficient to induce thermokarst activity. Mackay (1970), for example, describes how an Eskimo dog in the Mackenzie Delta was tied to a stake with a 1.5 m long chain. In the ten days of tether, the animal trampled and destroyed the tundra vegetation of that area. Within two years, the site had subsided like a pie dish by a depth of 18–23 cm and the active layer thickness had increased by more than 10 cm within the depression.

Without doubt, the most common cause of man-induced thermokarst on a large scale is the clearance of the surface vegetation for agricultural or construction purposes. If this occurs in an area underlain by a polygonal network of ice wedges, a distinctive hummocky microrelief forms (Fig. 16.1). This results from the general subsidence of the ground combined with preferential melt along the wedges. A classic example has been described from the Fairbanks region of Alaska where extensive areas were cleared for agriculture in the 1920s. The following 30 years saw the formation of mounds and depressions in the fields, the mounds varying from 3 to 15 m in diameter and up to 2.4 m in height (Rockie, 1942). Subsequently, these features were termed thermokarst mounds (Péwé, 1954). In the Former Soviet Union, similar undulating surfaces are common in clearings adjacent to small lumber camps in the taiga. In places, shallow troughs, 0.5–1.0 m deep, form hummocky terrain termed '*baydjarakhs*' or 'graveyard mounds' (Soloviev, 1973a, 1973b). In other areas underlain by extremely ice-rich sediments, widespread subsidence may lead to the formation of alas depressions. Adjacent to the village of Maya in central Yakutia, for example, a depression 5–8 m deep and between 200 and 300 m in diameter formed in historic times following deforestation and the beginning of the agricultural settlement (see Fig. 7.4).

These examples illustrate the extreme sensitivity of permafrost terrain to man-induced surface modifications. We can identify at least three controls over such permafrost degradation: first, the ice content of the underlying permafrost and, in particular, the presence or absence of excess ice; second, the thickness and insulating qualities of the surface vegetation; and third, the duration and warmth of the summer thaw period.

Several case histories illustrate the nature and rapidity of man-induced thermokarst. In all instances, the initial disturbance is associated with borrow pits, where material has been removed for road, airstrip, or construction purposes. Terrain disturbance at an exploratory wellsite in central Banks Island, in the western Canadian Arctic, was monitored for several years following initiation in 1973 (French, 1978). In August of that year, following the infilling of the waste pit, the site was abandoned and restoration undertaken. In an attempt to infill the kitchen waste pit, material was removed from an adjacent gravelly ridge and pushed into the depression. In all, an area of approximately 3000 m² was disturbed. Two years later, a crude polygonal system of gullies had developed at the site, reflecting preferential erosion along underlying ice wedges. After two further years, typical thermokarst topography had formed, consisting of unstable hummocks and mounds interspersed with standing water bodies.

This experience can be compared with the man-induced thermokarst which formed adjacent to the airstrip at Sachs Harbour, also on Banks Island (French, 1975a). This airstrip was constructed during the summers of 1959–62. In order to grade the proposed strip, thawed material was removed each summer from adjacent terrain and transported, via access ramps, to the site. In all, a total of 50 000 m² was disturbed and as much as 2 m of material removed in places. Subsequent surficial drilling revealed the underlying sediments to be ice-rich sand and gravel with excess ice values of 25–30 per cent and natural water (ice) contents of between 50 and 150 per cent. When examined in 1972 the borrow pits portrayed actively subsiding thermokarst mound topography (Fig. 16.1). Only in recent years has the terrain shown signs of stabilization.

These studies provide insight into the speed at which man-induced thermokarst develops. Stabilization only begins 10–15 years after the initial disturbance and probably is not complete until 30 years or more have passed.

In environments of greater summer thaw, an essentially similar sequence of thermokarst activity takes place, except that the amplitude of the thermokarst mounds is greater, reflecting the greater thaw depths.

(a)

(a)

Figure 16.2   Terrain disturbance associated with vehicle movement over ice-rich tundra: (a) old vehicle track, probably created in late 1940s or early 1950s in area of old United States Navy Petroleum Reserve-4 (NPR-4), Alaska North Slope (photo taken August 1977); (b) gully erosion along an old vehicle track made in the summer of 1970 near the site of Drake Point blow-out, Sabine Peninsula, Melville Island, NWT. The terrain is underlain by ice-rich shale. (Photo taken August 1976.)

A second major cause of man-induced thermokarst relates to the movement of vehicles over permafrost terrain. If this occurs in summer when the thawed surface is soft and wet, surface vegetation can be destroyed and deep trenching and rutting can occur. Probably some of the worst examples of this sort of activity exist on the Alaskan North Slope in the old US Naval Petroleum Reserve No. 4. There, in the late 1940s and early 1950s, the uncontrolled movement of tracked vehicles in summer associated with early well-drilling activities led to considerable trenching and thermokarst on account of the ice-rich subsoils.

In places subsidence along vehicle tracks has formed trenches as much as 1 m deep and between 3 and 5 m wide (Fig. 16.2 (a)). Large areas of the North Slope are permanently scarred by these tracks. Furthermore, the tracks favour continued thermokarst by collecting water and, if located upon a slope, promote gullying by channelling snowmelt and surface runoff.

In Canada, an unfortunate error was made in 1965 when a summer seismic line programme was undertaken in the Mackenzie Delta. Approximately 300 km of seismic lines were bulldozed and long strips of vegetation and soil, approximately 4.2 m wide and 0.25 m thick were removed. Thermokarst subsidence and erosion by running water subsequently transformed many of these lines into prominent trenches and canals over much of their length (Kerfoot, 1974). A more recent example of extensive vehicle track disturbance in Canada occurred during the summer of 1970 on the Sabine Peninsula of Eastern Melville Island. At that time a blow-out occurred at a wildcat well being drilled in the Drake Point area and vehicles were moved, of necessity, across tundra. Sensitive tundra lowlands underlain by soft ice-rich shale of the Christopher Formation were traversed, and substantial and dramatic trenching occurred (Fig. 16.2 (b)).

In general, however, severe disturbance associated with vehicle tracks is now rare and one must conclude that, for the most part, vehicle tracks present primarily aesthetic rather than terrain problems (French, 1978). Usually, vehicle operators prefer to traverse gently sloping terrain which does not provide the necessary gradient for subsequent deep gullying. Also, the differential settlement of the ground by thermokarst subsidence creates an irregular surface which precludes the development of an integrated drainage system. Furthermore, the introduction of vehicles equipped with special low pressure tyres, the restriction of movement of heavy equipment to the winter months by both Canadian and Alaskan authorities, and the initiation of various terrain sensitivity and biophysical mapping programmes in areas of potential economic activity, particularly in Canada (e.g. Kurfurst, 1973; Barnett *et al.*, 1977), are minimizing this sort of damage. In western Siberia, the lack of equivalent regulations until recently meant that significant terrain damage occurred in the Yamal oil and gas fields throughout the 1980s (Fig. 16.3).

Figure 16.3 Terrain disturbances adjacent to a staging area in the Bovanyanka gas fields, Yamal Peninsula, western Siberia. Photo taken in July 1989.

16.3 Engineering and construction problems

The thawing of permafrost and the heaving and subsidence caused by frost action result in serious damage to roads, bridges and other structures. In Alaska, following the realization of these problems in the 1940s, a determined effort was made by federal and state agencies to improve construction practices and to document permafrost problems (e.g. Péwé and Paige, 1963; Péwé, 1966a; Ferrians *et al.*, 1969). In Canada, where large-scale development projects in permafrost regions occurred slightly later, it was possible to benefit from Alaskan experience.

16.3.1 Housing and municipal services

With respect to construction in permafrost, a number of approaches are available, depending on site conditions and fiscal limitations. For example, if the site is underlain by hard consolidated bedrock, as is the case for some regions of the Canadian Shield, ground ice is usually non-existent and permafrost problems can be largely ignored. In most areas, however, this simple approach is not feasible since an overburden of unconsolidated silty or organic sediments is usu-

ally present. In the majority of cases, therefore, construction techniques are employed which aim to maintain the thermal equilibrium of the permafrost.

The most common technique is the use of a pad or some sort of fill which is placed on the surface (Fig. 16.4). This compensates for the increase in thaw which results from the warmth of the structure. By utilizing a pad of appropriate thickness the thermal regime of the underlying permafrost is unaltered. It is possible, given the thermal conductivity of the materials involved and the mean air and ground temperatures at the site, to calculate the thickness of fill required. Too little fill plus the increased conductivity of the compacted active layer beneath the fill will result in thawing of the permafrost. On the other hand, too much fill will provide too much insulation and the permafrost surface will aggrade on account of the reduced amplitude of the seasonal temperature fluctuation. In northern Canada and Alaska, gravel is the most common aggregate used since it is reasonably widely available and has low frost heave susceptibility.

In instances where the structure concerned is capable of supplying significant quantities of heat to the underlying permafrost, as in the case of a heated building or a warm oil pipeline, additional measures are frequently adopted. Usually the structure is mounted on piles which are inserted into the per-

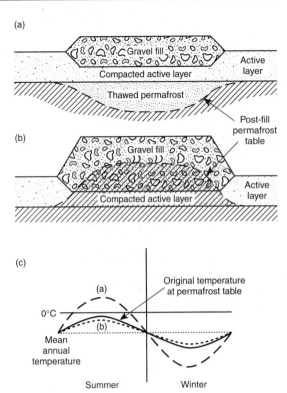

(a)

Gravel fill

Active layer

Compacted active layer

Thawed permafrost

Post-fill permafrost table

(b)

Gravel fill

Active layer

Compacted active layer

(c)

Original temperature at permafrost table

(a)

0°C

(b)

Mean annual temperature

Summer   Winter

Figure 16.4   Diagram illustrating the effects of a gravel fill upon the thermal regime and thickness of the active layer: (a) too little fill; (b) too much fill; (c) effects of cases (a) and (b) upon the thermal regime – too little fill increases the amplitude of seasonal temperature fluctuation at the permafrost table (*source*: Ferrians *et al.*, 1969).

mafrost. An air space left between the ground surface and the structure enables the free circulation of cold air which dissipates the heat emanating from the structure. Other techniques used include the insertion of open-ended culverts into the pad, the placing of insulating matting immediately beneath the pad and, if the nature of the structure justifies it, the insertion of costly refrigeration units or 'Cryo-Anchors' (e.g. Hayley, 1982) around the pad or through the pilings.

In Canada, the construction of the town of Inuvik in the Mackenzie Delta area in the early 1960s was an example of the careful manner in which large-scale construction projects need to be undertaken in permafrost regions. A major factor governing the location of the town was the presence of a large body of fluvioglacial gravel a few kilometres to the south. Rear-end dumping of these gravels was an

essential prerequisite to any heavy construction activity. The result was that the entire townsite was developed upon a gravel pad. Today, the gravel deposit has been exhausted and the future growth of the community is dependent upon the exploitation of more distant aggregate sources with their associated higher costs of haulage.

The provision of municipal services such as water supply and sewage disposal are particularly difficult in permafrost regions. Pipes to carry these services cannot be laid below ground beneath the depth of seasonal frost, as is the case in non-permafrost regions, since the heat from the pipes will promote thawing of the surrounding permafrost and subsequent subsidence and fracture of the pipe. At Inuvik, the provision of these utilities has been achieved through the use of utilidors – continuously insulated aluminium boxes which run above ground on supports and which link each building to a central system (Fig. 16.5). The cost of such utilidor systems is high and they involve a high degree of town planning and constant maintenance; as a consequence, they can only be justified in large settlements.

In Dawson City, Yukon, a slightly different approach has been taken by Parks Canada and the Yukon Government in the restoration and maintenance of historic buildings, and in the provision of utilities to the townsite. The city of Dawson is located on a restricted area of the flood plain of the Yukon River underlain by 2–4 m of silt over alluvial gravel. Despite nearly a century of occupation, warm (between –3 °C and –1 °C) permafrost is present to a depth of about 20 m. The occurrence of segregated ice lenses and ice wedges means that the soils are thaw-sensitive and subject to settlement if disturbed.

The earliest buildings in Dawson were log structures or frame buildings placed on large squared timbers laid at or near the surface. Virtually all the old buildings still remaining have settled differentially, necessitating periodic jacking and levelling with additional cribbing, and/or eventual abandonment (Fig. 16.6 (a)). Similar deformations in old structures placed directly upon ice-rich permafrost have been described from Alaska and Siberia (e.g. Péwé, 1983c, pp. 11–62). Since the early 1960s all new buildings in Dawson have been constructed on wooden piles or gravel pads. In restoring some of the historic buildings, Parks Canada has tried to maintain the original levels of the buildings with respect to the streets, ruling out the emplacement of thick gravel pads or the use of piles. Instead, the silty ice-rich material has been excavated and replaced by

Figure 16.5 At Inuvik, NWT, buildings are placed upon wooden piles. Services such as water and sewage are effected by a utilidor system which links each building to the central plant.

thaw-stable granular material to a depth of 5–7 m, and the historic buildings have been replaced in their original positions supported by adjustable jacks.

The provision of municipal services in Dawson has also been upgraded at considerable cost. The town uses water from infiltration wells situated near the bank of the Klondike River. Prior to 1980, the city water distribution and sewage systems were those that had been constructed in 1904. They consisted of woodstave pipes laid in gravel in the active layer; all were shallower than 1.2 m. In winter, the water was heated by electricity to +5.5 °C and enough flow was maintained to prevent freezing by bleeding into each house. At the end of the circulation system, the water temperature was about 1.1 °C. Needless to say, these water and sewage systems required frequent repairs owing to seasonal frost heave, settlement of the pipes through thaw, and frost deterioration of the pipes. During the winter and spring of 1979–80, a new system of underground services was installed in trenches that were excavated to a minimum depth of 2.0 m and backfilled with coarse (frost-stable) gravel fill (Fig. 16.6 (b)). Similar costly procedures are now regarded as inevitable in many of the smaller northern communities in Canada, if reliable and modern services are to be provided.

In the FSU, where cities with populations greater than 100 000 have been built in recent years on permafrost, utilidor systems constructed mainly of wood or cement are widely employed. In Yakutsk, for example, many of the recently completed high-rise buildings are connected to a central large utilidor system for sewage which runs beneath the main street and eventually empties into the large Lena River. As in North America, modern construction takes place on pilings, and airspaces are left between the buildings and the ground surface (Fig. 16.7).

The biggest disadvantage of pile foundations is their cost. This is especially the case for very small buildings, such as individual houses. Equally, in certain communities where good quality non-frost-susceptible aggregate is scarce, the cost of gravel pad construction is also high. As a result, new technologies are being tested. For example, in 1987, the National Research Council of Canada in association with the Yukon Government constructed two 350 m² multipurpose municipal buildings in the communities of Ross River and Old Crow, using heat pump chilled foundations (Goodrich and Plunkett, 1990). The aim was to prevent the thaw of permafrost beneath the buildings. Ross River has a mean annual ground temperature of greater than –0.5 °C and is typical of warm permafrost in the discontinuous

(a)

(a)

Figure 16.6 Dawson City, Yukon: (a) an abandoned building illustrating severe settlement due to permafrost degradation: (b) in May 1980, installation of new municipal services was by means of trenches excavated to a minimum depth of 2.0 m and backfilled with coarse gravel.

zone. Old Crow has a mean annual ground temperature of –5 to –7 °C and is more typical of cold permafrost in the continuous zone. The heat exchangers were placed in a sand layer within the granular fill used to level the sites (Fig. 16.8). Heat flowing down through the floor is captured by the heat exchangers and pumped back into the building. Thus, while the houses are being heated, the ground is being chilled. Comparisons of predicted and measured temperatures at the top and bottom of the gravel pad and at the top of the ice-rich silt layer (Fig. 16.8) for the first two years of operation at Ross River suggest that the system has worked well and that permafrost is being maintained beneath the structure.

16.3.2 Bridges, roads, railway and airstrips

Frost heaving of the seasonal frozen layer is a major engineering problem encountered in permafrost regions. Differential heave causes structural damage not only to buildings but also to roads, bridges, railways and airstrips. Equally important, frost heaving affects the use of piles for the support of structures.

While in warmer climates the chief problem of piles is to obtain sufficient bearing strength, in permafrost regions the problem is to keep the pilings in the ground since frost action tends to heave them upwards. Since heaving becomes progressively greater as the active layer freezes, it follows that the thicker the active layer, the greater is the upward heaving force. In the discontinuous permafrost zone, where the active layer may exceed 2 m in thickness, frost heaving of piles assumes critical importance. In parts of Alaska, for example, old bridge structures illustrate dramatically the effects of differential frost heave (see Péwé, 1983c). In these regions, it is not uncommon for a thawed zone to exist beneath the river channel. Thus, piles inserted in the stream bed itself experience little or no frost heave and piles inserted within permafrost on either side of the river are also unaffected. However, the piles adjacent to the river bank experience repeated heave since they are located in the zone of seasonal freezing. As a result, uparching of both ends of the bridge may occur.

In order to prevent these problems, alternative structures involving minimal pile support must be considered. A case in point is the recent construction of the Eagle River bridge on the Dempster Highway, northern Yukon (Fig. 16.9). The bridge consists of a single 100 m long steel span with the footings on the north side placed in ice-rich permafrost. Drilling prior to construction indicated that permafrost was present on the north bank to a depth of about 90 m and with a temperature of –3 °C. However, a deep near-isothermal talik existed beneath the main river channel while near the proposed south bridge abutment, permafrost had aggraded to depths of 8–9 m and was marginal in temperature (–0.4 °C).

In order to maintain the delicate permafrost conditions and to provide structural integrity, 15 steel piles were inserted at each abutment (Fig. 16.10). Conventional engineering adfreeze analysis indicated the optimum depth of emplacement of each pile was about 5 m. However, because of the very warm permafrost at the south abutment, the piles were driven to a depth of about 30 m. On the north abutment,

Figure 16.7 Modern construction techniques, Yakutsk, Siberia. Concrete piles are inserted into the permafrost and construction takes place above the ground surface.

where the permafrost was colder, the piles were installed in holes augered to a depth of 12 m. All were then backfilled with a sand slurry to promote adfreeze. A further complexity was that construction had to be carried out during the winter (1976–77), in order to minimize surface terrain damage. Subsequent monitoring indicates that the piles have experienced minimal heave, the thermal regime of the permafrost has been maintained and the bridge structure is performing satisfactorily (Johnston, 1980).

Several railways, constructed across permafrost terrain in Alaska and northern Canada, have also experienced costly maintenance problems on account of frost heave adjacent to bridge structures and thaw settlement along the railbed (e.g. Ferrians *et al.*, 1969; Hayley, 1988; Hayley *et al.*, 1983). In Tibet, a number of experimental studies have been undertaken to evaluate the same problems as essential background for an eventual railroad across the plateau (e.g. Research Group on Experimental Roadbed Research, 1979).

The Hudson Bay railway well illustrates the sorts of problems involved. After nearly 60 years of operation, thaw settlement of the railway embankment and destruction of bridge decks by frost heave have been perpetual problems. Test sections, now installed with heat pipes (Hayley, 1988), are proving effective but costly measures in minimizing thaw subsidence. However, the numerous transitions from frozen to unfrozen terrain in the discontinuous permafrost of northern Manitoba make installation of such techniques along the entire 820 km route impractical. In Alaska, the Copper River railway has also experienced similar maintenance problems, and other railway lines have been abandoned (e.g. Ferrians *et al.*, 1969).

The construction and maintenance of airstrips is also costly in permafrost regions since any slight heave or thaw settlement will affect the runway grade. In northern Alaska and Canada, gravel and rockfills are used for all-season airfields (e.g. Crory, 1988). In northern Canada, the airstrip at Inuvik has been black-coated following construction upon 2–3 m of crushed dolomite, and the progression of the frost-line is being monitored (e.g. Johnston, 1982). In Svalbard, and in northern Russia, airstrip maintenance is also a problem. Since airstrips are of vital importance to many northern settlements, to military usage, and for the supply of hydrocarbon and mineral exploration activities, the importance of permafrost engineering cannot be underestimated.

(a)

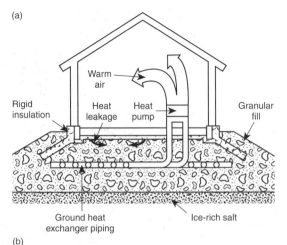

(b)

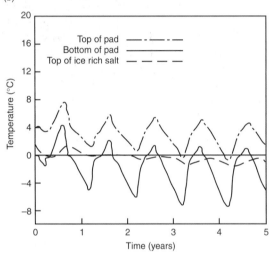

(c)

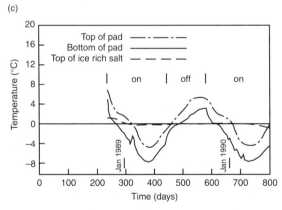

Figure 16.8 Ross River school, Yukon, Canada:
(a) design of insulated building using heat
pump chilled foundation; (b) calculated
temperatures; (c) measured temperatures
(from Baker and Goodrich, 1990).

16.3.3 Pipelines

The construction of warm oil pipelines through permafrost terrain further illustrates the complexity of frost heave and related permafrost problems. For example, the construction of the Trans-Alaska Pipeline System (TAPS) from Prudhoe Bay on the North Slope to Valdez on the Pacific Coast between 1974 and 1977 utilized many procedures designed to minimize permafrost problems (Metz *et al.*, 1982; Heuer *et al.*, 1982). Approximately half of the route was elevated on vertical support members (VSMs), many with cooling devices ('heat tubes') to prevent heat transfer from the warm pipe to ice-rich (i.e. thaw-sensitive) permafrost (Fig. 16.11).

In Canada, the recently completed small diameter Norman Wells pipeline did not have to address the problems of thaw subsidence to the same extent as the Alaska line, since it operates at or close to the prevailing ground temperature. Many of the terrain problems associated with this pipeline lie in the stability of wood-chip covered embankments along the right of way, and in the crossing of streams (Burgess and Harry, 1990).

The proposed construction of buried chilled gas pipelines presents more complex problems that are, as yet, not completely resolved. Here, the problem is one of prolonged frost heave adjacent to the pipe (e.g. see Smith and Williams, 1990) with the possibility of eventual rupture (Fig. 16.12). This might occur in the discontinuous permafrost zone wherever the pipe crosses unfrozen ground and where there would be relatively unlimited moisture migration towards the cold pipe. Equally, when the pipe passes from unfrozen (stable) to ice-rich (unstable) terrain, or vice versa, thaw settlement may result depending upon the situation.

In order to understand these problems, several natural scale experiments are currently in progress, at Calgary, Caen (France) and Fairbanks (Alaska), which aim to study the behaviour of soil around a refrigerated pipeline. The Calgary frost heave test facility has been in operation since 1974 and circulates air at –10 °C in a 1.2 m diameter pipe buried to represent a number of possible gas pipelines modes (Carlson *et al.*, 1982). Within a couple of years of operation, a 'frost bulb' had formed around the pipe and, in the deep burial mode, the pipe had heaved more that 60 cm while frost depths had penetrated to 3 m below the pipe. At Caen, a non-insulated pipe 2.7 m in diameter was buried in initially unfrozen soil

Figure 16.9 The Eagle River bridge, Dempster Highway, Yukon, is a single-span structure with minimal pile support in the river.

with a lateral transition from a frost-susceptible silt to a non-frost-susceptible sand, thereby simulating a major soil type boundary common to permafrost terrain. During a first freezing experiment, run in 1982–83 with a pipe temperature of –2 °C and a chamber temperature of –7 °C, the pipe heaved 11 cm on the 16 m long section, and frost penetrated 45 cm beneath the pipe in the sand and 30 cm beneath the pipe in the silt (Burgess, 1985). Results from the Fairbanks test facility (Fig. 16.13) are not yet published; preliminary data indicate that in the first 166 days of operation, the pipe heaved at least 10 cm at the critical permafrost/non-permafrost boundary.

One can be reasonably optimistic that solutions to these problems will be found. The observed magnitudes of frost heave and the frost penetration depths at the experimental sites relate well to values obtained via numerical simulation. They suggest that the amounts of heave and settlement that will be experienced by northern pipelines are predictable to engineering levels of accuracy using existing methods (Nixon, 1990).

16.4 Hydrological problems

The groundwater hydrology of permafrost regions is unlike that of non-permafrost regions since permafrost acts as an impermeable layer (Sloan and van Everdingen, 1988). Under these conditions the movement of groundwater is restricted to various thawed zones or taliks (see Chapter 5).

16.4.1 Water supply

Given these hydrological characteristics, a difficult problem in many permafrost regions is the provision of drinking water to settlements. Since supra-permafrost water is subject to contamination and usually small in amount, and intra-permafrost water is often highly mineralized and difficult to locate, the tapping of sub-permafrost water is vital. In the discontinuous permafrost zone, opportunities exist for groundwater recharge. In parts of central Alaska and

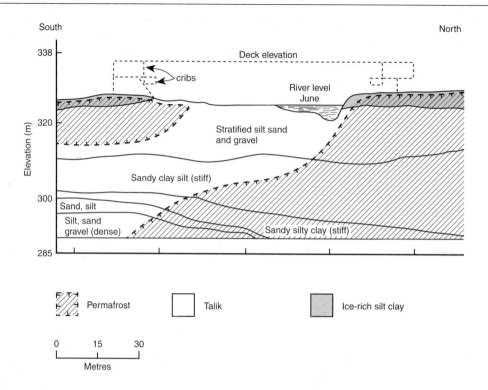

Figure 16.10   Plan and profile at Eagle River bridge, Northern Yukon, with stratigraphic and permafrost information determined by drilling during the 1976–77 winter (from Johnston, 1980).

Figure 16.11   The Trans-Alaska Pipeline near Fairbanks, Alaska. Note the elevation of the pipe, the cooling devices on the VSMs and the gravel access pad. Photo taken in May 1980.

parts of Siberia, the occurrence of perennial springs fed by sub-permafrost water assumes special importance to man since these may be the sole source of water available over large areas. However, in many areas of northern Canada (the Canadian Shield) the permafrost is several hundred metres deep and perennial springs are absent. In these situations, drilling is either not possible, since the hole would freeze, or too costly. As a result, surface water bodies, particularly those that do not freeze to their bottoms in winter, must be utilized and great care taken to prevent contamination. It follows that the supply of water is a severe limitation to any large-scale permanent settlement in much of the continuous permafrost zone. For example, the water supply problems at Sachs Harbour, a small Inuit community of approximately 250 people on southwest Banks Island, are reasonably typical of many situations. There, the water supply is derived from a lake approximately 3 km from the townsite. It is trucked, by water tanker, to individual homes which have indoor storage containers, every three or four days. Contamination is a problem and

the Mackenzie Valley, NWT, extensive alluvial deposits provide an abundant source of groundwater. In Fairbanks, houses rely on numerous small-diameter private wells (see Péwé, 1983c, pp. 67–85). In

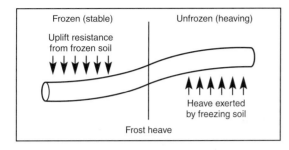

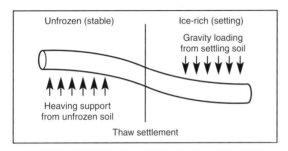

Figure 16.12   Conceptual illustration of the freezing and thawing effects of a pipeline crossing from unfrozen to frozen terrain, or vice versa, in the discontinuous permafrost zone in Canada (from Nixon, 1990).

the size of the lake, one of the few deep enough not to freeze to its bottom during winter, limits the growth of the community.

16.4.2   Icings

A different group of hydrological problems relates to the formation of icings. These are sheet-like masses of ice which form at the surface in winter where water issues from the ground, usually from a supra-permafrost talik. Icings are of great practical concern as regards highway and railway construction and in fact are a distinct hazard to any construction activity. These problems are most common in the discontinuous permafrost zone. Although sub- and intra-permafrost waters may be involved, the most frequently occurring icings are those associated with supra-permafrost water. A common occurrence is where a roadcut or other man-made excavation intersects with the supra-permafrost groundwater table. Seepage occurs and a sheet of ice forms, often several tens of square metres in extent.

In North America, icings were first encountered on a large scale during the building of the Alaskan Highway and they occur widely in Alaska (e.g. see

Figure 16.13   View of the frost heave test facility owned and operated by Northwest Alaskan Pipeline Company, at Fairbanks, Alaska. A series of cooling devices (Cryo-Anchors) are in the foreground.

Thomson, 1966; Péwé, 1983c, pp. 74–80). Unless precautions are taken, icings can occur on most northern highways which traverse sloping terrain. Counter measures to reduce icing problems include the avoidance of roadcuts wherever possible, the installation of high-arch culverts to divert water from the source of the icing, and the provision of large drainage ditches adjacent to the road. Icings may also block culverts placed beneath road embankments and, by diverting meltwater, initiate washouts in the spring thaw period. The costs of icing control and/or remedial measures can be considerable; for example, van Everdingen (1982) provides a conservative estimate of $20 000 for icing control at one locality studied on the Alaska Highway, Yukon, in the 1979–80 winter.

United States Geological Survey, Professional Paper 678, 37 pp.

French, H.M. (1987) Permafrost and ground ice. In: K.J. Gregory and D.E. Walling (eds), *Human activity and environmental processes*. Chichester: J. Wiley and Sons Ltd, pp. 237–269.

Hayley, D.W. (1988) Maintenance of a railway grade over permafrost in Canada. In: *Permafrost, Proceedings 5th International Conference, Vol. 3*. Trondheim: Tapir Publishers, pp. 46–48.

Johnston, G.H. (1981) *Permafrost. Engineering design and construction*. Toronto: J. Wiley and Sons Ltd, 540 pp.

Péwé, T.L. (1983) *Geologic hazards of the Fairbanks area, Alaska*. Special Report 15, Division of Geological Surveys, College, Alaska, 109 pp.

Further reading

Crory, F.E. (1988) Airfields in Arctic Alaska. In: *Permafrost, Proceedings 5th International Conference*, Vol. 3. Trondheim: Tapir Publishers, pp. 49–55.

Ferrians, O., R. Kachadoorian and G.W. Green (1969) *Permafrost and related engineering problems in Alaska*.

Discussion topics

1. Why do permafrost and intense seasonal frost pose problems to geotechnical engineering and construction?

2. How does permafrost affect man's economic activities?

CHAPTER 17   Global change and periglacial environments

This chapter examines the impact of predicted climate change upon periglacial environments. Emphasis is placed upon seasonal snow cover, permafrost and vegetation changes. All will be significantly affected by enhanced atmospheric concentrations of greenhouse gases.

The projected climate changes will most likely lead to decreases in the global aerial extent and masses of seasonal snow cover, ice and permafrost. This will affect both local and global hydrology (meltwater flow, peak discharge, seasonal distribution of runoff and sea-level rise), nature and distribution of plants and animals, and local and regional terrain instability (thermokarst, slope failures and other mass movements).

17.1 Global change and cold regions

The Intergovernmental Panel on Climate Change (IPCC) Scientific Assessment (Houghton *et al.*, 1990) predicts an increase of global mean temperature during the next century of about 0.3 °C per decade. This is based upon assumptions concerning present and future emissions of greenhouse gases, especially carbon dioxide (CO_2) and methane (CH_4). It is predicted that land surfaces will warm more rapidly than oceans, and high latitudes will warm more than the global mean, particularly in winter. Several general circulation models, based upon a doubling of CO_2, suggest that the changes for the months of December –January–February will be of the order of 8–12 °C (Houghton *et al.*, 1992) and that mean surface temperature may rise by 1.5–4.5 °C by the middle of the twenty-first century.

These anticipated changes are four to five times those that have occurred over the past century. As a result, the IPCC Impact Assessment Report (Tegart *et al.*, 1990) indicates that 'seasonal snow, ice and permafrost' is an important factor in global climate

change (Street and Melnikov, 1990). It follows that the periglacial environments will be critically affected by predicted global changes in the twenty-first century.

Not only are the periglacial environments of high latitudes sensitive to climate change but the changes that may occur there will have a profound influence upon the rest of the climate system. This is because a number of feedback mechanisms will come into play. These include (a) increased biomass production and decay in the tundra and taiga zones (e.g. Billings, 1987; Kolchugina and Vinson, 1993) and (b) increased methane flux due to the decomposition of organic matter frozen in the permafrost and the decomposition of methane hydrates (e.g. Kvenvolden, 1988; Judge and Majorowicz, 1992). There will also be impact upon alpine (mountain) environments of middle latitudes (e.g. Haeberli *et al.*, 1993).

The increased concentration of greenhouse gases in the atmosphere of northern periglacial regions will lead to general warming and precipitation (snow) increases. All aspects of the landscape will be affected, including various slope processes, runoff and all components of the water balance (e.g. Koster, 1993; Lewkowicz, 1992a; Woo, 1990a; Woo *et al.*,

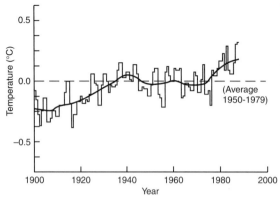

Figure 17.1 Global surface air temperatures (1900–88) plotted against 1950–79 average (from Slaymaker and French, 1993).

1992). The northern limits of the boreal forest, shrub-tundra and tundra eco-zones may shift latitudinally by several hundreds of kilometres. It is not surprising, therefore, that much recent research in periglacial geomorphology has concentrated upon the measurement of cryospheric parameters likely to be sensitive to climate change. These include the depth of the active layer, the temperature of permafrost, the extent and duration of seasonal snow cover, and the freeze-up and breakup of lakes and rivers. Also, research now emphasizes quantitative long-term field studies on the frequency and magnitude of certain cryogenic process which are controlled, to varying degrees, by climatic factors. There processes include thermal contraction cracking, thermokarst, active layer slope failures and solifluction.

17.2 Evidence from the present day

One of the problems in predicting global changes is that current trends and events may only be short-term fluctuations on a longer time scale around a stable mean. In addition, the data are variable in nature and quality, and highly dispersed. As a consequence, it is still difficult to generalize about global climate changes in the periglacial regions.

Figure 17.1 shows the annual average global surface air temperature since 1900 plotted against the 1950–79 average. These data indicate that temperatures have increased during the present century.

When one examines in detail, and on a regional basis, the data from which this graph is constructed, the complexity of the change becomes apparent. In northern Canada, for example, records at Norman Wells, NWT, give winter mean temperatures since 1944 that suggest a warming trend since 1966 (Fig. 17.2 (a)). Moreover, the data also demonstrate that the winters of 1988–86 and 1988–89 were the two warmest on record. There is also regional variability to consider. For example, summer records for the Mackenzie Valley during 1988 for Yellowknife and Inuvik, NWT (Fig. 17.2 (b)) suggest that while Inuvik experienced a warm summer, Yellowknife had a wet one. It is clear, therefore, that any evidence for climate change observed today must be evaluated very carefully.

17.2.1 Ground thermal regimes

A number of studies indicate that permafrost ground temperatures have been rising over the last 20–30 years. Whether they truly indicate global warming or whether they are just short-term fluctuations still remains to be determined.

In the European Arctic and subarctic of Russia, data from a number of permafrost monitoring stations indicate that, during the period 1970–90, there was a rise in the temperature of the permafrost at a depth of 3.0 m which, on average, amounted to 0.6–0.7 °C (Pavlov, 1994, table 2). Data from the Marre-Sale station in northeast Siberia also indicates that between 1980 and 1991 at a depth of 10 m, temperatures increased by 0.03 °C/year (Pavlov, 1994, table 3). Although these average values mask considerable regional and site variability, they appear to indicate a widespread warming of permafrost is underway. A similar trend is reported from the Qinghai-Xizang (Tibet) Plateau (Table 17.1). According to S. Wang (1993), temperatures at the 20 m depth have risen by 0.2–0.3 °C during the last two decades. At the same time, some permafrost bodies along the boundaries of the permafrost zone in Qinghai Province have thinned or disappeared and the lower altitudinal limit of permafrost in the Kunlun Shan and other adjacent mountains has risen. Since the Tibet Plateau is sparsely populated and human disturbances are minimal, this permafrost degradation is most likely caused by climatic amelioration. Recorded air temperatures at Wudaoliang indicate that the ten-year running means for 1971 and 1980

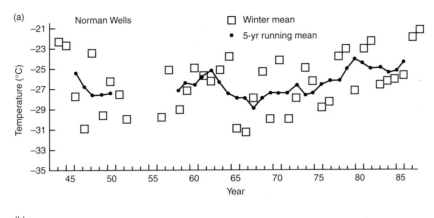

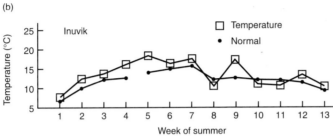

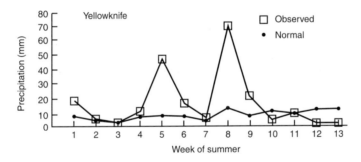

Figure 17.2 Regional variability of climate, Mackenzie Valley, NWT: (a) winter mean temperature, Norman Wells, NWT (1944–87) and five-year running means; (b) time series of temperature for Inuvik, NWT and of precipitation for Yellowknife, NWT, over 1988 summer (31 May–28 Aug.) (from Slaymaker and French, 1993).

are 0.5 and 0.7 °C warmer than those for 1961 and 1970, respectively (Wang, 1993).

In northern Canada, there is also evidence to support these trends. In Mayo Yukon, where the mean annual ground temperature at the depth of zero annual amplitude (10 m) is –1.3 °C, upward projection of the temperature gradient at depth suggests a former mean temperature at the surface of permafrost of approximately –2.0 °C (Burn, 1992). Geothermal modelling, assuming a previous equilib-

rium situation, suggests that a period of 20 years was required for the temperature change. According to Burn, increased snowfall and warmer winter temperatures probably caused the ground warming. However, the reverse trend is documented by Allard *et al.* (1995) following borehole measurements at various coastal sites in northern Québec. A cooling trend in the permafrost at the 20 m depth of approximately 0.05 °C/year has been monitored for the period 1988–93. This is related to thermohaline cir-

Table 17.1 Recent trends in ground thermal regimes, Qinghai-Xizang Plateau: (a) rise of mean annual ground temperature at Fenghuo Shan, 1962–89; (b) decrease in permafrost thickness along northern boundary of permafrost zone adjacent to the Qinghai-Xizang Highway

(a)

Year:	1962	1963	1967	1976	1979	1980	1984	1989
T (°C)	−3.5	−3.5	−3.5	−3.4	−3.3	−3.3	−3.3	−3.3

(b)

Year:	1974	1979	1985	1989
Average thickness (m):	15	14	12	10

Source: Wang (1993); from Wang and French (1994)

culation changes in the Arctic and North Atlantic oceans. Since the active layer thickness has not changed during the period of analysis, Allard *et al.* (1995) conclude that the climate cooling takes place principally through longer and colder winters. Until more data are available, over longer time periods, it is impossible to reconcile the apparently conflicting data from the eastern Arctic with interior Yukon.

17.2.2 Cryogenic processes

Climatic change will affect the magnitude and frequency of many of the geomorphic processes currently operating in periglacial environments. Evidence from thermal contraction cracking, thaw slumping and active layer detachments also suggest that some changes have occurred in historic time.

The frequency of thermal contraction cracking in the western Canadian Arctic, as measured by Mackay (1992, 1993a, 1993b) has been outlined earlier in Chapter 6. While cracking has been measured at Garry Island and Illisarvik, no cracking is recorded today from ice-wedge sites at Inuvik, some 100 km inland and where temperatures are several degrees warmer than on the Arctic coast. Anecdotal evidence is also provided by the sound of cracking (Mackay, 1993a). Older residents along the coast remember the audible sound of thermal contraction, as first reported by Leffingwell (1915) from northern Alaska. However, the sound of cracking is rarely reported from the mainland today and appears restricted to the more northerly islands such as Banks and Victoria, where winter temperatures are colder. Collectively, these observations support the conclusion that the climate of the western Canadian Arctic has warmed over the past 100 years and that

this is reflected in changes in the frequency of occurrence of thermal contraction cracking.

Two other processes which are likely to be immediately affected by climate warming are thaw slumping and active layer detachments. In the case of thaw slumps, the rate of ablation of the ice and the rate of headwall retreat is directly linked to energy imputs from the atmosphere (e.g. Lewkowicz, 1987, 1988). In the absence of long-term data, however, it is unclear whether present rates of ablation are significantly higher than those that occurred in the late nineteenth century. The same is true for active layer detachments which are triggered as the active layer deepens. Studies by Lewkowicz (1990, 1992b) on the Fosheim Peninsula of Ellesmere Island, demonstrate their frequent occurrence today, and also in the past. Whether the rate of current activity is greater or less than in the past, however, is open to debate, especially given the exceptionally hot summer of 1988 in the Canadian high Arctic (Edlund *et al.*, 1989).

17.3 Future responses

Following the IPCC Impact Assessment Report (Tegart *et al.*, 1990), we can summarize the potential changes which might occur within the periglacial environment under a number of headings.

17.3.1 Seasonal snow cover

The variability of periglacial climates makes it difficult to generalize. For example, if spring temperatures were to increase and early spring snowfall events became rain events, the duration of snow cover would decrease. If, however, the warming were to occur in regions of more severe periglacial climates where temperatures are projected to remain below or at freezing, the winters would become warmer but wetter. In this case, the snowpack would increase in depth and longevity. The latter scenario is probably the more appropriate for the majority of periglacial climates, especially those of the high Arctic and Continental type (see Chapter 3). Environments of deep seasonal frost and/or scattered or discontinuous permafrost may experience the former scenario.

Snow cover, through its influence on surface albedo, has an important impact upon the global climate system. Where climatic warming leads to decreased snow cover, a lowering of surface albedo will occur, resulting in increased warming (i.e. a positive feedback). In areas where climatic warming results in increased snow cover, surface albedo will increase, leading to a reduction in warming of the air and probably increased cloudiness. Finally, global warming may advance the melt season such that seasonal snow accumulations, which formerly provided late-season water sources required to maintain wetlands, may no longer exist. At the same time there may also be increased runoff from seasonal snowmelt.

All these considerations make the impact of global warming upon the seasonal snowcover complicated.

17.3.2 Glaciers, sea ice and sea level

Changes in the extent of the Greenland and Antarctic ice caps may lead to a world-wide sea-level increase of as much as 1.0 m. Of special concern to periglacial environments will be the coastal tundra lowlands of the western North American Arctic and the Siberian lowlands. A climate-induced rise in sea level will increase coastal erosion, flooding and inshore marine sedimentation. There are significant applied implications. In the Mackenzie Delta region, for example, Tuktoyaktuk and other coastal communities will experience repeated flooding. Elsewhere, industrial structures built at shoreline or offshore (e.g. drilling platforms and artificial islands for offshore oil or gas pipelines) will have to deal with changes in water depths, shoreline configurations, and sea ice conditions.

There is a strong possibility that the Arctic Ocean's ice cover, currently about 1.5 m thick on average and with a mean annual area of about $4\,000\,000$ km^2, will disappear. The change in net albedo, the increased source of atmospheric moisture from an ice-free ocean, and the consequent increase in cloudiness and precipitation will alter the environment of the high Arctic islands, many of which are technically deserts.

Since about 1840, when reliable observations on sea ice began in the northern hemisphere, its maximum extent has fluctuated by about 50 per cent. General experience suggests that rapid climatic warming would produce an almost instantaneous response of lighter sea-ice conditions in the marginal areas of the Arctic Ocean. Depending on storm patterns, cloudiness and precipitation, sea ice in the central Arctic Ocean might take a decade or more to respond; but warming of the amounts postulated would lead to instability and eventual disappearance of the ice.

These changes will have mixed economic implications. Reduction in thickness, extent and duration of sea ice in the southern Beaufort Sea would assist oil and gas exploration. Sea transportation routes along the Siberian coast, and northern Alaska, and in the Canadian high Arctic would also be open much longer. Iceberg generation, however, would be significantly expanded, interfering with marine transportation and, especially, any Canadian east coast offshore oil production.

17.3.3 Permafrost

Perhaps some of the most dramatic changes will be associated with permafrost (Smith, 1993). As explained in Chapter 5, an increase in ground temperature can lead to a decrease in permafrost thickness, and its elimination in certain instances. This will be accompanied by erosion, subsidence and extreme slope instability. A more general concern is that the thaw of permafrost will release methane, causing a positive feedback to enhance warming further.

Figure 17.3 illustrates the long-term effect of an air temperature rise upon the ground thermal regime at two sites representative of continuous and discontinuous permafrost. In the continuous permafrost, the active layer thickens and the thickness of permafrost decreases from both the top and bottom. In the discontinuous permafrost, the permafrost actually disappears. The increase in thickness of the active layer would take place at approximately the same time as the climate warmed; the change in permafrost thickness, however, may take hundreds to thousands of years. For example, Kane *et al.* (1991) have shown that a surface warming of 4 °C over 50 years in northern Alaska would result in an active layer

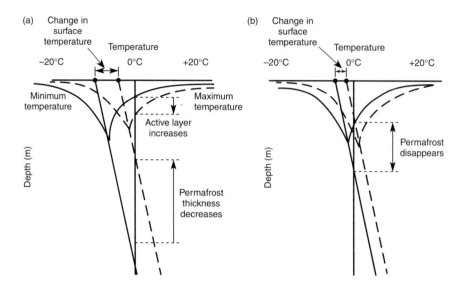

Figure 17.3 Equilibrium ground temperature profiles showing the long-term effect of a climatic warming of 4 °C in (a) continuous permafrost zone; (b) discontinuous permafrost zone.

increase in thickness of 0.50 to 0.93 m but permafrost temperatures at a depth of 30 m would have increased by only 1 °C. Lachenbruch *et al.* (1988) have also demonstrated that a 2 °C increase in the permafrost table temperature, which has occurred over the past 100 years in northern Alaska, has only penetrated to approximately 100 m to date.

Spatial changes in the extent of permafrost will be significant. Figures 17.4 and 17.5 provide some indications of the extent to which permafrost will ultimately degrade in Canada and Siberia, based upon warming scenarios of +4 °C and +2 °C respectively. In Siberia, studies predict that there will be a 10 per cent reduction in permafrost over a 50-year period. A similar scale of change is predicted for Canada. In all these scenarios, it must be emphasized that degradation will be gradual and restoration of a new ground thermal equilibrium may take several centuries.

Associated with these changes will be regional thermokarst activity. As described in Chapter 7, a complex range of interrelated processes will be involved, including subsidence, erosion, increased runoff and slope instability. As the active layer deepens, subsurface flow will increase in importance and with increased groundwater flow, more rainfall and less intense snowmelt, streamflow regimes will be altered.

17.3.4 Gas hydrates and methane

An important positive feedback associated with the degradation of permafrost relates to gas hydrates and the release of methane (CH_4) to the atmosphere.

Gas hydrates form where gas and water exist under high pressure and low temperature. These conditions exist within and beneath permafrost where solid crystals of gas hydrates can be found. Gas hydrates are a significant and important form of hydrocarbon. Large reserves occur in the Messoryakha gas field of western Siberia (Makogon *et al.*, 1972), in the Mackenzie Delta and Arctic islands (Judge, 1982), and on the Alaska North Slope (Collett, 1983). Since significant quantities of methane are trapped within gas hydrates, methane will be released to the atmosphere as permafrost degrades. This may lead to an additional 0.4 °C increase in global temperatures by 2020 and a 0.6–0.7 °C increase by 2050 (Street and Melnikov, 1990).

17.3.5 Seasonally frozen ground

Global warming will affect the areal distribution of seasonally frozen ground and the depth of frost penetration. Areas experiencing seasonal frost will be reduced in extent. For example, calculations based on

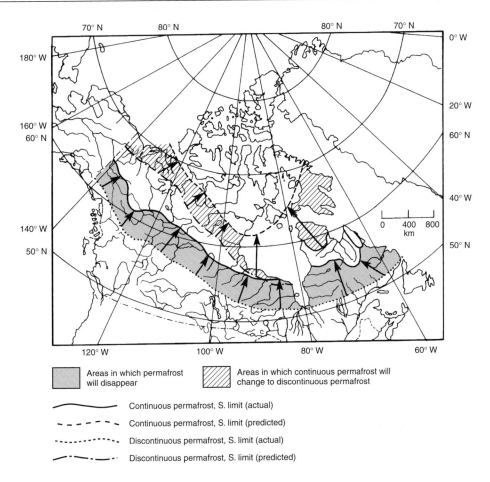

Figure 17.4 Predicted changes in permafrost in Canada as the result of a surface temperature increase of 4 °C (*source*: Atmospheric Environment Service, Canada).

degree days below 0 °C for Calgary and Toronto, two cities in Canada which experience seasonal frost, indicate that frost penetration will be reduced by 50–60 per cent and 75–85 per cent respectively as a result of an increase of 6 °C in the mean annual air temperature. Similar changes will occur in the northern United States, Sweden, northern Japan, Russian and China, and all areas where seasonal frost is widespread. It can be anticipated that frost damage to roads and structures will be reduced significantly.

17.3.6 Boreal forest, tundra and polar desert ecosystems

Higher temperatures in winter and changed precipitation patterns will significantly affect vegetation zonation and agricultural practices. In particular, the boreal forest and the northern treeline will move northward. For example, Fig. 17.6 (a) shows the possible shift in the position of the thermal boundaries of the forest for the Mackenzie valley lowlands, using the 600- and 1300-growing-degree-day isolines as approximations of the northern and southern boundaries of the boreal forest. While the shift in the northern boundary ranges from about 100 to 700 km, the shift in the southern boundary is much greater, about 250 to 900 km (Table 17.2). Such predictions are based on climate-change models assuming two-time CO_2 using data from the Goddard Institute for Space Studies (GISS) and data from the Geophysical Fluid Dynamics Laboratory (GFDL). One can question whether the rate of change of the forest will be a direct response to a

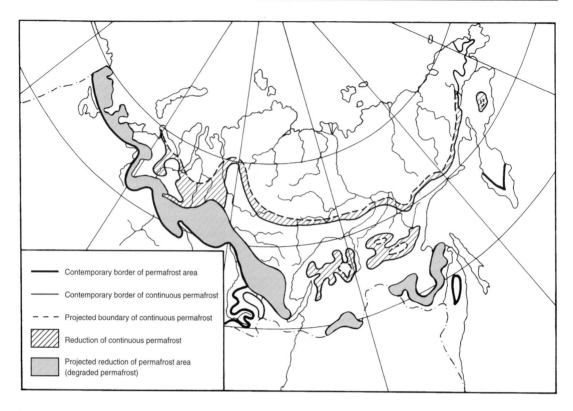

Figure 17.5 Predicted changes in permafrost distribution in Siberia as the result of a surface temperature increase of 2 °C (*source*: Anisimov, 1989; quoted in Street and Melnikov, 1990).

change in the thermal conditions and whether the growing-degree-day method is suitable for examining forest zone shifts, but such predictions highlight the major changes in vegetation, land use and agricultural practice which will follow warming in northern Canada. In the subarctic in particular, the potential for agriculture would increase in a warmer climate, with the growing season lengthening by 30–40 per cent. Growing conditions in Whitehorse and Yellowknife, for example, would become similar to those today in Edmonton and Calgary, approximately 1000 km to the south.

Similar scenarios are predicted for Scandinavia (Boer *et al.*, 1990) using the GISS model and a 3 °C mean annual temperature increase. One prediction indicates the northwards movement of oak trees, currently with a northern limit of 150 growing days (Fig. 17.6(b)) to a limit currently experiencing only 115 growing days. It is also predicted that the lower altitudinal limit of coniferous forest would rise by about 600 m and the boreal forest would disappear from all of Sweden except for elevations in excess of 1350 m a.s.l.

Limiting factors for viable plant communities in the polar deserts appear to be not severity of temperature but availability of nutrients and water. Climatic warming will thus influence arctic vegetation according to its effect on soil moisture and nutrients, especially nitrates. These vegetation changes are difficult to quantify at present, but we might expect a subtle but significant change in the distribution of tundra species, and their assemblages.

Closely linked to changes in vegetation zonation will be shifts in wildlife migratory patterns and aquatic and marine habitats. Settlements chosen for proximity to hunting or fishing grounds may no longer be well located for such activities. Warmer, wetter winters, for example, may decimate populations of caribou and muskoxen, since heavier snowfall will bury the tundra mosses and lichens on which these animals depend. In contrast, most marine life and migratory birds are expected to

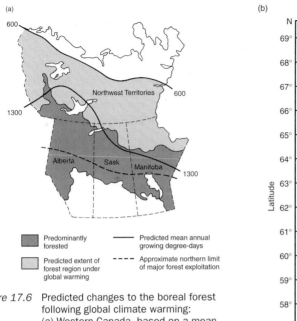

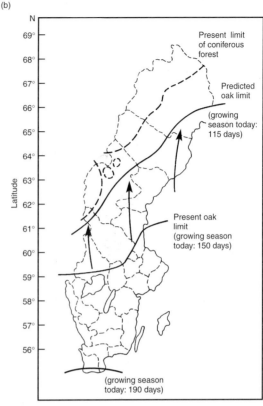

Figure 17.6 Predicted changes to the boreal forest following global climate warming:
(a) Western Canada, based on a mean annual growing degree days (above 5 °C). From Wheaton and Singh (1988);
(b) Sweden, based upon a 3° mean annual temperature increase showing northward movement of limit of oak, and the present limit of coniferous (boreal) forest, (from Boer *et al.*, (1990).

Table 17.2 Predicted changes in vegetation zonation for western and northwestern Canada, as implied by GISS and GFDL-based climate change models

(a) Northward shift (km) in northern and southern boundaries of boreal forest
(Delimited by 600- and 1300-growing-degree-day isolines)

	Climatic-change model	
Forest boundary	GISS	GFDL
Northern	80–720	100–730
Southern	470–920	250–900

(b) Changes in vegetation zonation according to GFDL-based model for three locations

Location	Present Zonation	GFDL Zonation
64°4'N, 120°W (southern NWT between Great Bear and Great Slave Lake)	Subarctic	Aspen parkland
59°9'N, 120°W (northeastern BC/northwestern Alta)	Boreal	Aspen parkland
55°5'N, 105°W (northern Sask)	Boreal	Boreal temperate

Source: from Wheaton and Singh (1988)

flourish while warmer temperatures would increase fish populations in rivers, lakes and the ocean. Native settlements which depends on hunting and fur trapping and coastal communities which exploit marine resources may all experience change as wildlife and mammal migratory patterns evolve.

Further reading

Boer, M.M. and E.A. Koster (eds) (1992) Greenhouse-impact on cold-climate ecosystems and landscape. *Catena Supplement*, **22**, 151 pp.

Boer, M.M., E.A. Koster and H. Lundberg (1990). Greenhouse impact in Fennoscandia – preliminary findings of a European workshop on the effects of climatic change. *Ambio*, **19**, 2–10.

Houghton, J.T., B.A. Callander and S.K. Varney (eds) (1992) *Climate Change 1992. The Supplementary Report to the IPCC Scientific Assessment*. Cambridge: Cambridge University Press. 199 pp.

Koster, E.A. (1993) Global warming and periglacial landscapes. In N. Roberts (ed.), *The changing global environment*. Oxford: Basil Blackwell, pp. 127–149.

Koster, E.A. (ed.) (1993) Permafrost and climate change. Special Issue. *Permafrost and Periglacial Processes*, **4**, 95–174.

Street, R.B. and P.I. Melnikov (1990) Seasonal snow cover, ice and permafrost. In W.J. McG. Tegart, G.W. Sheldon and D.C. Griffiths (eds), *Climate Change. The IPCC Impacts Assessment*. Canberra: Australian Government Publishing Service, pp. 7.1–7.33.

Vandenberghe, J. and J. Schwan (eds) (1993) Periglacial environments in relation to climatic change. Special Issue. *Geologie en Mijnbouw*, **72**, 101–235.

Vinson, T.S. and D.W. Hayley (eds) (1990) Global warming and climatic change. *Journal of Cold Regions Engineering*, **4**, 73.

Discussion topics

1. Why are periglacial environments particularly sensitive to predicted global changes?
2. What is the relationship between climate change and permafrost?

References

Academia Sinïca (1975) *Permafrost*. Lanzhou, China: Research Institute of Glaciology, Cryopedology and Desert Research. (National Research Council of Canada Ottawa, Technical Translation No. 2006, 1981, 224 pp.)

ACGR (Associate Committee on Geotechnical Research) (1988) *Glossary of permafrost and related ground ice terms*. Permafrost Subcommittee, National Research Council of Canada, Technical Memorandum 142, 156 pp.

Akagawa, S. and M. Fukuda (1991) Frost heave mechanism in welded tuff. *Permafrost and Periglacial Processes*, **2**, 301–309.

Akerman, J. (1993) Solifluction and creep rates 1972–1991, Kapp Liné, West Spitbergen. In: B. Frenzel, J. A. Matthews and B. Glaser (eds), *Solifluction and climatic variation in the Holocene*. Stuttgart: Gustav Fischer Verlag, pp. 225–250.

Akerman, J. and B. Malmstrom (1986) Permafrost mounds in the Abisko Area, Northern Sweden. *Geografiska Annaler*, **68A**, 155–165.

Aleshinskaya, Z. V., L. G. Bondarev and A. P. Gorbunov, (1972) Periglacial phenomena and some palaeo-geographical problems of Central Tien-Shan. *Biuletyn Peryglacjalny*, **21**, 5–14.

Alexandre, J. (1958) Le modèle quaternaire de l'ardennes Centrale. *Annales, Société Géologique de Belgique*, **81**, 213–331.

Allard, M., B. Wang and J. A. Pilon (1995) Recent cooling along the southern shore of Hudson Strait, Québec, Canada, documented from permafrost temperature measurements. *Arctic and Alpine Research*, **27**, 157–166.

Andersson, J. G. (1906) Solifluction; a component of subaerial denudation. *Journal of Geology*, **14**, 91–112.

André, M.-F. (1993) *Les versants du Spitsberg*. Nancy: Presses Universitaires de Nancy, 361 pp.

Andrews, J. T. (1961) The development of scree slopes in the English Lake District and Central Québec-Labrador. *Cahiers de Géographie de Québec*, **10**, 210–230.

Anisimov, O. A. (1989) Changing climate and permafrost distribution in the Soviet Arctic. *Physical Geography*, **10**, 282–293.

Anisimova, N. P., N. M. Nikitina, V. M. Piguzova and V. V. Shepelyev (1973) *Water sources of Central Yakutia*. Guidebook, Second International Conference on Permafrost, Yakutsk, USSR, 47 pp.

Anketell, J. M., J. Cegla and S. Dzulynski (1970) On the deformational structures in systems with reversed density gradients. *Rocznik Polskiego Towarzystwa Geologicznego*, **40**, 1–30.

Are, F. (1972) The reworking of shores in the permafrost zone. In: W. P. Adams and F. Helleiner (eds), *International geography*, Vol. 1. Toronto: University of Toronto Press, pp. 78–79.

Arnborg, L., H. J. Walker and J. Peippo (1967) Suspended load in the Colville River, Alaska. *Geografiska Annaler*, **49A**, 131–144.

Astakhov, V. I. (1992) The last glaciation in West Siberia. *Sveriges Geologiska Undersökning*, **81**, 21–30.

Astakhov, V.I. and L.L. Isayeva (1988) The 'Ice Hill': an example of 'retarded deglaciation' in Siberia. *Quaternary Science Reviews*, **7**, 29–40.

Avery, B.W. (1964) *The soils and landuse of the district around Aylesbury and Hemel Hempstead*. Memoirs, Soil Survey of Great Britain. London: HMSO.

Babb, T.A. and L. C. Bliss (1974) Effects of physical disturbance on Arctic vegetation in the Queen Elizabeth Islands. *Journal of Applied Ecology*, **II**, 549–562.

Baker, T. H. W. and L. E. Goodrich (1990) Heat pump chilled foundations for buildings on permafrost. *Geotechnical News*, **8**(3), 26–28.

Baker, V. R. (1983) Late Pleistocene fluvial systems. In: S. C. Porter (ed.), *Late Quaternary environments of the United States*, Volume 1. Minneapolis: University of Minnesota Press, pp. 115–128.

Balescu, S., Ch. Dupuis and Y. Quinif (1988) TL stratigraphy of pre-Weichselian loess from NW Europe using feldspar coarse grains. *Quaternary Science Review*, **7**, 309–313.

Balkwill, H. R., K. J. Roy, W. S. Hopkins and W. V. Sliter (1974) Glacial features and pingos, Amund Ringnes Island, Arctic Archipelago. *Canadian Journal of Earth Sciences*, **11**, 1319–1325.

Ballantyne, C.K. and C. Harris (1994) *The periglaciation of Great Britain*. Cambridge: Cambridge University Press, 330 pp.

Ballantyne, C. K. and G. Whittington (1987) Niveo–aeolian sand deposits on An Teallach, Wester Ross, Scotland. *Transactions of the Royal Society of Edinburgh*, **78**, 51–63.

Baranov, I. Y. (1959) Geographical distribution of seasonally frozen ground and permafrost. In: *General geocryology*. Moscow, USSR: V. A. Obruchev Institute of Permafrost Studies, Academy of Science, Part 1, Ch. 7, pp. 193–219. (National Research Council of Canada Technical Translation No. 1121, 1964.)

Barnett, D. M., S. A. Edlund and L. A. Dredge (1977) *Terrain characterization and evaluation from Eastern Melville Island*. Geological Survey of Canada, Paper 76–23, 18 pp.

Barr, W. (1976) Retreating coasts and disappearing islands in the Arctic. *Musk-Ox*, **18**, 103–111.

Barsch, D (1977) Eine Abschätzung von Schuttproduktion und Schuttransport im Bereich aktiver Blockgletscher der Schweizer Alpen. *Zeitschrift für Geomorphologie*, **28**, 148–160.

Barsch, D. (1978) Active rock glaciers as indicators of discontinuous permafrost. An example from the Swiss Alps. In: *Proceedings, 3rd International Conference on Permafrost*, Vol. 1. Ottawa: National Research Council, pp. 349–352.

Barsch, D. (1988) Rockglaciers. In: M. J. Clark (ed.), *Advances in periglacial geomorphology*, Chichester: J. Wiley and Sons Ltd., pp. 69–90.

Barsch, D. (1992) Permafrost creep and rockglaciers. *Permafrost and Periglacial Processes*, **3**, 175–188.

Barsch, D. (1993) Periglacial geomorphology in the 21st century. *Geomorphology*, **7**, 141–163.

Beck, N. (1989) Periglacial glacis (pediment) generation at the western margin of the Rhine Hessian Plateau. In: F. Ahnert (ed.), *Landforms and landform evolution in West Germany*, Catena Supplement No. 15, pp. 189–197.

Benedict, J. B. (1970) Downslope soil movement in a Colorado alpine region; rates, processes and climatic significance. *Arctic and Alpine Research*, **2**, 165–226.

Bennett, L. P. and H. M. French (1988) Observations on near-surface creep in permafrost, Eastern Melville Island, Arctic Canada. In: *Proceedings, 5th International Conference on Permafrost*, Vol. 2. Trondheim: Tapir Publishers, pp. 683–688.

Bennett, L. P. and H. M. French (1990) *In situ* permafrost creep, Melville Island, and implications for global change. In: *Proceedings, Fifth Canadian Permafrost Conference*, Québec City, Nordicana No. 54, pp. 119–123.

Berg, T. E. (1969) Fossil sand wedges at Edmonton, Alberta, Canada. *Biuletyn Peryglacjalny*, **19**, 325–333.

Beschel, R. L. (1966) Hummocks and their vegetation in the high Arctic. In: *Proceedings, 1st International Conference on Permafrost*. Ottawa: National Academy of Science – National Research Council of Canada, Publication 1287, 13–20.

Bik, M. J. J. (1969) The origin and age of the prairie mounds of southern Alberta. *Biuletyn Peryglacjalny*, **19**, 85–130.

Bird, J. B. (1967) *The physiography of Arctic Canada*. Baltimore: The Johns Hopkins Press, 336 pp.

Billings, W. D. (1987) Carbon balance of Alaskan tundra and taiga ecosystems: past, present and future. *Quaternary Science Reviews*, **6**, 165–177.

Billings, W. D. and K. M. Peterson (1980) Vegetational change and ice-wedge polygons through the thaw-lake cycle in Arctic Alaska. *Arctic and Alpine Research*, **12**, 413–432.

Black, R. F. (1952) Growth of ice wedge polygons in permafrost near Barrow, Alaska. *Bulletin, Geological Society of America*, **63**, 1235–1236.

Black, R. F. (1964) *Periglacial phenomena of Wisconsin, north central United States*. Report of INQUA Congress, Warsaw, 1961, Vol. IV, Lodz, pp. 21–28.

Black, R. F. (1969) Thaw depressions and thaw lakes; a review. *Biuletyn Peryglacjalny*, **19**, 131–150.

Black, R. F. (1973) Growth of patterned ground in Victoria Land, Antarctica. In: *Permafrost; North American Contribution, Second International Permafrost Conference, Yakutsk, USSR*. Washington, DC: National Academy of Science, Publication 2115, pp. 193–203.

Black, R. F. (1974) Ice-wedge polygons of northern Alaska. In: D. R. Coates (ed.), *Glacial geomorphology*, Publications in Geomorphology. Binghampton: State University of New York, Binghampton, pp. 247–275.

Black, R. F. and W. L. Barksdale (1949) Oriented lakes of northern Alaska. *Journal of Geology*, **57**, 105–118.

Boardman, J. (1978) Grèzes litées near Keswick, Cumbria. *Biuletyn Peryglacjalny*, **27**, 23–34.

Boch, S. G. and I. I. Krasnov (1943) O nagornykh terraskh i drevnikh poverkhnostyakh vyravnivaniya na Urale i svyazannykh s nimi problemakh. *Vsesoyuznogo Geograficheskogo obshchestva, Izvestiya*, **75**, 14–25. (English translation by A. Gladunova, 1994, On altiplanation terraces and ancient surfaces of levelling in the Urals and associated problems. In: D. J. A. Evans (ed.), *Cold climate landforms*. Chichester: J. Wiley and Sons Ltd, pp. 177–186).

Boelhouwers, J. (1991) Periglacial evidence from the Western Cape Mountains, South Africa: a progress report. *Permafrost and Periglacial Processes*, **2**, 13–20.

Boer, M.M., E. A. Koster and H. Lundberg (1990) Greenhouse impact in Fennoscandia – preliminary findings of a European Workshop on the effects of climatic change. *Ambio*, **19**(1), 2–10.

Borns, H. W. (1965) Late glacial ice-wedge casts in northern Nova Scotia. *Science*, **148**, 1223–1225.

Boulton, G. S. (1970) On the origin and transport of englacial debris in Svalbard glaciers. *Journal of Glaciology*, **9**, 213–229.

Bozhinskiy, A. N. and V. N. Konishchev (1982) *On the possible formation mechanism of inclined ice wedges in the Yedoma sequence of North Yakutia*. USSR Academy of Sciences, Section of Glaciology and Soviet Geophysical Committee and Institute of Geography, Data of Glaciological Studies, Publication 43, pp. 139–142 (in Russian).

Brakenridge, G. R. (1981) Late Quaternary floodplain sedimentation along the Pomme de Terre River, southern Missouri. *Quaternary Research*, **15**, 62–76.

Braun, D. D. (1989) Glacial and periglacial erosion of the Appalachians. *Geomorphology*, **2**, 233–256.

Brink, V. C., J. R. Mackay, S. Freyman and D. C. Pearce (1967) Needle ice and seedling establishment in southwestern British Columbia. *Canadian Journal of Plant Science*, **47**, 135–139.

Britton, M. E. (1967) Vegetation of the Arctic tundra. In: H. P. Hansen (ed.), *Arctic biology*. Corvallis: Oregon State University Press, pp. 67–130.

Brook, G. A. and D. C. Ford (1978). The nature of labyrinth karst and its implications of climaspecific models of tower karst. *Nature*, **280**, 383–385.

Brook, G. A. and D. C. Ford (1982) Hydrologic and geologic controls of carbonate water chemistry in the sub-Arctic Nahanni karst, Canada. *Earth Surface Processes and Landforms*, **7**, 1–16.

Brooks, I. A. (1971) Fossil ice-wedge casts in western Newfoundland. *Maritime Sediments*, **7**, 118–122.

Brown, E. H. (1969) Jointing, aspect and the orientation of scarp-face dry valleys, near Ivinghoe, Buckinghamshire. *Transactions, Institute of British Geographers*, **48**, 61–73.

Brown, J., W. Rickard and D. Vietor (1969) *The effect of disturbance on permafrost terrain*. US Army CRREL, Special Report 138, 13 pp.

Brown, R. J. E. (1960) The distribution of permafrost and its relation to air temperature in Canada and the USSR. *Arctic*, **13**, 163–177.

Brown, R. J. E. (1966) The relation between mean annual air and ground temperatures in the permafrost regions of Canada. In: *Proceedings, 1st International Conference on Permafrost*. Ottawa: National Academy of Science, National Research Council of Canada, Publication 1287, pp. 241–246.

Brown, R. J. E. (1967a) *Permafrost in Canada*. Map 1246a, Geological Survey of Canada, National Research Council of Canada, Ottawa.

Brown, R. J. E. (1967b) Comparison of permafrost conditions in Canada and the USSR. *Polar Record*, **13**, 741–751.

Brown, R. J. E. (1970) *Permafrost in Canada; its influence on northern development*. Toronto: University of Toronto Press, 234 pp.

Brown, R. J. E. (1972) Permafrost in the Canadian Arctic Archipelago. *Zeitschrift für Geomorphologie, Supplement 13*, 102–130.

Brown, R. J. E. (1973a) Influence of climate and terrain factors on ground temperatures at three locations in the permafrost region of Canada. In: *Permafrost; North American Contribution, Second International Permafrost Conference, Yakutsk, USSR*. Washington, DC: National Academy of Science, Publication 2115, pp. 27–34.

Brown, R. J. E. (1973b) Permafrost distribution and relation to environmental factors in the Hudson Bay lowlands. In: *Proceedings; Symposium on the Physical Environment of the Hudson Bay Lowland*. University of Guelph publication, pp. 35–68. (Research Paper No. 576, Division of Building Research, National Research Council of Canada, Ottawa.)

Brown, R. J. E. (1974) Ground ice as an initiator of landforms in permafrost regions. In: B. D. Fahey and R. D. Thompson (eds), *Research in polar and alpine geomorphology. Proceedings, 3rd Guelph Symposium on Geomorphology, 1973*. Norwich: GeoAbstract, pp. 25–42.

Brown, R. J. E. (1978) Influence of climate and terrain on ground temperature in the continuous permafrost zone of northern Manitoba and Keewatin District, Canada. In: *Proceedings, 3rd International Conference on Permafrost*, Vol. 1, Ottawa: National Research Council of Canada, pp. 15–21.

Brown, R. J. E. and T. L. Péwé (1973) Distribution of permafrost in North America and its relationship to the environment; a review 1963–1973. In: *Permafrost; North American Contribution, Second International Permafrost Conference, Yakutsk, USSR*. Washington, DC: National Academy of Science, Publication 2115, pp. 71–100.

Brown, R. J. E. and G. P. Williams (1972) *The freezing of peatlands*. Division of Building Research, Technical Paper 381. Ottawa: National Research Council of Canada, 24 pp.

Brunschweiller, D. (1962) The periglacial realm in North America during the Wisconsin glaciation. *Biuletyn Peryglacjalny*, **11**, 15–27.

Bryant, I. D. (1983) The utilization of arctic river analogue studies in the interpretation of periglacial river sediments from southern Britain. In: K. J. Gregory (ed.), *Background to paleohydrology*, Chichester: J. Wiley and Sons Ltd, pp. 413–431.

Büdel, J. (1944) Die morphologischen Wirkungen des Eiszeitklimas im geltscherfreien Gebiet. *Geologische Rundschau*, **34**, 482–519.

Büdel, J. (1951) Die klimazonen des Eiszeitalters. *Eiszeitalter und Gegenwart*, **1**, 16–26. (English translation: *International Geology Review*, **1**(9), 72–79, 1959.)

Büdel, J. (1953) Die 'periglazial' morphologischen Wirkungen des Eiszeitklimas auf der Ganzen Erde. *Erdkunde*, **7**, 249–266.

Büdel, J. (1960) *Die Frostschott-zone Südorst Spitzbergen*. Bonn: Colloquium Geographica, 6, 105 pp.

Büdel, J. (1963) Klimatische geomorphologie. *Geographische Rundschau*, **15**, 269–285.

Büdel, J. (1970) Pedimente, rumpfflächen und rückland Steihänge; deren aktive und passive ruckverlegung in verschiedenen klimaten. *Zeitschrift für Geomorphologie*, **14**, 1–57.

Büdel, J. (1982) *Climatic geomorphology*. Princeton, New Jersey: Princeton University Press, 443 pp. (translated by Lenore Fischer and Detlef Busche).

Bull, A. J. (1940) Cold conditions and landforms in the South Downs. *Proceedings, Geologist's Association*, **51**, 63–71.

Burbidge, G., H. M. French and B. R. Rust (1988) Water escape fissures resembling ice-wedge casts in Late Quaternary subaqueous outwash near St Lazare, Quebec, Canada. *Boreas*, **17**, 33–40.

Burgess, M. (1985) Permafrost: Large sale research at Calgary and Caen. *Geos*, **1985** (2), 19–22.

Burgess, M. and D. G. Harry (1990) Norman Wells pipeline permafrost and terrain monitoring; geothermal and geomorphic observations. *Canadian Geotechnical Journal*, **27**, 233–244.

Burn, C. R. (1988) The development of near-surface ground ice during the Holocene at sites near Mayo, Yukon Territory, Canada. *Journal of Quaternary Science*, **3**, 31–38.

Burn, C. R. (1989) Frost heave of subaqueous lake-bottom sediments, Mackenzie Delta, Northwest Territories. Geological Survey of Canada, Paper 89-1D, pp. 85–93.

Burn, C. R. (1990) Implications for palaeoenvironmental reconstruction of recent ice-wedge development at Mayo, Yukon Territory. *Permafrost and Periglacial Processes*, **1**, pp. 3–14.

Burn, C. R. (1992) Recent ground warming inferred from the temperature in permafrost near Mayo, Yukon Territory. In: *Periglacial geomorphology*. J. C. Dixon and A. D. Abrahams (eds), Chichester: John Wiley and Sons Ltd, pp. 327–350.

Burn, C. R. and F. A. Michel (1988) Evidence for recent temperature-induced water migration into permafrost from the tritium content of ground ice near Mayo, Yukon Territory, Canada. *Canadian Journal of Earth Sciences*, **25**, 909–915.

Burn, C. R. and M. W. Smith (1988) Thermokarst lakes at Mayo, Yukon Territory, Canada. In: *Proceedings, 5th International Conference on Permafrost*, Vol. 1. Trondheim: Tapir Publishers, pp. 700–705.

Burn, C. R., F. A. Michel and M. W. Smith (1986) Stratigraphic, isoptopic, and mineralogical evidence for an early Holocene thaw unconformity at Mayo, Yukon Territory. *Canadian Journal of Earth Sciences*, **23**, 794–803.

Burt, T. P and P. J. Williams (1976) Hydraulic conductivity in frozen soils. *Earth Surface Processes*, **1**, 349–360.

Butrym, J., J. Cegla, S. Dzulynski and S. Nakonieczny (1964) New interpretation of 'periglacial structures'. *Folia quaternaria*, **17**, 34 pp.

Cailleux, A. (1942) *Les actions eoliennes périglaciaires en Europe*. Memoire 46, Société Géologique de France, 176 pp.

Cailleux, A. (1956) Mares, mardelles et pingos. *Comptes Rendus, Académie des Sciences, Paris*, **242**, 1912–1914.

Cailleux, A. (1957) Les mares du sud-est de Sjaelland (Danemark). *Comptes Rendus, Académie des Sciences, Paris*, **245**, 1074–1076.

Cailleux, A. (1974) Formes précoces et albédos du nivéo-éolien. *Zeitschrift für Geomorphologie*, **18**, 437–459.

Cailleux, A. (1978) Niveo-eolian deposits. In: R. W. Fairbridge and S. Bourgeois (eds), *Encyclopedia of earth sciences, The Encyclopedia of Sedimentology*, Vol. 6, New York: Reinhold Book Corp., pp. 501–503.

Cailleux, A. and P. Calkin (1963) Orientation of hollows in cavernously weathered boulders in Antarctica. *Biuletyn Peryglacjalny*, **12**, 147–150.

Cailleux, A. and G. Taylor (1954) *Cryopédologie, études des sols gelés*. Paris: Expéditions Polaires Françaises, Hermann & Cie, 218 pp.

Caine, T. N. (1963) Movement of low angle scree slopes in the Lake District, northern England. *Revue de Géomorphologie Dynamique*, **14**, 171–177.

Caine, T. N. (1967) The tors of Ben Lomond, Tasmania. *Zeitschrift für Geomorphologie*, **11**, 418–429.

Calkin, P. and A. Cailleux (1962) A quantitative study of cavernous weathering (taffoni) and its application to glacial chronology in Victoria Valley, Antarctica. *Zeitschrift für Geomorphologie*, **6**, 317–324.

Capps, S. R. (1919) The Kantishna Region, Alaska. *United States Geological Survey, Bulletin*, **687**, 7–112.

Carey, K. L. (1970) *Icing occurrence, control and prevention, an annotated bibliography*. US Army Corps of Engineers, Cold Regions Research and Engineering Laboratory Special Report, 151 pp.

Carlson, L. E., J. R. Ellwood, J. F. Nixon and W. A. Slusarchuk (1982) Field test results of operating a chilled buried pipeline in unfrozen ground. In: H. M. French (ed.) *Proceedings, Fourth Canadian Permafrost Conference*. Ottawa: National Research Council of Canada, pp. 475–480.

Carson, C. E. and K. M. Hussey (1962) The oriented lakes of Arctic Alaska. *Journal of Geology*, **70**, 417–439.

Carson, C. E. and K. M. Hussey (1963) The oriented lakes of Arctic Alaska; a reply. *Journal of Geology*, **71**, 532–533.

Carson, M.A. and M. J. Kirkby (1972) *Hillslope form and process*. Cambridge: Cambridge University Press, 475 pp.

Carter, L. D. (1981) A Pleistocene sand sea on the Alaskan Arctic Coastal Plain. *Science*, **211**, 381–383.

Carton, A., F. Dramis and C. Smiraglia (1988) A first approach to the systematic study of the rock glaciers in the Italian Alps. In: *Proceedings, 5th International Conference on Permafrost*, Vol. 1. Trondheim: Tapir Publishers, pp. 712–717.

Castleden, R. (1977) Periglacial pediments in central and southern England. *Catena*, **4**, 11–21.

Chambers, M. J. G. (1966) Investigations of patterned ground at Signy Island, South Orkney Islands. II: Temperature regimes in the active layer. *Bulletin, British Antarctic Survey*, **10**, 71–83.

Chambers, M. J. G. (1967) Investigations of patterned ground at Signy Island, South Orkney Islands. III: Miniature patterns, frost heaving and general conclusions. *Bulletin, British Antarctic Survey*, **12**, 1–22.

Chandler, R. J. (1970a) The degradation of Lias Clay slopes in an area of the East Midlands. *Quarterly Journal of Engineering Geology*, **2**, 161–181.

Chandler, R. J. (1970b) A shallow slab slide in the Lias Clay near Uppingham, Rutland. *Géotechnique*, **20**, 253–260.

Chandler, R. J. (1972) Periglacial mudslides in Vestspitsbergen and their bearing on the origin of fossil 'solifluction' shears in low angled clay slopes. *Quarterly Journal of Engineering Geology*, **5**, 223–241.

Chandler, R. J., G. A. Kellaway, A. W. Skempton and R. J. Wyatt (1976) Valley slope sections in Jurassic strata near Bath, Somerset. *Philosophical Transactions of the Royal Society*, London, **A283**, 527–555.

Chatwin, S. C. and N. W. Rutter (1978) Upper Mackenzie River Valley. *Field Trip No. 2, 3rd International Conference on Permafrost, Edmonton, Alberta*, 53 pp.

Cheng, G. (1983) The mechanism of repeated-segregation for the formation of thick layered ground ice. *Cold Regions Science and Technology*, **8**, 57–66.

Cheng, G. and F. Dramis (1992) Distribution of mountain permafrost and climate. *Permafrost and Periglacial Processes*, **3**, 83–91.

Chueca, J. (1992) A statistical analysis of the spatial distribution of rock glaciers, Spanish Central Pyrenees. *Permafrost and Periglacial Processes*, **3**, 261–265.

Church, M. (1972) *Baffin Island sandurs; a study of Arctic fluvial processes*. Geological Survey of Canada, Bulletin 216, 208 pp.

Church, M. (1974) Hydrology and permafrost with reference to northern North America. In: *Permafrost Hydrology; Proceedings of Workshop Seminar*. Canadian National Committee, International Hydrological Decade, Environment Canada, Ottawa, pp. 7–20.

Church, M. and J. M. Ryder (1972) Paraglacial sedimentation: a consideration of fluvial processes conditioned by glaciation. *Bulletin, Geological Society of America*, **83**, 3059–3072.

Ciry, R. (1962) Le role du froid dans la speleogenese. *Spelunca Memoires*, **2**(4), 29–34.

Clark, G. M. and E. J. Ciolkosz (1988) Periglacial geomorphology of the Appalachian Highlands and Interior Highlands south of the glacial border – a review. *Geomorphology*, **10**, 475–477.

Clark, M. J. (1988) Periglacial hydrology. In: M. J. Clark (ed.), *Advances in periglacial geomorphology*. Chichester: John Wiley & Sons Ltd, pp. 415–462.

Clark, M.J., H. M. French and D. G. Harry (1984) Reconnaisance techniques for the estimation of Arctic coastal sediment budget and process. In: M. W. Clark (ed.), *Coastal research: UK perspectives*. Norwich: Geobooks, pp. 1–14.

Collett, T. S. (1983) Detection and evaluation of natural gas hydrates from well logs, Prudhoe Bay, Alaska. In: *Proceedings, 4th International Conference on Permafrost*. Washington, DC: National Academy Press, pp. 169–174.

Cook, F. A. (1967) Fluvial processes in the high Arctic. *Geographical Bulletin*, **9**, 262–268.

Cook F. A. and Raiche, V. G. (1962). Freeze–thaw cycles at Resolute, N.W.T. *Geographical Bulletin*, **18**, 64–78.

Corte, A. E. (1966) Particle sorting by repeated freezing and thawing. *Biuletyn Peryglacjalny*, **15**, 175–240.

Corte, A. E. (1971) Laboratory formation of extrusion features by multicyclic freeze–thaw in soils. In: *Étude des phénomènes périglaciaires en laboratoire*. Colloque International de Géomorphologie, Liège-Caen, 1971, Centre de Géomorphologie à Caen, Bulletin No. 13–14–15, pp. 117–131.

Corte, A. E. (1978) Rock glaciers as permafrost bodies with a debris cover on an active layer. A hydrological approach in the Andes of Mendoza, Argentina. In: *Proceedings, 3rd International Conference on Permafrost*. Vol. 1. Ottawa: National Research Council of Canada, pp. 263–269.

Corte, A. E. (1988) Geocryology of the Central Andes and rock glaciers. In *Proceedings, 5th International Conference on Permafrost*. Vol. 1. Trondheim: Tapir Publishers, pp. 718–723.

Coxon, P. (1986) A radiocarbon dated early post glacial pollen diagram from a pingo remnant near Millstreet, County Cork. *Irish Journal of Earth Sciences*, **8**, 9–20.

Crory, F. E. (1988) Airfields in arctic Alaska. In: *Proceedings, 5th International Conference on Permafrost*. Vol. 3. Trondheim: Tapir Publishers, pp. 49–55.

Cui, Zhijiu (1983). An investigaton of rock glaciers in the Kunlun Shan, China. In: *Proceedings, Permafrost, 4th International Conference on Permafrost*. Washington DC: National Academy Press, pp. 208–211.

Currey, D. R. (1964) A preliminary study of valley asymmetry in the Ogotoruk Creek area, Northwest Alaska. *Arctic*, **17**, 85–98.

Czeppe, Z. (1964) Exfoliation in a periglacial climate. *Geographia Polonica*, **2**, 5–10.

Czudek, T. (1964) Periglacial slope development in the area of the Bohemian Massif in Northern Moravia. *Biuletyn Peryglacjalny*, **14**, 169–194.

Czudek, T. (1985) Zum problem der talkryopedimente. *Acta Scientiarum Naturalium, Academiae Scientiarum Bohemoslovacae, Brno*, **19**(2), 1–47.

Czudek, T. and J. Demek (1970) Thermokarst in Siberia and its influence on the development of lowland relief. *Quaternary Research*, **1**, 103–120.

Czudek, T. and J. Demek (1973) The valley cryopediments in Eastern Siberia. *Biuletyn Peryglacjalny*, **22**, 117–130.

Dahl, R. (1966) Blockfields and other weathering forms in the Narvik Mountains. *Geografiska Annaler*, **48A**, 224–227.

Dallimore, S. R. and S. A. Wolfe (1988) Massive ground ice associated with glaciofluvial sediments, Richards Island, N.W.T., Canada. In: *Proceedings, 5th International*

Conference on Permafrost. Vol. 1. Trondheim: Tapir Publishers, pp. 132–137.

Danilova, N. S. (1956) Soil wedges and their origin. In: *Data on the principles of the study of the frozen zones in the Earth's crust*, Issue 111. Moscow, V. A. Obruchev Institute of Permafrost Studies, Academy Science. (National Research Council of Canada, Technical Translation No. 1088, Ottawa, 1964, pp. 90–99.)

Datsko, P. S. and V. V. Rogov (1988) Transformation of dispersed deposits under cycles of freezing-thawing. In: *Microstructure of frozen ground*. Moscow: Moscow University Press, pp. 132–149 (in Russian).

Dawson, A. G. (1980) Shore erosion by frost: an example from the Scottish Lateglacial. In: J. J. Lowe, J. M. Gray and J. E. Robinson (eds). *Studies in the Lateglacial of north-west Europe*. Oxford: Pergamon, pp. 45–53.

Dawson, A. G. (1986) Quaternary shore platforms and sea-levels in southern Britain: a speculative hypothesis. In: W. Ritchie, J. C. Stone and A. S. Mather (eds), *Essays for Professor R. E. H. Mellor*. Aberdeen: University of Aberdeen, pp. 377–382.

De Gans, W. (1988) Pingo scars and their identification. In: M. J. Clark (ed.), *Advances in periglacial geomorphology*. Chichester: John Wiley and Sons Ltd, pp. 299–322.

De Gans, W. and H. Sohl (1981) Weichselian pingo remnants and permafrost on the Drente plateau (The Netherlands). *Geologie en Mijnbouw*, **60**, 447–452.

De Groot, Th., P. Cleveringa and B. Klijnstra (1987) Frost-mound scars and the evolution of a Late Dryas environment (northern Netherlands). *Geologie en Mijnbouw*, **66**, 239–250.

De La Beche, H. T. (1839) *Report on the Geology of Cornwall, Devon, and West Somerset*. Memoirs, Geological Survey, United Kingdom.

Demek, J. (1964) Castle koppies and tors in the Bohemian Highland (Czechoslovakia). *Biuletyn Peryglacjalny*, **14**, 195–216.

Demek J. (1969a) Cryoplanation terraces, their geographical distribution, genesis and development. *Ceskoslovenski Akademie Ved Rozpravy, Rad Mathematickych A Prirodnich Ved*, Issue 79, 4, 80 pp.

Demek, J. (1969b) Cryogene processes and the development of cryoplanation terraces. *Biuletyn Peryglacjalny*, **18**, 115–125.

Demek, J. (1972a) Die pedimentation im subnivalen Bereich. *Göttingen Geographische Abhandlungen*, **60**, 145–154.

Demek, J. (1972b) *Manual of detailed geomorphological mapping*. Prague: Publishing House of the Czechoslovak Academy of Sciences.

Demek, J. (1978) Periglacial geomorphology. In: C. Embleton, D. Brunsden, and D. R. C. Jones (eds.), *Geomorphology, present problems and future prospects*, Oxford: Oxford University Press, Oxford, pp. 139–155.

Denny, C. S. (1936) Periglacial phenomena in southern Connecticut. *American Journal of Science*, **32**, 322–342.

Derbyshire, E. (1972) Tors, rock weathering, and climate in southern Victoria Land, Antarctica. In: *Polar geomorphology*, Institute for British Geographers Special Publication No. 4, pp. 93–105.

Derbyshire, E. (1973) Periglacial phenomena in Tasmania. *Biuletyn Peryglacjalny*, **22**, 131–148.

Derbyshire, E., M. A. Love and J. E. Martin (1985) Fabrics of probable segregated ground-ice origin in some sediment Cores form the North Sea Basin. In: J. Boardman (ed.), *Soils and Quaternary landscape evolution*. Chichester: John Wiley and Sons Ltd, pp. 261–280.

DeWolf, Y. (1988) Stratified slope deposits. In: M. J. Clark (ed.), *Advances in periglacial geomorphology*. Chichester: John Wiley and Sons Ltd, pp. 91–110.

Dijkmans, J. W. A. and E. A. Koster (1990) Morphological development of dunes in a subarctic environment, Central Kobuk Valley, Northwestern Alaska. *Geografiska Annaler*, **72A**, 93–109.

Dijkmans, J. W. A., E. A. Koster, J. P. Galloway and W. G. Mook (1986) Characteristics and origin of calcretes in a subarctic environment, Great Kobuk Sand Dunes, Northwestern Alaska, USA. *Arctic and Alpine Research*, **18**, 377–387.

Dines, H. G., S. E. Hollingworth, W. Edwards, S. Buchan and F. B. A. Welch (1940) The mapping of head deposits. *Geological Magazine*, **77**, 198–226.

Dingman, S. L. and F. R. Koutz (1974) Relations among vegetation, permafrost and potential insolation in central Alaska. *Arctic and Alpine Research*, **6**, 37–42.

Dionne, J.-C. (1971) Fente de cryoturbation Tardiglaciaire dans la région de Québec. *Revue de Géographie de Montréal*, **25**, 245–264.

Dionne, J. C. (1972) Caractéristiques des blocs erratiques des rives de l'estuaire du Saint-Laurent. *Revue de Géographie de Montréal*, **XXVI**, 125–152.

Dixon, J. C., C. E. Thorn and R. G. Darmody (1984) Chemical weathering processes on the Vantage Peak nunatak, Juneau Icefield, southern Alaska. *Physical Geography*, **5**, 111–131.

Dostovalov, B. N. and V. A. Kudryavtsev (1967) *Obszceje mierzlotowiedienije* (General Permafrost Science). Moscow: Moscow State University (in Russian).

Dostovalov, B. N. and A. I. Popov (1966) Polygonal systems of ice wedges and conditions of their development. In: *Proceedings, 1st International Conference on Permafrost*. Ottawa: National Academy Science, National Research Council of Canada, Publication 1287, pp. 102–105.

Douglas, G.R., W. Whalley and J. P. McGreevy (1991) Rock properties as controls on free-face debris fall activity. *Permafrost and Periglacial Processes*, **2**, 311–319.

Dramis, F. and A. Kotarba (1992) Southern limit of relict rock glaciers, Central Apennines, Italy. *Permafrost and Periglacial Processes*, **3**, 257–260.

Dredge, L. A. (1992) Breakup of limestone bedrock by frost shattering and chemical weathering, eastern Canadian Arctic. *Arctic and Alpine Research*, **24**, 314–323.

Dresch, J. (1982) *Géographie des régions arides*. Paris: Presses Universitaires du France, 277 pp.

Dubikov, G.I. (1982) Origin of tabular ice in permafrost in Western Siberia. In: A. I. Popov (ed.), *Tabular ice in the cryolithozone*. Yakutsk: Permafrost Institute, pp. 24–42.

Dunbar, M. and K. R. Greenaway (1956) *Arctic Canada from the air*. Ottawa: Queen's Printer, 541 pp.

Dury, G. H. (1959) *The face of the Earth*. London: Penguin Books, 226 pp.

Dyke, A. S. (1976) Tors and associated weathering phenomena, Somerset Island, District of Franklin. Geological Survey of Canada, Paper 76–1B, pp. 209–216.

Dyke, A. S. (1978) Qualitative rates of frost heaving in gneissic bedrock on Southeastern Baffin Island, District of Franklin. Geological Survey of Canada, Paper 78–1A, pp. 501–502.

Dyke, A. S. and S. C. Zoltai (1980) Radiocarbon-dated mudboils, Central Canadian Arctic. Geological Survey of Canada, Paper 80–1B, pp. 271–275.

Dyke, L. S. (1984) Frost heaving of bedrock in permafrost regions. *Bulletin Association of Engineering Geologists*, **XXXI** (4), 389–405.

Dylik, J. (1953) Periglacial investigations in Poland. *Bulletin, Société des Sciences et des Lettres de Lódz*, **4**, 1–16.

Dylik, J. (1956) Coup d'oeil sur la Pologne périglaciaire. *Biuletyn Peryglacjalny*, **4**, 195–238. (English translation by A. Guilcher, 1992: A general view of periglacial Poland. In: D. J. A. Evans (ed.) *Cold climate landforms*. Chichester: J. Wiley and Sons Ltd, pp. 45–81, 1994.)

Dylik, J. (1957) Tentative comparison of planation surfaces occurring under warm and under cold semi-arid conditions. *Biuletyn Peryglacjalny*, **5**, 175–186.

Dylik, J. (1960) Rhythmically stratified slope waste deposits. *Biuletyn Peryglacjalny*, **8**, 31–41.

Dylik, J. (1963) Periglacial sediments of the Sw. Malgorzata hill in the Warsaw–Berlin pradolina. *Bulletin, Société des Sciences et des Lettres de Lódz*, **14**, 1–16.

Dylik, J. (1964a) Eléments essentiels de la notion de 'périglaciaire'. *Biuletyn Peryglacjalny*, **14**, 111–132.

Dylik, J. (1964b) Le thermokarst, phénomène négligé dans les études du Pleistocene. *Annales de Géographie*, **73**, 513–523.

Dylik, J. (1966) Problems of ice wedge structure and frost fissure polygons. *Biuletyn Peryglacjalny*, **15**, 241–291.

Dylik, J. (1968) Thermokarst. In: R. W. Fairbridge (ed.), *Encyclopedia of geomorphology*. New York: Reinhold Book Co., pp. 1149–1151.

Dylik, J. (1969a) Slope development under periglacial conditions in the Lódz region. *Biuletyn Peryglacjalny*, **18**, 381–410.

Dylik, J. (1969b) Slope development affected by frost fissures and thermal erosion. In: T. L. Péwé (ed.), *The periglacial environment*. Montreal: McGill-Queen's University Press, Montreal, pp. 365–386.

Dylik, J. (1971) L'érosion thermique actuelle at ses traces figées dans le paysage de la Pologne Centrale. *Bulletin de l'Académie Polonaise des Science, Série des Sciences de la Terre*, **xix**, 55–61.

Dylik, J. (1972) Rôle du ruisellement dans le modèle périglaciaire. In: J. Hoverman and G. Oberback (eds), *Sonderdrück aus Heft 60 der Hans-Poser-festschrift*. Göttingen: Geographische Abhandlungen, Vol. 60, pp. 169–180.

Dylikowa, A. (1961) Structures de pression congélistatique et structures de gonflement par le gel de Katarzynów près de Lódz. *Bulletin de la Société des Sciences et des Lettres de Lódz*, **12**, 1–23.

Edelman, C. H. and G. C. Maarleveld (1949) De asymmetrische dalen va de Veluwe. *Tijdschrift Koninklijk Nederland Aardrijkskundig Genootschap*, **66**, 143–146.

Edelman, C. H., F. Florschütz and J. Jeswiet (1936) *Über spätpleistozäne und frühholozäne kryoturbate Ablagerungen in den östlichen Niederlanden*. Verhandelingen: Geologisch-Mijnbouwkundig Genootschap voor Nederland en Kolonien, Geologisch Series 11, pp. 301–360.

Eden, M. J. and C. P. Green (1971) Some aspects of granite weathering and tor formation on Dartmoor, England. *Geografiska Annaler*, **53A**, 92–99.

Edlund, S. A., B. T. Alt and K. Young (1989) Interaction of climate, vegetation, and soil hydrology at Hot Weather Creek, Fosheim Peninsula, Ellesmere Island, Northwest Territories. Geological Survey of Canda, Paper 89-1D, pp. 125–133.

Egginton, P. A. (1986) Active layer processes. In: H. M. French (ed.), *Focus: Permafrost geomorphology, The Canadian Geographer*, **30**, 364–365.

Egginton, P. A. and L. S. Dyke (1982) Density gradients and injection structures in mudboils in central District of Keewatin. Geological Survey of Canada, Paper 82-1B, pp. 173–176.

Egginton, P. A. and H. M. French (1985) Solifluction and related processes, eastern Banks Island, N.W.T. *Canadian Journal of Earth Sciences*, **22**, 1671–1678.

Egginton, P. A. and W. W. Shilts (1978) Rates of movement associated with mudboils, central District of Keewatin. Geological Survey of Canada, Paper 78-1B, pp. 203–206.

Eissmann, L. (1978) Mollisoldiapirismus. *Zeitschrift Für Angewandte Geologie*, **24**, 3, 130–138.

Eissmann, L. (1994) Grundzüge der Quartärgeologie Mitteldeutschlands (Sachsen, Sachsen-Anhalt, Südbrandengurg, Thüringen). *Altenburger Naturwissenschaftliche Forschungen*, **7**, 55–135.

Ershov, E. D. (1979) *Moisture transfer and cryogenic textures in fine grained soils*. Moscow: Moscow University Publication, 214 pp. (in Russian).

Ershov, E. D. (1984) Transformation of dispersed deposits under repeated freezing–thawing. *Engineering Geology*, **3**, 59–66 (in Russian).

Ershov, E. D., V. G. Cheverev, Yu P. Lebedenko and L. V. Shevchenko (1980) Water migration, formation of texture and ice segregation in freezing and thawing clayey soils. In: *Proceedings, Third International Conference on*

Permafrost, Part 1: English translations of twenty-six of the Soviet papers. Ottawa: National Research Council of Canada, Publication 18119, pp. 159–175.

Evans, J. G. (1968) Periglacial deposits on the Chalk of Wiltshire. *Wiltshire Archaeological and Natural History Magazine*, **63**, 12–26.

Everett, K. R. (1965) Slope movement and related phenomena. In: N. J. Wilimovsky (ed.,) *The Environment of the Cape Thompson Region, Alaska*. United States Atomic Energy Commission, PNE–481, pp. 175–220.

Everett, K. R. (1967) Mass-wasting in the Taseriaq area, West Greenland. *Meddelelser om Gronland*, **165**, pp. 1–32.

Everett, K. R. (1981) Landforms. In: D. A. Walker, K. R. Everett, P. J. Webber and J. Brown (eds), *Geobotanical atlas of the Prudhoe Bay Region, Alaska*. Hanover, New Hampshire: US Army CRREL.

Fahey, B. D. (1973) An analysis of diurnal freeze–thaw and frost heave cycles in the Indian Peaks region of the Colorado Front Range. *Arctic and Alpine Research*, **5**, 269–281.

Fahey, B. D. (1974) Seasonal frost heave and frost penetration measurements in the Indian Peaks region of the Colorado Front Range. *Arctic and Alpine Research*, **6**, 63–70.

Fahey, B. D. (1981) Origin and age of upland schist tors in Central Otago, New Zealand. *New Zealand Journal of Geology and Geophysics*, **24**, 399–413.

Fahey, B. D. (1985) Salt weathering as a mechanism of rock breakup in cold climates: an experimental approach. *Zeitschrift für Geomorphologie*, **29**, 99–111.

Fahnestock, R.K. (1963) *Morphology and hydrology of a glacial stream – White River, Mt Rainier, Washington*. United States Geological Survey, Professional Paper, 422-A, 70 pp.

Faucher, D. (1931) Note sur la dissymetrie des vallons de l'Armagnal. *Bulletin Societe H. N. Toulouse*, **61**, pp. 262–268.

Fernald, A.T. (1964) Surficial Geology of the Central Kobuk River Valley, Northwestern Alaska. *US Geological Survey Bulletin*, **1181–K**, 1–31.

Ferrians, O. J. (1965) *Permafrost map of Alaska*. United States Geological Survey, Miscellaneous Map, I-445.

Ferrians, O. J., R. Kachadoorian and G. W. Green (1969) *Permafrost and related engineering problems in Alaska*. United States Geological Survey, Professional Paper 678, 37 pp.

Flemal, R. C. (1976) Pingos and pingo scars: their characteristics, distribution, and utility in reconstructing former permafrost environments. *Quaternary Research*, **6**, 37–53.

Flemal, R.C., K. C. Hinkley and J. L. Hesler (1973) The Dekalb Mounds; a possible Pleistocene (Woodfordian) pingo field in north central Illinois. *Geological Society of America, Memoir*, **136**, 229–250.

Ford, D. C. (1984) Karst groundwater activity and landform genesis in modern permafrost regions of Canada. In: R. G. LaFleur (ed.), *Groundwater as a geomorphic agent*. London: Allen and Unwin Ltd, pp. 340–350.

Ford, D. (1987) Effects of glaciations and permafrost upon the development of karst in Canada. *Earth Surface Processes and Landforms*, **12**, 507–521.

Francou, B. (1988) Eboulis stratifiés dans les Hautes Andes Centrales du Pérou. *Zeitschrift für Geomorphologie*, **32**, 47–76.

Francou, B. (1990) Stratification mechanisms in slope deposits in high subquatorial mountains. *Permafrost and Periglacial Processes*, **1**, 249–263.

Fraser, J. K. (1959) Freeze–thaw frequencies and mechanical weathering in Canada. *Arctic*, **12**, 40–53.

Freidman, J. D., C. E. Johansson, N. Oskarsson, H. S. Svensson, S. Thorarinsson and R. S. Williams (1971) Observations on Icelandic polygon surfaces and palsa areas. *Geografiska Annaler*, **53A**, 115–145.

French, H. M. (1970) Soil temperatures in the active layer, Beaufort Plain. *Arctic*, **23**, 229–239.

French, H. M. (1971a) Ice cored mounds and patterned ground, southern Banks Island, western Canadian Arctic. *Geografiska Annaler*, **53A**, 32–38.

French, H. M. (1971b) Slope asymmetry of the Beaufort Plain, northwest Banks Island, N.W.T. Canada. *Canadian Journal of Earth Sciences*, **8**, 717–731.

French, H. M. (1972a) Asymmetrical slope development in the Chiltern Hills. *Biuletyn Peryglacjalny*, **21**, 51–73.

French, H. M. (1972b) Proglacial drainage of northwest Banks Island, District of Franklin, N.W.T. *Muskox*, **10**, 26–31.

French, H. M. (1973) Cryopediments on the Chalk of Southern England. *Biuletyn Peryglacjalny*, **22**, 149–156.

French, H. M. (1974a) Mass-wasting at Sachs Harbour, Banks Island, N.W.T., Canada. *Arctic and Alpine Research*, **6**, 71–78.

French, H. M. (1974b) Active thermokarst processes, eastern Banks Island, western Canadian Arctic. *Canadian Journal of Earth Sciences*, **11**, 785–794.

French, H. M. (1975a) Man-induced thermokarst, Sachs Harbour airstrip, Banks Island, NWT. *Canadian Journal of Earth Sciences*, **12**, 132–144.

French, H. M. (1975b) Pingo investigations and terrain disturbance studies, Banks Island, District of Franklin. Geological Survey of Canada, Paper 75-1, pp. 459–464.

French, H. M. (1976a) *The periglacial environment*. London and New York: Longman, 308 pp.

French, H. M. (1976b) Geomorphological processes and terrain disturbance studies, Banks Island, District of Franklin. Geological Survey of Canada, Paper 76-1, pp. 289–292.

French, H. M. (1978) Terrain and environmental problems of Canadian Arctic oil and gas exploration. *Muskox*, **21**, 11–17.

French, H. M. (1986) Periglacial involutions and mass displacement structures, Banks Island, Canada. *Geografiska Annaler*, **68 A** (3), 167–174.

French, H. M. (1987a) Periglacial geomorphology in North America: current research and future trends. *Progress in Physical Geography*, **11**, 569–587.

French, H. M. (1987b) Periglacial processes and landforms in the Western Canadian Arctic. In: J. Boardman (ed.), *Periglacial processes and landforms in Britain and Ireland*. Cambridge: Cambridge University Press, pp. 27–43.

French, H. M. (1987c) Permafrost and ground ice. In: K. J. Gregory and D. E. Walling (eds), *Human activity and environmental processes*. Chichester: J. Wiley and Sons Ltd, pp. 237–269.

French, H. M. (1988) The active layer. In: M. J. Clark (ed.), *Advances in periglacial geomorphology*. Chichester: J. Wiley and Sons Ltd, pp. 151–177.

French, H. M. and P. Egginton (1973) Thermokarst development, Banks Island, western Canadian Arctic. In: *Permafrost: North American Contribution, Second International Permafrost Conference, Yakutsk, USSR*. Washington, DC: National Academy of Science, Publication 2115, pp. 203–212.

French, H. M. and J. Gozdzik (1988) Pleistocene epigenetic and syngenetic frost fissures, Belchatow, Poland. *Canadian Journal of Earth Sciences*, **25**, 2017–2027.

French, H. M. and D. G. Harry (1983) Ground ice conditions and thaw lakes, Sachs River Lowlands, Banks Island, Canada. In: H. Poser and E. Schunke (eds) *Mesoformen des Reliefs im heutigen Periglazialraum*. Abhandlungen der Akademie der Wissenschaften in Gottingen, Math.-Phys. Klasse, No. 35, pp. 70–81.

French, H. M. and D. G. Harry (1988) Nature and origin of ground ice, Sandhills Moraine, southwest Banks Island, western Canadian Arctic. *Journal of Quaternary Science*, **3**, 19–30.

French, H. M. and D. G. Harry (1990) Observations on buried glacier ice and massive segregated ice, western Arctic coast, Canada. *Permafrost and Periglacial Processes*, **1**, 31–43.

French, H. M. and D. G. Harry (1992) Pediments and cold-climate conditions, Barn Mountains, unglaciated northern Yukon, Canada. *Geografiska Annaler*, **74 A**, 145–157.

French, H. M. and W. H. Pollard (1986) Ground-ice investigations, Klondike District, Yukon Territory. *Canadian Journal of Earth Sciences*, **23**, 550–560.

French, H. M. and O. Slaymaker (1993) Canada's cold landmass. In: H. M. French and O. Slaymaker (eds.), *Canada's cold environments*. Montreal: McGill-Queen's Press, pp. 3–27.

French, H. M., D. G. Harry and M. J. Clark (1982) Ground ice stratigraphy and late Quaternary events, southwest Banks Island, western Canadian Arctic. In: H.M. French (ed.), *Proceedings, 4th Canadian Permafrost Conference, Calgary, Alberta*. Ottawa: National Research Council of Canada, pp. 81–90.

French, H.M, S. A. Harris and R. O. van Everdingen (1983) The Klondike and Dawson. In: H. M. French and J. A. Heginbottom (eds), *Northern Yukon Territory and Mackenzie Delta, Canada. Guidebook to permafrost and related features*. 4th International Conference on Permafrost, Guidebook 3, Division of Geological and Geophysical Surveys, Fairbanks, Alaska, pp. 35–63.

Fristrup, B. (1952/53) Wind erosion within the Arctic deserts. *Geografisk Tidsskrift*, **52**, 51–56.

Fujino, K., K. Horiguchi, M. Shinbori and K. Kato (1983) Analysis and characteristics of cores from a massive ice body in Mackenzie Delta, N.W.T., Canada. In: *Proceedings, 4th International Conference on Permafrost*. Washington DC: National Academy Press, pp. 316–321.

Fujino, K., S. Sato, K. Matsuda *et al.* (1988) Characteristics of the massive ground ice body in the western Canadian Arctic. In: *Proceedings, 5th International Conference on Permafrost*. Vol. 1. Trondheim: Tapir Publishers, pp. 143–147.

Fukuda, M. (1983) The pore water pressure in porous rocks during freezing. In: *Proceedings 4th International Conference on Permafrost*. Washington, DC: National Academy Press, pp. 322–327.

Fulton, R. J. (ed.) (1989) *Quaternary geology of Canada and Greenland*, Geology of Canada No. 1. Ottawa: Geological Survey of Canada, 839 pp.

Furrer, G., F. Bachmann and P. Fitze (1971) Erdströme als Formelemente von Soliflukhousdecken im Raum Munt Chevagi/Munt Buffalora. *Ergebnisse der Wissenschaftern Untersuchungen im Schwizerischen Nationalpark*, **11**, 188–269.

Gamper, M. (1983) Controls and rates of movement of solifluction lobes in the Eastern Swiss Alps. In: *Proceedings, 4th International Conference on Permafrost*, Vol. 1. Washington, DC: National Academy Press, pp. 328–333.

Gerard, R. (1990) *Hydrology of floating ice*. National Hydrology Research Institute Science Report No. 1, pp. 103–134.

Gerasimov, I. P. and K. K. Markov (1968) *Permafrost and ancient glaciation*. Ottawa: Defence Research Board, Translation T499R, pp. 11–19.

Geukens, F. (1947) De asymmetrie der droge dalen van Haspengouw. *Natuurw. Tijdschr.*, No. 29, 13–18.

Gibbard, P. L. (1988) The history of the great northwest European rivers during the past three million years. *Philosophical Transactions, Royal Society of London*, **B318**, 559–602.

Gilichinsky, D. and S. Wagener (1995) Microbial life in permafrost: A historical review. *Permafrost and periglacial Processes*, **6**, 243–250.

Gleason, K. J., W. B. Krantz, N. Caine, J. H. George and R. D. Gunn (1986) Geometrical aspects of sorted patterned ground in recurrently frozen soil. *Science*, **232**, 216–220.

Gloriad, A. and J. Tricart (1952) Etude statistique des vallées asymmétriques de la feuille St. Pol, au 1:50,000. *Revue de Géomorphologie Dynamique*, **3**, 88–98.

Gold, L. W. and A. Lachenbruch (1973) Thermal conditions in permafrost – a review of North American literature. In: *Permafrost, North American Contribution, Second International Conference, Yakutsk, USSR*. Washington, DC: National Academy of Sciences, Publication 2115, pp. 3–26.

Gold, L. W., G. H. Johnston, W. A. Slusarchuk and L. E. Goodrich (1972) Thermal effects in permafrost. In: *Proceedings, Canadian Northern Pipeline Conference, Ottawa*, Associate Committee on Geotechnical Research, National Research Council of Canada, Technical Memorandum, 104, pp. 25–45.

Good, T. R. and I. D. Bryant (1985) Fluvio-aeolian sedimentation – an example from Banks Island, N.W.T., Canada. *Geografiska Annaler*, **67**, 33–46.

Goodrich, L. E. (1982) The influence of snow cover on the ground thermal regime. *Canadian Geotechnical Journal*, **19**, 421–432.

Goodrich, L. E. and J. C. Plunkett (1990) Performance of heat pump chilled foundations. In: *Proceedings, 4th Canadian Permafrost Conference*, Université Laval, Nordicana No. 54, 409–418.

Gorbunov, A. P. (1988) The alpine permafrost zone of the USSR. In: *Proceedings, 5th International Conference on Permafrost*. Vol. 1. Trondheim: Tapir Publishers, pp. 154–158.

Goudie, A. (1974) Further experimental investigation of rock weathering by salt and other mechanical processes. *Zeitschrift für Geomorphologie, Supplementband*, **21**, 1–12.

Goudie, A. (1995) *The changing earth, rates of geomorphological processes*. Oxford: Blackwell Publishers.

Gozdzik, J. (1973) Origin and stratigraphic position of periglacial structures in Middle Poland. *Acta Geographica Lodziensia*, **31**, 104–117.

Granberg, H. B. (1973) Indirect mapping of the snowcover for permafrost prediction at Schefferville, Quebec. In: *Permafrost; North American Contribution, Second International Permafrost Conference, Yakutsk, USSR*. Washington, DC: National Academy of Science. Publication 2115, pp. 113–120.

Grave, N. A. and I. A. Nekrasov (1961) Some observations of thermokarst in the vicinity of the settlement of Anadyr. *Problemy Severa*, **94**, 157–164.

Gravis, G. F. (1969) Fossil slope deposits in the northern Arctic asymmetrical valleys. *Biuletyn Peryglacjalny*, **20**, 239–257.

Gray, J. T. (1973) Geomorphic effects of avalanches and rock falls on steep mountain slopes in the central Yukon territory. In: B. D. Fahey and R. D. Thompson (eds), *Research in polar and alpine geomorphology*, Proceedings, Third Guelph Symposium on Geomorphology. Norwich: Geo Abstracts Ltd, pp. 107–117.

Grechishchev, S. W. (1970) *Basis of method for predicting thermal stresses and deformations in frozen soils* (in Russian). Ministerstvo Geologii SSSR, Vsesoyuznyi Nauchno-Issledovatel'skii Institut Gidrogeologii I Inzhenernoi Geologii (VSEGINGEO), Moscow. (English Translation, 1976, National Research Council Canada, Technical Translation 1986.)

Grechishchev, S. E., A. V. Pavlo and V. V. Ponomarev (1992) Changes in microstructure of fine-grained soils due to freezing. *Permafrost and Periglacial Processes*, **3**, 1–10.

Green, C. P., D. H. Keen, D. F. M. McGregor, J. E. Robinson and R. B. G. Williams (1983) Stratigraphy and environmental significance of Pleistocene deposits at Fisherton, near Salisbury, Wiltshire. *Proceedings, Geologist's Association*, **94**, 17–22.

Gregory, K. J. and D. E. Walling (1973) *Drainage basin form and process, a geomorphological approach*. London: Edward Arnold (Publishers) Ltd, 458 pp.

Grimberbieux, J. (1955) Origine et asymmétrie des vallees sèches de Hesbaye. *Annales, Société Géologique de Belgique*, **78**, 267–286.

Grosso, S. A. and A. E. Corte (1989) Pleistocene ice-wedge casts at 34°S, eastern Andes piedmont, south-west of South America. *Geografiska Annaler*, **71A**, 125–136.

Grosso, S. A. and A. E. Corte (1991) Cryoplanation surfaces in the Central Andes at latitude 35°S. *Permafrost and Periglacial Processes*, **2**, 49–58.

Guillien, Y. (1951) Les grèzes litées de Charente. *Revue Geographique de Pyrénées et de Sud-Ouest*, **22**, 154–162.

Gullentops, F. and E. Paulissen (1978) The drop soil of the Eisden type. *Biuletyn Peryglacjalny*, **27**, 105–115.

Guo, D., Y. Huang, S. Xu and L. Zhang (1982) Taliks in the Buqu river valley area, northern slope of Tangual Mountain (in Chinese). In: *Proceedings, First Chinese Conference on Glaciology and Geocryology*. Beijing: China Science Press, pp. 11–18.

Hack, J. T. and J. C. Goodlett (1960) *Geomorphology and forest ecology of a mountain region in the Central Appalachians*. United States Geological Survey Professional Paper 347, 65 pp.

Haeberli, W. (1973) Die Basis Temperatur der winterlichen Schneedecke als möglicher Indikator für die Verbreitung von Permafrost in den Alpen. *Zeitschrift für Gletschologie und Glazialgeologie*, **9**, 221–227.

Haeberli, W. (1978) Special aspects of high mountain permafrost methology and zonation in the Alps. In: *Proceedings, 3rd International Conference on Permafrost*, Vol. 1. Ottawa: Publication 18119, National Research Council, pp. 379–384.

Haeberli, W. (1985) *Creep of mountain permafrost; internal structure and flow of alpine rock glaciers*. Mittgeilugen der Versuchsanstalt fur Wassenbau Hydrologie and Glaziologie, No. 77, 142 pp.

Haeberli, W., G. Cheng, A. P. Gorbunov and S. A. Harris (1993) Mountain permafrost and climatic change. *Permafrost and Periglacial Processes*, **4**, 165–174.

Haesaerts, P. (1983) Stratigraphic distribution of periglacial features indicative of permafrost in the Upper Pleistocene loesses of Belgium. In: *Proceedings, 4th International Conference on Permafrost*. Vol. 1. Washington, DC: National Academy Press, pp. 421–426.

Haesaerts, P. and B. Van Vliet-Lanoë (1981) Phénomènes périglaciaires observés à Maisières-Canal, à Harmignies et à Rocourt (Belgique). *Biuletyn Peryglacjalny*, **28**, 291–324.

Hall, K. (1990) Mechanical weathering rates on Signy Island, Maritime Antarctic. *Permafrost and Periglacial Processes*, **1**, 61–67.

Hall, K. and A. Hall (1991) Thermal gradients and rock weathering at low temperatures: some simulation data. *Permafrost and Periglacial Processes*, **2**, 103–112.

Hall, K. and W. Otte (1990) A note on biological weathering on nunataks of the Juneau Icefield, Alaska. *Permafrost and Periglacial Processes*, **1**, 189–196.

Hall, K. J., A. Verbeek and I. A. Meiklejohn (1986) The extraction and analysis of solutes from rock samples with some comments on the implications for weathering studies: an example from Signy Island, Antartica. *British Antarctic Survey Bulletin*, **70**, 79–84.

Hallet, B. (1990) Self-organisation in freezing soils: from microscopic ice lenses to patterned ground. *Canadian Journal of Physics*, **68**, 842–852.

Hallet, B. and S. Prestrud (1986). Dynamics of periglacial sorted circles in Western Spitzbergen. *Quaternary Research*, **26**, 81–99.

Hallet, B., S. P. Anderson, C. W. Stubbs and E. C. Gregory (1988) Surface soil displacements in sorted circles, Western Spitzbergen. In: *Proceedings, Fifth International Conference on Permafrost*, Vol. 1. Trondheim: Tapir Publishers, pp. 770–775.

Hallet, B., J. S. Walder and C. W. Stubbs (1991) Weathering by segregation ice growth in microcracks at sustained subzero temperatures: verification from an experimental study using acoustic emissions. *Permafrost and Periglacial Processes*, **2**, 283–300.

Hamilton, T. D. and M. O. Curtis (1982) Pingos in the Brooks Range, Northern Alaska, U.S.A. *Arctic and Alpine Research*, **14**, 13–20.

Hamilton, T. D., J. P. Galloway and E. A. Koster (1988) Late Wisconsin eolian activity and related alluviation, central Kobuk River Valley. In: J. P. Galloway and T. D. Hamilton (eds), *Geologic studies in Alaska by the U.S. Geological Survey during 1987*. US Geological Survey Circular, 1016, pp. 39–43.

Harris, C. (1972) Processes of soil movement in turf-banked solifluction lobes, Okstindan, northern Norway. In: *Polar Geomorphology*. Institute of British Geographers Special Publication, No. 4, pp. 155–174.

Harris, C. (1977) Engineering properties, groundwater conditions, and the nature of soil movement on a solifluction slope in North Norway. *Quaternary Journal of Engineering Geology*, **10**, 27–43.

Harris, C. (1981) *Periglacial mass-wasting: a review of research*. BGRG Research Monograph 4. Norwich: Geo Abstracts, 204 pp.

Harris, C. (1985) Geomorphological applications of soil micromorphology with particular reference to periglacial sediments and processes. In: K. S. Richards, R. R. Arnett and S. Ellis (eds), *Geomorphology and soils*. London: Allen and Unwin, pp. 219–232.

Harris, C. (1987) Mechanisms of mass movement in periglacial environments. In: M. G. Anderson and K. S. Richards (eds.), *Slope stability*. Chichester: John Wiley and Sons Ltd, pp. 531–559.

Harris, C. and M. D. Wright (1980) Some last glaciation drift deposits near Pontypridd, South Wales. *Geological Journal*, **15**, 7–20.

Harris, S. A. (1979) Ice caves and permafrost zones in southwest Alberta. *Erdkunde*, **33**, 61–70.

Harris, S. A. (1983) Cold air drainage west of Fort Nelson, British Columbia. *Arctic*, **35**, 539–541.

Harris, S. A. (1988) The alpine periglacial zone. In: M. J. Clark (ed.), *Advances in periglacial geomorphology*. Chichester: J. Wiley and Sons Ltd, pp. 369–413.

Harris, S. A. and R. J. E. Brown (1978) Plateau Mountain: a case study of alpine permafrost in the Canadian Rocky Mountains. In: *Proceedings, Third International Conference on Permafrost*, Vol. 1. Ottawa: National Research Council of Canada, Publication 18119, pp. 385–391.

Harris, S. A. and R. J. E. Brown (1982) Permafrost distribution along the Rocky Mountains in Alberta. In: H.M. French (ed.), *Proceedings, Fourth Canadian Permafrost Conference*, Calgary. Ottawa: National Research Council of Canada, pp. 59–67.

Harris, S. A., R. O. van Everdingen and W. H. Pollard (1983) The Dempster Highway – Dawson to Eagle Plain. In: H. M. French and J. A. Heginbottom (eds), *Northern Yukon Territory and Mackenzie Delta, Canada. Guidebook to permafrost and related features*, 4th International Conference on Permafrost, Guidebook No. 3. Fairbanks, Alaska: Alaska Division of Geological and Geophysical Surveys, pp. 65–86.

Harry, D. G. (1988) Ground ice and permafrost. In: M. J. Clark (ed.), *Advances in periglacial geomorphology*. Chichester: J. Wiley and Sons Ltd, pp. 113–149.

Harry, D. G. and H. M. French (1983) The orientation and evolution of thaw lakes, southwest Banks Island, Canadian Arctic. In: *Proceedings, 4th International Conference on Permafrost*. Vol. 1. Washington, DC: National Academy Press, pp. 456–461.

Harry, D. G. and J. S. Gozdzik (1988) Ice wedges: growth, thaw transformation, and paleoenvironmental significance. *Journal of Quaternary Science*, **3**, 39–55.

Harry, D. G., H. M. French and M. J. Clark (1983) Coastal conditions and processes, Sachs Harbour, Banks Island, western Canadian Arctic. *Zeitschrift für Geomorphologie, Supplementband*, **47**, 1–26.

Harry, D. G., H. M. French and W. H. Pollard (1985) Ice wedges and permafrost conditions near King Point, Beaufort Sea coast, Yukon Territory. Geological Survey of Canada, Paper 85–1A, pp. 111–116.

Harry, D. G., H. M. French and W. H. Pollard (1988) Massive ground ice and ice-cored terrain near Sabine Point, Yukon Coastal Plain. *Canadian Journal of Earth Sciences*, **25**, 1846–1856.

Haugen, R. K. and J. Brown (1970) Natural and man-induced disturbances of permafrost terrain. In: D. R. Coates (ed.), *Environment geomorphology*, Binghamton: State University of New York, pp. 139–149.

Hawkins, A. B. and K. D. Privett (1981) A building site on cambered ground at Radstock, Avon. *Quarterly Journal of Engineering Geology*, **14**, 151–167.

Hayley, D. W. (1982) Application of heat pipes to design of shallow foundations on permafrost. In: H. M. French (ed.), *Proceedings, Fourth Canadian Permafrost Conference, Calgary*. Ottawa: National Research Council Canada, pp. 535–544.

Hayley, D. W. (1988) Maintenance of a railway grade over permafrost in Canada. In: *Proceedings, 5th International Conference on Permafrost*. Vol. 3. Trondheim: Tapir Publishers, pp. 43–48.

Hayley, D. W., W. D. Roggensack, W. E. Jubien and P. V. Johnson (1983) Stabilization of sinkholes on the Hudson Bay Railway. In: *Proceedings, 4th International Conference on Permafrost*. Vol. 1. Washington, DC: National Academy Press, pp. 468–473.

Heginbottom, J. A. (1973) *Effects of surface disturbance upon permafrost*. Report 73–16, Environmental-Social Committee Northern Pipelines, Task Force on Northern Oil Development, Information Canada, 29 pp.

Heginbottom, J. A. and L. K. Radburn (1993) *Permafrost and ground ice conditions of northwestern Canada*. Map 1691, Geological Survey of Canada, scale 1:1,000,000.

Helbig, K. (1965) Asymmetrische Eiszeittaler in Süddeutschland und Ostereich. *Wurzburger Geographisches Arbeiten*, Vol. 14. Wurzburg: Geographische Institut der Universität, 103 pp.

Hétu, B. (1995) Le tilage des éboulis stratifiés cryonivaux en Gaspésie (Québec, Canada); Rôle de la Sédimentation Nivéo-Éolienne et des Transits Surpranivaux. *Permafrost and Periglacial Processes*, **6**, 147–171.

Hétu, B., H. Van Steijn, and P. Vandelac (1994) Les coulées de pierres glacées: un nouveau type de coulées de pierraille sur les talus d'éboulis. *Géographie physique et Quaternaire*, **48**, 3–22.

Hétu, B., H. van Steijn and P. Bertran (1995) Le rôle des coulées de pierres sèches dans la genèse d'un certain type d'éboulis stratifiés. *Permafrost and Periglacial Processes*, **6**, 173–194.

Heuer, C. E., T. G. Krzewinski and M. C. Metz (1982) Special thermal design to prevent thaw settlement and liquefaction. In: H. M. French (ed.), *Proceedings, Fourth Canadian Permafrost Conference, Calgary*. Ottawa: National Research Council of Canada, pp. 507–522.

Higgins, C. G. *et al.*, (1990) Permafrost and thermokarst; Geomorphic effects of subsurface water on landforms of cold regions. In: C. G. Higgins and D. R. Coates (eds), *Groundwater geomorphology; the role of subsurface water in earth–surface processes and landforms*. Boulder, Colorado: Geological Society of America Special Paper, **252**, pp. 211–218.

Hodgson, D. A. (1982) *Surficial materials and geomorphological processes, Western Sverdrup and adjacent islands, District of Franklin*. Geological Survey of Canada, Paper 81–9, 44 pp.

Hoekstra, P. (1969) Water movement and freezing pressures. *Soil Science Society of America Proceedings*, **33**, 512–518.

Högbom, B. (1914) Über die geologische Bedeutung des Frostes. *Uppsala Universitet, Geological Institute Bulletin*, **12**, 257–389.

Hollingworth, S. E., J. H. Taylor and G. A. Kellaway (1944) Large-scale superficial structures in the Northampton Ironstone field. *Quaternary Journal Geological Society London*, **100**, 1–44.

Holmes, G. W., D. M. Hopkins and H. L. Foster (1968) Pingos in central Alaska. *United States Geological Survey Bulletin*, **1241-H**, 40 pp.

Hopkins, D. M. (1949) Thaw lakes and thaw sinks in the Imuruk Lake area, Seward Peninsula, Alaska. *Journal of Geology*, **57**, 119–131.

Hopkins, D. M., T. D. Karlstrom and others (1955) *Permafrost and ground water in Alaska*. United States Geological Survey, Professional Paper 264-F, pp. 113–146.

Horswill, P. and A. Horton (1976) Cambering and valley bulging in the Gwash valley at Empingham, Rutland. *Philosophical Transactions Royal Society, London, A*, **283**, 427–451.

Houghton, J. T., G. J. Jenkins and J. J. Ephraums (eds) (1990) *Climate change. The IPCC Scientific Assessment*. Cambridge: Cambridge University Press, 364 pp.

Houghton, J. T., B. A. Callander and S. K. Varney (eds) (1992) *Climate Change 1992*. The supplementary report to the IPCC Scientific Assessment. Cambridge: Cambridge University Press, 199 pp.

Hughes, O. L. (1969) *Distribution of open-system pingos in central Yukon Territory with respect to glacial limits*. Geological Survey of Canada Paper 69–34, 8 pp.

Hughes, O. L. (1972a) Surficial geology and land classification, Mackenzie Valley Transportation Corridor. In: *Proceedings, Canadian Northern Pipeline Research Conference, Canada*. Ottawa: National Research Council of Canada, Technical Memorandum 104, pp. 17–24.

Hughes, O. L. (1972b) *Surficial geology of northern Yukon Territory and northwestern District of Mackenzie, Northwest Territories*. Geological Survey of Canada, Paper 69-36, Map 1319 A.

Hughes, O. L. (1982) *Grey Hunter Peak, surficial geology and geomorphology*. Geological Survey of Canada, Map 3 (1:1 million).

Hughes, O. L., J. J. Veillette, J. Pilon, P. T. Hanley and R. O. Van Everdingen (1973) *Terrain evaluation with respect to pipeline construction, Mackenzie transportation corridor, central part, Lat. 64°–68°N*. Environmental-Social Committee Northern Pipelines, Task Force on Northern Oil Development, Report No. 73-37, 74 pp.

Hume, J. D. and M. Schalk (1964) The effects of beach borrow in the Arctic. *Shore and Beach*, **April**, 5 pp.

Hume, J. D. and M. Schalk (1967) Shoreline processes near Barrow, Alaska; a comparison of the normal and the catastrophic. *Arctic*, **20**, 86–103.

Hume, J. D., M. Schalk and P. W. Hume (1972) Short-term climatic changes and coast erosion, Barrow, Alaska. *Arctic*, **25**, 272–279.

Hunter, J. A., A. S. Judge, H. A. Macaulay, R. L. Good, R.M. Gagne and R. A. Burns (1976) *The occurrence of permafrost and frozen sub-seabottom materials in the southern Beaufort Sea.* Beaufort Sea Technical Report No. 22, Environment Canada, Ottawa, 174 pp.

Hussey, K. M. and R. W. Michelson (1966) Tundra relief features near Point Barrow, Alaska. *Arctic*, **19**, 162–184.

Hutchinson, J. N. (1974) Periglacial solifluxion; an approximate mechanism for clayey soils. *Géotechnique*, **24**, 438–443.

Hutchinson, J. N. and T. P. Gostelow (1976) The development of an abandoned cliff in London Clay at Hadleigh, Essex. *Philosophical Transactions Royal Society, London*, **A283**, 557–604.

Ives, J. D. (1966) Blockfields, associated weathering forms on mountain tops, and the nunatak hypothesis. *Geografiska Annaler*, **48A**, 220–223.

Iwata, S. (1977) Asymmetrical valleys in the Konsen Genya Plain, Eastern Hokkaido, Northern Japan. *Geographical Review of Japan*, **50-8**, 455–470 (in Japanese).

Iwata, S. (1987) Debris-mantled rectilinear slopes in the western Sor Rondane mountains, East Antarctica. In: *Proceedings, National Institute of Polar Research (NIPR), Symposium Antarctic Geoscience*, Vol. 1, pp. 178–192.

Jahn, A. (1960) Some remarks on evolution of slopes on Spitsbergen. *Zeitschrift für Geomorphologie, Supplement 1*, 49–58.

Jahn, A. (1961) Quantitative analysis of some periglacial processes in Spitsbergen. *Nauka O Ziemi II, Seria B*, **5**, 3–34.

Jahn, A. (1962) The origin of granite tors. *Czasopismo Geograficzne*, **33**, 41–44.

Jahn, A. (1975) *Problems of the periglacial zone*. Warsaw: PWN Polish Scientific Publishers, 219 pp.

Jahn, A. (1976) Contemporaneous geomorphological processes in Longyeardalen, Vestspitsbergen (Svalbard). *Biuletyn Peryglacjalny*, **26**, 253–268.

Jahn, A. (1983) Soil wedges on Spitsbergen. In: *Proceedings, 4th International Conference on Permafrost*. Vol. 1. Washington, DC: National Academy Press, pp. 525–530.

Jakob, M. (1992) Active rock glaciers and the lower limit of discontinuous alpine permafrost, Khumbu Himalaya, Nepal. *Permafrost and Periglacial Processes*, **3**, 253–256.

Jennings, J. N. (1971) *Karst*. Boston: MIT Press, 252 pp.

Jersak, J. (1973) Eemian and early Würmian soils in loess of Poland. *Biuletyn Peryglacjalny*, **22**, 169–184.

Jersak, J. (1977). Cyclic development of the loess cover in Poland. *Biuletyn Instytut Geologicznego*, **305**, 83–97.

Jerwood, L. C., D. A. Robinson and R. B. G. Williams (1990a) Experimental frost and salt weathering of chalk. *Earth Surface Processes and Landforms*, **15**, 699–708.

Jerwood, L. C., D. A. Robinson and R. B. G. Williams (1990b) Experimental frost and salt weathering of chalk – II. *Earth Surface Processes and Landforms*, **15**, 699–708.

John, B. S. and D. E. Sugden (1975) Coastal geomorphology of high latitudes. *Progress in Geography*, **7**, 53–132.

Johnson, D. W. (1932) Rock planes in arid regions. *Geographical Review*, **22**, 656–665.

Johnson, P. G. (1974) Mass movement of ablation complexes and their relationship to rock glaciers. *Geografiska Annaler*, **56A**, 93–101.

Johnsson, G. (1959) True and false ice wedges in southern Sweden. *Geografiska Annaler*, **41**, 15–33.

Johnsson, G. (1962) Periglacial phenomena in Southern Sweden. *Geografiska Annaler*, **44**, 378–404.

Johnsson, W. H. (1990) Ice–wedges and relict patterned ground in Central Illinois and their environmental significance. *Quaternary Research*, **33**, 51–72.

Johnston, G. H. (1980) Permafrost and the Eagle River bridge, Yukon Territory, Canada. In: *Proceeding, Permafrost Engineering Workshop*. Ottawa: National Research Council of Canada, Technical Memorandum 130, pp. 12–28.

Johnston, G. H. (ed.) (1981) *Permafrost: Engineering design and construction*. New York: J. Wiley and Sons Ltd, 340 pp.

Johnston, G. H. (1982) Design and performance of the Inuvik, N.W.T. airstrip. In: H. M. French (ed.), *Proceedings, Fourth Canadian Permafrost Conference*, Ottawa: National Research Council of Canada, pp. 577–585.

Johnston, G. H. and R. J. E. Brown (1964) Some observations on permafrost distribution at a lake in the Mackenzie Delta. *Arctic*, **17**, 162–175.

Jones R. L. and D. H. Keen (1993) *Pleistocene environments in the British Isles*. London: Chapman and Hall, 346 pp.

Jorré, G. (1933) Probleme des 'terrasses goletz' sibériennes. *Révue de Géographie Alpine*, **21**, 347–371.

Judge, A. S. (1982) Natural gas hydrates in Canada. In: H. M. French (ed.), *Proceedings, Fourth Canadian Permafrost Conference*. Ottawa: National Research Council of Canada, pp. 32–328.

Judge, A. S. and J. A. Majorowicz (1992) Geothermal conditions for gas hydrate stability in the Beaufort Mackenzie area: the global change aspect. *Global and Planetary Change*, **6**, 257–269.

Kachurin, S. P. (1962) Thermokarst within the territory of the USSR. *Biuletyn Peryglacjalny*, **11**, 49–55.

Kaiser, K. (1960) Klimazeugen des periglazialen dauerfrostbodens in Mittel- und West-Europa. *Eiszeitalter und Gegenwart*, **11**, 121–141.

Kallio, A., and S. Reiger (1969) Recession of permafrost in a cultivated soil of interior Alaska. *Proceedings, Soil Science Society of America*, **33**, 430–432.

Kane, D. L., L. D. Hinzman and J. P. Zarling, (1991) Thermal response of the active layer to climatic warming in a permafrost environment. *Cold Regions Science and Technology*, **19**, 111–122.

Kaplanskaya, F. A. and V. D. Tarnogradskiy (1986) Remnants of the Pleistocene ice sheets in the permafrost zone as an object for paleoglaciological research. *Polar Geography and Geology*, **10**, 257–266.

Karrasch, H. (1970) Das phanomen der klimabedingten reliefasymmetrie in Mitteleuropa. *Göttingen Geographische Abhandlungen*, **56**, 299 pp.

Karrasch, H. (1972) Flachenbildung unter periglazialen klimabedingungen. *Göttingen Geographische Abhandlungen*, **60**, 155–168.

Karte, J. (1979) Raumliche abgrenzung und regionale differenzierung des periglaziärs. *Bochumer Geographische Arbeiten*, **35**, 211 pp.

Karte, J. (1983) Grèzes litées as a special type of periglacial slope sediments in the German Highlands. *Polarforschung*, **53** (2), 67–74.

Karte, J. (1987) Pleistocene periglacial conditions and geomorphology in north and central Europe. In: J. Boardman (ed.), *Periglacial processes and landforms in Britain and Ireland*. Cambridge: Cambridge University Press, pp. 67–75.

Katasonov, E. M. (1969) *Composition and cryogenic structure of permafrost*. Ottawa: National Research Council of Canada, Technical Translation 1358, pp. 25–36.

Katasonov, E. M. (1973) Present day ground and ice veins in the region of the Middle Lena. *Biuletyn Peryglacjalny*, **23**, 81–89.

Katasonov, E. M. (1975) Frozen-ground and facial analysis of Pleistocene deposits and paleogeography of central Yakutia. *Biuletyn Peryglacjalny*, **24**, 33–40.

Katasonov, E. M. and M. S. Ivanov (1973) *Cryolithology of Central Yakutia*, Guidebook, Second International Permafrost Conference, Yakutsk, USSR, 38 pp.

Keen, D. H. (1985) Late Pleistocene deposits and mollusca from Portland, Dorset. *Geological Magazine*, **122**, 181–186.

Kellaway, G. A. (1972) Development of non-diastrophic Pleistocene structures in relation to climate and physical relief in Britain. In: *Proceedings, 24th International Geological Congress, Montreal*, Section 12, pp. 136–146.

Kerfoot, D. E. (1974) Thermokarst features produced by man-made disturbances to the tundra terrain. In: B. D. Fahey and R. O. Thompson (eds), *Research in Polar and Alpine Geomorphology*, Proceedings, Third Guelph Symposium on Geomorphology. Norwich: Geo Abstracts Ltd, pp. 60–72.

Kerney, M. P. (1963) Late glacial deposits on the Chalk of south-east England. *Philosophical Transactions Royal Society, London*, **B246**, 203–254.

Kerney, M. P., E. H. Brown and T. J. Chandler (1964) The late glacial and post glacial history of the Chalk escarpment near Brook, Kent. *Philosophical Transactions Royal Society, London*, **B248**, 135–204.

Kershaw, G. P. and D. Gill (1979) Growth and decay of palsas and peat plateaux in the Macmillan Pass – Tsichu River area, Northwest Territories, Canada. *Canadian Journal of Earth Sciences*, **16**, 1362–1367.

King, L. (1983) High mountain permafrost in Scandinavia. In: *Proceedings, 4th International Conference on Permafrost*. Washington, DC: National Academy Press, pp. 612–617.

King, L. (1986) Zonation and ecology of high mountain permafrost in Scandinavia. *Geografiska Annaler*, **68 A**, 131–139.

King, L. C. (1953) Canons of landscape evolution. *Geological Society of America, Bulletin*, **64**, 721–752.

Klassen, R. and W. Shilts (1987) *Bylot Island, Eastern Canadian Arctic*. XII INQUA Congress Field Excursion A.I. Guidebook. Ottawa: National Research Council of Canada, 54 pp.

Klatkowa, H. (1965) Vallons en berceau et vallées sèches aux environs de Lódz. *Acta Geographica Lodziensia*, **19**, 124–142.

Klatkowa, H. (1994) Evaluation du rôle de l'agent périglaciaire en Pologne centrale. *Biuletyn Peryglacjalny*, **33**, 79–106.

Kleman, J. and I. Borgström (1990) The boulder fields of Mt. Fulufjället, west-central Sweden – Late Weichselian boulder blankets and interstadial periglacial phenomena. *Geografiska Annaler*, **72 A**, 63–78.

Kolchugina, T. P. and T. S. Vinson (1993) Climate warming and the carbon cycle in the permafrost zone of the Former Soviet Union. *Permafrost and Periglacial Processes*, **4**, 149–163.

Kolstrup, E. (1980) Climate and stratigraphy in northwestern Europe betwen 30,000 BP and 13,000 BP with special reference to the Netherlands. *Mededelingen Rijks Geologische Dienst*, **32-15**, 181–253.

Kolstrup, E. (1987) Frost wedge casts in western Jutland and their possible implications for European periglacial research. *Zeitschrift für Geomorphologie*, **31**, 449–461.

Kondratjeva, K. A., S. F. Khrutzky and N. N. Romanovsky (1993) Changes in the extent of permafrost during the late Quaternary period in the territory of the Former Soviet Union. *Permafrost and Periglacial Processes*, **4**, 113–119.

Konishchev, V. N. (1982) Characteristics of cryogenic weathering in the permafrost zone of the European USSR. *Arctic and Alpine Research*, **14**, 261–265.

Konishchev, V. N. and V. V. Rogov (1985) *Methods of cryolithological investigation*. Moscow: Moscow State University Press (in Russian).

Konishchev, V. N. and V. V. Rogov (1993) Investigations of cryogenic weathering in Europe and Northern Asia. *Permafrost and Periglacial Processes*, **4**, 49–64.

Konischev, V. N., V. V. Rogov and G. N. Schurina (1976) Cryogenic factor influence on primary minerals (results of experimental investigation). *Problems of Cryolithology*, **5**, 50–61 (in Russian).

Köppen, W. V. (1923) *Die Klimate der Erde*. Berlin: De Gruyter, 369 pp.

Koster, E. A. (1988) Ancient and modern cold-climate aeolian sand deposition: a review. *Journal of Quaternary Science*, **3**, 69–83.

Koster, E. A. (1993) Global warming and periglacial landscapes. In N. Roberts (ed), *The changing global environment*. Oxford: Basil Blackwell, pp. 127–149.

Koster, E. A. and J. W. A. Dijkmans (1988) Niveo-aeolian deposits and denivation forms, with special reference to the Great Kobuk Sand Dunes, Northwestern Alaska. *Earth Surface Processes and Landforms*, **13**, 153–170.

Krantz, W. B., K. J. Gleason and N. Caine (1988) Patterned ground. *Scientific American*, **259** (6), 68–75.

Krigstrom, A. (1962) Geomorphological studies of sandur plains and their braided rivers in Iceland. *Geografiska Annaler*, **44**, 328–346.

Kudryavtsev, V. A. (1965) Temperature, thickness and discontinuity of permafrost. In: *Principles of geocryology (permafrost studies)*, Part 1, *General geocryology*, Chapter VIII. Moscow: USSR Academy of Sciences, 1959 pp. 219–273. (National Research Council of Canada, Ottawa, Technical Translation 1187.)

Kudryavtsev, V. A. (1978) *Obszceje mierzlotowiedienije (gyeokreologeya)* (General Permafrost Science – geocryology). Moscow: Moscow State University, 464 pp. (in Russian).

Kudryavtsev, V. A., K. A. Kondratyeva and N. N. Romanovsky (1978) Zonal and regional patterns of formation of the permafrost region in the USSR. In: *Proceedings, 3rd International Conference on Permafrost*, Vol. 1. Ottawa: National Research Council of Canada, pp. 419–426.

Kurfurst, P. J. (1973) *Norman Wells, 96E/7, map 22; Terrain Disturbance and Susceptibility Maps*. Environmental-Social Program, Task Force on Northern Oil Development. Ottawa: Information Canada.

Kvenvolden, K. A. (1988) Methane hydrates and global climate. *Global Biogeochemical Cycles*, **2**, 221–230.

Kwon, S.-S. (1978) Block field in the vicinity of Bomosa Temple. *Journal of Geography (Korea)*, **5**, 49–54. (in Korean).

Kwon, S.-S. (1979) Fossil periglacial phenomena on the southern parts of Geoje Island, Korea. *Journal of Geography (Korea)*, **6**, 151–153. (in Korean).

Lachenbruch, A. (1957) Thermal effects of the ocean on permafrost. *Bulletin, Geological Society of America*, **68**, 1515–1529.

Lachenbruch, A. (1962) *Mechanics of thermal contraction cracks and ice-wedge polygons in permafrost*. Geological Society of America, Special Paper 70, 69 pp.

Lachenbruch, A. (1966) Contraction theory of ice wedge polygons; a qualitative discussion. In: *Proceedings, 1st International Conference on Permafrost*. National Academy of Science, National Research Council of Canada, Publication 1287, pp. 63–71.

Lachenbruch, A. (1968) Permafrost. In: R. W. Fairbridge (ed.), *Encyclopedia of geomorphology*. New York: Reinhold Book Co., pp. 833–838.

Lachenbruch, A., G. W. Greene and B. V. Marshall (1966) Permafrost and the geothermal regimes. In: N. J. Wilimovsky (ed.), *The Environment of the Cape Thompson Region, Alaska*. Ottawa and Washington, DC: United States Atomic Energy Commission, PNE-481, pp. 149–163.

Lachenbruch, A., T. T. Cladouhous and R. W. Saltus (1988) Permafrost temperature and the changing climate. In: *Proceedings, 5th International Conference on Permafrost*, Vol. 3. Trondheim: Tapir Publishers, pp. 9–17.

Ladanyi, B. and G. H. Johnston (1973) Evaluation of *in situ* creep properties of frozen soils with the pressuremeter. In: *Proceedings, 2nd International Conference on Permafrost, Yakutsk, USSR*, Washington, DC: National Academy of Sciences, Publication 2115, pp. 310–317.

Lamothe, C. and D. A. St-Onge (1961) A note on a periglacial process in the Isachsen area, N.W.T. *Geographical Bulletin*, **16**, 104–113.

Lauriol, B. (1990) Cryoplanation terraces, northern Yukon. *The Canadian Geographer*, **34**, 347–351.

Lauriol, B. and L. Godbout (1988) Les terrasses de cryoplanation dans le nord du Yukon: distribution, genèse et age. *Géographie physique et Quaternaire*, **42**, 303–313.

Lauriol, B. and J. T. Gray (1980) Processes responsible for the concentration of boulders in the intertidal zone in Leaf Basin, Ungava. Geological Survey of Canada, Paper 80-10, pp. 281–292.

Lauriol, B. and J. T. Gray (1990) Drainage karstique en milieu de pergélisol: le cas de l'île d'Akpatok, T.N.O., Canada. *Permafrost and Periglacial Processes*, **1**, 129–144.

Lautridou, J.-P. (1982) La fraction fine des débris de gélifraction experimentale. *Biuletyn Peryglacjalny*, **29**, 77–85.

Lautridou, J.-P. (1988) Recent advances in cryogenic weathering. In: M. J. Clark (ed.), *Advances in periglacial geomorphology*. Chichester: J. Wiley and Sons Ltd, pp. 33–47.

Lautridou, J.-P. and P. Giresse (1981) Genèse et signification paléoclimatique des limons à doublets de Normandie. *Biuletyn Peryglacjalny*, **28**, 149–161.

Lautridou, J.-P. and J. C. Ozouf (1982) Experimental frost shattering: 15 years of research at the Centre de Géomorphologie du CNRS. *Progress in Physical Geography*, **6**, 215–232.

Lautridou, J.-P. and M. Seppälä (1986) Experimental frost shattering of some precambrian rocks, Finland. *Geografiska Annaler*, **68A**, 89–100.

Lawson, D. E. (1979) *Sedimentological analysis of the western terminus region of the Matanuska Glacier, Alaska*. Hanover, NH: Cold Regions Engineering and Research Laboratory, Report 79–9.

Lawson, D. E. (1983) Ground ice in perennially frozen sediments, Northern Alaska. In: *Proceedings, 4th International Conference on Permafrost*, Vol. 1. Washington DC: National Academy Press, pp. 695–700.

Leffingwell, E. K. (1915) Ground-ice wedges, the dominant form of ground-ice on the north coast of Alaska. *Journal of Geology*, **23**, 635–654.

Leffingwell, E. K. (1919) *The Canning River Region, Northern Alaska*. United States Geological Survey, Professional Paper 109, 251 pp.

Lefroy, General Sir J. H. (1889) Report upon the depth of permanently frozen soil in the polar regions, its geographical limits, and relations to the present poles of greatest cold. *Proceedings of the Geographical Section, Royal Geographical Society, London*, **1889**, 740–746.

Leonard, A. B. and J. C. Frye (1954) Ecological conditions accompanying loess deposition in the Great Plains region. *Journal of Geology*, **62**, 399–404.

Leopold, L. B., M. G. Wolman and J. P. Miller (1964) *Fluvial processes in geomorphology*. San Francisco, Freemans, 522 pp.

Leopold, L. B., W. W. Emmett and R. M. Myrick (1966) *Channel and hillslope processes in a semi-arid area, New Mexico*. United States Professional Paper 352-G, pp. 193–253.

Letavernier, G. and J. C. Ozouf (1987) La gélifraction des roches et des parois calcaires. *Bulletin de L'Association Française pour l'Etude du Quaternaire*, **3**, 139–145.

Lewis, C. A. (1988) Periglacial landforms. In: B. P. Moon and G. F. Dardis (eds), *The geomorphology of Southern Africa*. Johannesburg: Southern Book Publishers, pp. 103–119.

Lewis, C. A. (1994) *Field guide to the Quaternary glacial, periglacial and colluvial features of the East Cape Drakensberg*. Southern African Society for Quaternary Research, Field Guide No. 1, 52 pp.

Lewis, C. R. (1962) Icing mound on the Sadlerochit River, Alaska. *Arctic*, **15**, 145–150.

Lewkowicz, A. G. (1983) Erosion by overland flow, central Banks Island, western Canadian Arctic. In: *Proceedings, 4th International Conference on Permafrost*. Vol. 1. Washington, DC: National Academy Press, pp. 701–6.

Lewkowicz, A. G. (1985) Use of an ablatometer to measure short-term ablation of exposed ground ice. *Canadian Journal of Earth Sciences*, **22**, 1767–1773.

Lewkowicz, A. G. (1987) Nature and importance of thermokarst processes, Banks Island, Canada. *Geografiska Annaler*, **69A**, 1077–1085.

Lewkowicz, A. G. (1988) Ablation of massive ground ice, Mackenzie Delta. In: *Proceedings of 5th International Conference on Permafrost*. Vol. 1. Trondheim: Tapir Publishers, pp. 605–610.

Lewkowicz, A. G. (1990) Morphology, frequency and magnitude of active-layer detachment slides, Fosheim Peninsula, Ellesmere Island, N.W.T. In: *Proceedings, Fifth Canadian Permafrost Conference*, Québec City, Université Laval, Nordicana 54, pp. 111–118.

Lewkowicz, A. G. (1992a) Climatic change and the permafrost landscape. In: M. K. Woo and D. J. Gregor (eds), *Arctic environment: past, present and future*, Hamilton: Department of Geography, McMaster University, pp. 91–104.

Lewkowicz, A. G. (1992b) Factors influencing the distribution and initiation of active-layer detachment slides on Ellesmere Island, Arctic Canada. In: J. C. Dixon and A. D. Abrahams (eds), *Periglacial geomorphology*. Chichester: John Wiley and Sons Ltd, pp. 223–250.

Lewkowicz, A. G. (1992c) Slope hummocks on Fosheim Peninsula, Ellesmere Island, Northwest Territories. Geological Survey of Canada, Paper 92-1B, pp. 97–102.

Lewkowicz, A. G. (1994) Ice-wedge rejuvenation, Fosheim Peninsula, Ellesmere Island, Canada. *Permafrost and Periglacial Processes*, **5**, 251–268.

Lewkowicz, A. G. and H. M. French (1982a) The hydrology of small runoff plots in an area of continuous permafrost, Banks Island, N.W.T. In: H. M. French (ed.), *Proceedings, Fourth Canadian Permafrost Conference*, Calgary. Ottawa: National Research Council of Canada, pp. 151–162.

Lewkowicz, A. G. and H. M. French (1982b) Downslope water movement and solute concentrations within the active layer, Banks Island, N.W.T. In: H.M. French (ed.), *Proceedings, Fourth Canadian Permafrost Conference, Calgary*. Ottawa: National Research Council of Canada, pp. 163–172.

Linton, D. L. (1955) The problem of tors. *Geographical Journal*, **121**, 470–487.

Linton, D. L. (1964) The origin of the Pennine tors; an essay in analysis. *Zeitschrift für Geomorphologie*, **8**, 5–24.

Lorrain, R. D. and P. Demeur (1985) Isotopic evidence for relic Pleistocene glacier ice on Victoria Island, Canadian Arctic Archipelago. *Arctic and Alpine Research*, **17**, 89–98.

Loveday, J. (1962) Plateau deposits of the southern Chiltern Hills. *Proceedings, Geologist's Association, UK*, **73**, 83–102.

Lowe, J. J. and M. J. C. Walker (1984) *Reconstructing Quaternary environments*. Harlow: Longman, 389 pp.

Lozinski, W. von (1909) Über die mechanische Verwitterung der Sandsteine im gemässigten Klima. *Acad. Sci. Cracovie, Bull. Internat., Cl. Sci. Math. et Nat.*, **1**, 1–25.

Lozinski, W. von (1912) Die periglaziale Fazies der mechanischen Verwitterung. *Comptes Rendus, XI Congrès Internationale Géologie, Stockholm 1910*, pp. 1039–1053.

Luckman, B. H. (1972) Some observations on the erosion of talus slopes by snow avalanches in Surprise Valley, Jasper National Park, Alberta. In: H. O. Slaymaker and H. J. McPherson, (eds), *Mountain geomorphology*. Vancouver: Tantalus Research, pp. 85–110.

Luckman, B. H. (1988) Debris accumulation patterns on talus slopes in Surprise valley, Alberta. *Géographie physique et Quaternaire*, **42**, 247–278.

Maarleveld, G. (1960) Wind direction and cover sands in the Netherlands. *Biuletyn Peryglacjalny*, **8**, 49–58.

Maarleveld, G. (1976) Periglacial phenomena and the mean annual temperature during the last glacial time in the Netherlands. *Biuletyn Peryglacjalny*, **26**, 57–78.

Maarleveld, G. (1981) Summer thaw depth in cold regions and fossil cryoturbation. *Geologie en Mijnbouw*, **60**, 347–352.

Maarleveld, G. C. and J. C. van den Toorn (1955). Pseudo-solle in Noord-Nederland. *Tijdschrift Koninklijk Nederlands Aardrijkskundig Genootschap*, **72**, 334–360.

Mackay, J. R. (1962) Pingos of the Pleistocene Mackenzie Delta area. *Geographical Bulletin*, **18**, 21–63.

Mackay, J. R. (1963) *The Mackenzie Delta area*. Geographical Branch Memoir, No. 8, 202 pp.

Mackay, J.R. (1966) Segregated epigenetic ice and slumps in permafrost, Mackenzie Delta area, N.W.T. *Geographical Bulletin*, **8**, 59–80.

Mackay, J. R. (1970) Disturbances to the tundra and forest tundra environment of the western Arctic. *Canadian Geotechnical Journal*, **7**, 420–432.

Mackay, J. R. (1971) The origin of massive icy beds in permafrost, western Arctic coast, Canada. *Canadian Journal of Earth Sciences*, **8**, 397–422.

Mackay, J. R. (1972a) The world of underground ice. *Annals, Association of American Geographers*, **62**, 1–22.

Mackay, J. R. (1972b) Offshore permafrost and ground ice, southern Beaufort Sea, Canada. *Canadian Journal of Earth Sciences*, **9**, 1550–1561.

Mackay, J. R. (1973a) The growth of pingos, western Arctic coast, Canada. *Canadian Journal of Earth Sciences*, **10**, 979–1004.

Mackay, J. R. (1973b) Problems in the origin of massive icy beds, western Arctic, Canada. In: *Proceedings, 2nd International Conference on Permafrost, Yakutsk, USSR*, Vol. 1. Washington, DC: National Academy of Sciences, Publication 2115, pp. 223–228.

Mackay, J. R. (1973c) A frost tube for the determination of freezing in the active layer above permafrost. *Canadian Geotechnical Journal*, **10**, 392–396.

Mackay, J. R. (1974a) Measurement of upward freezing above permafrost with a self-positioning thermistor probe. Geological Survey of Canada, Paper 74-1B, 250–254.

Mackay, J. R. (1974b) Ice-wedge cracks, Garry Island, Northwest Territories. *Canadian Journal of Earth Sciences*, **11**, 1366–1383.

Mackay, J. R. (1974c) Reticulate ice veins in permafrost, Northern Canada. *Canadian Geotechnical Journal*, **11**, 230–237.

Mackay, J. R. (1975) The closing of ice-wedge cracks in permafrost, Garry Island, Northwest Territories. *Canadian Journal of Earth Sciences*. **12**, 1668–1674.

Mackay, J. R. (1977) Pulsating pingos, Tuktoyaktuk Peninsula, N.W.T. *Canadian Journal of Earth Sciences*, **14**, 209–222.

Mackay, J. R. (1978a) The use of snow fences to reduce ice-wedge cracking, Garry Island, Northwest Territories. Geological Survey of Canada, Paper 78-1, pp. 523–524.

Mackay, J. R. (1978b) Sub-pingo water lenses, Tuktoyaktuk Peninsula, Northwest Territories. *Canadian Journal of Earth Sciences*, **15**, 461–462.

Mackay, J. R. (1979a) Pingos of the Tuktoyaktuk Peninsula area, Northwest Territories. *Géographie physique et Quaternaire*, **33**, 3–61.

Mackay, J. R. (1979b) An equilibrium model for hummocks (non-sorted circles), Garry Island, Northwest Territories. Geological Survey of Canada, Paper 79-1A, pp. 165–167.

Mackay, J. R. (1980a) Deformation of ice-wedge polygons, Garry Island, Northwest Territories. Geological Survey of Canada, Paper 80-1A, 287–291.

Mackay, J. R. (1980b) The origin of hummocks, western Arctic coast. *Canadian Journal of Earth Sciences*, **17**, 996–1006.

Mackay, J. R. (1981) Active layer slope movement in a continuous permafrost environment, Garry Island, Northwest Territories, Canada. *Canadian Journal of Earth Sciences*, **18**, 1666–1680.

Mackay, J. R. (1982) Active layer growth, Illisarvik experimental drained lake site, Richards Island, Northwest Territories. Geological Survey of Canada, Paper 82-1A, 123–126.

Mackay, J. R. (1983) Downward water movement into frozen ground, western arctic coast, Canada. *Canadian Journal of Earth Sciences*, **20**, 120–134.

Mackay, J. R. (1984) The frost heave of stones in the active layer above permafrost with downward and upward freezing. *Arctic and Alpine Research*, **16**, 439–446.

Mackay, J. R. (1985) Pingo ice of the western Arctic coast, Canada. *Canadian Journal of Earth Sciences*, **22**, 1452–1464.

Mackay, J. R. (1986a) Fifty years (1935–1985) of coastal retreat west of Tuktoyaktuk, District of Mackenzie. Geological Survey of Canada, Paper 86-1A, pp. 727–735.

Mackay, J. R. (1986b) Growth of Ibyuk Pingo, Western Arctic Coast, Canada and some implications for environmental reconstructions. *Quaternary Research*, **26**, 68–80.

Mackay, J. R. (1986c) Frost mounds. In: H.M. French (ed.), *Focus: Permafrost geomorphology, The Canadian Geographer*, **30**, 363–364.

Mackay, J. R. (1986d) The first 7 years (1978–1985) of ice-wedge growth, Illisarvik experimental drained lake site, western Arctic coast. *Canadian Journal of Earth Sciences*, **23**, 1782–1795.

Mackay, J. R. (1988) The birth and growth of Porsild Pingo, Tuktoyaktuk Peninsula, District of Mackenzie. *Arctic*, **41**, 267–674.

Mackay, J. R. (1989a) Massive ice: some field criteria for the identification of ice types. Geological Survey of Canada, Paper 89-1G, pp. 5–11.

Mackay, J. R. (1989b) Ice-wedge cracks, western Arctic coast. *The Canadian Geographer*, **33**, 365–368.

Mackay, J. R. (1990a) Some observations on the growth and deformation of epigenetic, syngenetic and anti-syngenetic ice wedges. *Permafrost and Periglacial Processes*, **1**, 15–29.

Mackay, J. R. (1990b) Seasonal growth bands in pingo ice. *Canadian Journal of Earth Sciences*, **27**, 1115–1125.

Mackay, J. R. (1992) The frequency of ice-wedge cracking (1967–1987) at Garry Island, western Arctic coast, Canada. *Canadian Journal of Earth Sciences*, **29**, 236–248.

Mackay, J. R. (1993a) The sound and speed of ice-wedge cracking, Arctic Canada. *Canadian Journal of Earth Sciences*, **30**, 509–518.

Mackay, J. R. (1993b) Air temperature, snow cover, creep of frozen ground, and the time of ice-wedge cracking, western Arctic Coast. *Canadian Journal of Earth Sciences*, **30**, 1720–1729.

Mackay, J. R. (1995a) Active layer changes (1968 to 1993) following the forest-tundra fire near Inuvik, NWT, Canada. *Arctic and Alpine Research*, **27**, 323–336.

Mackay, J. R. (1995b) Ice wedges on hillslopes and landform evolution in the late Quaternary, western Arctic coast, Canada. *Canadian Journal of Earth Sciences*, **32**, 1093–1105.

Mackay, J. R. and S. R. Dallimore (1992) Massive ice of the Tuktoyaktuk area, western Arctic coast, Canada. *Canadian Journal of Earth Sciences*, **29**, 1235–1249.

Mackay, J. R. and L. M. Lavkulich (1974) Ionic and oxygen isotopic fractionation in permafrost growth. Geological Survey of Canada, Paper 74-1, pp. 255–256.

Mackay, J. R. and R. V. Leslie (1987) A simple probe for the measurement of frost heave within frozen ground in a permafrost environment. Geological Survey of Canada, Paper 87-1A, pp. 37–41.

Mackay, J. R. and D. K. MacKay (1976) Cryostatic pressures in nonsorted circles (mud hummocks), Inuvik, Northwest Territories. *Canadian Journal of Earth Sciences*, **13**, 889–897.

Mackay, J. R. and W. H. Mathews (1974) Needle ice striped ground. *Arctic and Alpine Research*, **6**, 79–84.

Mackay, J. R. and O. Slaymaker (1989) The Horton River breakthrough and resulting geomorphic changes in a permafrost environment, western Arctic coast, Canada. *Geografiska Annaler*, **71 A**, 171–184.

Mackay, J. R., V. N. Rampton and J. G. Fyles (1972) Relic Pleistocene permafrost, western Arctic, Canada. *Science*, **176** (4041), 1321–1323.

Mackay, J. R., J. Ostrick, C. P. Lewis and D. K. MacKay (1979) Frost heave at ground temperatures below 0°C, Inuvik, Northwest Territories. Geological Survey of Canada, Paper 79-1A, pp. 403–406.

Makogon, Y .F., F. A. Trebin, A. A. Trofimuk, V. P. Tsarev, and N. V. Cherskiy (1972) Detection of a pool of natural gas in a solid (hydrated gas) state. *Doklady Academy of Sciences of the USSR, Earth Science Section* (English translation), **196**, 199–200.

Malaurie, J. N. and Y. Guillien (1953) Le modèle cryo-nival des versants meubles de Skansen (Disko, Groenland). Interprétation général des grèzes litées. *Bulletin, Société Géologique de France*, **3**, 703–721.

Manley, G. (1959) The late glacial climate of northwest England. *Geological Journal*, **2**, 188–215.

Marsh, B. (1987) Pleistocene pingo scars in Pennsylvania. *Geology*, **15**, 945–947.

Matsuoka, N. (1989) Mechanisms of rock breakdown by frost action: an experimental approach. *Cold Regions Science and Technology*, **17**, 253–270.

Matsuoka, N. (1990) The rate of bedrock weathering by frost action: field measurements and a predictive model. *Earth Surface Processes and Landforms*, **15**, 73–90.

Matsuoka, N. (1991) A model of the rate of frost shattering: application to field data from Japan, Svalbard and Antarctica. *Permafrost and Periglacial Processes*, **2**, 271–281.

Matsuoka, N., K. Moriwaki and K. Hirakawa (1988) Diurnal frost-heave activity in the Sør-Rondane Mountains, Antarctica. *Arctic and Alpine Research*, **20**, 422–428.

McCann, S. B. (1972) Magnitude and frequency of processes operating on Arctic beaches, Queen Elizabeth Islands, N.W.T, Canada. In P. W. Adams and F. Helleiner (eds), *International geography*, Vol. 1. Toronto: University of Toronto Press, pp. 41–43.

McCann, S. B. and R. J. Carlisle (1972) The nature of the ice foot on the beaches of Radstock Bay, southwest Devon Island, N.W.T., Canada, in the summer of 1970. In: *Polar geomorphology*, Institute of British Geographers Special Publication No. 4, pp. 175–186.

McCann, S. B. and E. H. Owens (1969) The size and shape of sediments in three Arctic beaches, southwest Devon Island, N.W.T., Canada. *Arctic and Alpine Research*, **1**, 267–278.

McCann, S. B., P. J. Howarth and J. G. Cogley (1972) Fluvial processes in a periglacial environment; Queen Elizabeth Islands, N.W.T., Canada. *Transactions, Institute of British Geographers*, **55**, 69–82.

McDonald, B. C. and C. P. Lewis (1973) *Geomorphic and sedimentologic processes of rivers and coasts, Yukon Coastal Plain*. Report 73-39, Environmental-Social Committee Northern Pipelines, Task Force on Northern Oil Development, Information Canada, Ottawa, 245 pp.

McGreevy, J. P. and W. B. Whalley (1982) The geomorphic significance of rock temperature variations in cold environments: a discussion. *Arctic and Alpine Research*, **14**, 157–162.

McGreevy, J. P. and W. B. Whalley (1985) Rock moisture content and rock weathering under natural and experimental conditions: a comparative discussion. *Arctic and Alpine Research*, **17**, 337–346.

McKenna-Neuman, C. and R. Gilbert (1986) Aeolian processes and landforms in glaciofluvial environments of southeastern Baffin Island, N.W.T., Canada. In: W. G. Nickling (ed.), *Aeolian geomorphology*. Boston: Allen and Unwin, pp. 213–235.

McRoberts, E. C. and N. R. Morgenstern (1974) The stability of thawing slopes. *Canadian Geotechnical Journal*, **11**, 447–469.

McRoberts, E. C. and J. F. Nixon (1975) Reticulate ice veins in permafrost, northern Canada: discussion. *Canadian Geotechnical Journal*, **12**, 1509–1562.

Meinardus, W. (1912) Beobachtungen über Detritussortierung und Strukturböden auf Spitzbergen. *Gesell, Erdkunde Berlin Zeitschrift*, pp. 250–259.

Melnikov, P. I. and N. I. Tolstikhin (eds) (1974) *Obschcheye Merzlotovedeniye*. Izdatel'stvo 'Nauka', Novosibirsk, Sibirskoye Otdeleniye (in Russian).

Metz, M. C., T. G. Krzewinski and E. S. Clarke (1982) The Trans-Alaska Pipeline workpad – an evaluation of present conditons. In: H. M. French (ed.), *Proceedings Fourth*

Canadian Permafrost Conference, Calgary, Alberta. Ottawa: National Research Council of Canada, pp. 523–534.

Michaud, Y. and L. D. Dyke (1990) Mechanism of bedrock frost heave in permafrost regions. In: *Proceedings Fifth Canadian Permafrost Conference*. Université Laval, Nordicana No. 54, pp. 125–130.

Michel, F. A. and P. Fritz (1982) Significance of isotope variations in permafrost waters at Illisarvik, N.W.T. In: H.M. French (ed.), *Proceedings, Fourth Canadian Permafrost Conference, Calgary, Alberta*. Ottawa: National Research Council of Canada, pp. 173–181.

Miller, R. D. (1972) *Freezing and heaving of saturated and unsaturated soils*. Highway Research Record, 393-1-11.

Minervin, A. V. (1982) The role of cryogenic processes in forming of loess deposits. *Problems of Cryolithology*, **10**, 41–61 (in Russian).

Morgan, A. V. (1971) Polygonal patterned ground of late Weichselian age in the area north and west of Wolverhampton, England. *Geografiska Annaler*, **54A**, 146–156.

Morgan, A. V. (1972) Late Wisconsinan ice-wedge polygons near Kitchener, Ontario, Canada. *Canadian Journal of Earth Sciences*, **9**, 607–617.

Morgan, A. V. (1973) The Pleistocene geology of the area north and west of Wolverhampton, Staffordshire, England. *Philosophical Transactions Royal Society of London*, **B265**, 233–297.

Morgan, A. V. and A. Morgan (1980) Beetle bits – the science of paleoentomology. *Geoscience Canada*, **7**, 1, 22–29.

Morgan, A. V., A. Morgan, A. C. Ashworth and J. V. Matthews Jr (1983) Late Wisconsin fossil beetles in North America. In: S. C. Porter (ed.), *Late Quaternary environments of the United States*, Volume 1, The Late Pleistocene. Minneapolis: University of Minnesota Press, pp. 354–363.

Morgenstern, N. R. (1981) Geotechnical engineering and frontier resource development. *Géotechnique*, **31**, 305–365.

Morgenstern, N. R. and J. F. Nixon (1971) One dimensional consolidation of thawing soils. *Canadian Geotechnical Journal*, **8**, 558–565.

Mottershead, D. N. (1971) Coastal head deposits between Start Point and Hope Cove, Devon. *Field Studies*, **5**, 433–453.

Mottershead, D. N. (1977) *South West England; Guidebook for excursions A6 and C6, X INQUA Congress*. Norwich: GeoAbstracts Ltd, 59 pp.

Mullenders, W. and F. Gullentops (1969) The age of the pingos of Belgium. In: T. L. Péwé (ed.), *The periglacial environment*. Montreal: McGill-Queen's University Press, pp. 321–336.

Müller, F. (1959) Beobachtung uber pingos. *Meddelelser om Gronland*, **153**(3), 127 pp. (English Translation, National Research Council of Canada, Technical Translation TT-1073, 117 pp.)

Muller, S. W. (1945) *Permafrost or permanently frozen ground and related engineering problems*. United States Engineers Office, Strategic Engineering Study, Special Report No. 62, 136 pp. (Reprinted in 1947, Ann Arbor, Michigan: J. W. Edwards, 231 pp.)

Murton, J. B. and H. M. French (1993a) Sand wedges and permafrost history, Crumbling Point, Pleistocene Mackenzie Delta, Canada. In: *Proceedings, Sixth International Conference on Permafrost*. Vol. 1. Beijing: Science Press, pp. 482–487.

Murton, J. B. and H. M. French (1993b) Thaw modification of frost-fissure wedges, Richards Island, Pleistocene Mackenzie Delta, western Arctic Canada. *Journal of Quaternary Science*, **8**, 185–196.

Murton, J. B. and H. M. French (1993c) Thermokarst involutions, Summer Island, Pleistocene Mackenzie Delta, western Canadian Arctic. *Permafrost and Periglacial Processes*, **4**, 217–229.

Murton, J. B. and H. M. French (1994) Cryostructures in permafrost, Tuktoyaktuk coastlands, western Arctic, Canada. *Canadian Journal of Earth Sciences*, **31**, 737–747.

Murton, J. B., C. A. Whiteman and P. Allen (1995) Involutions in the Middle Pleistocene (Anglian) Barham Soil, eastern England: a comparison with thermokarst involutions from arctic Canada. *Boreas*, **24**, 269–280.

Muscoe, G. E. (1982) The origin of honeycomb weathering. *Geological Society of America Bulletin*, **93**, 108–115.

Natural Resources Canada (1995) *Canada permafrost. The national atlas of Canada*, 5th Edition. Ottawa, MCR 4177, scale 1:75,000,000.

Nekrasov, I. A. and P. P. Gordeyev (1973) *The Northeast of Yakutia*. Guidebook, Second International Permafrost Conference, Yakutsk, 46 pp.

Nichols, R. L. (1966) Geomorphology of Antarctica. In: J. C. F. Tedrow (ed.), *Antarctic soils and soil forming Processes*. American Geophysical Union, Antarctic Research Series No. 8, pp. 1–59.

Nicholson, F. H. and H. B. Granberg (1973). Permafrost and snowcover relationships near Schefferville. In: *North American Contribution, Second International Conference on Permafrost, Yakutsk, USSR*. Washington, DC: National Academy of Science, Publication 2115, pp. 151–158.

Nicholson, F. H. and B. G. Thom (1973) Studies at the Timmins 4 permafrost experimental site. In: *North American Contribution, Second International Conference on Permafrost, Yakutsk, USSR*. Washington, DC: National Academy of Science, Publication 2115, pp. 159–166.

Nickling, W. G. (1978) Eolian sediment transport during dust storms: Slims River Valley, Yukon Territory. *Canadian Journal of Earth Sciences*, **15**, 1069–1084.

Nixon, J. F. (1990) Northern pipelines in permafrost terrain. *Geotechnical News*, **8**, 25–26.

Nixon, J. F. and E. C. McRoberts (1973) A study of some factors affecting the thawing of frozen soils. *Canadian Geotechnical Journal*, **10**, 439–452.

Norris, K. (1977) *Blow River and Davidson Mountains, Yukon Territory – District of Mackenzie*. Geological Survey of Canada, Map 1516 A.

Nyberg, R. (1985) *Debris flows and slush avalanches in northern Swedish Lappland.* University of Lund, Sweden, Department of Geography, Avhandlingar XCVII, 222 pp.

Ollier, C. D. and A. J. Thomasson (1957) Asymmetrical valleys of the Chiltern Hills. *Geographical Journal*, **123**, 71–80.

Ostrem, G. (1963) Comparative crystallographic studies on ice from ice-cored moraines, snow-banks and glaciers. *Geografiska Annaler*, **45**, 210–240.

Owens, E. H. and S. B. McCann (1970) The role of ice in the Arctic beach environment with special reference to Cape Ricketts, Southwest Devon Island, N.W.T *American Journal of Science*, **268**, 397–414.

Palmer, J. and R. A. Nielson (1962) The origin of granite tors on Dartmoor, Devonshire. *Proceedings, Yorkshire Geological Society*, **33**, 315–340.

Palmer, J. and J. Radley (1961) Gritstone tors of the English Pennines. *Zeitschrift für Geomorphologie*, **5**, 37–52.

Paris, F. P., P. Cleveringa and W. de Gans (1979) The Stokersdobbe: geology and palynology of a deep pingo remnant in Friesland (The Netherlands). *Geologie en Mijnbouw*, **58**, 33–38.

Parmuzina, O. Yu (1978) The cryogenic structure and certain features of ice separation in a seasonally thawed layer. In: A. I. Popov (ed.), *Problems of cryolithology*, Vol. 7. Moscow: Moscow State University, pp. 141–163 (in Russian).

Pavlov, A. V. (1994) Current changes of climate and permafrost in the Arctic and Sub-Arctic of Russia. *Permafrost and Periglacial Processes*, **5**, 101–110.

Pearce, A. J. and J. A. Elson (1973) Postglacial rates of denudation by soil movement, free face retreat, and fluvial erosion, Mont St. Hilaire, Québec. *Canadian Journal of Earth Sciences*, **10**(1), 91–101.

Peltier, L. C. (1950) The geographic cycle in periglacial regions as it is related to climatic geomorphology. *Annals, Association of American Geographers*, **40**, 214–236.

Perov, V. F. (1969) Block fields in the Khibiny Mts. *Biuletyn Peryglacjalny*, **19**, 381–387.

Peteet, D. M., R. Daniels, L. E. Heusser, J. S. Vogel, J. R. Southon and D. E. Nelson (1994) Wisconsinan late-glacial environmental change in southern New England: a regional synthesis. *Journal of Quaternary Science*, **9**, 151–154.

Péwé, T. L. (1948) Origin of the Mima Mounds. *Scientific Monthly*, **46**, 293–296.

Péwé, T. L. (1954) Effect of permafrost upon cultivated fields. *United States Geological Survey Bulletin*, **989F**, 315–351.

Péwé, T. L. (1955) Origin of the upland silt near Fairbanks, Alaska. *Geological Society of America Bulletin*, **66**, 699–724.

Péwé, T. L. (1959) Sand wedge polygons (tesselations) in the McMurdo Sound region, Antarctica. *American Journal of Science*, **257**, 545–552.

Péwé, T. L. (1966a) Permafrost and its effect on life in the north. In: H. P. Hansen (ed.), *Arctic biology*, 2nd edition. Corvallis: Oregon State University Press, pp. 27–66.

Péwé, T. L. (1966b) Ice wedges in Alaska – classification, distribution and climatic significance. In: *Proceedings, 1st International Conference on Permafrost.* National Academy of Science: National Research Council of Canada, Publication 1287, pp. 76–81.

Péwé, T. L. (1969) The periglacial environment. In: T. L. Péwé (ed.), *The periglacial environment.* Montreal: McGill-Queen's University Press, pp. 1–9.

Péwé, T. L. (1970) Altiplanation terraces of early Quaternary age near Fairbanks, Alaska. *Acta Geographica Lodziensia*, **24**, 357–363.

Péwé, T.L. (1973). Ice-wedge casts and past permafrost distribution in North America. *Geoforum*, **15**, 15–26.

Péwé, T. L. (1975) *Quaternary geology of Alaska.* United States Geological Survey Professional Paper 835, 1–145.

Péwé, T. L. (1983a) Alpine permafrost in the contiguous United States: a review. *Arctic and Alpine Research*, **15**, 145–156.

Péwé, T. L. (1983b) The periglacial environment in North America during Wisconsin time. In: S. C. Porter (ed.), *Late Quaternary environments of the United States*, Volume 1, *The late Pleistocene.* Minneapolis: University of Minnesota Press, pp. 157–189.

Péwé, T. L. (1983c) *Geologic hazards of the Fairbanks area, Alaska.* Division of Geological and Geophysical Surveys, Fairbanks, Alaska, Special Report 15, 109 pp.

Péwé, T. L. (1991) Permafrost. In: G. A. Kiersch (ed.) *The heritage of engineering geology: the first hundred years.* Boulder, Colorado: Geological Society of America Centennial Special Volume 3, pp. 277–298.

Péwé, T. L. and A. Journaux (1983) *Origin and character of loesslike silt in unglaciated south-central Yakutia, Siberia, U.S.S.R.* United States Geological Survey Professional Paper 1262, 46 pp.

Péwé, T. L. and R. A. Paige (1963) Frost heaving of piles with an example from the Fairbanks area, Alaska. *United States Geological Survey Bulletin*, **1111-I**, 333–407.

Péwé, T. L., D. E. Rowan, R. H. Péwé and R. Stuckenrath (1982) Glacial and periglacial geology of northwest Blomesletta peninsula, Spitsbergen, Svalbard. Norsk Polarinstitutt, Skrifter 177, 32 pp.

Péwé, T. L., L. Tungsheng, R. M. Slatt and L. Bingyuan (1995) *Origin and character of loesslike silt in the southern Qinghai-Xizang (Tibet) Plateau, China.* United States Geological Survey Professional Paper 1549, 55 pp.

Pissart, A. (1953) Les coulées pierreuses du Plateau des Hautes Fagnes. *Annales, Société Géologique de Belgique*, **76**, 203–219.

Pissart, A. (1956) L'origine périglaciaire des viviers des Hautes Fagnes. *Annales, Société Géologique de Belgique*, **79**, 119–131.

Pissart, A. (1958) Les dépressions fermées dans la région parisienne; le problème de leur origine. *Revue de Géomorphologie Dynamique*, **9**, 73–83.

Pissart, A. (1960) Les dépressions fermées de la région parisienne; Les difficultés d'admettre une origine humaine. *Revue de Géomorphologie Dynamique*, **11**, 12 pp.

Pissart, A. (1963) Les traces de 'pingos' du Pays de Galles (Grande Bretagne) et du Plateau des Hautes Fagnes (Belgique). *Zeitschrift für Geomorphologie*, **7**, 147–165.

Pissart, A. (1964) Vitesses des mouvements du sol au Chambeyron (Basse Alpes). *Biuletyn Peryglacjalny*, **14**, 303–309.

Pissart, A. (1965) Les pingos des Hautes Fagnes; le problème de leur genèse. *Annales, Société Géologique de Belgique*, **88**, 277–289.

Pissart, A. (1966a) Etude de quelques pentes de l'île Prince Patrick. *Annales, Société Géologique de Belgique*, **89**, 377–402.

Pissart, A. (1966b) Le rôle géomorphologique du vent dans la région de Mould Bay (Ile Prince Patrick – TNO – Canada). *Zeitschrift für Geomorphologie*, **10**, 226–236.

Pissart, A. (1967a) Les pingos de l'île Prince Patrick (76°N– 120°W). *Geographical Bulletin*, **9**, 189–217. (English translation, National Research Council of Canada, Technical Translation TT-1401, Ottawa, 46 pp.)

Pissart, A. (1967b) Les modalités de l'écoulement de l'eau sur l'Ile Prince Patrick. *Biuletyn Peryglacjalny*, **16**, 217–224.

Pissart, A. (1968) Les polygons de fente de gel de l'île Prince Patrick (Arctique Canadien, 76° Lat. N.) *Biuletyn Peryglacjalny*, **17**, 171–180.

Pissart, A. (1970) Les phénomènes physiques éssentiels liés au gel; les structures périglaciaires qui en résultent et leur signification climatique. *Annales, Société Géologique de Belgique*, **93**, 7049.

Pissart, A. (1977) Apparition et évolution des sols structuraux périglaciaires de haute montagne. Expériences de terrain au Chambeyron (Alpes, France). *Abhandlungen der Akademie der Wissenschaften in Göttingen, Math.-Physik Klasse*, **31**, 142–156.

Pissart, A. (1987) Les traces de pingos et de palses en Belgique et dans le monde. In: *Geomorphologie périglaciaire. Textes des leçons de la Chaire Francqui belge*. Université de Liège, Belgique: Rijksuniversiteit Gent, Édition Laboratoire de Géomorphologie et de Géologie du Quaternaire, pp. 45–53.

Pissart, A. (1990) Advances in periglacial geomorphology. *Zeitschrift für Geomorphologie, Supplementband*, **79**, 119–131.

Pissart, A. and H. M. French (1976) Pingo investigations, north-central Banks Island, Canadian Arctic. *Canadian Journal of Earth Sciences*, **13**, 937–946.

Pissart, A. and P. Gangloff (1984) Les palses minérales et organiques de la vallée de l'Aneveau, près de Kuujjuaq, Québec subarctique. *Géographie physique et Quaternaire*, **38**, 217–228.

Pissart, A. and E. Juvigné (1980) Génèse et âge d'une trace de butte périglaciaire (pingo ou palse) de la Konnervenn (Hautes Fagnes, Belgique). *Annales, Société Géologique de Belgique*, **103**, 73–96.

Pissart, A. and J. P. Lautridou (1984) Variations de longueur de cylindres de pierre de Caen (calcaire bathonian) sous l'effect de sechage et d'humidification. *Zeitschrift für Geomorphologie*, **49**, 111–116.

Pissart, A., J. S. Vincent and S. A. Edlund (1977) Dépôts et phénomènes éoliens sur l'île de Banks, Territoires du Nord-Ouest, Canada. *Canadian Journal of Earth Sciences*, **14**, 2452–2480.

Podbornyi, E. (1978) Time and intensity of formation of frost induced cracks. In A. I. Povov (ed.), *Problems of cryolithology*, Vol. 7. Moscow: Moscow University Press, pp. 132–140 (in Russian).

Pollard, W. H. (1990) The nature and origin of ground ice in the Herschel Island area, Yukon Territory. In: *Proceedings, Fifth Canadian Permafrost Conference*, Université Laval, Nordicana No. 54, pp. 23–30.

Pollard, W. H. and H. M. French (1980) A first approximation of the volume of ground ice, Richards Island, Pleistocene Mackenzie Delta, Northwest Territories, Canada. *Canadian Geotechnical Journal*, **17**, 509–516.

Pollard, W. H. and H. M. French (1983) Seasonal frost mound occurrence, North Fork Pass, Ogilvie Mountains, northern Yukon, Canada. In: *Proceedings, 4th International Conference on Permafrost*, Vol. 1. Washington, DC: National Academy Press, pp. 1000–1004.

Pollard, W. H. and H. M. French (1984) The groundwater hydraulics of seasonal frost mounds, Northern Yukon. *Canadian Journal of Earth Sciences*, **21**, 1073–1081.

Pollard, W. H. and H. M. French (1985) The internal structure and ice crystallography of seasonal frost mounds. *Journal of Glaciology*, **31**, 157–162.

Popov, A. I. (1961) Cartes des formations periglaciaires actuelles et pleistocenes en territoire de l'U.R.S.S. *Biuletyn Peryglacjalny*, **10**, 87–96.

Popov, A. I. (1962) *The origin and development of massive fossil ice*. Issue 11, Academy of Sciences of the USSR, V.A. Obruchev Institute of Permafrost Studies, Moscow. (National Research Council of Canada, Technical Translation 1006, pp. 5–24.)

Popov, A. I., S. P. Kachurin and N. A. Grave (1966) Features of the development of frozen geomorphogy in northern Eurasia. In: *Proceedings, 1st International Conference on Permafrost*. Ottawa: National Academy of Science, National Research Council of Canada, Publication 1287, pp. 181–185.

Popov, A. V., N. A. Gvozdetskiy, A. G. Chiksishev and B. I. Kudelin (1972) Karst in U.S.S.R. In: M. Herak and V. T. Stingfield (eds), *Karst*. Amsterdam: Elsevier, pp. 355–416.

Popov, A.I. *et al.* (1985a) *Cryolithological map of the USSR*. Scale 1:4,000,000. Moscow: Moscow State University, Faculty of Geography. In Russian. (English translation available at Secretary of State, Ottawa and Geological Survey of Canada, Ottawa.)

Popov, A. I., G. E. Rozenbaum and N. V. Tumel (1985b) *Cryolithology*. Moscow: Moscow State University Press, 238 pp. (in Russian).

Popov, A.I. *et al.* (1990) *Cryolithological Map of North America*. Scale 1:6,000,000. Moscow: Moscow State University, Faculty of Geography. (English translation by D. Tedford and J. A. Heginbottom, Geological Survey of Canada, Ottawa.)

Porsild, A. E. (1938) Earth mounds in unglaciated Arctic northwestern America. *Geographical Review*, **28**, 46–58.

Porsild, A. E. (1955) The vascular plants of the western Canadian Arctic archipelago. *National Museum of Canada, Bulletin*, **135**, 226 pp.

Poser, H. (1948) Boden- und klimaverhältnisse in Mittel- und Westeuropa während der Würmeiszeit. *Erdkunde*, **2**, 53–68.

Potter, N. Jr (1972) Ice-cored rock glacier, Galena Creek, Northern Absaroka Mountains, Wyoming. *Bulletin, Geological Society of America*, **83**, 3025–3068.

Preece, R. C., R. A. Kemp and J. N. Hutchinson (1995) Late-glacial colluvial sequence at Watcombe, Ventnor, Isle of Wight, England. *Journal of Quaternary Science*, **10**, 107–121.

Prestwich, J. (1892) The raised beaches and 'head' or rubble drift of the south of England. *Quarterly Journal of the Geological Society*, **48**, 263–343.

Price, L. W. (1973) Rates of mass wasting in the Ruby Range, Yukon Territory. In: *Permafrost; North American Contribution, Second International Permafrost Conference, Yakutsk, USSR*. Washington, DC: National Academy of Science, Publication 2115, pp. 235–245.

Price, R. J. (1969) Moraines, sandar, kames, and eskers near Breidamerkurjokull, Iceland. *Transactions, Institute of British Geographers*, **46**, 17–43.

Price, W. A. (1968) Oriented lakes. In: *Encyclopedia of geomorphology*. New York: R.W. Fairbridge (ed.), Reinhold Book Co., pp. 784–796.

Prick, A., A. Pissart and J.-C. Ozouf (1993) Variations dilatométriques de cylindres de roches calcaires subissant des cycles de gel-dégel. *Permafrost and Periglacial Processes*, **4**, 1–15.

Priesnitz, K. (1981) Fussflächen und taler in der Arktis NW-Kanadas und Alaskas. *Polarforschung*, **51**, 145–159.

Priesnitz, K. (1988) Cryoplanation. In: M. J. Clark (ed.), *Advances in periglacial geomorphology*, Chichester: J. Wiley and Sons Ltd, pp. 49–67.

Priesnitz, K. and E. Schunke (1983) Periglaziale pediplanation in der Kanadischen Kordillere. In: H. Poser and E. Schunke (eds), *Mesoformen des reliefs im heutigen Periglazialraum*. Abhandlungen Akadem.Wissenschaften in Göttingen, Math.-Phys. Klasse, No. 35, pp. 266–280.

Prince, H. (1961) Some reflexions on the origin of hollows in Norfolk compared with those in the Paris region. *Revue de Géomorphologie Dynamique*, **12**, 110–117.

Pye, K. (1984) Loess. *Progress in Physical Geography*, **8**, 176–217.

Qui, G. and G. Cheng (1995) Permafrost in China: past and present. *Permafrost and Periglacial Process*, **6**, 3–14.

Rampton, V. N. (1974) The influence of ground ice and thermokarst upon the geomorphology of the Mackenzie–Beaufort region. In: B. D. Fahey and R. D. Thompson (eds), *Research in Polar and Alpine Geomorphology*, Proceedings, 3rd Guelph Symposium on Geomorphology. Norwich: GeoBooks, pp. 43–59.

Rampton, V. N. (1982) Quaternary geology of the Yukon Coastal Plain. *Geological Survey of Canada, Bulletin*, **317**, 49 pp.

Rampton, V. N. and R. I. Walcott (1974) Gravity profiles across ice-cored topography, *Canadian Journal of Earth Sciences*, **11**, 110–122.

Rapp, A. (1960a) Recent development of mountain slopes in Kärkevagge and surroundings, northern Sweden. *Geografiska Annaler*, **42**, 71–200.

Rapp, A. (1960b) Talus slopes and mountain walls at Tempelfjorden, Spitsbergen. *Norsk Polarinstitutt Skrifter*, No. 119, 96 pp.

Rapp, A. (1967) Pleistocene activity and Holocene stability of hillslopes, with examples from Scandinavia and Pennsylvania. In: *L'Évolution des Versants, Les Congrès et Colloques de L'Université de Liège*, **40**, Belgique, pp. 229–244.

Rapp, A. (1985) Extreme rainfall and rapid snowmelt as causes of mass movements in high latitude mountains. In: M. Church and O. Slaymaker (eds), *Field and theory: lectures in geocryology*. Vancouver: University of British Columbia Press, pp. 35–56.

Raup, H. (1966) Turf hummocks in the Mesters Vig District, northeast Greenland. In: *Proceedings, 1st International Permafrost Conference*. Ottawa: National Academy of Science, National Research Council, Publication 1287, pp. 43–50.

Ray, R. J., W. B. Krantz, T. N. Caine and R. D. Gunn (1983) A model for sorted patterned ground regularity. *Journal of Glaciology*, **29**, 317–337.

Reanier, R. E. and F. C. Ugolini (1983) Gelifluction deposits as sources of palaeoenvironmental information. In: *Proceedings 4th International Conference on Permafrost*, Vol. 1. Washington, DC: National Academy Press, pp. 1042–1047.

Reger, R. D. and T. L. Péwé (1976) Cryoplanation terraces; indicators of a permafrost environment. *Quaternary Research*, **6**, 99–109.

Reid, C. (1887) On the origin of dry valleys and of coombe rock. *Quarterly Journal Geological Society*, **43**, 364–373.

Research Group on Experimental Roadbed Research (1979) Experimental roadbed in an area with a thick layer of ground ice. In: *Proceedings, 3rd International Conference on Permafrost*, Vol. 2. Ottawa: National Research Council of Canada, Publication 18119, pp. 187–197.

Richard, P. J. H. (1994) Wisconsinan Late-glacial environmental change in Québec: a regional synthesis. *Journal of Quaternary Science*, **9**, 165–170.

Richardson, F. R. S. (1839) Notice of a few observations which it is desirable to make on the frozen soil of British

North America; drawn up for distribution among the Officers of the Hudson's Bay Company. *Journal Royal Geographical Society, London*, **9**, 117–120.

Richter, H., G. Haase and H. Barthel (1963) Die Goletzterrassen. *Petermanns Geogr. Mitteilungen*, **107**, 183–192.

Roberts, M. C. (1985) The geomorphology and stratigraphy of the Lizard Loess in south Cornwall, England. *Boreas*, **14**, 75–82.

Robitaille, B. (1960) Géomorphologie du sud-est de l'Ile Cornwallis, T.N-O. *Cahiers de Géographie de Québec*, **8**, 359–365.

Rockie, W. A. (1942) Pitting on Alaskan farms; a new erosion problem. *Geographical Review*, **32**, 128–134.

Rogov, V. V. (1987) The role of gas-liquid inclusions in mechanism of cryogenic disintegration of quartz. *Vestnik, Moscow University, Geography*, **3**, 81–85 (in Russian).

Romanovskii, N. N. (1980) *The frozen earth*. Moscow: Moscow University Press, 188 pp. (in Russian).

Romanovskii, N. N. (1985) Distribution of recently active ice and soil wedges in the USSR. In: M. Church and O. Slaymaker (eds), *Field and theory; lectures in geocryology*. Vancouver: University of British Columbia Press, pp. 154–165.

Romanovskii, N. N. (1993) *Principles of cryogenesis of lithozone*. Moscow: Moscow University Press, 344 pp. (in Russian).

Romanovskii, N. N., V. Zaitsev, O. Lisitrine and A. Tyurin (1989) *Kurums and cryolithogical facies*. Moscow: Moscow University Press, 152 pp. (in Russian).

Root, J. D. (1975) Ice-wedge polygons, Tuktoyaktuk area, N.W.T. Geological Survey of Canada, Paper 75-1, B, p. 181.

Rose, J., J. Boardman, R. A. Kemp and C. A. Whiteman (1985a) Palaeosols and the interpretation of the British Quaternary stratigraphy. In: K. S. Richards, R. R. Arnett and S. Ellis (eds.), *Geomorphology and soils*. London: George Allen and Unwin, pp. 348–375.

Rose, J., P. Allen, R. A. Kemp, C. A. Whiteman and N. Owen (1985b) The early Anglian Barham soil of eastern England. In: J. Boardman (ed.), *Soils and Quaternary landscape evolution*. Chichester: John Wiley & Sons Ltd, pp. 197–229.

Rösli, A. and A. B. Harnik (1980) Improving the durability of concrete to freezing and de-icing salts. In: P. J. Sereda, and G. G. Livan (eds), *Durability of building materials and components*. American Society for Testing Materials 691, pp. 464–473.

Rott, H. (1983) *SAR data analysis for an Alpine test site*. The European SAR-580 Experiment Investigation Preliminary Report. Publication JRC-ESA, Brussels, September 1983, pp. 1–14.

Rudberg, S. (1962) A report on some field observations concerning periglacial geomorphology and mass movement on slopes in Sweden. *Biuletyn Peryglacjalny*, **11**, 311–323.

Rudberg, S. (1963) Morphological processes and slope development on Axel Heiberg Island, N.W.T., Canada.

Abhandlungen der Akademie der Wissenschaften, Gottingen, KL.11, **14**, 218–228.

Rudberg, S. (1964) Slow mass movement processes and slope development in the Norra Storfjall area, southern Swedish Lappland. *Zeitschrift für Geomorphologie*, Supplementband.

Ruegg, G. H. J. (1983) Periglacial eolian evenly laminated sandy deposits in the Late Pleistocene of N.W. Europe, a facies unrecorded in modern sedimentological handbooks. In: M. E. Brookfield and T. S. Ahlbrandt (eds), *Eolian sediments and processes*. Amsterdam: Elsevier Science Publishers, pp. 455–482.

Ruhe, R. V. (1983) Depositional environment of Late Wisconsin loess in the midcontinental United States. In: S. C. Porter (ed.), *Late Quaternary Environments of the United States*, Vol. 1, *The late Pleistocene*. Minneapolis: University of Minnesota Press, pp. 130–137.

Salvigsen, O. and A. Elgersma (1985) Large-scale karst features and open taliks at Vardeborgsletta, outer Isfjorden, Svalbard. *Polar Research*, **3**, 145–153.

Savigny, K. W. and N. R. Morgenstern (1986a) Geotechnical conditions of slopes at a proposed pipeline crossing, Great Bear River valley, Northwest Territories. *Canadian Geotechnical Journal*, **23**, 490–503.

Savigny, K. W. and N. R. Morgenstern (1986b) *In situ* creep properties in ice–rich permafrost soil. *Canadian Geotechnical Journal*, **23**, 504–514.

Savigny, K. W. and N. R. Morgenstern (1986c) Creep behaviour of undisturbed clay permafrost. *Canadian Geotechnical Journal*, **23**, 515–527.

Schafer, J. P. (1949) Some periglacial features in central Montana. *Journal of Geology*, **57**, 154–174.

Schumm, S. A. (1964) Seasonal variations of erosion rates and processes on hillslopes in western Colorado. *Zeitschrift für Geomorphologie, Supplement*, **5**, 215–238.

Schunke, E. (1977) The ecology of thufurs in Iceland. In: *Berichte ans der forschurgsstelle Nedri As, Hveragerdi (Island)*, No. 26, pp. 39–69.

Schwan, J. (1986) The origin of horizontal alternating bedding in Weichselian aeolian sands in Northwestern Europe. *Sedimentary Geology*, **49**, 73–108.

Schwan, J. (1987) Sedimentologic characteristics of a fluvial to aeolian succession in Weichselian Talsand in the Emsland (F.R.G.). *Sedimentary Geology*, **52**, 273–298.

Séguin, M. K. and M. Allard (1984) Le pergélisol et les processus thermokarstiques de la région de la rivière Nastapoca, Nouveau-Québec. *Géographie physique et Quaternaire*, **XXXVIII**, 11–25.

Sekyra, J. (1969) Periglacial phenomena in the oases and the mountains of the Enderby Land and the Dronning Maud Land (East Antarctica). *Biuletyn Peryglacjalny*, **19**, 277–289.

Selby, M. J. (1971a) Salt weathering of landforms, and an Antarctic example. *Proceedings, Sixth Geography Conference*, New Zealand Geographical Society, Christchurch, pp. 30–35.

Selby, M. J. (1971b) Slopes and their development in an ice-free, arid area of Antarctica. *Geografiska Annaler*, **53**, 235–245.

Selby, M. J. (1974) Slope evolution in an Antarctic oasis. *New Zealand Geographer*, **30**, 18–34.

Sellman, P. V., J. Brown, R. I. Lewellen, H. McKim and C. Merry (1975) *The classification and geomorphic implications of thaw lakes on the Arctic coastal plain, Alaska.* United States Army, Cold Regions Research and Engineering Laboratory, Research Report, No. 344, 21 p.

Seppälä, M. (1971) Evolution of eolian relief of the Kaamasjoki-Kiell-ajoki River Basin in Finnish Lapland. *Fennia*, **104**, 543–562.

Seppälä, M. (1972a) Location, morphology and orientation of inland dunes in Northern Sweden. *Geografiska Annaler*, **54a**, 85–104.

Seppälä, M. (1972b) The term 'palsa'. *Zeitschrift für Geomorphologie*, **16**, 463.

Seppälä, M. (1974) Some quantitative measurements of the present-day deflation on Hietatievat, Finnish Lapland. *Abhandlungen der Akademie der Wissenschaften Göttingen, Math.-Phys. Kl, III*, **29**, 208–220.

Seppälä, M. (1982) An experimental study of the formation of palsas. In: H. M. French (ed.), *Proceedings, Fourth Canadian Permafrost Conference, Calgary, Alberta*, Ottawa: National Research Council of Canada, pp. 36–42.

Seppälä, M. (1988) Palsas and related forms. In: M. J. Clark (ed.), *Advances in periglacial geomorphology*, Chichester: John Wiley and Sons Ltd, pp. 247–278.

Shang, J. (1982) Some characateristics of permafrost along the Qinghai-Xizang Plateau (in Chinese). In: *Proceedings, First Chinese Conference on Glaciology and Geocryology*. Beijing: China Science Press, pp. 38–43.

Sharp, R. P. (1942a) Ground ice mounds in tundra. *Geographical Review*, **32**, 417–423.

Sharp, R. P. (1942b) Periglacial involutions in northeastern Illinois. *Journal of Geology*, **50**, 113–133.

Sharp, R. P. (1949) Pleistocene ventifacts east of the Big Horn mountains, Wyoming. *Journal of Geology*, **57**, 175–195.

Shearer, J. M., R. F. McNab, B. R. Pelletier and T. B. Smith (1971) Submarine pingos in the Beaufort Sea. *Science*, **174**, 816–818.

Sher, A. V., T. N. Kaplina, R. E. Giterman, A. V. Lozhkin, A. A. Arkhangelov, S. V. Kiselyov, Yu V. Kouznetsov, E. I. Virina, V. S. Zazhigin (1979) *Late Cenozoic of the Kolyma lowlands*, Guide book, XIV Pacific Science Congress. Moscow: Academy of Sciences, 115 pp.

Shi, Y. (ed.) (1988) *Map of Snow, Ice and Frozen Ground in China (1:4,000,000), with explanatory notes*. Beijing: China Cartographic Publishing House.

Shilts, W. W. (1974) Physical and chemical properties of unconsolidated sediments in permanently frozen terrain, District of Keewatin. Geological Survey Canada, Paper 74A, pp. 229–235.

Shilts, W. W. (1978) Nature and genesis of mudboils, central Keewatin, Canada. *Canadian Journal of Earth Sciences*, **15**, 1053–1068.

Shostakovitch, W. B. (1927) Der ewig gefrorene boden Siberiens. *Gessel. Erdkunde Berlin Zeitschrift*, **1927**, 394–427.

Shotton, F. W. (1960) Large scale patterned ground in the valley of the Worcestershire Avon. *Geological Magazine*, **97**, 404–408.

Shumskiy, P. A. and B. I. Vtyurin (1966) Underground ice. In: *Proceedings, 1st International Conference Permafrost*. National Academy of Science, National Research Council of Canada, Publication 1287, pp. 108–113.

Shur, Y. L. (1988) The upper horizon of permafrost soils. In: *Proceedings, Fifth International Conference on Permafrost*, Vol. 1. Trondheim: Norway, Tapir Publishers, pp. 867–871.

Sigafoos, R. S. (1951) Soil instability in tundra vegetation. *Ohio Journal of Science*, **51**, 281–298.

Sissons, J. B. (1981) The Loch Lomond Stadial in the British Isles. *Nature*, **280**, 199–203.

Slaymaker, O. and H. M. French (1993) Cold environments and global change. In: H. M. French and O. Slaymaker (eds), *Canada's cold environments*, Montreal: McGill-Queen's University Press, pp. 313–334.

Sloan, C. E. and R. O. van Everdingen (1988) Region 28, Permafrost region. In: W. Back, J. C. Rosenshein and P. R. Seaber (eds), *Hydrology. The geology of North America*, Vol. 0–2. Boulder, Colorado: Geological Society of America, pp. 263–270.

Small, R. J. (1970) *The study of landforms*. Cambridge: Cambridge University Press, 486 pp.

Small, R. J., M. J. Clark and J. Lewin (1970) The periglacial rock-stream at Clatford Bottom, Marlborough Downs, Wiltshire. *Proceedings, Geologist's Association*, **81**, 87–98.

Smith, D. I. (1972) The solution of limestone in an arctic environment. In: *Polar geomorphology*, Institute of British Geographers Special Publication No. 4, pp. 187–200.

Smith, D. J. (1987) Frost-heave activity in the Mount Rae Area, Canadian Rocky Mountains. *Arctic and Alpine Research*, **19**, 155–166.

Smith, H. T. U. (1949) Physical effects of Pleistocene climatic changes in non-glaciated areas; eolian phenomena, frost action and stream terracing. *Bulletin, Geological Society of America*, **60**, 1485–1516.

Smith, H. T. U. (1962) Periglacial frost features and related phenomena in the United States. *Biuletyn Peryglacjalny*, **11**, 325–342.

Smith, H. T. U. (1964) *Periglacial eolian phenomena in the United States*. Volume IV, VI INQUA Congress, Warsaw, 1961. Lodz: Lódzkie Towarzvstwn Naukowo, pp. 177–186.

Smith, M. W. (1977) *Computer simulation of microclimate and ground thermal regimes: test results and programme description*. ALUR 1975–76–72. Ottawa: Department of Indian Affairs and Northern Development, 74 pp.

Smith, M. W. (1985a) Models of soil freezing. In: M. Church and O. Slaymaker (eds), *Field and theory: lectures in geocryology*. Vancouver, BC: University of British Columbia Press, pp. 96–120.

Smith, M. W. (1985b) Observations of soil freezing and frost heave at Inuvik, Northwest Territories, Canada. *Canadian Journal of Earth Sciences*, **22**, 283–290.

Smith, M. W. (1993) Climatic change and permafrost. In: H. M. French and O. Slaymaker (eds), *Canada's cold environments*. Montreal: McGill-Queen's University Press, pp. 291–311.

Smith, M. W. and C. T. Hwang (1973) Thermal disturbance due to channel shifting, Mackenzie Delta area, N.W.T., Canada. In: *Permafrost: North American Contribution, Second International Conference, Yakutsk, U.S.S.R.* National Academy of Science, National Research Council of Canada, Publication 2115, pp. 51–60.

Smith, S. L. and P. J. Williams (1990) Ice lens orientation around a chilled buried pipe. *Proceedings, Fifth Canadian Permafrost Conference*, Université Laval, Nordicana, No. 54, 83–87.

Sollid, J. L. and L. Sörbel (1992) Rock glaciers in Svalbard and Norway. *Permafrost and Periglacial Processes*, **3**, 215–220.

Solomatin, V. I. (1986) *Petrology of underground ice.* Academy Nauka, Novosibirsk; 215 pp. (in Russian).

Soloviev, P. A. (1973a) *Alas thermokarst relief of Central Yakutia.* Guidebook, Second International Permafrost Conference, Yakutsk, USSR, 48 pp.

Soloviev, P. A. (1973b) Thermokarst phenomena and landforms due to frost heaving in Central Yakutia. *Biuletyn Peryglacjalny*, **23**, 135–155.

Soons, J. M. and L. W. Price (1990) Periglacial phenomena in New Zealand. *Permafrost and Periglacial Processes*, **1**, 145–160.

Souchez, P. (1966) Réflexions sur l'évolution des versants sous climat froid. *Revue de Géographie Physique et de Géologie Dynamique*, **VIII**, 317–334.

Souchez, P. (1967a) Gélivation et évolution des versants en bordure de l'Islandsis d'Antartides orientale. In: *L'Évolution des Versants. Les Congrès et Colloques de L'Université de Liège*, **40**, 291–298.

Souchez, P. (1967b) Le recul des verrous-gradins et les rapports glaciaire-périglaciaire en Antarctique. *Revue de Géomorphologie dynamique*, No. 2, 6 pp.

Sparks, B. W., R. G. B. Williams and F. G. Bell (1972) Presumed ground ice depressions in East Anglia. *Proceedings, Royal Society London*, **A327**, 329–343.

Stalker, A. (1960) Ice-pressed drift forms and associated deposits in Alberta. *Geological Survey of Canada Bulletin*, **57**, 38 pp.

Stalker, A. (1984) Ice age bones – a clue. *Geos*, **2**, 11–14.

Stalker, A. MacS. and C. S. Churcher (1982) *Ice Age deposits and animals from the southwestern part of the Great Plains of Canada.* Geological Survey of Canada, Miscellaneous Report No. 31.

Stangl, K. O., W. D. Roggensack and D. W. Hayley (1982) Engineering geology of surficial soils, eastern Melville Island. In: H. M. French (ed.), *Proceedings, Fourth Canadian Permafrost Conference, Calgary, Alberta*, Ottawa: National Research Council of Canada, pp. 136–147.

St-Onge, D. A. (1959) Note sur l'érosion du gypse en climat périglaciaire. *Revue Canadienne de Géographie*, **XIII**, 155–162.

St-Onge, D. A. (1965) La géomorphologie de l'Ile Ellef Ringnes, Territoires du Nord-Ouest, Canada. *Étude Géographique, Direction de la Géographie*, No. 38, Ottawa, 46 pp.

St-Onge, D. A. (1969) Nivation landforms. *Geological Survey Canada*, Paper 69-30, 12 pp.

Street, R. B. and P. I. Melnikov (1990) Seasonal snow cover, ice and permafrost. In: W. J. McG. Tegart, G. W. Sheldon and D. C. Griffiths (eds), *Climate Change, the IPCC Impacts Assessment*. Chapter 7. Report prepared for IPCC by Working Group II, Canberra: WMO-UNEP, Australian Government Publishing Service, 7-1 to 7-33.

Street, R. B. and P. I. Melnikov (1993) Terrestrial component of the cryosphere. In: W. J. McG. Tegart and G. W. Sheldon (eds) *Climate Change 1992, The Supplementary Report to the IPCC Impacts Assessment*. Ch. VIII. Canberra: WMO–UNEP, Australian Government Publishing Service, pp. 94–102.

Sutcliffe, A. J. (1985) *On the track of Ice Age mammals.* London: British Museum (Natural History), 224 pp.

Svensson, H. (1983) Ventifacts as paleowind indicators in a former periglacial area of southern Scandinavia. In: *Proceedings, Fourth International Conference, on Permafrost*, Vol. 1. Washington, DC: National Academy Press, pp. 1217–1220.

Svensson, H. (1988) Ice-wedge casts and relict polygonal patterns in Scandinavia. *Journal of Quaternary Science*, **3**, 57–67.

Sverdrup, H. V. (1938) Notes on erosion by drifting snow and transport of solid material by sea ice. *American Journal of Science*, **35**, 370–373.

Sweeting, M. M. (1972) *Karst landforms.* London: Macmillan Press Ltd.

Synge, F. M. (1981) Quaternary glaciation and changes of sea level in the south of Ireland. *Geologie en Mijnbouw*, **650**, 305–351.

Taber, S. (1929) Frost heaving. *Journal of Geology*, **37**, 428–461.

Taber, S. (1930) The mechanics of frost heaving. *Journal of Geology*, **38**, 303–317.

Taillefer, F. (1944) La dissymétrie des vallées Gasconnes. *La revue de Géographie de Pyrénnees et du Sud-Ouest*, **xv**, 153–181.

Tarnocai, C. (1973) *Soils of the Mackenzie River area.* Report No 72–36, Environmental-Social Program, Northern Pipelines, Task Force on Northern Oil Development, Indian and Northern Affairs Canada, Ottawa, 136 pp.

Tedrow, J. C. F. (1969) Thaw lakes, thaw sinks and soils in northern Alaska. *Biuletyn Peryglacjalny*, **20**, 337–345.

Tegart, W. J. McG., G. W. Sheldon and D. C. Griffiths (eds) (1990) *Climate Change. The IPCC Impacts Assessment.* Canberra: Australian Government Publishing Service.

Te Punga, M. T. (1956) Altiplanation terraces in southern England. *Biuletyn Peryglacjalny*, **4**, 331–338.

Te Punga, M. T. (1957) Periglaciation in southern England. *Tijdschrift Koninklijk Nederlands Aardrijkskundig Genootschap*, **74**, 400–412.

Thibaudeau, P., J. Roberge and B. Lauriol (1988) Agressivité chimique des eaux dans les massifs calcaires du north du Yukon – Canada. *Revue de géomorphologie dynamique*, **XXXVI**, 61–71.

Thie, J. (1974) Distribution and thawing of permafrost in the southern part of the discontinuous zone in Manitoba. *Arctic*, **27**, 189–200.

Thomasson, A. J. (1961) Some aspects of the drift deposits and geomorphology of southeast Hertfordshire. *Proceedings, Geologist's Association*, **72**, 287–302.

Thompson, E. C. and F. H. Sayles (1972) *In situ* creep analysis of room in frozen soil. *ASCE Journal of Soil Mechanics and Foundation Division*, **98**, 899–916.

Thompson, H. A. (1966) Air temperatures in northern Canada with emphasis upon freezing and thawing indices. In: *Proceedings, 1st International Conference on Permafrost*. National Academy of Science, National Research Council of Canada Publication, No. 1287, pp. 18–36.

Thomson, S. (1966) Icings on the Alaskan Highway. *Proceedings, First International Conference on Permafrost*. National Academy of Sciences, National Research Council of Canada Publication, No. 1287, pp. 526–529.

Thorn, C. (1976) Quantitative evaluation of nivation in the Colorado Front Range. *Geological Society of America Bulletin*, **87**, 1169–1178.

Thorn, C. (1979) Ground temperatures and surficial transport in colluvium during snow-patch meltout, Colorado Front Range. *Arctic and Alpine Research*, **11**, 41–52.

Thorn, C. (1988) Nivation: a geomorphic chimera. In: M. J. Clark (ed), *Advances in periglacial geomorphology*. Chichester: John Wiley and Sons Ltd, pp. 3–31.

Thorn, C. E. and K. Hall (1980) Nivation: an arctic-alpine comparison and reappraisal. *Journal of Glaciology*, **25**, 109–124.

Thorn, C. E. and D. S. Loewenherz (1987) Spatial and temporal trends in alpine periglacial studies: implications for paleo-reconstruction. In: J. Boardman (ed.), *Periglacial processes and landforms in Britain and Ireland*. Cambridge: Cambridge University Press, pp. 57–65.

Thorsteinsson, R. and E. T. Tozer (1962) *Banks, Victoria and Stefansson Islands, Arctic Archipelago*. Geological Survey of Canada, Memoir 330, 83 pp.

Tomirdiaro, S. V., and V. K. Ryabchun (1978) Lake thermokarst on the Lower Anadyr Lowland. In: *Permafrost: USSR Contribution, Second International Conference, Yakutsk, USSR*. Washington, DC: National Academy of Sciences, pp. 94–100.

Tong, B and S. Li (1983) Permafrost characteristics and factors affecting them, Qinghai-Xizang Plateau (in Chinese). In: *Professional Papers on Qinghai-Xizang Plateau Permafrost*. Beijing: China Science Press, pp. 1–11.

Trenhaile, A. S. and P. A. Rudakas (1981) Freeze–thaw and shore platform development in Gaspé, Québec. *Géographie physique et Quaternaire*, **35**, 171–181.

Tricart, J. (1968) Periglacial landscapes. In: R. W. Fairbridge (ed.), *Encyclopedia of Geomorphology*, New York: Reinhold Book Co., pp. 829–833.

Tricart, J. (1970) *Geomorphology of cold environments* (translated by E. Watson). New York: Macmillan, St Martin's Press, 320 pp.

Tricart, J., and A. Cailleux (1967) *Le modèle des régions périglaciaires*. Paris: Traité de Géomorphologie, SEDES, 512 pp.

Troll, C. (1944) Strukturböden, Solifluktion und Frostklimate de Erde. *Geologische Rundschau*, **34**, 545–694. (English translation, 1958: *Structure soils, solifluction and frost climate of the Earth*. Translation 43, United States Army Snow Ice and Permafrost Research Establishment, Corps of Engineers, Willmette, Illinois, 121 pp.)

Troll, C. (1962) 'Solle' and 'Mardelle'. *Erdkunde*, **16**, 31–34.

Tsytovich, N. A. (1973) *Mekhanika merzlykh gruntov* (The mechanics of frozen ground). Moscow: Vysshaya Shkola Press (in Russian), 446 pp.) (Translation by Scripta Techica, G. K. Swinzow and G. P. Tschebotarioff, Editors (eds), New York: Scripta/McGraw-Hill, 1975, 426 pp.)

Tufnell, L. (1972) Ploughing blocks with special reference to north-west England. *Biuletyn Peryglacjalny*, **21**, 237–270.

Twidale, C. R. (1987) Genesis of covered pediments: an alternative to Sakaguchi's climatic interpretation. *Bulletin, Department of Geography, University of Tokyo*, **19**, 71–74.

Tyrtikov, A. P. (1964) *The effect of vegetation on perennially frozen soil*. National Research Council of Canada Technical Translation, 1088, Ottawa, pp. 69–90.

Tyurin, A. J., N. N. Romanovskii and N. F. Poltev (1982) *Frost facies analysis of rock streams*. Moscow: Nauka, 148 pp. (in Russian).

Ugolini, F. C., J. G. Bockheim and D. M. Anderson (1973) Soil development and patterned ground evolution in Beacon Valley, Antarctica. In: *Permafrost; North American Contribution, Second International Permafrost Conference, Yakutsk, USSR*. Washington, DC: National Academy of Science, Publication 2115, pp. 246–254.

Urdea, P. (1992) Rock glaciers and periglacial phenomena in the Southern Carpathians. *Permafrost and Periglacial Processes*, **3**, 267–273.

Ushakova, L. F. (1986) Changing of intensity of weathering as function of depth. *Izvestiya VNII Gidrotechniky*, **193**, 79–82 (in Russian).

Vandenberghe, J. (1983) Some periglacial phenomena and their stratigraphical position in the Weichselian deposits in the Netherlands. *Polarforschung*, **53**, 97–107.

Vandenberghe, J. (1988) Cryoturbations. In: M. J. Clark, (ed.), *Advances in periglacial Geomorphology*. Chichester: J. Wiley and Sons Ltd, pp. 179–198.

Vandenberghe, J. (1993) Changing fluvial processes under changing periglacial conditions. *Zeitschrift fur Geomorphologie, Supplementband*, **88**, 17–28.

Vandenberghe, J. and L. Krook (1981) Stratigraphy and genesis of Pleistocene deposits at Alphen (southern Netherlands). *Geologie en Mijnbouw*, **60**, 417–426.

Vandenberghe, J., and A. Pissart (1993) Permafrost changes in Europe during the Last Glacial. *Permafrost and Periglacial Processes*, **4**, 121–135.

Vandenberghe, J. and P. Van den Broek (1982) Weichselian convolution phenomena and processes in fine sediments. *Boreas*, **11**, 299–315.

Vandenberghe, J., C. Kasse, S. Bohncke and S. Kozarski (1994) Climate-related river activity at the Weichselian–Holocene transition: a comparative study of the Warta and Maas rivers. *Terra Nova*, **6**, 476–485.

van Der Vinne, G., T. D. Prowse and D. Andres (1991) Economic impact of river ice jams in Canada. In: T. D. Prowse and C. S. L. Ommanney (eds.), *Northern hydrology: selected perspectives*. Saskatoon: National Hydrology Research Institute Symposium No. 6, pp. 333–352.

van Everdingen, R. O. (1978) Frost mounds at Bear Rock near Fort Norman, N.W.T. 1975–1976. *Canadian Journal of Earth Sciences*, **15**, 263–276.

van Everdingen, R. O. (1979) *Potential interactions between pipelines and terrain in a northern environment*. National Hydrology Research Institute, Inland Waters Directorate, Environment Canada, Paper No. 8, 7 pp.

van Everdingen, R. O. (1981) *Morphology, hydrology and hydrochemistry of karst in permafrost terrain near Great Bear Lake, Northwest Territories*. National Hydrology Research Institute, Paper No. 11, Inland Waters Directorate Scientific Series 114, 53 pp.

van Everdingen, R. O. (1982) Management of groundwater discharge for the solution of icing problems in the Yukon. In: H. M. French (ed.), *Proceedings, Fourth Canadian Permafrost Conference, Calgary, Alberta*. Ottawa: National Research Council of Canada, pp. 212–228.

van Everdingen, R. O. (1985) Unfrozen permafrost and other taliks. In: J. Brown, M. C. Metz and P. Hoekstra, (eds), *Workshop on Permafrost Geophysics, Golden, Colorado*. US Army, Cold Regions Research and Engineering Laboratories, Special Report 85-5, 101–105.

van Everdingen, R. O. (1990) Ground-water hydrology. In: T. D. Prowse and C. S. L. Ommaney (eds), *Northern hydrology: Canadian perspectives*. Saskatoon: National Hydrology Research Institute Report No. 1, pp. 77–101.

van Huissteden, J. (1990) Tundra rivers of the last glacial: sedimentation and geomorphological processes during the middle pleniglacial in Twente, eastern Netherlands. *Mededelingen rijks geologische dienst*, **44-3**, 3–138.

van Huissteden, J. and J. Vandenberghe (1988) Changing fluvial style of periglacial lowland rivers during the Weichselian Pleniglacial in the eastern Netherlands. *Zeitschrift für Geomorphologie, Supplementband*, **71**, 131–146.

van Steijn, H., P. Bertran, B. Francou, B. Hétu and J.-P. Texier (1995) Models for the genetic and environmental interpretation of stratified slope deposits: a review. *Permafrost and Periglacial Processes*, **6**, 125–146.

Van Vliet-Lanoë, B. (1982) Structures et microstructures associées à la formation de glace de ségrégation: leur conséquences. In: H. M. French (ed.), *Proceedings, Fourth Canadian Permafrost Conference, Calgary, Alberta*. Ottawa: National Research Council of Canada, pp. 116–122.

Van Vliet-Lanoë, B. (1985) Frost effects in soils. In: J. Boardman (ed.), *Soils and Quaternary landscape evolution*, Chichester: John Wiley and Sons Ltd, pp. 117–158.

Van Vliet-Lanoë, B. (1988) The genesis of cryoturbations and their significance in environmental reconstruction. *Journal of Quaternary Science*, **3**, 85–96.

Van Vliet-Lanoë, B. (1991) Differential frost heave, load casting and convection: converging mechanisms; a discussion of the origin of cryoturbations. *Permafrost and Periglacial Processes*, **2**, 123–139.

Van Vliet-Lanoë, B., J.-P. Coutard and A. Pissart (1984) Structures caused by repeated freezing and thawing in various loamy sediments. A comparison of active, fossil and experimental data. *Earth Surface Processes and Landforms*, **9**, 553–566.

Velichko, A. A. (1975) Paragenesis of a cryogenic (periglacial) zone. *Biuletyn Peryglacjalny*, **24**, 89–110.

Velichko, A.A. (1982). *Paleogeography of Europe during the last one hundred thousand years* (atlas monograph in Russian with abstract and legends in English). (I.P. Gerassimov, ed.). Moscow: Nauka. 156 pp.

Vernon, P. and O.L. Hughes (1966). Surficial geology of Dawson, Larsen Creek and North Creek map areas, Yukon Territory. *Geological Survey of Canada Bulletin*, **136**, 25 pp.

Viereck, L. A. (1965) Relationship of white spruce to lenses of perennially frozen ground, Mount McKinley National Park. *Arctic*, **18**, 262–267.

Veireck, L. A. (1973) Ecological effects of river flooding and forest fires on permafrost in the taiga of Alaska. In: *Permafrost; North American Contribution, Second International Permafrost Conference, Yakutsk, USSR*. Washington, DC: National Academy of Science, Publication 2115, pp. 60–67.

Vincent, J. S. (1982) The Quaternary history of Banks Island, N.W.T., Canada. *Géographie physique et Quaternaire*, **36**, 209–232.

Vincent, J. S. (1989) Quaternary geology of the northern Canadian Interior Plains. In: R. J. Fulton (ed.), *Quaternary geology of Canada and Greenland, Geology of Canada*, No. 1. Ottawa: Geological Survey of Canada, pp. 100–137.

Vtyurina, E. A. (1974) *The cryogenic structures of the active layer* (in Russian). Moscow: Nauka, 126 pp.

Wagner, S. (1992) Creep of alpine permafrost, investigated on the Murtel rock glacier. *Permafrost and Periglacial Processes*, **3**, 157–162.

Wahl, H. E., D. B. Fraser, R. C. Harvey and J. B. Maxwell (1987) *Climate of Yukon*. Environment Canada, Atmospheric Environment Service. Ottawa: Supply and Services Canada, 323 pp.

Walder, J. S. and B. Hallet (1985) A theoretical model of the fracture of rock during freezing. *Geological Society of America, Bulletin*, **96**(3), 336–346.

Walder, J. S. and B. Hallet (1986) The physical basis of frost weathering: toward a more fundamental and unified perspective. *Arctic and Alpine Research*, **18**, 27–32.

Walker, H. J. (1974). The Colville River and the Beaufort Sea: some interactions. In: J. C. Reed and J. E. Sater (eds), *The coast and shelf of the Beaufort Sea*. Washington, DC: The Arctic Institute of North America, pp. 513–540.

Walker, H. J. (1978) Lake tapping in the Colville River delta. In: *Proceedings, 3rd International Conference on Permafrost*, Vol. 1. Ottawa: National Research Council of Canada, Publication 18119, pp. 233–238.

Walker, H. J. (1983) Erosion in a permafrost-dominated delta. In: *Proceedings, 4th International Conference on Permafrost*. Washington, DC: National Academy Press, pp. 1344–1349.

Walker, H. J. (1991) Bluff erosion at Barrow and Wainwright, Arctic Alaska. *Zeitschrift für Geomorphologie, Supplementband*, **81**, 53–61.

Walker, H. J. and L. Arnborg (1966) Permafrost ice wedge effect on riverbank erosion. In: *Proceedings, 1st International Conference on Permafrost*. National Academy of Science, National Research Council, Publication 1287, pp. 164–171.

Wallace, R. E. (1948) Cave-in lakes in the Nebesna, Chisna and Tanana river valleys, eastern Alaska. *Journal of Geology*, **56**, 171–181.

Walters, J. C. (1994) Ice-wedge casts and relict polygonal patterned ground in north-east Iowa, USA. *Permafrost and Periglacial Processes*, **5**, 269–282.

Wang, B. and H. M. French (1994) Climate controls and high-altitude permafrost, Qinghai–Xizang (Tibet) Plateau, China. *Permafrost and Periglacial Processes*, **5**, 87–100.

Wang, B. and H. M. French (1995a) Frost heave and its implications for patterned ground, Tibet Plateau, China. *Arctic and Alpine Research*, **27**, 337–344.

Wang, B. and H. M. French (1995b) *In situ* creep of frozen soil, Fenghuo Shan, Tibet Plateau, China. *Canadian Geotechnical Journal*, **32**, 3, 545–552.

Wang, B. and H. M. French (1995c) Permafrost on the Tibet Plateau, China. *Quaternary Science Reviews*, **14**, 255–274.

Wang, S. (1993) Permafrost changes along the Qinghai-Xizang Highway during the last decades (in Chinese). *Arid Land Geography*, **16**, 1–8.

Wankiewicz, A. (1984) Analysis of winter heat flow in an ice-covered Arctic stream. *Canadian Journal of Civil Engineering*, **11**, 430–443.

Washburn, A. L. (1956) Classification of patterned ground and review of suggested origins. *Bulletin, Geological Society of America*, **67**, 823–865.

Washburn, A. L. (1967) Instrumental observations on mass wasting in the Mesters Vig District, Northeast Greenland. *Meddelelser om Gronland*, **166**, 318 pp.

Washburn, A.L. (1969) Weathering, frost action and patterned ground in the Mesters Vig District, Northeast Greenland. *Meddelelser om Gronland*, **176**, 303 pp.

Washburn, A. L. (1970) An approach to a genetic classification of patterned ground. *Acta Geographica Lodziensia*, **24**, 437–446.

Washburn, A. L. (1979) *Geocryology: a survey of periglacial processes and environments*, London: Edward Arnold, 406 pp.

Washburn, A. L. (1983) Palsas and continuous permafrost. In: *Proceedings, 4th International Conference on Permafrost*, Vol. 1. Washington, DC: National Academy Press, pp. 1372–1377.

Washburn, A. L. (1985) Periglacial problems. In: M. Church and O. Slaymaker (eds), *Field and theory. Lectures in geocryology*. Vancouver: University of British Columbia Press, pp. 166–202.

Washburn, A. L. (1989) Near-surface soil displacement in sorted circles, Resolute Area, Cornwallis Island, Canadian High Arctic. *Canadian Journal of Earth Sciences*, **25**, 941–955.

Washburn, A. L., D. D. Smith and R. H. Goddard (1963) Frost cracking in a middle-latitude climate. *Biuletyn Peryglacjalny*, **12**, 175–189.

Waters, R. S. (1962) Altiplanation terraces and slope development in west-Spitsbergen and southwest England. *Biuletyn Peryglacjalny*, **11**, 89–101.

Watson, E. (1971) Remains of pingos in Wales and the Isle of Man. *Geological Journal*, **7**, 381–392.

Watts, S. H. (1983) Weathering pit formation in bedrock near Cory Glacier, southeastern Ellesmere Island, Northwest Territories. Geological Survey of Canada, Paper 83-1A, pp. 487–491.

Wayne, W. J. (1967) Periglacial features and climatic gradient in Illinois, Indiana, and western Ohio, east central United States. In: E. J. Cushing and H. E. Wright Jr (eds), *Quaternary paleoecology*. New Haven: Yale University Press, pp. 393–414.

Wayne, W. J. (1991) Ice-wedge casts of Wisconsinan age in eastern Nebraska. *Permafrost and Periglacial Processes*, **2**, 211–223.

Weeks, A. G. (1969) The stability of slopes in south-east England as affected by periglacial activity. *Quarterly Journal of Engineering Geology*, **5**, 223–241.

Weigand, G. (1965) Fossile pingos in Mitteleuropa. *Wurzburger Geogr. Arbeiten*, **16**, 152 pp.

Weller, M. W. and D. V. Derksen (1979) The geomorphology of Teshepuk Lake in relation to coastline configuration of Alaska's coastal plain. *Arctic*, **32**, 152–160.

Werner, B. T. and B. Hallet (1993) Numerical simulation of self-organized stone stripes. *Nature*, **361**, 142–145.

West, R. G. (1977) *Pleistocene geology and biology*. Second edition, Harlow: Longman, 440 pp.

West, R. G. and M. Pettit (1993) Taphonomy of plant remains on floodplains of tundra rivers, present and Pleistocene. *New Phytologist*, **123**, 203–221.

West, R. G., F. R. S. Camilla, A. Dickson, J. A. Catt, A. H. Weir and B. W. Sparks (1974) Late Pleistocene deposits at Wretton, Norfolk II. Devensian Deposits. *Philosophical Transactions Royal Society of London*, **B267**, 337–420.

Wheaton, E. E. and T. Singh (1988) Exploring the implications of climatic change for the boreal forest and forestry economies of western Canada. *Climate Change Digest 89–02, Environment Canada*, 18 pp.

White, S. E. (1971) Rock glacier studies in the Colorado Front Range, 1961 to 1968. *Arctic and Alpine Research*, **3**, 43–64.

White, S. E. (1976) Is frost action really only hydration shattering? *Arctic and Alpine Research*, **8**, 1–6.

Whiteman, C. A. and R. A. Kemp (1990) Pleistocene sediments, soils, and landscape evolution at Stebbing, Essex, England. *Journal of Quaternary Science*, **5**, 145–161.

Williams, P. J. (1961) Climatic factors controlling the distribution of certain frozen ground phenomena. *Geografiska Annaler*, **43**, 339–360.

Williams, P. J. (1962) Quantitative investigtaions of soil movement in frozen ground phenomena. *Biuletyn Peryglacjalny*, **11**, 353–347.

Williams, P. J. (1968) Ice distribution in permafrost profiles. *Canadian Journal of Earth Sciences*, **5**, 1381–1386.

Williams, P. J. (1976) Volume change in frozen soils. In: *Laurits Bjerrum Memorial Volume*. Oslo: Norwegian Geotechnical Institute, pp. 233–346.

Williams, P. J. (1977) General properties of freezing soils. In: P. J. Williams and M. Fremond (eds), *Soil freezing and highway construction*. Ottawa: Carleton University, 702 pp.

Williams, P .J. (1986) *Pipelines and permafrost. Science in a cold climate*. Ottawa: Carleton University Press, 137 pp.

Williams, P. J. and M. W. Smith (1989) *The frozen earth. Fundamentals of geocryology*. Cambridge: Cambridge University Press, 306 pp.

Williams, R. B. G. (1964) Fossil patterned ground in eastern England. *Biuletyn Peryglacjalny*, **14**, 337–49.

Williams, R. B. G. (1968) Some estimates of periglacial erosion in southern and eastern England. *Biuletyn Peryglacjalny*, **17**, 311–335.

Williams, R. B. G. (1975) The British climate during the last Glaciation; an interpretation based on periglacial phenomena. In: A. E. Wright and F. Mosely (eds), *Ice ages-ancient and modern*. Liverpool: Seele House Press, pp. 95–120.

Williams, R. B. G. and D. A. Robinson (1981) Weathering of sandstone by the combined action of frost and salt. *Earth Surface Processes and Landforms*, **6**, 1–9.

Williams, R. B. G. and D. A. Robinson (1991) Frost weathering of rocks in the presence of salts – a review. *Permafrost and Periglacial Processes*, **2**, 347–353.

Wolfe, P. E. (1953) Periglacial frost–thaw basins in New Jersey. *Journal of Geology*, **61**, 113–141.

Woo, M.-K. (1986) Permafrost hydrology in North America. *Atmosphere-Ocean*, **24** (3), 201–234.

Woo, M. -K. (1990a) Consequences of climatic change for hydrology in permafrost zones. *Journal of Cold Regions Engineering*, **4**, 15–20.

Woo, M.-K. (1990b) Permafrost Hydrology. In: T. D. Prowse and C. S. L. Ommanney (eds), *Northern hydrology, Canadian perspectives*. NHRI Science Report No. 1, pp. 63–76.

Woo, M.-K. (1991) Arctic streamflow. In: Department of Geography, McMaster University, M.–K. Woo and D. J. Gregor (eds.), *Arctic environment: past, present and future*, Hamilton, Ontario: pp. 105–111.

Woo, M.-K. and J. Sauriol (1980) Channel development in snow-filled valleys, Resolute, N.W.T., Canada. *Geografiska Annaler*, **62A**, 37–56.

Woo, M.-K. and P. Steer (1982) Occurrence of surface flow on arctic slopes, southwestern Cornwallis Island. *Canadian Journal of Earth Sciences*, **19**, 2368–2377.

Woo, M.-K. and P. Steer (1983) Slope hydrology as influenced by thawing of the active layer, Resolute, N.W.T. *Canadian Journal of Earth Sciences*, **20**, 978–986.

Woo, M.-K. and Z. Xia (1995) Suprapermafrost groundwater seepage in gravelly terrain, Resolute, NWT, Canada. *Permafrost and Periglacial Processes*, **6**, 57–72.

Woo, M.-K., P. Marsh and P. Steer (1983) Basin water balance in a continuous permafrost environment. In: *Proceedings, Fourth International Conference on Permafrost*. Washington, DC: National Academy Press, pp. 1407–1411.

Woo, M.-K., A. G. Lewkowicz and W. R. Rouse (1992) Response of the Canadian permafrost environment to climatic change. *Physical Geography*, **13**, 287–317.

Wood, B. L. (1969) Periglacial tor topography in southern New Zealand. *New Zealand Journal of Geology and Geophysics*, **12**, 361–375.

Wright, H. E. (1961) Late Pleistocene climate of Europe; a review. *Bulletin, Geological Society of America*, **72**, 933–984.

Wright, H. E. and S. C. Porter (eds.) (1983) *Late Quaternary environments of the United States*. two volumes. Minneapolis, Minnesota: University of Minnesota Press, 407 pp and 207 pp.

Xing, Z., X. Wu, and R. Qu (1980) Determination of the ancient permafrost table, based on the variation in the content of clay minerals (in Chinese). *Bingchuan Dongtu*, **2**, 39–44. (English translation: 1984, National Research Council of Canada, Technical Translation 253, pp. 231–240.)

Young, A. (1972) *Slopes*. Edinburgh: Oliver and Boyd, 288 pp.

Young, A. (1974) The rate of slope retreat. In: E. H. Brown and R. S. Waters (eds), *Progress in geomorphology – papers in honour of David L. Linton*. Institute of British Geographers Special Publication 7, pp. 65–78.

Zhou, Y. and D. Guo (1982) Principal characteristics of permafrost in China (in Chinese). *Journal of Glaciology and Geocryology*, **4**, 1–19.

Zoltai, S. C. (1971) Southern limit of permafrost features in peat landforms, Manitoba and Saskatchewan. Geological Association of Canada, Special Paper No. 9, pp. 305–310.

Zoltai, S. C. (1972) Palsas and peat plateaus in Central Manitoba and Saskatchewan. *Canadian Journal of Forest Research*, **2**, 291–302.

Zoltai, S. C. (1973) Vegetation, surficial deposits and permafrost relationships in the Hudson Bay lowlands. In: *Proceedings, Symposium on the Physical Environment of the Hudson Bay Lowlands, University of Guelph*, pp. 17–34.

Zoltai, S. C. and W. W. Pettapiece (1973) *Terrain, vegetation and permafrost relationships in the northern part of the Mackenzie Valley and Northern Yukon*. Report 73–4, Environmental–Social Committee Northern Pipelines, Task Force on Northern Oil Development, Information Canada, Ottawa, 105 pp.

Zoltai, S. C. and C. Tarnocai (1974) *Soils and vegetation of hummocky terrain*. Report 74–5, Environmental–Social Committee Northern Pipelines, Task Force on Northern Oil Development, Information Canada, Ottawa, 86 pp.

Zoltai, S. C. and C. Tarnocai (1975) Perennially frozen peatlands in the western Arctic and Subarctic of Canada. *Canadian Journal of Earth Sciences*, **12**, 28–43.

Zoltai, S. C., C. Tarnocai and W. W. Pettapiece (1978) Age of cryoturbated organic materials in earth hummocks from the Canadian Arctic. In: *Proceedings, 3rd International Conference on Permafrost*, Vol. 1. Ottawa: National Research Council of Canada, pp. 325–331.

Index

Note: *Because of frequent repetition, Arctic, northern Canada, western Canadian Arctic and high Arctic islands are not indexed.*

active layer, 53, 54, 127–48, 153–4, 160, 161
    slope failures, 121, 139–40, 161–3, 298
aeolian sand, 207–9, 260–1, 262
agriculture, effect on permafrost, 282, 283
alas thermokarst relief, 113–16
Alaska, 8, 11, 25, 27, 52, 55, 56, 57, 65, 67, 78, 93, 97, 102, 116, 121–4, 132, 180, 191, 207, 208, 209, 259, 284, 288–94
Alaskan highway, 51, 293–4
alpine
    climates, 22, 23, 26, 63–4, 225
    permafrost, *see* permafrost mountain
altiplanation terraces, *see* cryoplanation terraces
anchor ice, 188
Anglian Barham soil, eastern England, 270
Antarctica, 26, 37, 40, 46–8, 56, 166, 172, 174, 205–6, 209, 213, 238
Arctic beaches, 210–12
artesian pore pressures, 77–8, 102–3, 146
aspect (orientation), effect of, 59, 63, 66, 78, 155–6, 223, 264
asymmetrical valleys, 14, 111, 183, 201, 202–3, 264, 265
atmospheric circulation, Pleistocene, 223–4
'aufeis', *see* icings
avalanches
    snow 162, 164, 171
    slush 163, 164–5

Badland thermokarst relief, 118–19
Baffin Island, NWT, Canada, 134, 190, 192, 194–7, 198, 201, 208
Banks Island, NWT, Canada, 13–15, 37, 66, 68–9, 76, 92, 105, 107, 111, 119, 120, 123, 124, 126, 140, 142, 151, 154, 156, 157, 160, 161, 173, 192, 199–200, 202–3, 206, 208, 209–12, 242, 269, 282, 283

Barn Mountains, Yukon Territory, Canada, 12, 14–18, 76, 170, 176–7, 183
Barrow, Alaska, 123, 210, 211, 212, 213
basin hydrology, 190–4
'baydjarakhs', *see* thermokarst mounds
Beaufort Plain, northwest Banks Island, NWT, Canada, 13–15, 18, 183, 200, 202–3
bedload sediment transport, 194–5, 198–9
bedrock
    frost-weathered, 41–2, 236
    heave, 133–5
biological evidence, Pleistocene reconstruction, 233–5
blockfields (rock-rubble; felsenmeer), 18, 41, 134, 236
Boreal forest (Taiga), 4, 21, 27, 67, 145, 159, 295, 296, 301–4
braided channels, 14, 198–9, 263–4
breakup, 186, 188–90, 191–2
breckland polygons and stripes, 268–9
BTS method, 64
'bugor', *see* frost mounds
bulgannyakhs, 102, 103, 104, 105, 115–16
buried glacier ice, 98–101

cambering and valley bulging, 169, 255
capillarity, 32
cave men, southern France, 233–4
chalk
    asymmetrical valleys, 267–8
    patterned ground, 268–9
    periglacial deposits, 266–7
        legacy, 270–1
        valleys (dells), 270
    rock streams, 268
    southern England, 235, 238, 239, 250–1, 260, 266–71
channel
    hydrology, 186–90
    morphology, 198–201
Charente region, southwest France, 238–9
China, 8, 61–3, 130, 230–1
Churchill, Manitoba, Canada, 67, 68
'classic' solifluction, *see* solifluction

coasts, 209–14
  Pleistocene, 231
coefficient
  of cryogenic contrast, 44
  of linear expansion, 39, 140
  of thermal expansion, 96
Colorado Front Range, USA, 39, 151, 156
Colville River and Delta, Alaska, 124, 195, 196,
  213–14
Coombe Rock, southern England, 239, 267
composite wedge casts, 247, 248
Cornwallis Island, NWT, Canada, 190–1, 193–4, 197
cover sand and dunes, 206, 209, 260–1
creep of permafrost, 7, 167, 242, 255–6
crop markings, 244
cryofacies, 84–5
cryofront, 129, 131
cryopediments, 16, 175–7, 181–2
cryoplanation, 181–2
  terraces, 18, 177–81, 236-8
cryosphere, 26–8
cryostatic (i.e. freezeback) pressures, 143
cryostratigraphy, 83–5
cryostructures, 81–6
cryosuction, 32–4
cryotextures, 81
cryotic and non-cryotic, 52
cryoturbation(s), 141, 143, 240, 241, 242

Dawson City, Yukon Territory, Canada, 22, 23, 24,
  61, 190, 286–7
debris flows, 162–5, 171–2, 239
deflation, 206
'degradation polygons', see polygons, high centred
degree-days, 34–5, 301–3
DeKalb Mounds, Illinois, USA, 253
deltas, cold-climate, 213–14
'denivation' forms, 208
desert pavement, 206, 262
'detachment failures', see active layer slope failures
dissolved organic carbon transport, 195, 197
'drunken forest', Siberia, 177
dry valleys (dells), 267, 272–3

Eagle Plain, Yukon Territory, Canada, 12, 16
Eagle River bridge, Yukon Territory, Canada, 288–9,
  291, 292
East Anglian
  chalky drift, 268–9
  stratigraphic record, 219
Ellef Ringnes Island, NWT, Canada, 48, 175, 180,
  192, 238

Ellesmere Island, NWT, Canada, 166, 191
engineering and construction problems, 285–91
England, southern, 154, 168, 213, 235, 236, 237,
  239–40, 250, 251, 255, 260, 262
experimentation
  field, 71, 91–7, 104–6, 160, 290–1
  laboratory, 34, 41, 42–3, 44–6, 133, 137–9

Fairbanks, Alaska, 22, 167, 207, 283, 292, 293
faunal and insect remains, see biological evidence,
  Pleistocene reconstruction
Fenghuo Shan, Tibet Plateau, 21, 22, 23, 24, 35–6,
  167, 298
Fennoscandia, 70, 26–7, 28, 63–4, 70, 302–3
fluvial
  cycle, Pleistocene, 263–4
  processes, 7, 13, 185–98, 224
fluvio-thermal erosion, 124–6, 197–8
forest fires, 25, 69, 111–12, 139
Former Soviet Union (FSU), 8, 55, 59–61, 230,
  282, 287
'fortress polygons', 117–18
Fosheim Peninsula, Ellesmere Island, NWT, Canada,
  161–2, 163, 298
fossil cryoturbations, see frost-disturbed soils and
  structures, Pleistocene
frazil ice, 188
freeze
  back, 36, 128
  –thaw cycles, 4, 35, 37–9, 221, 238, 239, 264
  -up, 186, 188–9
freezing
  front, 129, 131
  level, 33–4
  one-sided and two-sided, 151
  oxygen isotope composition, 86–7
  point depression, 32, 33
  process, 31–4
freezing and thawing indices, 34–5
frost
  action, 4, 5, 31–45, 235–43
    phenomena, Pleistocene, 224–5, 230, 235–42
  blisters/mounds, 78–9
  coated clast (debris) flow, 172, 239
  cracking, see thermal contraction cracking
  creep, 151–2, 239
  disturbed soils and structures, Pleistocene, 220,
    234, 235, 240–3
  fissures, Pleistocene, 243–50
    primary and secondary infill, 245
    pseudomorphs and casts, 228, 244–9
  heave, 5, 32–4, 54, 131–9, 282, 287, 288–91

primary, 34, 131–2
secondary, 34, 54, 132–3
differential, 135–6, 138, 143, 146
heaving; bridges, roads, railways and airstrips,
     288–9
mounds, 101–2, 106–8, 242, 249–53
sorting, 137–9
tube, 127
weathering (mechanical), 7, 40–6, 178, 179, 180,
     235, 236–8, 267, 270
'frost-stable', 287
'frost-susceptible', 34, 54, 135, 291
frozen
     and unfrozen ground, 5–6, 52–3
     ground, Pleistocene, 242–56
'frozen fringe', 132–3

Garry Island, NWT, Canada, 92, 97, 130, 139, 152,
     153, 154, 156
gelifluction, 151, 152–5
geotechnical and engineering problems, 281–94
geothermal gradient, 54–6, 60, 62, 65
glaciers, sea ice and sea level, 299
'glacis' ('erosion glacis'), see pediments
global warming (change), 26–8, 110, 295–304
goletz terraces, see cryoplanation terraces
Gora Sw Malgorzata, Poland, 273, 274
Greenland, 151, 154, 156, 201, 202, 205, 209, 213, 238
'grèzes litées', 161, 172, 238–9
ground ice, 54, 80–108, 281
     amounts, 89, 113
     classification, 87–8
     distribution with depth, 89–90
     epigenetic and syngenetic, 87
     isotopic composition, 85–7, 100
     slumps, see retrogressive thaw slumps
ground temperature (thermal) regime, 35–9, 128–30,
     296–300
ground veins, see soil wedges
groundwater, 73–8
     bedrock heave, 133
     chemical composition, 74–5, 86–7
     water supply, 291–3
Gruytviken, south Georgia Island, Antarctica, 23
'gulls', widened joints, 255, 271

'head' deposits, 239–40
heavemeters, 133
hillslope processes, 149–69
honeycomb weathering, 46–7, 205
housing and municipal services, 285–8
Hudson Bay railway, Canada, 289

hummock growth, equilibrium model, 143, 145
hummocks, see non-sorted circles
hydraulic potentials, high, 77, 147
hydrolaccoliths, see frost mounds
hydrology, permafrost, 54, 73–9, 242

Ibyuk Pingo, NWT, Canada, 105
ice
     amount, 89
     content, 80
     crystallography, 85–6
     distribution with depth, 89–90
     'excess ice', 80–1
     geochemistry, 86–7
     hardness, 205
ice-cored
     mounds, 101–8
     topography, 116–17
ice dykes, 100
ice-foot, 209
ice-jams, 186, 189–90
Iceland, 196, 201
ice-marginal (meltwater) channels, 15, 262, 264
'ice-rind', 89, 235
ice segregation, 5, 7, 33–4, 146, 242
ice wedges, 39, 89–98, 117–19, 122, 167, 212, 244–6,
     283, 298
     pseudomorphs (casts), 220, 230, 245–6, 247
     relief, 94–6, 98
     thermokarst terrain, 117–19
icings, groundwater, 75–7, 293–4
     river 188–90
Illisarvik drained lake, NWT, Canada, 92, 95–6, 128,
     130, 133
intrasedimental ice, 100–1
intrusive (injection) ice, 5, 88, 100, 103, 105–6
Inuvik, NWT, Canada, 12, 36, 69, 97, 111–12, 128,
     132, 286, 287, 289, 296, 297
involutions, 126, 234, 235, 240–2, 254

Jokulhlaupe, 192

Kärkevagge, Sweden, 162, 163, 164, 166, 171, 195
karstification, 47–50
Keewatin District, Canada, 147–8, 154
Klondike Plateau, Yukon Territory, Canada, 174–5
Koukdjuak, Great Plain of the, 123
'kurums', 41, 236

land ice and seasonal snow, 27
Lappland, Finnish, 71, 206, 208
latent heat, 33, 128

Late/Postglacial vegetation sucessions, 221–2
late Quaternary stratigraphy, 218
'*limons à doublets*', 260
liquefaction, 154, 240, 242
Lódź Plateau, Poland, 272–3
loess-like silt, 206–7, 259
loess, Pleistocene, 257–60
Longyeardalen, Spitsbergen, 164, 166, 172
Lozinski, Walery von, 3

Mackenzie (NWT, Canada)
    Delta, 13, 21, 22, 40, 68, 83, 87, 91, 99, 102,
        103–7, 120, 121, 123, 124, 126, 132, 133, 200,
        213–14, 283, 284, 286, 299, 300
    River, 8, 13, 168, 186–8, 189–90, 196, 197, 200
    Valley, 139, 145, 162, 167, 168, 292, 296, 297, 301
'macro-beaded' drainage, 116
mammals, Pleistocene, 233–5
mass wasting, 7, 149–66
massive ice
    creep and deformation, 117
    icy bodies, 81, 98–101, 119
Mayo, Yukon Territory, Canada, 81, 98, 297
Melville Island, NWT, Canada, 136, 140, 147, 161, 167
Mesters Vig, Greenland, 39, 132
methane (gas) hydrates, 295, 300
'mineral' palsas, 70, 251, 252
morpho-climatic reconstruction, Late Pleistocene,
    226–31
    China, 230
    Europe, 226–7
    FSU, 230
    North America, 227–9
morphogenetic region, periglacial, 21
mud
    boils, 138, 146, 147–8, 154
    hummocks, 152–3
mudbursts, 154

Nahanni Karst, NWT, Canada, 49–50
'nalyedi', *see* icings
needle ice, 137
nival
    flood, 191–2, 197–8
    stream flow regime, 14, 191, 198
nivation, 7, 159, 181
niveo-aeolian deposits, 206, 208–9, 239
non-diastrophic structures, Pleistocene, 169, 242,
    254–6, 271
non-sorted circles (hummocks), 143–6
Norway, 48, 154, 156, 164, 168

Ogilvie Mountains, Yukon Territory, Canada, 75, 174
oil and gas activities, 284, 285, 290–1
Old Crow, Yukon Territory, Canada, 12
oriented thaw lakes, 123–4

palaeo-reconstruction, problems, 221–6
palaeo-thaw layer, 85, 126, 234–5, 253–4
palsas, 58, 68, 70–1, 77, 102, 251
palynology, July max. air temperatures, 218–19, 233
paraglacial, proglacial and periglacial, 10–13
patterned ground, 140–7
    description, 141–2
    origins, 142–6
    palaeoclimatic significance, 146–7
peat plateaux, 58, 70–1
pediments, 16–18, 174, 176–7, 180–1
Peninsula Point, NWT, Canada, 100–1
perennial frost
    cracks, *see* thermal contraction cracking
    mounds, *see* pingos
perennially
    and seasonnally frozen ground, Pleistocene, 234–5
    cryotic ground, 6, 7, 52–3
periglacial
    climates, 8, 20–8
        alpine, 22, 26
        continental, 22, 25
        high Arctic, 22–5
        low annual temperature range, 22, 26
        Qinghai-Xizang (Tibet) Plateau, 22, 25–6
    concept, 3–6
    'cycle of erosion', 172, 181–2
    domain, 3–5, 6, 20
    geomorphology, 7–8
    involutions, *see* thermokarst involutions
    landscape, 10–18
    landscape modification, Pleistocene, 264–76
    processes, 5–7
    valleys, Pleistocene, 270, 272–3
    zone, 3–5, 8
permafrost, 4, 5, 27, 51–79, 299–300, 301, 302
    distribution, 55, 56–65
        Canada and Alaska, 56–9
        China, 56, 61–3
        Greenland, 56
        Mongolia, 56
        Russian and Siberia, FSU, 56, 59–61
    effects of fire, 69, 111–12
    effects of snow, 62, 64, 67, 71
    effects of terrain, 65–73
    effects of vegetation, 66–7
    geothermal regime, 54–6

hydrology, 54, 73–9, 281
mountain, 61, 62–4, 71–3
plateau, 61–3
Pleistocene, 65, 223
 cold and warm ice sheets, 230
 climatic fluctuation, 230
 degradation (thermokarst), 253–6
 effect of snow, 223
 extent, 227–31
 southern hemisphere, 230
relict, 4, 56, 60–1, 65
science (geocryology), 6, 8
subsea, 64–5
terminology, 52–3
thickness, 55, 58–9, 60–2, 65, 68
pile foundations, 288–9
pingos
 closed system, 103–6, 107
 open system, 77–8, 102–3, 251–3
 Pleistocene, 234, 249–53
Pingo 20, Tuktoyaktuk Peninsula, NWT, Canada, 107
pipelines, 290–1, 293
Pleistocene
 chronology and time scale, 217–21
 periglacial conditions,
  mid-latitudes, 217–32
  northern latitudes, 233–5
ploughing blocks, 156
'plug-like' flow, 151, 152–4
Poland, 238, 247, 258, 259, 271–6
polygons
 high-centred, 113, 117–18, 119
 low-centred, 95–7, 117–18
pore
 ice, 33–4, 87
 water convection, 146
Porsild Pingo, NWT, Canada, 104
pradolinas, 262, 273, 274
Prairie Mounds, southern Alberta, Canada, 253
precipitation, Pleistocene, 225
Prince Patrick Island, NWT, Canada, 106–7, 174, 175, 199
proglacial streamflow regime, 191, 198

Qinghai-Xizang (Tibet) Plateau, 12, 22, 23, 27, 37, 55, 61–3, 132, 167, 204, 205, 206, 207, 259, 296, 298
Quaternary-climatic curve, 219
 palaeo-magnetic time scale, 219
 time scale, 218

rapid mass movement, 7, 161–6
residual thaw layer, 73, 85

Resolute, NWT, Canada, 12, 13, 39, 142, 145, 158, 159, 210
reticulate ice vein network, 81–2
retrogressive thaw slumps, 119–21, 139, 298
Richter denudation-slope, 172, 181–3
river discharge, Northern Canada, 192–3
rock glaciers, 71–3
rockfalls, 7, 163, 165–6
Ross River, Yukon Territory, Canada, 190, 287–8, 290
Ruby Range, Yukon Territory, Canada, 155–6
Russia, 8, 51

Sachs Harbour, NWT, Canada, 12, 13, 22, 23, 210–11, 282, 283, 292–3
Sachs River lowlands, Banks Island, NWT, Canada, 68–9, 105, 122, 123, 209
sand dunes and sand sheets, 207–8, 209
sand wedges, 39–40, 83
 casts, 246–7
Sandar, periglacial, 200–1, 206
Schefferville, P.Q., Canada, 67
sea ice and wave generation, 209–11
sea level changes, Quaternary, 230
 global warming, 299
seasonal
 frost cracking, 40, 234
 frost mounds, 77–7, 86, 102, 106, 234, 250
 snow cover, ice and permafrost, 27
seasonally frozen ground, 234–5
 Pleistocene, 240–3, 250, 270
secondary thaw unconformity, 83, 85, 234
sediment movement (fluvial), 194–7
seepage, supra-permafrost groundwater, 161
segregated ice, 32–4, 86, 87–8, 98–101, 103–6, 107–8, 152
'self-developing' thermokarst, 110–11
Shingle Point, Yukon Territory, Canada, 12, 16
Siberia, 39, 41–2, 123, 124, 125, 130, 175, 177, 178, 180, 185–6, 201, 202, 205, 207, 209, 213, 282, 296
Signy Island, Antarctica, 37, 38, 39, 132
Sleepy Mountain, Yukon Territory, Canada, 16, 17, 164
slope failures, thawing soil, 7, 167–9
slopes
 evolution, 7, 180–3, 269, 273–6
 frozen, 167–9
 morphology, 170–84
  convexo-concavo debris-mantled slopes, 172–5
   free-face model, 170–2
   pediment-like forms, 175–7
   rectilinear debris-mantled slopes, 172
   stepped forms, 177–80

slopewash 7, 157–59, 174
  Pleistocene, 224, 269, 273
snow
  geomorphic effects, 159, 189–90, 243
  jams, 189–90
snowbank
  ablation and runoff, 159, 298–9
  hydrology, 158, 159–61
  snow patches, 7, 14, 157, 159, 174, 181, 203, 206,
    238, 264, 270
snowline, Pleistocene, 225
soft-sediment deformations, 126, 242, 254
soil wedges, 39–40, 234
solifluction, 7, 151–7, 163, 174
  lobes, 156–7, 174
  phenomena, 156–7
  Pleistocene, 239–40, 267–8
  rates, 155–6
  sheets, 156
solute transport, 47, 160, 163, 195, 196, 197
solution, 47–50, 160–1
southern hemisphere (excluding Antarctica), 230, 236
Spitsbergen (Svalbard), 8, 22, 23, 24, 48, 78, 89,
    145–6, 155, 156, 160, 164, 165, 166, 168, 170, 171,
    173, 175, 201, 202, 209, 213
spring thaw, 36, 128
spring-fed streamflow regime, 191
stone streams (*coulées pierreuses*), 236, 268
stone tilting, 7, 135–7
straight and meandering channels, 199–200
stratified slope deposits, 161, 238–9, 270, 274
stream flow regimes, 191–3
sub-river taliks, 58, 200
surface runoff, 75–7
Sweden, 150, 156, 164, 196, 208, 236, 302–3

Taele gravels, East Anglia, 267
'taffoni', *see* honeycomb weathering
taiga, 67, 111–12
taliks, 53, 54, 68, 73–5, 103, 115, 291–3
talus, 163, 164, 171–2
Tasmania, Australia, 230–1
temperature, annual cycle, 35–7
  diurnal range, 37–9
  short-term fluctuations, 37–9
temperature depressions, Pleistocene, 225
terrain disturbance, permafrost, 281–5
thaw
  consolidation, 139, 154, 281
  lakes (thermokarst), 121–4
  unconformity, 85
thaw 'sinks' and depressions, 121

thawing front, 129, 131, 139
'thaw-sensitive' sediments, 81, 290
'thaw-stable' sediments, 81, 287, 290
thermal
  conductivity, 33, 66
  contraction cracking, 5, 7, 39–40, 298
    evidence for Pleistocene frozen ground, 242–9
    palaeo-temperature inferences, 225
    seasonal or perennial, Pleistocene, 234
  diffusivity, 128
  erosion, 112–13
thermally induced mass displacements, 139–40
thermo-erosional niche, 111, 124, 197, 212, 274
thermokarst, 5, 109–26
  causes, 109–12
  depressions, Pleistocene, 253
  human-induced, 281–4
  involutions, 126, 242, 245, 246, 254
  mounds, 113–15, 116, 118–19, 283
  Pleistocene significance, 225, 242–6
  valleys, 115
Thompson, Manitoba, Canada, 61, 128–9, 167
Thomsen River, Banks Island, NWT, Canada,
    199–200
thufur, 142
timberline, 159
tors, 18, 174–5, 236–8
treeline, 20, 159
'Tuk 3' drained lake site, Pleistocene, Mackenzie
    Delta, NWT, Canada, 105
Tuktoyaktuk, NWT, Canada, 12, 24, 99, 100, 105,
    117, 213, 299
tundra, 3, 4, 20, 27, 295, 301–4
  rivers, 262–4

unfrozen water, 33–4, 131
upfreezing, 7, 134–7
  'frost-pull', 134
  'frost-push', 134
USSR, *see* Former Soviet Union (FSU)

vehicle tracks, tundra, 284
vein ice, 88
ventifacts, 205, 262
'Viviers', Hautes Fagnes, Belgium, 251–2

Walewice, central Poland, 238, 273–6
wash, surface and subsurface, 160–1
water
  balance, 193–4, 295
  supply, 291–3
weathering, chemical, 5, 40, 45–50, 205, 234

cryogenic, 5, 40–5
   frost, 41–3, 175
   physico-chemical, 5, 7, 45–6
   salt, 40, 45–7, 205
wetland streamflow regime, 191
wind action, 7, 204–9
   erosion, 47, 175, 205–6, 238
   deflation, 206
   indirect effects, 206–7

   Pleistocene, 224, 257–62
wind direction, Pleistocene, 223–4, 260, 262

Yakutsk, Siberia, 8, 22, 23, 24, 51, 113, 287, 289
Yukon, 48, 49, 72, 168, 175, 176–7, 180, 196, 207, 208, 213, 286, 287–90, 294
Yukon River, Alaska and Canada, 124, 190, 213, 286

'Zero curtain', 36–7, 128